CON

The DK Handbook

FOURTH EDITION

ANNE FRANCES WYSOCKI
University of Wisconsin, Milwaukee

DENNIS A. LYNCH
University of Wisconsin, Milwaukee

New!
2016
MLA
Updates

PEARSON

Boston   Columbus   Indianapolis   New York   San Francisco
Amsterdam   Cape Town   Dubai   London   Madrid   Milan   Munich   Paris   Montréal   Toronto
Delhi   Mexico City   São Paulo   Sydney   Hong Kong   Seoul   Singapore   Taipei   Tokyo

Text design, page layout,
and cover design:
**Stuart Jackman,
with Anne Frances
Wysocki**

Vice President and Editor-in-Chief: Joseph Opiela
Program Manager: Eric Jorgensen
Development Editor: Anne Brunell Ehrenworth
Product Marketing Manager: Allison Arnold
Content Specialist: Laura Olson
Project Manager: Shannon Kobran
Project Coordination, and Electronic Page Makeup:
    Cenveo® Publisher Services
Program Design Lead: Beth Paquin
Cover Art (clockwise from upper left): Anders Photo/Shutterstock, Kongsak/
    Shutterstock, Studio Vin/Shutterstock, Tuulijumala/Shutterstock,
    MPF Photographer/Shutterstock, Tischenko Irina/Shutterstock
Senior Manufacturing Buyer: Roy L. Pickering, Jr.
Printer/Binder: LSC Communications/Crawfordsville
Cover Printer: Lehigh-Phoenix Color/Hagerstown

Credits and acknowledgments borrowed from other sources and reproduced, with permission, in this text-book appear on the appropriate page within text and on pages 544–545.

Library of Congress Cataloging-in-Publication Data
Names: Wysocki, Anne Frances, date- author. | Lynch, Dennis A., date- author.
Title: The DK Handbook / Anne Frances Wysocki ; Dennis A. Lynch.
Description: Fourth Edition | Boston : Pearson, [2016] | Includes index.
Identifiers: LCCN 2015045026 | ISBN 9780134139869 (student edition) | ISBN
    0134139860 (student edition) | ISBN 9780134150949 (exam copy) | ISBN
    0134150945 (exam copy)
Subjects: LCSH: English language—Rhetoric—Problems, exercises, etc. |
    English language—Rhetoric—Handbooks, manuals, etc. | Report
    writing—Problems, exercises, etc. | Report writing—Handbooks, manuals,
    etc. | English language—Grammar—Problems, exercises, etc. | English
    language—Grammar—Handbooks, manuals, etc.
Classification: LCC PE1408 .W973 2016 | DDC 808/.042—dc23
LC record available at http://lccn.loc.gov/2015045026

2   17

www.pearsonhighered.com

Student ISBN-10:   0-13-470297-2
Student ISBN-13: 978-0-13-470297-1
A la Carte ISBN-10:   0-13-472410-0
A la Carte ISBN-13: 978-0-13-472410-2

PREFACE

This handbook originated in a visual communication class Anne has taught for many years. The final assignment asks people in class to bring manuals and textbooks they hate to class—and then to redesign pages from the books so that the pages encourage students to feel smart and invited to learn. The second-most-hated books students bring (after a thermodynamics text) are writing handbooks—and, from how students talk about what they need and how they learn, Dennis and I learned much that shaped *this* handbook, as you can see in how we two designed and laid out these spreads.

From this book's first edition, we have worked to be responsive to students, who want and need to learn with small frustration but with possibly some delight and satisfaction. The handbook underwent two different rounds of usability tests with undergraduates. Other students kept diaries of how they used the handbook and of what has worked—and not. We have been lucky to give workshops with the handbook around the country and at many different kinds of schools—and have watched and listened carefully and learned much from the participating teachers. From them, and from reviewers and focus groups, we have heard the need to help students evaluate and use new kinds of sources and learn even more how to think with and use sources responsibly and critically.

Our original vision and design principles continue from the first edition, but we have—with pleasure—made substantial revisions to both the content and organization of the book in response to all we learned. Our goal continues to be to offer a useful text to the growing community of teachers and students who use *The DK Handbook*.

NEW AND ENHANCED

1 Develop abilities to work well in a writing class: A new Part 1—Flourishing in a College Writing Class—supports students in learning both general academic habits and approaches as well as those specific to reading and writing thoughtfully.

2 Attend to the writing knowledge, practices, and attitudes that undergraduate students develop in first-year composition: Each part of this book now opens by addressing questions students often have about the part's content; each part also opens by describing which of the Council of Writing Program Administrators' outcomes is addressed by that part. Both teachers and students can better understand how the part helps them learn stronger writing abilities.

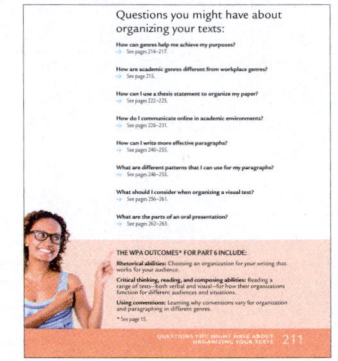

3 Learn more about ethics and plagiarism: Part 4, Using Sources with Integrity, brings together and expands coverage of ethics, plagiarism, and using sources to help students understand academic standards and the responsibilities of the writer in today's cut-and-paste culture.

4 Follow a student's composing process: In Part 2, an assignment sets a student to composing. Follow her as she writes about the assignment and develops and evaluates her research—and then as she writes a thesis statement, statement of purpose, annotated bibliography, rough draft, revision plan, and a research paper.

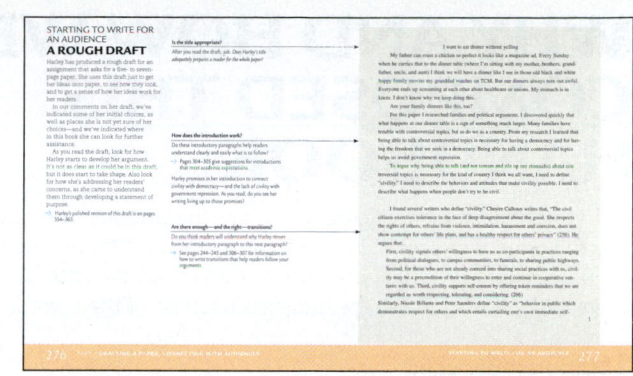

5 Read and write critically: Part 5 emphasizes connections between critical reading and using sources. A section on putting sources in dialogue with each other helps students synthesize multiple sources with differing points of view.

6 Compose multimodally: Material in Part 6 on "multimodal organization," and in Part 8 on "multimodal style" helps students apply rhetorical principles to visual texts and oral presentations.

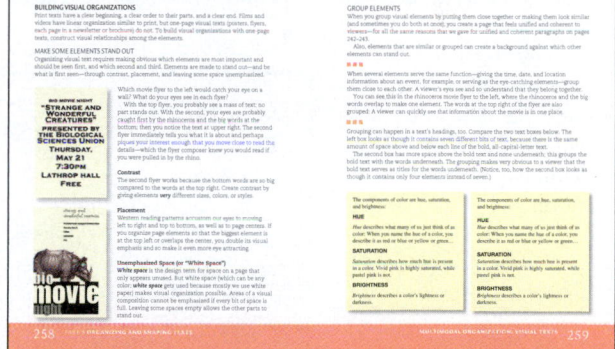

7 Work well with online sources: Instruction and sample citations in Part 9 show how to cite source types like Twitter posts, e-books, articles accessed via databases, and sources accessed on an iPad or mobile device.

WHY AND HOW WE COMPOSED THIS HANDBOOK

We wrote this handbook to be useful to a community that matters to us, the community of writing learners and writing teachers. We want those who use this book to use it with confidence and even delight—so that they can then write with confidence and take delight and satisfaction in the shape and effectiveness of their words.

1 Pages are designed to support the conceptual work of learning.

Our handbook's *layered structure* helps learners move from the general to the specific. Each new topic begins with a page that offers a *topic overview*; each overview helps students grasp quickly and visually the key steps of processes and concepts. Students can then turn to *detail pages* to learn more.

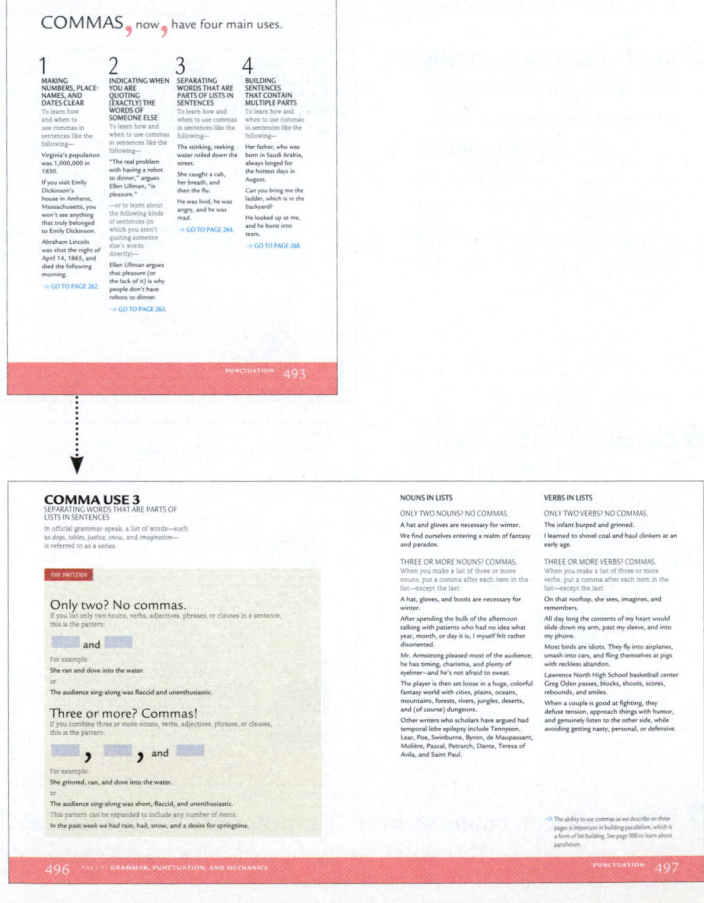

2 Consistent and uncluttered layouts help learners find what they need.

Each topic fits on its two-page spread, making information and ideas easily readable and accessible. The topic of every two-page spread appears dependably at its top left corner. Because finding and seeing information is made easy, students can focus on what they need to learn instead of on finding it.

3 Pattern pages help students search for—and easily remember—the visual and verbal concepts that match the problems they need to solve.

4 Processes are presented visually.

Many of our reviewers told us how frustrated students are by the details of documentation—as well as of revising and editing. We make visible the patterns of documentation so that students won't feel each citation requires starting anew, and we worked to make other details and patterns visible so that students can see and retain them.

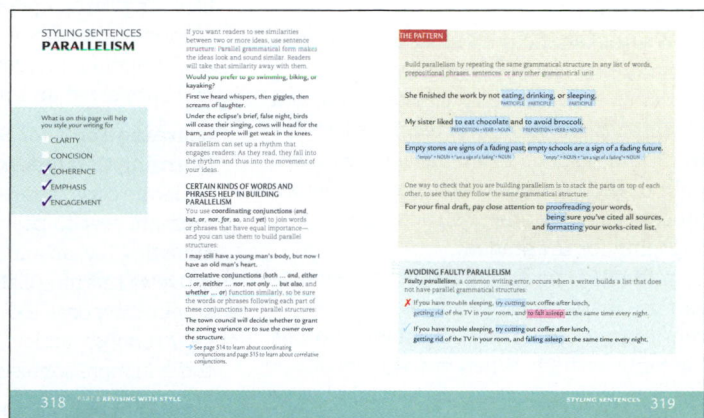

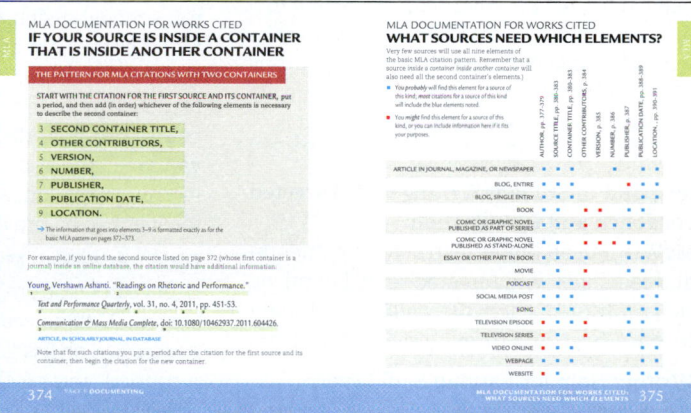

5 We work with students' desires for examples.

Our handbook's design puts examples front and center. We've included as many examples—of sentences, student writing, or source evaluation—as we could and we built explanations inductively from the examples. We want students to easily find the information that will help them solve their writing and editing concerns—and then we want them to remember the pattern of what they learn so they can apply it later.

MyWritingLab FOR COMPOSITION

MyWritingLab is an online practice, tutorial, and assessment program that provides engaging experiences for teaching and learning.

MyWritingLab includes most of the writing assignments from your accompanying textbook. Now, students can complete and submit assignments, and teachers can then track and respond to submissions easily—right in MyWritingLab—making the response process easier for the instructor and more engaging for the student.

In the Writing Assignments, students can use instructor-created peer review rubrics to evaluate and comment on other students' writing. When giving feedback on student writing, instructors can add links to activities that address issues and strategies needed for review. Instructors may link to multimedia resources in Pearson Writer, which include curated content from Purdue OWL. Paper review by specialized tutors through SmartThinking is available, as is plagiarism detection through TurnItIn.

Respond to Student Writing with Targeted Feedback and Remediation

MyWritingLab unites instructor comments and feedback with targeted remediation via rich multimedia activities, allowing students to learn from and through their own writing.

Writing Help for Varying Skill Levels

For students who enter the course at widely varying skill levels, MyWritingLab provides unique, targeted remediation through personalized and adaptive instruction. Starting with a pre-assessment known as the Path Builder, MyWritingLab diagnoses students' strengths and weaknesses on prerequisite writing skills. The results of the pre-assessment inform each student's Learning Path, a personalized pathway for students to work on requisite skills through multimodal activities. In doing so, students feel supported and ready to succeed in class.

Learning Tools for Student Engagement
Learning Catalytics

Generate class discussion, guide lectures, and promote peer-to-peer learning with real-time analytics. MyLab and Mastering with eText now provides Learning Catalytics—an interactive student response tool that uses students' smartphones, tablets, or laptops to engage them in more sophisticated tasks and thinking.

MediaShare

MediaShare allows students to post multimodal assignments easily—whether they are audio, video, or visual compositions—for peer review and instructor feedback. In both face-to-face and online course settings, MediaShare saves instructors valuable time and enriches the student learning experience by enabling contextual feedback to be provided quickly and easily.

Direct Access to MyLab

Users can link from any Learning Management System (LMS) to Pearson's MyWritingLab. Access MyLab assignments, rosters, and resources, and synchronize MyLab grades with the LMS gradebook. New direct, single sign-on provides access to all the personalized learning MyLab resources that make studying more efficient and effective.

Visit www.mywritinglab.com
for more information

ACKNOWLEDGMENTS

This fourth edition of *The DK Handbook* has bloomed under the guidance of Joe Terry and Anne Ehrenworth: What a joy, always, to work with smart people committed to thoughtful education! Shannon Kobran and Eric Jorgenson took care of production details with grace and amazing speed, as did the folks at Cenveo, with Lois Lombardo keeping the zillion details organized. And, with our great thanks, Ali Arnold shepherds our books into teachers' and students' hands with warm, smart, lively, and full understanding of writing classrooms.

As we continue with new editions of this book, responding to what we learn from teachers and students, we continue to thank those who helped early on: Lynn Huddon and Michael Greer are present on every page of this book, as is Joe Opiela. Tharon Howard's user testing with students continues to shape our designing.

We thank (and will continue to thank for a long time) all the above for the extraordinary efforts they have made on behalf of this book—but our most emphatic thanks go to our reviewers (listed on the right) and advisory board members (listed on the next page) and student diary participants (listed on the next page), whose generosity with their time and care for student learning has contributed to and strengthened every bit of this book.

Susan Achziger, Community College of Aurora; Allison Arnold, University of New Orleans; Lynn Atkinson, Everest College, Dallas; Richard E. Baker, Adams State College; Candace Barrington, Central Connecticut State University; Jessica Blezien, Hamline University; Shanti Bruce, Nova Southeastern University; Lisbeth Chapin, Gwynedd Mercy University; Jeff Cofer, Bellevue College; Mary Connerty, Penn State Erie, The Behrend College; Darren DeFrain, Wichita State University; Rebecca L. Fast, Ohio State University, Mansfield; Larry Giddings, Pikes Peak Community College; Cynthia Gribas, Hennepin Technical College; Emily Grigg, Spartanburg Community College; Kirk Hendershott-Kraetzer, Olivet College; Terri R. Hilgendorf, Lewis and Clark Community College; Anneliese Homan, State Fair Community College; Dr. Vickie Hunt, Northwest Florida State College; Peggy Jolly, University of Alabama at Birmingham; Roberta Kelly, Washington State University; Thomas M. Kitts, St. John's University; Amelia Lopez, Harold Washington College; Janie Pittendreigh, Middlesex Community College; Wesley Raabe, Kent State University; Sherry Schreiner, Mesa State College; Dianna Rockwell Shank, Southwestern Illinois College; Greta Skogseth, Montcalm Community College; Joyce Staples, Patrick Henry Community College; Verne Underwood, Rogue Community College; Bradley C. Watson, Franklin University; Leila Wells Rogers, Southern Crescent Technical College; Jo Wiley, Western Michigan University; Angela Wright, Patrick Henry Community College.

Students from seven campuses participated in our diary study and taught us much about how they used their handbooks. We are grateful to all of them, and to their teachers, who helped coordinate an extended survey process:

Susan Achziger, Community College of Aurora; Craig Bartholomaus, Metropolitan Community College - Penn Valley; Rosemary B. Day, Central New Mexico Community College; Uma Krishnan, Kent State University; Beverly Neiderman, Kent State University; Troy D. Nordman, Butler Community College; Josephine Walwema, Clemson University.

During development, members of our editorial advisory board provided ideas, enthusiasm, and constructive criticism, and we want to thank them again for all they contributed:

Kathryn Adams, Allan Hancock College; Diann Baecker, Virginia State University; Deborah Coxwell-Teague, Florida State University; Mark Crane, Utah Valley State College; David Elias, Eastern Kentucky University; Dan Ferguson, Amarillo College; Jacqueline Gray, St. Charles Community College; Ina Leean Hawkins, National Park Community College; Joel Henderson, Chattanooga State Technical Community College; Klint Hull, Lower Columbia College; John Hyman, American University; Ann Jagoe, North Central Texas College; Elizabeth Joseph, Eastfield College; Michael Knievel, University of Wyoming; Lydia Lynn Lewellen, Tacoma Community College; Sharon James McGee, Southern Illinois University, Edwardsville; James McWard, Johnson County Community College; Jeffrey Michels, Contra Costa College; Connie Mick, University of Notre Dame; Beverly Neiderman, Kent State University; Janet Kay Porter, Leeward Community College; Jane Rosecrans, J. Sargeant Reynolds Community College; Lisa Sandoval, Joliet Junior College; Joseph Scherer, Community College of Allegheny County, South Campus; Deidre Schoolcraft, Pikes Peak Community College; Bonnie Spears, Chaffey College; Kristine Swenson, University of Missouri, Rolla; Karen Taylor, Genesee Community College; Eula Thompson, Jefferson State Community College; Gina Thompson, East Mississippi Community College; Christopher Twiggs, Florida Community College at Jacksonville; Justin Williamson, Pearl River College; Geoffrey Woolf, Cincinnati State Technical and Community College.

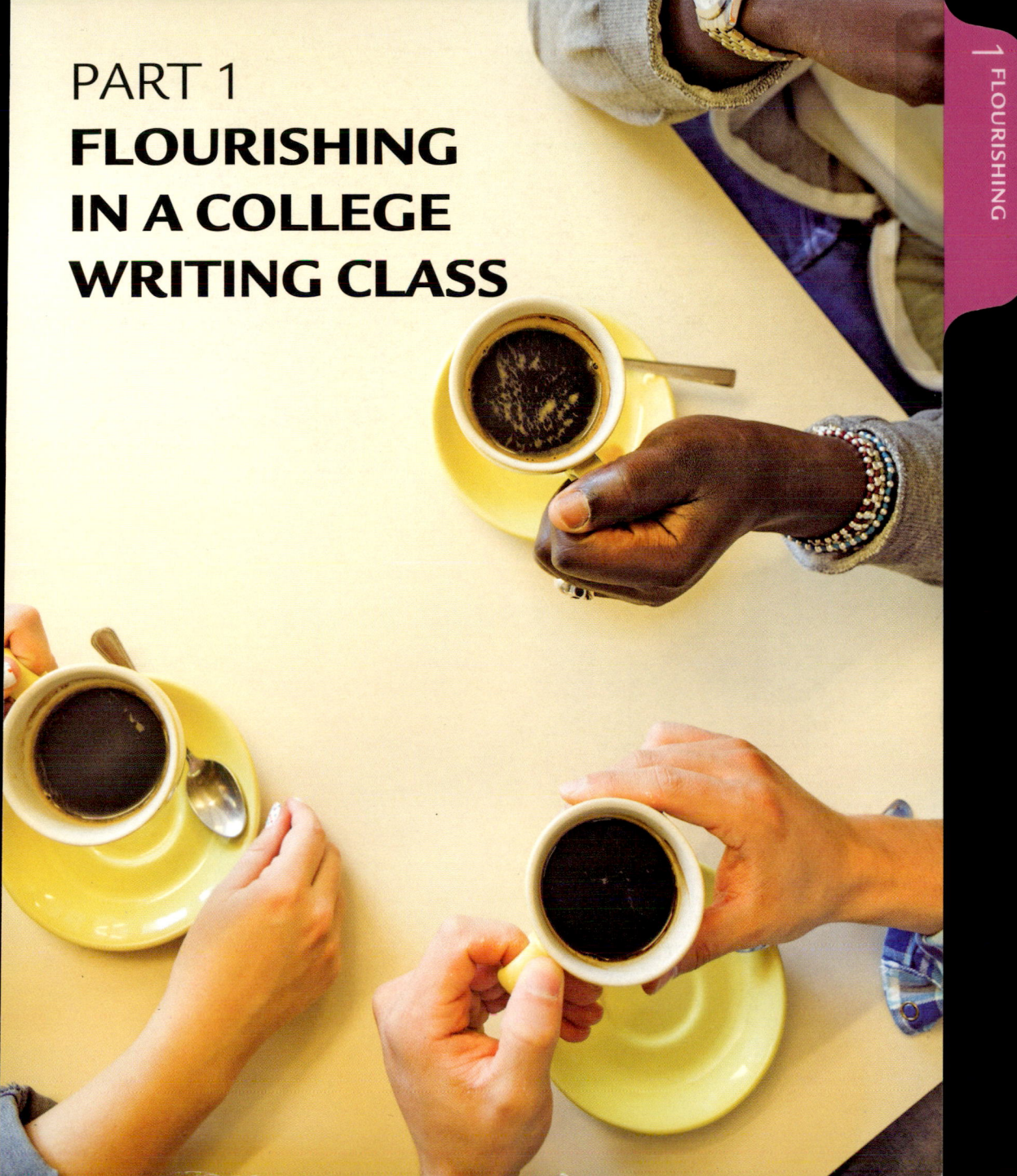

PART 1
FLOURISHING IN A COLLEGE WRITING CLASS

CONTENTS

LEARNING OUTCOMES FOR PART 1

You will learn qualities that help people do well in college, including:
- Setting goals and shaping your time to support your work.
- Becoming acquainted with the expectations and practices of college writing classes.

PART 1 **FLOURISHING IN A COLLEGE WRITING CLASS**

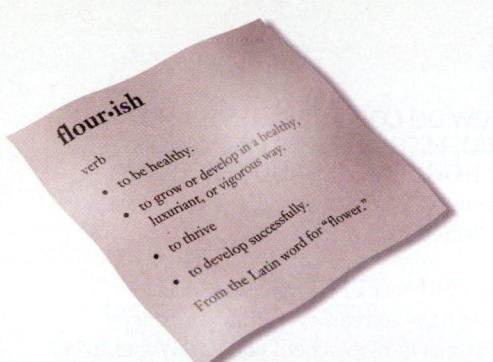

flour·ish

verb

- to be healthy.
- to grow or develop in a healthy, luxuriant, or vigorous way.
- to thrive
- to develop successfully.

From the Latin word for "flower."

FLOURISHING IN COLLEGE

To flourish is to grow into your potential.

Our book's opening section helps you help yourself: *What can YOU do to help yourself learn, succeed, and find pride in your work?*

QUALITIES OF PEOPLE WHO FLOURISH IN SCHOOL

- **They show up.** Just being there does not guarantee success, but you cannot succeed if you do not attend classes.

- **They cultivate patience.** Learning grows and builds in time, and college brings assignments that might span weeks if not months. Your results build over time.

- **They persevere and seek resilience.** Sometimes school is a breeze… and sometimes not. Like everyone else in the world, you will not get everything right all the time; you need to hang in even when you don't feel like it. Keep your eyes on the future, and cheer yourself with thoughts of past and future achievement.

- **They seek a confident and realistic attitude.** Know and trust your capabilities, and plan and dream accordingly—with trust in your ability to stretch.

- **They emphasize responsibility.** You have to do the work requested of you—by planning for it and making the time.

- **They learn how to get interested.** Learning does not result from someone pouring knowledge into you. You have to be actively engaged in thinking, questioning, and tying your current work to future goals.

- **They make friends.** Friends share information about campus, teachers, and resources, but—most importantly—they provide emotional support and human connection.

DIFFERENCES BETWEEN HIGH SCHOOL AND COLLEGE

If you know the differences between high school and college, you can more ably take on attitudes, knowledge, skills, and abilities for flourishing.

These two pages draw on the work of Drew C. Appleby, who has a PhD in psychology with a particular interest in how people learn. Dr. Appleby taught psychology for over forty years, and he paid attention to how people learn in school. The following information comes from a paper he presented at an annual meeting of the Midwestern Psychological Association.

Dr. Appleby described three kinds of understanding and activities that help people make the transition from high school to college, as we outline to the right.

1

HOW DO COLLEGE CLASSES AND PROFESSORS DIFFER FROM HIGH SCHOOL CLASSES AND TEACHERS?

Below we quote observations Dr. Appleby collected from people he taught.

DIFFERENCES BETWEEN CLASSES

"You have to read everything in college, whereas in high school you barely had to read anything at all."

"Even though you may not be in class as long as in high school, the amount of time you have to put in to complete the assigned work is doubled, even tripled."

"In high school, you learn the material in class. In college, most learning takes place outside the classroom."

"You did not have to do reading assignments in high school because your teacher taught you everything that was in your textbook that you had to know. ... You are much more on your own in college classes."

DIFFERENCES BETWEEN HIGH SCHOOL TEACHERS AND COLLEGE PROFESSORS

"College professors expect their students to read the syllabus, and the classroom ... is sink or swim. Do the work or fail. High school teachers reminded us about deadlines ... every day and tried to help us if we were struggling. It's really cool that college professors treat us like adults, but the down side of this is that we have to act like adults...!"

"In high school, teachers were supposed to learn our names and get to know us. In college, I have learned it is my responsibility to help my professors to get to know me."

2

WHAT KNOWLEDGE, SKILLS, AND ATTITUDES DO YOU NEED FOR COLLEGE?

WHAT DO YOU BRING WITH YOU?

What skills and attitudes do you already have that prepare you to do well in school? Look at the list of qualities on page 1; which do you have, and which do you need to develop? Look also at the following pages in this section, about setting goals, shaping your time, participating in class, and reading and writing: What do you already do—and where do you need to focus?

WHAT DOES YOUR COLLEGE OFFER?

Do you know the resources for learning that your college provides?

- Visit **your college library** and ask about library tours. Libraries offer many resources in addition to books: Reference librarians can help you with class projects, and there might be computers or cameras you can use or borrow, study rooms for group projects, and special collections. Check out the library website, too.

- Is there a **Writing Center** you can visit? Are there **Learning Centers** that might help you develop your skills and abilities?

- Are there **clubs and special interest groups** for you to join, to increase both your enthusiasm for school as well as your learning and friend connections?

- Finally, do you know **your professor's office hours**? Your professor will be happy to see you: Go to office hours with a question about class or an assignment.

3

HOW DO YOUR ASSIGNMENTS AND ACTIVITIES HELP YOU DEVELOP AND STRENGTHEN YOUR KNOWLEDGE, SKILLS, AND ATTITUDES?

Your professors design classroom assignments and activities to help you develop your knowledge, skills, and attitudes for flourishing—but you, as an active learner, should ask yourself (or the professor) how each assignment or activity is strengthening your knowledge, skills, and attitudes.

The more you reflect on what you learn and on how your actions help you learn, the more you can apply that learning usefully and help it grow.

SETTING GOALS

Learning challenges you to change your life. Learning challenges you to change your thoughts and opinions and to dig into the ideas of others. Learning challenges you to consider the assumptions you bring to your life and to choose the assumptions and beliefs on which you want to build the rest of your life.

Because of all that, learning can—and often *should*—be hard and uncomfortable.

If you are serious about learning, you will have moments when schoolwork gets tough and when you would so much rather do something (anything!) else.

Having clear goals for what you want to achieve in college helps you survive the hard moments and do well.

BEFORE YOU START SCHOOL: LONG-TERM GOALS

In a notebook or in a page you save on your computer, write down where you want to be in five and ten years. Imagine the best possible success and describe it.

AT THE BEGINNING OF EACH TERM

Review your long-term goals for the future, and then set goals for this year and for this school term. *What specifically do you want to learn? What new abilities do you want to acquire? What grade point average do you want?*

Then list the specific steps you need to take to get to what you want.

WEEKLY

Review your goals for the term to remind yourself of what matters to you. Draw up several goals for the week to keep yourself focused—and then use your goals to help you schedule your week (→ see pages 6–7).

WHEN SCHOOL GETS HARD

Review your long-term and short-term goals: Remind yourself why you are in school. Remind yourself of what you have achieved so far, and remind yourself of where you still want to go. Envisioning where you want to go can help you find the energy to persevere.

AND CELEBRATE!

Any time you check over your goals, re-evaluate them—but also appreciate what you have achieved.

SHAPING TIME

On *Reddit* recently, SerGarlan described why he flunked out of college:

It was my first time being on my own and being wholly responsible for my own actions. There was nobody to force me to get up, nobody to make sure I went to class, nobody to make sure I went to bed before 6 am. My second semester I had a class where I did not attend a single lecture. I was not ready for life on my own.

Given the differences between high school and college, you must figure out how to shape your time if you are to flourish.

MAKE A CALENDAR FOR THE TERM

Once you have a syllabus for each class, enter due dates for all the projects and major assignments into your calendar. After you have entered all the major work, break the projects and assignments down into the steps you need to complete them, and enter those into your calendar. Being able to see the due dates for important work helps you plan time in support of strong work.

MAKE A WEEKLY SCHEDULE—AND THEN MAKE DAILY TO-DO LISTS

At the beginning of each week, make a schedule of all you need to do during the week (at school, work, and home). This can be surprisingly soothing, for it can help you see time for relaxing while staying on track.

Then, each night just before you go to sleep, make a quick list of the tasks you need to accomplish the next day. This helps you remember what you need to do, and then you won't be troubled in your sleep worrying that you'll forget something. Having such a to-do list in mind keeps you from getting sidetracked and helps you feel more in control.

PRIORITIZE

When you make weekly schedules and daily to-do lists, prioritize what needs to get done—and then schedule what is most challenging for times when you know you will have the most energy and be most alert.

Prioritizing helps you avoid procrastination and instead focus on what is most important. It also helps you develop the important ability to say "No" to unplanned outings, tasks, or projects for which you simply do not have the time.

SCHEDULE TIME FOR STUDYING AND NOTHING BUT STUDYING

Schedule study time so that you are more likely to study. With such time, you can give your full attention to your work: You will not only do better work but you will work more quickly.

And do give your full attention to your work: Don't have the TV on in the background; turn off email and message notifications—and turn off your phone!

FOOL YOUR URGE TO PROCRASTINATE

If you know you procrastinate on big assignments, plan your schedule so that you start early on any such assignment: each day, give just a little bit of time to the assignment. (Often, just 20–30 minutes will be enough). Focus for just that amount of time, and then move on for a little while to a pleasant distraction. Shorter periods of working make the job seem more doable—and are less painful. In small regular chunks, big assignments can ease by.

BE WILLING TO COMPROMISE

At times in college (usually at mid- or end of term), you might simply have too much for any human to complete while staying healthy. Know your limits on sleep, so that you can put in the work time you can—but also know that sometimes good enough is good enough. If you have been working hard all term, you will be fine.

MAKE TIME FOR SLEEP—AND FOR PLAY

Research shows the necessity of a good night's sleep for health and for memory. Studying smaller chunks every day—rather than cramming all at once—helps you remember more easily because of both the repetition and the steady and better sleep.

And playtime—going out with friends, playing sports, walking outside, whatever brings you joy and delight—is also necessary for health and emotional balance.

FIND BALANCE

Of course, all that we describe here is easier said than done, given how many hours you work on top of going to school and being part of your family and group of friends. If you ever feel overwhelmed, take deep breaths and remind yourself of your goals and of how hard you work—and then figure out some fun time.

WHAT YOU NEED TO KNOW ABOUT WRITING CLASSES

Writing classes differ from many other classes you will take. On these two pages we list the differences as well as other expectations of writing classes, and—given all that—we discuss how you can flourish.

WRITING CLASSES ARE USUALLY SMALLER THAN LECTURE CLASSES.

Teachers will get to know you in a writing class—which matters, because they will be giving you personalized feedback.

Research also shows that, in any class, students who get to know their teachers—through attending office hours and through regular participation—always do better; they are more comfortable and engaged. So: *Go to office hours.* Read the syllabus, looking for where you have questions: It is appropriate to bring such questions to office hours. Bring questions about the assignment. Bring in writing drafts for feedback.

LEARNING TO WRITE REQUIRES LISTENING TO OTHERS' RESPONSES.

In high school, writing instruction can focus on mechanics and reports; this prepares you for the more sophisticated college-level work of addressing readers and attending to how a paper's details shape a reader's reading. High school writers sometimes think that if a reader doesn't understand writing it is the reader's fault—but consider how often misunderstandings happen even in face-to-face talk. In talking, you don't know if you've been understood until you hear your listener's response. Because writing is like conversation at a distance, more room exists for misunderstanding—and so feedback matters.

Effective writing develops from hearing how others read your words. If you've put care and effort into your writing, feedback can be hard to take—so develop abilities to hear and use feedback.

→ See pages 284–285 on reading and responding to feedback.

WRITING CLASSES OFTEN INCLUDE CLASS PARTICIPATION IN A GRADE.

Because writing requires thinking about readers and hearing others' thoughts, teachers want classes in which people talk with and listen to each other: They want people to participate. Your syllabus should specify what counts as participation; the following items are often included:

- Being prepared by having done all homework.
- Contributing to discussions by asking questions and making comments related to the topic (and by addressing others and not trying to be the only one talking).
- Showing interest in and respect for what others contribute.
- Taking active part in small group activities by doing the work and encouraging others.

You might be shy and not confident about speaking up. Getting to know the teacher and others in class helps tremendously in giving you the confidence to voice what matters to you. To get to know others in class, don't always sit in the same place: When you enter class, sit down next to someone new; introduce yourself and ask an opening question about the other's major, job, or what that person thought about the reading. You will not only help yourself be more comfortable in class, you will help others—and your teacher is likely to notice and appreciate you taking responsibility for helping make the class comfortable for everyone. (Most everyone in college is surprised to learn how many others fear they are not smart enough to speak out loud—so be generous toward your own and others' participation!)

COLLEGE WRITING DEMONSTRATES CRITICAL THINKING AND ANALYSIS.

Unlike report writing in high school, college writing asks you to consider others' positions, even positions with which you disagree. You analyze those positions by determining the pieces out of which they are built and how the pieces form a whole; you consider the validity and strength of the pieces and whole. In your writing, you are expected to respond fairly to those positions—and to consider your place among them.

→ See Part 5 on analysis.

COLLEGE WRITING NEEDS REVISION.

Hear "revision": to *re-vision*, to *re-see*, to *re-think*. Practiced writers expect to shift their thinking as they develop drafts and receive feedback, and so they expect to revise: They budget time for rearranging paragraphs, for writing new paragraphs, for finding new sources to help them consider possible new positions. Correcting spelling or fixing a few sentences is not revision—and so by itself does not make for successful college work.

→ See pages 290–297 and 434–435 on revision.

DOING WELL REQUIRES STAYING ON TOP OF ASSIGNMENTS.

Learning to write requires writing. A writing class will ask you to write regularly and to revise. Every teacher will tell you that you cannot make up several drafts in the last two weeks of class: You simply must keep up if you are to get the most out of class.

READING FOR A WRITING CLASS

All writing classes ask you to read. You read others' writing to learn how others write, but you also read to learn others' sources, positions, and thinking. Approach each class reading by asking what you need to achieve with the reading; also ask how you can use the reading to strengthen your own reading abilities: Do you want to learn to read with more attention and less distraction, or to read to increase your vocabulary, or . . .?

1

BEFORE READING

Digging into a reading with questions and concerns helps you read actively and critically. To develop questions and concerns about a reading, ask:

- What do you know about this text before you read it? What sounds interesting or useful or intriguing about it?

- Why have you been asked to read this text? What does the assignment tell you about how you might approach the reading?

2

PREVIEW THE READING

Consider the following features of the text, to help you develop new—and to deepen existing—questions and concerns:

- **The title.** What does the title suggest about how the writer(s) approach the topic?

- **The table of contents** (if the text has one). What do the chapter or section titles suggest about the text's overall purposes? What does the order of the chapters or sections suggest about what the writer(s) think is most important?

- **The introduction.** This might be the first paragraph or the first page or two. What does the introduction tell you about what the writer(s) hope the text will achieve?

- **The conclusion.** Read the last paragraph or any section labeled "Conclusion." Does this repeat what is in the introduction or shift in some way?

Previewing should take just a few minutes for a short reading and up to twenty minutes for a longer piece—but this time deepens your understanding and engagement and prepares you to read closely.

3

DURING READING

If you read a text on paper, use highlighters and make notes in the margins; if you read online, make notes in another document or on paper. With your notes, try to answer the following questions, highlighting what helps you respond:

- What are the most important words or phrases in the text? Why do you think so?
- What seem to be the main purposes the writer(s) had in composing this text?
- What other ideas or points does the writing present in order to build to the main purposes?
- What sticks out for YOU in this reading? What is new, odd, compelling, or weird?

Have a dictionary close by for looking up any new words.

4

AFTER READING

Prepare for class by writing the following:

- What seem to you to be the main purposes of the reading, and why?
- What do you need to understand or discuss to have a better hold on the reading and its main purposes?
- What general questions does the reading raise for you?

In addition, consider what you learned about your own abilities from reading this text:

- What hung you up in the reading? What can you do to keep this from happening with the next reading? Do you need to make more time for reading, talk to the teacher for advice, or visit the Learning Center on campus?
- How could you have read this text with even more engagement?

USING GOOGLE AS A DICTIONARY

Into Google's search box, type **define:** and then the word you do not know; press the return key. Google will respond with a dictionary definition and with links to help you learn more about the word.

IF YOU TAKE AN ONLINE WRITING CLASS

BEFORE YOU SIGN UP FOR AN ONLINE WRITING CLASS

Ask yourself the following:

- **Do I have easy access to the right technology?** Email the teacher to ask about required technologies; the teacher can answer your questions or direct you to someone who can. You cannot succeed in an online class if you do not have regular, reliable access to the needed technologies.

- **Am I disciplined enough?** Face-to-face classes have a scheduled time, meaning you are more likely to show up. Are you disciplined enough to make regular scheduled time to do work without a schedule or regular reminders?

- **Why do I want to take the class online?** Don't be tempted to take an online writing class because it might be easier—it won't be. Online writing classes require more writing of you than face-to-face classes, because all communication happens through writing. Because all communication happens through writing, your writing will for sure strengthen in an online class… but you must have the willingness and perseverance to be writing for many hours of the week.

- **Am I okay with missing the face-to-face aspects of a class?** Some people get lonely in online classes and miss interaction with others; some do not. If you think you benefit from chatting and joking with others face-to-face, then an online class will be hard for you.

TO FLOURISH IN AN ONLINE WRITING CLASS

- **Read the syllabus even more carefully than you would for a face-to-face class.** Understand and visualize the schedule and expectations thoroughly in order to know whether you can do this online. Put the schedule in your calendar.

- **Schedule regular time for the class, and then do course work during that time.** No one will remind you verbally about homework or about expected discussion postings or drafts. You will flourish if you make the class a regular habit.

- **Connect with the teacher.** Being in regular contact with the teacher is even more important than in a face-to-face class: Being comfortable with the teacher helps you connect to the class. Attend face-to-face or online office hours, by planning always to have regular questions to ask.

- **Pay attention to how you write to others online.** Participation matters as much online as in a face-to-face class (➜ see page 9). How you write online shows how well you have engaged with course materials and can help you encourage others to participate.

➜ See pages 226–231 for tips on writing most effectively online for classes.

- **Connect with others in class.** Online classes can be lonely without a face-to-face component, so e-mail others or set up a Facebook group. Arrange to meet face-to-face if you can, perhaps for a study group.

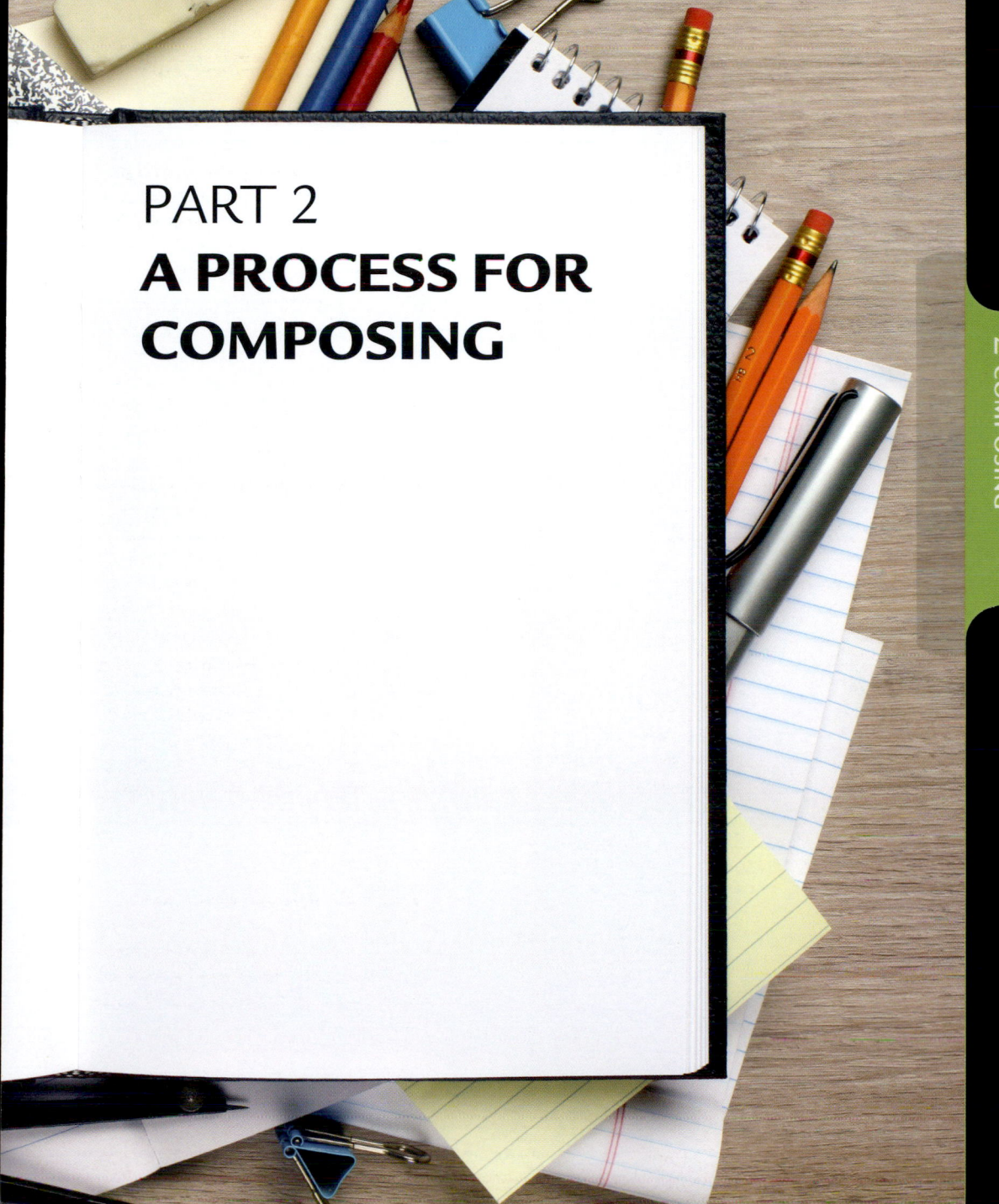

PART 2
A PROCESS FOR COMPOSING

CONTENTS

WHERE ARE WE IN A PROCESS FOR COMPOSING?
Understanding your project
Getting started
Asking questions
Shaping your project for others
Drafting a paper
Getting feedback
Revising
Polishing

2 A PROCESS FOR COMPOSING

Questions you might have about composing and rhetoric:

What is composing?
→ See pages 14–15.

What is rhetoric?
→ See pages 16–25.

How do writers think about the audiences who will read what they write?
→ See pages 20–21.

I just received a new assignment for a paper for my class. How do I figure it out so that I do well?
→ See pages 28–31.

THE WPA OUTCOMES* FOR PART 2 INCLUDE:

Composing processes: Understanding how writers have processes for developing their texts and that the steps of the process rarely happen in a neat, linear order.

Rhetorical abilities: Understanding that rhetoric is a method used by people who make texts, to take into consideration their audiences, purposes, and contexts as they compose.

* See page 15.

WHAT IS COMPOSING?

Composing a paper, you arrange words into sentences and into paragraphs, hoping to engage your readers. Composing a poster, you arrange words and photographs and colors, hoping viewers will want to look at the poster and heed its purposes. Composing a podcast, you arrange voices and other sounds, hoping others want to listen. In other words, composing—as we use it in this book—refers to any written, visual, oral, or otherwise mixed-media text you create.

The New London Group—British and American teachers who research how we learn to communicate—argues that composing requires three steps:

1 No matter the medium—written, visual, oral, or a mix—we compose with elements and arrangements already familiar within our cultures. These existing elements and arrangements are called **Available Designs** by the New London Group.

2 As we compose our texts out of available designs, we are **Designing**, trying out new shapes and combinations of what is available.

3 When we finish composing, we have made the **Redesigned**, something new out of past possibilities. The redesigned, in turn, becomes new available designs for our, or others', future composing.

This process shapes what we propose in this handbook. If you are to be an effective and satisfied composer, you need to learn the designs available to you—the conventions, grammars, and expectations—so you can design for your own purposes and make what helps you engage with your audiences.

COMPOSING: learning, practicing, experiencing, reasoning, nudging, deciding, adapting, reflecting...

Composing is a process that is always moving: it does not start when you type the first word of a paper and it does not stop when you turn in a paper. You are always composing:

1 As you talk with others, listen to music, watch videos, or read, you learn how others think; you are able to consider what concerns we share. You are always picking up on (consciously or not) available designs and attitudes and possibilities.

2 When you need to compose a text, your thinking (conscious or not) plays among the available designs, tinkering with possibilities. You learn as much as you can about the situations in which you compose (this is where **a rhetorical approach** comes in; ➜ see pages 16–25): For whom do you compose? Why are you composing?

3 You send whatever you compose—a brochure, an essay, a video—into the world. Whatever you compose moves among its audiences, perhaps catching their attentions, perhaps not... You can't control how others respond. But you learn from observing how your compositions move in the world, how they contribute to how others (and you yourself) think and feel and do: Through the ongoing activities of composing, you learn how to participate in the world in the ways that matter to you and your communities.

ABOUT WPA LEARNING OUTCOMES FOR FIRST-YEAR COMPOSITION

In beginning each part of this book (for example, ➜ see page 13), we list what you can learn in that part. The descriptions come from the Council of Writing Program Administrators (WPA), which researches how we learn to compose and participate in our worlds through composing.

The WPA has a statement describing the best current understandings of useful knowledge for people learning to compose. That statement addresses these four areas:

RHETORICAL KNOWLEDGE

Rhetorical savvy allows you to analyze the situations and audiences for whom you compose; that analysis helps you compose.

CRITICAL THINKING, READING, AND COMPOSING

Thinking critically involves analyzing, interpreting, and evaluating ideas and situations. You consider how and why others compose texts as they do and whether the ideas, values, and assumptions in a text are worth supporting. You approach your own texts with similar, critical, care.

PROCESSES

Composing in college and beyond involves many steps in a process. The steps happen in only a rough order, with composers often returning to earlier steps or using different steps for different kinds of compositions.

KNOWLEDGE OF CONVENTIONS

Conventions are expectations we all have about what should be in certain texts and how the texts should look or sound. Conventions develop over time and differ in different situations; college-level formal writing has conventions to learn and use.

WHAT IS RHETORIC?

Rhetoric is a method for understanding how communication happens.

Rhetoric developed in the western Mediterranean area over 2,000 years ago as political systems became democratic and as legal institutions came into being. People saw that audiences were moved by some speeches while other speeches not only failed but achieved the exact opposite of what their composers had hoped.

Some people—**rhetoricians**—started systematically studying why some speeches were more effective than others.

The result of the rhetoricians' studies was rhetoric. Rhetoric has developed over the centuries to consider writing and all other kinds of texts meant to communicate.

PURPOSE

The earliest rhetoricians realized that composers need to have purposes. This might seem so obvious as to be useless, but if composers cannot articulate their purposes in detail, then they cannot decide exactly what they need to say (or write) and in what order. (For example, one young woman went to court to appeal a ticket for driving through a red light. It was only after her appeal was denied that she realized her purpose needed to be persuading the judge that— truthfully—she didn't even know there was an intersection and a traffic light; instead, she had described how a truck was blocking the light and so a view of the intersection. The judge had assumed she knew there was an intersection and had told her she needed to stop, whether or not she could see the light.)

AUDIENCE

Rhetoric hinges on the understanding that writers (and composers of any kind of text) address audiences. Audiences are not mindless and automatically under a composer's sway; instead, audiences come to texts with understandings, beliefs, values, and ideas. Using rhetoric, composers consider the relationships they can build with audiences so that audiences will want to listen and engage with the composer around the matter at hand.

CONTEXT

Where and when do composer and audience meet? Is it face to face or through an essay? Late Saturday night or early Monday? How will recent events influence an audience's attitude? Rhetoricians recognize that composers need to consider the contexts of communication because the contexts shape how audiences attend and respond.

STRATEGIES

Once composers have a sense of audience, purpose, and context, they can begin making all the particular strategic decisions—big and small—that shape a composition. Composers need to consider how a choice of a particular word, just as much as a choice of what example or story comes first in a text, is likely to affect an audience's attitude toward a purpose.

■ ■ ■

RHETORICAL SITUATIONS

The combination of audience, purpose, and context makes up what rhetoricians (starting in the twentieth century) call **the rhetorical situation**. This term helps us keep in mind that communication is not a simple transfer of information but is rather an interaction of real, complicated people within the real, complex events of lives and cultures.

Even classrooms are rhetorical situations, where writing an essay involves people with different cultural and educational backgrounds: students and teachers. How do you use the audiences, purposes, and contexts of classrooms—and the strategies available to you—to learn to communicate as you hope?

■ ■ ■

THIS HANDBOOK

This book is about helping you discover as much as you can about your audiences, purposes, and contexts so that you can use the available strategies of writing (and also, to a lesser extent, of visual and oral communication) to construct the connections you want to build with your audiences.

WHAT IS RHETORIC?
PURPOSE

WHAT DO YOU WANT TO HAPPEN AS A RESULT OF YOUR COMPOSING EFFORTS?
What do you hope your audiences will think, feel, believe, or do after engaging with you through your text? What do you want to learn through engaging with your audiences?

PURPOSE IS NOT THESIS

A thesis is the idea—usually with reasons—you hope readers take away from argumentative writing. But when you compose such writing, you hope readers will **do** something with that idea: *Should they write to their national or state political representatives, buy energy-saving lightbulbs, or think differently about religion or women's lives?*

Purposes take into account the emotions and possible actions of readers as well as their thoughts.

PURPOSES ARE NEVER SIMPLE—AND THEY SHOW ASSUMPTIONS ABOUT AUDIENCES

Here are some purposes for composing:

"I hope my paper encourages readers to feel angry enough about teacher salaries in this state that they will join the demonstration to be held at the state capitol next month."

"Seeing my poster, my audience (I hope!) will look more carefully at how we treat pets, knowing there is a relation between pet abuse and child abuse."

"I want readers to be happy women's rights have advanced so much in the last century and to understand why it matters to protect those rights. I want them to see how what happened in that century connects with the improved health and lives of their mothers, sisters, daughters, and themselves."

Thinking about purpose, you think about what your composing needs to do. Notice that each of these purposes shows the composer making assumptions about what an audience already thinks or believes, as when the third assumes the audience doesn't know the history of women's rights and its connections to today's situation.

IMAGINING PURPOSE

As with audience, you need to imagine your purpose as closely as you can: If you picture for yourself exactly the response you hope the text you are composing brings about, you will be more likely to compose texts that appeal in concrete and engaging ways to audiences.

What emotions should your composing arouse or dampen in your audience?

Are you working to build connections with individuals by themselves or to bring people together?

Are you hoping people will take specific action—or quietly consider an issue in more depth?

→ Considerations of purpose weave throughout the rest of this book, but if you want specific help with purpose, see page 29 and pages 270–273.

WHAT IS RHETORIC?
AUDIENCE

WHO WILL BE READING, VIEWING, OR HEARING WHAT YOU COMPOSE?

WHAT ASPECTS OF YOUR AUDIENCE MATTER TO WHAT YOU HOPE TO ACHIEVE?

That a text you are composing has to be shaped for other people is the central concern of rhetoric.

THINKING ABOUT AUDIENCE TO DEEPEN YOUR WRITING ABILITIES

Perhaps the need to think about your audience when you compose seems obvious to you, but the understanding that we write and compose texts for others does not come with birth or, often, before college.

Before college, most writing education focuses on grammar, research, and the logical structures of writing. Before college, most people move in fairly small circles of friends and family, and so their communications are informal and relaxed: Most often, people in high school know well the people to whom they write and speak. After high school—when we go to college, start working to support ourselves, and start taking more active roles in our communities—we have to learn how to communicate with people we may not know as directly.

We need, in other words, to build upon what we learned about writing in high school: We need to start thinking about the wide range of people who read, view, or hear what we compose and about how those people are likely to respond to the many choices we make while composing.

AUDIENCES ARE NEVER FULL, REAL PEOPLE

Even when you are talking with your mother or best friend, you are addressing only some part of that person. Your mother is your mother, after all, and so you speak to her as *mother*; she may also be a boss, an employee, a sister, a daughter—but when **you** talk with her, you most often probably only address that part of her that is *mother*.

Likewise, when you write work memos, the memos go to your boss and coworkers insofar as they have the role of *boss* and *coworker*; you do not address the sides of them that are *parent*, *churchgoer*, or *novel reader*.

In addition, people have rich emotional and intellectual lives and different cultural backgrounds. When you compose texts for others, you focus on a particular topic and hope your audience will pay attention to your concerns. What emotions might others have around your topic—and how can you compose to arouse or to dampen those emotions? What possible opinions and values might your audiences hold on your topic—and how can you compose to focus their attentions on some particular aspect they might not have considered before or are likely to dismiss?

Audiences, in other words, are always a bit imaginary, in that you ask them to step into the roles and beliefs that the purposes and contexts of your composing require. You call audiences into being from where they really are.

→ Because the consideration of audience is so important, a whole part of this book—Part 7— is focused on shaping writing for audiences: See pages 265–288.

WHAT IS RHETORIC?
CONTEXT

WHERE ARE YOUR READERS AT THE MOMENT THEY ENGAGE WITH THE TEXT YOU ARE COMPOSING?

WHAT IS GOING ON AROUND THEM? HOW ARE THE PLACE AND TIME LIKELY TO AFFECT HOW THEY READ? How can you take those circumstances into account while composing so that the text fits its context and reaches its readers?

LOCAL AND IMMEDIATE CONTEXTS

When you write an essay for a class, the teacher has to respond to your essay as well as to the essays of everyone else in your class. Teachers respond to your work usually at night or on the weekend, at home. How is this likely to shape how your teacher reads?

When you write a memo at work, your boss or coworkers will receive the memo amid a pile of other paperwork, in the middle of distracting days. How is this likely to shape how they read?

When you design a flyer for a campus event, it goes up on walls or telephone poles alongside hundreds of others; it has to attract the attention of people who are hurrying by, ten feet away. How is this likely to shape how they read?

When you design a website for a nonprofit organization, readers will probably read it alone, at their computers. How is this likely to shape how they read?

Each of these circumstances, describing the particulars of how audiences come to texts, can help you consider composing. What do you need to do to show a tired, weary-eyed teacher that you've done what an assignment asked? How can you compose a memo so that your busy boss and coworkers will understand exactly what you need them to understand? What photographs and words— and what sizes, and how many—can help you attract the eyes of a passing poster audience? What words, colors, and photographs can help you take advantage of the intimacy of a computer screen reader?

The more you can imagine the time and place in which someone will read your text, the more you can shape the text to fit when and where the text will be read.

LARGER CONTEXTS

What are the values and concerns of your time and place? What has happened recently—in your town or country or in the world—that might affect how someone responds to a text?

For example, after September 11, 2001, no one could write an editorial about travel or world events without taking September 11 into account. It was a long time before people felt it was appropriate to tell jokes and be humorous about politics or world events.

But also imagine that your town is struggling over whether to allow Walmart to build a megastore or over how to find funding to keep the hospital open or the factory from shutting down. If you were to write a letter to the editor about a need for more school funding or for a new stoplight on your corner, taking into account those larger community concerns shows readers that you understand the consequences of what you argue—and so readers are more likely to listen.

Composing texts while mindful of the larger contexts in which your readers move can help you figure out the beliefs and values that shape how readers read and the mood your readers are likely to have. Considering all these details helps you understand how and why readers might respond and helps you build bridges to readers—and so helps you shape a text that readers are more likely to read, understand, and want to engage.

WHAT IS RHETORIC?
STRATEGIES

WHAT ARE THE CHOICES YOU CAN MAKE AS YOU COMPOSE A TEXT?

What words, tone of voice, or colors will you choose? What should come first? What examples will you use? Will you use photographs or charts? Which typefaces?

Every choice is a strategy affecting how your audience responds. Your choices depend on your purpose, context, and audience.

IN TERMS OF STRATEGIES,

becoming an effective composer of texts involves your ability to:

1 IDENTIFY THE WIDEST POSSIBLE RANGE OF CHOICES—OF STRATEGIES—AVAILABLE TO YOU IN YOUR RHETORICAL SITUATION.

When you first start considering a text you have to compose (or even when you are partly into composing it), if you list every choice you could make, you'll see how much room there is for you to experiment with possibilities; you're more likely, therefore, to achieve your purposes. (You'll also probably realize the impossibility of listing every possible strategy—but it's useful to try.)

2 SHAPE CHOICES TO ADDRESS YOUR AUDIENCE, GIVEN YOUR PURPOSE AND CONTEXT.

If you want your audience to write to their congressional representatives to support a bill funding more space exploration, don't begin with a discussion of where the money should come from: That starts your readers thinking about why space exploration might be too expensive. Start instead with a discussion of the wonders of space, and then describe the medical and industrial advances resulting from space exploration; your audience is more likely to approach your request with a positive point of view.

You can consider every possible strategy in light of how your readers are likely to respond, and how your choice will shape their attention and thus their receptiveness to your purpose.

THE STRATEGY OF ARRANGEMENT

In the example of space exploration, the strategy we discussed is arrangement. Arrangement is about what comes first in a composition, and what follows.

For some rhetorical situations, audiences expect certain arrangements. When you write a business letter, the letter starts with a date and a greeting, and then discusses the matter at hand, with (often) a final paragraph suggesting what the next actions should be. Scientific papers are usually arranged with an abstract first, then a description of experimental method, then a description of the results of the experiments, then a discussion of the results, and finally a list of other papers consulted during the research.

→ Because arrangement is such a crucial strategy in composing, a whole part of this book is devoted to it; see Part 6, on organizing, pages 211–264.

THE STRATEGY OF MEDIUM

Sometimes you enter a composing situation with all choices open to you, including that of the medium. If, for example, you have been asked to help a nonprofit organization improve its outreach to teenagers, would you recommend composing webpages or brochures, organizing a fair or school visits, or handing out printed T-shirts at the mall? Each of these media engages with the audience in different ways, and so can help you achieve your purpose in different—and differently effective—ways.

RHETORIC AND A PROCESS FOR COMPOSING

People who study writers and writing have learned that all effective writers have processes they follow to develop writing. These processes differ in their particulars from writer to writer, but generally—when it comes to composing a research paper—the processes contain the steps shown on the next page.

(Keep in mind that, although the process looks linear, writers often move back and forth through the steps, especially between revising and receiving feedback, as they produce several drafts of the work.)

With each step, you become more certain about audience, context, purpose, and—eventually—strategies, until it is time to declare a project finished.

Understanding your project

At this step, you develop your first tentative ideas of your audience, context, and purpose.

Getting started

Mulling over different ways of understanding audience, context, and purpose helps you determine what and where you need to research.

Asking questions

How does your research help you understand how your audience, context, and purpose relate to each other—and vice versa?

Shaping your project for others

Here, you focus on audience and how their understandings and expectations shape what and how you will compose.

Drafting a paper

Given your understanding of audience, context, and purpose, what strategies might help you compose most effectively?

Getting feedback

Once you have a draft, listen to how your audience reads and understands: What worked in your composition, and what didn't?

Revising

In response to feedback, how can you refine your strategies better to fit your audience, context, and purpose?

Polishing

Now you know exactly what your audience, context, purpose, and strategies are and can polish them into a solid, shining, finished composition.

UNDERSTANDING YOUR PROJECT OR ASSIGNMENT

To understand any new project or assignment—whether you are in school, at work, or anyplace else where you need to develop communication—you need to understand the rhetorical situation of the project or assignment:

❑ Who is your audience?

❑ What is the context?

❑ What is the purpose?

UNDERSTANDING A CLASS ASSIGNMENT

❏ Who is your audience?

In a writing class, you will often hear that the audience is your classmates—but probably your teacher will give you a grade on how well you address the concerns and beliefs of your classmates, so the teacher is also a very important part of your audience. (Sometimes teachers ask you to write for other audiences besides the class; you will have to ask how you are to learn about those audiences.)

❏ What is the context?

The classroom is the immediate context, of course—but so is your campus and its values and recent events. The values of the community around the school, current national and international events—how are these likely to shape how your audience will read? What has happened recently in their individual and shared lives that shapes how your audience thinks and feels, in general and on the topic you are considering?

➔ See a writing assignment—and a student's response to it—on the next page.

❏ What is the purpose?

Three levels of purpose shape class writing assignments:

- There are the teacher's purposes. You might be asked to demonstrate that you can produce polished prose; carry out research, integrate it into a paper, and document it; and develop and produce a persuasive argument. Look at each new assignment for explicit statements of what the teacher hopes you will learn; if they are not there, ask.

- You can have your own purposes for your own learning: If there are skills on which you need to focus (some particular aspect of grammar, or transitions, or writing complex paragraphs), how can you work them in?

- Your paper will have its particular purposes, such as *I want to persuade the people in class that replacing the lightbulbs in their houses with compact fluorescent bulbs is a useful thing to do* or *I would like to persuade people to write to their representatives about health care.*

When you wish to understand what a teacher hopes you will achieve, look for the following terms in an assignment:

summarize: to describe as concisely as possible the main points of writing

define: to explain a term or concept

inform: to tell others about an issue, with supporting examples and data

analyze: to break a process or object into its conceptual parts while showing how the parts relate to make a whole

persuade: to present your opinions on a topic using evidence, so that others might come to agreement with you

UNDERSTANDING YOUR PROJECT OR ASSIGNMENT
RESPONDING TO A WRITING ASSIGNMENT

On the opposite page is an assignment Harley received in her writing class. To the right, Harley writes about the assignment with the help of the questions on page 29.

In this book we show you the research, writing, and thinking Harley carries out for this assignment.

→ On page 45, see Harley choose and narrow a topic.

→ On page 95, see Harley's initial research questions.

→ On pages 140–141, see Harley's initial running list of the sources she finds.

→ On pages 204–205, see one page of Harley's annotated bibliography.

→ On pages 206–207, see how Harley puts her sources in dialogue with each other.

→ On page 273, see Harley's statement of purpose.

→ On pages 276–283, see Harley's first draft.

→ On page 293, see Harley's revision plan.

→ On pages 354–363, see Harley's final paper.

WRITING TO LEARN

Once you have read an assignment and thought about it through the questions on page 29, you will help yourself tremendously if you reflect on the assignment in writing, asking any questions that come up:

The assignment says I am to write an argumentative research paper on a topic of my choice, with the class as my audience. I've written research papers before, but I don't know what "argumentative" means with a research paper. I've got to pay attention to how the teacher means "argument." (And how can I start if I don't know what it means? I think I need to go talk to her.)

But "argument" sounds like the overall purpose for the teacher, to show that I know how to make research be an argument. (I'm also not sure what counts as evidence; I'll have to ask.)

And I don't really know the people in class yet, but they seem to be just like everyone else I know on this campus, so I can ask my friends to help me think about this paper.

The context? Well, it's this writing class—so I guess that means I also have to be careful about how I write.

A topic? Is there any way to write about how awful it is when everyone in my family talks about politics, like at dinner last night? Talk about argument!!! It's awful—and Jenna was saying it's just like that at her house.

RESEARCH PAPER ASSIGNMENT

Over the course of the semester you will produce an argumentative research paper on a topic of interest to you.

We will discuss "argument" as we proceed, so that you will develop an understanding of the characteristics of—and work that goes into—argumentative writing. For now, however, understand that arguments are always more complex than just pro/con; your research will help you explore the complexities of the topic you choose.

DETAILS OF THE PAPER

- The audience for your writing is your classmates.
- The paper will be 5–7 pages long.
- You will cite at least six sources in your writing, four of which must be academic sources.
- Based on your major, you will choose either MLA or APA style for your citations and Works Cited list or References list.

OBJECTIVES

I ask you to do this work to help you

- learn how to find and use authoritative and relevant sources.
- develop your critical thinking abilities through analyzing your sources' arguments.
- learn how to support and develop your ideas through engaging with your sources' arguments.
- learn scholarly disciplinary conventions for writing.

PROCESS

You will be developing and turning in the following documents on the way to producing the full paper. See the course calendar for due dates.

1 A short description of and rationale for your research topic
2 Your initial research questions
3 An initial running list of your sources
4 An annotated bibliography
5 Written responses to two of your sources, in which you analyze the sources and then consider how their thinking engages with your thinking
6 A statement of purpose
7 A rough draft
8 A revision plan
9 A final draft

UNDERSTANDING YOUR PROJECT OR ASSIGNMENT
UNDERSTANDING OTHER PROJECTS

Below are questions to help you start thinking about new communication projects. Later parts of this book will help you continue to develop your understanding of your rhetorical situation, as your questions and concerns become more focused with further work.

❏ **Who is your audience?**

What particular people will read, see, or hear the communication I am building? What are my relationships with those people? What values and beliefs do they hold concerning the topic of the communication? Why should this communication matter to them? What will be most important to them in this communication? Is there an immediate audience and then a secondary audience (as, for example, when someone writes a report for a boss, who will then pass the report on to the next boss)?

➜ Part 7 of this book goes into detail about audiences; see pages 265–288.

❏ **What is the context?**

Where and when will my audience receive the communication from me? How does that context shape them to respond? Are there any recent events that might affect how they respond?

❏ **What is the purpose?**

Why am I doing this? What am I hoping to achieve? What should my audience think, feel, or do when they are finished reading? What relationships am I hoping to build with my audience?

➜ Part 7 of this book goes into detail about audiences; see pages 265–288.

PART 3
FINDING
IDEAS

CONTENTS

3 FINDING IDEAS

WHERE ARE WE IN A PROCESS FOR COMPOSING?

Understanding your project
Getting started
Asking questions
Shaping your project for others
Drafting a paper
Getting feedback
Revising
Polishing

Finding a topic
Narrowing the topic
Developing research questions
Finding sources

PART 3 **FINDING IDEAS**

Questions you might have about finding ideas:

How can I develop an organized approach to research?
→ See pages 36–39.

How do I find and focus a topic?
→ See pages 42–51.

What kinds of sources do I need for my research?
→ See pages 54–65.

Is Google the best way to find sources? How do I use search engines like Google for academic searches?
→ Google can be an important part of any search, as you will see throughout these pages. To use Google and other search engines most effectively, see pages 66–75.

What are library databases and how do I use them?
→ See pages 78–87.

Are there sources other than books I can use?
→ See pages 60–65, 72–73, and 88–91.

What's the problem with Wikipedia?
→ See page 65.

THE WPA OUTCOMES* FOR PART 3 INCLUDE:

Critical thinking, reading, and composing abilities: Locating primary and secondary research materials, including journal articles and essays, books, scholarly databases or archives, and Internet sources.

Composing processes: Discovering ideas.

Conventions: Applying citation conventions in your own work

* See page 15.

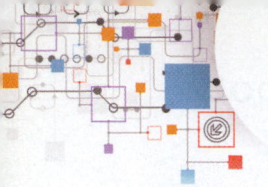

COMPOSING TO LEARN & COMPOSING TO COMMUNICATE

AS A WRITER, THE MOST IMPORTANT DISTINCTION YOU MUST MAKE IS: *When are you writing for yourself and when are you writing for others?*

This distinction is rarely taught in high school—but successful writers use it constantly.

To understand this distinction, understand that others usually won't get your ideas if those ideas fall directly out of your head onto paper. It's not that there's something wrong with your readers; it's that those readers don't live inside your head. Those readers don't know the same things you know; they don't know all you can take for granted when you first put words on a page or screen.

All writing—all composing—starts with your ideas, thoughts, and responses ... but then the writing has to be shaped for others: All composing, that is, starts as composing to learn but then has to be shaped if it is to communicate to others.

Effective and successful writers understand that they should first lose themselves in their own words to find what ideas matter to them. They also recognize that they need to look at their ideas from a little distance: This helps them make their ideas, and the connections between those ideas, explicit for readers.

COMPOSING TO LEARN

If you write, sketch, or read to figure out what you think, believe, or feel, then you are composing to learn. You have no one else in mind as you work: You simply work things out for yourself. In this stage, you don't think about audiences.

Composing to learn can take place on scraps of paper, in journals, on white boards, on dinner napkins, in dreams. This is writing meant to be read only by you. Only you will fully understand it

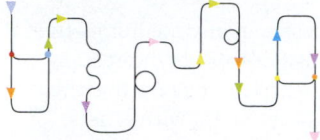

Writers usually move back and forth many times between composing to learn and composing to communicate as they move back and forth between figuring out their own ideas and figuring out how to make those ideas clear to others.

COMPOSING TO COMMUNICATE

When you alertly shape your ideas for others, you compose to communicate. You explain overtly how and why you move from one idea to the next; you consider how others might respond and address their concerns and perspectives.

Composing to communicate requires composing to learn. Until you have a good idea of what matters to you, you can't know what it is you want others to hear or see.

LEARN TO RECOGNIZE WHEN YOU ARE COMPOSING TO LEARN— AND WHEN YOU NEED TO COMPOSE TO COMMUNICATE

If you can recognize when you are composing to learn and when you are composing to communicate, or if you can recognize that sometimes you need to back off from shaping your ideas for readers in order to figure out your own ideas, your composing process will be smoother and will yield stronger results.

PART 3 OF THIS BOOK IS ABOUT COMPOSING TO LEARN

At the earliest stages of composing, you need to let yourself wander through a wide range of perspectives on a topic. By letting yourself wander, you are more likely to come upon ideas that resonate for you and your audience. That is why Part 3 of this book is set up to help you identify and narrow a topic and then find a wide range of supporting sources.

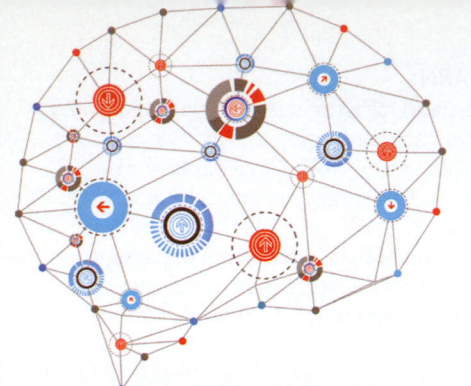

You know how you go to a party where you don't know anyone well and you have to listen first to figure out how to join in? Becoming an academic writer-researcher is like that: You do research as a way to figure out what is going on in the academic conversations already in place, so that you can join in.

And so what moves writers through a composing process is research.

A RESEARCH PROCESS

Writers—like composers in any medium—start by researching an idea or topic of interest. By doing initial broad research, they narrow their interest to concerns they share with others.

Once writers have a narrowed topic, they can generate questions about it. The questions help writers discover what further, focused research they need.

Through this research, writers move toward a thesis statement. A thesis statement arranges, logically, the parts of the developing argument.

With a thesis statement, writers can then build a statement of purpose; this statement uses a writer's knowledge about readers to describe strategies for reaching the audience.

With all that research behind them, writers are prepared to draft an effective and strong composition.

NO RESEARCH PROCESS IS LINEAR
In the graphic to the right, the research process looks straightforward. It isn't. You repeat steps and double-back as you find sources to take you in new directions or you discover more about what matters to you.

GENERAL TOPIC

the economy music war sports technology the draft
global warming video games immigration
politics education childcare
globalization healthcare the Internet

RESEARCH

how electronic voting can be manipulated in U.S. national elections

file sharing and the success of new bands

the effects of charter schools on local public schools

NARROWED TOPIC

RESEARCH

What is electronic voting? What makes electronic voting machines better (or worse) than other voting methods? Who oversees electronic voting machines? Who makes electronic voting machines? Who recommends electronic voting machines? Who owns electronic voting machines? Who says we shouldn't use electronic voting machines? How can someone tamper with electronic voting machines?

QUESTIONS TO GUIDE RESEARCH

RESEARCH

Voting machines developed and owned by private companies that tally the vote themselves are not accountable to the voting public; therefore, government-developed and -owned electronic voting machines that print receipts for voters have a higher degree of accountability.

THESIS STATEMENT

RESEARCH

Because I am writing to people in class, many of whom will not have ever voted, I need to explain about different kinds of voting machines—and how each one causes troubles in tracking and counting votes. I also need to show how electronic voting machines—given how they are now developed—seem more vulnerable to tampering and fraud than other existing kinds of voting, and why this should matter to all of us.

STATEMENT OF PURPOSE

RESEARCH

FINISHED WRITING

COMPOSING TO LEARN

COMPOSING TO COMMUNICATE

A RESEARCH PROCESS
RESEARCH BROADLY, THEN DEEPLY

GENERAL TOPIC

RESEARCH

NARROWED TOPIC

RESEARCH

QUESTIONS TO GUIDE RESEARCH

RESEARCH

THESIS STATEMENT

RESEARCH

STATEMENT OF PURPOSE

RESEARCH

FINISHED WRITING

During the early stages of research, *general and popular sources* help you research broadly for a general sense of what matters to people. Online sources like Google and Wikipedia and popular magazines like *Time* and *Newsweek* can provide help with this broader, preliminary inquiry.

During the later stages of research, *academic journals and other specialized sources* help you deepen your research and develop your thesis. In academic and other kinds of formal writing, audiences also expect you to provide multiple sources to support your main points.

→ See pages 54–55 and 60–65 for more on kinds of sources and the expectations audiences have about them.

A SKETCH OF ONE WRITER'S PROCESS

GENERAL TOPIC

file sharing

RESEARCH

NARROWED TOPIC

file sharing and the careers of new bands

RESEARCH

QUESTIONS TO GUIDE RESEARCH

Developing guiding questions can help you know what information you need and so what focused research to carry out. Doing this research helps you gain a better sense of what is at stake, for whom, and why—and so helps you understand how to shape your writing. *Who shares files? How many files are shared in a year? What is file sharing? What are different ways to file-share? What kinds of files are shared? Are there competing interpretations of what counts as file sharing? Who assigns different interpretations? Who decides whether file sharing is good or bad? What criteria do they use? Some people think file sharing is always theft; are there conditions under which it is beneficial? Who benefits from file sharing? Who doesn't? Do the effects of file sharing differ when different kinds of files are shared? What aspects of file sharing ought to be protected? When should file sharing be prohibited?*

RESEARCH

THESIS STATEMENT

A thesis statement is logic: It offers reasons for your position that will be persuasive to your intended audience. *Musicians who make their music freely available online attract new audiences; therefore, musicians who make their music available online sell more music than those who do not share their music online.*

→ See pages 160–161 and 222–225 for more on thesis statements.

RESEARCH

STATEMENT OF PURPOSE

Writers use statements of purpose to shape a thesis statement for a particular audience. A statement of purpose helps a writer think through the details (such as tone of voice, arrangement, or kinds of examples) of how to present a thesis to an intended audience.

→ Because a statement of purpose is usually several paragraphs long, we cannot give an example here; see pages 271 and 273 for examples.

GETTING STARTED WITH RESEARCH

GETTING STARTED—AND KEEPING GOING

To get started with writing and research, you just need to start. On the next pages we describe how you can find, narrow, and research a topic—but you do just need to start and to keep going.

Understand that all writers deal with all the stuff that gets in the way of writing: procrastination, fear that you are not good enough, distractions from what seems more immediately fun. Cheryl Strayed, the author of *Wild*, says,

When I am in a writing phase, I do all the things people do when they need to get something done that feels hard to do. I hem and haw. I think of every reason not to write (the dirty dishes in the sink, the newspaper, all the things to read on the Internet), and then I just tell myself to quit my bitching and write.

Similarly, on his *Tumblr*, Neil Gaiman has written, "Write the ideas down. . . . Finish the things you start to write. Do it a lot and you will be a writer. The only way to do it is to do it."

Keep in mind the future satisfactions of doing good work.

TIP

RESEARCHING ETHICALLY
→ See Part 4 to learn why and how to approach research with respect for others.

SETTING UP A SCHEDULE

Unless you do them just because you want to, research projects almost always have due dates—so part of getting started is figuring out how to schedule to be done on time. Making a schedule also reminds you of just how much work goes into a research paper that is worthy of your efforts and from which you will learn.

Below is one student's detailed schedule, given her assignment. She started with the due date and moved backward through *all* the steps she needs to take to do the work. Follow her model, applied to your due dates, to figure out how to fit the necessary steps into your school, work, and home schedule. This may look overwhelming because it includes almost every single step, but you will indeed do almost all this work on the way to a paper:

RESEARCH PAPER

Due date	12/15
Date assigned	11/1

STEPS	DATE TO COMPLETE STEP
Analyze project (pp. 14-17)	11/2
Find & narrow a topic (pp. 28-35)	11/6
Develop questions for guiding my research (pp. 36-39)	11/7
Figure out the kinds of research I need to do (pp. 40-45)	11/7
[Will I need to do any interviews, surveys, or observations? (pp. 76-77)]	
[Do I need to do archival research? (pp. 74-75)]	
Carry out my research (pp. 62-77)	
and start keeping running list of sources (pp. 126-127)	11/14
Evaluate sources, deciding what to include (pp. 88-101)	11/21
Develop working thesis (pp. 146-147 & 190-191)	11/22
Do further research required by my thesis	11/25
Develop statement of purpose (pp. 250-253)	11/28
Develop Works Cited list (pp. 342-343)	11/29
First draft due	12/1
Receive draft back with comments	12/8
If more research is necessary...	12/10
Revise first draft	12/13
Edit first draft	12/14
Proofread	12/14
FINAL DRAFT DUE	12/15

FINDING A TOPIC

WHAT IS A TOPIC?

A topic is a general area of interest. It's often just a name, a few words, or two ideas:

- computer game violence
- children's education
- automobiles
- racism
- women's rights
- sports and advertising
- health and aging
- politics
- viruses

A topic is a place to start, but it is too broad for a paper; you have to narrow it by doing research that helps you shape your topic for a particular audience in a particular context.

IF AN ASSIGNMENT GIVES A GENERAL TOPIC

You may be given broad guidelines within which to choose a topic. For example, in a history class you might be asked to *Write a short biography of a person who lived through World War I* or *Find two articles that take different positions on an event we've discussed and compare the articles' arguments.*

Start by identifying an area—a topic—within the parameters of the assignment, an area in which you want to do further research. If an idea does not immediately spring to mind, use the recommendations on the opposite page to help you choose.

What matters to you?

IF YOUR ASSIGNMENT ASKS YOU TO CHOOSE A TOPIC

In writing classes, you are often asked to write on a topic you choose. You want to pick a topic that matters to you, but if a topic does not immediately come to mind, try:

- **Asking yourself some questions.** What current issues bother or intrigue you—or are affecting a friend or someone in your family? What current events or issues do you not understand?

- **Talking to others.** Ask friends and family members what matters to them and why.

- **Going online.** Some library and writing center websites provide lists of current topics that are rich with research possibilities. In your favorite search engine, use terms like "essay idea generator" or "research paper topics."

Once you have possible topics, try these strategies to determine which you want to develop further:

- **Do a Google search on the topic.** Does it look like there's lots of interest in the topic? What are people's different positions on the topic? Do the webpages you visit suggest other, related topics or other directions for research?

- **Write a little bit on each possible topic.** Use these questions to help:

  Audience questions: Why might my audience care about this topic? What might they already know about it?

  Context questions: Does this topic seem rich enough to help me write a paper of the length asked by the assignment? Does it seem complex enough for the assignment? What is happening locally/nationally/internationally around this topic?

  Purpose questions: How does this topic help me address the assignment's purposes? Will this topic expand my learning? How can I shape this topic into a purpose that will interest my audience—*and me?*

→ See pages 16–25 to review the concepts of audience, purpose, and context.

GET STARTED EARLY

Given the time constraints of school—and of producing a solid research paper—you usually need to choose a topic quickly. If you start working early, you'll have time to explore possibilities and find an engaging topic.

Keep in mind, too, that a research paper develops in stages. Starting early gives you time to modify your topic and the research questions that grow out of it, if needed. Starting early also helps you stay sane.

NARROWING A GENERAL TOPIC

A TOPIC HAS TO BE NARROWED BEFORE IT CAN HELP YOU SHAPE RESEARCH AND WRITING

Imagine you want to write about the 1960s because your grandparents talk about those years all the time. You describe this interest to one of your slightly more obnoxious friends, who responds, "Groovy! Are you going to tell us about the Vietnam War and the draft and hippies and the free speech movement and the civil rights movement and the Black Panthers and Women's Rights and the deaths of Jimi Hendrix and Janis Joplin and then there's Woodstock and the Young Republicans…? And do you want to talk about the 1960s in Africa, Asia, and Europe?"

You probably already had some idea of where within that long list you wanted to focus, but until you can make your focus clear and specific to others, simply being able to name your topic sets you up to be unfocused. If you are unfocused, your writing will also be unfocused and you will find it hard to plan and organize a paper.

NARROW A GENERAL TOPIC THROUGH INITIAL, BROAD RESEARCH

To narrow a general topic, start researching it, using general and popular research sources. To the right we show how one writer, Harley Williams, starts to narrow her topic of how awful it is when her family argues about politics.

GENERAL TOPIC
"how awful it is when my family argues about politics"

narrowing a topic by
GOING ONLINE

GOOGLE SEARCH
The search terms "family political argument" turn up a review of the book *The Righteous Mind* by Jonathan Haidt, a social psychologist. According to the review (in the online *New York Times*), the book describes the psychology of why people of differing political values have trouble talking.

WEBSITE
The book review above contains a link to the website CivilPolitics.org, which says its mission "is to find and promote evidence-based methods for increasing political civility"; the site defines civility as "the ability to disagree with others while respecting their sincerity and decency."

REPORT
The website above offers a link to a report from the Pew Research Center for the People & the Press (an "independent, non-partisan public opinion research organization") on how in the United States "values and basic beliefs are more polarized along partisan lines than at any point in the past 25 years."

narrowing a topic by
CHATTING FACE-TO-FACE

TALKING TO FAMILY
Asked if family dinners were always this way, her grandmother reminisces about being a little girl during World War II. She describes the family sitting on the porch in the evenings, talking with neighbors about politics. She said sometimes people yelled but everyone kept talking to each other.

TALKING TO FAMILY
Asked if family dinners were always this way, her mother remembers a dinner during the Vietnam War when her older brother yelled at her father about what was happening politically, stormed away, and didn't come back for several years.

TALKING TO FRIENDS
Her friends describe family dinners where everyone agrees ahead of time not to talk about politics—and then the dinners are full of uncomfortable silences.

After such initial research, this writer could narrow her topic in these directions:

- The effects of political polarization on families
- Whether political polarization has increased in this country
- How to increase civility in political discussions (in families or more generally)

NARROWING A GENERAL TOPIC

HOW DO YOU KNOW WHEN YOU HAVE A NARROWED TOPIC?

A NARROWED TOPIC IS LINKED TO AN ISSUE OR CONTROVERSY THAT WILL INTEREST YOUR AUDIENCE

Given what you know about your audience, use your initial, broad research (as described on the previous page) to find possible areas that might be useful, surprising, or provocative to your readers.

For example, if you are writing about the 1960s for a class research paper, you probably already have some sense of how others in class think about what happened in the 1960s. If everyone else thinks of the 1960s in terms of free love and music, then imagine how you will catch their attention if you can narrow your topic to *How the current conservative movement in the United States is a response to the social movements of the 1960s.*

As you move forward in reading and thinking, keep in mind that your initial ideas might change. All writers experience changes in their thinking as they learn more—and that is how it should be!

TIP

KEEP YOUR MIND OPEN

The more widely you look for information on a topic, the more likely you are to be surprised by what you find—and being surprised helps you be more interested and engaged and thus write more strongly.

Also, don't look only for sources that support your initial thoughts on a topic. Seek a range of positions so that you have the widest sense of how people are thinking—and so that you become as capacious a thinker as possible.

NARROWED TOPICS

A narrowed topic usually relates a general topic to specific places, times, actions, or groups of people.

GENERAL TOPIC	NARROWED TOPIC
women in the workforce →	the number of women in politics in the United States the last fifty years
advertising →	advertising and democratic participation in the United States
water as a resource →	water management in the Middle East
the Internet →	how corporations shape Internet social networking sites
poetry →	poetry written by people rooted in two cultures
racial profiling →	racial profiling and law-enforcement policies
global climate change →	elementary school education about climate change
sports →	college sports training and men's body images
religion →	the tax-exempt status of churches and their role in political races
technology →	the development of the compass, gunpowder, and papermaking in China
the Civil Rights Movement →	organizational strategies of the Civil Rights Movement

USE GOOGLE TO TEST YOUR TOPIC

TIP

In two ways Google can tell you if your topic is narrow enough:

- If the first websites that Google suggests come from scholarly, academic sources or respected organizations, your topic is narrow enough to be worth further research. (Pages 55 and 60–65 can help you determine if the sources are scholarly.)
- If Google responds with hundreds of millions of possible links, your topic is not yet focused enough.

NARROWING A GENERAL TOPIC
OTHER STRATEGIES FOR NARROWING A TOPIC

BRAINSTORMING

Brainstorming lets your brain run loose. You just let your brain jump from one idea to whatever next idea appears.

Coming up with ideas that will engage an audience can sometimes happen when you think hard and with focus; other times you need simply to let your brain's associative abilities do what they will.

You can brainstorm alone or with others; with others, you have the advantage of playing off each other's ideas. In either case, work in the same way:

- Set aside five or ten minutes.

- Say your topic out loud, and then say out loud—but also write down—every single thought that comes to mind in response.

- Do not stop to judge. If an idea seems too absurd to record, record it nonetheless: It might lead to something you can use. (And let yourself laugh: The energy of laughter is part of what makes brainstorming work.)

- If you hit a dead end, go back to an earlier term and see what other associations you have with it. (Try thinking of synonyms or opposites to spur your thinking—or come up with as absurd an association as you can.)

- At the end, read your ideas out loud to see if anything else comes up. If one or two ideas seem useful or potentially fruitful now, hold on to them. Otherwise, put the list aside and look at it the next day.

FREEWRITING

Freewriting is a little like brainstorming on paper. Give yourself five minutes and just write on your topic. As with brainstorming, record whatever ideas come up: Let one idea lead into the next without stopping.

Freewriting becomes easier the more you do it; it's a good way to help your mind run more easily, and it's a practice of many successful writers.

At the end of your time limit, read over what you have written to see if any ideas stand out for development. If not, put the writing aside and go back to it later.

CLUSTERING

Like brainstorming and freewriting, clustering is a strategy for making your ideas visible to yourself—but instead of writing, you draw. Clustering helps you see relations among ideas, which can help you see arrangements you might use later when you start writing a paper.

To cluster, write your topic in the center of a page. Around the topic, write down as many related ideas as you can. Turn to each of those related ideas, and see what other ideas relate to them. If one idea suggests a chain of related ideas, follow it.

Below is the cluster Shelly made in thinking about body image, which led her to think about how the media shape our sense of our bodies and how our body image affects our health; by doing this clustering, and thinking about how pro ana sites work, she came up with this narrowed topic: *the effects of body images in the media produced for you by others—and of body images you produce about yourself.*

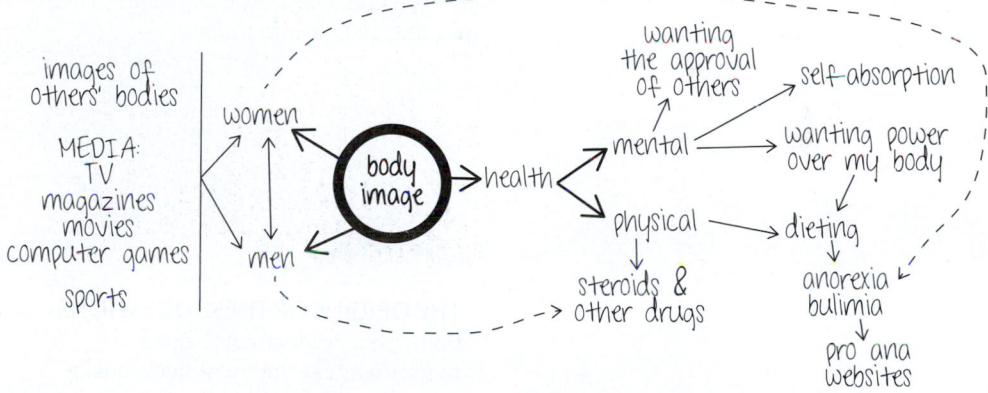

USE IDEA MAPPING TOOLS

There are free online applications that can help you cluster ideas (in information design and management, clustering is called *mapping*): try FreeMind <http://freemind.sourceforge.net/wiki/index.php/Main_Page> or CMapTools <http://cmap.ihmc.us/>.

QUESTIONS TO GUIDE RESEARCH

Once you have a narrowed topic, you can go online or to the library to start more focused research. But if you take time to carry out one more step—generating questions to help guide your research—you will have a better sense of what you need to find to write a solid paper and where to look for that information.

On the next page, we show you one way to generate questions on your topic. Doing this can help you see:

- areas of research you might not have considered otherwise.
- possible ways for shaping your purpose.
- questions your audience might have that you need to address.
- the specific research directions you need to take.

You may not need to address all the questions you develop, but you won't know for sure until you start using them to help you find and dig into sources.

THE ORIGINS OF THESE QUESTIONS

Courtroom observations helped rhetoricians see that most questions fit into a set of categories. Rhetoricians called the categories *stases*, the plural of *stasis*, the Greek word for *place*. Stasis questions—like the ones to the right— help communicators determine what is at stake in any argument and the complexity of what is at stake.

KINDS OF QUESTIONS TO GUIDE RESEARCH

These categories can help you not only invent questions to ask but also determine which questions are likely to lead to rich research, as we show on the next pages.

QUESTIONS OF FACT

- What happened?
- Who was involved?
- Where did it happen?
- When did it happen?

QUESTIONS OF DEFINITION

- What is the thing or issue under discussion? What is it made of?
- What is the expected way (in the particular context) of using the thing, word, title, or expression?

QUESTIONS OF INTERPRETATION

- How do we understand and make sense of what happened?
- How are we to incorporate facts and definitions into a story that makes sense to us?

QUESTIONS OF CONSEQUENCE

- What caused what happened? What changes—to which persons, processes, or objects—led to the issue at hand?
- What are the effects of what happened? What changes might result from what happened?

QUESTIONS OF VALUE

- Is what is at stake good, useful, worthy of praise, or worthy of blame?
- What audiences will value the matter at hand? What do people say about the issue?
- Which of our (or our audience's) values are called upon as we make judgments about what happened?

QUESTIONS OF POLICY

- Given the circumstances, what should we do?
- Given the circumstances, what rules should we make or enforce?
- Given the circumstances, what laws should we write?

QUESTIONS TO GUIDE RESEARCH

USING QUESTIONS TO GUIDE YOUR SEARCH FOR SOURCES

USING THE QUESTIONS

Use the research questions to generate as many questions as you can on your narrowed topic. Doing this helps you understand questions your audience might have, which are questions your research and composing need to answer. Generating questions also helps you see what research to pursue to gain authority on your topic.

Finally, generating questions helps you see whether your initial opinion on your topic is sufficiently informed. You learn whether your opinions really are the ones you want to hold.

When you use the research questions to generate more questions, just let the questions come: Let one question lead to another. The more questions you can generate, the more you will have a sense of what further research you need to do.

→ Pages 58-59 show how your questions help you determine useful kinds of sources.

→ In this section we've seen Harley start to narrow a topic on political discussions; on page 95 you can see how Harley uses these questions to help her find sources.

DEVELOPING SEARCH TERMS FOR ONLINE SEARCHES

From your questions, pick out words and phrases directly related to your topic, and use them in searching for sources.

The terms below come from all the questions Kwan generated to the right:

stem cell, stem-cell research, viable stem-cell treatments, stem-cell treatments, stem-cell controversy, stem-cell results, paralysis, stem-cell therapies, consequences of stem-cell research, stem-cell policy, stem-cell research in Europe, stem-cell research in Asia

USING THE RESEARCH QUESTIONS, EXAMPLE 1

Kwan chose the topic of stem-cell research for an argumentative research paper, and he has narrowed his topic to the possibilities of stem-cell treatments for paralysis. Using the research questions, he brainstorms the following questions:

QUESTIONS OF FACT
What are researchers able to do now with stem cells to help paralysis? How far away do viable stem-cell treatments seem?

QUESTIONS OF DEFINITION
What are stem cells? What is stem-cell research? What is paralysis?

QUESTIONS OF INTERPRETATION
Do stem-cell treatments cure paralysis? Should paralysis always be treated?

QUESTIONS OF CONSEQUENCE
What happens to people who have stem-cell treatments for paralysis? How do stem-cell therapies work in treating paralysis?

QUESTIONS OF VALUE
Who thinks stem-cell research is worthwhile, and who doesn't? Why? What values are called upon as people make judgments about stem-cell research? What values aren't called upon? Are the bad results of stem-cell research offset by the good results?

QUESTIONS OF POLICY
What are the different policies we could have toward stem-cell research and paralysis? What are the policies of other countries on stem-cell research?

USING THE RESEARCH QUESTIONS, EXAMPLE 2

Eva chose the topic of road building, and has narrowed her topic to the effects of road building on rural communities. Using the research questions, she brainstorms the following questions:

Questions of Fact
Who decides where and when roads are built? How expensive is a new road? What affects the cost of a new road? Who pays for roads in rural areas?

Questions of Definition
What counts as a new road? What, really, is a road?

Questions of Interpretation
What do new roads bring to a rural community? What do existing roads bring to a rural community?

Questions of Consequence
What happens when a new road is built in a rural community—or not? Who or what is affected when a new road is built, and how?

Questions of Value
Are the consequences of new roads good—or bad—for a community? For whom or what are new roads good or bad (including nonhumans)? What values are at stake in making judgments about whether roads are good or bad? What values underlie the different laws that exist about road building?

Questions of Policy
What laws already exist about the development of roads? How have laws and policies changed over the years?

KINDS OF SOURCES

You have a narrowed topic and a series of questions that can help you learn more about your topic in a focused and organized manner.

Now you need to determine where to look to find answers to your questions.

UNDERSTANDING DIFFERENT KINDS OF SOURCES

Sources are the texts—written, filmed, videotaped, recorded, photographed—from which you learn about your topic.

As you seek sources, seek a range of different ones—whose composers hold differing opinions—to help you learn a range of possible positions on your topic and so to push your own thinking and opinions.

Sometimes sources provide evidence and examples to use in your writing or other composing.

PRIMARY AND SECONDARY SOURCES

To determine whether a source is primary or secondary, ask yourself if you are reading someone's original words or reading *about* the person. In a paper about Ida B. Wells, for example, speeches and books by Wells are primary sources; commentary about Wells by other writers is a secondary source.

Examples of primary sources:

- Novels, poems, autobiographies, speeches, letters, diaries, blogs, e-mails.
- Eyewitness accounts of events, including written, filmed, and photographed accounts.
- Field research (surveys, observations, and interviews) that *you* conduct.

Examples of secondary sources:

- Biographies.
- Encyclopedias.
- News articles about events.
- Reviews of novels, poems, autobiographies, speeches, letters, diaries, e-mails, blogs.

Knowing the distinction between primary and secondary sources helps you seek out both kinds and cover all the bases in your research. For example, if you find a useful statistic in a newspaper (a secondary source), chances are the origins of the statistic and evidence supporting it will not be given; searching online and finding the primary source where the statistic was reported, with evidence, allows you to cite the most authoritative evidence.

SCHOLARLY AND POPULAR SOURCES

This distinction depends on the authority and reliability of the information in the sources.

In scholarly sources:

- Authors have academic credentials: they have studied the topic in depth and know how to weigh and present different sides of the topic.
- The sources used by the writer are listed so readers can check that the sources have been used fairly.
- Topics are examined at length.
- Their purpose is to spread knowledge. These sources are usually found in libraries; they contain little or no advertising.

In popular sources:

- Authors are journalists or reporters, usually without academic study in the topic.
- The sources are not listed.
- Topics are addressed briefly.
- Their purpose is to be quickly informative or entertaining. You find these sources at newsstands and stores, and they contain advertising.

Starting research with a range of popular sources can help you quickly get an overview of available perspectives on a topic. But the expectation for an authoritative research paper is that most of its sources are academic.

KINDS OF RESEARCH

Most research projects require you to do different kinds of research, seeking sources in different places and seeking different kinds of sources. On these two pages we describe general categories for kinds of research you can do.

ONLINE RESEARCH

Not everything is online—nor does Google link to all that is online.

Unspecialized search engines—like Google, Bing, and Yahoo!—are useful for the following, usually early in research:

- Developing a sense of popular opinion on topics.
- Finding popular sources on topics, in both popular magazines and in blogs.
- Finding person-on-the-street quotations.
- Finding links or references to academic sources.

Specialized search engines provide access to material to which popular search engines often don't have access. Google has the specialized search engines Google Scholar and Google Books, and your library probably provides you with search engines linked to databases of journals.

→ See page 72 for descriptions of two other specialized search directories; see pages 80–87 to learn how to use your library's databases.

LIBRARY RESEARCH

You can use most libraries these days in two ways: in person and online.

We encourage you to get to know, in person, a librarian. Being able to have a conversation with a librarian about a topic can help you open up new approaches you might not have considered on your own. A reference librarian can help you with both in-library and online uses of the library's resources.

In-library resources include the obvious books, journals, and reference materials. But some libraries also house historical or art archives, as well as map and government repositories. If you do not know how to find these—or even what materials are available—see if your library gives tours or workshops; knowing what is in your library can help you find creative possibilities for research.

Online library resources can include catalogs of the library's holdings and databases of newspapers and journals from across disciplines. (Later we discuss how to use such databases.)

Finally, libraries usually give you access to interlibrary loans: If your library does not have a book or journal you need, your librarians can usually order it for you from another library.

FIELD RESEARCH

Interviews, observations, and surveys are all forms of research. To carry them out, you have to go out **into the field**—which could be a suburban strip mall, urban nonprofit organization, classroom, or rural farm.

→ For more on carrying out interviews, observations, and surveys, see page 168.

RESEARCH IN ARCHIVES AND SPECIAL LIBRARY COLLECTIONS

Physical archives include local history associations or museums that have collections of old manuscripts, comics, furniture, clothing, or other items. Such archives are usually private or provide limited access in order to protect their collections; they have different access policies that you can learn by contacting the archive. To find archives that might be close to you, do an online search using *archive* or *museum* as a keyword along with the kind of information you seek, look in the phone book under *museum*, or ask a librarian.

Virtual archives are online collections of digitized materials such as letters, posters, photographs, or speeches.

Many libraries also have special collections of paintings and prints, films and video, maps, and/or sound recordings—often not digitized. If you are writing on a topic that has a historical dimension, or are just curious, such special collections can be fascinating.

→ For more information on finding and using both physical and virtual archives and special collections, see pages 88–89.

USE VISUAL AND AUDIO SOURCES

With any of the research sites we mention here you can do *visual research* and *aural research*. Almost all the kinds of research we mention access not only print sources but also photographs, videos, speeches, and historic printed matter such as brochures and posters. If any visual or aural sources can support your research, search for them online and ask librarians about them.

WHERE TO RESEARCH

WHAT SOURCES AND RESEARCH WILL HELP?

Almost all research writing starts by grounding its readers in definitions and facts on the topic, and then focuses on interpretation of the issue to show a problem (which could be a consequence of an event) or to argue for certain policies. Once you have focused questions, use this chart to choose kinds of sources and research.

	primary source	secondary source	academic sources	popular source	online research	library research	archival research	field research
QUESTIONS OF FACT								
encyclopedias, atlases, and other reference works		✓	✓		✓	✓		
statistics	✓				✓			
government or organizational documents	✓				✓		✓	
firsthand accounts (interviews, autobiographies)	✓							✓
photographs of events	✓						✓	
trial transcripts	✓						✓	
surveys and polls	✓				✓			✓
QUESTIONS OF DEFINITION								
dictionaries (for general audiences as well as specialized)		✓	✓	✓	✓	✓		
academic journal articles		✓				✓		
QUESTIONS OF INTERPRETATION								
editorials and opinion pieces	✓			✓		✓		
partisan news sources		✓		✓	✓			
people's stories	✓				✓		✓	✓
artwork (movies, novels, short stories, documentary photography)	✓				✓	✓	✓	
position statements		✓		✓	✓			
biographies		✓	✓		✓		✓	
academic journal articles		✓	✓		✓			

As you move forward with a research project and develop a thesis statement, you will know which of these categories of questions most guides your work. This will help you know where to focus your last research efforts as you gather the last evidence to support your work.

→ To develop a thesis statement, see pages 160–161 and 222–225.

→ To see how a thesis statement can help you shape a paper and help you determine the very last bits of evidence gathering to do, see pages 222–225.

	primary source	secondary source	academic sources	popular source	online research	library research	archival research	field research
QUESTIONS OF CONSEQUENCE								
statistics	✓		✓	✓	✓	✓		
historical accounts	✓				✓		✓	
photographs of the aftermaths of events		✓			✓		✓	
academic journal articles		✓	✓			✓		
the items listed under INTERPRETATION								
QUESTIONS OF VALUE								
organizational mission statements	✓				✓		✓	✓
voting results	✓				✓	✓		
surveys and polls	✓				✓	✓		
position statements	✓						✓	✓
academic journal articles		✓	✓			✓		
the items listed under INTERPRETATION								
QUESTIONS OF POLICY								
government decisions	✓				✓	✓	✓	
organizational policy statements and decisions	✓					✓	✓	✓
business records	✓					✓	✓	✓
trial decisions	✓				✓		✓	
academic journal articles		✓	✓	✓		✓		

CHOOSING SOURCES
THAT HELP YOUR RESEARCH AND SUPPORT YOUR ARGUMENTS

Compositions that audiences take seriously offer as much support as possible from a range of sources. The kinds of sources appropriate for your argument depend on the argument you are making, the audience to whom you make the argument, and your context.

CHOOSING SOURCES WISELY

- MOST IMPORTANT: Teachers want you to compare and think about a range of positions on your topic—so search for sources that present such a range. Thinking across many possible positions gives you background for contributing to community and civic decision making.

- Sometimes teachers give you guidelines for how many sources to cite. If you have not been given guidelines and you want to indicate that you have considered a good range of ideas, eight or more sources is reasonable for a 7- to 10-page research paper.

- Understand that—to find the right sources—you probably need to find and read many more sources than you will finally cite in your writing.

- Generally, use only one or two popular sources, perhaps to present the voices and opinions of others that show why an issue is a problem. The other sources should be academic, from journal articles and books.

- Avoid using only one kind of source. Having all your citations come from one magazine or reference work (whether that work is in print or online) indicates you have not done thorough research.

CHARACTERISTICS THAT DISTINGUISH SOURCES

On the next pages, we describe different commonly used sources so you can judge their appropriateness for your purposes. We use the following criteria:

- **AUDIENCE**

  If a source is aimed at a general audience, the information it offers will generally be broad but shallow.

  Sources for academic or other specialized audiences will usually be more developed and better supported.

- **WRITERS**

  When writers are paid by the company or organization for which they write, they might offer opinions and information that are in line only with the goals of the company or organization.

- **APPEARANCE**

  A professional appearance is a reflection of an overall ethic of care and attention to detail.

- **FORMAT**

  If information is presented alongside advertisements, it can mean the advertiser had some say in what information is presented.

- **LANGUAGE**

  Sources using informal language are for general audiences; although they are easier to read, such sources are considered less authoritative than sources that use the language and vocabulary of specialized disciplines.

- **REVIEW**

  If a source's information is reviewed by people who are unpaid and have no connection with the publisher, readers will grant it more authority.

- **BIBLIOGRAPHY**

  Your readers will consider most authoritative sources that themselves have a works cited list or other kind of bibliography, showing the source's sources.

- **WHEN TO USE**

  We make general suggestions for using sources in ways readers will trust—but keep in mind that you always need to consider your readers, your purposes, and your context in choosing your sources and how you use them. If you have questions about a source, ask several people from your intended audience how they would respond to your use of the source.

OTHER KINDS OF SOURCES

Almost any composition can be a source: You can cite song lyrics to show how hip-hop artists interpret current events differently than mainstream media; you can use a computer game screenshot to discuss representations of women; you can interview a neighbor about the history of local development. We cannot possibly list all the sources you might use because what you use is limited only by what will support your purposes given your audience.

THERE IS NO ONE PERFECT SOURCE

Do not search for sources thinking that there will be one—or even three—perfect sources that will answer all your questions. You want sources to encourage your thinking, so you want a range of sources that help you approach your project from multiple angles.

CHOOSING SOURCES
PRINT

	WHEN TO USE	AUDIENCE	WRITERS
PERIODICALS			
DAILY NEWSPAPERS	Examples and evidence from newspapers can be appropriate if you write for a general audience.	General public	Newspaper writers are paid; their credentials are rarely given, so you don't know their background.
POPULAR MAGAZINES	Examples and evidence from popular magazines can be appropriate if you write for a general audience.	General public	Employees of the magazines or freelancers are paid to write; their credentials may or may not be given.
ACADEMIC JOURNALS	Evidence from academic journals can help make your arguments as well-informed as possible.	Researchers, scholars, specialists	Experts or specialists write for no pay; their credentials are usually provided.
BOOKS			
NONFICTION BOOKS	Because of the publishing review process, such books tend to have authority for readers.	General public or specialists	Publishing companies solicit writers or accept proposals and choose what to publish.
REFERENCE BOOKS	Use these books to provide definitions of words or terms unfamiliar to an audience.	General public or specialists	Authorities on a topic usually write entries in reference books.
EDITED COLLECTIONS	Because of the publishing review process, such books tend to have authority for readers.	General public; specialists; scholars	Publishing companies solicit writers or accept proposals and choose what to publish.
CORPORATE AUTHOR	A company's reputation on the publication topic will shape its authority with your readers.	General public or specialists	Company employees, or people hired specifically for a project, produce these texts.
GOVERNMENT AUTHOR	Use such texts when your audience will accept the government's authority on your topic.	General public or specialists	Writers can be government employees or people hired because of their expertise.

→ See pages 54–55 if you want to learn more about these kinds of sources.

REVIEW	BIBLIOGRAPHY	EXAMPLES
Articles are assigned to writers and reviewed for content and mechanics by editors.	References might be mentioned, but there are few ways for readers to check sources.	*New York Times* *Chicago Tribune* *Kansas City Star* *Los Angeles Times*
Articles are assigned to writers and reviewed for content and mechanics by editors.	References might be mentioned, but there are few ways for readers to check sources.	*Newsweek* *Rolling Stone* *Harper's* *Sports Illustrated*
Reviewers who are recognized experts in the field review articles for no pay.	Articles end with lists of references (and/or contain footnotes or endnotes) so readers can check the sources.	*College English* *Computer Graphics Forum* *World Journal of Microbiology and Biotechnology* *European Journal of Public Health*
Publishers approve the writing and may arrange for fact-checking.	References are usually mentioned.	*The Mind's Eye* *Where Good Ideas Come From: The Natural History of Innovation* *Central Works in Technical Communication*
Publishers approve the writing and may arrange for fact-checking.	References are usually mentioned.	*World Book* *Longman Dictionary of Contemporary English* *Encyclopedia of China*
Publishers approve the writing and may arrange for fact-checking.	References are usually mentioned.	*The Best American Nonrequired Reading 2015* *Comics as Philosophy* *Learning from the Histories of Rhetoric: Essays in Honor of Winifred Bryan Horner*
Companies *may* set up reviews.	References *may* be mentioned.	*Mountains to Marshes: The Nature Conservancy Preserves in Maryland* *Publication Manual of the American Psychological Association*
The writing can be reviewed in the same or other government agencies.	References *may* be mentioned.	*Washington State Building Code* *Digest of Supreme Court Decisions Interpreting the National Prohibition Act and Willis-Campbell Act*

WEBPAGES AND OTHER ONLINE SOURCES

	WHEN TO USE	AUDIENCE	WRITERS
PERSONAL WEBPAGES AND BLOGS	If the writer is an expert on the topic, you can use the writing to support your points.	General public or readers interested in the particular topic of the pages.	Such pages can be produced by anyone.
GROUP BLOGS	If the writers are respected in their fields, citing their opinions can support your writing.	Group blogs usually focus on a shared set of interests; the audience will be drawn to those interests.	These writers want to be read; they tend to choose each other carefully on the quality of their writing.
CORPORATE WEBSITES AND BLOGS	These blogs are usually promotional; their words can be used to inform about the company.	General public, consumers, people interested in the topics covered.	Employees of the company or freelancers.
WEBSITES FOR NONPROFIT ORGANIZATIONS	Such websites can provide facts and figures as well as descriptions of the organizations.	Anyone interested in the work of the organization; organizations want to inform and attract donors.	Employees of the organization or freelancers.
GOVERNMENT WEBSITES	Use government websites for statistics or wording of policies.	General public; specialists looking for information the government compiles.	Government employees or freelancers.
ONLINE PERIODICALS	Use online periodicals as you would use their print counterparts, as described on pages 62–63.	The audience can be general or technical, depending on the periodical.	Writers can be paid employees, freelancers, or volunteers.
ONLINE NEWSPAPERS	Examples and evidence from newspapers can be appropriate if you write for a general audience.	General public	Newspaper writers are paid; their credentials are rarely given, so you don't know their background.
DATABASES OF JOURNALS	Any time you want to find a generally credible range of articles to help you narrow your topic or develop your arguments, use these databases, which should be available through your school library.		
WIKIPEDIA	*Wikipedia* is a particular kind of online reference work, developed by volunteers who write and edit on topics of interest to them. Teachers consider *Wikipedia* controversial because the entries can be shaped by nonspecialists and because there are no easy ways to check the authority of entries.		

→ See pages 54–55 to learn more about these categories of sources.

REVIEW	BIBLIOGRAPHY	EXAMPLES
No one reviews the materials except the writer.	Writings may be accompanied by source links or links to supporting webpages.	*stevenberlinjohnson.com* *camillaengman.com* *digbysblog.blogspot.com*
The writers on such blogs can run their writing by each other.	Writings may be accompanied by source links or links to supporting webpages.	*crookedtimber.org* *boingboing.net* *metafilter.com*
Company websites may be reviewed by lawyers to protect the company from lawsuits.	Writings may be accompanied by source links or links to supporting webpages.	*apple.com* *googleblog.blogspot.com* *panelfly.com*
The organization approves what is on the website.	Writings may be accompanied by source links or links to supporting webpages.	*anacostiaws.org* *commongoodradio.org* *standnow.org*
Government websites adhere to governmental accessibility and writing policies.	Writings may be accompanied by source links or links to supporting webpages.	*ca.gov* *nyc.gov* *whitehouse.gov*
Such websites might have review policies, which will vary.	Academic periodicals will provide sources; others may or may not.	*time.com* *americanscientist.org* *utne.com*
Articles are assigned to writers and reviewed for content and mechanics by editors.	References might be mentioned, but there are few ways for readers to check sources.	*nytimes.com* *chicagotribune.com* *mininggazette.com*

Unless you are writing about databases, you are not going to cite them; you will instead use them to find periodical articles—and so their authority is not at issue.

→ See pages 80–87 to learn more about using databases to find journals.

Wikipedia can be useful in the early stages of research, when you seek quick and preliminary information. You can learn how others think on a topic and might find links to more authoritative sources. Citing *Wikipedia* in a works-cited or reference list, however, shows readers that you have only done quick and shallow research.

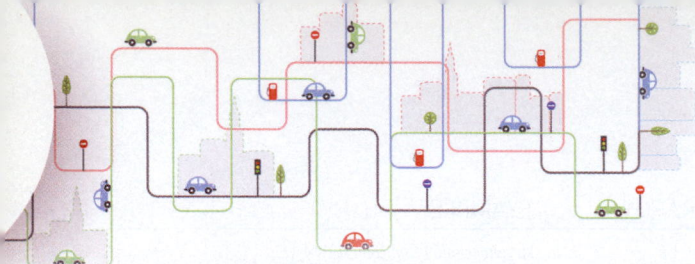

FINDING SOURCES

ONE PROCESS FOR FINDING PUBLISHED POPULAR AND ACADEMIC SOURCES

On the opposite page we outline one process for finding popular and academic sources. For this process to work well for you, you need to have your initial search terms and some sense of the kinds of sources you need.

We recommend starting online and then moving to your school library's resources. Many researchers work this way because using general search engines like Google or Bing is quick and brings up both popular sources as well as titles of academic sources: This is an easy way to get a sense of a range of positions people have on a topic but also a way to find titles of academic sources that you can then seek in a library.

→ Pages 60–65 help you determine the kinds of sources useful for your project.

DO YOU SEEK SOURCES IN ARCHIVES OR SPECIAL COLLECTIONS?
→ See pages 88–89.

ARE YOU CARRYING OUT FIELD RESEARCH?
→ See pages 90–91 and 168.

1 SEARCH ONLINE

THEN

Using the advice on pages 68–73 for online searches, enter your search terms (and their variations) in search engines like Google or Bing to find:

- **Popular (online) sources**
  newspapers
  magazines
  blogs
  organizational reports
  government websites
  videos
  photographs and illustrations

- **Titles of academic sources**
  journal articles
  books
  Because you will rarely find these actual sources on the public internet, be sure to record all source information you do find; then you can find the source in your school library.

Given the particulars of your research project, it might help you to look at the specialized websites listed on pages 72–73.

2 SEARCH USING YOUR LIBRARY'S RESOURCES

Go to your library's webpage and carry out each step below:

> **Search in the library's catalog for any books whose titles you found in your online search. Also search for books that might not have come up in your online search.**
>
> → Page 77 describes how to use a library's online catalog.

> **Use the library's database search features to look for the journal articles whose titles you found in your online search.**
>
> → Pages 78–85 describes how to do this.
> → Page 80 describes what databases are.

> **Use the library's database subject search features to look for journal articles (and other academic and popular sources) that didn't show up in your online search.**
>
> → page 82 describes how to do this.
> → Page 80 describes what databases are.

> **Search using specific databases if you need to.**
>
> → Page 83 describes how to do this.
> → Page 80 describes what databases are.

AS YOU FIND SOURCES...
EVALUATE THEM
→ Pages 102–115 describe how to do this.

AS YOU FIND SOURCES...
KEEP TRACK OF THEM
→ Pages 140–141 describe how to do this.

FINDING SOURCES
SEARCHING ONLINE

HAVING USED GOOGLE BEFORE ISN'T ENOUGH FOR KNOWING HOW TO DO ACADEMIC SEARCHES

A recent study by librarians and anthropologists found that many college students don't know how to use online search tools to find the best academic sources. Students often type just one or two words into Google or Bing—and then get frustrated because too many (or too few) responses appear.

By interviewing students and watching them search for sources, the researchers found that students did not know what they did not know. Students did not know:

- how search engines can help them do a focused search.

- that specialized search engines like Google Scholar and Google Books exist.

- how to narrow their search terms to find the most helpful sources and information.

- what databases to search for the most helpful sources and information.

- how to judge the relevance and credibility of what they found online.

- that librarians are willing to help them carry out helpful online searches.

ABOUT SEARCH ENGINES AND SEARCH DIRECTORIES

Search engines access large databases of websites; the information in the databases has been collected by automated programs called **spiders** or **robots**. Within the databases, the websites are indexed: Their words and phrases are compiled into lists structured for easy computer searching.

When you enter search terms into a search engine, it compares your terms to its indexes, and returns to you a list of websites containing your terms.

Search directories are similar to search engines because each compiles databases of websites—but a directory only searches through sites already inspected for their relevance.

Because each search engine or directory searches the Web differently, and indexes its terms differently, different search tools return different results for the same search terms—so using more than one search tool will help you find the most useful sources.

PREPARING TO SEARCH

HAVE SEARCH TERMS

If you generated research questions as we described on pages 50–53, you have multiple words and phrases to use in your searches—as we describe on the next pages.

DEVELOP ALTERNATE SEARCH TERMS

Daniel Russell, who works at Google, says of successful searches, "Part of the skill here is being fascinated about language. You've got to think about equivalent terms." If you cannot readily think up synonyms for the key terms of your narrowed topic, use a thesaurus, or ask someone else what other terms come to mind for your topic. You can also use reverse dictionaries: These are online resources into which you can type a concept and get back a list of words and phrases related to the concept. The more terms you can use, the more likely you are to find helpful sources.

SET ASIDE TIME TO SEARCH OVER SEVERAL DAYS

You need to search in multiple online places, using Google and its specialized tools but also your library's tools. You will also turn up new search terms and develop new search questions as you start to read through what you find.

BREATHE

Research succeeds not only in a final paper but in ideas that spark you to think. Stay open to finding ideas that tease you into engaging with ideas.

USING A SEARCH ENGINE SMARTLY

Since Part 2, we've been following Harley as she composes a paper on civility. Harley's questions prepare her for an online search. Below, we show how to use the particular logics of Google to carry out very focused searches—but every search engine offers approaches for such focusing of searches. Each search below helped Harley find useful searches and challenging ideas.

> site:nytimes.com   ~civility   2010..2015

site: tells Google to search on the specific website you name; be sure you type in the exact name of the site. Harley searches the *New York Times* because it is a respected newspaper.

~ (the tilde character, at the top left of your keyboard) instructs Google to search using not only the word typed after the tilde but also related terms like *politeness*, *decorum*, and so on.

The two periods between the dates tells Google to search between this date range—so you can do current searches or searches in a focused time frame.

> filetype:pdf intitle:civility polarization

filetype: tells Google to search for that specific kind of file only.

intitle: tells Google to search for documents that have that exact word in their title.

"polarization" at the end adds one of Harley's terms to guarantee the word will be on any page returned from the search.

> "civility is * in a *"

" " —putting any expression within quotations tells Google to find pages that have exactly that expression. First, Harley did a search for "civility is," which helped her find definitions; then she did a search with asterisks, as shown to the right, and found still more useful sites.

* — the asterisk is a "wildcard": It tells Google to find pages that use the this phrase with any words appearing where the asterisks are.

OTHER STRATEGIES FOR PRODUCTIVE ONLINE SEARCHES

BE SPECIFIC

A one-word search is usually useless, especially if the word is broad, like **cars**. Try two words and then three: **cars fuel** or **cars ethanol**—and then **cars alternate fuels**.

In library catalogs and databases, you can enter the key terms from your narrowed topic; you can also enter any synonyms for those terms.

In search engines like Google, you can enter the key terms from your narrowed topic—but you can also enter a question such as "Does ethanol provide better mileage than a hybrid car?" and receive the most focused information possible from the websites to which Google has access. Use the research questions you generated for such searches.

THINK ABOUT HOW SOMEONE ELSE WOULD WRITE ABOUT YOUR TOPIC

Successful searches depend on you finding your way to what other people have written in the areas that matter to you.

USE THE SEARCH ENGINE'S HELP TIPS AND ADVANCED SEARCH FEATURES

All search engines—the library's online catalog, a library database, or a general search engine—have a link to help or usage tips. These tips help you learn how to do a search for sources that contain a very specific phrase, for example, or to search using synonyms, or to search for sources within a particular time frame. Most search engines will also help you limit your search just to newspapers, peer-reviewed journal articles, or books.

USE A FAMILIAR SEARCH ENGINE TO FIND SOURCES YOU CAN THEN OBTAIN IN A MORE SPECIALIZED SEARCH ENGINE

Many people, including faculty, first use Google to find sources and then check to see if their library has them. For example, Google Scholar might turn up a reference to a useful-looking academic article; into your library's journal database you can then enter the journal name and article title to access the article in PDF form. (Similarly, some researchers use Amazon to find books because they can usually read some of the book and check reviews. If the book looks useful, they will then check their library.)

DO A PRELIMINARY EVALUATION OF SOURCES AS YOU FIND THEM

In Part 4 (see pages 102–115), we show how to evaluate sources for relevance and credibility, including checking the URL for what it indicates about a source. Online searches sometimes turn up numerous potential sources, so you need to decide which will be most useful. With any source that looks intriguing to you, always ask whether it looks relevant and will add to or challenge your thinking; only then should you add it to your collection of sources to read more slowly and critically later.

PERSIST

The more creative you are with search terms and the longer you search, the more ideas you will find that push you to weigh differing opinions and so to write what others want to read. And be sure to look beyond the first page of results: Often, the exact information you need will appear not on the first but on a later page.

FINDING SOURCES
ONLINE RESOURCES

Your library probably has a listing of online materials, longer than what we can include here—but on these pages we include widely used sources.

ONLINE REFERENCES

BARTLEBY.COM
<http://www.bartleby.com/>
This site offers dictionaries, quotations, thesauruses, and usage and style references.

THE INTERNET MOVIE DATABASE
<http://us.imdb.com/>
If you research movies, this site offers information on actors, directors, and writers.

ONELOOK
<http://www.onelook.com/>
This website links to over 1,000 dictionaries.

WIKIPEDIA
<http://en.wikipedia.org/wiki/Main_Page>
Wikipedia is controversial for teachers precisely because anyone can edit and contribute. But you can start research with *Wikipedia*: It gives you openings into a topic; just know that using it as a source in an academic paper will not give your paper the expected authority.

TWO USEFUL SEARCH DIRECTORIES

ACADEMIC INDEX
<http://www.academicindex.net>
A librarian developed this tool, which searches databases of information on topics of academic interest and quality, compiled or recommended by librarians, teachers, and researchers.

IPL2: INFORMATION YOU CAN TRUST
<http://www.lii.org>
The site is hosted by Drexel University's College of Information Science & Technology together with a consortium of colleges and universities whose information science programs maintain the directory.

ONLINE NEWSPAPERS

If your local or national newspapers require you to subscribe, access them through your library's databases. For wider searches, try:

ONLINENEWSPAPERS.COM
<http://www.onlinenewspapers.com/>
This website gives access to newspapers around the world (many in English).

ONLINE (OR VIRTUAL) ARCHIVES
→ See page 89.

GOVERNMENT SOURCES

Every government agency has a website, so if you seek educational or agricultural information, for example, check the websites of the Departments of Education or Agriculture. Be mindful that some information is shaped by the political ends of the current administration.

THE U.S. CENSUS BUREAU
<http://www.census.gov/>
The Census Bureau compiles statistics on the U.S. population and economic systems.

MEDLINE PLUS
<http://www.nlm.nih.gov/medlineplus/>
The U.S. National Library of Medicine and the National Institutes of Health provide nonspecialist health and medical information.

CONGRESS
<https://www.congress.gov>
This website helps you search Congress's bills and resolutions.

THE WORLD FACTBOOK
<https://www.cia.gov/library/publications/the-world-factbook/index.html>
The U.S. Central Intelligence Agency offers geographic, government, and other information about every country in the world.

PHOTOGRAPHIC AND OTHER VISUAL RESOURCES

Many museums have photograph collections; many U.S. government agencies also have such collections. For example, check the Great Images in NASA Library *<http://grin.hq.nasa.gov/>* or the National Oceanic and Atmospheric Administration's Photo Library *<http://www.photolib.noaa.gov/>*.

NYPL DIGITAL
<http://digitalgallery.nypl.org/nypldigital/index.cfm>
The New York Public Library offers this resource of "800,000 images digitized from the … Library's vast collections, including illuminated manuscripts, historical maps, vintage posters, rare prints, photographs…"

PERRY-CASTAÑEDA MAP COLLECTION
<http://www.lib.utexas.edu/maps/map_sites/map_sites.html>
The library of the University of Texas at Austin has produced this long list of links to all kinds of maps.

PRINTS AND PHOTOGRAPHS ONLINE
<http://www.loc.gov/pictures/>
Part of the U.S. Library of Congress, this website gives access to posters, photographs, maps, magazines; many are copyright free, but you need to check each entry.

WIKIPEDIA: PUBLIC DOMAIN IMAGE RESOURCES
<http://en.wikipedia.org/wiki/Wikipedia:Public_domain_image_resources>
This webpage contains a long, categorized list of mostly public domain online photograph and other visual text resources.

→ To cite photographs and other visual texts in your writing, see pages 387–392 for MLA style and page 419 for APA style.

FINDING SOURCES
USING YOUR LIBRARY'S RESOURCES

WHY USE YOUR LIBRARY'S RESOURCES?

- **Not everything is on the Internet.** Your library has books, videos, maps, posters, and other resources you will not be able to find online.

- **Not everything on the Internet is free.** While you might be able to find useful references to books and articles online, you probably won't be able to read them online—or read them for free; your library will provide you these resources. Not only can you check out physical books, magazines, and videos, but you can access articles from thousands of journals

- **Taking your thinking abilities seriously means engaging with the best resources.** Your library resources have been chosen by people who have evaluated the resources for their quality. Engaging with the sources you can find in or through your library will help you do better in all your courses.

GET TO KNOW A LIBRARIAN

Librarians know a tremendous amount about different kinds of sources and how to find them, in print and online—and they like to be useful. Whenever you have research questions, ask your librarian. (And studies show that students who seek library help do better with research.)

You can help your librarian help you if you have specific questions. "I need statistics about how many manufacturing jobs have been lost in the U.S. in the past 25 years. What can you suggest for finding that information?" will help the librarian find you useful and specific information. "I want to learn something about job loss in the U.S." is less likely to do so.

FINDING SOURCES IN THE LIBRARY

You probably know that every item in the library—whether a book, a journal issue, a DVD, a map—has a unique call number attached to it. Each call number contains numbers and perhaps letters that indicate a general category into which the item fits (philosophy, history, science, and so on) and then indicates finer classifications, such as the history of a particular country.

Librarians place items on the library shelves in the order of their call numbers.

When you use a library's search systems (➜ see pages 76–79) and find items you want to evaluate, record the call number. Then ask a librarian where to find the call number on the shelf; there should also be maps of the library to help you find call numbers.

USING LIBRARY PRINT INDEXES

If you think information you need will be in a print source that was published before the rise of networked computers (or, roughly, before the early 1990s), then you might be successful with the print indexes in your library for journal articles, newspapers, and books in several subject areas. A reference librarian can help you find the appropriate index.

SPECIAL LIBRARY COLLECTIONS

➜ See pages 88–89 to read more about special collections—both print and digital—that your library might have.

WHEN YOU FIND ITEMS ON LIBRARY SHELVES YOU CAN FIND OTHER USEFUL ITEMS NEARBY

Precisely because library items are arranged by their call numbers (as we described above), that means that items arranged together are all on the same (or very similar) topics.

If you find on your library shelves a book or journal that looks useful, look at the items immediately around it on the shelves. Because those items will be on the same topic, you might easily find other sources that will be highly useful to your project.

ADVICE FROM ANOTHER STUDENT

"In my first-year writing class we had a session in the library—and the librarian who led the session was pretty funny and friendly. When I was working on my research paper and felt a little lost I happened to see him behind the counter. I went and asked him for some help and he was great. He showed me some tricks for looking things up in the system so that I didn't waste my time looking through long lists of useless stuff.

Since then, I always ask a librarian for help if I start to get frustrated or lost. They've all been incredibly nice and helpful—and I feel so much more confident now about my own abilities to find things."

FINDING SOURCES
USING YOUR LIBRARY'S ONLINE RESOURCES

GET TO KNOW YOUR LIBRARY'S WEBPAGES—ESPECIALLY THE FIRST!

Because college and university libraries design their websites for *their* students, faculty, and programs, no two school websites are the same; still, you can count on the website's first page giving you access to certain features as we describe below.

Such tools on the first page help you do basic—broad—searches; they also enable you to click through to tools for more focused searches, as we describe on the next pages.

USING THE LIBRARY'S FIRST WEBPAGE TO CARRY OUT BASIC SEARCHES

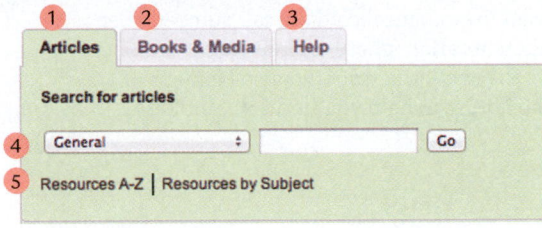

1 **Articles:** "Search for articles" searches databases for articles based on your search terms entered in the white box. These articles might be in journals the library has on its shelves or to which the library can give you electronic access.

2 **Books and media:** Enter title, keyword, or author terms for finding books *on the library's shelves.*

3 **Help:** Some libraries enable you to chat with a librarian or e-mail questions.

4 **Focus your search:** This pop-up enables you to choose databases related to academic topics—or you can do a search using several general databases. Under the Books tab, this pop-up enables you to search with keywords or a book's author or title.

5 **Resources A–Z and Resources by Subject:** Choose a database to search from an alphabetic list OR choose a subject and see useful databases on that subject.

USING LIBRARY CATALOGS

If you have narrowed search terms and questions, look for a **Catalog** or **Advanced Search** option on your library website's first page; such an option will lead you to a page with features similar to the box below. The features may appear in different places on screen or in checkboxes instead of pop-up menus—but they will work similarly. To prepare to use such a catalog, be sure you have a focused set of search terms, as we describe on page 52.

Portland State UNIVERSITY

Advanced Search   Search   Clear

Enter search terms in at least one of the fields below

1 Keyword: ⬍ [   ]

   Title: ⬍ [   ]

   Author: ⬍ [   ]

Popular Limits (optional)

2 ☐ Only return peer-reviewed articles

Narrow your search (optional)

3 Library: [Libraries Worldwide ⬍]
   Return only items owned by selected library(ies)

4 Year: [   ] to: [   ]
   Return only items published from   e.g. 1971   e.g. 1977

5 Audience: [Any Audience ⬍]
   Return only items for the audience

6 Content: [Any Content ⬍]
   Return only items with the content

7 Format: [All Formats ⬍]
   Return only items in the format

8 Language: [All Languages ⬍]
   Return only items in the language

1. **What search terms?** With these pop-up menus, you use a keyword or phrase or just the subject; you can combine searches, looking for a periodical title along with a word or phrase. Choose an option, then enter your terms in the boxes on the right.

2. **Peer-reviewed or not?** If you seek sources that have authority because they have been reviewed by authorities and found to be well-argued, use this option if it is available.

3. **Where to search?** Some university systems have multiple or specialized libraries; such an option allows you to search any of them—or, sometimes, to search libraries all over the world.

4. **What dates are most useful for your sources?** This option helps you search for sources published within a particular time frame, helpful if you need only very recent sources— or sources from years ago.

5. **What audience?** Such an option allows you to find sources written for young people or for adults.

6. **What content?** This option allows you to search specifically for fiction, nonfiction, biographies, or dissertations.

7. **What format?** If you know you want to search only for books, or for journals, or for video— or from a large range of other text formats— look for an option like this.

8. **What language?** To find sources in a specific language, use this option.

WHAT IS A "KEYWORD"?

A *keyword* is a word (usually a noun or noun phrase) that is significant to an article or book; this could be a word in a title or a word that appears often in a text. When digital records are created for texts, keywords are also recorded. Search tools in catalogs and databases can search the keywords just as they can search titles and author names.

FINDING SOURCES
GETTING YOUR HANDS ON ARTICLES YOU FIND THROUGH AN ONLINE SEARCH

Most scholarly journals (the kinds of journals you want to reference in your academic writing) are now online—but are not accessible through Google or other public Internet resources. You might find names and descriptions of potentially useful journal articles through a Google search, but then you will need to check whether your library has subscribed to the journal.

IF YOU FIND A JOURNAL OR ARTICLE REFERENCE THROUGH A GOOGLE SEARCH: HOW TO FIND THE SOURCE IN YOUR LIBRARY

As we described on pages 67 and 71, many researchers find references to specific articles or journals through Google but cannot access the article or journal on the public Internet.

If you do find a potential source this way, do the following:

1 Record the following information about the journal or article: the journal name, the author's name, article title, volume and issue numbers, and date. That is the most important information for finding the source through your library.

2 Go to your library's website. Look for a link named something like "Citation Linker" or "Looking for a Specific Journal?" That link will take you to a page with search tools looking something like those to the right.

3 Enter the information you recorded (or copy and paste from the webpage where you found the information). You do not need to enter information into each text field in search tools like these.

4 Click "Find It" or "Go."

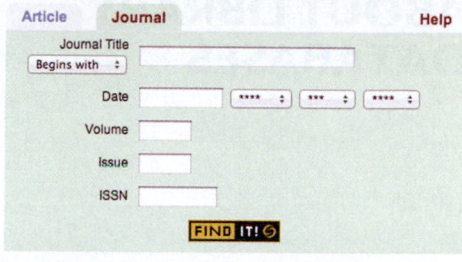

Citation Linker - Article

Article | Journal | Help

Exact Article Title

Journal Title | Begins with ⇕

Date | **** ⇕ | *** ⇕ | **** ⇕

Volume | Issue

Start page | End Page

ISSN | DOI

Author | Last Name | First Name | Initials

FIND IT! ⟳

Citation Linker - Journal

Article | Journal | Help

Journal Title | Begins with ⇕

Date | **** ⇕ | *** ⇕ | **** ⇕

Volume

Issue

ISSN

FIND IT! ⟳

Different library systems work slightly differently when you click "Find It" or "Go."

If your library has a subscription to the journal, you should be taken to another webpage that will give you the initial information about the article and either information for finding the journal on a library shelf or a link for retrieving the full-text article; you might also be taken to a webpage that gives you access to the journal and you will need to click links to get to the issue (and so the article) you need.

If your library does not have a subscription to the journal, you will be taken to a webpage telling you that the library doesn't have the journal; you can then probably order your article through Interlibrary Loan. If the webpage does not offer a link to Interlibrary Loan, ask a librarian for help.

RECORDING BIBLIOGRAPHIC INFORMATION

If you do an initial search on Google, be sure to record the bibliographic information of any potential sources you find: Record the title, author's name, and all information you find about the book, journal, or journal article. You need this information for finding the source in the library—as well as for your works-cited or references list in a research paper.

→ Part 3 explains what to record about any source you might use in your writing.

FINDING SOURCES
ABOUT LIBRARY DATABASES

WHAT IS A DATABASE?

When you have lots of data—journal articles, sports statistics, census numbers—it must be organized if it is to be searchable. In a computer database, journal articles can be organized by different tags—records—such as the title, author, date, keywords, and so on; the database software can then use your search terms to search through the records to find ones that match.

HOW LIBRARY DATABASES WORK FOR LIBRARIES—AND FOR YOU

Different companies build databases for academic journals, providing tags to the journal name and then to the particular volume and issue numbers and dates of each journal; they also record tags for each article title as well as the article's author(s) and any keywords. Different subscription services give access to databases in different disciplinary areas or to different newspapers. For example, some services provide access only to engineering or to humanities databases.

The databases sometimes provide only basic bibliographic information for a source—the article title, author's name(s), date and place of publication, and journal or periodical name—and an abstract giving a brief description. Once you find this information, you have to find out if your library has a subscription to the journal or periodical so that you can see the full article.

Often, however, these databases provide *full-text* versions of journal articles and periodicals you can read online. *Full-text* means that you can read the complete article online or download it, as a PDF, onto your computer to read later.

WHEN TO USE DATABASES— AND WHERE

Search using your library databases anytime you want to find the richest academic resources for your scholarly writing. You will find sources that you will not find through just a Google search—so after you carry out a general online search for sources, be sure to set aside several hours for using your library's databases.

Note, too, that almost all college and university libraries allow their patrons to search the databases from off-campus. That means you can do this research at home at any hour. (But do bring your search questions into the library to ask a librarian.)

HOW TO FIND YOUR LIBRARY'S DATABASES

More and more frequently now, using the search tools on the first page of your library's website will give you access to your library's databases without you even knowing it. Librarians work hard to make information access easy for you, and so they hide some of the more complex machinations that go on behind the scenes of their websites . . . but if you want to do thorough academic searches, you should know how to get to the databases directly.

To find the databases, look on the library's webpage for a link labeled something like *Search and Find*, *Research Tools and Collections*, *Resources for Research*, or, even, *Databases*.

Click the link, and then look for further links to *Databases A-Z* or *Databases by Subject*.

• ➤

Learn about the actual steps of using your library's databases on the next pages.

PATIENCE WITH DATABASES

Working with databases can help you find tremendously useful sources—but they require patience and persistence. Even teachers and graduate students can get frustrated with figuring out which databases to use and which search terms—but they persevere because they know that if they have patience and try different terms they will eventually find what they need.

FINDING SOURCES
USING LIBRARY DATABASES: DATABASES BY SUBJECT

SEARCHING JOURNAL DATABASES BY SUBJECT

There are hundreds of databases to which libraries can subscribe, and each database provides access to a shifting array of journals and other sources. Experienced researchers eventually learn which databases are most useful to them, but—as you start research—you can take advantage of your librarians' expertise: They have grouped databases by their usefulness to the research people carry out on your campus.

When you find databases listed by subject on your library's website, you will see a list something like that below. Click the subjects closest to your topic, and you will be taken to a screen like that shown on the opposite page.

Search by Subject

Search databases specific to your area of study.

- Africology
- Anthropology
- Architecture
- Art/Art History
- Astronomy
- Biological Sciences
- Business
- Chemistry
- Communication/Journalism/Public Speaking
- Computer Science
- Criminal Justice
- Dance
- Earth Sciences/Geography/Geology
- Economics
- Education
- Engineering
- Ethnic Studies
- Film/Television
- Fresh Water Sciences
- General
- Government Information
- Health Sciences, Biomedicine, and Informatics
- History, U.S.
- History, World
- Information Studies
- International Studies
- Journalism/Media Studies
- Law/Legal Research
- LGBT Studies
- Linguistics/Language
- Literature
- Math
- Music
- Music Education
- Musical Theater
- News
- Nonprofit Management
- Nursing
- Philosophy
- Physics
- Political Science
- Psychology
- Public Health
- Religious Studies
- Social Work
- Sociology
- Statistics
- Theater
- Urban Studies
- Women's Studies

SEARCH UNDER DIFFERENT SUBJECTS

Because different databases are grouped under each of the different listed subjects, you will get different results from trying different subject listings—so always search under each topic that has anything to do with your research project.

The picture below shows what you would see if you had clicked "Communication / Journalism / Public Speaking" on the screen shown to the left.

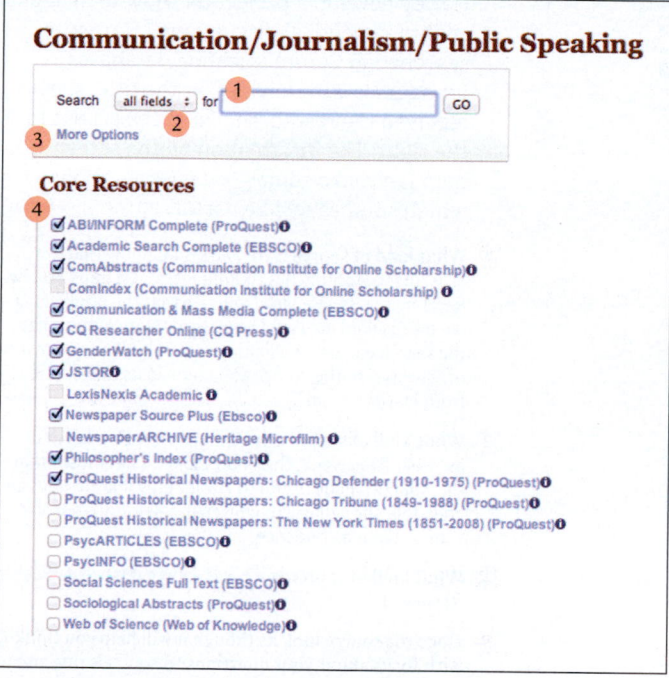

Learn what happens when you click "GO."

1 Enter your search terms here, in the white box.

2 From the pop-up menu, choose the kind of search you want to carry out: If you choose "All fields" from this pop-up menu, you will get results where your search terms show up in the title, author, or subject fields for articles in the database. For fewer but more useful results, choose the "Subject" option.

3 Click "More options" to do a more refined search: The options such a link provides depend on your library, but, minimally, this option will allow you to search for title and subject together, for example, or to search by subject and date together.

4 These are the databases you will be searching. The list shows the databases your librarians have decided are most likely to cover sources in the subject you chose. Notice, though, that you can click the checkboxes to search a narrower or broader range of databases.

→ See pages 86–87 to learn about the most popular databases for starting out.

FINDING SOURCES
USING LIBRARY DATABASES: EVALUATING DATABASE SEARCHES

WHICH RESULTS OF A DATABASE SEARCH WILL BE USEFUL?

Since page 45, we have been watching Harley develop a project on "How to increase civility in political discussions." Harley searched in Communication databases for sources with "civility" in the title; she received the results shown in the screen to the right. The information on the screen will help her make some good guesses about which sources will be useful.

1 **What kind of source is it?** The results show that "Discursive Approaches to Politeness" is **a book review**. Reading this source *might* indicate that the book being reviewed could be useful to Harley. (Notice, too, that the search engine automatically searched for synonyms of "civility," so this source has a term in its title different from Harley's term.)

2 **What kind of source is it?** Other sources are labeled as "Peer Reviewed"; this source *is not*. That means that this source will be useful to Harley only if it provides an anecdote she can use to enliven her writing—but she cannot use it as evidence.

3 **What kind of source is it?** This source *is* labeled "Peer Reviewed."

4 **Does the source look as though it will help you think with focus about your questions?** A source's title and short description help you determine how well the source fits your needs. In this case, this source will take Harley back several centuries—which makes the source unhelpful because she cares about the present.

5 **Does the source look as though it will help you think with focus about your questions?** This last source looks as though it will closely examine what "civility" means and why it matters—which Harley needs to know in order to start exploring how to increase civility.

6 **Do you have access to the source?** If the source is labeled "Full-Text" or "Full-Text Available," you can click that link to read the source online. If a source is not so labeled, ask a librarian for help accessing it.

Discursive Approaches to Politeness

① Book Review

The article reviews the book "Discursive Approaches to Politeness."

By: ,

Year: 2012

Published in: Language & Intercultural Communication

⟳ **Find It!**

🗀 **Save this record**

Rules of Civility

② Article

By: ,

Year: 2012

Published in: Entertainment Weekly

📄 **Full text available**

🗀 **Save this record**

"Tumbled into the Dirt": Wit and Incivility in Early Modern England

③ Article 🎓 Peer Reviewed

④ This paper considers notions of "wit" in early modern England. It deploys quantitative methodologies to trace the term's general discursive importance over time; it also looks at the use and conceptualisation of the terms by canonical writers—Robert Greene and William Shakespeare in the 1590s.

By: Withington, Phil

Year: 2011

Published in: Journal of Historical Pragmatics

🗀 **Save this record**

Why Civility Matters

Article 🎓 Peer Reviewed

⑤ Comments on the contemporary confusion over the informal rules of social interaction. Clarification on the concept of civility; Discussion on the three elements of civility; Recognition of the importance of civility for the sustenance of social capital in a community.

By: ,

Year: 2002

Published in: Policy

⑥ 📄 **Full-Text Available**

🗀 **Save this record**

TIPS

KEEP AN EYE OUT FOR PEER REVIEWED ARTICLES

Peer reviewed articles (as we discussed on page 55) have been judged credible by those knowledgeable in a research area; such articles have credibility with academic readers.

DO MULTIPLE SEARCHES

You can see that, of the four items Harley found in this search, only one is useful. Rewarding research requires trying different search terms but also requires trying different databases.

FINDING SOURCES
USING LIBRARY DATABASES: CHOOSING INDIVIDUAL DATABASES

Libraries can subscribe to hundreds of databases, so we cannot explain them all. But below we describe some of the most popular and useful ones, so that you can quickly decide which to search if your library requires that you choose one; note that some of the databases are for specific or a limited range of disciplines. Always try to search several.

ABI/INFORM
This database covers U.S. and international business and management topics, with information on companies and access to business journals.

ACADEMIC SEARCH
This database indexes thousands of journals across a range of scholarly disciplines, with full text for most. The database also gives access to scanned journal pages going back as far as 1887.

CSA ILLUMINA
This is a database of other databases, giving you access to more than 100 full-text and bibliographic databases in the arts and humanities, natural sciences, social sciences, and technology.

ERIC
The ERIC database focuses on education at all levels, indexing journals, books, theses, curricula, conference papers, standards, and guidelines.

GOOGLE SCHOLAR
Google Scholar searches across many disciplines to index scholarly texts such as articles, theses, books, and abstracts and court opinions. If you use Google Scholar, you will need to find the actual source through your library or elsewhere online.

JSTOR

JSTOR gives access to academic books and journals (dating back to 1665 in one case) in the arts and sciences; health, biology, and general science; and business. (Your library may not subscribe to all the areas JSTOR covers.) Importantly, note that for some journals JSTOR does not provide access to the most recent issues; instead, you can access all the issues up until a few years ago.

LEXISNEXIS ACADEMIC

This provides full-text access to news, business, legal, and reference information.

PROQUEST RESEARCH LIBRARY

This database indexes and provides broad full-text access to a mix of scholarly journals, trade publications, magazines, and newspapers.

PsycINFO

This database gives you access to citations and abstracts about worldwide research in psychology and related fields.

PUBMED/MEDLINE

PubMed is the National Library of Medicine's search service that provides access to over 14 million citations in MEDLINE, and other related databases, with links to participating online journals.

WEB OF SCIENCE (WEB OF KNOWLEDGE)

Web of Science includes three databases within the Web of Knowledge platform: Science Citation Index Expanded, Social Sciences Citation Index, and Arts & Humanities Citation Index. It indexes more than 8,000 peer-reviewed journals, providing complete bibliographic data and author abstracts.

TIPS

USING DATABASES

BE PATIENT AND PERSISTENT

You can't do one database search and be done. One search might give only one useful source. Give yourself time to search several databases and to try different search terms and different kinds of searches (title, keyword, general).

LOOK AT ALL THE RESULTS

The list resulting from a database search (→ as on page 85) will have the order the software designer thinks matches your search terms—but that person can't read your mind. A source that will delight you might not appear until page 3 or 5—so check over the full list, determining the potential usefulness of a source in the ways we describe on page 85.

HOW MANY SOURCES?

An assignment might require five or eight sources, but you need to find more: The first five or eight sources will not answer all your questions. And you won't know a source's usefulness until you read it. You may also get into your project, reading your sources and determining your arguments, only to discover new questions and concerns that require new sources.

KEEP IN MIND WHAT COMES NEXT

Once you have sources, you need to read, evaluate, and analyze them (→ see pages 102–115 on evaluating sources and pages 146–187 on analyzing their arguments). You must also track the bibliographic information that enables you to cite your sources conventionally.

→ See pages 140–141 to learn about keeping track of the sources you find.

FINDING SOURCES
ARCHIVAL AND SPECIAL LIBRARY COLLECTION SOURCES

SPECIAL LIBRARY COLLECTIONS

Duke University has special collections related to women's history and culture, to African and African American documentation, and to the history of sales, advertising, and marketing. Haverford College has special collections of materials related to the Quakers. The University of Idaho and the University of Utah have special collections on the history of their states.

Check your library's website to see what special collections it holds. These collections can be fascinating to visit on their own, but they might also provide engaging support for your project.

PHYSICAL ARCHIVES

Archives store documents of historic interest such as letters, diaries, newspapers, sermons, and postcards. Archives can store the documents of a town or county, a church or synagogue, or a person or family; they can be about labor history, African American music, or the development of the telephone.

Many small museums, historical organizations, and libraries have archives of local materials. Some archives collect materials related to the life of a political, literary, or cultural figure who was from or lived in the area.

To find archives in your area, do an online search using your town or city name and **Historical Organizations** and **Museums**.

To learn about archives at your university, check the library website, which will list the library's collections.

Archival research can be captivating: Holding a pioneer woman's diary from the 1860s will give you an exciting sense of differences in lives then and now—and using the diary's words in your writing will give your writing life and authority.

VIRTUAL ARCHIVES

Many physical archives have digitized their materials and made them available online. (If you use a virtual archive, keep in mind that digitization is time-consuming and costly; an archive may have only a small portion of its collection online, so you may still want to try to visit the physical archive if possible.) Each archive will have its own system for searching its collection. Individual archives might also tell you how they would like to be cited if you use their materials in your work.

Some rich virtual archives are:

THE INTERNET ARCHIVE
<http://www.archive.org/index.php>
This is an archive of video, music, sound, software, and texts from across the years the Internet has existed.

THE LIBRARY OF CONGRESS'S AMERICAN MEMORY PROJECT
<http://memory.loc.gov/ammem/index.html>
This collection provides "free and open access … to written and spoken words, sound recordings, still and moving images, prints, maps, and sheet music that document the American experience."

THE NATIONAL ARCHIVES OF THE UNITED STATES
<http://www.archives.gov/>
The Archives are a tremendous collection of materials (primarily government related) about this country. You have to go to the archive to look at most materials, but some are available digitally. If you are carrying out research in genealogical, social, political, or economic areas, check out the archives that have been put in searchable databases: *<http://aad.archives.gov/aad/>*

THE UNIVERSITY MUSEUMS AND COLLECTIONS
<http://publicus.culture.hu-berlin.de/umac/>
This is an international database linking you to museums in 45 countries.

→ On page 390 you can see a works-cited listing (in MLA style) for a chart from an online archive.

FINDING ARCHIVES OUTSIDE YOUR LOCAL AREA

Go online if historical materials will answer your research questions and there are no useful local archives.

Using your search terms, do at least three searches:

your topic + **archive**
your topic + **special collection**
your topic + **museum**

Try out variations on your topic, too, because you cannot know how websites describe themselves and so are cataloged by search engines.

For example, if you were researching organizational strategies used in the civil rights movement, you could do a search with the terms **civil rights movement** and **archive**. Among other useful links, this search turns up a link to the "Voices of Freedom" website at Virginia Commonwealth University, where you can listen to a recording of Dr. Joyce E. Glaise speaking about the church's role in organizing.

Keep in mind that such searches may not turn up materials you can access digitally, but they may suggest books you can find in your library or order through your library's interlibrary loan service.

FINDING SOURCES
FIELD RESEARCH SOURCES

Field research can be performed in more depth than we can describe here. Your teacher or a librarian can help you find further information.

→ See page 168 on evaluating field research.

INTERVIEWS

You can interview experts on your topic, people who have lived through an event central to your research, or those who have opinions about your topic.

Here is an email requesting an interview:

Dear Professor/Ms./Mr./Dr. [Name],
For my writing class, I am researching [your topic] and would like to interview you, informally, on this topic.

If you are willing, I would need only 30 minutes of your time. I would like to use a sound recorder during the interview.

If an interview is amenable to you, here are several times in the next two weeks when I could come to your office: [list times here].

Sincerely, [your name]

PREPARE FOR AN INTERVIEW

• What would you like to learn from this person? Write down questions that can draw that information out of the person. (You can use the guiding questions for research you developed.)

AT THE INTERVIEW

• Start by thanking the person.

• Explain your research.

• Ask your questions, and don't hesitate to ask other questions that come to you as you listen.

• End with a "Thank you!" Ask if you can contact the interviewee for clarifications.

AFTERWARD

• Send a thank-you e-mail or note.

• Call or e-mail for clarifications.

OBSERVATIONS

If you are researching the effects of video games on men's social relations, you could observe a group of friends playing a game together and then observe a group playing softball, to watch for differences in the friends' interactions. If you are researching cellphone use among teenagers and adults, you could go to the mall and count the teenagers and adults using cellphones.

PREPARE FOR AN OBSERVATION

- Consider where you can observe without others being aware of you so they don't change their behavior because of you.
- Determine what kinds of actions or behaviors you want to observe and record.
- Determine how you will record what you see. (If you do multiple observations, set the same time limit for each.)

WHILE OBSERVING

- Start your records with the time and date.

AFTERWARD

- If you have not learned what you thought you would, have you learned something else? Do you need to change your overall purpose, or do you need to do another observation, one set up slightly differently?
- Think about how you will justify your observations to your readers; you will need to include this in your writing.

SURVEYS

Small, focused surveys (the kind you can carry out, instead of state or national surveys) help you learn others' opinions about events or policies.

Small surveys can take two forms:

YES-OR-NO QUESTION SURVEYS

For example: *Do you think there should be a traffic light at the intersection of Bridge and Montezuma Streets?* Such surveys:

- Solicit quick decision making, leaving no room for gray areas.
- Allow you to tabulate results into claims: *Ninety percent of respondents favor a traffic light.*
- Tend to get more responses because they are quick and easy to take.

OPEN-ENDED QUESTION SURVEYS

For example: *What additional school programs would better prepare elementary school students to use developing technologies?* Such surveys:

- Solicit more thoughtful responses, usually with reasons.
- Require interpretation. Sometimes answers group together and sometimes you get a range of responses. You need to present explanations of what you learned.

Before giving a survey, test questions on a few people to be sure they understand the questions and can answer easily. Also consider how many people to survey so that your results are well supported.

GETTING PERMISSION FOR FIELD RESEARCH

Almost all colleges and universities have an *Institutional Review Board* (IRB), a committee to ensure the ethical treatment of subjects in research studies. Such boards were started to oversee medical and other kinds of technological research, but their responsibility spread to the humanities and social sciences. Every campus's IRB has policies for field research in writing classes. If you will use the results of your field research only in a classroom paper, you might not need IRB permission—but the only way to know is to ask your teacher.

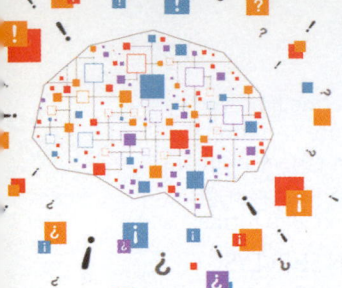

WHAT IF YOU CAN'T FIND ANYTHING ON YOUR NARROWED TOPIC?

If you are not finding information on your narrowed topic, there are several possible reasons:

- You have a creative and original topic.
- Your topic might not yet be narrow enough.
- You haven't yet found the right search terms or combination of search terms.
- You haven't yet found the right places to search.
- You have not yet learned how to use search tools comfortably.
- You are not putting in enough time.

IF YOU HAVE A CREATIVE AND ORIGINAL TOPIC

You have a decision to make: Find a new topic, or continue searching with your original topic.

Making effective arguments around creative and original topics is challenging and can teach you much. You still need to find supporting evidence for the points you want to make, so you have to get creative with finding sources that inform you about others' positions; you also have to be creative and careful with weaving those sources together into supporting evidence for the position you ultimately take. The following suggestions for generating search terms can still help you.

IT'S POSSIBLE YOUR TOPIC IS NOT YET NARROW ENOUGH

If a search engine returns millions of responses on your topic—none of which seems to address what matters to you—go back to pages 44–49 to work on further narrowing your topic.

IF YOU HAVEN'T YET FOUND THE RIGHT SEARCH TERMS

- Be open to what you find: Remember that, at this stage of producing a research paper, you are trying to gather as much information as you can on a topic. You might need to shift the focus of your topic as you learn what information is available.

- Develop lists of synonyms for your terms. For example, if you are searching the topic of childhood obesity and its relationship to food advertising using cartoon characters, you'll want to search with different combinations of the following:

  childhood, youth, young
  obesity, overweight, weight
  food, junk, diet, cereal, candy
  advertising, commercials
  cartoons, animation

  To find other words for searching, look for terms people use in the articles and websites you do find; ask others—teachers, librarians, and anyone you know who is good with words or reads a lot—what terms come to mind when you describe your topic.

- Keep track of other terms that come up as you search. In any article or webpage that seems at all close to your concerns, note what terms the authors use to describe your topic, and use those for further searches.

- Try a different search tool. Because each search tool works differently, different search tools will give you different results.

KNOWING IF YOU HAVE FOUND THE RIGHT PLACES TO SEARCH

If you have tried only one search engine or database, you need to try others. If you have tried multiple databases without luck, talk to your teacher or a librarian: They can help you determine other databases that might be fruitful.

But perhaps you are searching online when you need to be interviewing others or looking in an archive. Again, talking to a teacher or librarian about your narrowed topic—and about what you are hoping to learn—can help you determine where to look.

IT'S POSSIBLE YOU ARE NOT USING SEARCH TOOLS COMFORTABLY ENOUGH

If every time you do your research you get frustrated or confused, it is definitely time to make an appointment with your teacher, a librarian, or someone from your campus's Writing (or Learning) Center. Be specific about the help you need: First, describe your narrowed topic and what you are hoping to learn, and then describe the research you have carried out so far. Finally, ask for someone to sit by you while you search, to guide you and give advice.

IT'S POSSIBLE YOU ARE NOT GIVING YOUR RESEARCH ENOUGH TIME

If you expect research to take fifteen minutes or even an hour one night, you are wrong. Effective research requires patience, spread out over hours and days: It takes time and persistence to find the information that will help you be smart.

STARTING A PAPER

ONE STUDENT'S EXPERIENCE

The night before Harley received an assignment to write a research paper, her family had yet another bitter political fight over dinner. Her mother and brother were barely talking with each other, and her sister and uncle had stopped talking. When she received the research paper assignment, she also remembered chats she had had with friends about the same problems in their families—especially at Thanksgiving or other holiday meals when everyone got together.

HARLEY'S GENERAL TOPIC

When she received her assignment, Harley decided to learn more about why families—and people more generally—can't talk about politics without fighting. Some of her initial research work is shown on page 45.

This initial research taught her that (at least) two issues need to be considered in the fighting she observed: *political polarization*, when there is no middle ground available for political positions but only extreme positions; and *civility*, which a website she found (*Civilpolitics.org*) defined as "the ability to disagree with others while respecting their sincerity and decency."

HARLEY NARROWS HER TOPIC

Harley decides that she will research **how to increase civility in political discussions (in families or more generally)**.

HARLEY'S QUESTIONS FOR RESEARCH

Based on what she had learned from her initial research, Harley brainstormed questions to guide her further research:

Questions of Fact
How do schools teach people about discussion and argument? How do schools teach people about politics? Are there statistics available on political polarization in our country?

Questions of Definition
What is civility? What is discussion—and what is argument? What is political polarization?

Questions of Interpretation
Must political arguments always have winners? Why have political arguments become so polarized? Will learning to be more civil really help us not be polarized over politics? Who benefits from different definitions of civility?

Questions of Consequence
What are the purposes of political discussion? What are the best possible results of political discussions? Who benefits from political discussion? How does what happens in family political arguments affect what happens in communities and other larger groups? What happens to families—and communities—when families can't talk about politics?

Questions of Value
Why should we value political discussions? Why value listening carefully to others? Should families talk about politics at all?

Questions of Policy
Are there any laws or other policies that affect how people argue—especially about politics?

HOW HER QUESTIONS HELP HARLEY FIND SOURCES

From her initial work, Harley realized that her first Google searches were helping her begin to answer questions of definition but not other types of questions.

Because she is concerned to see what would result from people increasing their concern for civility, the questions that matter most to her are questions of consequence and values; this helped her use the charts on pages 58–59 to determine where to search: While editorial and opinion pieces (including on blogs) might help her show how others have similar experiences around the family dinner table, she saw that statistics and academic journal articles and books about political polarization and civility might give her more in-depth and well-researched perspectives on these matters.

After she had done her initial Google searches she turned to her library databases. She found that general database searches for **family argument politics** didn't help her find much (she found only popular sources this way)—but when she performed a title search for **civility** (meaning that she searched for articles that had **civility** in the title) and a subject search for **political polarization** she found sources that appeared to be useful.

Some of the suggested sources were books, so she looked them up on Amazon to learn more about them—and on the Amazon pages for each book she found recommendations for similar books.

HINTS & TIPS FOR FINDING IDEAS

HOW DO YOU KNOW IF YOU HAVE FOUND ENOUGH SOURCES?

In the earliest stages of research, you won't know, exactly, if you have all the sources that will help you develop an argument that will satisfy readers.

But you are researching broadly enough—finding enough sources—if you can answer most of the research questions you've generated.

HOW DO YOU KNOW IF YOUR MIND IS OPEN?

You might think that you should have definitive answers to all your research questions. But—*especially for questions of consequence, interpretation, value, and policy*—if your research makes you hesitate over deciding between two or three possible responses, then you are keeping an open mind. If you can offer good reasons for several differing possibilities, then you are researching as you should.

Academic writing is rarely about offering final solutions to anything: There are few situations in life where the available evidence supports one final conclusion. Instead, you need to acknowledge the differing possibilities and offer the best evidence and arguments you can for the position (or positions) you believe to be best.

HOW CAN YOU KEEP A TOPIC FRESH AND INTERESTING? HOW DO YOU STAY MOTIVATED?

If you get bored with your topic, you won't enjoy writing, your writing will reflect your emotion, and your readers will pick up on it.

Because there are different ways to get bored with a topic, there are different approaches for becoming unbored:

- Perhaps you've chosen a topic that isn't controversial or challenging enough to keep you engaged. Talk with a teacher or someone who knows about the topic to determine if you can make the topic more challenging . . . or if you need a new topic.

- Sometimes topics become boring when you've done a lot of research and feel you know all there is to know. If this happens, remember that not everyone knows what you do: If you talk to others and lay out why the topic should matter, you might just see how writing about your topic can help others learn important information.

- Sometimes boredom is a safe way to be nervous. If you don't want to work on your paper, ask yourself if you are worried about the work or a possible grade—and remind yourself that writing projects exist to help you learn and that learning is not comfortable. All that sounds clichéd—but it is true. Learning does require stretching yourself beyond what is easy and what you already know, and so of course writing a paper will have moments of nerves and worry. Remind yourself that all writers experience these emotions.

PART 4
USING SOURCES WITH INTEGRITY

CONTENTS

WHERE ARE WE IN A PROCESS FOR COMPOSING?

Understanding your project
Getting started
Asking questions
Shaping your project for others
Drafting a paper
Getting feedback
Revising
Polishing

Evaluating sources
Tracking sources

4 USING SOURCES WITH INTEGRITY

Questions you might have about working with sources:

What are the steps of working with sources?
→ See pages 100–101.

I've found sources that look good—but how do I evaluate them?
→ See pages 102–115.

How do I tell whether a source is relevant for my purposes?
→ See pages 104–107.

How do I tell whether a source will be credible for my readers?
→ See pages 108–115.

What is plagiarism? Why should I care about plagiarism?
→ See pages 116–121.

What are good practices for avoiding plagiarism?
→ See pages 120–121 and page 141.

What information do I need to track for different kinds of sources?
→ For books (print or digital), see pages 124–127.
→ For parts of books (print or digital), see pages 128–129.
→ For print or digital periodicals (like magazines, journals, and newspapers), see pages 130–137.

THE WPA OUTCOMES* FOR PART 4 INCLUDE:

Critical thinking, reading, and composing abilities: Evaluating primary and secondary research sources for relevance and credibility.

Using conventions: Exploring the concepts of intellectual property—such as fair use and copyright—that underlie the conventions of documentation; applying citation conventions in your own work

* See page 15.

WORKING WITH SOURCES

USING SOURCES WITH INTEGRITY GROUNDS ACADEMIC WRITING

Readers respect academic writing—and take actions based on it—because academic writers seek to use evidence fairly and provide balanced thinking. Using evidence fairly means using it fully and not hiding or ignoring what does not fit with what one wants; providing balance means considering all honest, informed, and thoughtful positions.

To achieve those values, academic writers show integrity toward their sources. They read sources carefully, to evaluate them for *their* integrity, and they acknowledge in their writing where they found ideas.

The sources that help you think (which you started finding in Part 3) stay with you throughout your writing; you have to interact with them in these two main ways:

- You need to read, evaluate, and analyze your sources. These processes help you decide whether a source is appropriate for your work and help you think about the issues that matter in your writing.

- You need to keep track of the sources' bibliographic information—their titles, authors, and publication information— so that you can cite the sources in your writing. As we describe in following pages, citing sources—telling readers where you got your ideas—is a convention of academic writing in the United States and other western countries.

HOW SOURCE WORK WEAVES INTO A PROCESS FOR COMPOSING

Because (as we describe on the opposite page) the two main ways of interacting with sources—thinking with them, tracking them—run throughout a composing process for research, they weave throughout the parts of this book, as the diagram below indicates.

→ See the next three pages for more details on working with sources.

Understanding your project

Getting started

Deciding on kinds of sources—and finding them.
→ PART 3

Asking questions

Evaluating your sources for relevance and credibility, the initial step to decide if your sources are useful. → PART 4

Collecting citation information about your sources, so that you can use it later when you write your paper. → PART 4

Analyzing your sources' arguments, to further decide their usefulness—and to help you think about them. → PART 5

Engaging with your sources—summarizing, paraphrasing, and quoting them—to put your ideas in dialogue with theirs and to put them in dialogue with each other. → PART 5

Shaping your project for others

Drafting a paper

Creating in-text citations for any sources whose words you quote, summarize, or paraphrase in your writing. → PART 9

Creating works cited lists, references lists, and bibliographies to go at the end of a paper. → PART 9

Getting feedback

Revising

Polishing

STEPS FOR WORKING WITH SOURCES

There are four styles for citing sources: MLA, APA, CMS, and CSE. Each style is used by a different set of disciplines. As we note on the opposite page, we devote separate pages of this book to each of these styles.

1

EVALUATING SOURCES FOR RELEVANCE AND CREDIBILITY

Before you use a source in your writing, how do you know whether it will be persuasive to your audience? Evaluate it for its relevance to your argument and its credibility to your audience.

→ See pages 102–115.

2

COLLECTING THE CITATION INFORMATION YOU NEED FOR ANY SOURCE YOU USE

After you have evaluated a source and decided you will use it in your writing—by quoting, summarizing, paraphrasing, or otherwise referencing it in your writing—you need to give readers information about the source. (Sources can include photographs, drawings, charts, and graphs—any text by another person that you reference in your writing.)

For different sources you need to collect different information.

→ To learn the information to collect, see pages 124–139.

→ To determine the kinds of sources you have, see pages 54–55 and 60–65.

3

ANALYZING OTHERS' ARGUMENTS

To begin deciding whether you want to be persuaded by a source's arguments— and deciding how you want to respond—you need to analyze the source: What is its main argument? What are implications of the argument?

→ To learn more, go to pages 146–187 in Part 5.

4

USING SUMMARY, QUOTATION, OR PARAPHRASE TO INTEGRATE OTHERS' IDEAS INTO YOUR ARGUMENTS

By working with others' ideas and words, you develop your position.

SUMMARIZING

Pollan's book describes origins of four different meals, helping us question how our eating embeds us in social, economic, political, and ecological webs.

QUOTING

"We started making videos to send home to show what life here was like," says Wright in an e-mail from his Antarctic base.

PARAPHRASING

Sabido describes how his *telenovelas* should reach his audience's limbic brain, which governs emotions.

→ To learn more, go to pages 188–203 in Part 5.

5

CREATING IN-TEXT CITATIONS

When you use the words or ideas of someone else, provide information to help readers find those words themselves. Each style provides ways for you to give this information.

MLA STYLE

Monroe reminds us that there is no generic access to computers: Access at home is not the same as access at work or school (19–20, 26–27).

APA STYLE

Whalen (1995) analyzed how the talk of operators responding to 911 calls was organized by the task of filling in required information on a computer screen with a specific visual structure.

6

CREATING WORKS-CITED LISTS, REFERENCE LISTS, AND BIBLIOGRAPHIES

Each style has its own name for the list of sources at the end of a piece of writing, but all of them require writers to list all the sources used in their writing.

APA STYLE

Panofsky, E. (1970).
Meaning in the visual arts.
Harmondsworth, England:
Penguin.

CSE STYLE

20. Latchman DS. From genetics to gene therapy: the molecular pathology of human disease. London: Bios Scientific Publishers; 1994. 362 p. (UCL molecular pathology series).

Because each style for in-text citations and works-cited lists is different, we provide separate sections for each style.

→ For **MLA style**, see pages 350–392.

→ For **APA style**, see pages 393–419.

→ For **CSE style**, see pages 420–424.

→ For **CMS style**, see pages 425–428.

ONE relevance

TWO credibility

EVALUATING SOURCES
WITH AUDIENCE AND PURPOSE IN MIND

Part 3 gave you information for narrowing your research directions and finding supporting sources.

On the next pages we describe how to carry out an initial evaluation of any sources you've found, so that you can decide how useful they will be to the further development of your ideas.

WHY EVALUATE SOURCES?

FOR RELEVANCE

After you narrow your topic and search for sources, you probably intuitively evaluate sources for whether they are relevant to your immediate writing purposes. You judge sources for whether they are on topic and fit in the time frame of your questions. In addition, for your sources to be rhetorically and academically relevant, you also need to ask whether your readers will make the same judgments you do. For your sources to support your own growth, you need to ask whether they help you think in more depth and from new perspectives about your topic.

FOR CREDIBILITY

The tradition of academic writing grounds its integrity in sources that are credible, that (in other words) use evidence carefully and fairly (even evidence that might counter the source's arguments) and that enable readers to check a source's own sources.

Learning how to evaluate sources for their credibility helps you deepen your own integrity toward others work as well as toward your own thinking.

HOW WILL THE NEXT PAGES HELP YOU WITH YOUR RESEARCH?

1 *Your sources will be relevant to your audience and purpose.* The sources will supply appropriate support for what you are arguing.

2 *Your sources will be credible to your audience.* Your audience ought to trust the sources, and thus they will be more likely to trust any arguments you build based on those sources.

Because you need to know that your sources are *both* relevant and credible, the process of evaluating sources has two steps—one for evaluating relevance and the second for evaluating credibility.

ARE YOU READY TO APPLY THE INFORMATION IN THE NEXT PAGES?

IF THIS IS YOUR SITUATION, THE ANSWER IS **NO**.

Midnight: Your eyes hurt, and your database search has returned 5,652 items.

Go back to pages 44–49 and 52–53 for help in narrowing your topic and search terms so that you get fewer but more focused results.

IF THIS IS YOUR SITUATION, THE ANSWER IS **YES**.

You've got good research questions and you've got a pretty good initial sense of the audience you want to address. (If you are unsure about your research question, check pages 50–53. If you want to think about your audience a bit more, check pages 266–269.)

Apply what we present in the next few pages to develop a list of sources you know to be relevant and credible.

APPLY THE CRITERIA IN ORDER

While the criteria of relevance and credibility are equally important, use the steps on the next pages in order. Determining credibility often takes more effort than determining relevance, so you can save yourself some time by checking relevance first.

EVALUATING SOURCES
FOR RELEVANCE

☑ ONE
relevance

☐ TWO
credibility

1

IS THE KIND OF SOURCE RELEVANT TO YOUR AUDIENCE?

❑ **Given your research questions and purposes, what kinds of sources are likely to be most appealing and persuasive to your particular audience?** When you write an academic research paper, your audience is academic readers, who tend to respect books published by academic presses, academic journal articles, and specialized encyclopedias.

Academic audiences also respect the use of primary sources. (→ See page 55 on primary sources.)

Depending on your purposes, however, you might need to supplement such sources. For example, if you are writing about the role of women in space exploration, you might want to begin your essay with one woman's personal story about how she got into the U.S. space program; in such a case, you could look in popular periodicals or blogs for such stories—and those sources would be appropriate for your purposes.

2

IS THE SOURCE RELEVANT TO YOUR ARGUMENT?

❑ **Is the source on topic?** This might seem too obvious a question to ask, but you can save yourself lots of time if, with each possible source, you ask yourself whether the source really does provide information focused on your topic.

❑ **Does the source have a publication date appropriate to your research?** If you are writing about the current state of a rapidly changing topic—such as AIDS research—you need sources dated close to the moment you write; if you are writing about a past event or about past situations that have led to a current event, then you need sources from those time periods as well as from people in the present who analyze the past event.

❑ **Does the source bring in perspectives other than those of the sources you've already collected?** You do not want to collect sources that all take the same position, for two reasons. First, if all you can find are sources that take the same perspective on your topic, then your topic is probably not controversial or interesting enough for an academic paper. Second, your audience is not likely to be persuaded by writing that does not consider multiple perspectives.

❑ **Does the source provide something interesting?** Your audience wants to be intellectually engaged with your writing. As you consider a new source, ask yourself if it contains ideas or information that are interesting because they are funny, provocative, puzzling, or otherwise provide a new or unexpected perspective. Quoting or citing such ideas or information in your writing helps you write a more engaging paper.

❑ **Does the source bring in data or other information different from the sources you have already collected?** This criterion is similar to the one preceding, but it asks you to consider how much data or other information is useful for you to collect in order to construct a persuasive position in your writing.

❑ **Does the source suggest other possible directions your research could take?** We want you to stay on track in your research as much as you want to stay on track, given that you have a deadline—but we also want you to stay open to the possibilities of reshaping or retouching your research questions and purpose as you discover potentially new and exciting approaches.

TIP

IF A SOURCE MEETS MOST OF THE CRITERIA ABOVE, HOLD ON TO IT.

When you evaluate a source's *relevance*, you are determining how likely most readers are to believe that what the source presents is appropriate to your arguments.

Finding sources that meet all the criteria doesn't guarantee that they'll end up in your works-cited list at the end of your paper—but sources that meet all the criteria are much more likely to help you write a solid, strong, and persuasive argument.

EVALUATING SOURCES
FOR RELEVANCE:
SAMPLE SOURCES

✓ ONE
relevance

☐ TWO
credibility

Here are examples showing how to judge the relevance of a source based on your research questions and audience.

Harley's narrowed research topic is

how to increase civility in political discussions (in families or more generally).

Harley is writing for her classmates and teacher.

Zak's narrowed research topic is

how family dinner habits affect young people's political participation.

Zak is writing an article for his college newspaper in a series about increasing students' political participation.

Julier, Alice P. *Eating Together: Food, Friendship, and Inequality*. Champaign: Illinois UP, 2013. Print.

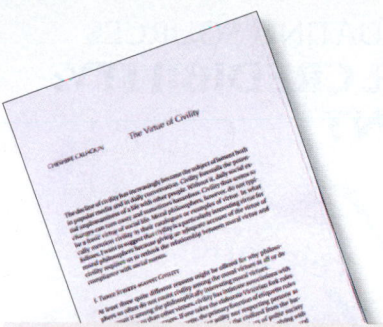

Calhoun, Chesire. "The Virtue of Civility." *Philosophy and Public Affairs* 29.3 (2000): 252–75. Print.

This source is **NOT RELEVANT**, given Harley's purposes. The book offers research into a century's worth of etiquette books from the last century as well as results from interviews and observations of people eating together; based on that research, the book discusses how people do or do not feel included in social groups. Although the book discusses how social relations form among people, the book does not discuss how to increase civility and so will not help Harley in her writing.

This source is **RELEVANT**, given Harley's purpose. This article defines civility carefully, in the context of many different writers' definitions of the term. This article will help Harley better understand the term central to her concerns.

This source is **RELEVANT**, given Zak's purposes. This book discusses how relations of economics, gender, and ethnicity develop through how people eat together, and so this book's arguments and research can help Zak better understand how people do or do not feel politically connected as a result of the meals they share with others.

This source is **RELEVANT** for Zak. This article defines civility as behavior necessary for participation in democratic processes, and so—if he thinks that he accepts the definition offered—it will provide him concepts for arguing what behaviors need to be cultivated over family dinners if young people are to learn how to participate politically.

EVALUATING SOURCES
FOR CREDIBILITY: PRINT

ONE
relevance

TWO
credibility

A NOTE ON THE GENERAL CREDIBILITY OF PRINT SOURCES

Some people are nostalgic for pre-Internet days because the institutions of print publication seemed then to make evaluating a source's credibility easy. The costs and complexities of print publication and distribution are behind that perception.

Printing books, magazines, and newspapers is expensive. Those who provide the money want return on their investments, so they want readers to trust what is published. Print publishing therefore developed systems of editors and fact-checkers: Often when you buy a print text, its credibility has been checked in different ways. (Libraries contribute to this system, too, because librarians often buy only books recommended to them by trusted sources.)

But, as you know, not all print texts are credible. Think of supermarket tabloids, for example, or of how some publishers have political motivations. You cannot therefore count on something you find in print to be absolutely reliable—and you also have to consider what criteria your audience will use for judging credibility.

IF A SOURCE MEETS MOST OF THE CRITERIA ABOVE, HOLD ON TO IT.

When you evaluate a source's *credibility*, you decide whether most of your readers will accept the source's facts and arguments.

Finding sources that meet all the criteria for credibility doesn't guarantee they will end up in your works-cited list or bibliography—but sources that meet all the criteria are much more likely to help you write a well supported and persuasive argument.

DETERMINING THE CREDIBILITY OF A PRINT SOURCE

❏ **Who published the source?** Look at page 61, on Characteristics that Distinguish Sources, to read about the motivations behind different kinds of publishers. A publisher's motivations can help you decide the level of credibility the source will have for your audience.

❏ **Does the author have sufficient qualifications for writing on the topic?** Most print publications tell you something about the author; you can also search online to learn about the author. If you cannot find an author or sponsoring agency, is that because no one wants to take responsibility?

❏ **What evidence is presented?** Does the evidence support the claims? What evidence would be stronger?

➔ See pages 162–171 on evidence.

❏ **Does the evidence seem accurate?**

❏ **Do the claims seem adequately supported by the offered evidence?**

❏ **Does the source try to cover all the relevant facts and opinions?** If you are at the beginning of your research, this might be hard to answer, but as you dig deeper into your research, you'll have a sense of the range of perspectives one can take on your topic, and you'll be able to judge how widely a source engages with the issues at stake.

❏ **What is the source's genre?**
Is the source an advertisement (or does it contain advertisements)? Advertisers sometimes try to influence what is published near their advertisements to keep their appeal strong.

But it also matters if the source is an opinion piece, a thought-experiment or essay, or a piece of scholarship: Writers and readers have different expectations for different genres regarding how much (unsupported) opinion is appropriate.

❏ **Does the source make its position, perspective, and biases clear?**
When writers do not make their own biases clear, they often do not want readers to think about how those biases affect the writers' arguments.

❏ **Does the source make a point of seeking out different perspectives?** If so, this is an indication that a writer is trying to understand a topic fully and not just giving a narrow view.

❏ **Does the writing seek to sound reasonable and thoughtful?**
Inflammatory language in a piece of writing is a sign that the writer is trying to move you solely through your emotional responses without engaging your thoughtfulness.

IF A SOURCE MEETS MOST OF THE CRITERIA ABOVE, CHECK ITS BIBLIOGRAPHY.
If you find a relevant and credible source that helps you think, look in its bibliography: Often, the bibliography can point you to new and useful sources.

EVALUATING SOURCES
FOR CREDIBILITY:
SAMPLE PRINT SOURCES

ONE
relevance

TWO
credibility

Here are examples of how to judge the credibility of a print source based on your research question and audience.

Harley's narrowed research topic is

how to increase civility in political discussions (in families or more generally).

Harley is writing for her classmates and teacher.

Zak's narrowed research topic is

how family dinner habits affect young people's political participation.

Zak is writing an article for his college newspaper in a series about increasing students' political participation.

Weinstein, Miriam. *The Surprising Power of Family Meals: How Eating Together Makes Us Smarter, Stronger, Healthier and Happier*. Westminster: Steerforth, 2006. Print.

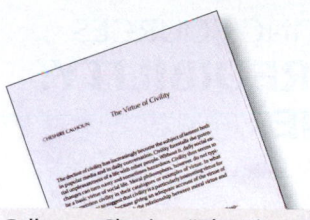

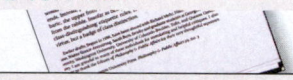

Calhoun, Chesire. "The Virtue of Civility." *Philosophy and Public Affairs* 29.3 (2000): 252–75. Print.

This source is **NOT CREDIBLE** for Harley's audience and purpose. This book was published by a popular press, not an academic press; the author is a documentary filmmaker and journalist and not a research specialist. Although the book cites studies across many fields, it also offers stories and other non-academic approaches to its topic. Harley *could* use this source for anecdotes and stories; she could also track down its original sources and perhaps use them. For an academic paper, however, this source will not have the credibility of a source published by an academic press through the process of peer review.

This source is **CREDIBLE** for Harley's audience and purposes because it was published in a peer-reviewed academic journal. The writing is careful and precise, keywords are defined, all sources are cited, and inflammatory language is carefully avoided.

This source could be **CREDIBLE** for Zak's audience and purposes because it was published by a credible popular press and allows Zak to refer to other studies about family meals. The book focuses on the broad benefits of families eating together, including the respect people gain for others and an ability to talk well with others; given Zak's purposes, he would therefore probably not make this a major source because he will have to connect such results with political participation.

This source is **CREDIBLE** for Zak's audience and purpose. For all the reasons mentioned above, this source will carry weight with Zak's audience.

EVALUATING SOURCES
FOR CREDIBILITY: ONLINE

✔ ONE relevance

✔ TWO credibility

DETERMINING THE CREDIBILITY OF AN ONLINE SOURCE

Use the same criteria as for evaluating print sources, with the following additions:

❑ **Who published the source?**

The domain name in the URL can indicate something about a publisher's credibility. (Example domain names are microsoft.com, whitehouse.gov, or lacorps.org.)

Look at the domain name's last letters:

.gov   A website created by an office of the U.S. federal government

.com   A website created for a company that is seeking to publicize itself or sell products

.org   A nonprofit organization—but anyone can register for the .org domain

.edu   Colleges and universities

.mil   U.S. military websites

.me.us   A website for one of the fifty U.S. states: The first two letters are the abbreviation of the state name

.de   A website created in a country other than the U.S.—but websites created outside this country can also use .com, .net, and .org

.net   The most generic ending; Internet Service Providers (ISPs) as well as individuals can have websites whose URLs end in .net

What sorts of websites will your audience think are most appropriate and credible, given your purpose?

☐ **Does the author have qualifications for writing on the topic?** With some websites you won't be able to answer this because you won't be able to determine who the author is, either because no name is given or a pseudonym is used.

If you cannot find the name of an author or sponsoring agency, perhaps no one wants to take responsibility; perhaps someone is worried about the consequences of publishing the information. If you are writing on a controversial topic, you could use information from such a site to describe the controversy and support the fact that there is a controversy—but you couldn't use the site to offer factual support for anything else.

☐ **What evidence is offered?** In the most credible print sources, authors list the sources of their evidence; the same holds true for websites. If you cannot find the source of the evidence used, the site is not as credible as a site that does list sources.

→ See pages 162–171 on evidence.

☐ **Does the source make its position, perspective, and biases clear?** Approach websites just as you approach print sources with this question, except that with websites you can also check where links on the site take you. A website may give the appearance of holding a middle line on a position, but if the other websites to which it links support only one position, then question the credibility of the original site.

☐ **What is the source's genre?** Some online genres, such as newspapers and magazines, mimic print genres; approach them with the same questions as you would their print equivalents.

But webpages can easily be made to look like any genre. For example, some websites look like the informational material you pick up in a doctor's office. Just as when you receive such material in a doctor's office, however, you need to look carefully: Is the website actually advertising a company's treatments or products?

Keep in mind that blogs are a tricky genre to use as sources. There are many well-respected blogs published by experts; if you want to cite such a blog, you will need to give evidence why that particular blog is respected by other experts. On the other hand, if you are citing words from a blog solely to show a range of opinions on a topic, the blog's credibility will not be an issue.

ALSO:

☐ **How well designed is the website or webpage?** A site that looks professionally designed, is straightforward to navigate, and loads quickly suggests that its creators put time and resources into all the other aspects of the site; these characteristics could also indicate that the site was published by an organization rather than an individual. Do any of these factors matter for your purpose and audience?

EVALUATING SOURCES
FOR CREDIBILITY:
SAMPLE ONLINE SOURCES

ONE
relevance

TWO
credibility

Here are examples of how to judge the credibility of an online source based on your research question and audience.

Harley's narrowed research topic is

how to increase civility in political discussions (in families or more generally).

Harley is writing for her classmates and teacher.

Zak's narrowed research topic is

how family dinner habits affect young people's political participation.

Zak is writing an article for his college newspaper in a series about increasing students' political participation.

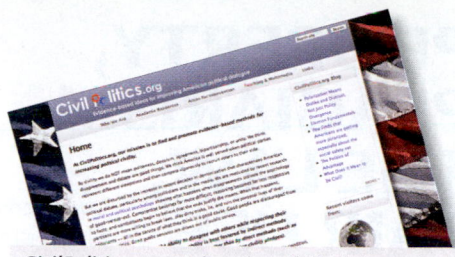

Fishel, Anne. "The Most Important Thing You Can Do with Your Kids? Eat Dinner with Them." Washington Post. *Washington Post*, 12 Jan. 2015. Web. 26 Nov. 2015. Web. 26 Nov. 2015.

CivilPolitics.org. University of Virginia and University of Southern California, n.d. Web. 26 Nov. 2015.

This source is **NOT CREDIBLE** for Harley's audience if Harley wanted to use this as a source for her main arguments. While the *Washington Post* is a well respected newspaper, it is not an academic source; while the author is a respected academic from a well-respected school, she has written this piece for a popular audience. In the article, however, the author has included links to academic studies, and Harley could use those studies; she could also use anecdotes and other examples from this writing to supplement academically credible sources.

This source *might* be **CREDIBLE** for Harley's audience. This website is a collaboration among many academic researchers from a range of disciplines (law, political science, psychology, sociology) and is sponsored and overseen by researchers at two very respected universities. The site is a compendium of sources for studying civility, and as such has introductory written material that gives definitions and gives links to sources. Harley can perhaps draw on this site for definitions, but her thinking and writing will be pushed to develop more if she follows the links to articles, videos, and books.

This source is **CREDIBLE** for Zak's audience. Even though Zak is writing for a popular audience, which will not expect Zak to use academic sources as thoroughly as Harley's audience does, Zak's audience still expects good evidence to be offered for any claims Zak makes. For the same reasons that Harley should not base her main arguments on this article—that its writing is based only on one person's experiences and opinions— neither should Zak.

This source is **CREDIBLE** for Zak's audience. Those who have put the site together show their background and sources, and their writing is careful and strives to approach the issue from multiple perspectives. Given Zak's audience and purposes, this site gives him reasonable depth for what he needs to do—but, like Harley, his research and thinking would be well served by digging into the additional sources suggested by this site.

PROPERTY, PLAGIARISM, THE LAW, FAIR USE

To understand the ethical use of sources, including why plagiarism is a legal issue, you need to understand basic principles of copyright. These principles underlie how people in the United States think about sources; such thinking starts in different categories of **property**:

PROPERTY

PROPERTY YOU CAN TOUCH WITH YOUR HANDS	PROPERTY YOU CANNOT TOUCH WITH YOUR HANDS
REAL PROPERTY land or buildings **PERSONAL PROPERTY** objects you can carry with you.	**INTELLECTUAL PROPERTY** The ideas embodied in writing, drawing, musical compositions, performances; intellectual property is divided into:

CREATIVE PROPERTY
Literary, academic, and artistic works

INDUSTRIAL PROPERTY
Industrial inventions and trademarks like company logos

Creative property is covered by **copyright law.** Copyright law developed over several hundred years, in a push-pull between those who make and those who publish and distribute creative property. Copyright gives legal protection to creators so that they have some control over how their creations get used.

Plagiarism occurs when a person uses another's creative property without the maker's consent or knowledge. This can involve using a part of another's work or passing off the whole as one's own. Plagiarism is unethical and can be illegal.

➜ See pages 118–121 and page 141 for more on plagiarism.

SHARED CULTURE, ACADEMIC RESEARCH, AND FAIR USE

If we had to pay the creator every time we told a fairy tale, sang an old lullaby, or repeated the story of George Washington chopping down the cherry tree, we probably wouldn't share these ideas often and would therefore have no shared ideas to bind us together as a culture.

In recognition of this need for shared culture, the law says that, after a set number of years, creators' copyright control over their productions passes into the **public domain**. When a creative production is in the public domain, others can use it freely, as when the Disney Company makes a movie about Pocahontas or the Little Mermaid.

But academic research—in all the disciplines of the sciences, social sciences, and the humanities—cannot wait the length of time it takes for ideas to pass into the public domain. Academic research depends on being able to use and build on the ideas of others *now*, as does artistic development. In recognition of such conditions, there is a doctrine in U.S. copyright law called **fair use**.

FAIR USE

Fair use, a doctrine in copyright law, allows *certain* uses of others' copyrighted material without permission. Fair use does not specify how much of another's work one may use; instead, four factors are considered, in legal cases, to determine if a use is fair:

1 **The purpose and character of the use.** Is the use commercial or is it for nonprofit and educational purposes (such as criticism, parody, or art)? Fair use is meant to support public, not personal, enrichment. If the use transforms the copied work, making something new of it, that is also more likely to be considered fair use.

2 **The nature of the copyrighted work.** Generally, uses of published nonfiction works are considered to benefit the public—and not harm the rights of a copyright holder—more so than uses of unpublished or fictional works.

3 **The amount and substantiality of the portion used in relation to the copyrighted work as a whole.** The less one copies, the more likely the copying is to be considered fair use.

4 **The effect of the use upon the potential market for or value of the copyrighted work.** If the use will not cause the copyright holder to lose income, it is more likely to be considered fair use.

The doctrine of fair use underpins academic uses of the words of others—as in research writing—which is what we discuss in this part of this book. Fair use protects most academic uses of intellectual property—but as soon as you use that property for personal gain or commercial ends, the use is no longer protected.

WHY CITE AND DOCUMENT SOURCES?
CONSIDERING PLAGIARISM— AND HOW TO AVOID IT

Do you want to live and work in communities—school districts, neighborhoods, cities, countries—where people respect each other and each other's ideas? Do you want to live and work where people try to persuade you and each other based on the best possible evidence?

If you do, you can contribute to shaping such communities: You need to know how to show respect in spoken or written deliberations—even when you disagree. You are also responsible for understanding how to determine and use the best possible evidence; you need to let others know where that evidence comes from so they can judge and check it themselves.

Many people think that using, citing, and documenting sources is only for academic writing. Academic conventions for doing such work certainly exist (see the following pages and Part 9). But these conventions exist because people who write academic papers, no matter what discipline, want to use the best possible evidence and make that evidence available to others to check—no matter whether they are writing academic papers or blog posts.

Citing and documenting sources shows that you want to take part in ongoing cultural and academic deliberations while being respectful of the research and thinking others have done before you. It shows that you want others to understand the good reasons and thinking from which your own work grows.

It shows that you value yourself as a thinker.

WHAT IS PLAGIARISM?

Plagiarism is using the ideas or words of others without acknowledgment, as though they were your own.

At one extreme, plagiarism involves putting one's name on someone else's paper. But plagiarism happens in smaller doses, too. Writers who do not show the source of ideas in a paper plagiarize: By not using the conventional indications of attribution—quotation marks or other signs of using other's ideas together with in-text citations and endnotes—such writers let readers think all the ideas come from the writer. Finally, summaries and paraphrases that follow the original too closely are also plagiarism (➔ see pages 190–193 and 200–201).

Plagiarism can happen inadvertently: While doing research, you might take notes or copy some text from a webpage and, in the rush to finish a paper, you lose track of where you found the sources and you put them straight into your paper.

Plagiarism can also happen when you don't have enough confidence in your own ideas or the quality of your research to take your own positions; you let others' words stand in for your own.

Whether plagiarism is inadvertent, purposeful, or the result of not enough confidence, it is considered wrong in the United States.

PLAGIARISM—OR MISUSE OF SOURCES?

Sometimes students and other novice writers are accused of plagiarism because they did not cite all their sources or did not cite their sources conventionally. This can happen when writers are inexperienced with or simply do not know the conventions.

To avoid this happening to you, take the following steps:

- If you receive an assignment that asks you to use sources, be sure you know what citation style your teacher wants you to use. If an assignment does not specify a style, ask.

- Ask your teacher or someone in a Writing or Learning Center to look at a draft of your writing: Are you using citation styles as conventions ask?

- Pay close attention to the conventions as they are presented in this handbook. The conventions are detailed and can seem tedious to learn, but the conventions are detailed precisely because it is a cultural practice in the United States to be very careful with the words and ideas of others.

➔ In Part 3 we guide you through keeping track of bibliographic information so that you can then document your sources conventionally when you write—as we show in Part 9.

CULTURAL ATTITUDES TOWARD THE WORDS AND IDEAS OF OTHERS

In some cultures, one is supposed to know and use the words of respected elders without attribution; everyone is supposed to know those words and where they came from. In some cultures, students use the words of their teachers and other authorities as their own to indicate that they have learned what they were supposed to. In the United States, however, concern for the value of property—and a belief that words and ideas can be individual property (➔ see pages 116–117)—has led to a valuing and the development of conventions for acknowledging uses of others' words or ideas.

WHY CITE AND DOCUMENT SOURCES?
AVOIDING PLAGIARISM

The best way to avoid plagiarism is to have integrity toward your sources and toward yourself as a researcher: *Respect the words and ideas of others as you would like your own words and ideas respected.*

KNOW WHAT WORDS AND IDEAS DON'T NEED TO BE CITED

- **Common and shared knowledge.** You don't need to cite a source when you write common knowledge, such as that there are seven days in a week or that Maryland's capital is Annapolis. To be sure whether you need to cite a source, ask yourself if everyone in your audience will know the information. If your answer is **yes**, then you need not cite a source. If you're unsure whether your information is common knowledge, find and cite a source for it.

- **Facts available in a wide range of sources.** If every encyclopedia or newspaper you find states that Joan of Arc died in 1431 or that between 22 and 26 inches of snow fell in upstate New York on Monday, then you can include these facts without citations.

- **The results of your own field research.**

KNOW WHAT WORDS AND IDEAS ALWAYS NEED TO BE CITED

- **Someone else's exact words** that you copied from a book, website, or interview.

- **Your paraphrase or summary of another's words or ideas.** (→ See pages 190–193 and 200–201.)

- **Facts not known or accepted by everyone in your audience.** For example, while global climate change is accepted by almost all scientists, some nonscientific audiences are still unsure. If you write to such an audience, provide sources for any evidence you offer that the climate is changing.

- **Photographs, illustrations, charts, or graphs.** Give the source (with permission from the text's copyright holder, if possible) for any visual object you use.

WORK HABITS FOR AVOIDING PLAGIARISM

- Keep a running source list or a working bibliography of all sources you might use. This will help you have at hand the information you need to cite sources as others expect.

  → See pages 140–141.

- If you record someone else's words because you might use them later, mark that they *are* someone else's words; this will keep you from using them as though they were yours.

  If you copy words from a webpage into your notes, color-code the notes or put quotation marks around them; always record the information you need for citing the words.

  → See pages 132–135 for the information you need to record to cite webpages.

- If you record words from print sources, put quotation marks around them and record the source information.

  → See pages 124–131 for the information to record to cite print texts.

- If you work online, use websites like *diigo.com* or *citeulike.org*—or use *Zotero*—to track your sources. Similarly, make copies of print sources you might use so that you can check—after you've finished your writing—that you have cited with integrity.

- Understand how to quote, summarize, and paraphrase.

  → See pages 188–203.

- Understand how to cite the words of others in your text.

  → For MLA in-text citations, see pages 364–367; for APA, see pages 399–401; for CSE, see page 422; for CMS, see pages 425–428.

- Understand how to build accurate and appropriate works-cited or reference list pages.

  → For sample sets of MLA works-cited pages, see pages 362–363; for a sample APA reference list, see page 398.

HOW TO CHECK THAT YOU HAVE CITED ALL YOUR SOURCES

When you are almost finished with a paper, give it to a friend who is a careful reader—along with two differently colored highlighters. Ask the friend to mark your ideas in one color and everyone else's ideas in the other. If your friend highlights the ideas correctly, then your paper should be good to go. If not, follow the links mentioned above to make it clear when your paper's ideas and words are not your own.

KNOW KINDS OF SOURCES

Knowing that there are five kinds of sources and that each requires different citation information helps you use sources with integrity.

1

BOOKS

For the purposes of academic documentation, the category of books includes the following:

- edited collections and anthologies
- novels
- graphic novels
- computer documentation and software instructions bound like books
- conference proceedings
- textbooks and handbooks

→ See pages 124–127 to learn what you need to find for documenting books.

2

PARTS OF BOOKS

If you are summarizing, paraphrasing, or quoting from any of the following—

- an essay in a book that contains essays written by different authors (and this could include one story in a collection of graphic stories, for example)
- a single chapter in a book written by one author
- an article in a reference collection
- one poem in a collection of one author's poems
- one poem in a collection of many authors' poems
- the preface, introduction, foreword, or afterword in a book

—then you need to find the same information you would find for the book in which you found the part you are citing, as well as additional information.

→ See pages 128–129 to learn what additional information to find to cite a part of a book.

3

PERIODICALS

Periodicals are published regularly: every day, every week, every month, four times a year, or on some other schedule. Every issue of a periodical has the same name and similar formatting.

If you summarize, paraphrase, or quote from any of the following materials—

- a newspaper or newsletter
- a letter to the editor
- an editorial
- a popular journal, such as a magazine published once a month or even weekly
- an academic journal
- an article on microfilm
- a government booklet, pamphlet, or brochure
- a comic book that is published in a series

—then you are working with a periodical.

→ See pages 130–131 to learn what information to find in order to cite print periodicals.

4

WEBPAGES

If you are documenting an article in an online database,

→ See pages 136–137 to learn what information to find to create a citation.

For documenting any other kind of webpage,

→ See pages 132–135 to learn what information to find to create a citation.

→ To determine the kind of webpage you are using, see pages 64–65.

5

EVERYTHING ELSE

If you wish to cite a source other than the four kinds listed here,

→ See pages 138–139.

ABOUT SOURCES YOU READ ON A DESKTOP COMPUTER, LAPTOP COMPUTER, TABLET COMPUTER, OR CELL PHONE

It doesn't matter the device on which you read a source. A webpage that you read on a laptop is cited exactly as a webpage you read on a cell phone. A book you read on an e-reader requires (for MLA style) that you record the kind of software (**Kindle file, Nook file,** or just **Digital file**)—but not the device itself.

COLLECTING CITATION DATA FOR BOOKS

YOU FIND A BOOK'S CITATION INFORMATION IN TWO PLACES:

- On the Title page, which is usually a book's second or third page and has the title, the author's name, and the publisher's name and location.

- On the Copyright page, which usually is the back of the Title page. (In some books, this information is on the very last page.)

No matter what citation style you use, record the five pieces of information described on the next page. Some of this information you use for in-text citations and all you use for your paper's works cited section. All the styles require this information; they just use it differently.

If you cite a book you read in any digital or online format, you still need to record all this information.

YOU MIGHT ALSO NEED...

→ See page 387 for the additional information you need for dissertations, translations, multiple-volume series, and second (or later) editions.

→ See pages 126–127 for the additional information you need if the book is a collection of essays or articles written by different authors, a chapter in a reference work, or a poem in an anthology.

THIS BOOK'S MLA CITATION
Leith, Sam. *Words Like Loaded Pistols: Rhetoric from Aristotle to Obama.* Basic Books, 2012.

THIS BOOK'S APA CITATION
Leith, S. (2012.) *Words like loaded pistols: Rhetoric from Aristotle to Obama.* New York, NY: Basic Books.

❏ BOOK'S TITLE

Record the book's title exactly as it appears on the book's Title page, including punctuation (also record the subtitle if there is one). If the book's title is not in English, copy it exactly, including any punctuation.

❏ AUTHOR'S NAME

Record the author's name exactly as it appears on the book's Title page.

→ See pages 112–113 for what to record in cases of no or multiple authors, if a company or organization is listed, or if the author is described as an editor.

❏ PUBLISHER'S NAME

Record the publisher's name exactly as it appears on either the Title or the Copyright page. (For the sample to the right, you would record *Basic Books*; the other corporate information is not used in citations.)

❏ PLACE OF PUBLICATION

Record the city and state, or the city and country if the book was not published in the United States. (This information can be on either the Title or the Copyright page.) If you cannot find a place of publication, make a note of this. If more than one place is listed, use the first.

❏ DATE OF PUBLICATION

Record the year listed on the Copyright page (sometimes it is also on the Title page). If no year is listed, record that there is no date. Record the latest date if more than one is listed.

WORDS LIKE LOADED PISTOLS

RHETORIC FROM ARISTOTLE TO OBAMA

SAM LEITH

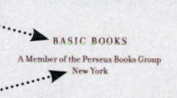

BASIC BOOKS
A Member of the Perseus Books Group
New York

TITLE PAGE

Copyright © 2012 by Sam Leith

Published by Basic Books,
A Member of the Perseus Books Group

All rights reserved. Printed in the United States of America. No part of this book may be reproduced in any manner whatsoever without written permission except in the case of brief quotations embodied in critical articles and reviews. For information, address Basic Books, 387 Park Avenue South, New York, NY 10016-8810.

Books published by Basic Books are available at special discounts for bulk purchases in the United States by corporations, institutions, and other organizations. For more information, please contact the Special Markets Department at the Perseus Books Group, 2300 Chestnut Street, Suite 200, Philadelphia, PA 19103, or call (800) 810-4145, ext. 5000, or e-mail special .markets@perseusbooks.com.

Designed by Trish Wilkinson
Set in 11 point Minion Pro

Library of Congress Cataloging-in-Publication Data

Leith, Sam.
  [You talkin' to me.]
  Words like loaded pistols : rhetoric from Aristotle to Obama / Sam Leith.
    p. cm.
  Previously published as: You talkin' to me.
  Includes bibliographical references and index.
  ISBN 978-0-465-03105-4 (alk. paper) — ISBN 978-0-465-03107-8 (e-book)
  1. Persuasion (Rhetoric) 2. English language—Rhetoric. 3. Rhetoric—History.
4. Rhetoric. I. Title.
P301.5.P47.L45 2012
808.5—dc23   2012005866

10 9 8 7 6 5 4 3 2 1

COPYRIGHT PAGE

COLLECTING CITATION DATA FOR BOOKS

WHAT TO DO WHEN THERE IS NO SINGLE PERSON LISTED AS AUTHOR

❑ **If you cannot find an author's name,** make a note of this.

❑ **If there is not a person's name but instead the name of a government organization,** record the information exactly as it appears.

❑ **If there are two author names listed,** record them all exactly as they appear, in the order they appear. For the example below, you would record, ***Ellington, Laura J., and Patricia J. Sotirin***.

AUNTING
CULTURAL PRACTICES THAT SUSTAIN FAMILY AND COMMUNITY LIFE

Laura L. Ellingson & Patricia J. Sotirin

BAYLOR UNIVERSITY PRESS

❑ **If there are three or more authors**

→ See page 378 to record this information in the MLA format.

→ See pages 423–424 to record this information in the APA format.

→ See page 444 to record this information in the CSE format.

→ See page 449 to record this information in the CMS format.

Images of an Era: the American Poster 1945-75

National Collection of Fine Arts Smithsonian Institution Washington, D.C. 1975
Distrubuted by The MIT Press Cambridge, Massachusetts London, England

Aesthetic Computing

edited by Paul Fishwick

THE ELEMENTS OF STYLE

by
WILLIAM STRUNK, JR.

*With Revisions, an Introduction, and
a New Chapter on Writing*

by E. B. WHITE

❏ **If no person's name is listed but there is instead the name of an organization or business,** you have what is called a **corporate author**. Record the name exactly as it appears on the Title page. For example, for the book above, you would record and cite "National Collection of Fine Arts."

❏ **If the person listed on the Title page is described as an editor** (as on the left), record the person's name and that the person is the editor. (If more than one person is listed, record the names just as you would record multiple authors' names, as indicated in the cross-references on the bottom of page 126.)

❏ **If the book has an author listed as well as the name of someone who revised that person's work** (as on the left), record the name of the author as well as the name of the person who revised the book, indicating that the second person did a revision.

COLLECTING CITATION DATA FOR PARTS OF BOOKS

When you cite part of a book—

- a poem in an anthology
- one essay or article from an edited collection of essays or articles
- a chapter in a reference work
- the preface, foreword, introduction, or afterword to a book

—collect the same information you would for a book, as shown on pages 124–125.

Also collect the information shown on the page to the right.

If you cite part of a book you read in any digital or online format, you still need to record all the information described here.

AN MLA CITATION FOR THIS ESSAY FROM AN EDITED COLLECTION

Brasseur, Lee E. "Contesting the Objectivist Paradigm: Gender Issues in the Technical and Professional Communication Curriculum." *Central Works in Technical Communication,* edited by Johndan Johnson-Eilola and Stuart A. Selber, Oxford UP, 2004, pp. 64-80.

THIS ESSAY'S APA CITATION

Brasseur, L. E. (2004.) "Contesting the objectivist paradigm: Gender issues in the technical and professional communication curriculum." In J. Johnson-Eilola and S. A. Selber (Eds.), *Central works in technical communication* (pp. 64–80). New York, NY: Oxford University Press.

In addition to collecting the information for a book as shown on pages 124–125, also collect:

❑ **ESSAY OR ARTICLE TITLE**
Include a subtitle, if there is one.

❑ **NAME OF THE PERSON WHO WROTE THE ESSAY OR ARTICLE**

❑ **ARTICLE OR ESSAY PAGE NUMBERS**

32

CONTESTING THE OBJECTIVIST PARADIGM

*Gender Issues in the Technical and
Professional Communication Curriculum*

LEE E. BRASSEUR

When I wrote this article, I was excited about the class that I describe because it illustrated how a gender-centered pedagogy could inform an entire course in technical communication. At the time I was frustrated with the lack of cultural sensitivity in technical communication textbooks. Other motivations were my own reading of feminist scholars such as Donna Haraway, who examined the work of female physical and social anthropologists who studied primates in the field. These anthropologists initially found it difficult to have their theories of primate behaviours accepted because their interpretations were in direct opposition to the prevailing theory of the male dominance hierarchies in primate societies (91).

I was also affected by Beverly Sauer's work on miners and, in particular, her description of women's testimonies in mining disaster trials (73-5). One woman's testimony, for example, included information about the number of times she had to wash her husbands work clothes, indicating that mines were not properly rock dusked (74). Yet because this testimony did not fit within the discourse of the dominant legal culture, it was rejected.

Works like these were influential in leading me to design a course and write an article that focused on issues of gender and technology. Today many technical communications textbooks now include both cultural and ethical issues and at times gender issues. In addition, the early work of technical communication scholars Mary Lay and Jo Allen on gender has been extended with an increased focus on gender and cultural issues in the field's journals and scholarship. My own scholarship and teaching continues to be inflected with cultural issues, particularly as they affect visual communication. For example, I am working on a project that exp...
tio...
bas...

lea...
for...
pr...
cul...
of...
im...

64   ©1
36.

CENTRAL WORKS IN
TECHNICAL COMMUNICATION

Edited by

JOHNDAN JOHNSON-EILOLA
Clarkson University

STUART A. SELBER
Penn State University

New York · Oxford
OXFORD UNIVERSITY PRESS
2004

COLLECTING CITATION DATA FOR PERIODICALS

The seven pieces of information listed to the right are used by every citation style, with minor shifts.

IF YOU ARE WORKING WITH THE FOLLOWING...

❏ If you are citing a letter to the editor, an editorial, a published interview, a review (of a book, movie, CD, performance, or anything else), or a microfilm, **record the kind of publication** (that is, along with all the other information listed to the right, record *letter to the editor* or *review*).

❏ If you are citing a daily newspaper, **record the newspaper's name**; if a local (not national) newspaper does not include the city name in its title, record the city name. For the date, **record day, month, and year**. When you **record page number(s), include any letters** that designate the newspaper section. If the article is on multiple pages, **record all of its pages, even if they are not sequential.**

❏ If you are citing a periodical that is published every week or every other week, **record its volume and issue numbers**. For the date, **record day, month, and year**. If the article is on multiple pages, **record all of its pages, even if they are not sequential.**

THIS ARTICLE'S MLA CITATION

Bieze, Katie. "Military Malfeasance: Exposing the 'Invisible War.'" *Documentary,* vol. 31, no. 3, 2012, pp. 16–17.

THIS ARTICLE'S APA CITATION

Bieze, K. (2012). Military malfeasance: Exposing the "Invisible War." *Documentary 31*(3), 16–17.

□ **ARTICLE TITLE**

Record the title exactly as it appears, including the subtitle. If the title is not in English, copy it exactly, including the punctuation.

□ **AUTHOR'S NAME**

Record this exactly as it appears. In some periodicals, the author's name is at the end of the writing.

□ **PAGE NUMBERS**

Record the page numbers for all the pages, even if the article is not on sequential pages. The example to the right is on pages 16–17, but you might have an article that goes from pages 72–75 *and* from 120–123; record all the pages, even if the range jumps.

□ **PERIODICAL NAME**

Record the name exactly as it appears on the periodical's Table of Contents or in the header or footer.

□ **VOLUME AND ISSUE NUMBER**

Record the volume and issue number from the Table of Contents. Sometimes this information is at the top of the page, but it might be at the bottom or on a second page. Look carefully—but know that some periodicals do not include this information. Record what you can find.

□ **DATE OF PUBLICATION**

Record the exact date: It may be a month and year, two months, or a specific day. The date can appear in a page header or footer, but it is always on the Table of Contents page. In this example, the date is *2012*.

COLLECTING CITATION DATA FOR WEBPAGES

For the purposes of citation, figure out the kind of webpage you want to cite.

→ See pages 64–65.

Is the webpage you want to cite...

- a personal webpage or blog?
- a group webpage or blog?
- a corporate website or blog?
- a website for a non-profit organization?
- a government website?

→ See pages 134–135.

- a page from a database of journal articles?

→ See pages 136–137.

- an article in an online periodical?

→ See pages 130–131.

- part of a book?

→ See pages 128–129.

Many kinds of webpages exist; on the following pages we show other examples.

THIS WEBSITE'S MLA CITATION
Sterkenberg, Tessa. "What is the Future of Communication? Let's Ask the Experts." *Media*, 15 July 2012, thenextweb.com/media/2012/07/15/whats-the-future-of-communication-lets-ask-the-experts.

THIS WEBSITE'S APA CITATION
Sterkenberg, T. (2012, July 15). What is the future of communication? Let's ask the experts. *Media*. Retrieved from http://thenextweb.com/media/2012/07/15/whats-the-future-of-communication-lets-ask-the-experts.

❏ WEBSITE NAME
If there is a name for the overall webpage or website, record it exactly.

❏ TITLE OF ARTICLE (OR OF WEBPAGE)
Record the title exactly as it appears, with any punctuation.

❏ PUBLICATION DATE
This can be near the author's name or at the end of the text or the bottom of the page. If you find only a year, record that. If you find nothing, note that, too.

❏ AUTHOR'S NAME
Record this exactly.

❏ PUBLISHER
If there is a company or organization name, copy it exactly. If this information is not obvious at the top of the page, look at the bottom. If you cannot find a sponsoring organization, make a note of this.

❏ DATE ACCESSED
Record the date on which you visited the page. You will use this information if the site has no other date or if the information is likely to change.

❏ URL
Record the URL.

LOOK EVERYWHERE!
This information can be anywhere on a webpage.

COLLECTING CITATION
DATA FOR WEBPAGES
EXAMPLES

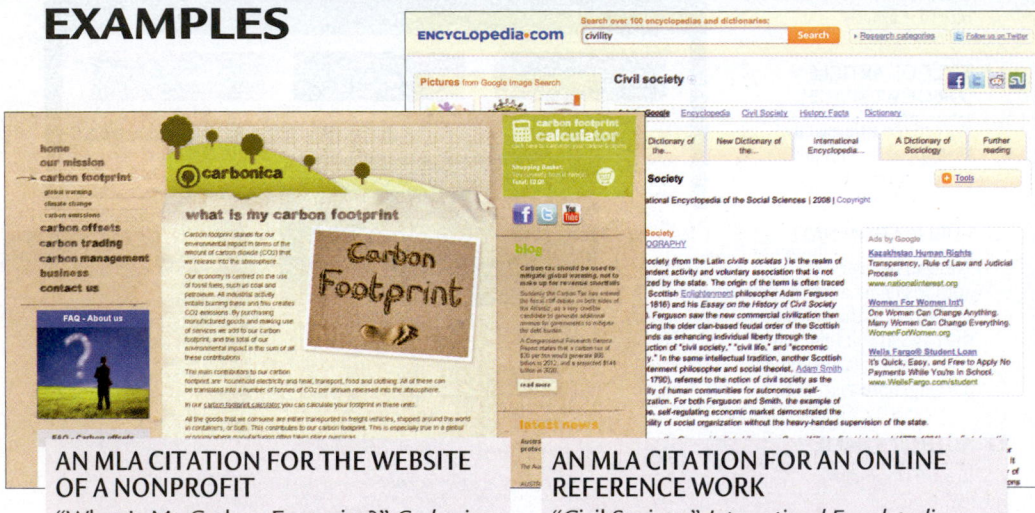

AN MLA CITATION FOR THE WEBSITE OF A NONPROFIT

"What Is My Carbon Footprint?" *Carbonica*.
2012, www.carbonica.org/carbon-
footprint.aspx.

THIS WEBSITE'S APA CITATION

"What is my carbon footprint?" (2012).
Carbonica. Retrieved from http://www
.carbonica.org/carbon-footprint.aspx

This webpage does not give an individual
writer for the article being cited; the date
was at the very bottom of the page. The
sponsoring organization is the same as the
website name.

AN MLA CITATION FOR AN ONLINE REFERENCE WORK

"Civil Society." *International Encyclopedia
of the Social Sciences*, 2008, www.
encyclopedia.com/topic/Civil_society.
aspx#3carbonica.org/carbon-footprint.
aspx.

THIS WEBSITE'S APA CITATION

"Civil society." (2008). *International
Encyclopedia of the Social Sciences*. Retrieved
from http://www.encyclopedia.com
/topic/Civil_society.aspx#3carbonica.
org/carbon-footprint.aspx

GROUP BLOGS AND CORPORATE AUTHORS

For group blogs, follow what is shown on page 135 for an individual blog; for the author
name, put the name of the person who wrote the particular blog post you cite. For
corporate authors, follow what is shown on page 135 for government websites, using the
corporation name instead of the government agency.

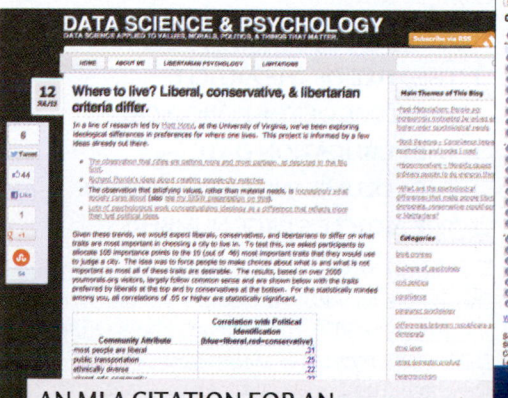

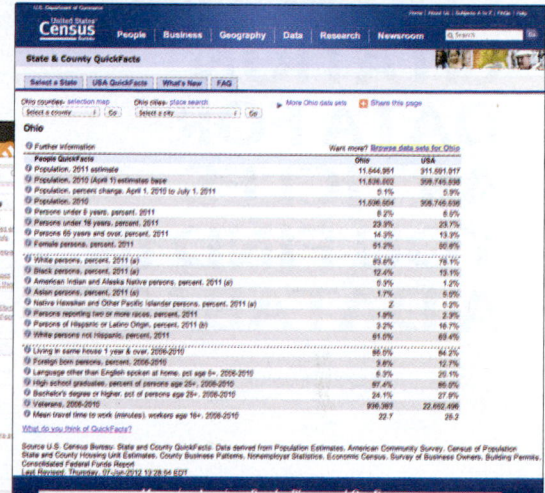

AN MLA CITATION FOR AN INDIVIDUAL'S WEBSITE OR BLOG

Iyer, R. "Where to Live? Liberal, Conservative, and Libertarian Criteria Differ." *Data Science & Psychology*, 2012, www.polipsych.com/2012/07/12/where-to-live-liberalsconservatives-libertarians.

THIS WEBSITE'S APA CITATION

Iyer, R. (2012, July 12). Where to live? Liberal, conservative, & libertarian criteria differ. [Web log post]. *Data Science & Psychology*. Retrieved from http://www.polipsych.com/2012/07/12/where-to-live-liberalsconservatives-libertarians/

Sometimes a personal website or blog will list a publisher or other sponsoring organization, but often it won't, as above. Note that the website does have a name, different from the text; you can find the writer's name by clicking "About Me."

AN MLA CITATION FOR A GOVERNMENT WEBSITE

United States Census Bureau, U.S. Dept. of Commerce. "State and County Quick Facts: Ohio." 7 June 2012, quickfacts. census.gov/qfd/states/39000.html.

THIS WEBSITE'S APA CITATION

United States Census Bureau. (2012). "State & county quick facts: Ohio." U.S. Dept. of Commerce. Retrieved from http://quickfacts.census.gov/qfd/states/39000.html

This webpage has no author name—but does list the government agency responsible for the information (as well as the name of the larger department within which that agency sits). Notice that the title in the citation includes the state name, to make clear to a reader exactly what page was referenced.

COLLECTING CITATION DATA FOR ARTICLES YOU FIND IN A DATABASE

→ See pages 80–87 to learn how to use databases.

FIRST, collect the same information as you would for any periodical article; this will usually be in one place on the page the database provides about the article, as in the example to the right.

- ❏ **THE NAME(S) OF THE AUTHOR(S)**
- ❏ **THE TITLE OF THE ARTICLE**
- ❏ **THE NAME OF THE PERIODICAL**
- ❏ **THE PUBLICATION DATE**
- ❏ **THE VOLUME AND ISSUE NUMBERS**
- ❏ **THE ARTICLE'S PAGE NUMBERS**

—but note that some databases will give you the article as a PDF and some will not. *When the article is a PDF*, the page numbers will be the same anywhere, and so you can copy the page numbers exactly as they are given. *When the article is **not** a PDF*, copy only the first page number, however it is presented.

THEN, collect information about the database and your use of it, being aware that MLA and APA citation tyles require different information, as shown to the right.

THIS ARTICLE'S MLA CITATION

Edwards, Kari, and Edward Smith. "A Disconfirmation Bias in the Evaluation of Arguments." *Journal of Personality & Social Psychology*, vol. 71, no. 1, 1996, pp. 5-24. *PsycARTCLES*, doi: 10.1037/ 0022-3514.71.1.5.

THIS ARTICLE'S APA CITATION

Edwards, K., & Smith, E. (1996). A disconfirmation bias in the evaluation of arguments." *Journal of Personality & Social Psychology 71*(1), 5-24. doi: 10.1037/0022-3514.71.1.5

❏ MLA: THE NAME OF THE DATABASE

This is usually at the top left. Be careful to distinguish between the database vendor (EBSCOHost here) and the database, *PsycARTICLES*.

❏ MLA: THE DATE YOU ACCESSED THE ARTICLE

❏ MLA and APA: THE DOI

The digital object identifier (→ see pages 390 or 416) is usually listed mid-way down the page; if you cannot find it, look for a "stable url" and record that.

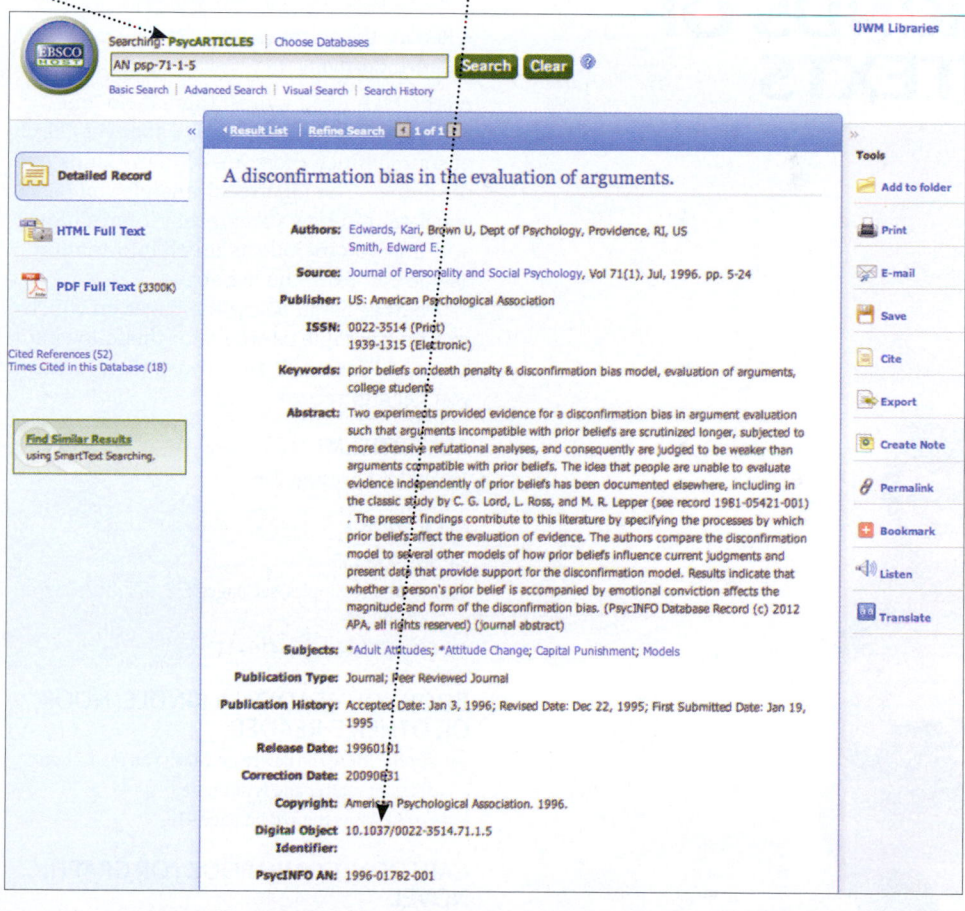

COLLECTING CITATION DATA FOR OTHER KINDS OF TEXTS

IN GENERAL...

- Record the author's name or names, if you can find any.
- Record the title.
- Record any information you can about who published the source, where, and when.
- Record any sort of page information for the whole piece or any part you cite.
- Record the source's medium (such as *DVD*, *Chart*, *Cartoon*).

As the MLA itself writes, there is no "one complete and correct format" for every kind of source, since there are so many kinds of sources. The MLA recommends you be consistent in how you present information and that you include as much information as you can from the list above.

We have listed below the pages on which we show sample citations for the following kinds of sources, so that you can see what you need to record.

ADVERTISEMENTS
→ For MLA, see page 376.

BLOG POST
→ See page 135.
→ For MLA examples, see pages 372, 377, 387, 389, and 390.
→ For APA, see pages 416–417.

BOOK YOU READ ON A KINDLE, NOOK, OR OTHER E-READER
→ For the MLA, the device on which you read a book does not matter and is not noted.
→ For APA, see the TIP on page 418.

CARTOON, COMIC BOOK , OR GRAPHIC NOVEL
→ For MLA examples, see pages 379, 384, 385, and 386.

FACEBOOK POST

→ For an MLA example, see page 389.
→ For APA, see page 417.

FILM, TELEVISION, OR VIDEO (INCLUDING ONLINE)

→ For MLA examples, see pages 377, 378, 379, 385, 386, and 387.
→ For APA, see pages 418–419.

INTERVIEW IN PRINT, ONLINE, OR ON TELEVISION OR RADIO

→ For MLA examples, see page 383 and 388.

INTERVIEW YOU CONDUCT

→ For APA, see page 419.

MAGAZINE OR JOURNAL ARTICLE YOU READ ON A KINDLE, NOOK, OR OTHER E-READER

→ For the MLA, the device on which you read an article does not matter and is not noted.
→ For APA, see the TIP on page 418.

MAP, GRAPH, CHART (PRINT OR ONLINE)

→ For MLA examples, see pages 389 and 390.
→ For APA, see page 419.

PAINTING, DRAWING, OR PHOTOGRAPH (PRINT OR ONLINE)

→ For MLA, see pages 382 and 391.
→ For APA, see page 419.

MUSICAL, DRAMATIC, DANCE, POETIC, OR OTHER ARTISTIC PERFORMANCE

→ For an MLA example, see page 391.

PUBLIC TALK

→ For an MLA example, see page 391.
→ For APA, see page 419.

SOUND RECORDING (INCLUDING AUDIOBOOKS AND PODCASTS)

→ For MLA examples, see pages 383 and 389.
→ For APA, see page 418.

SOFTWARE

→ For APA, see page 418.

TELEVISION OR RADIO PROGRAM

→ For MLA, see page 382.
→ For APA, see pages 418–419.

TWEET

→ For MLA examples, see page 378 and 383.
→ For APA, see page 417.

YOUTUBE OR OTHER ONLINE VIDEO

→ For MLA examples, see pages 377 and 378.
→ For APA, see page 417.

THIS WHOLE RESEARCH AND WRITING PROCESS MEANDERS

Because we present all this information on all these pages in a book, the process looks neat, as though it follows the linear order of book pages—but all people who call themselves "writers" will tell you that the process is not like that at all. Writers' ideas shift as they learn more; they need to rethink earlier ideas or find new sources. So don't worry if your process so far (and in the future) looks more like this:

KEEPING TRACK OF YOUR SOURCES

STARTING A RUNNING SOURCE LIST

As you find sources that are useful to you or that contain phrases or sentences that will attract your readers' attention, keep track of both the sources and the quotations. You can do this on paper or online.

Keep all this information in order to produce writing that meets current academic expectations. As we described earlier in these pages, writers producing academic texts acknowledge the sources from which they draw their ideas and they make it easy for readers to check those sources. There are standard forms for showing this information in a research paper.

→ For information on the forms for documenting sources, see Part 9.

WHEN YOU FIND A SOURCE YOU MIGHT USE

Enter any source you might use into a running list—like the sample to the right—recording the information you need for that kind of source:

→ For a book or part of a book, see pages 124–129 for the information you need.

→ For a newspaper, magazine, or journal article, see pages 130–131.

→ For a webpage or website, see pages 132–135.

→ For an article you find in a database, see pages 136–137.

IF YOU THINK YOU MIGHT QUOTE WORDS FROM ANY SOURCE

In addition to the information for the source, record the exact words you might quote, along with the number of the pages on which the words appear (if there are page numbers).

HELPING YOURSELF AVOID PLAGIARISM

Because respecting the work of others and therefore acknowledging when you use their work is so important in academic writing, find strategies to keep track of when you copy the words of others. Whenever you copy words off a website into your notes or into a paper, color-code or otherwise mark those words.

→ See pages 104–107 to learn more about plagiarism.

EXAMPLE OF A RUNNING SOURCE LIST

November 15, 2016

Haidt, Jonathan. The Righteous Mind: Why Good People are Divided by Politics and Religion. Pantheon, 2012.

Schwind, Christina, et al. "Preference-inconsistent Recommendations: An Effective Approach for Reducing Confirmation Bias and Stimulating Divergent Thinking?" Computers & Education, vol. 58, 2012, pp. 787-796. Elsevier, doi: dx.doi.org.ezproxy.lib.uwm.edu/10.1016/j.compedu.2011.10.003.

"Home." CivilPolitics.org University of Virginia and University of Southern California, www.civilpolitics.org. Accessed 10 Nov. 2016.

KEEP A PAPER TRAIL

If you have the slightest feeling that you might use a source—to paraphrase or quote—keep track of it. It is awful to finish a paper only to realize you have a quotation whose source you don't remember: Either you have to remove the quote or you have to find the source.

ORGANIZE YOUR LINKS

If you don't already know about them, take a look at websites like Diigo, Delicious, or Mendeley, or at software like Zotero, for tracking your online sources. These websites can also help you see the research other people have carried out on your topic.

CITE VISUAL SOURCES

If you use visual material made by others—such as charts, graphs, posters, photographs, and so on—you need to document the source.

→ For citing visual materials in MLA style, see pages 376, 378, 379, 389, 390, and 391. For APA style, see pages 439–440.

HINTS & TIPS FOR COLLECTING CITATION INFORMATION

COLLECT IT NOW!

If there is any possibility that you might use a source, record its citation information immediately. Nothing will vex you more than having to find a source at the last minute as you are putting the finishing touches on a paper.

COLLECT INFORMATION ABOUT ONLINE SOURCES

Even though you can bookmark webpages and go back to them later, two problems will confront you if you do not collect citation information immediately:

- You have to wade through all your other bookmarks to find the ones you want.
- The information on the page might have changed from when you first visited it.

If you are publishing your paper online, you might think that you do not need to provide a works cited list because you can provide links directly to the webpages you cite. But many readers will still want to see the full list of all your citations in one place. In addition, because websites can change quickly (or disappear), a citation will reference when you saw the site so that readers won't be lost if a link takes them to a site different from the one you referenced.

KEEP ALL YOUR SOURCE INFORMATION IN ONE PLACE

Get in the habit of having a notebook or folder or single online document in which you keep track of all your sources.

You want to be able to put together your final, formal list of works cited all at once, and you want to be able to check your in-text citations all at once.

IF YOU KNOW THE STYLE EXPECTED FOR YOUR FINAL PAPER, PUT YOUR SOURCES INTO THAT FORMAT RIGHT AWAY

This will save you time when you are finishing your paper.

→ For MLA style, see pages 329–394.
→ For APA style, see pages 395–440.
→ For CSE style, see pages 441–445.
→ For CMS style, see pages 446–450.

KEEP IN MIND THAT YOU MIGHT NOT USE ALL THE SOURCES YOU COLLECT

Until you have the absolute, final version of a paper, you will not know exactly which sources you will need. Sometimes you can become attached to a source, or to all your sources, because of the time and energy you put into researching—but this doesn't mean you will need the source.

Remember that you cite only the sources that you quote, paraphrase, summarize, or otherwise reference in your writing.

PART 5
ANALYZING ARGUMENTS AND ENGAGING WITH SOURCES

CONTENTS

5 ANALYZING ARGUMENTS

WHERE ARE WE IN A PROCESS FOR COMPOSING?

Understanding your project
Getting started
Asking questions
Shaping your project for others
Drafting a paper
Getting feedback
Revising
Polishing

Critical thinking and questioning
Summarizing, quoting, and paraphrasing sources
Developing a thesis statement

Questions you might have about analyzing arguments and engaging with sources:

What does it mean to "engage with sources"?
→ See pages 144–145.

What is analysis? Why should I do analysis?
→ See pages 146–147.

How do I read arguments analytically and critically?
→ See pages 158–187.

How—and why—do I quote, summarize, and paraphrase sources?
→ See pages 188–203.

Why is summarizing one of the most important academic abilities I need?
→ See page 191.

What is an annotated bibliography?
→ See pages 204–205.

How do I put sources in dialogue with each other?
→ See pages 206–207.

How do I develop a working thesis statement?
→ See pages 208–209.

THE WPA OUTCOMES* FOR PART 5 INCLUDE:

Rhetorical abilities: Learning and using rhetorical concepts through analyzing a variety of texts.

Critical thinking, reading, and composing abilities: Using reading and writing for inquiry and critical interpretation; reading a range of kinds of texts, attending to relations between assertion and evidence and between verbal and nonverbal elements.

* See page 15.

ENGAGING WITH SOURCES

> Authentic research is all about playing with ideas. You notice something odd: two things that are strangely similar, something that doesn't behave the way you expect, or something that makes you think, "What's up with that?" Maybe you see something that's broken, and you want to work out a way to fix it, or you hear something that makes you so mad and you need to explain why it's messed up. You don't know where it's leading when you start, and you might change your mind before you're done, but that's how it goes.

WE HOPE PART 5 HELPS YOU INCREASE YOUR CONFIDENCE

The words above come from Barbara Fister, a professor and Academic Librarian at Gustavas Adolphus College in Minnesota; she spoke them in an interview with Project Information Literacy. (You can read the interview at http://projectinfolit.org/st/fister.asp). In the interview, Fister goes on to say:

> I have read wonderful undergraduate papers, ones that are creative, insightful, and original—and perceptive about what an academic audience expects and values. Those students have made a shift in self-perception that makes a huge difference. They see knowledge as constructed by people like them; they have a genuine question and a genuine itch to see how they might answer it. And they have figured out how to present their ideas in an academic form that doesn't desiccate their insights or silence their individual voice.

We quote Fister because we'd like you to gain or strengthen the attitude, sense of play, and confidence toward sources and ideas she describes.

WRITING THAT ENGAGES WITH SOURCES...

SEEKS INTEGRITY AND ACCURACY

Engaged writing respects the hard work of a source's author. Such writing shows that a writer tried hard to understand the source on its own terms and to represent it truthfully in all references to the source.

→ See pages 148–157 to learn about analyzing sources for understanding.

→ Learn how to quote, summarize, and paraphrase accurately on pages 188–203.

IS PROPELLED BY SOURCES

Writing that engages with sources doesn't simply repeat what a source says. Although such writing quotes, summarizes, or paraphrases sources, it explains why it uses the sources and how sources move the writer's own thinking.

→ See sample analytic writing on pages 156–157, 180–183, and 206–207.

DOESN'T JUMP TO AGREEMENT WITH A SOURCE

Using sources is not about finding those that agree with what a writer believes. Instead, sources should help thicken and make subtle a writer's thinking and should help a writer see the complex relations that shape our lives together.

→ See sample analytic writing on pages 156–157, 180–183, and 206–207.

APPROACHES SOURCES WITH QUESTIONS

In Part 3 we showed strategies for developing questions to bring to sources. Writers engaged critically with sources approach the sources with many questions in mind: They want to read to learn.

→ On pages 174–179 and 186–187 you can see writers approaching sources with questions.

USES SOURCES TO GENERATE MORE QUESTIONS

As writers analyze sources to build understanding of their arguments, they use that understanding to generate further questions: questions for the source itself but also new questions for the issue being considered.

→ An annotated bibliography on pages 204–205 shows a writer summarizing sources and asking questions.

ENGAGES WITH SOURCES—NOT SENTENCES

Engaged writing does not draw only on single sentences from sources; instead, it shows that it understands the full argument of a source and draws on the ideas developed in the source.

→ To write summaries, see pages 190–193.

→ See Haley's final draft in Part 9, on pages 354–363.

WHAT IS ANALYSIS?

Analysis breaks something into its pieces to help us learn how the pieces fit into a whole.

To learn about and prevent diseases, doctors analyze bodies' organs and functions. They analyze skeletal or muscular systems, the organs of digestion or sight, and the cellular processes of those systems and organs. Once doctors understand how these parts fit together, they can question how a change in one part affects others, how (for example) a liver disease affects the stomach.

Similarly, social scientists analyze crises resulting from human action (such as wars and economic depressions) and crises resulting from a mix of human and natural causes (deaths from heatwaves or hurricanes). They try to understand the political, social, economic, and technological structures of cities, countries, and regions so they can ask how actions and events affect those structures. They hope to learn how similar crises might be avoided in the future.

Similarly, communication specialists analyze the texts we all give each other. They can specialize in analyzing political speeches, television advertising, film, literature, or digital communications. These specialists use different analytic tools; in this book, we use the analytic tools of rhetoric.

WHY DO ANALYSIS FOR WRITING?

The diagram below shows what writers can do with analysis of others' texts: Analysis helps you understand how a text works, which then helps you determine whether you want to be persuaded by its arguments.

In addition, analyzing others' texts helps you sharpen your thinking in general—and you can apply observations about others' writing to help you with your own.

In the upcoming pages, we follow the analytic scheme below, to help you move from *analyzing to understand* to *analyzing to ask questions of a text.*

ANALYSIS helps us to...

Break a text down into its parts and identify its main strategies. Then we can...

understand.

If we can describe the parts of a text and how they fit together into a whole, then we can say we understand the text and what its composer's purpose might have been in producing it.

ask questions.

Once we understand a text, we can question it:

Does the text achieve the composer's purpose?

- Do the strategies used in the text fit with its purpose?

- Is the intended audience likely to be persuaded by the strategies used?

What do I think about that purpose and the strategies used to achieve it?

- Can I support the purpose?

- Are the strategies used valid?

- Do I accept those strategies, or think they are ethical?

- Do I think the text's composer respects the text's audience?

UNDERSTANDING AND ANALYZING TEXTS

RHETORICAL ANALYSIS

Rhetorical analysis begins with two steps:

STEP 1

NAMING A COMPOSER'S CHOICES IN DEVELOPING A TEXT.

A rhetorical approach assumes that composers make choices as they compose. A writer chooses a topic, words, word order, kinds of sentences, and paragraph order—among many other possible choices. A videographer chooses a script, actors, lighting, music and other audio effects, what to shoot, and so on.

The first step in rhetorical analysis is identifying the choices you see in any text. Simply list them, and then move on to the next step.

STEP 2

CONSIDERING HOW THOSE CHOICES HELP COMPOSERS ACHIEVE THEIR PURPOSES WITH THEIR AUDIENCE.

A second assumption underlying a rhetorical approach is that a composer's choices connect to how a composer hopes to persuade a particular audience.

For example, the music in a video documentary can tell you whether the maker wanted the audience to feel like dancing or like sitting back observantly—which can tell you whether the maker wanted the audience simply to be carried away by the documentary's arguments or to be alert and thinking about the arguments.

THE ADVERTISEMENT'S TEXT:

Almost 50 percent of all landmine victims are children.

Help us to help: www.ishr.org

STEP 1, FOR THE AD TO THE LEFT

In the next pages we do a rhetorical analysis of the ad to the left, carrying out step 2. For step 1, here are the choices we see in the ad:

- one photograph on the whole page, showing the inside of a house (but no people) from the Middle East or Africa
- the use of tick marks and handwriting to show a growing child's height
- the use of a girl's name, "Mariam," next to the tick marks
- the use of very few words
- the use of the International Society of Human Rights logo at the bottom right

STEP 2, RHETORICAL CHOICES: APPEALS

In carrying out the analysis of the ad on the next pages, we introduce you to strategies rhetoricians believe to exist in all texts:

- Appeals to emotion, called *pathos appeals*.
- Appeals based on the arrangements of a text, called *logos appeals*.
- Appeals based on the character of the text's author, called *ethos appeals*.

In the next pages you'll see these appeals in action.

UNDERSTANDING AND ANALYZING TEXTS
UNDERSTANDING APPEALS TO EMOTIONS

PEOPLE COMPOSE TEXTS TO MOVE OTHERS

Every text is composed for a purpose—and for that purpose to be achieved, the audience has to shift. The audience can simply have their attention shifted from one object to another; more often, however, the shift is larger, from passivity to engagement, from not knowing or caring about a topic to knowing and caring, from feeling hopeless to wanting to act.

In all of this, there is a shifting in the audience's emotion.

What emotions does an audience hold on a topic before they read, see, or hear a text—and what emotions does the composer hope the audience will hold afterward?

And—given the emotion a text's composer hopes an audience will feel after engaging with the text—what compositional strategies should the composer choose?

In rhetoric, a composer's use of strategies to shift an audience's emotions is called

PATHOS.

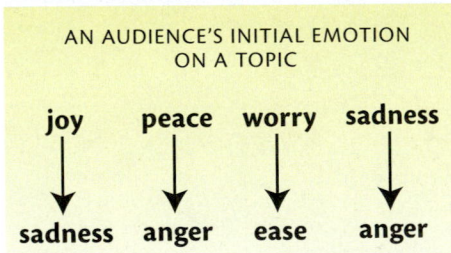

AN AUDIENCE'S INITIAL EMOTION ON A TOPIC

joy	peace	worry	sadness
↓	↓	↓	↓
sadness	anger	ease	anger

THE EMOTION YOU HOPE THEY WILL HOLD AFTER ENGAGING WITH YOUR TEXT

PATHOS IN ADVERTISEMENTS

In both these advertisements, intended for magazines, pathos is large. Both ads help viewers fill in what is missing and so move from not knowing or feeling much about land mines' effects to feeling sadness and loss at the effects.

In the first ad, the single large photograph pulls viewers into a house, looking toward the front doors. The house is empty, but people and their once happy actions are implied: The tickmarks on the wall imply that parents and a child live here, with the parents proudly tracking the child's growth. But the photograph also shows the child has lost height—which raises the emotion of confusion in viewers. When they read the words at the bottom of the page about child victims of land mines, viewers will sadly understand what happened to the child who lives in this house; they will understand why the space now feels empty and quiet.

The second ad, from Physicians Against Land Mines, does show us a person and it fills in what is missing in two ways: The ad shows us a young woman, and where her leg should be there are words. The words tell exactly how the woman lost her leg at five while playing in a field; the words also tell how every 22 minutes someone is killed or maimed by a land mine left from a past conflict, and that over sixty million mines remain buried in almost seventy countries.

The second ad is more abstract and flatter than the first: It is black and white, and the woman is photographed as though she is no place, with her being helped to stand by a leafless branch (perhaps implying what the field looked like after the mine detonated?). The photograph implies that the young woman's life is now colorless, and she looks directly at viewers with a serious expression, as though to ask that viewers not let this happen to anyone else.

UNDERSTANDING AND ANALYZING TEXTS
UNDERSTANDING ARRANGEMENT
(including logic)

EVERY TEXT UNFOLDS IN TIME

Even in short texts like advertisements, we see some elements first and some second: Some elements are big or at the top. With novels, essays, films, or video games, we have to look longer to see the arrangements: We may read a book's conclusion first, but in the table of contents we see that the composer put the chapters into a particular order. On a website we can look at individual pages in any order, but we see that the designers have designated one page as the home page—and we still have to look at each page starting at the top.

To move audiences, composers make choices about the order in which audiences experience their work.

Choices about order can concern the:

- **Large scale of a text.** What introduces someone to the text and what concludes it? What does someone see first, then second, and so on?

- **Middle scale.** How are intermediate parts of a text given shape, such as sections or paragraphs in writing, the arrangements of one photograph in an advertisement that contains ten photographs, and so on?

- **Small scale.** In writing, how does the order of words in a sentence shape how readers read? In sound recordings, how do background music or ambient sounds play behind main sounds but still shape a listener's overall experience?

In rhetoric, a text's arrangements (including its logical arguments) are referred to as the strategy of

LOGOS.

LOGOS IN ADVERTISEMENTS

When viewers first encounter the ISHR ad, they probably see the photograph first, because of how it fills the whole page; after eyeing the page they see the words. This order matters because this order sets up an intellectual puzzle: Viewers see the tickmarks on the wall and are puzzled by why Mariam got shorter; if they saw the words first there would be no puzzle to figure out and the order would not engage readers as much.

The Physicians Against Land Mines poster is also mostly one big photograph—but it is presented so that viewers see the young woman and the words-that-fill-in-her-leg at the same time. Viewers see a space where the young woman's leg used to be, but the space is already filled with explanatory words. Nothing is left to the imagination with this ad's arrangements: The arrangement of elements shows viewers the stark black-and-white results of land mines, and the last words of the missing leg inform readers about the ongoing danger.

THE BREADTH OF LOGOS

Logos might make you think of **logic**, and that is appropriate: Both words developed from the same Ancient Greek word.

Logos, as a name for a strategy that looks at the arrangement of a text, includes logic. Logic is about how ideas are structured—arranged—to have a very specific kind of effect.

So when you hear the word **logos**, it is fine to think about all kinds of arrangements that are used to structure texts, including the particular arrangements we call **logic**.

UNDERSTANDING AND ANALYZING TEXTS
DEVELOPING A SENSE OF THE AUTHOR

WE MAKE ASSUMPTIONS ABOUT THE COMPOSERS OF TEXTS

Whenever you engage with a text, you develop a sense of the text's maker.

Listening to talk radio, you probably develop—without thinking—a sense of any speaker's gender and age, and probably also a sense that the person is serious, funny, or well informed. You could be wrong in all your assumptions—but that doesn't stop you from making such assumptions.

We make the same assumptions when we read and even when we look at photographs, posters, or video games: We develop, consciously or not, a sense of who made the text and whether the person is trustworthy, authoritative, knowledgeable, intelligent, and so on. We develop a sense of how a text's maker thinks of the audience: Does the maker respect the audience and believe they can think for themselves, or does the maker think the audience has to be hit over the head with information?

WE NEVER KNOW A REAL PERSON THROUGH OUR ASSUMPTIONS

Text producers choose how they want to appear in texts: Writers (for example) choose tone of voice, evidence, and how they describe others. Because the evidence is limited—and can be carefully crafted—the sense we develop of composers is always limited and partial; we never get to know a **real** person through a text.

Composers can use any available strategy available to shape how audiences understand who the composers are. In traditional rhetorical terms, the sense that audiences develop about composers is called

ETHOS.

ETHOS IN ADVERTISEMENTS

In both ads, viewers see quickly that the makers of each want them to be engaged with the serious topic of land mines. This suggests that the ad designers are serious and concerned—and so worthy of a listen. But each ad engages viewers very differently with this issue, and so their different strategies suggest some differences between the ethos of each poster's maker.

The poster on the left shows no people. It shows only an empty space. The markings on the wall suggest that people—a family with a child—live in the space. The first ad's makers suggest what they want viewers to be thinking because they do not tell them any of this. The whole ad works this way, asking viewers to fill in empty spaces. The tickmarks on the wall can pull viewers in by confusing them: How does a child

get smaller? Only by reading the words at the bottom of the ad—the statement that 50 percent of land mine victims are children—can viewers understand what the photograph is about: Viewers cannot see the child but must imagine that she has lost her legs because of a land mine. These logos strategies suggest that the ad's makers think viewers are smart enough to figure this all out.

In contrast, the second ad fills in what is missing: The ad shows a young woman, and where her leg should be there are words. Those words name the woman, tell viewers what happened to her, and ask viewers to help Physicians Against Land Mines. The logos strategies of the second ad suggest that the ad's makers believe viewers need to be addressed directly and told explicitly about what has happened if they are to care.

UNDERSTANDING AND ANALYZING TEXTS
A SAMPLE ANALYSIS ESSAY

As we wrote earlier, the first step of doing analysis is to *analyze for understanding*. Can you describe what you think the purpose of the text is, and for whom it was intended? Can you find evidence from the text—your observations about how ethos, pathos, and logos are used—that supports your understanding? If you can do all that, then you understand a text.

   Your understanding may differ from others', but as long as you can use as evidence the strategies you have noted, then you have built your own understanding. Listen to how others analyze, and notice how they use the evidence they see

   On the opposite page is a written rhetorical analysis of one of the advertisements we examined on the previous pages, as an example of how you can write such an analysis for understanding.

■ ■ ■

You'll notice that the writing uses some of the descriptions from the preceding pages. This is one way to develop an analysis: Write down your observations, and then use them to build a more formal analysis (such as one required by a class assignment).

The introduction

The essay's introduction gives readers the context, telling that the essay is about a particular advertisement and who produced the ad. The introduction also acts like a signpost to what is to come, helping readers understand that the essay will explain how the ad is like a puzzle.

The body: Evidence

The essay's body fills in the promise of the introduction: The body gives evidence from the advertisement, describing exactly what is in the ad and offering readers an interpretation of how the different parts of the ad work together to create an experience for viewers.

The conclusion

In the conclusion to the essay, the writer summarizes the points made in the body of the paper and suggests future application in his own work.

A citation

Unless a teacher says you do not need to, always include a citation for any source about which you write. Because the ad was found in an odd place online, this writer had to do his best to follow the MLA citation style for ads (➔ see page 390).

The advertisement about landmines and children produced by the International Society for Human Rights (ISHR) contains only one photograph, fourteen words, and a logo. Even with so few elements, the advertisement creates a deep feeling of emptiness and loss. The few elements have been designed like a puzzle: viewers must think and use their imaginations to understand the ad—and so they feel involved and connected.

How viewers are pulled in starts with the one photograph in the ad, which takes up the whole ad. The photograph places viewers on the inside of a house, at the entryway facing the doors to the outside. On the wall to the side of the doors are hand drawn tickmarks, the kind families use to mark the height of growing children. The space and the tickmarks encourage viewers to imagine a family: parents and a girl named Mariam. The parents proudly follow Mariam's growth, and we can imagine them gathered together happily to record how she grows. From the top down, the tickmarks record *Mariam, 7*, then *Mariam, 6*, and, finally, *Mariam, 8*. In other words, the tickmarks show Mariam getting shorter rather than taller. How can that be?

The only other words in the ad explain. These words are small and at the very bottom of the ad, the last place viewers look as their eyes move from top to bottom; they only see these words after looking at the photograph, imagining Mariam and her family and wondering why Mariam got shorter. The words say "Almost 50 percent of all landmine victims are children." Mariam got shorter, viewers will infer, because Mariam lost her legs to a landmine. That is the intellectual jump viewers have to make.

This ad doesn't ask viewers to actually **do** much of anything; instead, the final words are simply "Help us to help: www.ishr.org." Engaged viewers should go to the website to find out what they might do—but in the meantime their minds and hearts are full of the empty space they have filled in with the sounds of what should be a happy family but is no longer.

This ad shows the power of getting viewers involved by not showing or explaining everything but instead by designing a puzzle that asks viewers to figure things out themselves. The ad asks viewers to figure things out intellectually (why Mariam is shorter) and emotionally (filling in the hallway with the once happy family). The ad therefore gets viewers to think and to use their imaginations actively: It pulls viewers into the life of the not-shown family, and so probably pulls people into being more likely to want to learn and do more. I want to remember this approach for my own composing.

Works Cited

International Society for Human Rights. Advertisement. 3 June 2014, www. gutewerbung.net/international-society-human-rights-child-measurement.

ANALYZING ARGUMENTS

Once you understand a text, you can make judgments about it.

- Do you agree with the arguments the text is making?
- Is there enough evidence to persuade you to agree? Does the evidence offered truly support the arguments being made?
- What are consequences of the arguments being made?

Experienced researchers and scholars do not respond only to isolated chunks of a text but instead try to be fair to the whole text and to how its various strategies build to a whole.

On the next pages we show steps for taking apart arguments to see whether enough evidence is offered (and so we also discuss kinds of evidence and how to judge them). We suggest questions you can ask of texts to support your analysis.

TIP

BEING CRITICAL
In the next few pages on analysis, we help you judge the evidence offered in a text: Such judgments help you decide whether you want to accept the evidence and thus the arguments built on the evidence. (Earlier, in Part 4, we offered strategies for an initial analysis of a source's relevance and credibility.)

Judging the evidence of a text for yourself will help you decide later if your readers will see the text as a credible source that supports the arguments you build.

Be careful to evaluate carefully all texts—including and especially those with which you agree. It's easy to be critical when you disagree. The challenge is to think critically about sources with which you agree.

This editorial was published in the *San Francisco Chronicle* in March 2007:

Food Ad Blitz

IT CAN'T be healthy for a 9-year-old—or any child—to be bombarded with an average of 21 food ads on television each day.

That's especially the case when most of the products being peddled don't come close to meeting the ordinary definition of the word "food."

According to the most exhaustive study yet done on advertising to children by the Kaiser Family Foundation in Menlo Park, one-third of all "food" ads are for candy and snacks. Just under a third are for cereals (almost all of them loaded with sweeteners). Ten percent are for fast foods.

Of the 8,854 ads reviewed, none was for fruits or vegetables.

All those commercials add up. So-called "tweens"—kids between the ages of 8 and 12—see some 7,600 food ads each year. On average, teenagers see slightly fewer—6,000 a year, or 17 a day, while 2-to-7-year-olds see 4,400, or 12 ads a day.

To view these ads as an inevitable, and even normal, part of childhood in America is not acceptable. As an authoritative report last year by the Institute of Medicine concluded, food ads have a direct impact on children's health. "Television advertising influences the food preferences, purchase requests and diets, at least of children under 12, and is associated with the increased rates of obesity among children and youth," the report found.

What's more, food ads swamp public-service advertising that promote fitness and nutrition. Children between ages 2 and 12 see a pitiful 164 such messages each year, or one every two or three days. Teenagers see one such PSA, on average, once a week.

Marketers of food products can, and must, do better. Last year, 10 of the top 10 food companies formed the "Children's Food and Beverage Advertising Initiative," and promised to devote at least half of their ads to healthier food messages that encourage fitness and nutrition.

This must be a serious effort on the part of the food industry—and must embrace more than just the major food companies. Given the high stakes—the health of future generations of Americans—it would not be premature for Congress to begin to exercise more oversight over the glut of food advertising intruding into the lives of children.

On the next pages, we offer strategies for questioning the arguments offered in this editorial. The strategies will help you analyze the editorial but also:

- **Make judgments about sources you are considering using in support of your own composing.** If you question a source and find its arguments to be poorly made, you do not want to base your arguments on that source.

- **Make judgments about the validity and strengths of your own composing.** You can use the strategies we offer to be sure your arguments are well supported and are therefore more likely to be taken seriously by others.

ANALYZING ARGUMENTS
THESIS STATEMENTS

THE FORM OF A THESIS STATEMENT

Sometimes people use *thesis statement* very generally, to mean any short statement about what a writer hopes to achieve.

In this book, however, when we use *thesis statement* we mean a statement with the specific, informal, logical form described to the right. The ideas here about thesis statements come from the work of mid-twentieth-century philosopher Stephen Toulmin. Through his studies into the structure of argument, Toulmin developed an understanding of an argument's **evidence, claim,** and **warrant**.

When you approach a thesis statement in this way—whether you are figuring out the thesis statement in someone else's writing or shaping a thesis statement for your own writing—the thesis statement's form is what helps you figure out whether you want to be persuaded by an argument or whether your own argument is solid.

FINDING A THESIS STATEMENT IN OTHER'S WRITING

When you read another's writing, you can analyze it to pull out a thesis statement and its claim, warrant, and evidence—as we do on the right. By more directly seeing what an argument asks you to accept, you are in a better position to decide whether you agree.

USING A THESIS STATEMENT TO ORGANIZE YOUR OWN WRITING

Thesis statements structured as we describe help writers make decisions: They help writers organize their writing, decide what evidence is strongest, and determine where to focus their energies in writing.

→ See pages 222–225 for using a thesis statement to organize writing.

A THESIS STATEMENT FOR "FOOD AD BLITZ" (from page 159)

Below is the article's thesis statement:

> Food advertising on TV is affecting the future health of young people; *therefore*, Congress should have oversight of food advertising.

A THESIS STATEMENT IS COMPOSED OF THREE PARTS:

1 EVIDENCE

The evidence in a thesis statement provides the main reason the claim should come to pass: **Food advertising on TV is affecting the future health of young people.** In a thesis statement, evidence will be offered in a general form, but in writing developed from a thesis statement, usually more—and more specific—evidence is offered.

2 CLAIM

A claim is the condition, policy, or event that a writer wants to persuade the audience to desire: **Congress should have oversight of food advertising.**

3 WARRANT (which is implied by the evidence and claim)

The warrant is what a writer thinks the audience already believes—and so the warrant will not be stated explicitly in the argument or in the thesis statement. But *the whole argument depends on the warrant* precisely because the warrant is what the audience must believe for the evidence to persuade them to accept the claim.

To construct a warrant, first construct the thesis statement; then, combine the ideas that are not repeated in the evidence and the claim. For the thesis statement above, that gives us this warrant: **Congress should have oversight of the future health of young people.**

Sometimes a warrant can seem obvious but it is only by figuring out the warrant that you can determine what values or beliefs a writer is hoping you will accept without thinking.

Given the evidence offered by "Food Ad Blitz" and its warrant, do you want to accept the article's claim?

ANALYZING ARGUMENTS
WHAT COUNTS AS EVIDENCE

Evidence is what you offer audiences to persuade them that your position on a topic is worth considering.

There are many kinds of evidence composers can use to support their warrants; on these pages we consider:

1 EXPERT TESTIMONY
2 PERSONAL EXPERIENCE
3 ANALOGIES
4 FACTS (AND STATISTICS)
5 FIELD RESEARCH
6 SHARED VALUES
7 EXAMPLES

EXPERT TESTIMONY

An expert has special and thorough knowledge on a particular topic because of education, profession, study, or experience. Experts can be individuals or groups. Because of their knowledge, we believe we can rely on experts' judgments in the areas in which they know more than the average person.

Text composers can use the words of experts—their testimony—as authoritative backing on the topics about which the expert is knowledgeable.

EVALUATING EXPERT TESTIMONY

If you are wondering whether to accept expert testimony:

❑ Do an online search on the person or organization. Does the person have credentials—education and experience—for offering the evidence? Does the organization specialize in the topic? Does the person or organization have an affiliation indicating potential bias?

❑ Ask others what they know about the person or organization.

When you compose your own texts:

❑ Ask people from your audience if they know and trust the experts you are citing.

❑ If your audience might not know an expert you are citing, include descriptions of the expert, saying why the expert has authority for you.

PERSONAL EXPERIENCE

Personal experience is what we know through living. Each of us has experienced families, schools, jobs, and romance; we've paid taxes, driven cars, eaten, shopped, and seen our communities change. Every experience—and especially repeated experiences—shapes our sense of how the world works.

Personal experience is limited evidence precisely because it is personal. Without considerable research, you cannot know how many other people share your experiences; you cannot know if they draw the same knowledge from their experiences as you do from yours.

Because personal experience is limited, it ought to play only a small part in formal writing. It can serve as a single example in support of a point. An introductory anecdote about your experiences working in a fast-food restaurant can draw readers emotionally into an argument about the moral satisfactions of low-paying jobs, but you would need much more evidence to show that others enjoy the same satisfactions.

The same holds true for using others' experiences as evidence. A friend who has been to Burundi on a missionary trip might have interesting observations about how donations are spent in that country, but those observations have little place in your writing unless your friend is also an expert on the economics of donations or unless the observations are backed up by other evidence.

Personal experience can become facts or statistics when it is joined with and examined alongside the experiences of others through field research.

EVALUATING PERSONAL EXPERIENCE

When you see others using personal experience as examples in their writing, whether the experiences are their own or belong to others, ask:

❑ Is the experience used as evidence in support of the composer's ability to discuss this topic (ethos) or as an emotional appeal (pathos)?

❑ If the experience is used as evidence, does the writer acknowledge that the experience is necessarily limited? Is other evidence also given as support?

❑ If the experience is used to show that the composer has relevant experience for taking on the topic at hand, is the experience sufficient? Does the experience indicate that the composer has any bias on the topic?

❑ If the experience is used as an emotional appeal, does the emotion draw the audience away from what is at issue or does it help show why the issue might be worth the audience's attention?

When you compose your own texts, keep in mind the following:

❑ Be wary of generalizing from your own experiences. Always try to find out if your audience has shared the same experiences—and, if they have, ask if they have drawn conclusions similar to yours.

❑ When you use the experiences, observations, anecdotes, or opinions of others, use them only to illustrate examples and then offer other evidence of the kinds we describe on these pages.

ANALOGIES

Analogies are quasi-logical structures: When you use an analogy, you compare—usually at length—two objects, events, or processes so that the more familiar can explain the less familiar. For example, a long description of how the brain is like a computer would be an analogy in which the composer relies upon the audience's knowledge of computers to explain how the brain works.

Similarly, to call the Internet the *Information Superhighway* is to use an analogy: We are to understand the abstract Internet networked system as being like a highway. Most people in the United States have experienced highways, and so can think of the Internet as a series of roads and interchanges with information traveling between locations in packets just like cars.

But analogies work more than descriptively. They carry assumptions from the more familiar object to the less familiar. For example, the *Information Superhighway* analogy carries the assumption that the Internet should be a public resource as highways are, and that the Internet should be regulated, supported, and repaired with public funds just as highways are.

Analogies can be used in small, focused ways, or can shape the argument of a whole book: The writer Malcolm Gladwell, for example, one of whose short essays we examine later, has used a whole book to consider how *ideas can be contagious exactly as a virus is.*

An athlete offers the following analogy, drawing personal lessons from geese flying:

Geese have always been a role model for me as an athlete. They embody teamwork, loyalty, and a great sense of aerodynamics. When geese migrate south in the fall, they make a V formation—each bird takes turns leading, breaking the wind so that the geese behind can draft like in a bicycle race and conserve their energy. Each goose also takes turns pulling, The other geese honk and squawk from behind as a sign of encouragement. Each goose pulls his own weight over the long haul by taking a turn at the front....

To me, geese and the V formation symbolize teamwork.

If you do a Google search, you will find many such examples of geese flying in a V-formation as an analogy for how teams should work together and how business managers should lead. If you do carry out such a search, be sure to read any comments about the analogy; the comments often point out its shortcomings: If you carry out the analogy, it would be appropriate for a company's top managers to drop out of the lead positions and for some others either to die or recover; the V-formation is a pattern learned over the millions of years of evolution and so not easy for humans to learn or apply; there is no scientific evidence for the geese's honks being offered as support for the others.

Der Mensch als Industriepalast

Aus Kahn, DAS LEBEN DES MENSCHEN / Franckh'sche Verlagshandlung, Stuttgart /

Visual analogies are also possible. The above poster—from 1926—asks us to think of the human respiratory and digestive systems as an "industrial palace" or chemical plant. What might be consequences of thinking of humans as machines, or of the brain as composed of managers making decisions about how the rest of a body functions?

EVALUATING ANALOGIES

In reading and developing analogies, consider:

❑ Analogies prove nothing and do not guarantee that a situation will play out as the analogy suggests. Composers use analogies to shape an audience's attitudes: A compelling analogy can persuade audiences to consider an object or process in a positive light, which is a large part of any successful argument. A compelling analogy is therefore both a pathos appeal and a form of logos.

❑ When it is compelling, an analogy can so focus your perceptions that you cannot think outside the analogy. When you see an analogy being used as evidence in an argument, or want to use one yourself, try carrying out the implications of the analogy, as those commenting on the bird–human leadership example (on the opposite page) did.

By coming up with alternative analogies, you can also explore how an analogy shapes thinking. For example, consider how the *Internet as a Superhighway* analogy asks us to think of the Internet as roads and exchanges and implies that the Internet should be built and supported with public funds as our highways are. To consider an alternative, ask what implications accompany thinking of the Internet as a marketplace or huge library.

FACTS AND STATISTICS

A fact is a statement about an event or condition that exists or has happened. Facts are true or false, with no gray areas.

Facts are verifiable: They can be checked. If someone claims that it is a fact that cold climate turtles hibernate, we ought to be able to go see such hibernating turtles for ourselves.

Facts can be presented in words and through numbers, firsthand experience, illustrations, charts, and graphs.

Facts can be presented in diagrams, as in this explanation of swimmer's itch:

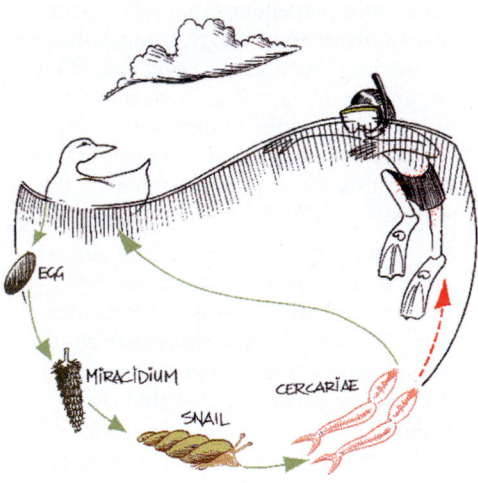

This diagram brings together small facts about a parasitic flatworm's life cycle in order to build a larger fact about how swimmers get infected with the worm.

Facts can be about historical events—

In the late 18th century, Haiti's nearly half million slaves revolted under Toussaint L'Ouverture. In 1804, after a prolonged struggle, Haiti became the first black republic to declare its independence.

—more recent events—

He graduated from Aurora College in 2015.

—or natural objects and events:

Jupiter is the largest planet.

The maximum age of a snapping turtle recorded in nature is 24 years.

STATISTICS—A KIND OF FACT

Statistics result from manipulations of number sets. Statistics can be in tables—

Table 1241.
Household Pet Ownership: 2006

	DOGS	CATS	BIRDS
Total companion pet population (millions)	72.1	81.7	11.2
Number of households owning pets (millions)	43.0	37.5	4.5
Average number owned per household	1.7	2.2	2.5

Source: U.S. Census Bureau, *Statistical Abstract of the United States: 2012*

—be written—

In June 2012, developer PopCap released the results of its third annual survey of mobile game consumption in the United States and United Kingdom. According to this survey, more than 4 in 10 (44%) of adults surveyed had played at least one mobile game in the past month, an increase of 29 percent compared to just a year ago.

—or presented in charts or graphs:

HIGH SCHOOL SPORTS in the U.S.
Rate of Injuries in 2014–2015 School Year

(rate is per 1,000 times athletes participated in one practice, competition, or performance; counts injuries where athletes lost 1 or more days participation)

Rate	Sport
1.27	Girls' volleyball
1.34	Boys' basketball
1.67	Boys' ice hockey
1.74	Boys' soccer
1.82	Boys' lacrosse
1.84	Girls' basketball
1.95	Girls' field hockey
2.23	Boys' wrestling
2.70	Girls' soccer
3.94	Boys' football

SOURCE: National High School Sports-related Injury Surveillance Study

EVALUATING FACTS AND STATISTICS
To evaluate these, ask the following:

❑ Are sources given for the facts and statistics? If so, are they authoritative? If not, do you trust the author enough to accept the facts?

❑ Do the facts and statistics support the conclusions that are based on them?

❑ Can you find other facts that contradict those you are questioning?

When you are using facts and statistics in your own compositions, consider:

❑ Will your audience accept the authority of the sources from which you've drawn the facts or statistics?

❑ Have you made clear how the facts support the points you are making?

❑ If you are working with a source that offers a wide range of facts or statistics—census data, for example—are you using the facts responsibly, using them fully, and not choosing only those that support your points?

USE FACTS, NOT OPINIONS

Pele—Edson Arantes do Nascimento—is the greatest male soccer player of all time.

The sentence above is an opinion: People can argue about who is the greatest soccer (or baseball or football) player of all time.

In 2014, Hannah Short of East Tennesee State University scored the most total goals in Division I soccer.

The sentence above gives a fact: It can be verified by checking data collected about college soccer in 2014.

FIELD RESEARCH

If researchers are fair and open-minded, honestly researching what others think, their interviews, observations, and surveys create facts. When researchers compile information, they can demonstrate what a group of people think or believe in a particular place and time. For example, they can provide statistics about how many people desire a particular policy or, through interviewing older people in an area, show what Sunday activities were popular in 1950.

You can use the following questions both to evaluate field research carried out by others and to help you shape field research you might perform.

EVALUATING INTERVIEWS

❑ Did the interviewer ask open-ended questions, allowing those being interviewed to provide their opinions and beliefs?

❑ Did the interviewer present the interview fairly, showing where the words of the person interviewed were cut or edited?

❑ What sort of relationship does the interviewer appear to have had with those being interviewed? Does the interviewer seem hostile, or overly friendly?

EVALUATING OBSERVATIONS

❑ Does the researcher describe the methods and goals of the observation, and how those methods and goals may have shaped the research?

❑ Does the researcher appear to have approached the observation seeking particular results—or been open to whatever happened?

❑ Are the researcher's results only positive, in support of the researcher's goals, or does the researcher note any observations that went against expectations?

EVALUATING SURVEYS

❑ Did the survey ask open-ended questions, allowing the person or people being interviewed to provide their opinions and beliefs?

❑ Was the number of people surveyed sufficient for providing support for any assertions a researcher is making based on the research? (To learn how many people need to be surveyed depending on what a researcher is trying to find out, see the article "Sample Size: How Many Survey Participants Do I Need?" <http://www.sciencebuddies.org/science-fair-projects/project_ideas/Soc_participants.shtml?from=Blog>.)

❑ Did the researcher seek information from an appropriately wide group of people, or only from those likely to give responses the researcher wanted?

SHARED VALUES

The editorial on page 159 relies on the warrant that *Congress should have oversight of the future health of young people.* (as shown on page 161). This warrant presumes the article's readers are concerned about living safe and peaceful lives as citizens. The editorial's writer does not argue for this value or offer evidence for it; the writer instead assumes that readers readily accept that value.

Composing an argument that does not rely on readers' values in this way is impossible. Even simple arguments such as *Don't do that—you'll get hurt!* work only if the person at whom they are directed believes that getting hurt is bad. The person making the statement doesn't have to explain this.

Longer and more complex arguments about going to war or about health care, for example, will appeal to shared values about patriotism, nationalism, the right of people to a doctor's care, or the right not to suffer.

Because the composers of texts rely on such shared values to encourage readers to accept their arguments, these values work to support arguments just as other kinds of evidence do.

EVALUATING SHARED VALUES

When you are questioning shared values or using them in your own work, keep in mind:

❑ Using shared values to support arguments depends on what the audience believes— so you must look at the values you assume as you argue and ask if audiences truly do believe the assumptions. Under what conditions does an audience accept them?

❑ People can hold contradictory values or accept some values only under certain conditions, as when some are against violence except in response to aggression. When you consider the values underlying an argument, ask if the assumptions hold in all cases or only in some.

❑ When you compose your own texts, be aware of the values you assume you and your readers share. If you do not make those values explicit to yourself, you will not be able to use them alertly in your writing—and so you may be surprised when your audience responds negatively.

EXAMPLES

Examples can make general or abstract arguments specific and concrete for audiences. Detailed examples can help audiences visualize what might otherwise be only conceptual.

Examples can be in a sentence—

Classes at our college emphasize personal attention, especially in the first year, when all classes are limited to fifteen students.

—or a paragraph:

What always amazed me about my father was how multifaceted he was. He was an intellectually curious physician living in a small town who had traveled the world, read at least a book a week up until he died, could continually kick my ass in Scrabble even though he didn't learn English until he was 23, and knew practically everything there was to know about classical music, Spanish wines, and French cinema. All I wanted to be when I grew up was as smart as my dad.

In each example above, a general statement comes first—*Classes at our college emphasize personal attention* and *What always amazed me about my father was how multifaceted he was*—followed by examples to show concretely what the terms **personal attention** and **multifaceted** mean to the writers.

Like analogies, examples do not prove anything. Rather, they help audiences better understand a point or concept, and so can enhance an audience's engagement with your work. Like analogies, they are logos and pathos appeals.

USING VISUAL EXAMPLES

Notice how the following selection uses both written and visual examples:

By immersing players in political or economic structures, the makers of *serious games* hope to encourage critical thinking and even activism. For example, in *Bacteria Salad* from Persuasive Games, players learn about agribusiness because they have to (in the words of the Persuasive Games website) "Harvest mass amounts of cheap produce and sell it for as much profit as possible. But watch out for floods and animal waste, or your greens might turn, uh—brown—and your customers will get E. Coli." As you can tell from the description, the game is humorous and, as the screenshot below shows, has lighthearted graphics, all to seduce players to engage critically with serious issues. I wonder, however, if the playfulness encourages or distracts from that purpose.

Screenshot of *Bacteria Salad* from Persuasive Games website.

EVALUATING EXAMPLES

Whether you analyze others' examples or use them in your own work, consider:

❑ Do the examples make clear the point they are meant to explain? Do they distract from the point, or will audiences easily understand why you use the examples?

❑ How do the examples support the general or abstract points being made? Are the examples too specific, causing the general points to get lost?

❑ If more than one example is used to clarify a general or abstract point, are all the examples appropriate? Are the examples ordered to move from least complex to most, or from most known to least known?

In addition, for **visual examples**, consider the following:

❑ Are the examples used only to support and explain general points, or do they distract from the purpose?

❑ Are the examples labeled, both to give proper attribution and to help readers understand their relationship to the words?

CHOOSING KINDS OF EVIDENCE FOR YOUR COMPOSITIONS

The research questions you developed in Part 2 can help you choose useful evidence. Decide which questions most guide your research; use the information below to help you develop evidence or find it in sources. Use what we've written in Part 4 to evaluate your evidence.

QUESTIONS OF FACT: FACTS!

QUESTIONS OF DEFINITION: Expert testimony (from a person or authoritative text) can help.

QUESTIONS OF INTERPRETATION: Expert testimony, analogies, personal experience, and field research can help persuade audiences to consider the interpretation you offer.

QUESTIONS OF CONSEQUENCE: Expert testimony, analogies, facts about what has already happened, and field research can be persuasive about what might result from a proposed action.

QUESTIONS OF VALUE: Expert testimony, personal experience joined with field research, shared values, and facts about people's behaviors help identify values.

QUESTIONS OF POLICY: Use expert testimony and facts.

ANALYZING ARGUMENTS
FURTHER QUESTIONS TO GUIDE CRITICAL READING

In the previous pages, we have been focusing on paying critical attention to logical elements of texts. Here, we offer you questions to help you consider an even broader range of choices composers make in their texts.

Once you have done preliminary analysis to be sure you understand a text, ask these questions to help you decide if you want to be persuaded by a text:

QUESTIONS ABOUT AUDIENCE
❏ Whom does the composer include in the audience? Who is excluded from the audience—and why?

❏ To what is the composer drawing the audience's attention? What might the composer be able to overlook by focusing the audience's attention in this way?

❏ What does the composer assume the audience knows or believes?

QUESTIONS ABOUT PURPOSE
❏ Why does this purpose matter at this time and in this place?

❏ Are there secondary purposes as well as a main purpose?

❏ Is the purpose clearly stated or easy to determine? If not, why might the composer have decided not to make the purpose obvious?

TIP

USING STYLE TO SUPPORT ANALYSIS
When you are analyzing writing, use Part 8 of this book, on style, to help you identify a writer's choices. Part 8 will help you name the strategies a writer uses for emphasizing parts of an essay and thus will help you figure out what is emphasized (logos) as well as how to describe the writer's ethos and pathos strategies. Such identifications help you see a writer's purposes more easily.

QUESTIONS ABOUT CONTEXT

❏ Where does the audience encounter the text? How might this shape their responses?

❏ When is an audience likely to encounter the text? How might this shape their responses?

❏ What events at the time of the text's production are likely to shape an audience's expectations about the topic?

QUESTIONS ABOUT ETHOS

❏ Does the composer have the appropriate background or experience for pursuing this purpose?

❏ Does the composer seem open to multiple perspectives? Is the composer treating those perspectives fairly?

❏ What cultural backgrounds and expectations shape the composer's positions?

❏ Is the composer using a tone of voice appropriate to the purpose?

❏ What role does the composer take toward the audience? Is the composer acting as a teacher, a lecturer, a parent, a peer, a friend? Is this role appropriate for the purpose?

❏ Is the composer respectful of the audience, treating them as intelligent, thoughtful people?

QUESTIONS ABOUT PATHOS

❏ What emotion is the intended audience likely to have about the issue? How does the text acknowledge that emotion, and try to shift it?

❏ Do the emotional appeals seem reasonable to you—or overblown?

❏ Are the emotional appeals appropriate to the issue?

QUESTIONS ABOUT LOGOS

❏ What claims, reasons, and warrants are explicit or implied in the text? (→ See pages 160–161.)

❏ What kinds of evidence does the composer use? (→ See pages 162–171.) Is that evidence relevant, credible, and sufficient? (→ See pages 88–101.) Do you know of or can you find evidence that points to different conclusions?

❏ Are the sources cited so that the audience can check them? If so, are the sources relevant and credible? (→ See pages 88–101.)

❏ Why might a composer start with particular examples or evidence? To what will these draw the audience's attention? (And from what will these examples distract attention?)

❏ How does the composition end? How will the end affect how the audience looks back on the rest of the composition?

GIVING EVIDENCE

If you are using these questions to do the preliminary analysis for writing a paper, include with your responses any evidence in the text that supports your responses. For example, when taking notes about ethos, you might write: *It feels as though the author is yelling at readers. All the sentences are short, emphatic, addressed to "**you!**" written as though readers know nothing about the topic.*

ANALYZING ARGUMENTS
AN EXAMPLE OF CRITICAL READING

To the right is a short argumentative essay about zero-tolerance policies in schools.

Read it through once, ignoring the questions we've put next to it. Come to your own understanding of the purpose, audience, and context for this text.

Then use the questions we've put here, which draw on the analytic approaches we've described in the last pages, to help you further develop your critical reading.

The beginning: Pathos and an example as evidence

The first sentences give an example and encourage readers to sympathize with the student before knowing anything else about him. Why might Gladwell start with an introduction dependent on pathos?

Naming

Why might Gladwell tell us the name of the tutor but not the student?

Evidence: A second example

What attitude does Gladwell want readers to have toward Bomar? Toward students now? How has Gladwell prepared his readers to have those attitudes?

Pathos: How readers are addressed

Why do you think Gladwell addresses readers directly here? How might a reader respond to these questions?

ANNOTATING WHAT YOU READ

The comments we've added to this article suggest how you can mark up your own reading, to keep track of your own questions and comments. By annotating, you see patterns in what you read, patterns that can help you determine purpose and other strategies. By annotating, you also see patterns in your responses—patterns that can suggest an overall analysis.

No Mercy
Malcolm Gladwell

In 1925, a young American physicist was doing graduate work at Cambridge University, in England. He was depressed. He was fighting with his mother and had just broken up with his girlfriend. His strength was in theoretical physics, but he was being forced to sit in a laboratory making thin films of beryllium. In the fall of that year, he dosed an apple with noxious chemicals from the lab and put it on the desk of his tutor, Patrick Blackett. Blackett, luckily, didn't eat the apple. But school officials found out what had happened, and arrived at a punishment: the student was to be put on probation and ordered to go to London for regular sessions with a psychiatrist.

Probation? These days, we routinely suspend or expel high-school students for doing infinitely less harmful things, like fighting or drinking or taking drugs—that is, for doing the kinds of things that teenagers do. This past summer, Rhett Bomar, the starting quarterback for the University of Oklahoma Sooners, was cut from the team when he was found to have been "overpaid" (receiving wages for more hours than he worked, with the apparent complicity of his boss) at his car dealership. Even in Oklahoma, people seemed to think that kicking someone off a football team for having cut a few corners on his job made perfect sense. This is the age of zero tolerance. Rules are rules. Students have to be held accountable for their actions. Institutions must signal their expectations firmly and unambiguously: every school principal and every college president, these days, reads from exactly the same script. What, then, of a student who gives his teacher a poisoned apple? Surely he ought to be expelled from school and sent before a judge.

Suppose you cared about the student, though, and had some idea of his situation and his potential. Would you feel the same way? You might. Trying to poison your tutor is no small infraction. Then again, you might decide, as the dons at Cambridge clearly did, that what had happened called for a measure of leniency. They knew that the student had never done anything like this before, and that he wasn't well. And they knew that to file charges would almost

Evidence: Examples

How do we know anyone is *incorrigible* or a *decent kid*? Gladwell seems to believe that these are obvious characteristics of people, but who gets to make these decisions, and based on what evidence?

Evidence: Research

How might readers respond to this move from the made-up stories of Jimmy and Bobby to the Tennessee study? Is there enough evidence given in this essay for us to check on the Tennessee study ourselves, to see if we agree with how it was conducted or with Gladwell's characterization of it?

Pathos: How readers are addressed

Gladwell now refers to himself and the audience together as *we*. By assuming we are all in agreement with what he writes, what might he be trying to achieve?

Evidence: Examples

Because of when this essay was published, Gladwell assumes his readers know he refers here to events in Iraq and at Guantanamo; he also assumes his readers share his interpretation of the events. Why would he insert such a serious example in parentheses here, when all his preceding examples have involved students?

certainly ruin his career. Cambridge wasn't sure that the benefits of enforcing the law, in this case, were greater than the benefits of allowing the offender an unimpeded future.

Schools, historically, have been home to this kind of discretionary justice. You let the principal or the teacher decide what to do about cheating because you know that every case of cheating is different—and, more to the point, that every cheater is different. Jimmy is incorrigible, and needs the shock of expulsion. But Bobby just needs a talking to, because he's a decent kid, and Mary and Jane cheated because the teacher foolishly stepped out of the classroom in the middle of the test and the temptation was just too much. A Tennessee study found that after zero-tolerance programs were adopted by the state's public schools, the frequency of targeted offences soared: the firm and unambiguous punishments weren't deterring bad behavior at all. Is that really a surprise? If you're a teenager, the announcement that an act will be sternly punished doesn't always sink in, and it isn't always obvious when you're doing the thing you aren't supposed to be doing. Why? Because you're a teenager.

Somewhere along the way—perhaps in response to Columbine—we forgot the value of discretion in disciplining the young. "Ultimately, they have to make the right decisions," the Oklahoma football coach, Bob Stoops, said of his players, after jettisoning his quarterback. "When they do not, the consequences are serious." Open and shut: he sounded as if he were talking about a senior executive of Enron, rather than a college sophomore whose primary obligation to Oklahoma was to throw a football in the direction of young men in helmets. You might think that the University of Oklahoma was so touchy about its quarterback being "overpaid" it ought to have kept closer track of his work habits with an on-campus job. But making a fetish of personal accountability conveniently removes the need for institutional accountability. (We court-marshall the grunts who abuse prisoners, not the commanding officers who let the abuse happen.) To acknowledge that the causes of our actions are complex and muddy seems permissive, and permissiveness is the hallmark of an ideology now firmly in

Evidence: Analogy

Gladwell takes an analogy about Christ and the Crucifixion and turns it around. This analogy concerns an event many take seriously and would not want to see used lightheartedly. Do you think Gladwell's overall purpose justifies his use of this analogy? What sort of reader, holding what sort of beliefs, would be likely to accept this analogy and find it appropriate? (And why might Gladwell use such a serious analogy here?)

The end

Why might Gladwell wait until his essay's end to mention the name of the student whose actions he described back at the very beginning of the essay? (Robert Oppenheimer was one of the people responsible for the atom bomb.)

ANALYZING GLADWELL'S EVIDENCE, CLAIM, AND WARRANT

To the right is one possible way of analyzing Gladwell's evidence, claim, and warrant. By separating these elements, you can have a better sense of whether you agree with each, whether you think they really do fit together logically, and whether you think the evidence works.

disgrace. That conservative patron saint Whittaker Chambers once defined liberalism as Christ without the Crucifixion. But punishment without the possibility of redemption is even worse: it is the Crucifixion without Christ.

As for the student whose career Cambridge saved? He left at the end of the academic year and went to study at the University of Göttingen, where he made important contributions to quantum theory. Later, after a brilliant academic career, he was entrusted with leading one of the most critical and morally charged projects in the history of science. His name was Robert Oppenheimer.

New Yorker, September 4, 2006, pp. 37–38.

EVIDENCE: *Zero-tolerance* policies potentially prevent good people from developing to their full productive potential.

THEREFORE

CLAIM: We should apply discretion rather than *zero-tolerance* policies when responding to the bad behavior of youth.

WARRANT: Discretion in response to the bad behavior of youth will help good people develop to their full productive potential.

DETAILED EVIDENCE: *Facts:* The people who apply zero tolerance apply the policy outside their rightful realm, as the University of Oklahoma case shows. *Shared values:* Zero tolerance does not take into account the differences in people, as the Bobby and Jimmy examples show. Zero tolerance does not take into account the moral development of youth. Zero tolerance removes the need for institutional responsibility. *Appealing to readers' experiences:* Readers are likely to agree, based on their own experiences, that Robert Oppenheimer would perhaps not have gone on to do his important work if *zero tolerance* had been in use in 1925.

ANALYZING ARGUMENTS
A SAMPLE RHETORICAL ANALYSIS

On the opposite page, we show a written rhetorical analysis—a critical analysis—of the article we examined on the previous pages, Malcolm Gladwell's article "No Mercy." You should be able to see how this essay grows from responding to the questions asked of Gladwell's essay in the previous pages—as well as how this essay cuts to the heart of Gladwell's argument by questioning his warrant.

This rhetorical analysis is one example of how you can write such an analysis.

The beginning: Ethos and a summary

This writer starts with a quick summary of Gladwell's article, to show that she has worked to understand it. This builds her ethos positively, so her questioning will be more persuasive to readers.

Then this writer gives her readers a sense of what is to come by quickly summarizing her main concern about the Gladwell article; in the following paragraphs, she gives evidence for this concern.

Analyzing ethos

The writer analyzes Gladwell's ethos: He is "confident … but not bullying" and wants to inspire others to think critically.

Logos: Evidence

Here the writer uses direct quotations from the Gladwell article to show that she has read carefully and is responding to specific Gladwell arguments.
→ See pages 194–199 and 524–525 for help with including direct quotations in your writing.

Ethos and pathos: The writer asks questions

After showing her readers the specific parts of Gladwell's writing that concern her, this writer can then raise the questions that motivate her concern.

Ethos: Adding authority by using other sources

After searching online, this writer found a report to demonstrate that her worry is real. This source ought to carry authority with readers because it is published by a government source—and also because the writer describes the detailed research on which the report is based.

No Justice, No Mercy?
Responding to Malcolm Gladwell

In his essay "No Mercy," published in the September 4, 2006, issue of the *New Yorker*, Malcolm Gladwell argues implicitly that current "zero-tolerance" policies hurt people more than we realize. For example, Gladwell tells about the brilliant physicist Robert Oppenheimer, who under today's policies probably would have been expelled from college and denied his important career because of dangerous actions he took as a graduate student. With this example Gladwell suggests that current students who are expelled for lesser offenses are losing future careers in which they might contribute to society. While there is much in Gladwell's argument with which I agree, his examples raise for me the question of who is to judge others, and how.

I appreciate the tone of Gladwell's writing. He is a confident writer, but not bullying. There is nothing in his writing to suggest that he thinks anyone who disagrees is somehow stupid or unthoughtful. Instead, Gladwell's writing seems more of a provocation, asking us to think on these matters because they have consequences. I appreciate being drawn into this issue by the range of examples and ideas Gladwell brings into his writing—but those examples lead me to my concerns.

As a possibility for how we might treat the poorly considered actions of the young, Gladwell uses the notion of "discretion," which he describes as being based in an awareness that "every cheater is different" (119). Therefore, Gladwell argues, we need to approach each case with an awareness of who has done the action, and why, in order to decide consequences: "Jimmy is incorrigible, and needs the shock of expulsion," Gladwell writes, but "Bobby just needs a talking to, because he's a decent kid" (119). But how does anyone know these things? What would someone have to do to get to know Jimmy or Bobby well enough to make these decisions with any certainty? And what sort of person would we want to make such decisions that have so much effect on the lives of others? To live together using the discretion that Gladwell asks us to have, we would need to find people who have the time and sensitivity to look carefully into the lives of others, and who have considerable training in understanding the patterns of someone's life so as to make valid decisions.

Meanwhile, however, many examples exist of discretion that is biased. For one, the United States Department of Justice's Office of Juvenile Justice and Delinquency Prevention published a report in 1995 in which the Office analyzed the available literature on the treatment of minority youth in the juvenile justice system; after analyzing 250

Ethos: Adding authority by quoting the words of others

This writer could have summarized the findings of the report she is citing, but by quoting from it she is able to let the report speak for itself, which can be more persuasive to readers.

Concluding

After giving her own evidence in the preceding paragraphs, the writer now summarizes her position so that her readers finish with a clear idea of her argument. (→ See pages 302–303 on conclusions.)

Notice, too, how she shapes her words: She neither dismisses Gladwell nor insists she knows it all. How does this shape her ethos? What sort of emotional room does this leave for reader response?

Citing sources

→ See Part 9 for help with citing sources.

THIS WRITER'S USE OF LOGOS...

To the right is one possible analysis of this writer's use of evidence, a claim, and a warrant. If you think that this writer has written a persuasive short essay, consider:

1 In what order are the evidence, claim, and warrant presented in the writing? Why might they be in that order?

2 Notice that other strategies weave into the writing, in support of both the logic of the claim, reason, and evidence, but also to persuade readers to have a sympathetic lean toward the writer's position: Logos matters tremendously, but it cannot stand alone.

published articles, with 47 being particularly relevant, the report argues that "processing decisions in many State and local juvenile justice systems are not racially neutral" (7).

Whether or not the juvenile justice system is the same now as it was in 1995, what the report shows is that racial bias can enter the system—even from people who are supposed to be professionals in deciding whether a young person committed an offense and how it should be treated. Other kinds of bias—based on class or gender, for example—also seem possible. If we do want discretion as the basis for responding to youth behavior, as Gladwell argues, how do we keep it fair?

I may sound as though I disagree with Gladwell. I do not. I think zero-tolerance policies in high schools harm the futures of people who are still too young to make certain decisions. But until an argument addresses how discretion can be applied knowledgeably and justly, without bias, I will sit uneasily with my beliefs.

Works Cited

Gladwell, Malcolm. "No Mercy." *New Yorker,* 4 Sept. 2006, pp. 37–38.

United States, Dept. of Justice, Office of Juvenile Justice and Delinquency Prevention. "Minorities and the Juvenile Justice System: Research Summary." 1995.

EVIDENCE: **Discretion is often neither fair nor offered equally.**

THEREFORE

CLAIM: **Discretion is not enough for making decisions about the lives of young people.**

WARRANT: **Young people deserve fair and equal treatment.**

DETAILED EVIDENCE: *Facts:* The writer also uses the expert testimony of the U.S. Department of Justice's Office of Juvenile Justice and Delinquency Prevention, and facts supported by that testimony. *Appealing to readers' experiences:* This writer appeals to the reader's own experiences by asking questions about how we make decisions.

ANALYZING ARGUMENTS
QUESTIONS TO GUIDE CRITICAL LOOKING

In the previous pages, we have been focusing primarily on alphabetic texts—but questioning photographs, graphic novels, advertisements, films and videos, and similar texts is equally important.

In our earlier discussions of how to understand what some posters do rhetorically (→ see pages 148–155), we analyzed the covers in terms of the rhetorical choices made by their designers. You can analyze any visual text that way—and then can ask **the same questions on pages 172–173** to help you consider whether you think the text has been designed ethically.

Because visual texts often function differently in society than print texts, you can also ask questions like the following:

QUESTIONS ABOUT AUDIENCE

❑ Who can see this text? How does the placement of the text (in a museum, on the Internet, in a magazine) shape who can see it? Who won't be able to see it?

❑ What knowledge is required for an audience to understand the text? Does a viewer have to know something about the history of art, about consumer culture, or about celebrities?

QUESTIONS ABOUT PURPOSE

❑ Is the primary purpose of the piece to encourage people to buy or to enjoy? Keep in mind that in either case, you need to say more: If the purpose were simply to sell or to delight for all advertisements or cartoons (for example), then there would be no variety among these texts because they could all achieve their purposes in the same way. If the primary purpose is to encourage people to buy, then there will be secondary purposes such as making people feel they lack something, or that they too can have endless fun, or....

❑ Why might the text's composers have used a visual text instead of an alphabetic text to achieve their purposes?

QUESTIONS ABOUT CONTEXT

❑ Are you seeing the text in the context for which it was designed? Where was it designed to be seen?

❑ How would the text be different if you saw it someplace else? If you are analyzing a painting in a museum, how would it be different in your bedroom? If you are analyzing a comic book, how would the pages be different if you saw them in a formal newspaper like the *New York Times*?

❑ How would seeing this text change if the number of people around you changed?

QUESTIONS ABOUT ETHOS

❑ Was this text made by one person or by many? Is it attributed to an organization?

❑ What knowledge and abilities did the maker(s) of this text need in order to design or produce the text?

QUESTIONS ABOUT PATHOS

❑ Would you describe this text as simple or complex? Is it cheery or morbid? Active or calm? What features of the text encourage these responses?

❑ Does this text use pathos as its primary appeal to your attention?

❑ Where does this piece require you to stand or sit to see it well? Do you need to be close or far away?

❑ Do you feel that this piece is inviting you to come closer or do you feel as though it is yelling at you to move away? Why?

❑ How would this piece be different if the colors were different?

QUESTIONS ABOUT LOGOS

❑ What is made visible in this text? On what people, objects, or processes does this text ask you to focus your eyes?

❑ What arguments are made by the text?

❑ What are the parts of this text? Name every element you can visually differentiate.

❑ What elements of this text do you see first? Which second, which third? Why?

A SAMPLE ANALYSIS OF A VISUAL TEXT

The poster to the right was produced by the World Health Organization as part of a Global Campaign for Violence Prevention.

The questions we ask here come from the questions on pages 172–173 and 184–185. The questions help you consider why this poster's composers chose the strategies they did.

Purpose
What do you think the people who designed this poster were hoping its audience would think, feel, or do after seeing the poster? Why?

Pathos
What do you think when you see these scratches? What sort of movement—inspired by what sort of emotion, using what sort of tool—would make them? What sort of emotional response might viewers have to seeing these scratches? Why do you think most of the scratches are over the eyes?

Context and pathos
The poster is simple: it has a photograph of a woman, a few lines of type, and some scratches. If we could see the original poster, the woman would be almost life-size. The poster situates its viewers as though they were sitting across the table from her, as though they could touch her. What emotional relationship might this physical closeness encourage viewers to have with the woman and so the poster?

Pathos: Color
Why might the photograph be black and white, with red text over it?

Audience
What does the age of the woman in the photograph—and what she is doing, and how she is dressed and made up—suggest about how the designers imagined the poster's audience?

Logos: Arrangement
Why might these words and the different logos be at the bottom of the poster rather than at the top? Why might the white space behind them have been made to look like torn paper?

Logos: Evidence and ethos
The poster gives one fact. What evidence is offered in its support? Whose authority is offered in support? Who might be interested in this fact?

GLOBAL CAMPAIGN FOR VIOLENCE PREVENTION
CAMPAGNE MONDIALE POUR LA PRÉVENTION DE LA VIOLENCE

1 IN 4 WOMEN EXPERIENCE SEXUAL ABUSE BY AN INTIMATE PARTNER IN THEIR LIFETIME.

WWW.WHO.INT/VIOLENCE_INJURY_PREVENTION

SUMMARIZING, QUOTING, AND PARAPHRASING

SHOWING THAT YOU ARE ENGAGED WITH OTHERS' IDEAS

Whenever you summarize, quote, or paraphrase, you show readers that you are engaging with others' ideas; you show readers that you are working to make sense of and build on available ideas and information. This is a hallmark of academic writing, as well as of any deliberative writing (writing that is about considering with others the choices we might make as citizens and community members).

SUMMARIZING

- focuses readers on the main points of a source's argument.
- shows that you are considering others' extended arguments.
- is a central ability for producing effective academic writing.

QUOTING

- emphasizes the exact words being used, which helps you emphasize ideas you want to highlight because they support your arguments or provide important counterpositions.
- carries the authority of the quoted person into your writing.
- can bring vibrant and memorable language into your writing.

PARAPHRASING

- allows you to turn language your readers might not understand (technical language, perhaps) into language they will.
- allows you to bring in others' opinions if their ideas are not presented succinctly or memorably.

EXAMPLE PASSAGE

So that we can explain how to work with the conventions of summarizing, quoting, and paraphrasing, we present below a passage to which we will refer on the following pages. The passage comes from page 787 of the article, "Preference-inconsistent recommendations: An effective approach for reducing confirmation bias and stimulating divergent thinking?" by Christina Schwind, Jürgen Buder, Ulrike Cress, Friedrich W. Hesse, published in the journal *Computers and Education* in 2012.

When learners inform themselves about relevant facts, arguments, or explanations on a controversial issue, they frequently fail to take dissenting information into account. This effect is referred to as selective exposure (Knobloch-Westerwick & Meng, 2009), congeniality bias (Hart et al., 2009), or confirmation bias (Jonas, Schulz-Hardt, Frey, & Thelen, 2001). This bias can be driven either by defense motives because the individual's focus is on being validated or by accuracy motives because the individual's focus lies on finding a correct solution (Hart et al., 2009). The classical, defense-motivated explanation for confirmation bias is based on Festinger's (1957) dissonance theory. Information which contradicts an individual's position leads to cognitive dissonance. As dissonance is a negative and uncomfortable state, individuals try to avoid it—or at least reduce it—and therefore prefer information which supports their own position. According to a more recent, accuracy-motivated explanation, confirmation bias may occur because individuals cognitively evaluate supporting information differently from dissenting information (Fischer, Jonas, Frey, & Schulz-Hardt, 2005). Since preference-consistent information appears convincing by itself (Lord, Ross, & Lepper, 1979), individuals do not feel any need for justification (Edwards & Smith, 1996). In contrast, preference-inconsistent information appears less valid, and this leads to a deliberate search for further information to refute dissenting arguments (Ditto & Lopez, 1992).

→ When you quote, paraphrase, and summarize, you have to show the sources for the words and ideas you are using. Each citation style handles this differently.

For MLA style, see pages 364–367.

For APA style (which the passage above uses), see pages 399–401.

For CSE style, see page 422.

For CMS style, see pages 425–428.

SUMMARIZING, QUOTING, AND PARAPHRASING
SUMMARIZING THE WORDS OF OTHERS

A summary condenses the main points of someone else's words and ideas. When you summarize, you leave out illustrations, examples, and details not necessary for your arguments. You go for the main points.

Here is a summary of the journal article excerpted on page 189:

In their article, "Preference-inconsistent recommendations," Schwind, Buder, Cress, and Hesse discuss how people tend to accept without question information that confirms what they already believe; the authors also discuss how people resist information that does not support what they believe.

WHAT A SUMMARY DOES

A useful and honest summary:

- is much shorter than the original.
- focuses on the excerpt's main point, drawing on information from the whole excerpt.
- tells whose ideas are being summarized.
- names the source of the information.

→ For citing in MLA style, see pages 364–367; for APA style, see pages 399–401; for CSE style, see page 422; and for CMS style, see pages 425–428.

WHAT A SUMMARY DOES NOT DO

- The summary's words do not repeat the exact words used in the excerpt (although it is fine to use a short quotation in a summary).
- The summary does not include any sources, statistics, facts, or commentary from the article (although you might include such information in the sentences or paragraphs that follow the summary if it were necessary to support your own developing arguments).

IF YOU CANNOT SUMMARIZE A SOURCE, YOU DO NOT YET UNDERSTAND IT

Sandra Jamieson and Rebecca Moore Howard, two professors who research how students use sources, have stated, "It is in summary that writers demonstrate comprehension of the larger arguments of a text, working from ideas rather than sentences."*

If you cannot summarize the whole of a source's arguments, you do not yet have a hold on the major ideas—and, importantly, on how the ideas build from one to the next. If you cannot summarize a source's arguments, take that as a signal that you need to return to the source and make it your own.

As you work, keep in mind that summarizing is an ability that gets easier with practice—and that it helps your thinking and writing become richer.

→ To avoid plagiarism when writing summaries, see pages 192–193.

TIPS

SUMMARIZING WELL

- A summary should almost always be considerably shorter than the original.

- Weave summaries into your writing using the same sorts of introductory phrases and strategies you use with quotations. (→ See pages 197–199.)

- Use the same sorts of strategies for alerting readers to the authority of the authors of the piece you summarize as you use for quotations. (→ See page 197.)

- A summary should be truthful to the ideas of the piece being summarized and focus on main points instead of on details, facts, and examples.

USING SUMMARY AND PARAPHRASE AS LEARNING STRATEGIES

Use summary and paraphrase to help you understand others' arguments: If you make yourself summarize several paragraphs or a whole article in a few sentences, or paraphrase the extended details completely in your own words, you will hold others' arguments in ways that both support your understanding and push you to expand your thinking.

→ See pages 200–201 for paraphrasing.

*See http://projectinfolit.org/smart-talks/item/110-sandra-jamieson-rebecca-moore-howard

SUMMARIZING, QUOTING, AND PARAPHRASING
SUMMARIZING TO AVOID PLAGIARISM

WATCH FOR PATCHWRITING

Patchwriting names the practice of patching together a summary from the words in the original.

For example, here is a patchwritten summary of the passage on page 189:

Schwind, Buder, Cress, and Hesse argue that learners who inform themselves about a controversial issue frequently fail to take dissenting information into account. This effect is called selective exposure, congeniality bias, or confirmation bias. This bias can be defensive because the individual wants to be validated. The defensive bias can result because an individual feels cognitive dissonance, which is a negative and uncomfortable state. People want to avoid it and therefore prefer information which supports their own position.

Even though this paragraph names the source's authors, this is still plagiarism.

What makes this patchwriting and so plagiarism? Notice how this patchwritten passage is almost as long as the passage it is supposed to summarize, and it does the following:

- It uses many of the exact same words as the original.

- It changes only a few of the words into the writer's own.

- It uses the same word order and order of ideas as the original.

WHAT CAUSES PATCHWRITING?

Writers who are unsure of themselves and their abilities to summarize patchwrite. Because they worry that they do not yet understand the ideas well enough, or perhaps worry that they do not have the authority to shorten the ideas presented, they stick too closely to the original

PATCHWRITING CAN BE A STEP TOWARD SUMMARY

Patchwriting can be a transition from the source's words to your own. If you see signs of patchwriting in your summary, step back, take a breath, and ask yourself what you don't yet understand.

If what you don't understand is the phrasing in a sentence, try writing the sentence with synonyms or dividing the sentence into several shorter sentences.

If what you don't understand is how the source gets from one idea to the next, step back and ask yourself what possible connections might get from one idea to the next—and see if that is in the source.

Trust yourself to figure it out. This is part of learning, and you can be proud of yourself for doing this.

WRITING SUMMARIES THAT AVOID PLAGIARISM

- Read the piece you want to summarize several times, jotting down the ideas and points that stick out for you—using your own words. (Use a thesaurus to look up synonyms for important terms.)

- Without looking at the piece, try to say out loud what you think the main point of the piece is. (This is easier to do if you can say it out loud to someone else.)

- Write down what you said, and check it against the piece to be sure you are accurate.

- Have confidence that you can do this. All it takes is practice and care.

SUMMARIZING, QUOTING, AND PARAPHRASING
QUOTING THE WORDS OF OTHERS

Here is one way to quote from the words of the journal excerpt on page 189:

In their 2012 article from *Computers and Education*, **researchers Schwind, Buder, Kress, and Hesse argue that, when people consider controversial topics, "they frequently fail to take dissenting information into account" (787).**

When you quote others' words, you bring both the sense of speaking and the authority of the speaker into your writing.

Because of this, use the exact words of others in your writing when those words add something to your argument that you cannot provide with your own words.

- Use words from those whom your readers are likely to recognize either by name, work, or affiliation or whose source will carry authority. This will give readers more reason to accept your points.

- Quote words that will be funny, poignant, striking, or otherwise memorable for your readers. This will help readers better remember your points.

- When in your writing you are considering the positions of people with whom you disagree, it can be useful to quote their words. This shows your audience that you are being fair by letting others speak for themselves.

BUT!

Always ask yourself whether you are quoting a source because you do not feel you have the authority to speak or because you don't think you understand the passage well enough to summarize or paraphrase. If so, turn to summarizing or paraphrasing to make yourself more confident about your use of the source.

THE PARTS OF QUOTING WELL

Here we repeat the example from the opposite page—with color coding—to show the conventions that readers of formal texts now expect for quotations:

In their 2012 article from *Computers and Education,* researchers Schwind, Buder, Kress, and Hesse argue that, when people consider controversial topics, "they frequently fail to take dissenting information into account" (787).

Conventionally, all direct quotations are indicated by quotation marks.

→ See page 196 for details on using quotation marks.

Quote a passage exactly.

→ Sometimes, however, you do need to modify the words you are quoting—perhaps to shorten the quotation, to give an explanation readers might need, or to correct spelling; see page 197.

Using a title or affiliation of the person you are quoting, or the source of the quote, can help your audience understand why they should pay attention to these words.

→ See page 197 for ways to do this.

It is a fairly consistent convention to give the name of those responsible for the words you quote.

→ See page 197 for ways to do this.

Signal to your readers that you are quoting others' words with a verb to introduce the quote; use such verbs to weave the quotation into your writing.

→ See page 198–199 for a list of signal words and for hints on weaving others' words into yours.

Each citation style specifies how to reference the page or paragraph of a citation's source. Readers can then find the exact place from which you drew your citation.

→ For MLA style, see pages 364–367.
→ For APA style, see pages 399–401.
→ For CSE style, see page 422.
→ For CMS style, see pages 425–428.

The points to the right can be a checklist for when you are quoting another's words, to be sure you stay with the conventions.

USING QUOTATION MARKS

Quotation marks are an immediately visible indicator to readers that you are using someone else's exact words—and there are many conventions regarding their use.

→ See pages 581–583 for the specific details of using quotation marks. Pay close attention to using quotation marks with other punctuation; this is an area where many lose track of the details.

WHEN WORDS YOU QUOTE CONTAIN THEIR OWN QUOTATION MARKS

Suppose you want to quote the words below, from marketing author and blogger Seth Godin, on how the expression *global warming* shapes how we talk about environmental change:

If the problem were called "Atmosphere cancer" or "Pollution death" the entire conversation would be framed in a different way.

The U.S. convention for quoting words that are already within quotation marks is to change the double quotation marks to single quotes:

As marketing author Seth Godin suggests, the general public might be more alarmed about global warming if "the problem were called 'Atmosphere cancer' or 'Pollution death.'"

Notice how this use of quotations means that the passage ends with a single quotation mark followed immediately by a double quotation mark.

WHEN NOT TO USE QUOTATION MARKS

If your quotation will take up more than four lines in your paper, make it into a **block quotation**. Introduce the quotation as you would any other, but:

- Make the quotation its own paragraph.
- Indent the paragraph one half inch from the left margin of your writing (but don't additionally indent the first line).
- Put the parenthetical information at the end of the quotation, following the style you have been asked to use.
- Put the parenthetical information outside the punctuation mark that ends the quotation.
- Follow a long quotation with words of your own.

Marie Vassiltchikov, a Russian refugee, worked in Berlin during World War II with a group that tried to kill Hitler. Her diaries give the only eyewitness account. In her diaries she also describes the night bombings of Berlin; after one such bombing, a friend of hers stopped by:

> During the night's raid (which I had described as "nothing serious") his driver had been killed and he himself had been buried in the cellar of his house, which had caved in; he had only managed to crawl out in the morning. He announced—and this is typical for our times!—that he had just bought one hundred oysters. (121)

Another time she tried on a new hat while buildings burned around her. Her diaries give a sense of how people try to hold on to what's normal during horrible times.

→ See page 357 for an example of a block quotation in a paper showing MLA formatting.

WHEN AND HOW TO MODIFY THE WORDS YOU ARE QUOTING

IF YOU NEED TO REMOVE WORDS FROM A QUOTATION

If you need to remove words to emphasize the main information, use an ellipsis punctuation mark:

In a recent article on tapeworms, science writer Carl Zimmer describes how some tapeworms called monogeans that live inside fish "give birth to offspring without releasing them from their bodies. Their offspring mature inside them and give birth as well .... A monogenean may contain twenty generations of descendents inside its body!"

→ See page 513 on ellipses.

IF YOU NEED TO ADD AN EXPLANATORY COMMENT TO A QUOTATION

Put the explanation in square brackets:

Leslie Collins (1976: 620) notes that "over 1000 women leaders were killed in China in 1927 by [members of a center-right political party opposed to the Communists]; many of [the women] were not Communists but simply active participants in the women's movement."

→ See page 517 for more on using brackets.

WHEN THERE IS AN OBSOLETE SPELLING OR A MISSPELLING IN THE WORDS YOU ARE QUOTING

If you are quoting an old text in which the spelling differs from what current readers expect, use the original spelling; including the words' date or providing an explanatory preface will help readers understand:

"Terrour," reasoned Thomas Churchyard in 1579, "made short warres."

USING TITLES, AFFILIATIONS, OR SOURCES IN SUMMARIES, QUOTATIONS, AND PARAPHRASES

If you know that your readers know the person you quote, then you probably do not need to explain who the person is. But if you think your readers won't know why it is worth quoting a particular person, then introduce the person with a title, affiliation, or other relevant information such as the source of the quotation so that readers understand the authority behind the person's words.

Douglas White, a University of Pittsburgh bioethicist and researcher, talks about "the powerful desire not to be dead."

USING THE NAME OF THE PERSON BEING CITED

When you cite someone for the first time, giving the full name of the person is a convention in formal writing. It is a way of acknowledging that ideas are always connected to thinkers.

The sports historian James Riordan suggests that after the revolutionary stirrings of 1905, factory owners introduced soccer to their workers "as an attempt to encourage a form of civil loyalty and to divert their employees from revolutionary and other disruptive actions" (27).

In later references to that person, use the person's last name:

Riordan believes that the factory owners' strategies were largely successful.

Not:

James believes that the factory owners' strategies were largely successful.

SIGNALLING THAT YOU ARE SUMMARIZING, QUOTING, OR PARAPHRASING: CHOOSING AN INTRODUCTORY VERB

It is a convention to introduce others' words with phrases that:

- signal to readers that you are about to summarize, quote, or paraphrase.

- weave the quoted words into your writing so that they fit the structure of your own sentence.

CHOOSING SIGNALLING VERBS

Many verbs signal to readers that they are about to read quoted words; at right, we list many for you to choose from.

Note, however, that the verb you choose not only signals that you are about to quote another's words; your verb choice can also signal to readers your position about the quoted words. Consider the examples below, looking at how they ask you to think about what Paulk says.

In his article about interior design in the computer game *The Sims*, Charles Paulk says that the Sims are "hard-wired social climbers."

In his article about interior design in the computer game *The Sims*, Charles Paulk charges that the Sims are "hard-wired social climbers."

In his article about interior design in the computer game *The Sims*, Charles Paulk complains that the Sims are "hard-wired social climbers."

SIGNALLING VERBS

Depending on how you use them, the verbs below can help you signal that you agree or disagree with the words you cite, or they can help you make a claim using the cite. Look carefully at others' writing to learn how to introduce summaries, quotations, and paraphrases persuasively.

acknowledges	adds	admits
advises	agrees	analyzes
answers	argues	asks
asserts	believes	charges
claims	comments	complains
concedes	concludes	concurs
condemns	confirms	considers
contends	criticizes	declares
denies	describes	disagrees
disputes	emphasizes	explains
expresses	finds	holds
illustrates	implies	insists
interprets	lists	maintains
notes	objects	observes
offers	opposes	points out
predicts	proposes	refutes
rejects	remarks	replies
reports	responds	reveals
says	shows	speculates
states	suggests	thinks

WEAVING QUOTED WORDS INTO YOUR WRITING

Anytime you quote, watch that:

- Your own words weave together with the quoted words to make a sentence that is **logical**.

    "Poverty is more than a problem of economics," Farah claims, because it is also a public health problem.

    The words that follow the quotation do not explain why Farah thinks poverty is a public health problem. Here is a fix:

    "Poverty is more than a problem of economics," Farah claims, because it is also a public health problem: Falk explains that poverty can adversely affect how the brain functions and so affect how people are able to live with each other.

- Your own words weave together with the quoted words to make a sentence that is **grammatical**.

    If poverty can "literally damage our brains," as Farah asserts, then it is "directly affecting the biological substrate of who we are and what we can become."

    Because the verb forms used above are inconsistent, the sentence is ungrammatical. Here is a fix:

    If poverty can "literally damage our brains," as Farah asserts, then it damages also "the biological substrate of who we are and what we can become."

TIPS

QUOTING WELL

- For formal academic writing, there are no hard-and-fast conventions for how many quotations are acceptable—but even though quotations can memorably and powerfully support your points, do not use so many (or such long ones) that they lose their strength. Check your drafts with readers to see if they think you are using too many (or too few) quotations.

- To ensure that you are respecting others' words, make it part of your final proofreading to check your quotations against the originals.

- Anytime you quote the words or ideas of others, ask yourself if you are being honest to the other person's intent and meaning. Build thoughtful and respectful communities by using the words and ideas of others as you would want them to use your words and ideas.

IMPORTANTLY!

Ask yourself:

- *Are you quoting because you don't trust your understanding of the source?* If this is the case, turn to summary and paraphrase to force yourself to gain understanding.

- *Are you quoting because you are not confident in your own ideas and arguments?* All writers worry about this at one time or another. You simply have to push through, trusting that you will learn from this work and gain confidence—and trusting that others will respect your efforts.

SUMMARIZING, QUOTING, AND PARAPHRASING
PARAPHRASING THE WORDS OF OTHERS

A paraphrase restates the original *in your own words*. You paraphrase when you need to rely closely on a source's argument or explanation. Here is a paraphrase of the journal article excerpt on page 189:

In their article, "Preference-inconsistent recommendations," Schwind, Buder, Cress, and Hesse describe how people learning about controversial topics do not pay attention to information that does not fit what they already believe. Psychologists have named this behavior "selective exposure," "congeniality bias," or "confirmation bias." People have such biases perhaps because they want what they already believe to be defended or because they are focused on finding what seems accurate, given what they already believe. The understanding tied to defense goes back to 1957 when a researcher named Festinger proposed that when people are confronted with information that goes against what they believe they are made uncomfortable and don't want to be. The understanding tied to accuracy is more recent and says that people evaluate information that agrees with them differently from information that disagrees; what agrees seems already correct and so doesn't need to be further evaluated; in contrast, what disagrees seems less correct.

Notice that this paraphrase:

- Retells in new words all the points of the passage's sentences—and so is often almost as long as the original passage.

- Makes the passage more accessible to a nonspecialist audience, often a reason for paraphrasing.

- Is more detailed than a summary would be: Summaries tend to be about whole arguments; paraphrases are usually of parts of arguments.

AVOIDING PLAGIARISM IN PARAPHRASES

This paraphrase—

In their article, "Preference-inconsistent recommendations," Schwind, Buder, Cress, and Hesse describe how those learning about controversial issues fail to take dissenting information into account. This effect is referred to as "selective exposure," "congeniality bias," or "confirmation bias." This bias can be caused by defense motives or accuracy motives. Defense motives are when an individual's focus is on being validated; accuracy motives are when the individual's focus lies on finding a correct solution. The classical explanation for confirmation bias is based on Festinger from 1957: Information that contradicts an individual's position leads to cognitive dissonance, which is an uncomfortable state and so individuals try to avoid it and prefer information that supports their position. The more recent accuracy-motivated explanation says confirmation bias happens because individuals evaluate supporting information differently from dissenting information. Because preference-consistent information appears convincing by itself, individuals do not feel any need for justification; in contrast, preference-inconsistent information appears less valid, and this leads to a deliberate search for further information to refute diissenting arguments.

—is plagiarism. Compare the passage to the original to see that it plagiarizes:

- It uses many of the original passage's exact words.
- When it doesn't use the exact words, this paraphrase simply removes a few words from the original, rearranges a few others, and replaces some words with synonyms.

TIPS

HOW TO PARAPHRASE TO AVOID PLAGIARISM

- Read several times the passage you want to paraphrase.
- On a piece of paper, break the passage up into its parts: What are the main points of the passage?
- Without looking at the passage or your notes, write down what you understand the passage to be communicating.
- Check your writing against the original to be sure you have the main ideas and have not inadvertently used the same words and structures in the original.

PARAPHRASING WELL

- A paraphrase is usually about as long as the original.
- Weave paraphrases into your writing using the same sorts of introductory phrases and strategies you use with quotations. (➜ See pages 197–199.)
- Use the same sorts of strategies for alerting readers to the authority of the authors of the piece you are paraphrasing as you use for quotations. (➜ See page 197.)
- The point of a paraphrase is to present the ideas of another as you think that writer wants others to understand them—so don't offer your interpretation or any comments until after you have finished a full and honest paraphrase.

➜ See pages 116–121 for more on plagiarism.

SUMMARIZING, QUOTING, AND PARAPHRASING
WAYS TO USE OTHERS' WORDS AND IDEAS WELL

On these two pages we give solid examples of how different student writers use words and ideas from sources. The examples grow in academic sophistication from the first to the last.

→ For more examples of using other's words and ideas well, see the following:
- The annotated bibliography on page 205.
- The use of sources on page 207.
- The final draft of Harley's paper, starting on page 354.

→ For some examples of how NOT to use sources, see Harley's first draft, starting on page 276.

USING OTHERS' WORDS FOR DEFINITIONS

Sometimes writers feel the need to rely on others' authority for a definition at the beginning of writing.

The people at the Critical Thinking Community website define critical thinking as "that mode of thinking—about any subject, content, or problem—in which the thinker improves the quality of his or her thinking by skillfully analyzing, assessing, and reconstructing it."

USING OTHERS' WORDS TO SUPPORT AN ARGUMENT

To "prove" that high school teachers have been struggling for a while to get people in their classes to read books, this writer turns to a source's words:

In her 2000 book on how to interest students in classic literature, Carol Jago wrote that, "Living in an age that glorifies the screen rather the printed page, it can be very hard work to persuade young people to turn off MTV and pick up a book" (6). This shows that getting students engaged in reading books is not a new challenge for teachers.

USING OTHERS' WORDS TO SET UP A PROBLEM

This writer uses quotations from two different sources to set up the problem that the rest of his paper considers:

In 1789, in a letter, Thomas Jefferson wrote that, "wherever the people are well informed they can be trusted with their own government." Similarly, PBS news anchor Jim Lehrer has said that, "If we don't have an informed electorate we don't have a democracy. So I don't care how people get the information, as long as they get it" (Barrett). Unfortunately, both statements only hold true if the information is impartial and if people know how to and want to evaluate it. If the information we receive is not impartial, and if people don't know or want to evaluate it, then can we have a democracy?

Here's another writer beginning a paper by summarizing an article and then a book to set up her concerns:

In "Motivation, Engagement, and Student Voice," Toshalis and Nakkula argue that much standardized education strips personality from students. Similarly, in their book *A New Culture of Learning*, Thomas and Brown argue that most education systems treat students as though they were machines. These authors must all love the Internet, where you can log onto Facebook, Twitter, or Tumblr right now and see creativity and self-expression bursting at the seams. Kids are resonating with song lyrics, waxing poetic on plots of their favorite television shows, and participating in new, growing forms of literature.

USING OTHERS' WORDS TO THINK

The person who wrote this passage found a distinction in a source; she quoted and analyzed the distinction to help her think about why she and others might want to own fewer things:

If one wants to own less stuff, one needs to think carefully about spending—and so such a desire seems to require the values of being thrifty or being frugal. The distinction between being thrifty and being frugal might seem unimportant, but the difference demonstrates something about the values of desiring less.

Sociologist David Evans defines "thrift" as "doing more (consumption) with less (money) and so thrifty practices are practices of savvy consumption, characterized by the thrill and skill of 'the bargain'" (551). Being thrifty is about spending carefully: For example, one might decide to spend less on clothes in order to go on a big trip. And so Evans argues that thrift is about consuming; it is about caring for those with whom you live and helping them have better lives by being careful about where your money goes.

Someone who is frugal, on the other hand, doesn't want to consume. Instead, according to Evans, such a person "values work over leisure; saving over spending; restraint over indulgence; deferred over immediate gratification and the satisfaction of 'needs' over the satisfaction of wants and desires" (552). And so frugality is about trying to consume as little as possible because one cares about the environment and how the shape of the environment affects everyone (and not just those with whom one lives).

If we desire to own less stuff, then we need to decide if it's because we want to spend our money more wisely or because we want to make time to live more thoughtfully.

AN ANNOTATED BIBLIOGRAPHY

A *bibliography* is a listing of the sources you use in a research project. An *annotated bibliography* lists sources using the format you would in a bibliography but also includes a summary of each source—and might also include quotations or paraphrases you think might be useful to your argument or might include your questions and comments about the sources.

Annotated bibliographies help you summarize and reflect critically on your sources—and so are useful preparation for well-developed research projects.

ABOUT WRITING ANNOTATED BIBLIOGRAPHIES

- Each entry starts with a citation for the source being annotated. Cite the source in the style you are using for your paper.

  → See Part 9 for citation syles.

- The annotation starts immediately after the citation, *not* on a new line.

- The annotations are presented in alphabetical order according to the last names of the authors of the sources.

- A basic annotation gives only a summary of the source, but annotations can also go on then to include evaluation after the summary (following the steps of analysis we presented on pages 146–147). The first sample here shows the writer giving a little evaluation; both samples show the writer thinking about the source in response to her topic.

A student's annotated bibliography
....
To the right, Harley summarizes and comments on two of her sources.

→ To see how Harley uses this work in her draft and final paper, go to pages 276–283 and 354–363.

ANNOTATED BIBLIOGRAPHY

Calhoun, Cheshire. "The Virtue of Civility." *Philosophy & Public Affairs*, vol. 29, no. 3, 2000, pp. 251-75. *JSTOR*, doi: 10.1111/j.1088-4963.2000.00251.x. Philosopher Calhoun argues that civility is a social virtue. When we are civil we display respect and tolerance for others and so "acknowledge the value of others' lives" (258). By being civil, we "safeguard the possibility of a common social life together" (272) because we make it possible for others to participate in discussing difficult issues. I worked hard to understand this article because his main argument—that civility is about the display of respect and tolerance rather than actually feeling respect and tolerance—seems like it's saying it's okay not to really believe that others are valuable as long as we act as though they are. But Calhoun offers examples of how it can actually be a good thing to be civil even when one doesn't truly respect another: Civility is about helping us live together and so requires us to act well towards each other no matter what we might individually feel. I did work hard to understand this, and it was kind of fun to follow his careful distinctions and figure it out.

Haidt, Jonathan. *The Righteous Mind: Why Good People Are Divided by Politics and Religion*. Pantheon, 2012. Haidt is a psychologist who studies the moral attitudes of people all over the world. He argues that people in different places uphold different "moral languages" that result from different combinations of six foundational categories: care, fairness, loyalty, authority, sanctity, and liberty. He claims that conservatives and liberals uphold different sets of these categories and that those differences are what can get in the way of us talking well together; he also argues, though, that both political positions are "necessary elements of a healthy state of political life" (312). Finally, he analyzes how belonging to groups helps us take care of each other—and that happiness comes from being in relationship with others. But being in groups also makes it harder for us to understand those outside the group. Early in the book he brings up the psychological notion of "confirmation bias." This notion names how people have a "tendency to seek out and interpret new evidence in ways that confirm what [they] already think" (78); Haidt brings in this tendency to help explain why people hold so tightly to their beliefs and opinions. I didn't know about confirmation bias before reading this book, and I want to learn more about it and think about how it affects how we argue.

PUTTING SOURCES IN DIALOGUE WITH EACH OTHER

Strong academic writing puts sources in dialogue with each other: Rather than using each source alone to make one point, strong academic writing asks what would happen if one source could talk to another.

Putting sources in dialogue, you might:

- Discover how sources that seem very different actually agree. In such cases, note exactly how the sources agree—as well as where they still disagree.

- Find that similar sources actually disagree. In such cases, note how the sources disagree—as well as how they still agree.

- Synthesize across sources to find a more encompassing solution or perspective—as happens in the writing to the right.

- Determine that disagreeing sources each still hold plausible positions. In such cases, do not erase differences. Instead, try to understand why each position seems plausible to you.

A student puts sources in dialogue

To the right, Harley considers the sources she summarized (on page 205) and thinks her way to new understanding on her topic.

→ See pages 276–283 for Harley's first draft and pages 354–363 for her final paper.

PUTTING SOURCES IN DIALOGUE

- Put sources in dialogue only after you have summarized them. Understanding different sources' main ideas prepares you to put those sources in dialogue.

- Even if you are asked to do such work formally, in class, start by just writing. Jot down what might happen if the sources could talk to each other. After you have an idea or two, give the writing formal shape.

The Idea of Civility and the Idea of Confirmation Bias

I've been reading a lot about civility, what the term means and how civil attitudes toward each other are necessary for all of us to have discussions about difficult topics. I've also been reading a lot about "confirmation bias," a psychological term (sometimes called "selective exposure"); the term names how people seek or interpret new information that confirms what they already know. When I thought about the different sources I'd been reading, and what the sources about civility discussed and what the sources about confirmation bias discussed, I realized that there should be connections between the two, but there aren't.

Haidt is the one writer who suggests a possible connection, but it's only a suggestion. In his book, *The Righteous Mind: Why Good People Are Divided by Politics and Religion*, he discusses confirmation bias. He references many sources to show that psychologists have believed in this concept a long time. He brings in the term to support his argument that people believe they are being rational in arguments when really they aren't. He wants to make clear that we make decisions usually not based on the best or the widest range of evidence but instead based on what we have come to believe given how we grew up. Haidt brings this up to make clear that we shouldn't think other people are stupid for what they believe. Instead, he argues that better thinking comes from many people bringing ideas to the table rather than from any one person's beliefs. Haidt implies, then, that we should be humble about our own beliefs and should seek out differing opinions and reasons.

Those who write about civility claim we need to have civil attitudes toward others precisely because we need to think together. So they are in agreement with Haidt that we think better in a democracy when we can think together. But their focus is on our attitudes toward each other, rather than on our attitudes toward ourselves—and that is where I think I can draw on Haidt's suggestions about confirmation bias. If we know about confirmation bias, then—in addition to trying to be civil toward others—we need to be humble about our own beliefs.

Civility is about how we think about and act toward others; if we are civil only, we can still think that our ideas are all the right ones, meaning we still won't really be listening. Bringing awareness of confirmation bias together with civility helps us be aware that our own ideas are rarely as well-informed as we think. If we are aware of that, then maybe we will listen more closely to others and really be able to figure out together how to solve our problems.

USING ANALYSIS TO COMPOSE A WORKING THESIS STATEMENT

Harley has done initial online and library research into civility in political discussions (in families and generally).

→ See how Harley first found her topic, on page 45.

→ Harley's initial research questions are on page 95.

→ You can see how Harley evaluated several sources on pages 106–115.

→ On pages 204–207 you can see Harley work with her sources.

USING ANALYSIS TO DEVELOP A TOPIC

Because Harley asked the research questions she did (→ see page 95), she was able to
read her sources analytically. She looked specifically for how others define civility and why civility matters in arguments; in one source, she found reference to the concept of "confirmation bias," which led her into learning more about that concept.

Her questions also helped her read to find connections between civility and political arguments. Her sources argue that broad conversations about difficult topics are necessary for a democratic government; they argue, in fact, that the best decision-making happens when the broadest range of differing ideas are brought into any discussion. For that to happen, people need to be civil to each other so they can feel comfortable laying out all their ideas.

By having read analytically and critically, Harley sees that she can start making an argument about civility.

FIRST THESIS STATEMENT

A thesis statement has this basic form, as described on pages 160–161: **EVIDENCE + CLAIM**

And so, based on her research, Harley first writes:

> Being civil in discussion helps us get along better; therefore, being civil in discussion is good.

EVALUATING THE FIRST THESIS STATEMENT

Effective and engaging papers are most likely to develop from thesis statements that

1 Have evidence supported by credible and relevant sources—but the statement of evidence is vague.

2 Have a concrete and focused claim.

3 Make an argument that is debatable.

Using those three points, here's an evaluation of Harley's first try:

1 Harley does have relevant and credible sources to support her evidence.

2 The claim that *being civil in discussion is good* is vague and not focused. What does **good** mean here? **Good** for whom and under what circumstances? Does Harley mean any kind of discussion whatsoever?

3 Because Harley's claim is so vague, it's hard to see who would find this thesis statement debatable.

SECOND THESIS STATEMENT

After evaluating her first try, Harley returns to her sources to develop a more concrete statement:

> Preventing government repression and supporting a healthy democracy depends on us being able to discuss controversial ideas and beliefs civilly; therefore, we should learn how to discuss our controversial ideas and beliefs civilly.

EVALUATING THE SECOND THESIS STATEMENT

1 The evidence part of Harley's thesis statement now connects specific results with a specific cause, and so her intentions are much clearer.

2 In her paper, Harley will have to define *civilly* in more detail than a thesis statement has room for. Her claim in this second thesis statement is concrete and focused because it states precisely the sort of discussions about which she intends to write.

3 Harley knows from chatting with classmates that few of them connect our style of argument with larger governmental concerns—and so she knows her thesis statement is debatable (and so probably interesting to her readers).

SEEING HARLEY USE HER THESIS STATEMENT

→ To see how Harley uses her thesis statement to organize for her first draft, see pages 222–225.

→ To see the draft that Harley develops out of this thesis statement, see pages 276–363.

HINTS & TIPS FOR ENGAGING WITH SOURCES AND ANALYZING ARGUMENTS

ASK: "WHAT SORT OF THINKER AND WRITER DO I WANT TO BE?"

Because cutting and pasting from the Web is so easy, writing teachers worry that people in their classes are not respecting the capabilities of their own minds to think deeply. Teachers worry that people in their classes write papers by stringing together short quotations found online; they worry that people build papers using only the ability to make quick associations rather than deep, extended connections.

Your teachers want you to ask yourself: *What do you value about your mind? How do you want to use your mind to participate in your community and culture? Do you want to learn how to think in more depth about issues that matter?*

If you want to develop your thinking abilities further, you need to make time to do so and you need to challenge yourself. We all suffer from not enough time and have to choose our priorities—but we all also know the satisfactions of taking on a new and challenging task, such as becoming a richer thinker.

Becoming a richer, serious thinker—one who wants to understand deeply and with integrity how the world works—requires approaches like those in the next column.

- **Remember that confidence in engaging with sources develops over time.** As with all learning, fluidity and comfort come with repeated practice.

- **Trust yourself as a thinker.** You have a mind and you can think and analyze.

- **Give yourself time to think and write.** When you finish reading a source for the first time, ask yourself what you don't understand and write down any questions—and then think about all that as you fall asleep or wake up, when your mind is relaxed. Going back over ideas and going back to the best sources stretches you mind.

- **Approach sources with questions.** The questions you generate in Part 3 (→ see pages 50–53) set you up to read your sources with purpose and focus.

- **Read generously.** Try to understand each source fully on its own terms before criticizing it.

- **Use key words and terms from one source to help you consider another source's arguments.** Comparing definitions and concepts among sources helps you better see what's at stake in the issues that matter to you.

- **Look for multiple perspectives on an issue.** In your sources, look for unexpected or new perspectives, so that you stretch your thinking and can write fully about a topic.

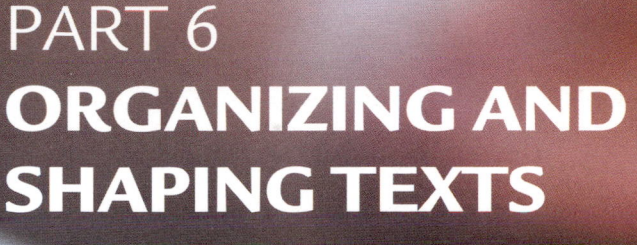

PART 6
ORGANIZING AND SHAPING TEXTS

CONTENTS

WHERE ARE WE IN A PROCESS FOR COMPOSING?

Understanding your project
Getting started
Asking questions
Shaping your project for others
Drafting a paper
Getting feedback
Revising
Polishing

Choosing a genre
Choosing an overall organization
Arranging paragraphs
Multimodal organization

PART 6 **ORGANIZING AND SHAPING TEXTS**

6 ORGANIZING

Questions you might have about organizing your texts:

How can genres help me achieve my purposes?
→ See pages 214–217.

How are academic genres different from workplace genres?
→ See page 215.

How can I use a thesis statement to organize my paper?
→ See pages 222–225.

How do I communicate online in academic environments?
→ See pages 226–231.

How can I write more effective paragraphs?
→ See pages 240–255.

What are different patterns that I can use for my paragraphs?
→ See pages 246–255.

What should I consider when organizing a visual text?
→ See pages 256–261.

What are the parts of an oral presentation?
→ See pages 262–263.

THE WPA OUTCOMES* FOR PART 6 INCLUDE:

Rhetorical abilities: Choosing an organization for your writing that works for your audience.

Critical thinking, reading, and composing abilities: Reading a range of texts—both verbal and visual—for how their organizations function for different audiences and situations.

Using conventions: Learning why conventions vary for organization and paragraphing in different genres.

* See page 15.

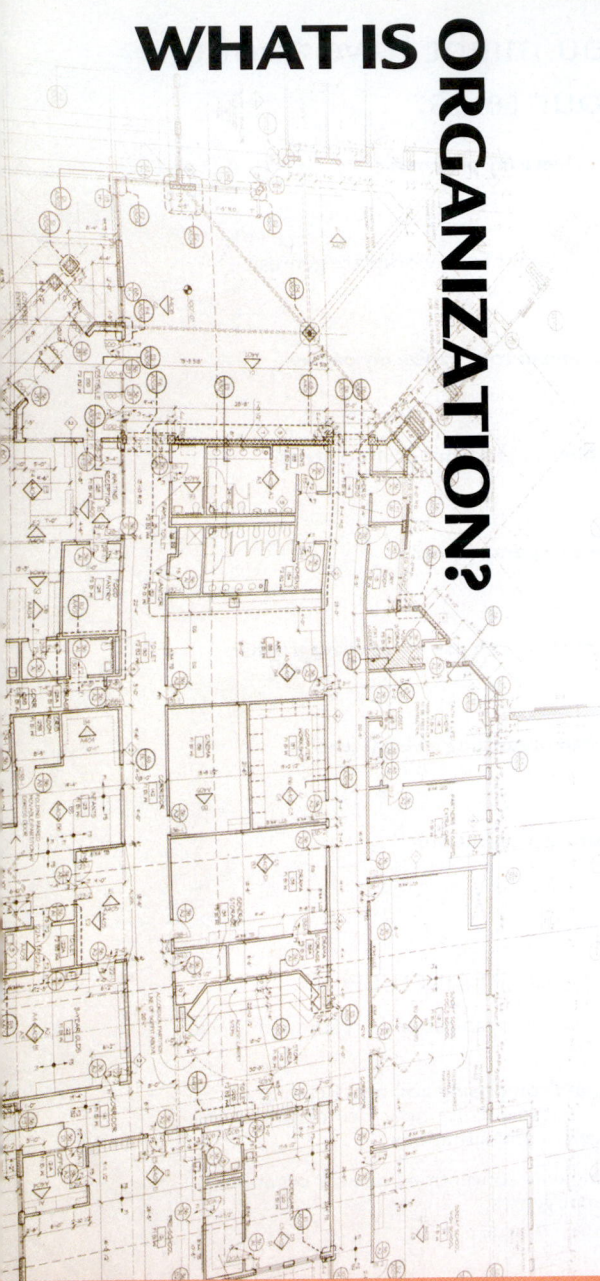

WHAT IS ORGANIZATION?

BUILDING A TEXT IS LIKE BUILDING A BUILDING

When you compose any text, your composing choices shape your audience's experience similarly to how people experience buildings.

Think of when you first visited a new acquaintance. You went to the person's apartment or house, and from the street you got a sense of the building's age. Seeing the overall style of the building—Victorian, modern, suburban ranch, or fifties apartment block—you sensed what you would see inside. Once inside, you got a sense of the organization of the rooms—of the layout and floorplan—which indicated how you could move through the rooms. Then there were the individual rooms with their furnishings, which told you about how comfortable it was to live in this place and what people did there. There was also the color of the walls, and what was on the walls, and what was on the shelves.

As you moved from the outside to the inside, you moved from seeing large structures to seeing smaller ones, from big shapes to small objects.

MOVING THROUGH A TEXT IS LIKE MOVING THROUGH A BUILDING

First, you see the whole, which sets up expectations about the smaller parts. As you read, listen, or look, you see the overall structure, and then you notice the parts, such as chapters, section headers, or paragraphs. Finally, you notice the details, such as tone of voice, sentence length, word choice, and so on.

In this part of the book, we focus on the major elements, the overall structure, and paragraphs.

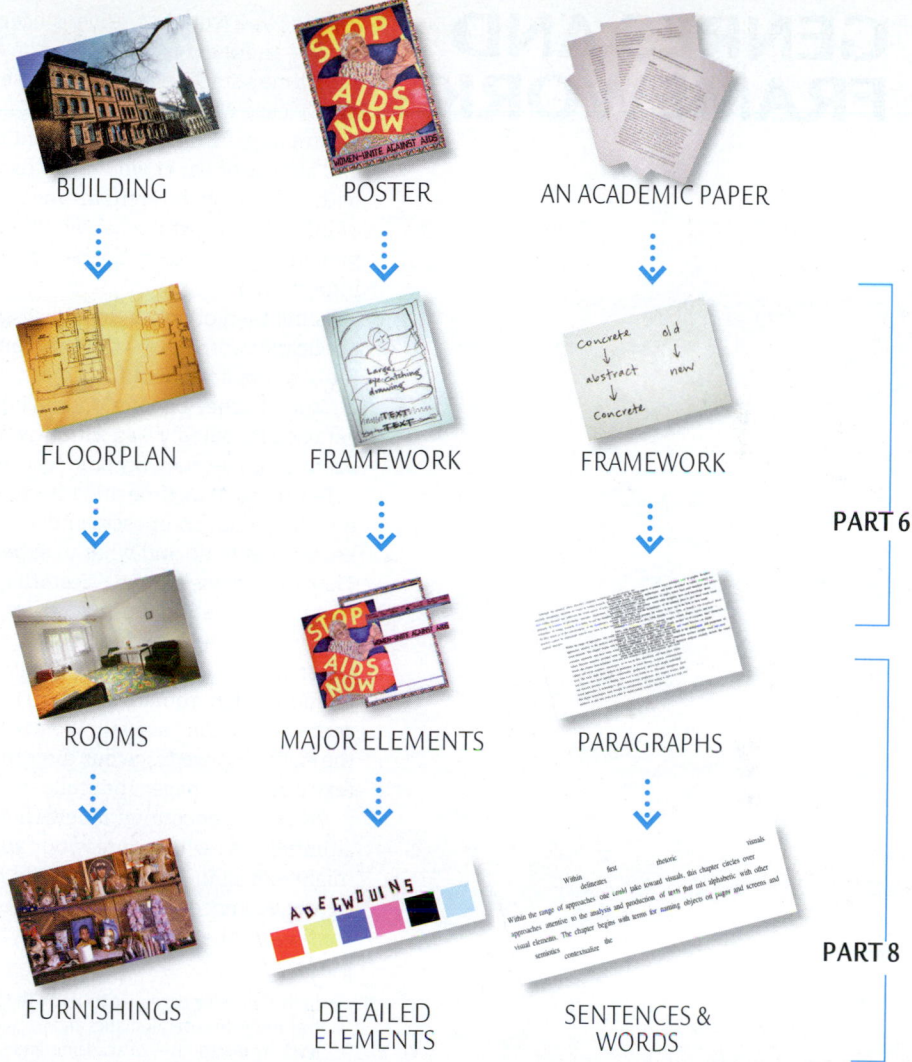

BUILDING → FLOORPLAN → ROOMS → FURNISHINGS

POSTER → FRAMEWORK → MAJOR ELEMENTS → DETAILED ELEMENTS

AN ACADEMIC PAPER → FRAMEWORK → PARAGRAPHS → SENTENCES & WORDS

PART 6

PART 8

ORGANIZATION IS ABOUT HOW YOU WORK AT EACH OF THESE LEVELS

At each level, you have many choices about how to place the relevant elements in relation to each other in order to achieve your purpose, for your audience, given your context. After considering large-scale organization, you are ready to draft—that's Part 7—and then you are ready to consider small-scale organization.

GENRES AND FRAMEWORKS

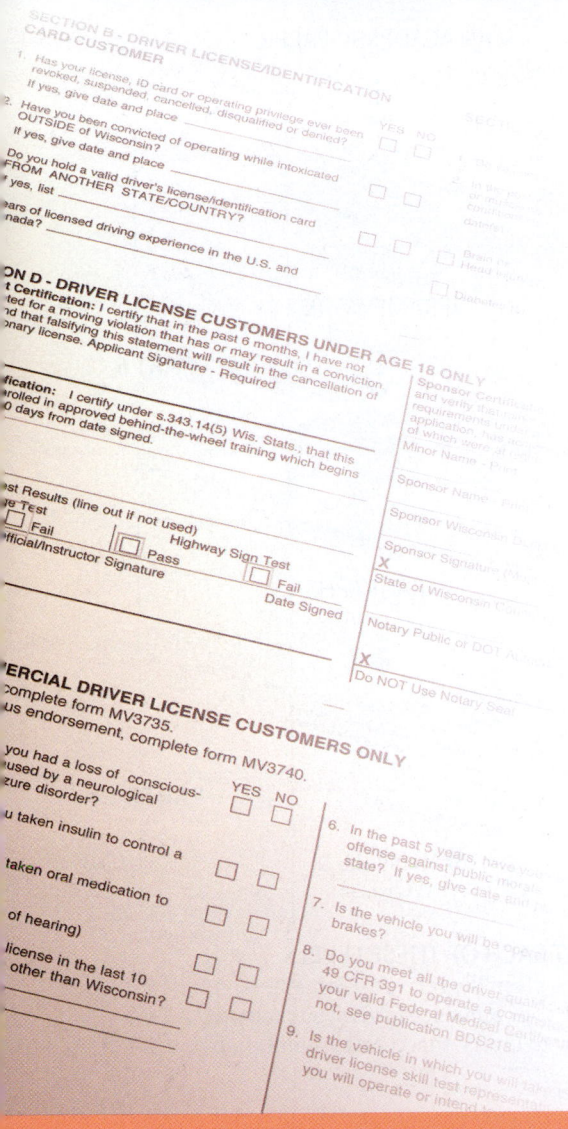

Imagine you work in a driver's license office—and there is no application form. Each time someone needs a license, you say, "Please write down the necessary information." How many different sizes and shapes of paper would you receive, with how many different arrangements of information—and what would each person consider to be "the necessary information"?

Think then of how a driver's license application form saves time and energy for both applicants and workers.

When frameworks for organizing texts get used repeatedly—as with driver's license forms—they become "genres."

Genres save us time and effort because they help both composers and audiences know what to do and what to expect. There are movie genres (Westerns, romantic comedies, horror movies), videogame genres (first person shooters, quests), and fiction genres (fantasy, science fiction, romance). There are genres for writing as well: We list two to the right, and we trace out their major features in the pages that follow.

When you encounter a new rhetorical situation, ask what genres your audience might expect in the situation and how tightly you need to stay within the confines of the genre to achieve your purposes.

→ In the following pages, we focus on the larger features—the overall shapes and paragraph-level organizations—of academic and workplace genres; to learn more about the styles of these genres—their sentence-level features—see Part 8.

ACADEMIC GENRES

WORKPLACE GENRES

	ACADEMIC GENRES	WORKPLACE GENRES
TEXTS	Academic papers, reports, articles in scholarly journals—also academic blogs	Memos, proposals, resumés, project plans, progress reports, white papers, executive summaries
AUDIENCES & PURPOSES	Academic genres help specialists build and share knowledge that is widely useful across the humanities, social sciences, sciences, engineering, and medicine.	Workplace genres help people get work done quickly and efficiently—and so such genres address how people work together as well as the products, services, and processes they use and produce.
AUDIENCE EXPECTATIONS	Academic audiences expect academic texts to be: • serious • direct • explicit • objective and unbiased • supported with evidence • respectful of previous knowledge • cautious in their claims, only making claims that can be supported by evidence	Workplace audiences generally expect workplace texts to be: • short • focused • to-the-point • easy-to-read • full of immediately useful information supported by some degree of research

ACADEMIC GENRES

THE VALUES OF ACADEMIC GENRES

As you will see in the following pages, different academic disciplines have different expectations about how writing within the discipline is organized, but all disciplines share these general expectations:

ACADEMIC WRITING IS ABOUT BUILDING KNOWLEDGE.

Academic audiences expect that you approach writing seriously because through writing you add to our understanding of the world and each other. This means you have to take existing arguments seriously, research and gather evidence methodically and honestly, and make only the arguments you can support with evidence.

ACADEMIC WRITING USES LOGICAL DEVELOPMENT OF IDEAS AND TRIES TO BE OBJECTIVE AND UNBIASED.

Logic is about ideas that relate to each other because of their structure or form—as thesis statements do and as papers that are organized around thesis statements do.

→ See pages 160–161 for an introduction to thesis statements.

→ See pages 222–225 on using a thesis statement to organize a paper.

The point of view of academic writing is rarely personal, rarely focused on the writer. Instead, the emphasis is on the argument being made and on ideas that benefit as many people as possible.

ACADEMIC WRITING LOOKS SERIOUS.

→ For formatting in MLA style, see pages 354–363; for formatting in APA style, see pages 394–398.

ACADEMIC WRITING GETS TO AND STAYS ON THE POINT.

An introduction moves quickly to stating what the paper is about. The writer can explain how each and every sentence helps move a reader to the conclusion. Any digression must fit with the purpose.

→ See pages 304–305 on writing introductions to academic papers.

→ See pages 240–255 to learn about paragraphs that move arguments forward.

ACADEMIC WRITING IS EXPLICIT.

Academic writers say directly what their writing is about. In fiction and creative nonfiction, writers use figurative language frequently to pull readers in and suggest an overall point without ever stating the point; academic writing rarely does this.

Academic writers also give full definitions of their terms because they understand that many readers have differing understandings.

→ See pages 314–315 and 322–329 for more on the characteristics of explicit writing.

ACADEMIC WRITING ALWAYS HAS AN ELEMENT OF DOUBT.

Academic writers accept that there are very few thoughts and ideas that apply to everyone, everywhere, at all times. Instead, academic writers consider a range of reasons and opinions.

To this end, academic writers often use phrases like *These facts suggest …* or *Given the available evidence, it would seem that …*

ACADEMIC WRITING IS NOT CONVERSATIONAL.

Academic writers strive for a thoughtful tone of voice and rarely tell jokes or use emotional language or colloquialisms. In some disciplines, writers use the pronoun *I* and use their own experiences as evidence or examples; reading examples of writing in a discipline will help you learn the discipline's particulars. (For help with writing assignments in classes in disciplines that are new to you, ask your teacher.)

→ See pages 312–313 for more on creating an academic tone.

Academic writing usually uses longer words and sentences, more vocabulary, and more complex grammar than spoken language. Some of the more complex grammatical forms that academic writing uses are

→ dependent clauses, described on page 449.

→ complex, compound, and complex–compound sentences, described on pages 486–491.

ACADEMIC WRITERS ARE RESPONSIBLE FOR THEIR ARGUMENTS AND TO OTHER WRITERS.

Academic writers can't just say anything. They take responsiblity for their claims by giving supporting evidence and by helping readers check that evidence. In addition, they are responsible for showing when the evidence they offer comes from others: Academic writers give careful and full acknowledgment when they use the words and ideas of others.

→ Parts 4 and 5 of this book are all about using the words and work of others.

WRITING IN THE HUMANITIES

Writing in the humanities can be creative, theoretic, or analytic. We focus on analytic writing, for you will be asked to produce such writing in literature, film, rhetoric, modern languages, art, philosophy, history, and gender studies classes.

When you write analytically, you focus on a text like a short story or film or on a topic as we described in Part 3. Whether you analyze a text or a topic, you analyze to understand **how** and **why** values and decisions come to be and their effects.

ANALYZING TEXTS

When you analyze texts, you can focus on one text alone, describing its parts and arguing how the parts create an overall effect. You might show how a poem's line lengths and soft vowel sounds evoke a reader's reflections.

You can also analyze a text by comparing it with other texts or by explaining how it (and perhaps other similar texts) embodies cultural values, events, and structures. You might compare contemporary graphic novels and short stories, to show how both use quick, pictorial description and argue that this echoes the timing of fast food or video edits.

ANALYZING TOPICS

When you analyze a topic, you do the work we describe in Parts 5, 6, and 7 of this book. You look to texts—books, journals, films, interviews—to help you learn about the topic and, using what you have learned from those other texts as evidence, you develop an argument focused on some aspect of the topic's values, ideas, or effects.

ORGANIZING ANALYTIC PAPERS

1 **A TITLE.** Examples: "Counterfeit Motion: The Animated Films of Eadweard Muybridge" or "'To Protect and Serve': African American Female Literacies"

2 **AN INTRODUCTION.** In humanities papers, an introduction can begin with a relevant quotation or example to pique interest, but the introduction's purpose is to draw readers' attention to the question or problem being discussed and to make clear why it should matter to them.

THESIS: The main argument is usually explicitly stated in the introduction and is probably also repeated in the conclusion. Writers rarely leave readers to infer the argument. Subsequent ideas and information are related to the thesis; nothing is put into the text that doesn't support or further the thesis.

3 **BODY.** This contains the writer's analysis of the text or topic. Evidence supports the analysis: In the analysis of a text, the evidence is drawn from the text itself, through quotation; in the analysis of topics, evidence comes from a range of sources.

→ See pages 162–171 on the kinds of evidence used in humanities writing.

ARRANGEMENT OF IDEAS: Writers state the main argument in the beginning of the paper and then provide evidence for it; they do not lead the reader to the main argument.

→ Pages 160–161 and 222–225 explain some aspects of the logic used in academic writing.

Each paragraph usually picks up on and develops a point from the preceding paragraph, moving readers forward with little repetition.

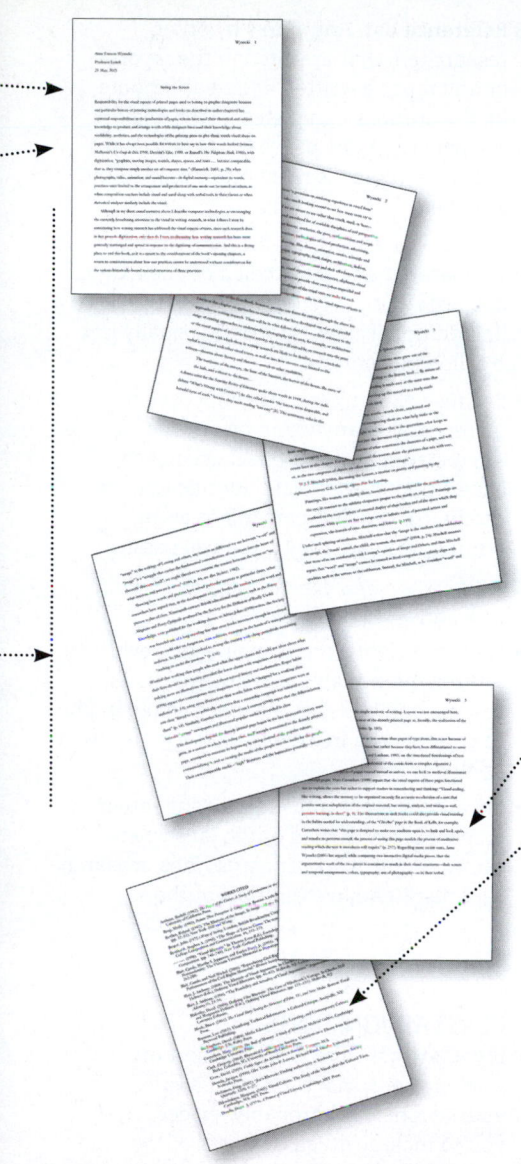

Writers consolidate or group issues that are related to make their writing less repetitive. They also signal the progression of their ideas using headings, transition sentences, and connecting words.

→ Pages 244–245 and 306–307 discuss transition sentences and connecting words.

EVIDENCE IN SUPPORT OF THE ARGUMENT. Evidence is given to support the main argument. Different disciplines will value different types of evidence and will use it in specific ways; but, in general, academic writers tend to avoid using only stories or examples to support a thesis.

→ See pages 162–171 for the types of evidence used in academic and technical writing.

→ See pages 220–221 to see the kinds of evidence valued in other disciplines.

The body of the writing is composed almost exclusively of evidence. Statistics, examples, and facts support any generalizations used in the argument.

4 A CONCLUSION. The conclusion summarizes the paper's argument while offering no new information.

5 WORKS-CITED LIST. At the end of the paper, list any works by other writers that are cited in the paper. (→ See pages 362–363 to learn MLA style, most often used in the humanities.)

In addition, if the writer's purpose and the context of the writing make it appropriate, writing in the humanities can be expressive: Writers can use **I**, draw on their own personal experiences or those of others, and use narratives as evidence. Check with your teacher if you are considering doing any of this for a class assignment.

WRITING IN THE SCIENCES

Research reports by scientists and engineers usually follow a specific arrangement of parts and a specific writing style. The arrangement directs readers' attention to how an experiment was performed; readers can then judge the results and perhaps replicate the experiment.

The arrangement that scientists and engineers have developed to support communications about experiments asks that any report have these parts, in order:

1 **A title.** The title describes the experiment. One example: *The Physiological Effects of Pallidal Deep Brain Stimulation in Dystonia.*

2 **An abstract.** This is a short and concise summary of the paper; abstracts allow readers to see quickly if a paper is relevant to their work.

3 **An introduction.** This states why the research was done, what was being tested, and the predicted results—the hypothesis. There might also be a review of earlier relevant research here.

4 **Methods.** Researchers describe the procedures they undertook to perform their experiments, including the materials and equipment used.

5 **Results.** Researchers describe what they learned from the experiment.

6 **Discussion.** Here, the researchers discuss their understanding of the results. Did the results support the hypothesis? Why—or why not?

7 **A conclusion.** In this section, the researchers describe possible implications of their experiment as well as possible further research.

8 **Reference list.** Any works by other researchers that are cited in the report—or any reports written at an earlier time by the authors—are listed at the end of the paper. (➔ See pages 420–424 to learn CSE style, which is most often used in the sciences.)

In a scientific report, all the above sections are separated and are labeled by the names listed above.

In addition, scientific writing usually has the following features:

- Because experiments are supposed to be repeatable anywhere by anyone, the experiment is emphasized, not the experimenter—and so scientific writers rarely use the first person *I* or **we** in writing; instead, they often use passive voice.

  ➔ See pages 308–309 and 445.

- Because scientific and engineering evidence is often quantifiable, writers use charts, graphs, and tables as evidence. Photographs of objects used in experiments are also used as evidence.

- Because science and engineering research is most often carried out in labs where many people work, or across labs, research reports often have multiple authors.

CLASS ASSIGNMENTS

If you are asked to write a report in a science or social sciences class, your teacher will probably expect you to include at least several of the parts described on these pages. If the organization or features are not described in the assignment, ask.

WRITING IN THE SOCIAL SCIENCES

As the term *social sciences* suggests, the disciplines that come under this name apply scientific methods to studying people as social groups and as individuals within social groups. The social sciences include anthropology, economics, education, geography, linguistics, political science, psychology, sociology, and speech communication. (At some schools, history and gender studies might be listed as social sciences, if those areas use primarily quantitative approaches to support their research.)

In writing papers for the social sciences, the arrangements that have developed over time follow the overall pattern of science writing as on the opposite page, but within the steps are some differences:

1 **A title.** This describes the study being reported in the paper. One example: *What Determines Cartel Success?*

2 **An abstract.** Abstracts contain 100–200 words that summarize the purpose of the study, its methods, and its results.

3 **An introduction.** This defines the problem that was studied, reviews previous writing on the problem, notes the gaps in the previous writing that the current study will address, and gives an overview of the methods used. Writers also tell readers why the research being described matters.

4 **Methods.** Evidence used in the social sciences is usually observational because social scientists are making and testing claims about human behavior. The sorts of methods for gathering this evidence are surveys and questionnaires, observations, interviews, and fieldwork (→ see page 168). In the methods section of the paper, the writer describes which of these methods was used and the details of how the method was carried out (how many people were interviewed or surveyed, for example, and what questions were asked).

5 **Results.** A description of what can be learned from the research.

6 **Discussion.** The researchers argue how the results of the study do (or do not) help with the problem described in the introduction.

7 **A conclusion.** The researchers summarize the problem, the research carried out, and what was learned.

8 **Reference list.** Any works by other researchers that are cited in the writing are listed at the end of the paper.

If the social sciences paper is longer than about five pages, the above sections are labeled by the names listed.

Because the social sciences seek as much objectivity as possible, additional features of social science writing echo what we have described for science writing:

- Use of passive voice.

- Use of charts, graphs, tables, and photographs as evidence.

- Multiple authors.

APA STYLE

The American Psychological Association (APA) has established the publishing and citation conventions most used in the social sciences.

→ See pages 393–419 to see a sample paper in APA style and to learn APA citation conventions.

USING A THESIS STATEMENT TO ORGANIZE AN ACADEMIC PAPER

You know that a paper needs an introduction, a body, and a conclusion, but what goes into those sections—and why?

If a reader cannot figure out why one paragraph or section follows another in a piece of writing, the reader will be confused—and the writing will lose its force.

But **the reader** won't be able to figure out why one paragraph or section follows another if **the writer** hasn't figured it out. Writers must be able to say why each paragraph is where it is in a composition, why one paragraph comes before or follows another. To do this, writers need a conceptual framework.

A framework (which we introduced on page 214) is like a skeleton: It is a bare-bones idea about organization, a sense of what generally needs to come first, second, and third in a piece of writing.

Having a thesis statement for a piece of writing helps writers develop a conceptual framework. A thesis statement can show the major steps a writer needs to take and in what order; a statement of purpose helps the writer begin to flesh out those steps.

→ On pages 224–225, see how one writer uses a thesis statement to develop an organization for her paper.

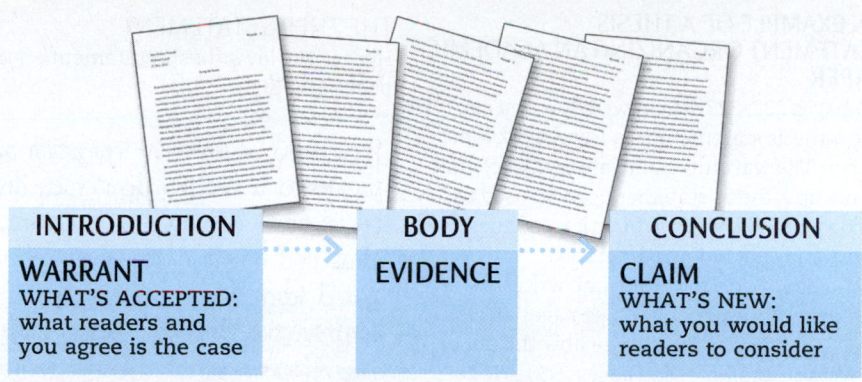

INTRODUCTION	BODY	CONCLUSION
WARRANT	**EVIDENCE**	**CLAIM**
WHAT'S ACCEPTED: what readers and you agree is the case		WHAT'S NEW: what you would like readers to consider

THESIS STATEMENTS, PERSUASION, AND ORGANIZING A PAPER

Those who developed the rhetorical method in ancient Greece noted that speeches were more likely to be persuasive when speakers started by discussing something about which they and the audience agreed: When speakers start by being in agreement with their audiences, audiences feel more generous toward the speakers and so are more likely to listen generously.

Because persuasive (or argumentative) research writing is about moving audiences to consider a different position than they may otherwise have held, those observations about persuasion led to the pattern diagrammed above for organizing persuasive compositions, following the parts of a thesis statement as we discussed it on pages 160–161:

1 INTRODUCTION: Use your warrant.
Start by discussing something around which you and your audience hold the same values or opinions.

2 BODY: Give your best evidence.
Offer your evidence for a new perspective on what you hold in common with the audience.

3 CONCLUSION: Make your claim explicit.
Make your claim: Tie together for your audience how what they already accepted (the warrant), when seen through the lens of your evidence, points to the conclusion of your claim. (Note that your conclusion is the concluding part of your paper; this could be the last paragraph, but in a five-page paper is more likely the last two or three paragraphs; in a seven-page paper, this could be the whole last page.)

AN EXAMPLE OF A THESIS STATEMENT ORGANIZING AN ACADEMIC PAPER

On pages 222–223 we showed how you can use a thesis statement as a framework for a paper: The warrant, claim, and evidence that make up a thesis statement can be used to guide what you write in your introduction, body, and concluding paragraphs.

We have been following one writer, as she develops a paper. (→ See pages 45, 95, 106–115, and 204–207; to see how the paper develops from here, see pages 273, 276–287, 293, and 354–363.) On these pages, we show how she uses her thesis statement to organize the paper she is about to write.

THE THESIS STATEMENT

Here is Harley's thesis statement (→ See pages 208–209).

> Preventing government repression and supporting a healthy democracy depends on us being able to discuss controversial ideas and beliefs civilly; therefore, we should learn how to discuss our controversial ideas and beliefs civilly.

THE WARRANT

Based on her thesis statement, Harley's warrant goes something like this:

> We should learn both how to prevent government repression and how to support a healthy democracy.

Remember—from page 161—that a warrant shows what a writer thinks her audience already believes. Given that Harley is writing to her classmates, do you think others in classes like yours would accept her warrant readily?

A STRUCTURE FOR A PAPER

Following what we've written on pages 222–223, Harley draws up the this conceptual framework, the large-scale organization for her paper:

1   In my introduction I will describe how most people DO NOT want government repression and DO want a healthy democracy (since my warrant shows that I think most people will believe this).

2   I need to spend the largest part of my writing presenting evidence to show how being able to discuss controversial topics civilly supports democracy and helps prevent government repression. This means I need to define civility. But it also means I am going to have to work hard to show how being civil in discussion helps prevent repression, because I think that connection will be new and surprising to people.

3   I can conclude by stating that, given my evidence, we all ought to support everyone learning how to discuss controversial topics civilly.

→ See pages 276–283 to learn how Harley blended this conceptual framework with a statement of purpose, to compose a first draft.

NOT LOGIC ALONE

A thesis statement can help you considerably in making some of the big choices about organizing a paper. Because persuasion does not happen based on logic alone, however, you still need to make other very important choices in your writing. Writing a statement of purpose helps you make these other choices about word choice, transitions, paragraph length, and so on.

→ See pages 270–273 for help with developing a statement of purpose.

ONLINE ACADEMIC GENRES

Not all of us but many. For example, who
ing in the background. No matter what you're
e an effect on whether or not I remember the
ost always print things out to read depending on the
was short so I did not have to print it, but the I
e minute I saw how long it was because a reading that
t was on the screen. I wouldn't be able to write and the
ing trees later so I always use the backside of the paper
e used it up.
hought this reading was interesting also because I saw
om the library since I was in high school. It's very rare
s kind of sad, but when I go to the library I go to study
round people who are USUALLLY there for the same

▶ **REPLY**

Reply by Senator Green on March 7, 20
You made a a statement that I find intere
me, nor does it apply to the group of peop
really have many friends.) You said you he
school and that it is rare that people do so
member. My boyfriend and best friend (wh
friends I have,) are also very active librar
I ended our night last night being curled
and are arguably from two different gene
tions about how technology was used
opposed to how it was used in my sta
I was thinking though, that our use of t
friends we make. In the most obvious
with people who we would otherwise
to that though, it helps shape who
wouldn't want to be friends with

FIRST: ETHOS ONLINE

Online, others usually experience you only through your words—as you experience them only through their words. Online, therefore, we all need to be particularly sensitive to how the self we create in words shapes how others read and listen.

Luckily, when you write for online genres you always have time to consider your writing before you send or publish it—and you have time to observe and reflect upon how others respond. Before you post any writing online, take a breath and look over your writing. Ask: *If someone else reads this, what sense will they develop of me, the writer? If that sense is not what I want, how do I modify what I've written to create the ethos I desire?*

Consider also how your words invite (or not) response. Again, read your words as though you were someone else, to ask: *How would I respond to these words? How can I modify my words so that others will be encouraged to respond and think more?*

Another advantage of online writing: You can go back and observe patterns. After several weeks in a class, go back and look over your words and the responses they elicited. Which of your posts received the most thought-encouraging responses— and why? What might you change—what experiments with writing ethos can you try—to shape the ethos and environment you think best?

Also look at how you responded to others' writing. If you responded negatively, figure out why. Could the other person have written in a way that would have encouraged a more positive response from you? Consider too why you responded positively when you did.

ACADEMIC BLOGGING, BLOGGING FOR CLASS

WHY ARE YOU BLOGGING?

Teachers might ask you to keep a blog for journaling, recording research on the way to a paper, posting reading responses, or still other reasons. You might also just want to have your own academic blog. Because you can blog for so many different reasons, you need to be very clear about your own particular reasons.

If you blog because of teacher request, pay particular attention to assignments. Are you expected to post polished, well-argued prose of a particular length—or short, informal, conversational reflections on what happened in class?

ENGAGING READERS

Perhaps one of your purposes with your blog is to learn how to write words that engage readers online; if so, having a specific and narrow purpose for each post can help you focus on producing well-shaped and engaging writing.

→ The pages on paragraphs in this part—pages 240–255—can help you develop focused posts.

→ Pages 314–315 offer suggestions for shaping focused, quick, and to-the-point sentences.

SHAPING WRITING FOR ONLINE

Be alert to differences between reading on paper and reading onscreen. Many people still find it easier to read longer prose on paper rather than screen. When you write onscreen, then, writing shorter paragraphs, putting spaces between paragraphs rather than indenting the first line, and using heads and subheads help readers track your words more easily.

USING PHOTOGRAPHS, ILLUSTRATIONS, AND VIDEO

Only if you can be certain your audience for an academic blog will understand your choice easily should you post a photograph or illustration without explanation; a video without accompanying explanation will only make sense if the video explains itself.

When you use photographs and illustrations, consider their placement within the text. Do they make sense at the beginning of the post, in the middle, or at the end?

CHOOSING WHERE YOU WRITE

Some bloggers write within their chosen blog software, but some use word processors because word processors offer a bigger writing screen and more tools for checking grammar and spelling. Unfortunately, copying from word processing software and pasting into blogging software can interfere with formatting. If this happens to you, try writing in Notepad or TextEdit (or pasting what you wrote into Notepad or TextEdit) and then copying and pasting into your blog software.

RESPONDING TO OTHERS' BLOG POSTS

→ See page 229.

E-MAIL IN ACADEMIC SETTINGS

Writing e-mail in academic contexts is just like writing e-mail in workplace contexts.

→ See page 235.

CONTRIBUTING TO ONLINE DISCUSSIONS IN A CLASS

SETTING THE TONE

Online, you probably have even more ability to shape discussion environments than in face-to-face classrooms. Being civil in online discussions—showing respect for others and their opinions and encouraging honest and full consideration of ideas even when you disagree—helps us all learn and grow.

- What word choices, tone of voice, and kinds of responses and questions encourage all to participate?

→ The research we show Harley developing throughout this book is about civility. Read her final paper on pages 354–363.

PREPARING TO CONTRIBUTE

- **Focusing.** What is the assignment or prompt? What is it asking you to learn? What kinds of contributions are you being asked to make? Look over the assignment to be sure you understand what's expected of you. If you don't understand, ask in an e-mail or in a post.

- **Referencing.** If you are supposed to engage with a class text when you respond, be prepared to summarize, paraphrase, and quote as needed to support your points.

- **Grounding yourself in the discussion.** If you are not the first to respond, read others' posts closely. If another's response sparks your thinking, ask yourself why; this helps you respond. Also look for where posts agree and disagree with your current ideas, to start thinking about a response. Reading others' posts also helps you *not* repeat already existing observations and arguments.

CONTRIBUTING

- **Contextualizing.** Being online is unlike in-class discussions where you can see who responds and why. Online, how can you shape your response to help others understand why you write? Do you need to quote from another's post or a class reading so others understand your response? Do you need to name the person to whom you respond? Try to read your response as though you were someone else: *What additional information does your post need to help others read?*

- **Staying on topic.** Although some informal conversation helps create community in online discussions, you do not want to distract from the discussion's purpose.

- **Being academic, 1.** If the person leading the discussion has not specified the level of formality expected, ask. Before posting your comments, check that your spelling and mechanics meet the expectations.

- **Being academic, 2.** How long does your post need to be to show that you have thoughtfully engaged with the topic? What other features of academic genres are expected in this writing?

→ See pages 216–221 on expectations of academic genres.

- **Deepening the discussion.** A firm statement of opinion often stops discussion: Not wanting to hurt others' feelings, we can feel that our only possible responses are to agree or be silent. If you end a post with invitations or questions—"I am curious whether anyone else sees the argument in the same way" or "Why do you think the reading's author would leave us uncertain about her opinion?"—you encourage response and deepen the discussion.

COMMENTING ON OTHERS' WRITING IN A BLOG OR DISCUSSION

Responding to others' posts offers opportunities to help others learn, to encourage engaged discussion, and to learn stronger communication abilities yourself.

→ See pages 286–287 on responding to drafts of papers; the suggestions there can also be useful for responding to online writing.

- *Being respectful to the writing.* To give yourself the best possible understanding and be most respectful (and also to avoid looking impatient or worse) read a whole post or comment before responding.

- *Being clear.* Written communication is never perfect—and online we can't see people's facial expressions or body language; as a result, we can misinterpret their emotional intentions. If at any time you are unclear about another's intentions, tell the other: Describe what you do not understand or where you find trouble. Offer others the patience and generosity you would like them to give your words.

- *Validating and encouraging.* We all do better when we feel respected. If you start a response with a positive statement, you encourage others to push their thinking:

  I see you making some very clear decisions about your technology uses, Sarah, but without yet saying WHY the decisions matter to you. This makes me very curious why you think books and paper are better for you than writing on the computer. Can you say more?

- *Asking questions:* Questions encourage others to think further and respond in turn.

- *Disagreeing.* Disagreeing can be hard for many of us, but our ideas develop more when we consider differing positions. Formulate disagreement by focusing on the poster's argument or points: Start by validating some aspect(s) of the original post and showing that you understand the whole argument or the part in question—and then articulate your disagreement:

  Brian, your reading summary really helps me understand how the author relies only on examples from the U.S. even though his argument is supposed to cover the whole world. But when you talk about videotaping in public, I don't think you are correct when you say people in the U.S. can't videotape the police. Here's a link to a website that explains…

- *Making connections.* If you point out similarities or differences among posts, or synthesize others' comments into a new observation, you help the conversation:

  Martha, based on the reading, you emphasize the positive aspects of privacy— but Harris, you emphasize the negative! I notice, though, that everything Martha says is about physical privacy in our homes— while everything Harris says is about online privacy (and how we don't seem to have any!). This makes me wonder whether we have to shift our notions of privacy for being online, or change our laws about what can be private online. Does anyone know more about how legal notions of privacy are shifting because of the Internet?

- *Remembering the purpose of the discussion.* Classroom online discussions exist to help you learn to discuss and think; they are not about being right!

WRITING IN A CLASS WIKI

Wikis consist of linked webpages, designed to be easy for anyone to create and modify. Anyone with access to the pages can edit any existing page to change the writing, comment, or add pictures, video, or links. You likely know the wiki *Wikipedia*.

Wikis encourage collaboration precisely because of their ease and openness to anyone editing. Because many workplaces require collaborative writing, and because networked digital spaces also tend to encourage collaboration, a teacher might ask you to write in a wiki.

In addition, because wikis are easy to use and encourage collaboration, teachers see them as writing spaces that students can take over. When no one person owns the writing and the audience can be anyone who finds the pages, the act of writing can become more engaging for students as they negotiate what is presented in the wiki.

LEARNING THE SOFTWARE

Different wiki software works differently in its particulars, but all will have tutorials. You will want to learn how to edit a page, comment on a page, make a new page, and link between the wiki pages and to webpages outside the wiki.

BEING CLEAR ABOUT THE ASSIGNMENT

As with all assignments, you will want to ask questions about an assignment that uses the wiki: *What are you being asked to write, and why? What level of academic formality does your teacher expect? How much are you expected to contribute, and on what sort of schedule? What support does the teacher describe for helping you learn the wiki?*

GETTING STARTED WITH OTHERS

Try to meet (face-to-face or through chat or e-mail) with your wiki collaborators. Agree that the final project is what matters; make clear you each understand that the project is a collaboration. For the project to be most successful, you each need to feel a valued and respected part, understand that your words can be edited, and contribute consistently. It can help for your group to state, out loud, your trust in each other to do the best possible work on this project and to support each other. (Giving your group a name can help you establish group spirit.)

Remember that this project will develop over time. You simply need to get started writing; you can discuss and figure out procedures as you go along.

Also discuss what you each hope to learn from the project, and then help each other achieve that learning.

WRITING

When adding a new page or paragraphs to an existing page, start writing as you would for any similar "regular" assignment. Over time, you and your class colleagues will figure out how to negotiate editing and needs for new content.

EDITING

Jump in and do it—even though editing another's writing can be touchy because you do not want to hurt anyone's feelings.

If the assignment does not specify that all writing on the wiki have a consistent voice, you need to negotiate with your colleagues about what approach to consistency fits your rhetorical purposes. Sometimes having one person do a final edit can help the wiki sound as though it has a consistent voice, if that is what you seek.

BEING EDITED

Remember that the whole project is what matters. If you disagree with another's edits of your writing, you can use the wiki comments or e-mail to negotiate over the writing—but face-to-face discussions in such circumstances usually are safest. When you talk, describe clearly what you disagree about and why—and then listen carefully to the other's reasons for editing. Often, the best solution is to figure out how to apply both approaches, since you probably both have good reasons. As you discuss, remember your group's goals for the assignment or project—and remember that you are learning valuable negotiation and collaboration abilities.

RESPONDING

Respond to each other's writing and comments as you would to other writing.

→ See pages 286–287.

COLLABORATING

Collaborating can be joyful and it can be the pits. You have some control because of how your enthusiasm and efforts shape the situation for others—but you cannot have complete control precisely because you are working with others. Do your work and be honest and respectful with others—but do talk to the teacher if your group needs help working together.

CHECKING IN

Every few days or weeks, depending on the project's length, check in with your colleagues. *What could make the collaboration stronger? What approaches can keep you all engaged in the writing?*

Also be sure to ask how well the wiki-in-progress moves toward the assignment's goals. *What more do you need to do—as individuals and as a group—to finish the assignment as you desire?*

ALLOWING FOR CREATIVITY

No small part of the collaboration's pleasure is learning approaches new to you. Early in a wiki project, you can try out all sorts of approaches, to see what new possibilities you can develop and to have fun together (which builds group trust and identity). As deadlines approach, look over all that you have produced and determine together what approaches—in writing or in design of the site and of pages—most help you surpass your goals.

FINISHING WITH PRIDE

When the project is complete, make sure to reflect on what worked and what you will do differently the next time you collaborate with others. Take delight in having learned and worked hard.

→ For more suggestions on how to write with others (advice that works for most on-paper writing as well), see the Wikipedia Etiquette page: <http://en.wikipedia.org/wiki/Wikipedia:Etiquette>

WORKPLACE GENRES

THE VALUES OF WORKPLACE GENRES

When you write for workplace audiences, keep the following considerations in mind:

THE PLACES IN WHICH WE WORK DEVELOP THEIR OWN CULTURES.

Communities develop shared habits and expectations, and workplaces are no exception. Learning to write well professionally means learning the habits and expectations of a workplace: Is the workplace formal or informal, focused particularly on getting things done quickly or on group discussions aimed at consensus?

WRITING IN WORKPLACES NEEDS TO FIT THE CULTURE OF THE WORKPLACE.

All our advice in this book about audiences applies to workplace writing, but writing in workplaces is tied to how people in the organization solve problems, attend meetings, organize projects, manage tasks, evaluate documents and performance, use computer technologies, give presentations, run training sessions, and so on.

Connected to these activities is a range of specialized forms of communication with which you need to become familiar; each has general characteristics that you can recognize across various places of work and that also become adapted to specific workplaces. For example, workplace audiences all know the general form of a memo, but they also know the specific ways memos are written—and read—in *their* workplace.

OFTEN IN WORKPLACES YOU WILL BE WRITING FOR TWO (OR MORE) AUDIENCES.

In workplaces, where you may be writing a brochure or an instruction set to be read by potential consumers, it can be useful to keep in mind that you often have two audiences, a foreground audience and a background audience. The foreground readers are the customers or clients; the background audience is those in the business or organization who will be looking at what you produce and making comments or suggestions along the way.

LARGER WORKPLACES CAN HAVE STYLE GUIDES YOU NEED TO FOLLOW WHEN YOU WRITE FOR CLIENTS OR CUSTOMERS.

Companies have such style guides to be sure all the documents they produce are consistent and represent the company professionally. Style guides can include guidelines for using the company's logo, formats for different kinds of writing, and specific phrases to use in writing (for example, a software company could specify that writers tell customers to *click a link* rather than to *click on a link*). If you are not given a style guide, ask if one exists.

BECAUSE WORKPLACES ARE ABOUT GETTING WORK DONE, PEOPLE AT WORK EXPECT WRITING TO HAVE A SINGLE PURPOSE AND BE EFFICIENT AND TO THE POINT.

For the sake of efficiency, workplace writers most often produce texts focused on a single purpose—and so the purpose is usually stated directly and clearly, usually in the beginning of the text.

Workplace texts are therefore usually short, with a formal but courteous tone.

This doesn't mean the writing is mechanical (it still needs to address its human audiences), but it needs to be very focused.

→ See pages 314–315 for suggestions on how to shape sentences that are focused, quick, and to the point.

TIP

GENRES FOR INTERNATIONAL WORKPLACES

The conventions of workplace genres are very much related to national culture. If you land a job with a company that has international offices, you may receive training in the forms of communication the company expects; if not, ask coworkers about the expected ways communication happens in the company.

If your company is in the United States but you must communicate with people in other countries, ask if the company will pay for you to take a workshop in cross-cultural communications or will hire a consultant who knows about communication expectations in the other countries.

MEMOS

Workplace memos are brief communications used for announcements and questions, setting up meetings, making requests, or confirming agreements. They can be on paper or sent through e-mail, and they are rarely longer than a page.

April 22, 2016

to: Video Project Team
Print Project Team
Interactive Project Team
Advertising Team
from: Erin Margaret Knight
subject: Finishing up the year—and preparing for next year!

Thank you all for your hard work this past year! On the bulletin board in our offices I've put all the cards we've received from various clients thanking you for your creativity and solid projects.

I want to remind you of what you need to do to finish up the year as professionally as possible.

FINISHING UP THE YEAR, step 1
If you are still finishing up a project before you head off for summer, set up a meeting with me within the next week. We need to confirm your final schedule and make sure that we can find staff to fill in should we need to. I will be checking in with each small project group, but do not wait for me to come to you—email me immediately if you have any work remaining.

FINISHING UP THE YEAR, step 2
All project reports are due by May 15.

PREPARING FOR NEXT YEAR
If you are continuing next year, do put into your calendars that we will have a kick-off meeting on Monday, September 9th, at 3pm. Please bring to that meeting any other students you think would be good additions to our team.

FINALLY, PARTY!
Don't forget our End-of-Year Celebration Party on Friday, May 17th. The party starts at 6pm. We'll have dinner (being provided by the Union) and then awards!

Thanks again for all your hard work. Do not forget to set up meetings with me if you have unfinished projects and to send in your project reports.

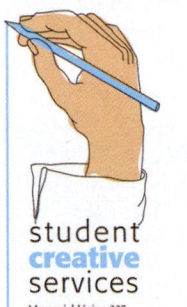

student
creative
services

Memorial Union 327
University of Wisconsin–
Milwaukee
Milwaukee, WI 53201
410-555-1212
scs@schooluwm.edu
www.scs.schooluwm.edu

Readers have come to expect memos to have the following parts:

1 **A heading:** At the top, on separate lines, memos have:
- the date
- the recipient's name(s) (and titles if appropriate)
- your name (and title if appropriate); sometimes writers initial their names
- a subject line

2 **An introduction:** Describe—quickly—your main purpose in writing.

3 **A body:** Give the information that supports or explains your purpose. If this information breaks into two or more parts, as in this example, consider using bold headings to make these parts easier to see.

4 **A closing:** Provide a one- or two-sentence summary, with contact information (if necessary). (Unlike letters, memos do not end with a signature.)

```
Dear Ms. Fisher:

I wanted to double-check that you are set for our class to visit the Keweenaw
National Historic Park Library on Thursday, the 5th. We're planning on arriving
around 4, and staying for about an hour; there will be 17 of us.

Thanks again for encouraging this visit: the people in class look forward to it.

Sincerely,
Anne Frances Wysocki
```

E-MAIL (ONLINE MEMOS)

When writing e-mails within workplace settings, or to people in workplaces, follow the same considerations as for memos, but also keep the following in mind:

- **Have a neutral-sounding e-mail address.** squirrlygrrrl@hotmail.com is fine for friends—but not for formal communication. Consider getting an e-mail account that uses your initials and last name. If your company or school gives you an e-mail address, use that for communicating with professors, staff, employers, and colleagues.

- **Write a subject that is descriptive but short and professional.** "Wanna meet?" is descriptive and short—but sounds like party time. For formal situations, "Budget meeting Tuesday 3 pm?" is more appropriate.

- **Start with a salutation.** Until you have a relaxed relationship with others, the expected way to show respect is to start with a formal salutation such as "Dear Professor:" or "Dear Dr. Murthy:" or "Dear Mo Folk:" (if you do not know someone's gender or title, write out the person's first and last names). Notice also that, in workplaces, the expected punctuation following the salutation is a colon. When others end messages to you with their first names, then you can write back to them using their first names. Otherwise, in any follow-up messages, address others in the way they signed their e-mails.

- **State your purpose following the salutation.** Put two returns after the salutation, and then state your purpose.

- **Write the e-mail in short paragraphs separated by two returns.** Readers can rarely see whole messages at once, and e-mail software is rarely designed to support easy reading. Others can read more easily if they can see your paragraphs—so arrange your paragraphs to be short and easy to see.

- **Avoid smiley faces.** They are appropriate for informal e-mails.

- **Sign your message.** Even though your name is in the header, it is still considered polite to type your full name at the end—until you know the person to whom you write.

- **Keep in mind how easily others can forward your messages.** If you do not want to risk the world knowing something, do not put it in e-mail.

RESUMÉS

Resumés summarize the experiences and education that make you appropriate for a job. Because a resumé (and cover letter; → see pages 238–239) is often how a potential employer first encounters an employee, it deserves time and attention. And because employers often receive hundreds of resumés, they look at them quickly. Therefore, a resumé needs to be:

- short, to the point, and easy to read.
- focused on the position for which it is being sent.
- accurate.

THE FORMAT OF A RESUMÉ

(1)
Shawnelle Ponder
sponder@mtu.edu

(2)
Address until 5/15/16	Permanent Address
29401 Woodmar Drive Apt. Q	4577 Pertin Drive
Huffton, Michigan 49938	Detroit, MI 48221
(096) 270-8187	(313) 688-1239

(3) **OBJECTIVE**
To acquire an internship designing and developing educational materials in biological sciences/health

(4) **EDUCATION**
Michigan Technological University, Houghton, Michigan
Bachelor of Science in Scientific and Technical Communication
Expected graduation date: May, 2016
Cumulative G.P.A. 3.75/4.00

(5) **EMPLOYMENT**
Design Assistant, MTU First-Year Programs, Houghton, MI (Summers 2014, 2015)
- Developed overall theme for and designed print materials (1- and 4-color) for Student Orientation
- Managed scheduling and production of print materials
- Oversaw development of related online materials

Communications Assistant, MTU Plant Biotechnology Research Center, Houghton, MI (2013-present)
- Perform educational outreach for the Center
- Design, develop, and maintain educational component of Research Center website based on my research; website visits increased by 125%

(6) **OTHER RELEVANT EXPERIENCE**
Writing Coach, MTU Writing Center, Houghton, MI (Fall 2014-Present)
- Meet with individual students to help develop their writing
- Participate in on-going research projects and presentations on student wrriting

(7) **RELEVANT COURSEWORK**
Technical Writing and Editing, Information Design, Interactivity Design, Usability, Graphic Design, Biology, Chemistry, Anatomy, Journalism, Creative Writing

(8) **COMPUTER SKILLS**
Operating Systems: Windows, Macintosh, Linux
Language: C++, Java, HTML, CSS
Software: InDesign, Photoshop, Dreamweaver, Acrobat Professional, Microsoft Professional Suite

(9) **HONORS**
Dean's List (2014, 2015)
Susan Lewis Anthony Memorial Award (2014)
University Student Award (2013)

(10) **EXTRACURRICULAR ACTIVITIES**
Scientific and Technical Communication, student association, president (2014–2015)
Black Student Association (BSA) (2012-present)
BSA Big Brother/Big Sister Mentoring Program (2012-present)
ExSEL Peer Mentoring Program (2013-Present)

(11) **REFERENCES**
Available upon request

1. **Name:** Center your name at the top. Do not use nicknames. Bold your name, and put it in a slightly larger size (14 or 16 points).

2. **Contact information:** Be sure your address will be current for several months; if you are still in school or planning to move, put a permanent address. Most companies contact you by phone or e-mail, so include both—and have a professional-sounding voice mail message. Your e-mail address should be your name or initials; hotdude@hotmail.com does not suggest a reliable, focused employee.

3. **Objective:** Fit this on one line. If you are responding to an ad, use the job title as part of the objective.

4. **Education:** Don't include high school unless there is something about your high school education that is relevant to the position.

5. **Employment:** Put your most recent employment first. Start an entry with the title, followed by the place of employment and the length of time you held the position.

   List your main accomplishments and responsibilities underneath the job title. Use action verbs in the past tense for past positions; use present tense for ongoing positions. If you have an accomplishment an employer will value, include it (such as *website visits increased by 125% after my redesign*).

6. **Other relevant experience:** In the same format as for employment, list experiences for which you received no pay but from which you gained abilities relevant to the position for which you apply. You can include hobbies if they are relevant.

7. **Relevant coursework:** List only those classes that are directly applicable for the position.

8. **Computer skills:** List these if the position requires computer skills.

9. **Honors:** List any awards, in the order received.

10. **Extracurricular activities:** List any clubs or societies relevant to the position.

11. **References:** It is fine to say these are *Available upon request*—but do check with your references that they don't mind being contacted.

COMPOSING A RESUMÉ

- For entry-level positions, a one-page resumé enables employers to scan quickly.

- Look at your first draft: For each line in the body of the resumé, ask yourself, *Does this help an employer see my suitability for this position?* If the answer is no, remove or replace the information.

- If possible, get feedback from someone who works in or supervises the sort of position for which you apply: *Does this person find your resumé readable, appropriately formatted, and strong?*

- Always have someone else proofread for you. Because employers receive so many resumes, they look for reasons to exclude applications; don't give them such a simple reason as a typo.

- Do not lie or pad your experiences.

PRINT GUIDELINES FOR RESUMÉS

- Use white or cream paper. Use good-quality paper, but don't use papers such as parchment or vellum unless they are appropriate for the position (graphic designer, for example).

- Use black ink.

- Use a typeface such as Times or Helvetica. (Times takes up less space and so fits more information on a page.)

- Use 11- or 12-point type.

- Use headings, bullets, and indents so that readers can see the parts quickly.

→ See pages 259 and 341 on using headings.

COVER LETTERS

Unless a job advertisement requests only a resumé, always send a cover letter with your resumé. A resumé lists your accomplishments; in a cover letter you address an employer directly, to describe why you are a fit for the job.

THE FORMAT OF A COVER LETTER

(1) March 1, 2016

(2) Dr. Louisa Williams
Community Education Director, Toivola Health Services
500 Campus Drive
Toivola, MI 49956

(3) Dear Dr. Williams:

(4) A professor you know at my university, Dr. Richard Otherly, suggested I write. He heard that I desire an internship in health education, and he said I would be a perfect fit for your organization because of my knowledge and background. He did not know if you have any internships starting in early June (which is when I will be available, for three to six months), but I write in hopes you will keep me in mind.

(5) From looking at your website, I see that your hospital provides a range of materials for helping people learn healthy habits or manage ongoing health issues. My attached resumé shows my experience in both the technical and scientific aspects of designing online educational materials for general audiences. In my position working at the Plant Biotechnology Research Center, my education in biology and chemistry helped me communicate with the scientists whose work I translated into educational materials; my technical knowledge and communication abilities allowed me to suggest strategies for developing creative and effective learning materials. (When I redesigned the Center's educational website, visits to the website increased by 125%.) I know how to make interactive animations that help people understand how plants uptake water, and I can imagine how useful (for example) an interactive animation about how insulin works would be on your diabetes education webpages. I also have experience developing print materials.

What my resumé doesn't show is that I am a solid and cheerful team player who gets things done on time. All my previous employers have commented on my responsibility and energy. I would be excited to be part of the good educational efforts your hospital is making.

(6) I would appreciate the opportunity to discuss an internship with you. I will contact you within the next ten days to see if you might have an opening and to see if you need any other information from me such as an application form, recommendations, or transcripts. Thank you for your time and consideration.

(7) Sincerely,

(8) *Shawnelle Ponder*

Shawnelle Ponder
29401 Woodmar Drive Apt. Q
Huffton, Michigan 49938
(096) 270-8187
sponder@mtu.udu

1. **Date**

2. **Name and address of recipient:** A job listing should give you a name and address. If you are writing to inquire whether a company has job openings, do some research first: Call to ask a receptionist for the name of the person who hires in the department where you would work; you might also find this information online.

3. **Salutation:** Use *Dear* and the title of the person being addressed; if there is no title, use *Ms.* or *Mr.* Be sure to spell the name accurately.

4. **Introduction:** Each of the two kinds of cover letters requires a different introduction
   - For letters written in response to job advertisements, include the name of the job—exactly as it is listed in the job ad—and any job number.
   - For letters expressing interest in a company if you don't know whether there is an opening, explain why you are writing to the particular company and how you learned about them, and describe the position you desire. If someone has recommended you to the company, say so.

5. **Body:** Use your research into the company to show how your abilities fit the company's goals and values. Don't just repeat what's listed in your resume but flesh it out: Give concrete examples, describe achievements, and help the potential employer see how you are suitable; be positive and enthusiastic.

6. **Sum up:** Let the person know you will be contacting the company to request an interview.

7. **Closing:** *Sincerely* or *Sincerely yours* are the formal options.

8. **Signature and contact information:** Leave four lines after the closing for your signature, and sign in blue or black ink. Type your name and full contact information, including your phone number and e-mail address.

GENERAL FEATURES OF COVER LETTERS

- Because employers receive many job letters and are always pressed for time, make your cover letter no more than one page long.

- Research the company by reading their website carefully or talking with people who work there; you need this knowledge for an effective letter.

- Put the cover letter on the same kind of paper as your resume, and send originals, not copies.

- When you send a cover letter and resume, put the cover letter on top. You can fold the two together to go into a business-size envelope, or you can send them in a large envelope so that they remain uncreased.

- Make it perfect. Many employers will use even one typo as a reason for discarding a letter and resume.

TIP

FORMATTING FOR PRINT OR ONLINE

Consider the following when you format a memo, resume, or cover letter:

- Because screen sizes are usually smaller than paper and so slow down reading, you can help readers online by using shorter paragraphs and sentences.

- Readers gain a stronger sense of a text's organization when they can see the visual divisions in the text. Online, separating paragraphs by two returns rather than with an indent helps readers see the organization and read more easily. Using headers also helps readers see the organization online.

SHAPING PARAGRAPHS FOR AUDIENCE AND PURPOSE

In the preceding pages we've discussed the larger-scale organizational structures of different kinds of texts, and how and why to use them.

Now we discuss the next level of written organization: paragraphs.

PARAGRAPHS

Academic and workplace writing are rarely about conveying random individual ideas to others. Instead, writing is meant to convey the structure and relations of the ideas that have led writers to hold the beliefs, opinions, and values they do.

Paragraphs break reading—conceptually and visually—into units a reader can easily see. And because readers can see them, paragraphs help readers remember and so think about the structure and relations of the ideas in a text.

Readers' expectations about paragraphs have developed over several centuries. What we present on the next pages are current expectations about paragraphs in formal writing.

PURPOSES OF PARAGRAPHS

There are three main categories of paragraphs:

1 Introductory paragraphs, which orient readers to the general concerns of a paper.

2 Body paragraphs, where the main arguments of the writing are developed.

3 Concluding paragraphs, which summarize the paper's argument and add nothing new to the argument.

In the next pages, we focus on body paragraphs. Such paragraphs can function to

- describe.
- define.
- narrate.
- give examples.
- give context.
- compare.
- classify.
- use analogies.
- analyze through division or through giving claims and evidence.

Paragraphs can also mix these functions.

In the coming pages, we give examples of and discuss some of these paragraph functions. Once you understand how paragraphs perform functions like these, you can shape paragraphs to function as you need for your own purposes.

→ Pages 302–305 address introductory and concluding paragraphs.

QUALITIES THAT READERS EXPECT IN PARAGRAPHS

UNITY

In the twenty-first century, readers expect a paragraph to contain sentences focused around only one idea or point.

COHERENCE

Readers expect the sentences of a paragraph to grow out of each other.

DEVELOPMENT

Readers expect paragraphs not to repeat the same idea over and over, but instead to add to their understanding of the idea being discussed as it relates to the writing of which the paragraph is a part.

■ ■ ■

In the next pages we go over these qualities in order.

SHAPING PARAGRAPHS FOR AUDIENCE AND PURPOSE

UNIFIED AND COHERENT PARAGRAPHS

Whether you write for an academic journal or a music blog, readers these days expect paragraphs to be unified and coherent.

To be unified, each sentence of a paragraph is on the same topic.

To be coherent, each sentence of a paragraph will seem to a reader to follow directly from the sentence that preceded it. Writers use strategies like the following to achieve coherence:

• Repeating crucial words and phrases.

• Repeating crucial concepts by using synonyms for the concepts.

• Using pronouns to show that successive sentences refer to the same topic.

• Using parallel structures (➔ see pages 318–319).

• Using words that show relations and connections among sentences (➔ see pages 244–245).

• Having a consistent point of view.

• Using the same tense throughout.

When a paragraph is coherent, a reader should be able to draw connections between various parts of the paragraph, as the examples to the right show.

UNIFIED BUT INCOHERENT

It is possible to have paragraphs that are unified but not coherent:

Dolphins are highly intelligent mammals that live in the oceans. They are closely related to whales. Some people think they are gentle and cute. Dolphins are predators who can act violently. Dolphins can hear better than people. Some people think dolphins are a symbol of freedom and joy. The Dolphins are a football team in Miami.

The paragraph is unified because each sentence is on the topic of *dolphins.* The paragraph is incoherent because nothing else connects one sentence to the next. Instead, the paragraph offers random facts about dolphins—and the Dolphins.

seas of the continental shelves, where they seek schools of fish and squid to eat.

Of these oceanic dolphins, bottle-nose dolphins are the most common and well-known to humans. These dolphins will curiously examine boats and the people on them, and they have been known to raise injured human divers to the surface, just as they will raise injured dolphins. Also making bottle-nose dolphins seem friendly are their curved mouths, which look like smiles. They are smart (with more nerve cells in their brains than humans) and they travel in social groups, communicating through sounds and body language. They work together to herd fish, and research suggests that mother dolphins teach their offspring how to use sponges to protect their undersides when they must search the sea bottom for their food.

Because they are so smart and alert to humans, such

ground were the result of deep and personal individual reactions to a new environment.

The knottiest mystery of survival is how one unequipped, ill-prepared seventeen-year-old girl gets out alive and a dozen adults in similar circumstances, better equipped, do not. But the deeper I've gone into the study of survival, the more sense such outcomes make. Making fire, building shelter, finding food, signaling, navigation—none of that mattered to Juliane's survival. Although we cannot know what the others who survived the fall were thinking and deciding, it's possible that they knew they were supposed to stay put and await rescue. They were rule followers, and it killed them.

In the World Trade Center disaster, many people

UNITY

Every sentence in the central paragraph to the left is about bottle-nose dolphins and the writer keeps a scientfically descriptive tone in each sentence.

COHERENCE

Notice the varying ways the writer refers to *bottle-nose dolphins*, and how each sentence or clause begins with a noun or pronoun that specifically references this kind of dolphin. In addition, each sentence is in the present tense.

■ ■ ■

UNITY

In this paragraph, the first sentence describes a *mystery*— and then every following sentence works to explain that mystery.

COHERENCE

In this paragraph, the writer has chosen a straightforward, emphatic tone throughout. The writer repeats *survival* often because that is the paragraph's unifying idea. The writer refers to a young woman in two different ways. After a first reference to those who did not survive the airplane crash that the young woman did, the writer uses pronouns to refer to them.

LINKING WORDS THAT BUILD COHERENCE IN PARAGRAPHS

If you use words from the following list in a paragraph's sentences, you will help your readers understand why the sentences belong together. When you use the words below, you can repeat them to build parallel structures (→ see pages 318–319) that also show how the sentences belong together. If you do use such repetition, read your paragraph aloud to be sure you have not built a boring, singsong rhythm (unless a boring, singsong rhythm supports your purpose).

To show that information in one sentence adds to information in a preceding sentence: *additionally, also, and, besides, equally important, furthermore, in addition, moreover, too*

To emphasize the information in a sentence: *indeed, in fact, of course*

To help readers understand that you are building a sequence of events or a description of a process: *again, also, and, and then, besides, finally, first…second…third, furthermore, last, moreover, next, still, too*

To build sentences to describe events that take place over time: *after a few days, after a while, afterward, as long as, as soon as, at last, at that time, at the same time, before, during, earlier, eventually, finally, immediately, in the future, in the meantime, in the past, lately, later, meanwhile, next, now, simultaneously, since, soon, then, thereafter, today, until, when*

To help readers compare information in one sentence with that in another: *also, in the same manner, in the same way, likewise, once more, similarly*

To help readers see any important differences between your sentences: *although, but, despite, even though, however, in contrast, in spite of, instead, nevertheless, nonetheless, on the contrary, on the one hand… on the other hand…, otherwise, regardless, still, though, yet*

To indicate to readers that a sentence contains an example: *for example, for instance, indeed, in fact, of course, specifically, such as, to illustrate*

To help readers see cause and effect: *accordingly, as a result, because, consequently, for this purpose, hence, so, then, therefore, thus, to this end*

To make clear to readers the spatial relations among objects you are describing: *above, adjacent to, behind, below, beyond, closer to, elsewhere, far, farther on, here, in the background, near, nearby, opposite to, there, to the left, to the right*

To concede that your arguments are open to question: *although it is true that, granted that, I admit that, it may appear that, naturally, of course*

To show that sentences are summarizing or concluding: *as a result, as I have argued, as mentioned earlier, consequently, in any event, in conclusion, in other words, in short, on the whole, therefore, thus, to summarize*

STRATEGIES FOR BUILDING COHERENCE

The paragraph below shows how each sentence connects to the next through one or more of the following three strategies:

- repetition of words and phrases, as we noted on page 243.
- linking words.
- parallelism.

You can see that only a few linking words are used in the paragraph below; too many linking words can fragment a paragraph, so, generally, writers use only a few but combine them with the other strategies we described on page 223 to link sentences.

"war"

War is used in four out of the seven sentences of this paragraph, helping keep the paragraph unified around its topic of how the Civil War changed the United States without destroying it.

It is a remarkable fact about the United States that it fought a civil war without undergoing a change in its form of government. The Constitution was not abandoned during the American Civil War; elections were not suspended; there was no coup d'état. The war was fought to preserve the system of government that had been established at the nation's founding—to prove, in fact, that the system was worth preserving, that the idea of democracy had not failed. This is the meaning of the Gettysburg Address and of the great fighting cry of the north: "Union." And the system was preserved; the union did survive. But in almost every other respect, the United States became a different country. The war alone did not make America modern, but the war marks the birth of a modern America.

parallelism

This sentence has three clauses, each of which has the same structure; the clauses are linked with semicolons. This structure shows that the three ideas have equal weight.

"in fact"

In fact precedes an explanation here and emphasizes the explanation. In this way, *in fact* indicates that the words following it amplify the words that precede it.

"This"

This refers to "that the system was worth preserving, that the idea of democracy had not failed." The pronoun carries those concepts into the next sentence, linking them.

"And"

And indicates to readers that the sentence it begins adds information to the sentence before it.

"But"

But signals to readers that there will be a change from what the preceding sentences were arguing.

SHAPING PARAGRAPHS FOR AUDIENCE AND PURPOSE

PARAGRAPHS THAT DEVELOP

WHAT DOES "DEVELOPMENT" MEAN FOR PARAGRAPHS?

No matter its specific purpose, all writing is meant to move readers: It might move them from knowing nothing about a proposal in an upcoming election to understanding why some people are against the proposal, or it might move them out of daily routines into stopping to savor the pleasures of breathing.

If writing is to move readers, it has to begin with ideas familiar to them and then, from paragraph to paragraph and within paragraphs, develop those ideas in new or unexpected directions.

Effective paragraphs thus start with a sentence that grows out of the preceding paragraph—and then each following sentence develops or adds to the idea that is the focus of the first sentence.

You can shape this development from the familiar to the unfamiliar in many ways; in the next pages, we describe patterns— moving from simpler to more complex—for developing paragraphs.

The simpler kinds of paragraphs (such as description, definition, and narrative) usually appear near the beginning of a composition because they help writers lay out the ideas and terms at stake. Later, when a writer is trying to persuade readers to make particular connections among ideas, the more complex kinds of paragraphs (classification and division, comparison and contrast, cause and effect, syllogistic, analogical, and other kinds of paragraphs that do analysis) are more useful because these kinds of paragraphs are about considering the relations among ideas.

→ Because introductory and concluding paragraphs have specific stylistic functions, we discuss them in Part 8 on style; see pages 302–305.

PARAGRAPHS THAT DESCRIBE

Descriptive paragraphs give details about people, places, or things.

Descriptive paragraphs serve two functions. First, because they appeal to our senses, they make what is being described more immediate and so they engage readers' attention. Second, such paragraphs help writers set the scene: They provide the background within which discussions, controversies, and experiments occur. Because they engage readers and set the scene, writers often use descriptive paragraphs at the beginning of a piece—but whenever writers need to make a scene clear or describe a situation that affects their arguments, they can use descriptive paragraphs.

DARK NIGHT in the mountains and no drums beating. No flute music like birdsong from the forest above the village—the men controlled the flutes and this was women's business, secret and delicious, sweet revenge. In pity and mourning but also in eagerness the dead woman's female relatives carried her cold, naked body down to her sweet-potato garden bordered with flowers. They would not abandon her to rot in the ground. Sixty or more women with their babies and small children gathered around, gathered wood, lit cooking fires that caught the light in their eyes and shone on their greased dark skins. The dead woman's daughter and the wife of her adopted son took up knives of split bamboo, their silicate skin sharp as glass. They began to cut the body for the feast.

New Guinea was the last wild place on

The paragraph to the left is the first paragraph of a book about certain neurological diseases.

The writer's descriptions appeal to ears and eyes, and they also describe skin sensations. Attention to a range of senses helps writers make descriptions as vivid as possible—and here the descriptions set the scene for the rest of the book and help pull readers into that scene.

PARAGRAPHS THAT NARRATE

Paragraphs that narrate tell stories. When we hear stories, we imagine ourselves in those situations. We know what feelings must be involved and might feel them ourselves. Stories can thus build emotional connections—positive or negative—between readers and topics.

Because stories are always about the experiences of one person or a few people, rarely can they stand alone as evidence: Readers will question a writer's attempts to generalize from limited experience. But stories can be useful in introductory or concluding paragraphs to engage readers emotionally with a topic or to make the topic memorable.

To write a narrative paragraph, tell what happened, in order. Include details—where the event took place, who was involved—but keep the narrative focused on your purpose: What is the main idea or feeling you want readers to remember?

(Note that stories based on real experiences are more effective than made-up stories; readers will not accept made-up stories as evidence because such stories are not real.)

The paragraph to the right introduces an article on the dangers of sitting in a tilted-back front seat of a car. The author's own story makes the topic real—and scary. In the paragraphs that follow in the article, the writer describes what she learned about tilted front seats through research and offers much more evidence than her own experience to argue that the dangers of riding in a reclined front car seat ought to be more well known.

Death Nap
THE DANGERS OF TILTING BACK THE FRONT SEAT—DON'T DO IT!

By Emily Bazelon

Posted Friday, Sept. 7 2007, at 4.24 PM ET

A couple of weeks ago, I was sleeping in the front passenger seat of our car when it slammed into the vehicle in front of us. We were on the highway coming home from a family trip. The other three people in our car weren't hurt. But I'd reclined my seat, and my seat belt, which was riding high, left a long welt around my rib cage and along my stomach. As it turned out, I had internal bleeding from a lacerated spleen and three cracked ribs. I spent the next two days in intensive care.

I've recovered nicely, thank you. But the more I thought about my accident, the more I wondered whether I'd inadvertently done myself in by tilting my car seat back—as I do on just

PARAGRAPHS THAT DEFINE

If you are unsure whether your readers will understand a particular term or concept, give a definition. If you use a term or concept special to a discipline or field, chances are you need to define it for a general audience. And if the term or concept is central to your argument, then defining it allows you and your readers to be in agreement about its meaning.

Because writers and readers need a shared understanding of terms and concepts if discussion and argument are to be possible, definitions of new or contested terms usually comes early in a text or early in a section that first uses the term or concept.

Sometimes a one-sentence definition is all you need—but if a term or concept is complex or central to your purpose, then use a whole paragraph to build a detailed definition.

meat and milk) than anyone had ever thought possible.

Grass farmers grow animals—for meat, eggs, milk, and wool—but regard them as part of a food chain in which grass is the keystone species, the nexus between the solar energy that powers every food chain and the animals we eat. "To be even more accurate," Joel has said, "we should call ourselves sun farmers. The grass is just the way we capture the solar energy." One of the principles of modern grass farming is that to the greatest extent possible farmers should rely on the contemporary energy of the sun, as captured every day by photosynthesis, instead of the fossilized sun energy contained in petroleum.

For Allan Nation, who grew up on a cattle ranch in Mississippi, doing so is as much a matter of sound economics as environ-

The paragraph to the left comes from a book arguing that food in the United States is now a petroleum product because of how crops and livestock are raised. This paragraph comes from a chapter in which the author describes Joel Salatin's farm in Virginia. The author uses this farm as an example of how crops and livestock can be raised without petroleum.

Notice how the first sentence gives a general definition of **grass farmer** (which itself includes a quick definition of **keystone species**). The following sentences add further detail and description—and use the words of an expert to support the definition being offered.

PARAGRAPHS THAT GIVE EXAMPLES

If you write, *No wonder people don't watch television news—there are so many commercials!*, readers might respond, *Sure, sure….* But imagine you wrote this:

No wonder people don't watch television news—there are so many commercials! Last night, I counted 12 commercials during one thirty-minute local newscast and 15 during a thirty-minute national newscast.

Examples give readers vivid, concrete evidence, and so give them reason to consider the situation you are discussing.

→ The evidence you offer as examples can be of different kinds; see pages 162–171.

The paragraph to the right comes from a newspaper magazine article about a breakdown in the social structures of elephant groups. The article describes how elephants now perform violent acts against other animals, other elephants, and humans; young elephants suffer from what looks to researchers like post-traumatic stress syndrome. To argue that we should therefore treat elephants differently than we currently do, the writer needs readers to think of elephants as complex beings who deserve our sympathies, respect, and awe.

This paragraph lists examples of concrete elephant behaviors, shaped to encourage readers to think of elephants differently.

When an elephant dies, its family members engage in intense mourning and burial rituals, conducting weeklong vigils over the body, carefully covering it with earth and brush, revisiting the bones for years afterward, caressing the bones with their trunks, often taking turns rubbing their trunks along the teeth of a skull's lower jaw, the way living elephants do in greeting. If harm comes to a member of an elephant group, all the other elephants are aware of it. This sense of cohesion is further enforced by the elaborate communication system that elephants use. In close proximity they employ a range of vocalizations, from low-frequency rumbles to higher-pitched screams and trumpets, along with a variety of visual signals, from the waving of their trunks to subtle anglings of the head, body, feet and tail. When communicating over long distances—in order to pass along, for example, news about imminent threats, a sudden change of plans or, of the utmost importance to elephants, the death of a community member—they use patterns of subsonic vibrations that are felt as far as several miles away by exquisitely tuned sensors in the padding of their feet.

PARAGRAPHS THAT GIVE CONTEXT

When writers give context, they give readers background for understanding a situation. The background might come from other times or other places, but whatever its origins, it helps readers see a situation more broadly or in a new light.

Paragraphs that give context can come at the beginning of a paper, to help readers understand why the situation being discussed matters. Paragraphs that give context can also come in a paper's body, to deepen readers' sense of why a particular question needs to be asked.

Are you curious about the origins of school vouchers? Rewind in time to 1953. The U.S Supreme Court was planning to make a decision in the case of *Brown v. Board of Education*; this lawsuit charged that racially segregated public schools led to inferior education for African American students and the lawsuit asked for schools to be integrated. In that year, Herman Talmadge, the governor of Georgia, proposed "an amendment to empower the general assembly to privatize the state's public education system." In proposing such an amendment, Talmadge said that "We can maintain separate schools regardless of the U.S. Supreme Court by reverting to a private system, subsidizing the child rather than the political subdivision" (Williams 17). Talmadge recognized that, if the Supreme Court were to decide that segregated schools are unequal, he could have the state close all public schools and issue vouchers to allow white parents the choice to enroll their children in segregated private schools. And so, as Barbara Miner notes, in her 2013 book *Lessons from the Heartland: A Turbulent Half-Century of Public Education in an Iconic American City* about how vouchers have been used in Milwaukee supposedly to help poor parents have school choice, "Ironically, the first use of vouchers was not by poor black parents but by whites hoping to escape desegregation" (167).

This paragraph comes toward the end of a paper written by a Milwaukee college student. The paper questions connections between private corporations and school vouchers. By putting school vouchers into historical context, along with his other arguments, this writer hopes his readers will ask questions of vouchers that they might not otherwise.

PARAGRAPHS THAT USE ANALOGY

To explain to children why cars need gasoline, you can talk about eating: Children probably understand that they need to eat because food gives them energy—so they can understand that cars need gasoline because otherwise the cars won't run. This explanation is an **analogy**: It uses a concept an audience already understands to explain a concept they don't.

Popular science writing uses analogies frequently, because the writing's purpose is usually to explain complex concepts to people who don't have a technical background; using analogies that draw on an audience's experiences bridges their unfamiliarity.

You can use paragraphs based on analogies when you need to make what is complex seem simpler. When you use an analogy, whatever associations your audience has with the more well-known concept will shape their attitudes toward the new or more complex concept. With the above analogy of food and gasoline, for example, it is likely that, because the audience probably likes food, they will think gasoline is a good thing. If you did not want children to have that attitude toward cars or gasoline, the analogy could get you into trouble.

→ For more on using and evaluating analogies, see pages 164–165.

The paragraph to the right draws on an audience's basic understanding of what computers are in order to help them understand how and why humans can be physically but not socially adept, as with conditions like autism (which, as you can see, is what the paragraph following the example is about).

individual, they later expect the individual to approach the character that helped it and to avoid the one that hurt it.

Understanding of the physical world and understanding of the social world can be seen as akin to two distinct computers in a baby brain, running separate programs and performing separate tasks. The understandings develop at different rates: the social one emerges somewhat later than the physical one. They evolved at different points in our prehistory; our physical understanding is shared by many species, whereas our social understanding is a relatively recent adaptation, and in some regards might be uniquely human.

That these two systems are distinct is especially apparent in autism, a developmental

PARAGRAPHS THAT DIVIDE AS A FORM OF ANALYSIS

Paragraphs that define can easily become or lead into paragraphs that divide: A definition establishes a criterion that names what something is (or is not); once you have done that, you can use the criterion to categorize and divide.

Academic writing often hinges on such division because such division is **analysis**. Analysis allows us to name and so to sort through the components of a process or event. We do that to learn what happened or to learn what stands in our way of accomplishing what we desire.

Paragraphs that divide are often followed by paragraphs that compare and contrast—because it is possible to compare and contrast two objects, processes, or events only when we can see that the objects, processes, or events are divided, or different.

(The opposite kind of paragraph—a paragraph that unites—is also central to academic work. Just as it is important to show that what had seemed the same is really different, it helps us when we can see that what had seemed different is really the same.)

Danah Boyd, a Senior Researcher at Microsoft Research, and a Research Assistant Professor in Media, Culture, and Communication at New York University, researches how young people use social networking software like MySpace and Facebook. In a blog article she uses sociologist Nalini Kotamraju's definition of "class" to consider differences between MySpace and Facebook. Kotamraju argues that in the United States class isn't about money but rather about social connection: Who you know is going to shape your life and what you can do more than how much money you make. Based on that distinction, Boyd argues that the difference between who uses Facebook and who uses MySpace is one of class: Facebook is where the "goodie two shoes, jocks, athletes, or other 'good' kids" go, while MySpace

> is still home for Latino/Hispanic teens, immigrant teens, burnouts, alternative kids, art fags, punks, emos, goths, gangstas, queer kids, and other kids who didn't play into the dominant high school popularity paradigm.

Boyd argues that marketers and the military have figured out this distinction and are making decisions on it; Boyd hopes that teachers and social workers will figure this out, too, in order to talk with young people about how cultural structures and decisions shape individual lives.

In the paragraph to the left, the writer summarizes part of another writer's arguments about youth culture. The summary shows how the original writer—Danah Boyd—starts with a definition of **class**. She then uses that definition to show a division: Many people had thought that all social networking sites that use profiles are the same, but Boyd shows how they are divided, or different.

By using the definition to show a division in an area that hadn't seemed to have any differences, Boyd can point to problems we might not otherwise see.

PARAGRAPHS THAT GIVE A CLAIM AND EVIDENCE AS A FORM OF ANALYSIS

Another kind of paragraph structure used frequently in academic writing starts with a claim necessary to the overall argument; that claim is then followed by evidence; the evidence in turn is followed by a discussion of how the claim and evidence contribute to the overall argument.

Such paragraphs generally come in the body of a paper, after an introduction to the paper's purposes and paragraphs that describe and define what is at stake.

This paragraph starts with a claim about unconscious bias. It then offers evidence from an academic website and two other academic sources to back up the claim. Finally, the paragraph discusses how unconscious bias might develop, as a way to lead into the following paragraphs about how we might work against our unconscious biases.

We might not like to admit it, but most of us probably unconsciously judge skin color, gender, or age. For example, on the Project Implicit website (run by an international network of university researchers), one can take a test to check one's attitudes toward black or white faces: one pushes a button to associate positive or negative terms with a photograph of a black or a white person. The compiled results for everyone who has taken the test indicate that "more than 70% associated 'good' with White faces more easily than with Black faces" (Nosek, Hawkins, & Frazier). Other researchers test implicit beliefs by sending resumés to employers and university science faculty; the resumés are the same except that one will have an African-American name at the top and the other a white-sounding name, or one a female and the other a male name. The employers and faculty make judgments based on that name only:

> Job applicants with African-American names get far fewer call-backs for each resume they send out. (Bertrand & Mullainathan 1011)

and

> Our results revealed that both male and female faculty judged a female student to be less competent and less worthy of being hired than an identical male student, and also offered her a smaller starting salary and less career mentoring. (Moss-Racusin et al.)

Such judgments probably result from enculturation: they result from our growing up within particular families and neighborhoods, from all the conversations we've ever had with others, from all the television shows, movies, or videos we've ever watched, and from all the classrooms in which we've been taught.

PARAGRAPHS THAT BLEND ORGANIZATIONS

Depending on your arguments, paragraphs can get complex: Writers need them to perform multiple functions.

(Keep in mind, though, that even when paragraphs blend several kinds of organizations, the paragraph will still have one main function in the overall argument of which it is a part: It needs to move the argument forward one step.)

beauty salons and restaurants, auto factories and welding shops. And I've been struck by the intellectual demands of what I saw.

Consider what a good waitress or waiter has to do in a busy restaurant. Remember orders and monitor them, attend to an ever-changing environment, juggle the flow of the work, make decisions on the fly. Or the carpenter: To build a cabinet, a staircase, or a pitched roof requires complex mathematical calculations, a high level of precision. The hairstylist's practice is a mix of scissors technique, knowledge of biology, aesthetic judgment, and communication skills. The mechanic, electrician, and plumber are trouble-shooters and problem-solvers. Even the routinized factory floor calls for working smart. Yet we persist in dividing labor into the work of the hand and the work of the mind.

Distinctions between blue collar and white collar do exist. White-collar work, for example,

The example to the left comes from a newspaper editorial, published on Labor Day, in which writer Mike Rose argues that we should "honor the brains as well as the brawn of American labor."

In this paragraph, Rose lists examples of the mental work that different kinds of blue-collar work require.

But this paragraph is not only examples. The examples ground Rose's argument that we need to unite rather than divide: We need to see that blue-collar and white-collar work have much in common.

Rose thus combines examples and analysis—unifying disparate elements—in this one paragraph.

TIP

MANY MORE KINDS OF PARAGRAPHS

In the last few pages, we described some of the most used paragraphs. But there are also paragraphs that classify, that explain processes, that show cause and effect, and that function in other ways depending on a writer's particular purposes. As you read others' writing, try to classify their paragraphs and to determine why they used a particular kind of paragraph when they did; such observations will help you expand your tool kit of paragraphs and strengthen your argumentative choices.

MULTIMODAL ORGANIZATION: VISUAL TEXTS

As our chart on pages 213 suggests, written and visual texts can both be analyzed for their overall conceptual framework, their major elements, and their detailed elements.

Just as with written texts, we will consider the conceptual frameworks and major elements of visual texts in these pages; in Part 8 we will consider the detailed elements of visual texts.

We start here by discussing the major elements of visual texts that mix words and visual pieces, and then we consider the organizational frameworks built from them.

MAJOR ELEMENTS OF TEXTS THAT MIX WORDS, PICTURES, AND OTHER VISUAL PIECES

You might have been taught about paragraphs so long ago that you don't realize you are creating major organizational elements as you write. When you work with texts that mix words and visual elements, you similarly have to create (or at least choose) the elements you will organize and build into larger elements.

When you work with photographs, paintings, drawings, charts, and graphs, your choices shape readers' and viewers' possible responses.

→ If in your composition you use a photograph, painting, drawing, chart, diagram, graph, or table made by someone else, you need to cite the source. For citing visual materials in MLA style, see pages 390–392 and 399; for APA style, see pages 418–419.

PHOTOGRAPHS

Use photographs to document how a person, place, or object looks or looked. (Because of digital technologies, however, you might need to assure readers that you have not manipulated photographs you use.)

Use photographs to create emotional connections between readers and a topic: Seeing a person or place encourages readers to feel physically, and so emotionally, closer than words.

When you use photographs, keep in mind that how the elements within a photograph are organized or cropped affects how readers respond. In the two photographs to the left, one creates a more intimate relation between viewer and photographed subject than the other because of how it has been cropped.

PAINTINGS AND DRAWINGS

Kehinde Wiley composed the painting to the left. Wiley asks Black men to look at paintings of saints from the Renaissance and Baroque periods and to choose poses from the paintings; Wiley paints the men in those poses.

Paintings—and drawings—show a composer's imagination. Like photographs, paintings and drawings are arranged to direct your visual attention and shape your attitude toward the subject.

Photographs, because they come out of cameras, seem more direct and less abstract than paintings or drawings. Use paintings and drawings, then, to present or illustrate abstractions.

Shmuel Yosef, copyright © 2011 Kehinde Wiley. Used by permission.

PHOTOGRAPHS, PAINTINGS, DRAWINGS—AND WORDS

How would you respond to the family photograph at the top of the page if it were titled "The Scientist as a Girl, with Her Family"? What if it were titled "From the W.E.B. Du Bois albums of photographs of African Americans in Georgia exhibited at the Paris Exposition Universelle in 1900"? What would you think about the Wiley portrait if our writing didn't tell you that its pose was derived from a Renaissance painting?

When photographs, paintings, or drawings come without words, viewers use their own experiences to interpret the text; when words are added—as a title or explanation—the words limit how freely a viewer can interpret; they instead start to shape the viewer's interpretation.

BUILDING VISUAL ORGANIZATIONS

Print texts have a clear beginning, a clear order to their parts, and a clear end. Films and videos have linear organization similar to print, but one-page visual texts (posters, flyers, each page in a newsletter or brochure) do not. To build visual organizations with one-page texts, construct visual relationships among the elements.

MAKE SOME ELEMENTS STAND OUT

Organizing visual text requires making obvious which elements are most important and should be seen first, and which second and third. Elements are made to stand out—and be what is first seen—through contrast, placement, and leaving some space unemphasized.

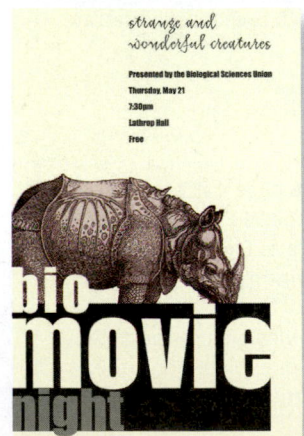

Which movie flyer to the left would catch your eye on a wall? What do your eyes see in each flyer?

With the top flyer, you probably see a mass of text; no part stands out. With the second, your eyes are probably caught first by the rhinoceros and the big words at the bottom; then you notice the text at upper right. The second flyer immediately tells you what it is about and perhaps piques your interest enough that you move close to read the details—which the flyer composer knew you would read if you were pulled in by the rhino.

Contrast

The second flyer works because the bottom words are so big compared to the words at the top right. Create contrast by giving elements *very* different sizes, colors, or styles.

Placement

Western reading patterns accustom our eyes to moving left to right and top to bottom, as well as to page centers. If you organize page elements so that the biggest element is at the top left or overlaps the center, you double its visual emphasis and so make it even more eye attracting.

Unemphasized Space (or "White Space")

White space is the design term for space on a page that only appears unused. But white space (which can be any color; *white space* gets used because mostly we use white paper) makes visual organization possible. Areas of a visual composition cannot be emphasized if every bit of space is full. Leaving some spaces empty allows the other parts to stand out.

GROUP ELEMENTS

When you group visual elements by putting them close together or making them look similar (and sometimes you do both at once), you create a page that feels unified and coherent to viewers—for all the same reasons that we gave for unified and coherent paragraphs on pages 242–243.

Also, elements that are similar or grouped can create a background against which other elements can stand out.

■ ■ ■

When several elements serve the same function—giving the time, date, and location information about an event, for example, or serving as the eye-catching elements—group them close to each other. A viewer's eyes see and so understand that they belong together.

You can see this in the rhinoceros movie flyer to the left, where the rhinoceros and the big words overlap to make one element. The words at the top right of the flyer are also grouped: A viewer can quickly see that information about the movie is in one place.

■ ■ ■

Grouping can happen in a text's headings, too. Compare the two text boxes below. The left box looks as though it contains seven different bits of text, because there is the same amount of space above and below each line of the bold, all-capital-letter text.

The second box has more space above the bold text and none underneath; this groups the bold text with the words underneath. The grouping makes very obvious to a viewer that the bold text serves as titles for the words underneath. (Notice, too, how the second box looks as though it contains only four elements instead of seven.)

The components of color are hue, saturation, and brightness: **HUE** *Hue* describes what many of us just think of as color: When you name the hue of a color, you describe it as red or blue or yellow or green… **SATURATION** *Saturation* describes how much hue is present in a color. Vivid pink is highly saturated, while pastel pink is not. **BRIGHTNESS** *Brightness* describes a color's lightness or darkness.	The components of color are hue, saturation, and brightness: **HUE** *Hue* describes what many of us just think of as color: When you name the hue of a color, you describe it as red or blue or yellow or green… **SATURATION** *Saturation* describes how much hue is present in a color. Vivid pink is highly saturated, while pastel pink is not. **BRIGHTNESS** *Brightness* describes a color's lightness or darkness.

UNIFY ELEMENTS THROUGH REPETITION

The boldness of a typeface can repeat the boldness of a line elsewhere on a page; the shape of a box on the page can repeat the shape of the page. If the title of a presentation being advertised on a flyer is "Four Aspects of Educational Success," the flyer could have four photographs about education on it.

When you repeat the elements of a composition, whether visual or written, the resulting organization will be unified and coherent for your audience.

The top flyer to the left has sufficient contrast, expected placement, and appropriate grouping to enable viewers easily to see the major elements of the flyer. But the elements still do not seem as though they belong together. Each grouping is in a different typeface, and the elements seem randomly placed horizontally.

The redesign of the flyer, below left, adds a photograph to the top to make the title even more visually engaging. But notice, too, what is now repeated in the new flyer's organization:

- Only two typefaces are used: a big bold one at the top and for the speaker's name, and a more traditional serifed typeface repeated for everything else.

  → See page 340 to learn about the typeface classifications of serif and sans serif.

- The typefaces are modern typefaces, repeating the concept of the twenty-first century mentioned in the talk's title.

- The left alignment is repeated for all the text elements.

- A gray square is repeated down the left side of the composition, helping separate the type groups.

- The gray of the square repeats the gray and the rectangular shapes of the buildings in the photograph.

ALIGN ELEMENTS

Aligning each element of a visual composition with at least one other element will help a layout look coherent and unified. Elements are aligned when you can draw straight lines along the edges of elements:

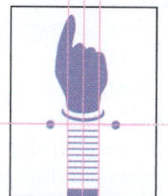  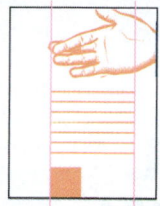

The top pink flyer to the right has sufficient contrast, expected placement, and appropriate grouping and typefaces to enable viewers to see the major elements of the flyer; it also has a photograph appropriate to the presentation topic.

But the bottom flyer feels still more unified and coherent because the composition is now organized around two (imaginary) vertical lines, one on the left and one on the right.

Notice that the title of the presentation stretches between both the lines, as do the bottom lines of text; this reinforces the unity the alignment brings.

(Notice also that the design repeats the photograph twice, first at the top and then smaller and flipped upside down at the bottom; notice also how the two photographs are aligned, a form of repetition.)

TIP

PHOTOGRAPHIC INTEREST

You've probably noticed in each redesigned flyer that a photograph is added. Photographs—especially of people—attract eyes. If you add a photograph to a composition, eyes will be drawn to start there.

MULTIMODAL ORGANIZATION: ORAL PRESENTATIONS

If they need to figure out their place in a printed text, audiences can look over the pages in their hands; audiences for oral presentations cannot do this.

When you compose oral presentations, therefore, your biggest consideration about organization should be helping your audience hear and remember the parts of your presentation: If they can remember the organization, they will remember the main points and argument attached to that organization.

REPEAT... AND KEEP IT BRIEF

- As our advice on these two pages suggests, repeating your purpose and main points in your introduction, as you move from paragraph to paragraph, and in your conclusion helps audiences follow your arguments. Repeat similar words, too.

- Pare it down. These days, we rarely receive instruction in how to listen well, so audiences usually benefit from straightforward, focused presentations.

TIP

VISUAL AIDS FOR ORGANIZATION

If you use visual aids such as slides, overheads, or handouts, include an opening screen or page that sketches or outlines the overall organization of the presentation; this helps keep your audience oriented in your talk.

As you move through the parts of your presentation, use screens that name the parts; such screens also help keep your audience oriented.

→ For more on making supporting slides, see pages 346–347.

THE PARTS OF AN ORAL PRESENTATION

Like papers, oral presentations have the basic structure of introduction, body, and conclusion. But as you prepare, use strategies that make the organization audible to your audience.

1 INTRODUCTION

You can start with an anecdote, quotation, or another attention-getting strategy (just as with introductory paragraphs, → see pages 304–305)—but then tell your listeners what your presentation is about; describe the parts that make up its structure. You want your audience to hear your purpose and organization clearly and several times so that they remember.

Vary the sentence patterns you use to describe your purpose and organization, so that you keep your audience engaged (→ see pages 300–301 about sentence patterns)—but then repeat the same or similar noun phrases to describe your purpose and organization so that audiences remember them well (→ see pages 478 and 480–481 on noun phrases).

2 BODY

Choose an easy-to-remember structure—and then tell your audience as you move from one point in the structure to the next.

Easy-to-remember structures have few parts: In a five-to ten-minute presentation, audiences can remember three to five steps. Easy-to-remember structures are:

- *Chronological.* Audiences can easily follow presentations that present events in the order in which they occurred.
- *Logical.* Use your thesis statement (→ as we describe on pages 222–225) to organize the body into three parts: one for the warrant, one for the reason, and one for the claim.
- *Problem-Solution.* Describe the problem and then argue for your favored solution.

- *Comparative.* If you are recommending one approach to a problem over another, present the approach you least favor then the one you want audiences to remember.

Keeping your audience aware of your movement from one point to the next involves phrases like the following:

- **My third point is…**
- **Now that I have described the problem, let me tell you what I think the best solution is.**
- **I've described what microcredit is, so let me tell you why economists think it is so important.**
- **Finally… or In conclusion…**
  - → The phrases on page 244 can help you move your audience from one point to the next.

3 CONCLUSION

Remind your audience of your argument and main points. If you can find one that fits well with your purposes, use an anecdote, story, or quotation to end memorably, so that your listeners hold on to your talk.

HINTS & TIPS FOR ORGANIZING TEXTS

BE WARY OF SETTLING ON AN ORGANIZATION TOO QUICKLY

To produce writing that is smart, complex, and creative, let your writing guide you. Although you may have a thesis statement that suggests an organization for your writing, it is in writing that you really test out and find your ideas.

All experienced writers will tell you of times when they came to different or more focused conclusions than they had originally planned. Because they listened to their words, and followed the logic of their initial ideas or of new evidence, their writing found new organizations.

So don't try to force an organization on your ideas. Listen to your ideas and the directions they take you. You can always reorganize a paper once you have found a new or shifted argument.

HOW OTHERS CAN HELP YOU CHECK ORGANIZATION

When you have a draft, cut it apart so that each paragraph is on its own piece of paper. Shuffle the pieces and give them to a friend or classmate; ask the person to tape the paragraphs back into a whole, leaving out any paragraphs that don't make sense or marking any places where it is impossible to tell what should come next.

Sometimes the other person will hand you back something with a clearer order, and sometimes you will learn where you need to make clarifications, insert transitions, or make other additions or subtractions.

CHECKING ORGANIZATION THROUGH AN AFTER-THE-FACT OUTLINE

Once you are confident in your arguments and know that your conclusion is exactly what you want (→ see pages 302–303), check back over all your other paragraphs: Does each logically follow what precedes it and does each lead to what comes next?

Experienced writers often make outlines for their papers *after* they have a first (or later) draft. Follow these steps when making such an outline:

- Summarize each paragraph in one sentence. (If you cannot summarize a paragraph in a sentence, then you might need to break the paragraph into two or more new paragraphs.)

- On a piece of paper, put each paragraph sentence summary in order. There's your outline.

- Does this outline step you logically from the introduction to the conclusion? If not, you may need to add, take out, or clarify paragraphs.

PART 7
DRAFTING A PAPER, CONNECTING WITH AUDIENCES

CONTENTS

DRAFTING

7

WHERE ARE WE IN A PROCESS FOR COMPOSING?

Understanding your project

Getting started

Asking questions   Thinking in depth about audience

Shaping your project for others   Developing a statement of purpose

Drafting a paper   Writing a rough draft

Getting feedback   Receiving feedback to drafts

Revising

Polishing

PART 7 DRAFTING A PAPER, CONNECTING WITH AUDIENCES

Questions you might have about drafting a paper:

What questions should I ask about my audience before I start drafting?
➜ See pages 266–269.

What is a statement of purpose? How do I develop one?
➜ See pages 270–273.

How do I know if I'm ready to write a rough draft?
➜ See page 274.

What are good practices for while I draft a paper?
➜ See page 275.

What questions should I be asking myself when working on my rough draft?
➜ The questions that annotate the sample draft on pages 276–282 suggest how you can be careful about many of the details of an academic paper.

How do I use feedback others give me on my draft?
➜ See pages 284–285.

What are some approaches for responding helpfully to others' writing?
➜ See pages 286–287.

THE WPA OUTCOMES* FOR PART 7 INCLUDE:

Rhetorical abilities: Learning rhetorical concepts for analyzing and composing a variety of texts.

Critical thinking, reading, and composing abilities: Composing for different audiences.

Writing processes: Developing a writing project through multiple drafts; developing flexible strategies for drafting and responding; learning to give and to receive productive feedback to works in progress.

* See page 15.

UNDERSTANDING YOUR AUDIENCE

WHY YOU NEED TO UNDERSTAND YOUR AUDIENCE

In the preceding parts, we have followed Harley as she develops her ideas on family arguments and civility. As you saw, Harley has done enough research and thinking to put together a thesis statement: *Preventing government repression and supporting a healthy democracy depends on us being able to discuss controversial ideas and beliefs civilly; therefore we should learn how to discuss our controversial ideas and beliefs civilly.*

But who needs to know this? For whom does this argument matter—and why?

Through her research, Harley has accumulated some supporting evidence for her thesis, but what of that evidence will be most persuasive? Into what order should she put her evidence? What tone of voice should she use in her writing?

Harley can answer these questions only if she has some sense of the attitudes and beliefs of those who will read her writing. Harley can say, *I write to people who don't like family arguments about politics*—but that level of understanding of audience is still vague; it does not help her make the choices posed by the questions above.

How can Harley develop a discerning and useful sense of her readers so she can make specific writing choices? How can she develop a sense of how her audience's needs and habits connect to her purpose and concerns?

WHAT DO YOU NEED TO KNOW ABOUT YOUR AUDIENCE?

One common way to begin considering audiences is through general characteristics: age, ethnicity, gender, level of education, sexual orientation, place of work, class, living place, and so on. Such characteristics can sometimes help you think about how your purpose and your audience entwine: Go through the above list of characteristics one by one, asking yourself how each characteristic might impinge on how your audience thinks or feels about your topic.

However, as you dig into research and make your purpose more detailed, you may discover that you need to think differently about your readers. For example, your purposes may require you to think not of "young people" but of "young people worried about the job market when they graduate"; you may need to think not of "people who live in the United States" but of "people who live in the United States at a time when discussions about race and ethnicity are not easy."

TO BRING AUDIENCE AWARENESS INTO YOUR WRITING:

FIND OUT what your audience knows, thinks, and feels about your topic
➡ See pages 268–269.

Develop A STATEMENT OF PURPOSE that helps you connect what you understand about your audience with specific writing strategies
➡ See pages 270–273.

YOU MIGHT THINK YOU ALREADY KNOW YOUR AUDIENCE…

Perhaps you are writing for your classmates (which, as you know, also means you write for your teacher). Or perhaps you are writing a memo to your boss to propose new procedures.

In each case, you think you know these people. After all, you live and work with them; you spend considerable time in varying degrees of contact.

But do you know their concerns and opinions *on your topic*? Do you know *why* they hold those concerns and opinions?

If your writing is to catch and hold these readers' attention, you need to understand what they think about your topic and why.

…OR MAYBE YOU DON'T KNOW THEM AT ALL

Perhaps you are writing a letter to the editor of your city's newspaper. Or you are putting together a grant application for a nonprofit. Or you are composing webpages for a new business.

In such cases, you probably don't know your audiences. Newspaper audiences are broad; people from diverse positions make grant decisions; businesses want to reach wide audiences. How do you shape your writing in such cases?

Even when you write to audiences with whom you are not in regular contact, you can still make judgments about why they will read what you offer and how their concerns and opinions will shape their reading. Imagine differing individuals in these audiences—give them names and characteristics—and then ask yourself what they might believe and think about your topic.

UNDERSTANDING YOUR AUDIENCE

WHAT DO PEOPLE KNOW, THINK, AND FEEL ABOUT YOUR TOPIC?

READERS AS PEOPLE WITH OPINIONS AND ATTITUDES

Move your focus from general characteristics to what people really do feel about a topic or issue. Talk to potential audience members, asking them about:

❑ what they know about the topic.

❑ their emotions around the topic.

❑ how they learned what they know about the topic.

❑ personal connections they might have to the topic.

❑ values/beliefs/commitments related to the topic.

❑ questions they might have about the topic.

❑ their self-identity as it connects them to the topic. How do they see themselves connected to the topic because of their specific relations to others? That is, does it matter that a reader is a mother, a daughter, unemployed, a Republican or a leftist, rich or not, a boss or a worker, a student or a teacher, ambitious or laid back, or...?

❑ recent events—locally, nationally, or internationally—that might shape their responses to the topic.

If you cannot talk directly with your audience, ask yourself the same questions while imagining how people with different backgrounds would respond.

FOR EXAMPLE...

If you were writing to argue that it might be time to build more nuclear power plants in the United States, you might learn that many people are opposed. You might learn that most people learned about the science of nuclear power in high school textbooks; they also learned about nuclear power from reading newspapers and magazines about cancer rates and animal mutations following the problems with the nuclear power plants in Japan after the tsunami of 2011 and how, because of radiation, people can no longer live in communities near those power plants. And, silly as it may seem, all the science fiction movies people have seen about radiation mutations do underlie general perceptions, further adding to a general emotional climate of fear and uncertainty around nuclear power.

In addition, people who have children are perhaps more resistant to nuclear power because they do not want their children to be in danger. On the other hand, businesspeople (or children of businesspeople) might be more concerned about the future costs of power because of how those costs affect their ability to keep their businesses running.

These observations can help writers understand that, for most readers these days, making decisions about nuclear power is not simply a matter of coolly weighing numeric, scientific evidence; it is also about fear of mutations, cancer, and the destruction of communities. This tells writers that they probably should not compose a list of facts but will have to address people's emotional concerns about radiation and its potential long-term effects.

FOR EXAMPLE...

Harley writes about what she learned from her classmates:

> I learned that lots of people in class feel the same way I do about big family dinners when politics come up: They want out! They hate it when everyone starts arguing and yelling and then leaves with upset stomachs.
>
> What I learned that most surprised me, though, is that people think the problem affects only them. They might think the problem is caused just by their relatives' personalities or in some way because of the current political climate—but they think the problem stays at the dinner table (or in their stomachs). They don't think about what I learned in my research, that not being able to argue about controversial issues causes troubles for our democracy.
>
> When I mentioned the connection, everyone thought it was cool and interesting. This shows me that I need to make really clear in my paper how our being able to argue about controversial topics is important to democracies.
>
> I also learned that most people don't like the current political climate, either. They'd like it if people spoke with more civility about politics. I learned that most people in class want to be more politically engaged but don't like how national talk can be like a big angry family dinner. So I can add some of that to my paper, too, about how learning to be more civil in argument might make it easier to be politically engaged.

STARTING TO WRITE FOR AN AUDIENCE
DEVELOPING A STATEMENT OF PURPOSE

WHAT IS A STATEMENT OF PURPOSE?

A **statement of purpose** weaves together the logical purpose of a thesis statement with what a writer learns about readers from doing the thinking and research we described on the preceding pages.

A thesis statement, as we described in Part 5, is a short statement summarizing the logic of your argument. But because humans respect logic at the same time that that they are, well, human, you need to consider more than just the potential logic of your writing. You need to consider how your writing will be emotionally persuasive to a particular audience and how your readers will construct a sense of you the writer— your authority, believability, and general character—based on your words. (→ See pages 150–151 and 154–155 for more on these strategies of pathos and ethos.)

A statement of purpose helps you do all of that. A statement of purpose is informal writing, but helps you move from writing-to-learn to writing-to-communicate (→ see pages 34–35). A statement of purpose saves you time by helping you make important decisions about your writing before you start it and before you get yourself too committed to a first draft.

A statement of purpose is thinking-on-paper, a way to help you consider what you really want your readers to think, feel, or do as they read your writing and then when they look up, finished, moved by your words.

FOR EXAMPLE...

This thesis statement is for a research paper:

> Nuclear power plants have become safer and more reliable; therefore, we can build new nuclear power plants in the United States to help take care of our energy needs and reduce reliance on foreign oil.

One possible statement of purpose from that thesis statement is this:

> My audience is a general audience, of different ages and backgrounds. They've heard or read about Chernobyl, Three Mile Island, Fukushima, and the government's tests in Utah in the 1950s. So they'll probably start reading with some real fears that nuclear energy, not carefully handled, can result in horrible children's cancers, as in Chernobyl. They also probably have some fears based in the science fiction movies they've seen.
>
> Because of those fears, I doubt I can change their minds completely—but I'm hoping to persuade them just *to look again* at nuclear power. I think recent scientific and technical developments might help.
>
> My readers also share concerns that might encourage them to be more open. They are concerned about how current energy sources—oil, coal, fracking—affect the environment. They are concerned about the costs of power production and use. So if I can show how nuclear power might just be cleaner and less expensive, they are likely to look at it again.
>
> Should I start by addressing their fears, or should I start by talking about a form of energy that's cleaner and less expensive?

WHAT YOU CAN LEARN FROM A STATEMENT OF PURPOSE

Here's how the statement of purpose to the left helps the writer make certain decisions:

ETHOS

Because his statement of purpose helps this writer realize he needs to encourage others to accept something they fear, he needs to have a careful tone of voice in his writing and admit that he doesn't have all the answers. If he came across as a know-it-all, how do you think his readers might respond?

PATHOS

Because he realizes that he is trying to shift people's thinking about something frightening to them, he now understands that he needs to acknowledge the fear and not pretend it doesn't exist. If he made fun of the fear, or made it sound as though only stupid people are afraid, chances are he'd lose his audience.

EXAMPLES AND EVIDENCE THAT WILL BE USEFUL, GIVEN THE AUDIENCE

This writer now understands that he needs to give many—and very credible—examples and other strong evidence to persuade readers that nuclear power can be cleaner and less expensive than oil, coal, or fracked natural gas.

HOW MUCH MORE RESEARCH TO DO

This writer has done enough research to understand that he needs to do more: He needs to find the credible sources—probably impartial academic sources and not industry sources—that will help him provide the examples and evidence his audience needs.

WRITING A STATEMENT OF PURPOSE

TO PREPARE TO WRITE, YOU NEED TO:

- have a thesis statement that you've developed following the guidelines on pages 160–161 and 222–225.

- have thought about your audience in the ways we've described on pages 266–269.

- set aside some time (thirty minutes to one hour) when you can be relaxed and can write without distractions.

THEN WRITE IN RESPONSE TO THESE QUESTIONS:

- Who, to the best of your ability to describe them, are your readers? What do they know—or not—about your topic?

- Given what you know about your audience, will they accept your warrant with little discussion? What sort of immediate responses are they likely to have to your evidence and claim?

- When they finish reading your writing, what would you like them to think, feel, or do?

- What sort of shifts—in emotion, in opinion—will your audience have to make from their initial position if they are to accept what you offer?

WHAT CAN YOU ACHIEVE?

Has your mind ever been changed *completely* on a topic (especially a controversial topic such as marriage equality or genetic engineering) by one article written by a stranger?

Most often, when we change our minds on such topics (or on almost any topic), it's because we've talked with people we know and trust. The writing of strangers—even of respected, experienced strangers—might give us a nudge to reconsider but will rarely change our minds.

When you write a statement of purpose, therefore, shape a purpose you can achieve. Don't expect to "*Convince my readers that gun control is bad*" or "*Make my readers finally understand how harmful our dependence on oil is.*" Instead, verbs like the following in your statement of purpose help you design achievable purposes:

inform	suggest	propose	acknowledge	offer
recommend	consider	attempt	understand	ask
introduce	reflect	look again	reconsider	invite

FOR EXAMPLE...

Here is Harley's thesis statement:

> Preventing government repression and supporting a healthy democracy depends on us being able to discuss controversial ideas and beliefs civilly; therefore, we should learn how to discuss our controversial ideas and beliefs civilly.

Here is her statement of purpose.

My audience is others in class and, of course, my teacher. From talking with the others in class, I know that they do not like family dinners that erupt when politics comes up; they do not like the anger and yelling and bad feelings. And I learned that most people think that such bad emotions only affect their families—when my research shows that not being able to talk at any time or in any place about controversial topics is a problem for democracies. If we cannot talk about these difficult issues, we do not learn the wide range of opinions that help us make the best decisions. So I know that my arguments will be interesting to them...

But this also helps me think about how I need to approach my topic.

I really need to emphasize the connection between civil discussion and strong democracies. I think I need to find still more evidence about that connection.

I also probably need to demonstrate civility in my own writing. That means I need to show respect to those who disagree—but writing that makes me realize that I haven't yet encountered anyone who disagrees. Everyone I talked to hated messy family political arguments and seemed open to learning about civility. I mean, who wants people in families to hate each other? But maybe when I lay out my evidence or discuss civility someone could disagree. This shows me again that I need to be very careful about my evidence and to discuss civility in a way that doesn't seem all namby-pamby. But I guess, too, that this shows me I need to be very careful in how I write, so that I don't come across as saying that my solution is the only one, suck it up or be stupid, something like that. I'll need to acknowledge where there are places others could disagree.

And then I think about my readers' emotions: When I bring up the topic everyone responds with a mess of anger and unhappiness about their families and they feel like they're stuck with the mess—and it's the same with the current political climate. I'd like them to go from that mess to hope. I'd like them to end by believing that they can do something at the dinner table—and in other political discussions, too. So perhaps I need to give some concrete examples of what civility looks like and how you keep it going? Would that help people feel more optimistic?

STARTING TO WRITE FOR AN AUDIENCE
WRITING A ROUGH DRAFT

WHAT IS A ROUGH DRAFT?

A rough draft is a testing ground. It is a first attempt to shape a coherent argument, knowing that it will later be strengthened through feedback and revision.

Successful writers write rough drafts, often many rough drafts. Such writers do not expect any piece of writing to be finished in one sitting. Instead, they allow themselves time to produce writing they know will be rough but that is necessary to help them figure out their final thoughts.

Even though such writers might have a pretty good idea of what they want to write before they sit down (by having developed a thesis statement and then a statement of purpose), they know that as they write, their ideas might shift or that they'll write something that doesn't quite do what they want it to.

ARE YOU READY TO WRITE A FULL ROUGH DRAFT?

You are not ready until you:

- have a thesis statement and have gathered evidence to support your claim.
- have a statement of purpose so you know how to shape your thesis for *your* readers.

TIP

HOW DO YOU FIND YOUR STARTING WORDS?

If you have prepared a thesis statement and statement of purpose, you should have a good idea of what your paper needs to include... but if you are stuck about how to start writing, look at the suggestions for introductions in Part 8 (➡ see pages 304–305). Pick any of the introductions that catch your fancy and just start writing—you just need to start! (You can always change an introduction later if the work of the draft or feedback suggests a more appropriate introduction.)

PREPARING TO WRITE A DRAFT

- Review any notes you have from reading and analyzing your sources.

- Keep your sources (or copies of your sources) nearby so you can check that you are summarizing, paraphrasing, or quoting according to academic conventions.

  → See pages 188–203 on how to summarize, paraphrase, and quote in academic papers.

- Set up your writing area so you have few distractions.

- Arrange your time so that you have at least an hour, but preferably two or three hours, to write at any one sitting.

- Do not expect to complete a five- to seven-page draft in one sitting. Plan for at least two or three different times to write.

USING YOUR THESIS STATEMENT TO ARRANGE YOUR DRAFT

→ See pages 222–225 for suggestions on how to use your thesis statement to arrange your draft.

WHILE WRITING

- Don't stop the flow of your ideas by fixating on grammar or spelling; instead, focus on writing. Because this is a draft, you have time later to revise and edit.

  → If English is not your home language, however, see the advice below.

- If you get stuck in your writing, you have at least three options:

  1 Get up and walk away. Come back to the writing later, after you've had a chance to rest, go for a walk, chat with some friends, or otherwise refresh your mind.

  2 Reread your writing from the beginning; that might spark your thinking.

  3 Review your thesis statement and statement of purpose to see if you've missed anything you need to include.

- If you summarize, paraphrase, or quote (→ see pages 188–203) any source, be sure to include the expected in-text citation in the format you are using. Also be sure to put any such sources into a running bibliography list at the end of your draft.

  → For MLA style, see pages 350–392.

  → For APA style, see pages 393–419.

  → For CSE style, see pages 420–424.

  → For CMS style, see pages 425–428.

IF YOU GREW UP SPEAKING A LANGUAGE OTHER THAN ENGLISH . . .

Start proofreading as soon as you have any writing that seems solid to you; don't wait until the paper is finished. If you leave all the proofreading until the end, you may not have enough time or you may find it overwhelming. If you know someone whose proofreading abilities you respect, ask that person to proofread and to note each change (and reason for change) while you watch and listen.

STARTING TO WRITE FOR AN AUDIENCE
A ROUGH DRAFT

Harley has produced a rough draft for an assignment that asks for a five- to seven-page paper. She uses this draft just to get her ideas onto paper, to see how they look, and to get a sense of how her ideas work for her readers.

In our comments on her draft, we've indicated some of her initial choices, as well as places she is not yet sure of her choices—and we've indicated where in this book she can look for further assistance.

As you read the draft, look for how Harley starts to develop her argument. It's not as clear as it could be in this draft, but it does start to take shape. Also look for how she's addressing her readers' concerns, as she came to understand them through developing a statement of purpose.

→ Harley's polished revision of this draft is on pages 354–363.

Is the title appropriate?

After you read the draft, ask: *Does Harley's title adequately prepares a reader for the whole paper?*

How does the introduction work?

Do these introductory paragraphs help readers understand clearly and easily what is to follow?

→ Pages 304–305 give suggestions for introductions that meet academic expectations.

Harley promises in her introduction to connect civility with democracy—and the lack of civility with government repression. As you read, do you see her writing living up to those promises?

Are there enough—and the right—transitions?

Do you think readers will understand why Harley moves from her introductory paragraph to this next paragraph?

→ See pages 244–245 and 306–307 for information on how to write transitions that help readers follow your arguments.

I want to eat dinner without yelling

My father can roast a chicken so perfect it looks like a magazine ad. Every Sunday when he carries that to the dinner table (where I'm sitting with my mother, brothers, grand-father, uncle, and aunt) I think we will have a dinner like I see in those old black and white happy family movies my granddad watches on TCM. But our dinners always turn out awful. Everyone ends up screaming at each other about healthcare or unions. My stomach is in knots. I don't know why we keep doing this.

Are your family dinners like this, too?

For this paper I researched families and political arguments. I discovered quickly that what happens at our dinner table is a sign of something much larger. Many families have trouble with controversial topics, but so do we as a country. From my research I learned that being able to talk about controversial topics is necessary for having a democracy and for hav-ing the freedom that we seek in a democracy. Being able to talk about controversial topics helps us avoid government repression.

To argue why being able to talk (and not scream and rile up our stomachs) about con-troversial topics is necessary for the kind of country I think we all want, I need to define "civility." I need to describe the behaviors and attitudes that make civility possible. I need to describe what happens when people don't try to be civil.

I found several writers who define "civility." Chesire Calhoun writes that, "The civil citizen exercises tolerance in the face of deep disagreement about the good. She respects the rights of others, refrains from violence, intimidation, harassment and coercion, does not show contempt for others' life plans, and has a healthy respect for others' privacy" (256). He argues that:

> First, civility signals others' willingness to have us as co-participants in practices ranging from political dialogues, to campus communities, to funerals, to sharing public highways. Second, for those who are not already coerced into sharing social practices with us, civil-ity may be a precondition of their willingness to enter and continue in cooperative ven-tures with us. Third, civility supports self-esteem by offering token reminders that we are regarded as worth respecting, tolerating, and considering. (266)

Similarly, Nicole Billante and Peter Saunders define "civility" as "behavior in public which demonstrates respect for others and which entails curtailing one's own immediate self-

1

Can I use quotations without introduction or attribution?

Rarely in academic writing do writers use quotations without introducing them in some way—but they always attribute others' words.

→ Pages 198–199 have suggestions for weaving quotations into your writing.

→ Pages 364–367 explain how to give the expected attributions for quotations in MLA style (which Harley uses here).

When is a quotation too long?

Harley has correctly followed the standard MLA format for quotations that take more than four lines.

→ See the information on block quotations on page 196.

But how might readers respond to Harley using so many long quotations (there's another on page 1)? Does this long quotation suggest that Harley isn't yet confident in her own understanding?

Is there sufficient evidence?

In her statement of purpose, Harley described how she needed to be particularly persuasive about connections between civil discussion and democracy. Do you think Harley has offered enough evidence for this? If you don't think she has, what more might she offer or how might she reframe her evidence to make it more compelling?

When should I summarize my own argument?

Here, Harley summarizes what she has written above to help keep her readers following what is most important as she builds her overall argument.

interest when appropriate" (33). A virtue that "aids social cooperation," and is an "alternative to repression." Without civility there is a danger of repression because

> different individuals will always want and desire different and incompatible things, and their unfettered pursuit of their own objectives will inevitably bring them into conflict. The question, therefore, is how (as well as how far) individual liberties are to be restricted or restrained. In the end, this will either be done by external political agencies of the state, or it will be achieved through enlightened self-regulation. (34)

Calhoun argues that "A principal point of having norms of civility is to regulate discussion of controversial subjects so that dialogue among those who disagree will continue rather than break down" (269). So according to Calhoun if we do not have an ability to talk with each other, there is danger of society breaking down; Billante and Saunders argue that if we want a society with "individual liberties" we either have civility—where we respect each other's opinions no matter whether we agree—or we have a repressive government that forces people to live together in one country under imposed rule.

If we don't want our country to fall apart into chaos, or to become a place where the government tells us what we can or cannot say to each other, then we have to learn to be civil to each other.

The definitions I gave above of civility imply what we each need to do in order to be civil to each other. Billante and Saunders describe that being civil requires: (1) respect for others; (2) behaving well in public; (3) self-regulation. In terms of respect for others, even George Washington, when he was 16, described what we should do in order that we get along; as Calhoun restates Washington's words, "The civil person refrains from humming, finger drumming, nail biting, bedewing others with spittle, eye rolling, lolling out the tongue, gaping, killing fleas and lice in others' sight, wearing foul clothes, and falling asleep while others speak" (257). Instead, we should act toward others in such a way to show that we believe they are worthy of respect—even if we disagree. In terms of behaving well in public, this depends on "a generalised empathy and sense of obligation which we feel with all who share our society with us" (33). Finally, self-regulation "involves holding back in the pursuit of one's own immediate self-interest—we desist from doing what would be most pleasing to us for the sake of harmonious relations with strangers" (33).

For the sake of living in one country (or eating a family dinner without an upset stomach), these definitions and descriptions show that we need to learn how to respect what other

2

How do summaries and transitions help readers?

Harley helps readers by providing this paragraph that summarizes her preceding writing and explicitly explaining her transition to talking about "confirmation bias" and "selective exposure."

→ Pages 244–245 and 306–307 have suggestions for helping readers stay oriented in your writing.

Why define terms?

Here is an example of a paragraph that defines, as we discussed in Part 6 (→ see page 249). For Harley to be able to use "confirmation bias" and "selective exposure," she first has to define them. Do you think she has defined them so her readers can understand them? Could you rewrite this paragraph to make the definitions clearer?

How do I introduce quotations to support my arguments?

Here Harley makes explicit a quotation's source, offering the writers' qualifications to demonstrate why they are worth quoting.

→ On page 197 we describe how to give a title to or explain the authority of those you quote.

How do I help readers check sources?

To check a source, readers usually need the name of the person(s) responsible for the words (so that they can find the source in the works-cited or references list at the paper's end) and a page number. Because the name of the person who wrote these words preceded this quotation, Harley needs only to give a page number.

→ Pages 364–367 explain how to show the sources of your quotations and evidence in MLA style (which Harley uses here).

people believe, even if we disagree. From what I've seen at our table, this means listening and nodding rather than telling others they don't know what they're talking about. In the course of my research, though, I came across articles that described a psychological concept that should help us be able to do this. This concept is called "confirmation bias" or "selective exposure."

"Confirmation bias" and "selective exposure" are terms that come from psychological research. This notion names how people have a "tendency to seek out and interpret new evidence in ways that confirm what [they] already think" (Haidt 78). In their article, "Preference-inconsistent recommendations," Schwind, Buder, Cress, and Hesse also discuss how people resist information that does not support what they already believe. A result is that "confirmation bias is detrimental to unbiased opinion formation" (788). It sounds to me as though if people aren't aware of this that they get caught in a vicious circle, only looking for and believing information that confirms what they already know.

Writers claim that cognitive bias affects all we believe, not just politics. For example, three researchers in behavioral and political sciences from Stony Brook University claim that "cognitive biases influence a wide range of health-related attitudes, from broad, national decisions about health reform to individual decisions about caffeine consumption and smoking" (Strickland, Taber, and Lodge 1). "Although fair-mindedness and objectivity are desirable qualities of thought, particularly for weighty issues such as gun control, health care reform, and affirmative action, evidence has shown that human information processing often does not operate in that manner" (6). I found other writers who discuss this, too (see, for example, Edwards & Smith; Balcetis & Dunning; or Nickerson). Researchers Taber and Lodge, for example, claim that, "In the extreme, if one distorts new information so that it always supports one's priors, one cannot be rationally responsive to the environment; similarly, manipulating the information stream to avoid any threat to one's priors is no more rational than the proverbial ostrich" (767). What "confirmation bias" and "selective exposure" show us is that none of us is perfect. Unless we have been very careful and purposefully sought out the broadest possible information on any topic, our information will be biased.

What my research has shown me is that civility is necessary if we are to be able to talk together about what matters to us as families and as a country. But civility isn't enough. Civility is about how we think about and act toward others; if we are civil only, we can still

3

How do I conclude?

Harley uses this last paragraph to summarize and restate her main argument. Academic readers expect this in essays. But what they don't expect in a conclusion is new information, such as Harley's claim about confirmation bias, which she did not discuss at all in her introduction.

→ Pages 302–303 contain ideas for shaping conclusions to academic writing.

Are there enough sources?

If you think Harley has not yet offered enough evidence for her arguments, then she probably needs more or other sources. Notice that her last two sources share two of the same authors. Would you recommend that Harley find some new sources with different authors so that her evidence doesn't seem to come from the same people?

Do the sources have appropriate credibility?

As you scan over the journal titles in this listing, do they carry for you sufficient credibility for the arguments Harley is making?

→ Pages 108–115 explain how you can judge a source's credibility.

TIP

CONSTRUCTING AN MLA WORKS-CITED LIST

For a rough draft, it is all right to start a works-cited list on the same page as the rest of the paper. For a final draft, however, the works-cited list should start on its own page.

→ See pages 362–363 and 368–369 for help in constructing a works-cited list in MLA format.

TIP

MLA STYLE FORMATTING

For formatting the body of a paper
→ See pages 354–361.

For formatting the works-cited list
→ See pages 362–363 and 368–369.

think that our ideas are all the right ones, meaning we still won't really be listening. Bringing awareness of confirmation bias together with civility helps us be aware that our own ideas are rarely as well-informed as we think. If we are aware of that, then maybe we will listen more closely to others and really be able to figure out together how to solve our problems.

Works Cited

Balcetis, Emily and David Dunning. "See What You Want to See: Motivational Influences on Visual Perception." *Journal of Personality and Social Psychology,* vol. 91, no. 4, 2006. *PsycARTICLES*, doi: 10.1037/0022-3514.91.4.612.

Calhoun, Cheshire. "The Virtue of Civility." *Philosophy and Public Affairs,* vol. 29, no. 3, 2000, pp. 251-75. *JSTOR*, doi: 10.1111/j.1088-4963.2000.00251.x.

Edwards, Kari and Edward E. Smith. "A Disconfirmation Bias in the Evaluation of Arguments." *Journal of Personality and Social Psychology,* vol. 71, no. 1, 1996, pp. 5-24. *Westlaw*, doi: dx.doi.org.ezproxy.lib.uwm.edu/10.1037/0022-3514.71.1.5.

Haidt, Jonathan. *The Righteous Mind: Why Good People Are Divided by Politics and Religion.* Pantheon, 2012.

Nickerson, Raymond S. "Confirmation Bias: A Ubiquitous Phenomenon in Many Guises." *Review of General Psychology,* vol. 2, no. 2, 1998, pp. 175-220. *PsycARTICLES*, doi: dx.doi.org.ezproxy.lib.uwm.edu/10.1037/1089-2680.2.2.175.

Schwind, Christina, et al. "Preference-inconsistent Recommendations: An Effective Approach for Reducing Confirmation Bias and Stimulating Divergent Thinking?" *Computers and Education,* vol. 58, 2012, pp. 87-96. *Elsevier*, doi: dx.doi.org.ezproxy. lib.uwm.edu/10.1016/j.compedu.2011.10.003.

Strickland, April A., et al. "Motivated Reasoning and Public Opinion." *Journal of Health Politics, Policy and Law,* Dec. 2011. *CINAHL Plus*, doi: dx.doi.org.ezproxy.lib.uwm. edu/10.1215/03616878-1460524.

Taber, Charles S. and Milton Lodge. "Motivated Skepticism in the Evaluation of Political Beliefs." *American Journal of Political Science,* vol. 50, no. 3, 2006, pp. 755-69. *Academic Search Complete*, doi: 10.1111/j.1540-5907.2006.00214.x.

4

RECEIVING FEEDBACK TO A DRAFT

→ See Harley's paper, revised to account for this and other feedback, on pages 354–363.

To the right is feedback Harley received from her teacher, with Harley's responses.

The feedback summarizes the teacher's understanding of Harley's argument; now Harley can understand whether readers are hearing what she hopes they will hear.

Receiving such feedback can be hard if you've put a lot of effort into writing: You might not want to hear that you have more work to do. But it's important to know how to receive feedback, because feedback is what helps you strengthen your writing so that it communicates what you want.

Read feedback as soon as you get it but then put it aside for a day or two. Read it again with a little distance, and you'll be in a better position to understand it.

Feedback is what most helps you move your words from writing-to-learn to writing-to-communicate (→ see pages 34–35).

When you receive feedback, keep in mind:

- The feedback of others helps you become a stronger writer. Only by hearing how others read and understand do you learn how your words communicate.

- If readers do not understand your argument, or believe it to be other than you intended, don't blame the readers. If readers miss or misinterpret your argument, ask them why they see the argument they do. Ask readers to go through your writing sentence by sentence, explaining out loud what they understand, so you can learn the particular effects your words have—and so you can learn how to revise your words to do what you hope.

→ To learn more about revising a paper, see Part 8, beginning with pages 290–291.

Harley-

This is a fine start. I can see that you have
found a good range of sources and are using
them to help you think through issues that
matter to you. I hope you are intrigued to see
how what at first seemed a personal, family
issue expands out into larger social issues.

In defining "civility," you are working out
how to weave together a range of sources to
make a larger point. This definitional section
still wanders a bit, though; I think you could
tighten this by using fewer quotations and
more of your own summary across the various
sources you use.

By tightening up that definition of "civility,"
though, I think you could open up space to do
more with an argument I see you just starting
to develop in your paper. If you look in your
last paragraph, notice how you have written
a pretty succint argument about how civility
is not enough to address the problems you
describe in your opening paragraphs. It's not
at all unusual in a first draft for writers to
write themselves into discovering a new, more
developed argument -- which often shows up in
the final paragraph when tying up is required!

In your revision, then, you could reframe your
argument, and pick up on really addressing how
civility is necessary but not enough. You've
got some smart ideas there, and you piqued my
thinking with how you ended.

Finally, though, I want to mention that I
have to admit that I am not yet persuaded by
the evidence you offer that connects lack of
civility with government repression. If you
want to stay with that idea, I think you need
to spell this out more explicitly and perhaps
offer more evidence.

I look forward to seeing your revisions of
this paper. You should take confidence from
the strengths.

Please come talk if you have any questions.

Thanks! Professor Komova

Okay—I was worried
that my own
summary wouldn't
have enough
authority, but I'll
give it a try.

How funny—I was
worried that I might
need to drop the
"confirmation bias"
stuff—but it really is
interesting to me. I
think I can see how
I might use it to
make a stronger
argument...?

Dam. I need to go
digging to see if I
can find more
evidence. Or is there
a way to present
what I have in a
different way?

Harley writes notes in the
margins to help her think
about this feedback.

RESPONDING TO THE WRITING OF YOUR PEERS

When you are asked to respond to someone else's writing, consider the following:

WHAT IS THE MOST USEFUL, RESPECTFUL FEEDBACK YOU'VE EVER RECEIVED?

Keep a collection of useful feedback, and analyze what makes it useful. This will not only help you give good feedback to others, but will help you develop a stronger eye for reading your own words.

WHAT KIND OF FEEDBACK DOES THE WRITER NEED?

Perhaps the writer only needs help checking grammar and spelling—but perhaps instead the writer needs feedback on the order of ideas, in which case for you to correct spelling is useless because the words you correct might go away in the revision. If a writer asks for help and does not specify what kind, ask. (By asking, you also help the writer to articulate what the writing needs.)

HAVE YOU READ TWICE BEFORE RESPONDING?

Take notes during a first reading, while you get a sense of what the writer is trying to do. Then reread, looking for what in the writing most supports what the writing is trying to do and for the parts that aren't as supportive. Then write comments.

HAVE YOU PRIORITIZED YOUR FEEDBACK?

You know how unhelpful it is to get a long, unordered list of feedback. When you are preparing feedback for another, pick the two to five most important observations you have—the observations that you think will most help the writer revise toward the best paper—and present only those.

Dear Harley,

I like how your paper starts with a family dinner. I've so been there. I hate it. And so your opening starts with something I care about—and so I am interested as you start to talk about civility, especially in how you connect it to larger political issues.

Almost all your writing is about civility, what it is and its consequences. I can follow the paragraphs of the writing, and see that it argues that if we are not civil to each other then bad consequences follow. But I have to honestly say that I am not yet seeing what the good benefits of civility are. I mean, your writing helps me see how being civil would make the dinner table easier. But I am not yet seeing how being civil really helps us as a country. I am not really seeing how being civil prevents government repression—that seems like a huge jump to me, sorry!

As I read, too, I get a little lost with the turn to the psychology stuff. I was following the civility arguments just fine, but the confirmation bias stuff came up pretty quickly and I had trouble connecting it back to civility. Some more explanation of the connection might have helped me.

I hope this is helpful to you. Let me know.
Matt

Do tell writers what you like about their writing, and why.

Writers (like any person) need to know what they do well. When we have a sense of what we do well, it gives us confidence for moving ahead.

If you are asked to give feedback to the main argument, say what you think the argument is.

You may see a different main argument from what the writer intends—and the writer needs to know. The writer can then try to strenghten the original or go in the direction you suggest. But if you give feedback on a different argument than what the writer intends, the writer will revise at cross (and confusing) purposes.

Respond to the writing, not the writer.

Respond with "This introduction didn't help me understand what the paper was about," not with "You can't do introductions." The first response helps a writer understand what revisions are needed; the second just makes the writer feel incompetent and unwilling to move forward.

Respond by talking about how you read.

All writers need help understanding how others understand their words, and so a good way to give feedback is to say something like, "The first sentence of this paragraph made me think that what would follow would be about x, but instead it was about y—so I got confused." This is much more helpful than, "This paragraph confused me."

Give reasons for your comments.

If instead of, "I get lost in this paragraph," you say, "In this paragraph you started out writing about the effects of video game violence on children but then you ended by writing about television cartoons, and I couldn't see what connected those two ideas," you give the writer information useful for revision. (And if you work to state feedback in this way, you'll find it easier to look at your own writing just as carefully; teachers of writing often talk about how useful to their own writing it is to have to give feedback to people in their classes.)

HINTS & TIPS FOR CONNECTING WITH AUDIENCES

IF YOU GET NERVOUS THINKING ABOUT AUDIENCES

Sometimes writers can get hung up if they think about audiences while they compose: Picturing people—whether it is people you know or the unknowns of a general audience—can sometimes make you hesitant, worried that you might say the wrong thing.

If this happens to you, keep in mind the following two approaches:

- Let yourself write to learn before you write to communicate (➔ see pages 34–35). Put all notions of readers out of your head; just write. Write down your ideas until you feel you have a thesis statement. Use the thesis statement to structure your writing (➔ as we describe on pages 222–225). Only when you have that solid amount of writing, put together a statement of purpose: Thinking about audience when you can take confidence from a solid argument makes the task easier—and you might very well find that it's pleasurable to shape writing for others once you have your argument.

- Remind yourself that nerves are a sign of caring about your work. Can you talk yourself into turning that nervous energy into excitement for your project, into the knowledge that you are thinking and learning and taking risks?

HINTS & TIPS FOR DRAFTING

ASK FOR FOCUSED FEEDBACK TO YOUR WRITING

Because getting feedback from readers is the main way to strengthen your writing, you must get useful feedback. But others have to learn how to give feedback, and many readers won't automatically know how to give you useful feedback.

When you are ready for feedback, tell readers what you need: For example, ask them to focus on your argument and to try to describe your thesis statement back to you. Or ask them to read the paper to see whether you offer enough evidence or your transitions help them understand why you move from one paragraph to the next.

Choose only one or two areas for them to focus on in their reading.

BE SURE YOU UNDERSTAND FEEDBACK

If you hear something you don't understand from a reader, ask for clarification. If you don't understand feedback, it can't help you.

GET FEEDBACK FROM YOURSELF

Put your writing aside for at least several hours to get some distance from it, and then reread it. Reread it once to see if your argument seems sufficiently developed, read it again to check your transitions, and so on.

You need to learn to be your own audience, because the paper you turn in is yours. You have the final responsibility for it.

PART 8
REVISING WITH STYLE

CONTENTS

WHERE ARE WE IN A PROCESS FOR COMPOSING?

Understanding your project
Getting started
Asking questions
Shaping your project for others
Drafting a paper
Getting feedback
Revising
Polishing

Learning how to make large-scale changes to your writing to shape it more effectively for your purposes

Paying attention to style—to the effects for your audience of your individual sentences and words

Questions you might have about revising and styling a paper:

How is revising different from editing and proofreading?
→ See pages 290–291.

How do I know what to revise in my paper?
→ See pages 292–293.

What can I do to make my writing more interesting and engaging?
→ See pages 294–329.

How do I strengthen my introduction and conclusion?
→ See pages 302–305 and 348.

How do I compose academic sentences?
→ See pages 312–313.

How do I make my writing more inclusive and nonbiased?
→ See pages 330–339.

What can I do to make my text look better?
→ See pages 340–343.

How do I create style in an oral presentation? How do I make sure my slides support an oral presentation?
→ See pages 344–347.

THE WPA OUTCOMES* FOR PART 8 INCLUDE:

Rhetorical abilities: Understanding how to shift voice, tone, and levels of formality according to audience expectations.

Writing processes: Developing strategies for revising.

Using conventions: Understanding why conventions for structure, paragraphing, tone, and mechanics vary.

*See page 15.

REVISING YOUR WRITING

WHAT IS REVISION?

To revise, focus on your argument: How well do readers (and you) understand it? To strengthen your writing at this stage of your composing process, you might need to move paragraphs, find new evidence and write new paragraphs to hold that evidence, rewrite your introduction, or turn your conclusion into your introduction (➔ see page 348).

You will most strengthen your writing if you don't get distracted by grammar, spelling, and mechanics at this stage but instead let yourself be open to large changes.

REVISING

When you revise, you attend to large-scale persuasive aspects of a text: organization and style. You start revising once you have close to a full draft.

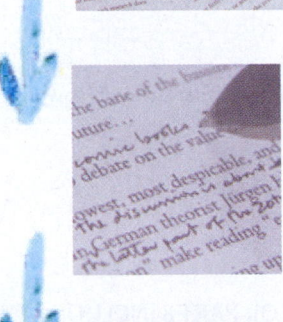

EDITING

In editing, you attend to sentences and other large details: Are sentences readable? Have you documented all your sources?

➔ See pages 429–460 (especially page 435).

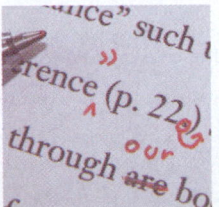

PROOFREADING

A proofreader checks spelling, punctuation, and other mechanics.

➔ See page 435 for more on proofreading.

TO REVISE, ASK YOURSELF:

- Am I clear about my argument? Can I state it as
  a thesis statement?
  → See pages 160–161, 208–209, and 222–225.

PART 5

- Did I offer well-supported and accurate evidence
  for each of my claims?
  → See pages 162–171.

- Have I been fair and respectful toward the differing positions
  one could take on my arguments?
  → See pages 105 and 204–207 for considering how you work with others'
  positions in your sources.

PART 6

- Will my readers understand the purpose of each paragraph?
  → See pages 240–255.

- Can I say why my paragraphs are ordered as they are?
  Can I describe the steps of my argument?
  → See pages 222–225.

PART 8

- Will my writing engage readers?
  → See pages 294–329.

- Does my introduction engage readers with my argument
  and initial concerns?
  → See pages 304–305.

- Have I given appropriate emphasis to the main parts
  of my arguments?
  → Look through Part 8 for pages checked for helping with emphasis.

- Do my transitions help readers move from one paragraph
  to the next?
  → See pages 244–245 and 306–307.

- Does my conclusion sum up my argument and
  end memorably for readers?
  → See pages 302–303 and 348.

REVISING YOUR WRITING
DEVELOPING
A REVISION PLAN

→ See Harley's revised paper on pages 354–363.

→ See the feedback she received on pages 284–287.

A REVISION PLAN

After you receive feedback to a draft, develop a revision plan. A revision plan is informal, just for you: Making such a plan helps you focus and list what you need to do in revising, and so helps you plan your time and stay on track.

To the right, Harley's plan lays out how she understands the feedback she received and how she plans to respond.

The feedback you receive from others, as well as the list on page 291, can help you determine how to focus your revision efforts.

PLAN FOR REVISING, NOT EDITING OR PROOFREADING

Notice that in her revision plan Harley doesn't mention anything about spelling or grammar: That's because revising is about focusing on your argument and how well readers understand it, not on the details of spelling and grammar.

GO TO THE WRITING CENTER!

If your school has a Writing Center, the staff will be happy to help you at any stage of your writing process—but know that visiting them while you revise is particularly smart.

Writing Center staff are well trained in helping writers revise and strengthen drafts. After you have a first draft, talking with someone in your Writing Center will help you speed your process and figure out and focus on the most important revision steps you can make.

→ When you are ready to edit and proofread, see page 435.

Given the feedback I've received from Professor Komova and everyone in class, I don't think I really yet have the evidence I need in support of my thesis statement—but I probably need to modify my thesis statement anyway so that I am clear about what I am doing. I really want to do more with the notion of confirmation bias. So how about this:

> Civility—which is about helping us discuss controversial matters with others—focuses only on our attitudes toward others and not on our attitudes toward our own ideas; therefore, to achieve the goals of civility, civility needs to have awareness of our own confirmation bias added to it.

That seems to get me more focused on civility and confirmation bias together—and means I need to rethink my organization a bit.

With my new thesis statement and feedback, I think I also need the following revisions:

- A shift in how I discuss civility. I don't think I need to connect it to repression any more—but I do need to show why we should want it.
- That means I still need more sources to show how civility and democracy are connected.
- Work on how I am using my sources: I need more summary and less quotation!
- Figure out how to give better examples about civility and democracy, so people get it better.
- My introduction seems to be working, but my conclusion isn't yet doing what it needs to.
- Experiment with my transitions, since I need to help people see better the connections I am making.

Rethinking a thesis statement

Because writing is thinking on paper, a draft often helps writers come to new understandings—and that can mean needing to rethink a thesis statement.

Organization and arrangement

→ See Part 6.

Working with sources

→ See Parts 3, 4, and 5.

Working with examples

→ See Part 5.

Conclusions, transitions, and other matters of style

→ See Part 8.

REVISING, STYLE, AND AUDIENCE

TWO ASPECTS OF REVISION

As we mentioned a few pages back, when you revise, you attend to large-scale persuasive aspects of a text:

1   ORGANIZATION. Are your paragraphs arranged so that readers understand why one paragraph follows the next? Can they follow the steps of your argument?

> → For more on working with paragraphs and the arrangements of paragraphs, see pages 240–255.

2   STYLE. Here in Part 8 we help you revise your writing so that it is clear, concise, coherent; puts emphasis on the points where you want emphasis; and engages your readers.

Style is not about being fancy; it is about the detailed choices you make to design your ideas for your audience.

We focus on style here, in these pages about revision, because—once you have the organization of your argument in place—it is through attending to the paragraphs, sentences, and words of your writing that you can be most persuasive.

ALL COMMUNICATIONS HAVE STYLE

In a book about the senses we read:

One scent can be unexpected, momentary, and fleeting, yet conjure up a childhood summer beside a lake in the Poconos, when wild blueberry bushes teemed with succulent fruit and the opposite sex was as mysterious as space travel; another, hours of passion on a moonlit beach in Florida, while the night-blooming cereus drenched the air with thick curds of perfume and huge sphinx moths visited the cereus in a loud purr of wings; a third, a family dinner of pot roast, noodle pudding, and sweet potatoes, during a myrtle-mad August in a midwestern town, when both of one's parents were alive.

On a webpage describing the work of two scientists who won the Nobel Prize, we read:

All the odorant receptors are related proteins but differ in certain details, explaining why they are triggered by different odorous molecules. Each receptor consists of a chain of amino acids that is anchored into the cell membrane and traverses it seven times. The chain creates a binding pocket where the odorant can attach. When that happens, the shape of the receptor protein is altered, leading to G protein activation.

The paragraphs differ because the writing is aimed at different audiences:

- The first paragraph (one long sentence!) is for a general audience. This paragraph opens a chapter and leads into passages of somewhat technical information. The paragraph's style suggests to readers that even though what the chapter covers is technical, they will still enjoy it because the information is sensuous and concrete.

- The second paragraph was written by scientists for an audience of scientists. Individual words are not defined; the writers assume readers know them. The sentences are much shorter than in the first example, and they focus on describing processes as directly as possible, with few adjectives.

Although the second paragraph may not seem to have much style, many choices went into it, choices about individual words, the length of sentences, and the grammatical construction of the sentences—choices all aimed to meet readers' expectations.

OVERALL STYLE—AND FINELY DETAILED STYLE

You can probably imagine the source of each example paragraph above: The first comes from a book of lush descriptions; the second comes from a short, to-the-point, descriptive article. Notice, then, what style is about:

- **The overall feel a piece has for a reader.** Does the piece feel lush and detailed, or quick and precise? In what contexts and for what purposes will audiences expect writing like the first example paragraph or like the second?

- **The feel of individual words, sentences, and paragraphs.** The overall style of a piece is built from the choices writers make with words and sentences. We've already pointed out the differences in sentence length and word choice between the two examples; what other differences can you see?

REVISING, STYLE, AND AUDIENCE
STYLES READERS EXPECT IN DIFFERENT SETTINGS

To the right are samples of writing on the same topic but aimed at different kinds of audiences.

ACADEMIC WRITING

Today nearly every job requires good performances on more than one task. Employees have to deal with several simultaneous demands, and good job performance is therefore linked to good multitasking performance. This holds true for many jobs, as shown by data from the Occupational Information Network (O*NET; cf. Peterson, Mumford, Borman, Jeanneret, & Fleishman, 1999) and other job analyses (e.g., Maschke & Goeters, 1999, for airline pilots). In terms of personnel selection, therefore, it would appear to be essential to identify future employees with adequate multitasking abilities.

Bühner, M., et al. (2006). Working memory dimensions as differential predictors of the speed and error aspect of multitasking performance. *Human Performance, 19,* 253-275.

The numbered lists to the right describe the stylistic features readers generally expect in writing for these different audiences and contexts.

1 Uses technical terms: *good multitasking performance, personnel selection.*

2 Has long noun phrases: *several simultaneous demands, adequate multitasking abilities.*

3 Has long sentences.

4 Uses verbs that refer to unchanging conditions (such as mental or bodily states): is ... *linked, requires.*

5 Has an element of doubt: *nearly every job, it would appear.*

6 Has a neutral tone.

7 Shows respect for the ideas and work of others by citing names and sources.

WORKPLACE WRITING

Meyer offers the following tips to reduce workplace stress:

- Set aside time for mindful work. Ignore or turn off your email signal and don't answer your phone so you can focus on the project at hand. Multitasking can make us less productive and it may be helpful to set aside time for focused effort each day.

- Revisit timelines. Assess whether your timelines are realistic. Working toward deadlines you cannot meet is self-defeating. Readjust the timeline when necessary.

Illinois Manufacturers' Association. (2007, August 29). *HR Memo.* Retrieved from http://www.ima-net.org/library/hrmemo/hr082907.cfm

1 Mixes popular words and expressions (*don't, set aside time*) with technical terms appropriate to the particular workplace (*timelines, deadlines*).

2 Has few long noun phrases; instead, if nouns are modified, it is usually with one adjective.

3 Has short sentences.

4 Uses action verbs: *ignore, revisit.*

5 Makes confident and direct recommendations, with explanations.

6 Has a confident tone.

7 Cites sources as needed.

POPULAR WRITING

Although we think we're doing several things at once—multitasking—this is a powerful and diabolical illusion. Earl Miller, a neuroscientist at MIT and one of the world experts on divided attention, says that our brains are "not wired to multitask well... When people think they're multitasking, they're actually just switching from one task to another very rapidly. And every time they do, there's a cognitive cost in doing so." So we're not actually keeping a lot of balls in the air like an expert juggler; we're more like a bad amateur plate spinner, frantically switching from one task to another, ignoring the one that is not right in front of us but worried it will come crashing down any minute.

Levitin, Daniel. (2015, January 18). Why the modern world is bad for your brain. *theguardian.com.* Retrieved from http://www.theguardian.com/science/2015/jan/18/modern-world-bad-for-brain-daniel-j-levitin-organized-mind-information-overload

1 Mixes popular words and expressions (*we're not actually, frantically*) with formal vocabulary (*neuroscientist, divided attention*).

2 Has few long noun phrases; instead, if nouns are modified, it is usually with one adjective.

3 Has shorter sentences.

4 Uses action verbs: *switching, ignoring.*

5 Can make confident and wide-ranging claims: *a powerful and diabolical illusion.*

6 Can have a playful, even sarcastic, tone.

7 Tells who spoke quoted words, but not where .

STYLE IN WRITING

What is on this page will help you style your writing for

✓ CLARITY

✓ CONCISION

✓ COHERENCE

✓ EMPHASIS

✓ ENGAGEMENT

STYLING FOR CLARITY, CONCISION, COHERENCE, EMPHASIS, AND ENGAGEMENT

If you construct your writing to be clear, concise, coherent, emphatic, and engaging, your writing will work for present-day readers in most contexts.

Your readers may not be able to name those five values, but in the United States we are a culture that desires information to come quickly and easily as well as with some pleasure. (Or, to look at it in another way, no one likes having to work hard for boring information.)

USING THE NEXT PAGES

On the next pages you will see boxes like that to the left, checked to show the style values that page can help you achieve. To apply these values, you must know your purposes in writing:

- Where do you want readers to pay particular attention? What are the central parts of your argument? What parts of your writing do you want your readers to walk away remembering? For any parts like those, use the strategies that help you provide emphasis and engagement.

- Where do you want to be absolutely sure readers can follow with no problems? Where do you present complex ideas that you need readers to follow clearly? Obviously, in academic writing you always want readers to follow easily, and so all the strategies related to clarity, concision, and coherence matter—but there will be parts of your writing where you want to pay particular attention to these.

CLARITY

Clarity comes from Latin and means *clear*, as when the air is clear on a bright day. When you strive for clarity in writing, you shape sentences to help readers see easily what is most important.

CONCISION

Being concise means getting to the point. To be concise in writing, use as few words as possible. Concision supports clarity.

COHERENCE

When writing is coherent, it feels as though all its parts weave together. Readers see connections between all the parts of the writing, and they can grasp easily the overall purpose. Coherence is built through repetition, sometimes of exact words but also of concepts.

EMPHASIS

To persuade others to listen to your concerns, you need to make your purposes clear and offer reasons. Some reasons will be more persuasive to readers than others, and so the following pages offer strategies for emphasizing the parts of writing that you want your audience most to notice.

Keep in mind that when you want to emphasize parts of your writing, you cannot emphasize every single word or phrase. That would be like yelling continually at your audience—and, as you know, when someone yells at you continually, you stop listening. Instead, emphasis is when someone has been talking in a regular tone for a while and only now and then raises (or lowers) her voice.

ENGAGEMENT

We humans are lively, energetic, social beings. We like to tell jokes. We like to hear about odd events in others' lives. We need to learn the practical details of living well and healthily. We need to learn how others live with the sorrows of death and pain.

We learn best from each other when our minds are active and engaged.

Writing that helps readers feel and understand someone else's delight or sorrow will be more effective than writing that doesn't. Writing that helps readers understand concretely and comfortably how to put together a stereo system will be more effective than writing that doesn't. Writing that helps readers understand the consequences of a melted polar ice cap is much more likely to bring readers to action than writing that lists sterile facts.

■ ■ ■

The following pages discuss strategies you can use to shape your writing to include all these values.

Because style is present in all levels of writing, the following pages consider style in three parts:

PARAGRAPHS
SENTENCES
WORDS

STYLING PARAGRAPHS

In Part 6 we discussed the expectations readers have about paragraph organization; we also discussed the different functions paragraphs can perform. (→ See pages 246–255.)

In the next pages, we consider smaller-scale decisions you can make about paragraphs: How do you keep readers engaged and at the same time help them follow your argument?

VARY SENTENCE LENGTH

If every sentence in a paragraph is the same length, readers (or listeners) might fall into a lulling rhythm and stop paying attention. The paragraph below shows—with the last sentence a contrast to all that precedes—one strategy for avoiding such rhythms:

In the Web 2.0 model, we have thousands of services scrutinizing each new piece of information online, grabbing interesting bits, remixing them in new ways, and passing them along to other services. Each new addition to the mix can be exploited in countless new ways, both by human bloggers and by the software programs that track changes in the overall state of the Web. Information in this new model is analyzed, repackaged, digested, and passed on down to the next link in the chain. It flows.

What is on this page will help you style your writing for

☐ CLARITY

☐ CONCISION

✓ COHERENCE

✓ EMPHASIS

✓ ENGAGEMENT

VARY SENTENCE PATTERNS

In Part 11 we describe the four patterns of sentences. (➡ See pages 479–491.) Varying a paragraph's sentence patterns can keep readers engaged:

In the thirties, Harold Gray's comic strip *Little Orphan Annie* had 47 million readers. Then it languished until the 1970s when Martin Charnin thought it would make a good stage musical. It did. For the film, fresh songs and scenes were added, and 8,000 girls auditioned for the part of Annie. Director John Huston wanted "a girl who can sing, dance and act, with tons of personality, so that for two hours audiences won't take their eyes off her." Aileen Quinn's high spirits in the role have caused children to say, after seeing the film, that they too want to be orphans.

You don't have to use all four patterns in every paragraph; just be aware that, if a paragraph's sentences sound repetitive to you, varying the patterns is one solution.

VARY SENTENCE ORDER

In English, readers expect sentences to have the order of subject-verb-object. (➡ See pages 480–483.) Because this expectation is so widespread, you can create emphasis in a paragraph by reversing a sentence's word order. Just be careful to do this infrequently, only when you want special emphasis. The following paragraph would be less strong if the first sentence were *Potential homebuyers should check basements first.*

Basements are where potential homebuyers should go first. The most expensive home repairs come up from weak and shaky foundations, and after you buy a house you do not want the surprise of thousands of dollars in bills for digging out and replacing the stone or cement block that is supposed to support your house. Only a detailed inspection by a foundation specialist can tell you whether a crack results from simple settling or the foundation breaking in two.

VARY PARAGRAPH LENGTH

Audiences expect different paragraph lengths, depending on medium and genre. For example, because many people are still becoming accustomed to reading online, paragraphs in online genres such as newspapers are often only two or three sentences each, much shorter than paragraphs in print. Paragraphs in academic genres, on the other hand, can extend over a page or two in a twenty-page paper. (In a paper shorter than ten pages, readers expect paragraphs to be shorter than a whole page.)

In general, all the paragraphs in any text will be of similar length, just long enough to develop and make clear the concept the writer needs to make at that point. But when you want to emphasize one point, you can use a paragraph that is much shorter than the others.

Readers will see visually and will feel through the change in reading rhythm that the paragraph's content matters.

STYLING PARAGRAPHS
CONCLUDING PARAGRAPHS

Why talk about concluding paragraphs before introductory paragraphs?

Because you cannot have a shining, strong introductory paragraph until you know the exact end toward which that paragraph points readers.

FUNCTIONS OF CONCLUDING PARAGRAPHS FOR READERS

1 Concluding paragraphs are logical: They sum up the arguments of the paper.

2 Concluding paragraphs carry emotional weight: Because readers read them last, concluding paragraphs are often what readers remember most.

FUNCTIONS OF CONCLUDING PARAGRAPHS FOR WRITERS

Once they are drafted, concluding paragraphs provide surprisingly useful suggestions to writers about revising.

→ See page 348.

What is on this page will help you style your writing for

✓ CLARITY

☐ CONCISION

✓ COHERENCE

✓ EMPHASIS

✓ ENGAGEMENT

STRATEGIES FOR CONCLUDING

As you write, you cannot separate the two functions of concluding paragraphs. As you read the following examples, look for how they mix functions, but also try to imagine what preceded the conclusion; a strong conclusion should enable you to do that.

SUMMARIZING YOUR ARGUMENT

Provide a crisp summary, not a rote repetition. You can include a question, quotation, or recommended action:

In sum, the globalization of English does not mean that if we English-speakers just sit back and wait, we'll soon be able to exchange ideas with anyone else anywhere: We can't count on much more than a very basic ability to communicate. Outside of certain professional fields, if English-speaking Americans hope to exchange ideas with people in a nuanced way, we should do as people elsewhere are doing: become bilingual.

RECOMMENDING ACTION

The problem at hand is so huge it requires a response like our national mobilization to fight—and win—World War II. To move our nation off of fossil fuels, we need inspired, Churchillian leadership and sweeping statutes à la the Big War or the Civil Rights Movement. So, frankly, I feel a twinge of nausea each time I see that predictable "10 Things You Can Do" sidebar in a well-meaning magazine or newspaper article. In truth, the only list that actually matters is the one we should all be sending to Congress *post haste*, full of 10 muscular clean-energy statutes that would finally do what we say we want: rescue our life-giving Earth from climate catastrophe.

SUGGESTING NEEDS FOR FURTHER RESEARCH

This research into freecycling, bartering, and other alternative consumer networks shows that most researchers have too simple an idea of how consumption and citizenship can work together. As the examples I highlighted in this study showed, connections people make through sharing economies *can* help them develop stronger civic connections— which stands in strong contrast to how most of the sources I found tied consumption to a decrease in civic connections. We need, therefore, further research that asks specifically what kinds of consumption build communities and strengthen civic connections.

REFLECTING ON HOW YOUR WRITING HAS AFFECTED YOU

Using your own voice pulls readers closer, making your observations more compelling:

In the interviews I conducted for this paper, I learned that men and women learn to be men and women by experiencing all the photographs, movies, magazine covers, and popular songs that portray what men and women are supposed to be and do. I've also learned how the simplest of tossed-off sentences can shape someone's sense of what counts as proper behavior. I heard how a teacher's comments are remembered for a long time. As an education major, it's that last observation I will carry with me, to help me think about the responsibilities I'll be taking on.

STYLING PARAGRAPHS
INTRODUCTORY PARAGRAPHS

What is on this page will help you style your writing for

✓ CLARITY

☐ CONCISION

☐ COHERENCE

✓ EMPHASIS

✓ ENGAGEMENT

FUNCTIONS OF INTRODUCTORY PARAGRAPHS FOR READERS

1 Introductory paragraphs engage readers with the topic.

2 Introductory paragraphs focus readers' attention on the particular aspects of the topic that matter to you.

WHAT TO AVOID

- **Broad and vague Introductions.** *From the beginning of time, humans have …* or *Life is amazing …* start papers that make readers impatient for or uncertain about the paper's focus. You might need such phrases to get your writing going, but—in revising—make your introduction more focused by instead stating as explicitly as you can what matters.

- **Starting with a dictionary definition.** With such a start, readers think you are not confident enough about your own arguments to put them in your own words.

- **Excuses.** Don't make excuses about not being an expert. Readers don't expect experts to be writing college papers. Instead, they expect well-researched arguments that acknowledge other possible positions.

STRATEGIES FOR INTRODUCTIONS

BE DIRECT AND EXPLICIT

Many believe that microcredit can end poverty as we know it. In what follows, I will argue that microcredit instead can exacerbate poverty, especially for women and others of the most poor.

USE A QUOTATION

In the 1820s, Fanny Trollope, that perceptive, sharp-tongued traveller, described North America as "a vast continent, by far the greater part of which is still in the state nature left it, and a busy, bustling, industrious population, hacking and hewing their way through it." That hewing, hacking, and shooting was to cause a lot of environmental damage.

USE A QUESTION

Millionaire Steve Fossett has been missing since last Monday, when he took off from a Nevada airstrip on a short flight. Rescue crews have yet to find the famous adventurer or his plane, but according to news reports, they've discovered at least *six uncharted wrecks* across a 17,000-square-mile swath of the Sierra Nevada—or nearly one a day since the search began. Why are there so many undocumented crash sites around the Sierra Nevada?

MAKE A SURPRISING CLAIM

Strange but true: Energy-efficient light bulbs and hybrid cars are hurting our nation's budding efforts to fight global warming.

MAKE A COMPELLING CLAIM

The rate of bipolar disorder diagnoses in children and adolescents seen as outpatients by physicians shot up dramatically between 1994 and 2003, raising new concerns about possible overdiagnosis of this severe mood disorder among young people.

PAINT A VISUAL PICTURE

Lady, an Australian shepherd mix who had been lounging in a sunny window seat at the Bothell Regional Library, pricked up her ears and wagged her tail when she saw 10-year-old Nicholas Goodman. When he sat down next to her with the book *Down in the Subway* and started to read aloud, she leaned against him, eyes closed, and appeared to listen intently. Her expression never changed, not even when Nicholas stumbled over tricky words like "guava."

That's the whole idea behind "Reading with Rover," a summer program for children at the Bothell and Kenmore branches of the King County Regional Library System.

HOW LONG?

In a five- to ten-page paper, an introduction, like a conclusion, should rarely take up more than two-thirds of a page. A longer introduction will have readers wondering, midway through, when they will actually get to the paper; a longer conclusion will have readers wondering if a new paper or argument is starting.

WHAT'S YOUR DISCIPLINE?

Writers in the humanities frequently do not explicitly state their thesis; instead, they develop it through the writing. Writers in the sciences and social sciences are expected to be explicit about their thesis and to announce a paper's structure. If you have any questions about what is appropriate, ask your teacher.

STYLING PARAGRAPHS
TRANSITIONS BETWEEN PARAGRAPHS

In Part 6, we discussed creating coherence *within* paragraphs; here we discuss creating coherence *between* paragraphs.

Most writers need to learn how to provide transitions between paragraphs; learning how to do this will help your writing be confident and effective. When you use the strategies we discuss here, you tell readers why one paragraph follows another and you enable readers to follow and so better understand your arguments.

STRATEGIES FOR BUILDING TRANSITIONS

- Repeat crucial words, phrases, or concepts from one paragraph to the next.
- Repeat crucial concepts by using synonyms.
- Use the linking words listed on page 244 to show relationships between your paragraphs.

LINK THE LAST SENTENCE OF ONE PARAGRAPH TO THE FIRST SENTENCE OF THE NEXT

In constructing transitions from one paragraph to the next, choose the most important words, phrases, or concepts in one paragraph's last sentence; then weave those words, phrases, or concepts into the first sentence of the next paragraph.

The paragraphs to the right use the strategies above to build transitions.

What is on this page will help you style your writing for

✔ CLARITY

☐ CONCISION

✔ COHERENCE

✔ EMPHASIS

✔ ENGAGEMENT

ozone in Mexico City have exceeded the country's air-quality standards 284 days per year, on average. Geography doesn't help: Mexico City lies on a broad basin ringed by tall mountains that can block the movement of air masses that might clear out pollution.

Furthermore, the city's rapid spread in recent decades has aggravated its pollution problems. Mexico City now covers about 1,500 square kilometers—about 10 times as much as it occupied

In this example, the writer uses the first paragraph to discuss connections between pollution in Mexico City and the city's geography; in the second paragraph, he turns to discussing how the city's size contributes to its pollution problems. **Furthermore** tells readers that additional information is being added, and **city** and **pollution** carry the topic from one paragraph to the next.

■ ■ ■

On one side were those, like Edwards and the Mather family, who believed in an anointed elect and in salvation through God's grace alone. They tended to have a religious fervor, a sense of social class, and hierarchy, and an appreciation for exalted values over earthly ones. On the other side were the Franklins, those who believed in salvation through good works, whose religion was benevolent and tolerant, and who were unabashedly striving and upwardly mobile.

Out of this grew many related divides in the American culture, and Franklin represents one strand: the side of pragmatism versus romanticism, of practical benevolence versus moral crusading. He was on the side of religious tolerance rather than evangelical faith.

From a biography of Benjamin Franklin, this example's first paragraph makes a distinction between the beliefs of different families of that time. The second paragraph begins with **Out of this**: the writer keeps readers' minds on the distinction from the first paragraph so that he can show how it gives rise to different ways citizens of the United States think and act now.

■ ■ ■

the same thing he does, you do it using plain words without instruments. Words are like music. Well-reasoned thoughts, conveyed with well-chosen words, can touch us deeply as a moving symphony or a driving drum beat.

But Maggie Simpson doesn't possess language and doesn't speak. In the twentieth century, philosophers concerned with humanity's place in the universe have turned to the relationship between words and thoughts. How do we think if

In this example, the writer argues first that words matter in communication; in the second paragraph, the discussion shifts to focus on a character who doesn't use words. **But** signals this shift to readers. The two paragraphs are still strongly connected by the repetition of concepts concerning words and language.

STYLING PARAGRAPHS
PASSIVE VOICE

Passive voice is a feature of individual sentences, and we define it in Part 10 (→ see page 445).

Even though passive voice is a feature of sentences, we discuss it here because it is in paragraphs that passive voice has its largest effects. Readers will rarely notice the use of passive voice in one or two sentences within several paragraphs or sections; when a whole paragraph is in passive voice, however, what readers take from the paragraph will be affected because their whole sense of the paragraph is affected.

In addition, as we point out to the right, writing some sentences in passive voice can constrain your other sentences.

What is on this page will help you style your writing for

☐ CLARITY

☐ CONCISION

☐ COHERENCE

✓ EMPHASIS

✓ ENGAGEMENT

PASSIVE VOICE IN SCIENTIFIC AND TECHNICAL WRITING

By using passive voice, writers can shift readers' focus away from who performs an action to the object acted upon. Because science writing is meant to be objective—that is, to imply that the actions (experiments, surveys, observations) being described could be performed by anyone—scientific writing often uses passive voice:

The behavior of fiber reinforced polymer (FRP) strengthened reinforced concrete beams subjected to torsional loads has not been well understood, compared to other loads. Interaction of different components of concrete, steel, and FRP in addition to the complex compatibility issues associated with torsional deformations have made it difficult to provide an accurate analytical solution. In this paper an analytical method is introduced for evaluation of the torsional capacity of FRP-strengthened RC beams. In this method, the interaction of different components is allowed by fulfilling equilibrium and compatibility conditions throughout the loading regime while the ultimate torque of the beam is calculated similarly to the well-known compression field theory. It is shown that the method is capable of predicting the ultimate torque of FRP-strengthened RC beams reasonably accurately.

PASSIVE VOICE—OR NOT?—IN WRITING FOR NONSCIENTIFIC AUDIENCES

Compare this paragraph—

During the last couple weeks, American snouts have increased dramatically in my garden and the surrounding area. But that is nothing like the masses that were recorded farther south in Texas a few weeks ago. An estimated 7.5 million snouts were reported in the Alamo area of the Lower Rio Grande Valley on September 5. And there is a chance that our numbers will continue to build over the next few weeks, at least until the really cold weather sets in.

—with this:

In the last few weeks, I thought American snouts had taken over my garden. On September 5, however, observers farther south in Texas recorded numbers that make my garden seem empty: They saw almost 7.5 million snouts in the Alamo area of the Lower Rio Grande Valley. And until the cold weather sets in, these small butterflies might very well overwhelm us with their numbers.

When they wish to sound scientific—which often requires longer and less direct grammatical constructions—writers often carry the patterns of passive voice into their other sentences, making all of them longer and more complex than they need to be.

If an occasional passive voice sentence supports your purposes, be alert to keeping your other sentences in the active voice.

STYLING SENTENCES

Style is all about how you connect with audiences in order to achieve your purposes.

On the next pages, we consider sentence style from two angles:

1 How do you construct sentences with the grammatical structures that readers expect in a formal, academic style of writing?

2 How do you construct sentences that readers want to read and that help you make your points?

Perhaps you think these two angles are really the same. After all, if sentences have the structures audiences expect, doesn't that mean readers will want to read them? Doesn't that mean the sentences will help writers make their points?

Consider this paragraph:

I must be real. Hear what I'm saying. We ain't going nowhere, as the boys in the hood be saying. Nowhere. If you promote all the surviving Afghans to the status of honorary Americans, Mr. President, where exactly on the bus does that leave me. When do I get paid. When can I expect my invitation to the ranch. I hear Mr. Putin's wearing jingle-jangle silver spurs around his dacha. Heard you fixed him up with an eight-figure advance on his memoirs. Is it true he's iced up to be the Marlboro man after he retires from Russia. Anything left under the table for me. And mine.

That paragraph breaks just about every rule one can imagine for formal writing. The writer uses periods instead of question marks. There are sentence fragments. The writer uses what some would call **colloquial phrasing**.

The paragraph's writer is John Edgar Wideman, who has won many prestigious awards for his writing and has taught writing at the university level. The paragraph comes from an essay, "Whose War," that appeared in the highly respected collection *The Best Essays of 2003*.

Given what he understood about his purposes—questioning the U.S. government's use of resources in the opening years of the twenty-first century—Wideman *chose* to write as he did. He chose to go against formal expectations so that his essay could convey anger and frustration, so that his essay would read as though it were being spoken, passionately.

Wideman chose to break expectations because he could. He is a practiced writer who knows and can use the expectations and standards of formal writing when he wants and also because he is a well-known writer. Because he is a well-known writer, others know that he usually does write in more expected formats and that he must therefore have had reasons for writing differently.

As you style your sentences, then, keep in mind the expectations of *your* readers for your words. Will your readers expect a formal piece? Do your readers know you well enough to know that, if you break expectations, you chose to do so? If you break expectations, how do you let readers know that you did so for a reason?

On the next pages, we offer angles for learning the expectations readers have for formal, academic writing.

Learn these well so that you can use them but also so that you can modify them as your purposes demand.

STYLING SENTENCES
ACADEMIC SENTENCES

CHECKLIST FOR FORMAL, ACADEMIC SENTENCES

❏ Your sentences have positive structures.

→ See the opposite page to learn about sentences without double negatives.

→ See the opposite page to learn about sentences that are positive rather than negative.

❏ Each sentence fits one of the four sentence patterns.

→ See pages 479–491.

❏ You use no sentence fragments—except, rarely, for emphasis.

→ See pages 446–449.

❏ Your sentences do not shift among grammatical forms.

→ See pages 436–439 to learn about shifts in person and number.

→ See pages 440–441 to learn about shifts in verb tense.

→ See page 445 to learn about shifts in voice.

→ See page 444 to learn about shifts in direct and indirect discourse.

→ See page 444 to learn about shifts in levels of formality.

❏ Your sentences are easy to read.

→ See pages 314–315.

SENTENCES DO NOT USE DOUBLE NEGATIVES

In formal writing, convention requires using only one negative in a sentence.
The negatives are *barely, hardly, neither, no, not, never, none, nobody, nothing,* and *scarcely.*

Sometimes two fixes are possible for a double negative:

✗ Bob did **not** have **no** solution for the problem.
TWO NEGATIVES

✓ Bob had **no** solution for the problem.
ONE NEGATIVE

✓ Bob did **not** have a solution for the problem.
ONE NEGATIVE

Sometimes a double negative offers only one obvious solution:

✗ **Nobody** said **nothing** about how to make quotations in a paper.
TWO NEGATIVES

✓ **Nobody** said anything about how to make quotations in a paper.
ONE NEGATIVE

SENTENCES ARE POSITIVE, NOT NEGATIVE

The following two sentences are both grammatically correct—but the second sentence
is easier to read and understand: Its information is presented positively.

Classic gangster films were not without a message, showing audiences that if a gangster's
life had no order, it was because society had no order.

Classic gangster films had a message, showing audiences that the chaos of a gangster's life
mirrored the chaos of society.

READ!

Formal, academic writing—even in
scientific disciplines—leaves considerable
room for working with style. Reading
widely respected writers in a discipline is
the best way to learn the leeway you have.

WHERE TO FOCUS?

You are probably already in good control
of several of these features of academic
sentences. Ask someone who is familiar
with your writing—a teacher or someone
in your Writing Center—which of these
features needs your attention, and then
focus your attention just on those.

STYLING SENTENCES
SENTENCES THAT ARE EASY TO READ

What is on this page will help you style your writing for

✓ CLARITY

✓ CONCISION

✓ COHERENCE

  EMPHASIS

✓ ENGAGEMENT

Easy-to-read sentences have the following six qualities:

SENTENCES ARE NOT WORDY

Due to the matter of the final report, which was turned in after the due date, I did not acquire the grade I hoped for in class and now therefore I appeal for a second chance to succeed.

Because of a late final report, I failed the class; I hope to retake the class.

Wanting to sound formal or legal, writers often stretch for long phrases and complex vocabulary; the resulting sentences often stutter and resist easy reading.

Those who study writing know that writers' language gets wordy and awkward precisely when writers are trying hard, perhaps because of a challenging or emotionally touchy project (like a grade appeal). If your project does make you nervous, or if you worry about wordiness, ask a trusted reader to check.

SENTENCES AVOID EXPLETIVES

An expletive can be a swear word, but it can also be a phrase that adds length but no meaning to a sentence, such as **There is …**, **There are …**, or **It is necessary …**.

Using one or two such phrases in several pages of writing is not a disaster, but learn to be on the lookout for expletives and replace them when you find more than a few:

It takes time to write.

Writing takes time.

If we are to end global warming, one thing people must do is get out of their cars and walk.

To end global warming, people must get out of their cars and walk.

SENTENCES USE FEW PREPOSITIONAL PHRASES

One argument of the parents from the neighborhood was that all parks in the city should be child-friendly.

Neighborhood parents argued that all city parks should be child-friendly.

Too many prepositions block readers from seeing your ideas.

When you can, convert prepositional phrases into adjectives (which you then place before the noun being modified):

the girl with red hair
the red-haired girl

the ambition of the senator
the senator's ambition

SENTENCES USE FEW RELATIVE PRONOUNS

The relative pronouns *who*, *which*, *whom*, *whose*, and *that* can slow readers:

Childhood is the audience sector which is most exposed to media seduction.

Childhood is the audience sector most exposed to media seduction.

Children who are breast-fed usually have stronger immune systems.

Breast-fed children usually have stronger immune systems.

If you can remove a relative pronoun without upsetting your sentence, do so, or try changing a relative clause (*who are breast-fed*) into an adjective.

SENTENCES FOCUS ON ACTION

A carefully chosen active verb can make sentences come alive for readers:

The never-ending war brought on a reduction in the morale of citizens.

The never-ending war demoralized citizens.

New parking regulations caused great confusion among commuters.

New parking regulations confused commuters.

SENTENCES AVOID NOMINALIZATIONS

When you change a verb or adjective into a noun, you nominalize the verb or adjective:

difficult → difficulty

destroy → destruction

investigate → investigation

analyze → analysis

Nominalizations shift a sentence's focus from verbs and adjectives to abstract nouns—and thus deaden sentences.

Change nominalizations back to verbs or adjectives to enliven sentences:

In this paper I give an analysis of the difficulty of the task of the crash investigation of the space shuttle.

In this paper I analyze the difficult task of those who investigated the space shuttle crash.

My observation was of the locals' table in a busy local restaurant.

I observed the locals' table in a busy local restaurant.

STYLING SENTENCES
USING COORDINATION AND SUBORDINATION

What is on this page will help you style your writing for

✓ CLARITY

CONCISION

✓ COHERENCE

✓ EMPHASIS

ENGAGEMENT

When you have two ideas to express, do you want the ideas to have equal weight in readers' minds—or is one idea less important than the other?

When the ideas are equal, they are **coordinate**.

When one idea is less important than another, it is **subordinate**.

As you build sentences out of multiple independent clauses, you relate the clauses through coordination or subordination.

Both coordination and subordination are signs of formal, academic writing.

TO COORDINATE OR TO SUBORDINATE?

It's up to you: What understanding do you want readers to take from a sentence?

For example, if you want readers to consider knitting's traditional role to be equal to its more recent role, use **coordination**:

Knitting has traditionally been a domestic activity for women, but in the last decades it has been turned into a fine art.

Knitting has traditionally been a domestic activity for women; however, in the last decades it has been turned into a fine art.

If, however, you want to emphasize the recently growing importance of knitting over its past role, use **subordination**:

Although knitting has traditionally been a domestic activity for women, in the last decades it has been turned into a fine art.

→ To learn more about independent and dependent clauses, see pages 449, 485–491, and 502–507.

→ To learn more about conjunctions, see pages 474–477.

COORDINATION

You can choose from two patterns for building a sentence using coordination:

1 | **independent clause** + **,** + **coordinating conjunction** + **independent clause** •

Stone insulates poorly, but it makes a tight wall that radiates stored heat for hours.

2 | **independent clause** + **;** + **conjunctive adverb** + **,** + **independent clause** •

With normal communication channels cut down during the war in Bosnia, the only news came by word of mouth; consequently, posters became a cheap and easy way to spread information.

SUBORDINATION

The one pattern for building a sentence that uses subordination has a reversible order:

independent clause + **,** + **subordinating conjunction** + **dependent clause** •

OR

subordinating conjunction + **dependent clause** + **,** + **independent clause** •

My grandmother would sift sugar on top of a cupcake to make a lacy pattern, after she had placed a doily on top of the cupcake.

After she placed a doily on top of a cupcake, my grandmother would sift sugar on top to make a lacy pattern.

The coordinating conjunctions are *and, but, for, nor, or, so,* and *yet.*

The conjunctive adverbs are *consequently, furthermore, however, moreover, otherwise, therefore, thus,* and *nevertheless.*

The subordinating conjunctions are *after, although, as, because, before, if, since, that, though, unless, until, when, where, whether, which, while, who, whom,* and *whose.*

STYLING SENTENCES
PARALLELISM

If you want readers to see similarities between two or more ideas, use sentence structure: Parallel grammatical form makes the ideas look and sound similar. Readers will take that similarity away with them.

Would you prefer to go swimming, biking, or kayaking?

First we heard whispers, then giggles, then screams of laughter.

Under the eclipse's brief, false night, birds will cease their singing, cows will head for the barn, and people will get weak in the knees.

Parallelism can set up a rhythm that engages readers: As they read, they fall into the rhythm and thus into the movement of your ideas.

CERTAIN KINDS OF WORDS AND PHRASES HELP IN BUILDING PARALLELISM

You use **coordinating conjunctions** (*and*, *but*, *or*, *nor*, *for*, *so*, and *yet*) to join words or phrases that have equal importance—and you can use them to build parallel structures:

I may still have a young man's body, but now I have an old man's heart.

Correlative conjunctions (*both … and*, *either … or*, *neither … nor*, *not only … but also*, and *whether … or*) function similarly, so be sure the words or phrases following each part of these conjunctions have parallel structures:

The town council will decide whether to grant the zoning variance or to sue the owner over the structure.

→ See page 474 to learn about coordinating conjunctions and page 475 to learn about correlative conjunctions.

What is on this page will help you style your writing for

CLARITY

CONCISION

✓ COHERENCE

✓ EMPHASIS

✓ ENGAGEMENT

PARALLELISM

Build parallelism by repeating the same grammatical structure in any list of words, prepositional phrases, sentences, or any other grammatical unit.

She finished the work by not eating, drinking, or sleeping.
PARTICIPLE   PARTICIPLE   PARTICIPLE

My sister liked to eat chocolate and to avoid broccoli.
PREPOSITION + VERB + NOUN   PREPOSITION + VERB + NOUN

Empty stores are signs of a fading past; empty schools are a sign of a fading future.
"empty" + NOUN + "are a sign of a fading" + NOUN   "empty" + NOUN + "are a sign of a fading" + NOUN

One way to check that you are building parallelism is to stack the parts on top of each other, to see that they follow the same grammatical structure:

For your final draft, pay close attention to proofreading your words,
being sure you've cited all sources,
and formatting your works-cited list.

AVOIDING FAULTY PARALLELISM

Faulty parallelism, a common writing error, occurs when a writer builds a list that does not have parallel grammatical structures:

✗ If you have trouble sleeping, try cutting out coffee after lunch, getting rid of the TV in your room, and to fall asleep at the same time every night.

✓ If you have trouble sleeping, try cutting out coffee after lunch, getting rid of the TV in your room, and falling asleep at the same time every night.

As you move through this book, you'll see (as in the example above) the ✗ and ✓ symbols; when you see them, be mindful of how context shapes language use:

✓ = what readers expect in formal writing

✗ = what readers do not expect in formal writing but which may be fine for other contexts

STYLING SENTENCES
FIGURATIVE LANGUAGE

When you want readers to understand or remember a crucial concept, use figurative language. *Figurative language* refers to a range of strategies that make concepts stand out.

FIGURATIVE COMPARISONS

As we said when we discussed analogy in Part 5 (➔ see pages 164–165), you can help readers understand new or complex ideas by describing the ideas in terms readers already know. Similarly, you can make ideas more vivid—and so more memorable—with unexpected comparisons.

COMPARISONS TO MAKE NEW IDEAS FAMILIAR

This passage uses concepts of building blocks and atoms to explain mathematical concepts:

Prime numbers, such as 17 and 23, are those that can be divided only by themselves and 1. They are the most important objects in mathematics because, as the ancient Greeks discovered, they are the building blocks of all numbers—any of which can be broken down into a product of primes. (For example, 105 = 3 x 5 x 7.) They are the hydrogen and oxygen of the world of mathematics, the atoms of arithmetic.

HOW MUCH?

As with spices, figurative language works best in small quantities. Because figurative language can heighten readers' attention to important points in your writing, using it a lot would diffuse its effects.

What is on this page will help you style your writing for

- CLARITY
- CONCISION
- COHERENCE
- ✓ EMPHASIS
- ✓ ENGAGEMENT

COMPARISONS TO MAKE IDEAS MEMORABLE

Microsoft is a middle-aged company struggling to figure out how to dance with the teenagers, and its body simply can't keep up with its intentions, no matter how correct they may be.

The passage could instead read, *Microsoft is having trouble attracting young audiences*—but would that have created such a funny picture in your head?

Michael Ondaatje's *The English Patient* is a novel whose nervous system connects books, visual art, and war.

By giving the novel it discusses a **nervous system**, the example above compares the novel to a living being, giving it a vibrancy it wouldn't otherwise have.

"Goya's Last Works," at the Frick, isn't large, but neither are grenades.

The one little word **grenades**—emphasized by its placement as the last word of the sentence—suggests that the exhibit of paintings being described is explosive and even somehow dangerous.

"I think of her as the human embodiment of Wal-Mart," said Kevvy Schlaucher, a 25-year-old engineer from Calgary, Canada, who used to watch the show with his mother. "The Oprah Empire is everywhere. She makes sure you don't get out of the system."

Saying that Oprah Winfrey's empire is a big business is not as memorable as making you hold her and Wal-Mart in your head at the same time.

FIGURATIVE PATTERNS

Experiments with familiar language patterns can make memorable figurative sentences:

On Monday, engineers repaired the ruptured 17th Street Canal levee in New Orleans and floodwaters receded a bit as some suburban residents, carrying suitcases and heavy hearts, briefly returned to their homes and sifted through the sodden debris.

When you read **carrying suitcases and**..., you might expect the next words to be **backpacks** or **boxes**. **Heavy hearts** can slow your reading, making palpable the residents' emotions.

Experiment with any language pattern, such as those of conjunctions:

All day I keep the Shabbos. This means I do not turn on a light or tear paper or write or bathe or cook or sew or do any of the hundred kinds of work involved in building the Holy Temple.

The **or**'s stretch out the list of actions to emphasize the number of items.

Just as you can multiply conjunctions, you can also take them away:

I smiled. We smoked. We looked up at the stars. We shook from cold.

Grammatical disconnection and emotional disconnection between people are shown by a lack of conjunctions.

NEED INSPIRATION?

Listen to country-western music. Figurative language abounds there, sometimes funny, sometimes not, as when Julie Roberts sings, "Men and mascara always run."

STYLING WORDS

Compare these two sentences:

What did the first settlers of Easter Island eat when they were not eating the local equivalent of maple syrup?

What did the first settlers of Easter Island eat when they were not glutting themselves on the local equivalent of maple syrup?

Which sentence gives you a clearer and sharper sense of action? Why? When might you use one sentence rather than the other?

Compare these two sentences:

The Canadian Rangers protect the Canadian Arctic, an area of Precambrian earth covered with 1,000-year-old Inuit settlements and ice.

The Canadian Rangers protect the Canadian Arctic, an old hunk of Precambrian earth, ice carpeted and spotted with Inuit settlements dating back 1,000 years.

The differences are subtle—but the second sentence (we think) asks you to think about the Canadian Arctic as a familiar, almost living, piece of the earth.

In what writing contexts would the second sentence be appropriate for shaping an audience's relations to the topic?

■ ■ ■

In the following pages we offer strategies to help you make your words as vivid and concrete as your purposes demand.

WHAT ARE YOUR MOST USED WORDS?

Go to www.wordle.net and follow the instructions to paste in an essay. You will see, in a pleasing way, the words you use most—which might show that you are emphasizing topics you don't mean to or are not offering readers enough variety.

The dictionary defines cancer as "A malignant growth of cells caused by their abnormal and uncontrolled division." Chances are, however, that you cannot read *cancer* without some fear; it's possible you read the word with memories of someone close to you who has had cancer.

The definition of *cancer* is what we call the **denotation** of the word. The denotation of any word is simply its analytic definition, what we can count on most anyone else knowing.

Connotation, on the other hand, is what individuals bring to a word because of their personal or cultural background. Connotation describes the ideas or mental pictures that come to people's minds— unbidden from their memories and experiences—when they hear a word.

As you choose words, consider what associations—the ideas and mental pictures—your readers are likely to have. Do you want your readers to have positive or negative associations?

Most importantly—and especially if you are writing for an audience you do not know very well—you want to avoid using words that will have associations opposite to those that will help you achieve your purposes.

FIND A READER
To be sure your word choices do not encourage readers to think of connotations that will undermine your purpose, have people from your audience read drafts of your writing.

What is on this page will help you style your writing for

✔ CLARITY

☐ CONCISION

☐ COHERENCE

☐ EMPHASIS

✔ ENGAGEMENT

STYLING WORDS
THE NAMES WE USE

DEFINITIONS AND
ASSOCIATIONS
WITH WORDS

What is on this page will help
you style your writing for

✓ CLARITY

☐ CONCISION

☐ COHERENCE

☐ EMPHASIS

✓ ENGAGEMENT

If the problem were called *Atmosphere cancer* or
Pollution death, the entire conversation would
be framed differently.

The writer of the above sentence is
discussing **global warming**, and argues that
we might, as individuals and as a culture, be
less sanguine about global warming if the
concept had been named more compellingly.

The words used to name a condition, a
syndrome, or a place carry considerable
weight through their connotations
(→ discussed on page 323). Consider how
the following terms ask readers to think
about the person or position named:

pro-choice	pro-abortion
right-wing	conservative
heterosexual	straight
gun rights	gun control
affirmative action	racial preferences
illegal alien	undocumented immigrant

Readers respond to the names you use based
on how they interpret the names. Someone in
favor of affirmative action, for example, will
likely be less amenable to writing that uses
racial preferences.

KNOW YOUR AUDIENCE
Ask people from your audience about any
terms you are considering so that you can
learn how they respond. This will help
you decide which terms help you make
the arguments you desire.

Jump. Giggle. Estimate. Play. Clarify. Balance. Sing. Compare. Interpret.

These are action verbs: They name actions readers can imagine themselves taking. (This is connotation at work again.) Because action verbs encourage readers to imagine doing what a sentence describes, action verbs help readers connect with writing.

Action verbs describe concrete actions and so clarify what is going on:

He is enjoying performing.

He revels in performing.

The second sentence uses an action verb instead of **is**. **Revels** carries associations of energetic delight, and so will likely convey that emotion to readers.

Here are other examples:

The wasp put her stinger through the roach's exoskeleton and directly into its brain.

The wasp slipped her stinger through the roach's exoskeleton and directly into its brain.

The second sentence helps a reader understand more precisely what the wasp did—and makes the wasp's action scarier and more compelling.

STYLING WORDS
ACTION VERBS

What is on this page will help you style your writing for

✔ CLARITY

☐ CONCISION

☐ COHERENCE

✔ EMPHASIS

✔ ENGAGEMENT

REPLACING "IS"

When you want your writing to connect with readers, underline every use of **is** (including its variations, such as **are** and **was** and **will be**) in your writing, and if you see more than a few, replace those words with action verbs.

STYLING WORDS
CONCRETE NOUNS

What is on this page will help you style your writing for

✓ CLARITY

　 CONCISION

　 COHERENCE

　 EMPHASIS

✓ ENGAGEMENT

When you hear the word **it**, what picture comes into your head? Any?

In the sentence *After he ordered his lunch he had to wait 30 minutes for it to be delivered,* **it** clearly refers to **his lunch**—and readers can make concrete connections with the word. But when you read the sentence below, what associations can you make with the **It** at the beginning?

It is wasteful of their energies if full-grown orangutans move randomly through trees looking for food.

It in the sentence above refers to nothing. Here is a revised sentence:

Full-grown orangutans can't afford to lumber along randomly through the trees, hoping to blunder upon food.

The replacement of **is wasteful** with **can't afford to** and the movement of **full-grown orangutans** to the front of the sentence make this sentence concretely descriptive and thus clearer and more engaging.

When you want readers to have concrete (and hence compelling) pictures in their heads about what you are writing, start your sentences with words that refer to specific people, animals, or objects.

REPLACING "IT IS"

Sometimes you need to use **it is** (or **there are**). But when you want your writing to connect with readers, underline every use of **is**, **it is**, and **there are**, and if you see more than a few, replace those phrases with concrete nouns and verbs.

Playing with fire. No place like home. Have a field day. From bad to worse. Bad hair day. Like a breath of fresh air.

Clichés are phrases that once stood out because they were—at one time—new and funny or compelling. Because they were new and stood out, however, people used them, and used them ... and used them until they stopped being new and compelling.

Because clichés have been used so much, they have become just part of language—and so they come to mind easily when you are writing. Readers will notice them, however, and because they've seen them before, the writing will seem tired and boring.

TO CATCH AND FIX CLICHÉS

To catch clichés, read your writing aloud; you can often hear clichés.

To fix clichés, be clear about your purpose: You need to explore wording that carries the meaning and emotion of your purpose. For example, instead of *His proposal was dead as a doornail*, you could write *His proposal received no response* or, more emotively, *Given how little attention others gave his proposal, he might as well never have spoken.*

CLICHÉS IN A NEW LANGUAGE

If you are not writing in your home language, clichés can be hard to hear because you are not familiar enough with them in the new language. Ask someone who grew up with your new language to read your writing and identify—and explain—clichés.

What is on this page will help you style your writing for

☑ CLARITY

☐ CONCISION

☐ COHERENCE

☑ EMPHASIS

☑ ENGAGEMENT

STYLING WORDS
JARGON

Jargon can describe the specialized language of an organization or a profession; it can also describe fancy-sounding words someone else uses that you don't understand. Jargon, then, is useful when you are writing to those inside your profession and need to be precise; it is bad to use outside the profession because readers can't follow your writing.

To a reader immersed in computer culture, this probably makes sense:

In architecting our software, build systems, and engineering processes, we have given considerable thought to how our code will be able to evolve alongside the Mozilla code, without forking it.

Most readers know **architect** and **fork** as nouns, not verbs, and probably do not know what a **build system** or **Mozilla** is. A general audience is more likely to understand:

In developing our software and engineering processes, we have considered how our code will be able to evolve alongside the existing code with which it must work—without making a mess.

What is on this page will help you style your writing for

✔ CLARITY

✔ CONCISION

☐ COHERENCE

☐ EMPHASIS

✔ ENGAGEMENT

TIP
KNOW YOUR AUDIENCE
If you are writing for people who share a vocabulary, use that vocabulary to be precise. If you do not know your audience, err on the side of caution: Use only words almost anyone would understand. Check this by having someone else read your writing.

As far as we can see, it is a fact that there are a whole lot of ways you can end up with way too many words in your sentences and, as a result of the too many words, make your readers bored or make it too hard for them to figure out your purpose.

When we see sentences like the above, it is usually a sign that the writer isn't sure what to say and is fumbling for a way to say it; sometimes people write like that when they aren't confident.

The sentence above is characterized by both empty words (words that add nothing to the purpose of the sentence) and redundant words (words that repeat uselessly what has already been said).

If we modify the sentence, we can end up with this, which is more concise and hence clearer for readers:

You can easily have too many words in a sentence, boring your readers and blocking their understanding.

To compose focused sentences, ask yourself, *What is it exactly that I want readers to take from this sentence?*

What is on this page will help you style your writing for

✓ CLARITY

✓ CONCISION

◻ COHERENCE

◻ EMPHASIS

✓ ENGAGEMENT

REREAD

Put your writing aside for a while, and then reread it: Looking at your writing anew will help you see where you have used more words than you need. You can also ask others to read it, to help you find the sentences that need tightening to clarify your points.

USING INCLUSIVE LANGUAGE

> My name is Jane Takagi-Little. Little was my dad, a Little from Quam, Minnesota. Takagi is my mother's name. She's Japanese. Hyphenation may be a modern response to patriarchal naming practices in some cases, but not in mine. My hyphen is a thrust of pure superstition. At my christening, Ma was stricken by a profound Oriental dread at the thought of her child bearing an insignificant surname like Little through life, so at the very last minute she insisted on attaching hers. Takagi is a big name, literally, comprising the Chinese character for "tall" and the character for "tree." Ma thought the stature and eminence of her lofty ancestors would help equalize Dad's Little. They were always fighting about stuff like this.
>
> "It doesn't mean anything," Dad would say. "It's just a name!," which would cause Ma to recoil in horror. "How can you say 'justa name'? Name is very first thing. Name is face to all the world."

This passage from Ruth L. Ozeki's novel *My Year of Meats* describes how the main character comes to be named and, in so doing, describes how we use words to shape our relations with those who have grown up in cultures different from ours. Jane's mother is alert to the social weight of words, of how the words we use to describe ourselves—and others—shape how we are seen and treated by others. She insists that her daughter carry a name that gives her importance and so respect in others' eyes.

This matter of how we are named comes up elsewhere in Ozeki's novel, as in the following exchange:

> Then, at the pancake breakfast where we had been filming, a red-faced veteran from WWII drew a bead on me and my crew, standing in line by the warming trays, our plates stacked high with flapjacks and American bacon.
>
> "Where are you from, anyway?" he asked, squinting his bitter blue eyes at me.
>
> "New York," I answered.
>
> He shook his head and glared and wiggled a crooked finger inches from my face. "No, I mean where were you *born?*"
>
> "Quam, Minnesota," I said.
>
> "No, no ... *What* are you?" He whined with frustration.
>
> And in a voice that was low, but shivering with demented pride, I told him, *"I ... am ... a [!@*!] ... AMERICAN!"*

Neither the questioning man nor Jane comes across well: they are each insistent, unwilling to back off. Precisely because our identities—the words we use to describe who we are—carry so much weight, this scene matters.

But Jane's position is the one with which Ozeki asks us to sympathize in the end, because Jane, in spite of her expletives, is defending herself. The man wants to judge her based only on how she looks.

Jane insists on naming herself, on choosing to be seen through a word that belies the assumptions the man holds.

Who does not want the right to be known by a name that speaks truthfully to and respectfully of one's background and experiences?

■ ■ ■

We need to grant each other the right to choose the names by which we are called and understood by others.

When others write or talk about us using names we believe do not reflect our backgrounds or experiences accurately or respectfully—or when they write or talk about us in ways we believe to be disrespectful—they show us either that they have made mistakes about us or that they do not see us as worthy of the same respect that they themselves expect.

When we write about others, it would seem only right that we grant to them the same respect we want. If your readers feel excluded because of your word choices, because of how you refer to them, then they will either stop reading or they will read your words with hostile, sad, or distanced attitudes.

Writing that connects with readers connects because readers feel respected by it. When you write, it is not about you. It is about your readers and about giving them the same respect and courtesy you deserve.

HOW DO YOU SHOW RESPECT TO YOUR READERS?

Here are general guidelines:

- **Ethnicity, gender, sexual orientation, age, religion, and mental and bodily ability are sensitive characteristics in our time. Anytime in your writing you refer to one of these areas, check that your word choice is both necessary and respectful of those to whom you are referring.** Educate yourself about why these issues are sensitive, because knowing the reasons behind these issues will help you make good decisions about how to write.

  How we refer to each other will shape how we think of and treat each other. How are the following sentences likely to affect a reader's attitude toward the people being described?

  Given how she finished the race before so many others who had two real legs, you would almost think she was a real athlete.

  A pert woman in a short leather skirt, the prime minister spoke about the financial relations between our countries.

  He has two children and a daughter adopted from China.

  Equally important, how are readers likely to think about the person who wrote these sentences?

- **Have you referred to people by the names they have chosen for identification?** If you are writing a description of a person you have interviewed, for example, ask the person what terms to use. Avoid using names that people find offensive; again, ask if you are unsure or do not know.

  As political and social changes affect our lives, the names people prefer may change; you will have to ask or do research to stay current. Members of a group may disagree about their preferred name; you can acknowledge this in your writing.

- **Do you refer to a person's characteristics only if your purpose requires it?** Imagine that the following sentences began newspaper articles about speeches given on a college campus.

  The speaker, a cute blonde, talked at length about world hunger.

  The speaker, a feisty old guy, lectured on parenting mishaps.

  From his wheelchair, the speaker argued against current tax policies.

  Do the descriptions in the sentences help you learn about the content of the speeches? Do they have anything to do with the speeches?

  The descriptions turn our attention away from the speeches and from the hard work done by the speakers, instead asking us to focus on qualities of the speakers that are incidental to their abilities as serious speakers.

- **Have you made assumptions about the lives of others based on your own experiences?** Only one team wins in a big sporting event, but different people experience that win differently: One set of fans will be jubilant and one will be frustrated. It is the same with elections, judicial cases, and world happenings: While everyone might agree on the facts of the outcome, different people, because of their different backgrounds, will respond differently.

This is also true of reading. You might read one set of words and think they are just fine, but the person across the table from you might be annoyed, hurt, or angered by the same words.

If you have a lot in common with others, you can make some predictions about their responses to different events, but in all cases, if you find yourself writing statements like these—

Who could possibly believe that?

All reasonable people will take this action.

Only an uninformed person could respond in this way.

—then you are making assumptions based on your own particular experiences and beliefs. You should not be surprised when some or many readers are turned off by how you characterize those who have different beliefs than you.

- **Have you avoided stereotyping?** Stereotyping happens when you focus on only one of a person's characteristics, with that characteristic being a negative or limited belief about a group.

Just like a man!

He's acting like an old lady!

What else could you expect from a teenage girl?

- **Have you expected one person's experience to represent everyone's?** To expect one woman to be an expert about the lives of all other women can result in creating stereotypes—just as it is to expect one African American man to speak for all African Americans or all men, one teenager who is a lesbian to speak for all teenagers or all lesbians, or one Christian to speak for all Christians.

FOLLOWING THESE SUGGESTIONS WON'T FIX EVERYTHING

The word choice issues we discuss here matter—but keep in mind that they interact with your writing's tone, attitude, and the other positions you consider to give readers an overall sense of your fairness and integrity.

USING INCLUSIVE LANGUAGE
INCLUDING ALL ETHNICITIES

"ETHNICITY" OR "RACE"?

Scientists argue that *race*—as a genetic basis for categorizing humans—does not exist. We have defined race based on physical appearances, but science shows that similar appearance does not necessarily mean common heritage. Because there is controversy over *race*, and because *race* focuses our attention on physical characteristics, it is more respectful—when we must refer to others through such lenses—to use the term *ethnicity*. *Ethnicity* refers to a people's common ancestry, language, or religion.

CHECKING YOUR WRITING

- **Have you referred to a person's ethnicity or national origin only when it is relevant to your argument?**

- **Have you used names that people from an ethnicity prefer for themselves?** As political and social changes affect people of different ethnicities, their preferred names can change; you will have to ask or do research to find preferred names. Members of a group may disagree about their preferred name for different reasons; you can acknowledge this in your writing.

- **Have you been as specific as you can in naming an ethnic group?** The more specific you can be, the less likely you are to slip into stereotyping. For example, use *Ojibwa* or *Cherokee* instead of *American Indian;* use *Bahraini* or *Saudi* instead of *Arab*.

- **Have you capitalized the names of ethnicities?** For example, write *Polish American* or *Filipino American*.

- **Have you NOT used hyphens in multiword names?** Write *Japanese American*, not *Japanese-American:* The hyphen implies dual citizenship (which may not be the case) and that one is not completely American.

- **Have you assumed that your readers share the same ethnicity or experiences as you?** Take care not to assume your readers hold your beliefs. This can be hard since much of what we believe, think, and feel is implicit; when in doubt, ask someone not of your ethnicity and who has grown up differently from you to read your writing.

- **Have you avoided phrases that use ethnically tied terms?** You may have grown up with phrases that seem to you just part of language, such as *Latin lover* or *Jewish mother*—but these terms stereotype.

- **Have you checked that any adjectives you put before the name of an ethnic group are appropriate?** To write that someone is (for example) *a quiet American* can imply that all Americans are loud.

CONSIDERING "RACE"

For centuries *race* has been used to justify unequal treatment of different peoples. We need to keep this historical fact in mind because, sadly, it still shapes people's relationships and livelihoods. Therefore, unless you write about *race* as a topic, use *ethnicity* to encourage your readers to enact more thoughtful relationships.

USING INCLUSIVE LANGUAGE
INCLUDING ALL GENDERS

SEXISM

Language is sexist when it implies that women are not only different from men but also somehow inferior.

CHECK YOUR WRITING

- **If you have described someone's gender—or used terms that are culturally gender-related—ask if the description is necessary.** Check by rewriting the sentence, changing the gender. For example, if you have written, *The musician, a pretty redheaded girl, played the piece effortlessly* but would not write, *The musician, a pretty redheaded boy, played the piece effortlessly,* then change the sentence to *The musician played the piece effortlessly.*

- **Have you used unequal terms to refer to men and women in equal positions?** If you write about the presidents of two countries, do not write *Mrs. Rousseff and President Obama*; write *Presidents Rousseff and Obama.* If you write *the girls' team*, refer to the boys' team as *the boys' team*; to call one *the team* and the other *the girls' team* implies that the first is the standard, the second a deviation.

- **Have you used any words that stereotype behavior according to gender?** If you are describing a group made up only of women or only of men, check that your sentences do not use words that belittle some members. You can check this by rewriting the sentence for the other gender. For example, if you've written, *The women were gossiping about the senatorial candidate,* see if *The men were gossiping about the senatorial candidate* sounds right. If it does not, then change the original sentence to *The women were discussing the senatorial candidate.*

- **Have you used *man, men, he,* or *him* to refer to a group that might include women?** Some claim these words include both men and women, but consider:

  On this form, everyone should add the name of his husband or wife.

  When pregnant, men need more sleep.

  Because *man, men, he,* and *him* are not inclusive, revise any such uses so that your words don't exclude women.

  To revise: Substitute gender-neutral nouns for *man* or *men*: For example, instead of *chairman*, use *chairperson.* Make a sentence plural so that you can use the gender-neutral *they* and *them*: *Everyone should bring his own umbrella* can become *All visitors should bring their own umbrellas.*

- **Have you avoided stereotyped uses of occupations?** *Each computer programmer has his own style of coding* and *A teacher can have a tremendous impact on her students* imply that these occupations are for one gender only. Plural sentences avoid stereotypes: *All computer programmers have their particular styles of coding* and *Teachers can have a tremendous impact on their students.*

- **Have you used salutations that include all members of an audience?** Do not start correspondence with *Dear Sirs* if you do not know your audience; you can start with *To whom it may concern* or *Dear Colleagues.*

INCLUDING ALL ABILITIES

> It is recommended that the word *disability* be used to refer to an attribute of a person, and handicap to the source of limitations. Sometimes a disability itself may handicap a person, as when a person with one arm is handicapped in playing the violin.
>
> However, when the limitation is environmental, as in the case of attitudinal, legal, and architectural barriers, the disability is not handicapping—the environmental factor is. . . . Thus, prejudice handicaps people by denying access to opportunities; inaccessible buildings surrounded by steps and curbs handicap people who require the use of a ramp.

ABLEISM

The American Psychological Association's language use guidelines, extracted above, acknowledge what people with disabilities have been working to counteract: People with disabilities are often seen as defined by their disabilities. For example, *a crippled woman* or a *wheelchair-bound teenager* focus our attentions not on people, their intelligence, and their abilities, but rather on their disability—a form of prejudice called **ableism**.

CHECK YOUR WRITING

- **Have you emphasized the person, not the disability?** This practice, known as *person-first language*, is called for by the 1990 Americans with Disabilities Act (ADA). This practice encourages language use that treats all people as having a complex and wide range of strengths, abilities, and skills. To practice person-first language, describe the person before you describe the disability. For example, write, *person who has AIDS* rather than *AIDS sufferer,* or *child who uses a wheelchair* rather than *wheelchair-bound child.* Also, use adjectives rather than nouns to describe someone with a disability. To call someone *a mute,* *a cripple,* or *an epileptic* is to imply that the person is completely swallowed up by the disability; to say, instead, *a child who cannot speak, a doctor with an amputation,* or a *musician who has epilepsy* lets the person—who has many other characteristics besides the disability—come forward.

- **When you refer to someone's disability in your writing, is it necessary to your purpose?** As with sexist and ageist writing, try rewriting the passage in question without the reference; if your purpose is still clear, then omit the reference.

- **Have you avoided asking your readers to think of the person as deserving only of sympathy?** If you use emotional words to describe someone with a disability (*the poor child with the limp* or *the helpless quadriplegic*), you are asking readers to see the person as incapable of doing anything but passively accepting our concern.

- **Have you used *disability* and *handicap* according to accepted uses?** The quotation at the top of this page describes how to use these terms.

- **Does your writing emphasize that people with disabilities contribute widely and in multiple ways to their communities?**

USING INCLUSIVE LANGUAGE
INCLUDING ALL AGES

AGEISM

In some cultures, gray hair and wrinkles are respected signs of the knowledge and understanding that can come with years. In the United States, however, most people want to stay young, and one result is that older people can be stereotyped as frail, rigid, reactionary, and incompetent—or as soft, kindly, and powerless. Meanwhile, young people are often stereotyped as reckless, selfish and self-absorbed, unambitious, sex-crazed, and lazy.

If you think about all the people you know who are younger than you and all the people who are older than you, however, your experiences ought to give you many counter-examples to these stereotypes. **Ageism**, the stereotyping of people because of their age, is therefore—like racism and sexism—a form of prejudice because it shapes our understanding of others in negative, limiting, and rarely true ways.

CHECKING YOUR WRITING

- **Have you referred to the age of a person only when your purpose requires it?** To check the necessity of referring to age in your writing, try taking it out; if your readers can still understand your purpose, then remove the reference. If, for example, in an article about poker you have written, *Ms. Jucovy, who is 63, won the final pot,* change the sentence to *Ms. Jucovy won the final pot* and ask others to read the article. If they still understand your article, then stay with the second version.

- **Have you used ageist terms to describe others?** Terms to avoid for people who are older include the following: *geriatrics, over the hill, ancient, old-timers, matronly, well preserved.* Terms to avoid for young people include the following: *punk, gangbanger, thug.*

- **Don't refer to older people as "our seniors" or "our elders."** The use of *our* implies that the group of people being discussed is the writer's property or possession instead of individual humans.

- **Have you used terms that patronize people because of their age?** Treat older—and younger—people with the same respect, using the same titles. The standard in Anglo culture in the United States, then, is not to call an old man *Grandpa* (unless he really is your grandfather) or to refer to an older woman as *Honey, Dear,* or *Auntie:* These terms imply a level of familiarity you wouldn't assume with people of other ages.

- **Have you referred to older people as the vital, interesting, productive people they are?** People who are retired do not share any common characteristic other than retirement: Some retire in their forties, and others retire in their seventies; some retire from one career to take up another while others take on active volunteer work. The more you learn about what a range of older people does, the more you are likely to write respectfully, fairly, and accurately about them.

USING INCLUSIVE LANGUAGE
INCLUDING ALL SEXUAL ORIENTATIONS

HETEROSEXISM

To write as though all readers have the same sexual orientation is to risk losing their attention and respect just as much as writing as though all readers are male, European American, or of one age risks losing their attention and respect.

CHECK YOUR WRITING

- **When you refer to someone's sexual orientation in your writing, is it necessary to your purpose?** If you would not write, *The heterosexual engineer was fluent with both the aesthetic and the technical aspects of design,* then do not write, *The gay engineer was fluent with both the aesthetic and the technical aspects of design.* As we have recommended on previous pages, if you are unsure about the appropriateness of including references to sexual orientation in your writing, remove the references. If readers still understand your purpose, then you can omit the references.

- **Have you used *sexual orientation* rather than *sexual preference*?** To write *sexual preference* is to imply that sexuality is the result of conscious choice, a view that neither scientific research nor the reported experiences of lesbians, gays, or heterosexuals support.

- **Have you avoided assuming heterosexuality?** The sentence *All employees are encouraged to bring their wives to our yearly events* is a problem because it assumes all employees are married heterosexual males. In contrast, *All employees are encouraged to bring their partners or significant others to our yearly events* includes employees of all genders and sexual orientations as well as those who are not married.

- **Have you used terms that those you are describing themselves prefer?** Currently, *gay* is the preferred term for homosexual men and *lesbian* is the preferred term for homosexual women; people whose sexual orientation includes both men and women prefer *bisexual. Transgendered* is preferred for those whose sex is not congruent with their gender identity.

  Homosexual emphasizes sexuality over relationships and in the past has been associated with mental illness and criminality. It has also been used primarily to refer to male sexuality, and thus erases lesbians from the discussion. Many people thus avoid using *homosexual.*

  Keep in mind that, in the twenty-first century, *lesbian* and *gay* are primarily about communities of people rather than sexual activity. This is important because some people have sex with others of the same gender but do not consider themselves *lesbian* or *gay.*

  If you have any concerns about the terms you use, ask and do research. As with all your writing, ask a range of people to read what you write, to be sure no one feels pushed away by your word choices.

USING INCLUSIVE LANGUAGE
INCLUDING ALL RELIGIONS

EXCLUSIONARY LANGUAGE ABOUT RELIGION

While there is no name for language that promotes one religion over others, religion is just as sensitive in our time as any other aspects of people's identities. As with other aspects of identity, our beliefs about deities and religions matter deeply to each of us—and so, as on the preceding pages, the main guideline for writing when you want to build common ground is to respect others' beliefs as you would want yours respected.

CHECK YOUR WRITING

- **Have you referred to someone's religion only when it is central to your purpose?** Whenever you include a reference to someone's religion, try taking it out and having others read your writing. If your readers still understand your purpose, then leave the reference out. We recommend this not because we believe religion should be excluded from all writing but rather because, given the weight of religious beliefs in people's lives, particular care is warranted.

- **When you write about religion in general, have you used terms that reflect a range of religions?** For example, if you are writing about how varying communities construct special buildings for religious observances, you should not write *All over the world, people build churches;* instead, write *All over the world, people build mosques, temples, churches, and other buildings specially named to signify their importance.* Similarly, be alert to the names religions use for their members and leaders. *Rabbi, priest, reverend, imam,* and *bishop* are only some of the possibilities. Doing a little research helps you show respect.

- **Have you avoided assuming your readers hold the same religious beliefs as you?** Many who believe in a deity do not belong to an established church, and many do not believe in a deity; the names of deities in different religions are different. If you wish to reach a broad audience—locally or globally—be careful that any references you include about your own faith and religion do not imply that everyone else does or should believe as you do.

- **Have you used the terms the people you are describing use for their beliefs?** When you want your writing to be read by a wide audience, be careful about your use of terms like *cult* instead of *religion,* or *myth* instead of *religious belief.* If you need to describe religious practices and beliefs, do research. Have a range of others read your writing to be sure it is respectful.

- **Have you acknowledged the broad beliefs held by people in the same religion?** When you write about a religion, do not assume all its members hold the same beliefs. Catholics, for example, hold a range of views on abortion, the death penalty, birth control, and the status of women. The same is true of Muslims, Jews, Baptists, and the members of any other religion you can name, on any topic.

MULTIMODAL STYLE: VISUAL TEXTS

TYPOGRAPHY
SERIF AND SANS SERIF TYPEFACES

This distinction between kinds of typefaces helps you choose typefaces to fit your purposes.

serif   sans serif

Serif (the French word for *tail*) describes typefaces that have little swashes (circled above) added to the ends of letters. **Sans** is French for *without*; thus **sans serif** typefaces have no serifs.

Serifed typefaces generally look more classical or old-fashioned than sans serif typefaces. Audiences in the United States are accustomed to seeing serifed typefaces in long sections of text.

DECORATIVE TYPEFACES

Typefaces that look like this are called "**DECORATIVE.**" They are not easy to read in anything but short phrases, and so they are most often used for short pieces of text like titles and headers. OCCASIONALLY A PARTICULAR PURPOSE JUSTIFIES USING THEM FOR BLOCKS OF TEXT YOU WANT PEOPLE TO READ, BUT ONLY OCCASIONALLY.

SOME NOTES ON USING TYPEFACES

Since the invention of the printing press in the fifteenth century, conventions for type in different genres have developed.

- Academic and other texts that are meant to be serious or formal almost always use only one size of a single, serifed typeface. For example, teachers might expect you to use the typeface Times in 12-point type for papers; at most, then, you would use the plain, italic, and bold versions of Times.

  Occasionally, writers use a second typeface in such writings: A plain, sans serifed typeface such as Helvetica or Arial in its bold version, can provide sufficient contrast for headings, as described to the right.

- The most formal visual design in our time values simplicity and unity—hence, in such designs, composers rarely use more than two typefaces. Even in genres that have considerable wiggle room in choice of type—genres such as posters or brochures—designers most often use only two or three typefaces: one for the title or main head, another for the information or body text, and perhaps a third if there is another text function that needs to be differentiated visually.

HEADINGS

When you chunk a text by inserting headings, you allow readers to better see the text's sections. This can help readers both comprehend and remember your arguments.

- Headings should be short, taking up only one line if possible, so that readers see them at a glance.
- Headings should have space above them so that readers see a heading as part of the text below it.
- The typeface of a heading should be different (in size, thickness, or style) from the typeface used in the body of the text, again so that readers can see and read the heading easily.

To create a conservative look in a heading
Use a bold version of the same typeface you use for the body of text.

To create a more modern look in a heading
Use a sans serif typeface heading with a serifed typeface for the body of the text. Usually, you will have to use a bold version of the sans serif typeface to create an easy-to-see contrast between the heading and the body.

NOTE: Unless a heading is very short, use upper- and lowercase letters. Using only uppercase letters is hard to read for more than just a few words.

COLOR TERMINOLOGY

To use color in support of your purposes, you need to know why you are choosing one color over another—and to do that, you need to know color terminology.

HUE

Hue describes what many of us think of as color. When you name the hue of a color, you say whether it is red or blue or yellow or green or purple or …

Hue, saturation, and brightness are present in all colors. In the examples above, the leftmost color is red-hued, with as much saturation and brightness as possible. The middle color is not very bright, but is still a fairly saturated red hue. The color on the right has a hue of blue, is fairly bright, but is not very saturated.

COLOR CONNOTATIONS

Colors and color combinations have connotations just as words do (→ see page 323). For example, we often associate bright red, blue, and yellow with childhood, while combinations of highly saturated red and green or orange and blue will remind some of concert posters from the 1960s.

When you choose colors to use in composing, keep in mind that the connotations we have with certain colors will be affected by the shape of the color and what is around it. For example, blue can suggest cold when used with **ice** or **winter**, but warmth and relaxation when used with **Caribbean summer afternoon**.

BRIGHTNESS

Brightness (sometimes also referred to as **value**) describes how light or dark a color is. In the bar above, the color at the extreme left has no brightness; the color at the extreme right is as bright as it can be.

SATURATION

Saturation describes how much of a hue is present in a color. In the bar above, the color at the far left is unsaturated; it has no blue in it. As you move to the right, the color becomes more saturated: It has more blue.

USING COLOR

CHOOSING HARMONIOUS COLORS

- Choose colors close to each other on the color wheel:

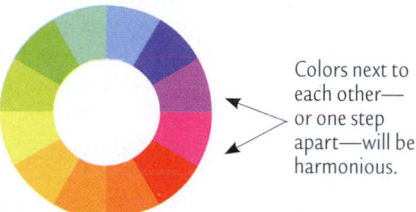

Colors next to each other— or one step apart—will be harmonious.

- Choose one color that supports your purpose, and then increase or decrease its saturation or brightness to create a set of harmonious colors to use:

- Choose a range of different hues, but give each the same brightness and saturation:

COLOR AND TYPE

Type is easiest to read when its color contrasts with the color behind it. The contrast between the colors can be a contrast in hue, saturation, or brightness.

STRONG CONTRAST
WEAK CONTRAST

STRONG CONTRAST
WEAK CONTRAST

STRONG CONTRAST
WEAK CONTRAST

STRONG CONTRAST
WEAK CONTRAST

Sometimes, however, you can create a very strong contrast in hue, but if the colors are very saturated and very bright, they can hurt our eyes rather than be easy to read:

STRONG CONTRAST
BUT HARD TO READ.

STRONG CONTRAST
BUT HARD TO READ.

MULTIMODAL STYLE:

ORAL PRESENTATIONS

In oral presentations, the main component of style is you. Your voice and gestures are your main strategies for creating emphasis and engagement.

CONNECTING WITH AN AUDIENCE

Public speaking might make you anxious. In addition to remembering to breathe deeply before and during a talk, making eye contact with people in your audience and even addressing them directly can help you relax. These actions are also style decisions.

As you prepare, decide how to connect with your audience. Few presentation contexts and purposes require formality. Rather, in almost all circumstances, you can engage your audience—and thus encourage their generosity toward your arguments—by asking them questions, speaking directly to them while looking into their faces, or smiling.

SPEAKING STYLES

Your voice—its volume, speed, and tone—gives you a wonderful range of style choices. To take advantage of your voice, have your presentation organized in time so you can practice. Seek a conversational style and avoid reading.

Identify the words or sentences you wish to emphasize. Then experiment with different ways of saying them: Exaggerate volume and tone, playfully, and make yourself laugh. This helps you relax—but also helps you find what works best for the real presentation.

BODY LANGUAGE

For most presentations, you need to use your body language—expressions and gestures—to put your audience at ease and to emphasize your major points.

Look over what you have written for your presentation, and decide what facial expressions (and where) support your arguments. In years past, audiences expected almost theatrical gestures and expressions; now, simple smiles, frowns, nods, or occasional head shakes are enough.

Similarly, current audiences do not expect grand hand gestures. You will make audiences uncomfortable if you nervously wring your hands, but you can instead keep your hands clasped in front of or behind you, placed on the lectern, or holding your notes.

Do check over your words, seeing where a gesture will emphasize what needs emphasizing. And then practice.

Practicing your presentation over and over will help your your body language become relaxed and friendly.

PARALLELISM IN ORAL PRESENTATIONS

Apply to your presentation the same guidelines for building parallelism in sentences that we described on pages 318–319. Paragraphs that use parallelism create rhythmic and emotionally compelling paragraphs, as in this Convocation Address by Nikki Giovanni:

We are Virginia Tech.

The Hokie Nation embraces our own and reaches out with open hearts and hands to those who offer their hearts and minds. We are strong, and brave, and innocent, and unafraid. We are better than we think and not quite what we want to be. We are alive to the imaginations and the possibilities. We will continue to invent the future through our blood and tears and through all our sadness.

We are the Hokies.

We will prevail.

We will prevail.

We will prevail.

We are Virginia Tech.

USING VISUAL SUPPORTS

Visual supports can be slide presentations (using software like PowerPoint or Keynote), overheads, handouts, or physical objects.

Use visual supports to help your audience see your presentation's main points.

Use objects that help you demonstrate procedures you discuss or that illustrate your main points: A stretched-out plastic bag holding the amount of trash an average American throws out in one day will make a point about resource use much more strongly than a spoken statistic.

Whatever your visual aids, practice with them. You need to be able to use them comfortably so that your audience focuses on your points rather than on you trying to use a projector. Also, using visual aids slows down a presentation; if you have a time limit, practicing with your visuals helps you stay within it.

→ See pages 346–347 to learn about designing slides to support oral presentations.

MULTIMODAL STYLE: ORAL PRESENTATIONS
SLIDES TO SUPPORT ORAL PRESENTATIONS

The title to the left gives the most important advice for designing slides: Slides should rhetorically *support* the arguments you make. Slides should not stand alone but should only come to life with your words and explanations.

Go easy on bullet points. If you must use them, keep them short and do not use more than 3–4. Go easy on text, in general. (Remember point 2 on the facing page.)

Choose typefaces that are easy to read— and make your type a size readable at the distance your audience will sit. Make sure that the type color contrasts crisply with the slide background so that the type will be readable to your audience. Test your slides ahead of time by projecting them and trying to read them from your audience's distance.

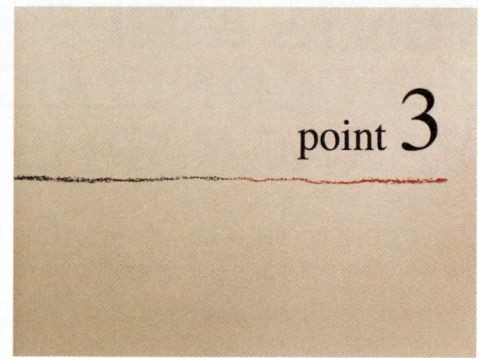

Only put on a slide the absolute minimum for making your point. You want the slide to be memorable for your audience—and so you do not need to decorate the slide (although a relevant graphic can help explain or make information memorable). If your slides are full of stuff, audiences will read them, not listen to you.

Choose (or make) and stay with a slide template that works with your purposes. Unless incoherence suits your purposes, using the same theme throughout gives your presentation coherence.

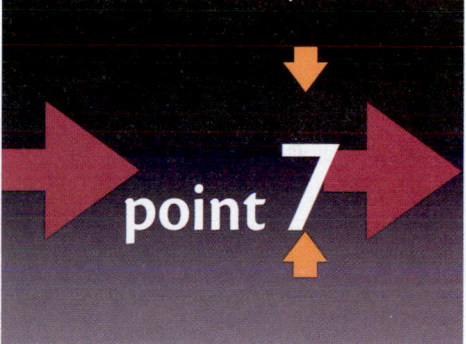

Photographs that are large and uncluttered generally are the most easy for audiences to understand—and all photographs should relate to your purposes.

Slide transitions are fun—but can make audiences dizzy. Transitions *between* slides should support your argument's movement: For example, does your argument seem to move up, or down, or sideways? Transitions *on* a slide (as bullet points come on, for example) should also tie to your purposes.

HINTS & TIPS FOR CONCLUDING PARAGRAPHS

USING CONCLUDING PARAGRAPHS TO HELP YOU REVISE

For many writers, a first draft's conclusion often provides crucial information:

- Often, a conclusion is when you realize what your argument really is. Experienced writers know that a first draft is only a beginning and that often they don't know what they really want to argue until they write the last paragraph. Sometimes writers use the concluding paragraph of a first draft—because it is often a succinct and passionate statement of an argument—as the first paragraph of the next draft.

- If you do feel that the concluding paragraph is an accurate and strong statement of your argument, go back through the rest of the paper to ask yourself: Do all the other paragraphs lead up to and support the conclusion?

- Because most writers intuitively know that concluding paragraphs should include a little passion, they include passion—but often there is no passion in the rest of the writing, making the conclusion seem abruptly out of place. When you finish a conclusion, check that its emotional tone is supported by the rest of the writing, just as you check to make sure its logical claims are likewise supported.

- Use the concluding paragraph to help make your introductory paragraph as strong and engaging as possible. Knowing the end point where you want to take readers, what might be the most effective starting point?

- Once you have a strong conclusion that satisfies you, revise your introduction—as well as the body of your paper—to use some of the same words and phrases as your conclusion: This will help give your whole paper pleasing coherence for your readers.

PART 9
MLA DOCUMENTATION

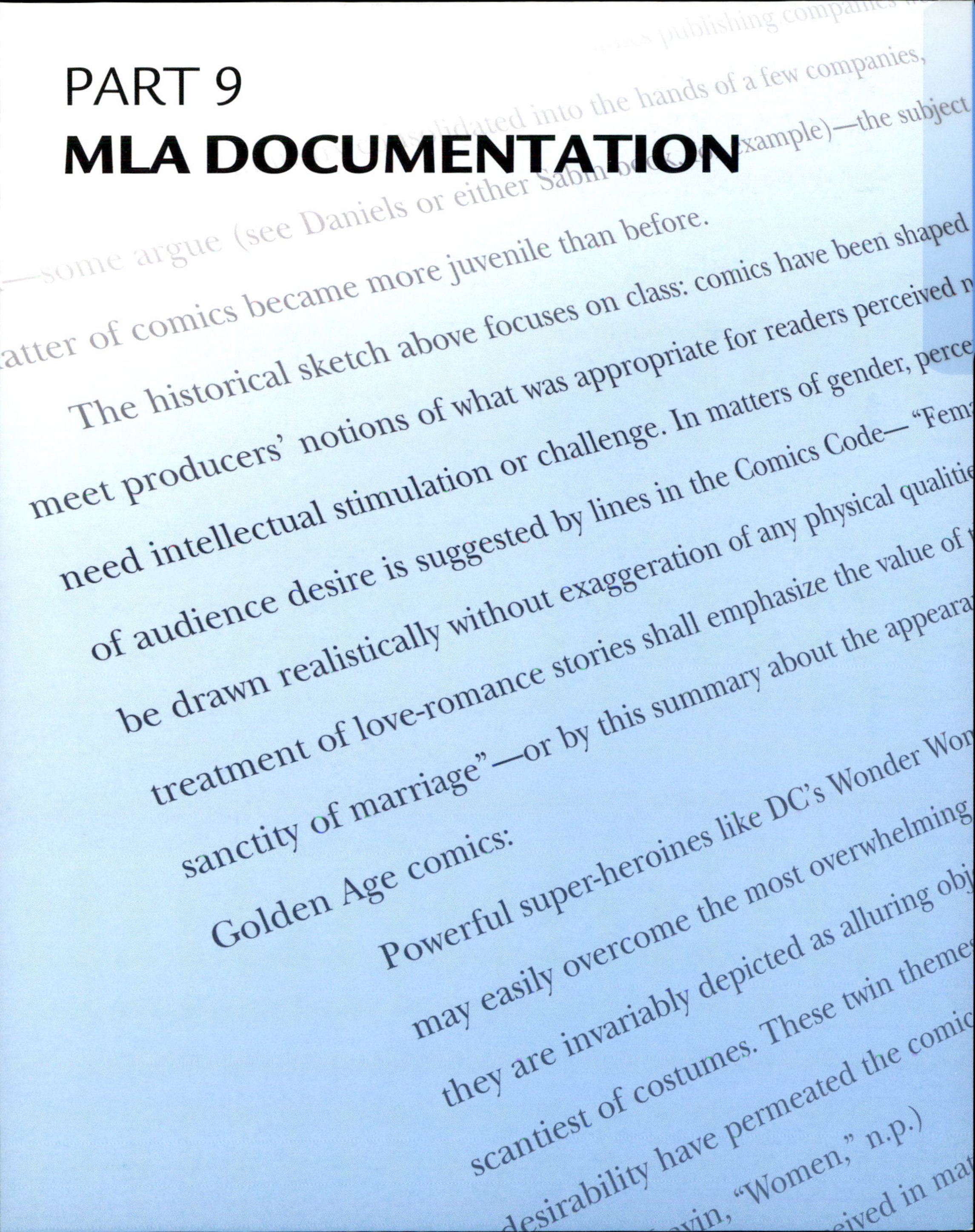

—some argue (see Daniels or either Sabin, for example)—the subject matter of comics became more juvenile than before.

The historical sketch above focuses on class: comics have been shaped to meet producers' notions of what was appropriate for readers perceived not to need intellectual stimulation or challenge. In matters of gender, perceptions of audience desire is suggested by lines in the Comics Code— "Females shall be drawn realistically without exaggeration of any physical qualities" and "The treatment of love-romance stories shall emphasize the value of the home and the sanctity of marriage" —or by this summary about the appearance of women in Golden Age comics:

Powerful super-heroines like DC's Wonder Woman may easily overcome the most overwhelming odds, but they are invariably depicted as alluring objects clad in the scantiest of costumes. These twin themes of power and desirability have permeated the comic ... ("Women," n.p.)

CONTENTS

WHERE ARE WE IN A PROCESS FOR COMPOSING?

Understanding your project

Getting started

Asking questions

Shaping your project for others

Drafting a paper

Getting feedback

Revising

Polishing

Ensuring that you have used your sources with integrity: Using MLA style to cite sources conventionally and build bibliographies

Questions you might have about documenting sources:

What are the steps for documenting sources?

➔ See pages 100–101 as well as (for MLA style) pages 352–353.

How do I formally format a paper?

➔ For MLA style, see pages 354–363.
➔ For APA style, see pages 394–398.

How do I format the page where I list all the sources I used?

➔ For MLA style, see pages 362–363.
➔ For APA style, see page 398.

What are in-text citations?

➔ For MLA style, see pages 364–367.
➔ For APA style, see pages 399–401.

What are the patterns for creating the citations I put on my works-cited or references page?

➔ For MLA style, see pages 370–377.
➔ For APA style, see pages 404–407.

How do I cite sources I find online?

➔ For MLA style, see pages 372–375, 383, and 388–389.
➔ For APA style, see pages 416–417.

THE WPA OUTCOMES* FOR PART 9 INCLUDE:

Using conventions: Practicing using citation conventions in your own work.

*See page 15.

MLA DOCUMENTATION

GUIDE TO MLA DOCUMENTATION MODELS

CAN'T FIND THE EXACT CITATION EXAMPLE YOU NEED?

→ Construct your citation following the patterns on pages 372–374—but also read page 376.

MLA

MLA: STEPS FOR DOCUMENTING SOURCES

On pages 100–101 we offered all the steps below for working with sources:

1 **EVALUATING SOURCES** → See pages 102–115.

2 **COLLECTING CITATION INFORMATION** → See pages 124–139.

3 **ANALYZING OTHERS' ARGUMENTS** → See pages 148–187.

4 **WORKING WITH OTHERS' IDEAS** → See pages 188–203.

In Part 9, we focus on steps 5 and 6.

5

WHEN WRITING A DRAFT OR FINAL PAPER
CREATING IN-TEXT CITATIONS FOR YOUR SOURCES

When you write, any time you summarize, paraphrase, quote, or otherwise reference a source, you need to provide certain information within the writing to help readers find the source in the works cited listing, as below.

→ See pages 364–367.

Williams 2

civility similarly, with slightly different details. For example, philosopher Chesire Calhoun writes that the "civil citizen exercises tolerance in the face of deep disagreement about the good. She respects the rights of others, refrains from violence, intimidation, harassment and coercion, does not show contempt for others' life plans, and has a healthy respect for others' privacy" (256). What all the definitions I read share is the importance of listening to others with respect, which means acting toward others' words and ideas as though you trust others to have good reasons for their beliefs and opinions.

Why does such civility—showing such respect to others in discussions about difficult topics—matter in a democracy?

Historically, democracies shifted political to citizens. Although the United States is a repr democracy (where we would all vote on every rather than electing legislators to represent us), to political deliberations. We need to be inform where we stand on certain issues and why. Acc journal Theory and Society) on different kinds "ultimate goal is a public sphere in which bette of the strength of these ideas rather than the str 301). Manuel Gómez, the former Vice Chancel of California–Irvine, writes that our First Amer protected for us—is based on "the concept of A ideas,' in which ideas compete for acceptance"

IN-TEXT CITATION
the quoted person's name
the page number of the quoted piece

RELATED WORKS CITED LISTING

Williams 5

Works Cited

Balcetis, Emily and David Dunning. "See What You Want to See: Motivational Influences on Visual Perception." *Journal of Personality and Social Psychology*, vol. 91, no. 4, 2006. *PsycARTICLES*, doi: 10.1037/0022-3514.91.4.612.

Calhoun, Cheshire. "The Virtue of Civility." *Philosophy and Public Affairs*, vol. 29, no. 3, 2000, pp. 251-75. *JSTOR*, doi: 10.1111/j.1088-4963.2000.00251.x.

Davetian, Benet. *Civility: A Cultural History*. Toronto UP, 2009.

Edwards, Kari and Edward E. Smith. "A Disconfirmation Bias in the Evaluation of Arguments." *Journal of Personality and Social Psychology*, vol. 71, no. 1, 1996, pp. 5-24. *Westlaw*, doi: dx.doi.org.ezproxy.lib.uwm.edu/10.1037/0022-3514.71.1.5.

Ferree, Myra, et al. "Four Models of the Public Sphere in Modern Democracies." *Theory

6

WHEN WRITING A DRAFT OR FINAL PAPER
CREATING AN MLA WORKS-CITED LIST

Such a list starts on its own page at the end of an MLA-style paper. To compose such a list:

first
COLLECT THE INFORMATION YOU NEED FOR EACH OF YOUR SOURCES.

To know what information to collect, you need to know whether your source is a stand-alone source, is a source inside a container—or is a source inside a container inside a container.

→ See pages 370–371 about stand-alone sources and containers.

→ See pages 124–139 for the information to collect for your source.

second
CONSTRUCT A CITATION FOR EACH SOURCE, FOLLOWING THE MLA PATTERN.

Follow the pattern to construct your listing element by element, starting with the author, moving on to the title, and so on, step by step, until you have a full citation.

→ The pattern is on pages 372–373.

→ The pattern for sources in containers inside other containers is on page 374.

third
CONSTRUCT YOUR WORKS CITED PAGE

When you have all your individual citations, put them together into the Works Cited page.

→ See pages 362–363 for how to format the Works Cited page.

A PAPER IN MLA FORMAT

The Modern Language Association (MLA) is an organization of scholars and teachers of languages and literature. The MLA publishes the *MLA Handbook for Writers of Research Papers,* which is now in its seventh edition and from which we take the formatting used here. The MLA style is used primarily in English studies, comparative literature, languages, literary criticism, and other humanities fields.

MLA FORMATTING

To format in MLA style, use the margins we show in blue to the right and:

- Double-space the paper throughout (To fit the sample paper on these pages, we could not use double spacing.).

- Put your last name at top right of every page, with the page number.

- Center the title above the paper's body on the first page.

- Use a readable typeface (like Times or Arial) in a readable size, such as 12 point.

- Look through the pages of Harley's paper to see how to format quotations and citations as well as how to create the final page of works cited.

How you can read this paper

Try reading this paper all the way through first, without reading any comments. Analyze the paper for yourself: *How persuasive do you find it? Which of Harley's main strategies (the order of her arguments, her questioning tone of voice, her use of evidence) are most—or least— persuasive for you? Why?*

How does the introduction work?

After you finish reading Harley's final draft, come back to this introduction: Has it encouraged the appropriate expectations for what is to come in this revision? How does this introduction compare to the introduction in Harley's first draft (→ see pages 276–283)? Why do you think she made the changes she did?

How do I make connections between ideas?

From responses to her first draft, Harley learned of the weakness of the connections she was trying to build between civility, democracy, and government repression. For this final draft she has completely revised how she has connected civility and democracy and has dropped talking about repression. Instead, she uses the history of civility to show its longstanding connections with democracy. How well does this work for you?

Harley Williams

Professor Komova

ENG102

15 Dec. 2016

Civility is Not Enough

My father can roast a chicken so perfectly it looks like a magazine ad. Every Sunday when he carries the chicken to the table I picture us in a dinner like those in the old happy family movies my granddad watches on TCM. But our dinners always turn out awful. Everyone ends up screaming at each other about healthcare or unions. I don't know why we keep doing this.

Are your family dinners like this, too?

For this paper I researched families and political arguments. I discovered that what happens at our table is a sign of something larger. Many families have trouble with controversial topics, but so do we as a country. From my research I learned that being able to talk about controversial topics—which requires being civil to each other—is necessary for having a democracy and its freedoms. I also learned from my research, however, that civility isn't enough.

In a book on the history of the idea of civility, sociology professor Benet Davetian writes that notions of civility were "born at a time when the Western world was overwhelmed by violence and in sore need of communal reconstruction and cooperative restraint" (8). Davetian writes about civility in its development as a concept in Europe starting approximately 800 years ago. He shows how the spread of civility helped individuals in societies move away from believing that violence should solve all problems; instead, the rise of belief in civility as a virtue parallels the rise of more democratic (and peaceful) forms of government.

Davetian defines "civility" as "the extent to which citizens of a given culture speak and act in ways that demonstrate a caring for the welfare of others as well as the welfare of the culture they share in common" (9). I found many other writers who defined civility similarly, with slightly different details. For example, philosopher Chesire Calhoun writes that the "civil citizen exercises tolerance in the face of deep disagreement about the good. She respects the rights of others, refrains from violence, intimidation, harassment and coercion, does not show contempt for others' life plans, and has a healthy respect for others'

Why define terms?

After introducing a short history of civility, Harley uses short quotations followed by a short summary to define *civility*. Compare this paragraph to how Harley defined *civility* in her first draft (→ see pages 276–283); in this final draft, does her approach to definition sound more coherent and confident to you than in the earlier draft? How does her definition of *civility* help her move her argument?

Why use a question as a transition?

This question keeps Harley's readers focused on her argument, prepares them for the next paragraph, and helps them keep in mind the connections between civility and democracy that Harley needs to make, given the feedback to her earlier draft (→ see pages 285, 287, and 293). How would the writing be different if she had phrased this as a statement rather than a question?

Using analogies as evidence?

In this paragraph, Harley uses two sources that use analogies: one describes democracy as a "marketplace of ideas," the other describes humans deliberating together as being like neurons in our brains. You might not have noticed these analogies as you read, but how do the analogies ask you to think of democracies and humans? What features of marketplaces and neurons are you expected to accept positively and without question? How do these analogies help Harley make her argument? (→ See pages 164–165 on analogies.)

How does explaining your points help readers?

Harley summarizes the preceding paragraph about what civility helps us accomplish. How might these last two sentences help readers follow the argument Harley builds?

privacy" (256). What all the definitions I read share is the importance of listening to others with respect, which means acting toward others' words and ideas as though you trust others to have good reasons for their beliefs and opinions.

Why does such civility—showing such respect to others in discussions about difficult topics—matter in a democracy?

Historically, democracies shifted political power away from kings and other royalty to citizens. Although the United States is a representative democracy and not a direct democracy (where we would all vote on every single issue that mattered to the country rather than electing legislators to represent us), our country still depends on us contributing to political deliberations. We need to be informed voters and to let our representatives know where we stand on certain issues and why. According to the writers of an article (in the journal Theory and Society) on different kinds of public spheres, for such democracies, the "ultimate goal is a public sphere in which better ideas prevail over weaker ones because of the strength of these ideas rather than the strength of their proponents" (Ferree et. al. 301). Manuel Gómez, the former Vice Chancellor for Student Affairs at the University of California–Irvine, writes that our First Amendment—in which freedom of speech is protected for us—is based on "the concept of American democracy as a 'marketplace of ideas,' in which ideas compete for acceptance"; it depends on "the virtues of competition between, and the open interrogation of, ideas" (13). Psychologist Jonathan Haidt uses an analogy to describe why this matters when he compares each of us to the kind of cell called a neuron: "A neuron by itself isn't very smart. But if you put neurons together in the right way you get a brain; you get an emergent system that is much smarter and more flexible than a single neuron." Together—building upon a wide range of perspectives—we come up with the best solutions. This means that everyone needs to be able to participate. By being civil, we not only encourage everyone to participate, we ensure that the widest range of ideas can be considered and used to make the best decisions.

Some of my sources pointed out that sometimes civility is inappropriate. Law professor Geoffrey R. Stone, for example, writes that

> incivility may be necessary to make a point effectively, to shake complacency, or to rouse "the people." A burning flag, a well-aimed insult, a scream of protest may be just what the doctor ordered to stir people to anger and awaken their consciences. As the Supreme Court has said, our nation has made a "profound commitment to the principle

1 ½"
for block
quotations

LEARN FROM ANOTHER'S PROCESS

The paper to the right is the final draft of Harley's paper, which we've shown developing throughout this book.

→ On page 30 in Part 2 you can see Harley's very first thoughts on this assignment.

→ Pages 45 and 95 in Part 3 show Harley's initial research.

→ In Part 4, you can see how Harley found, evaluated, and tracked sources in her initial work toward this paper.

→ In Part 5, we show Harley's annotated bibliography for two of her sources. We also show her putting two of her sources in dialogue with each other. If you look back at Harley's earlier writing, you can see how she used that writing in her papers.

→ In Part 6, you can see how Harley developed a thesis statement for organizing her paper. You can also see her statement of purpose that she developed through studying her audience.

→ Also in Part 7, pages 276–287 show Harley's first draft and the feedback from some of her readers. Look for differences between the two drafts to learn choices you can make to strengthen your writing.

→ On page 293 of Part 8, you can see Harley's revision plan for her first draft.

How to respond to objections?

In the sources she found after writing her first draft, Harley found new arguments about incivility, such as the one she quotes in this paragraph. Notice how Harley acknowledges this objection to her argument and takes it seriously—but also notice how she responds to it directly.

How do you use your own thinking to help readers?

In this sentence, Harley simply states what happened in her own thinking: As you can see in her writing where she put her sources in dialogue with each other (→ see pages 206–207), Harley was struck by how civility focused on others' ideas and left out considering one's own. By stating what happened in her own thinking, she helps readers follow why her writing moves from point to point. Watch for other spots in the writing where she describes her own thinking process.

Quotations—or summary, paraphrase, or your own explanations?

In her earlier draft (→ see pages 276–283), Harley had troubles because she strung together several long quotations instead of summarizing their points or making clear her position. In this paper, Harley uses two block quotations. Do you think Harley needs to use them? Do you think she has woven them well enough into her own arguments?

that debate on public issues should be uninhibited, robust, and wide-open, and that it

may well include vehement, caustic, and sometimes unpleasantly sharp attacks."

As Stone acknowledges, however, "a general presumption against incivility is sensible"

because incivility "can be counterproductive and seriously destructive of the larger values

of the community." So while incivility—not showing respect to others in discussion—is

sometimes warranted in extreme cases, it is civility that is warranted for family dinners and

probably most political discussions. As Chesire Calhoun (the philosopher I quoted earlier

when defining civility) writes,

> I am inclined to weigh civility heavily in the scales because I find something odd, and
>
> oddly troubling, about the great confidence one must have in one's own judgment (and
>
> lack of confidence in others') to be willing to be uncivil to others in the name of a
>
> higher moral calling. (275)

It is that question of one's attitude towards one's own ideas that leads me to question

whether civility alone is enough as we seek for us all to be able to discuss difficult topics

together.

If the goal of civility is to support democracy and help us come to understand the

broadest possible range of perspectives on difficult issues so that we can make the best

decisions together as a country, the definitions and descriptions above show that we need to

learn how to respect what other people believe, even if we disagree. From what I've seen at

our family dinner table—and in classrooms and on television and the Internet—this means

really listening, and nodding, rather than telling others they don't know what they're talking

about. But the words I quoted above from Calhoun about confidence make me turn to some

writing that came up almost by accident in my research, when I came across articles that

described a psychological concept that should help us consider how much confidence we

ought to have in our ideas when we talk with others. This concept is called "confirmation

bias" or "selective exposure."

"Confirmation bias" and "selective exposure" come from psychological research. They

name how people have a "tendency to seek out and interpret new evidence in ways that

confirm what [they] already think" (Haidt, ch. 4). In the article, "Preference-inconsistent

recommendations," Schwind, Buder, Cress, and Hesse discuss that people not only seek

evidence that confirms what they already believe but that they also resist information that

goes against what they already believe. A result is that "confirmation bias is detrimental to

unbiased opinion formation" (788). It sounds to me as though people who aren't alert to

REFLECTIVE WRITING

In class on the day Harley turned in this paper, her teacher asked everyone to write informally in response to these questions: *What made them proud of their papers? What helped them make the revisions they did? What will they do differently on a next paper—or what do they want to remember from this writing?* Here is Harley's writing:

I am happy with this paper! I learned a lot from sticking with the research and from giving myself time to think. I am proud of how I came up with a new idea when I put those two sources in dialogue with each other and then figured out how to write an argument that was all mine. I wasn't just repeating what I'd read.

Getting the feedback I did on my first draft about not really having an argument about civility and government repression is what I think made me work harder on this. I got stuck for a while when I thought I needed to write about incivility — then I saw how I could use Calhoun's argument about incivility and confidence to make a bridge to confirmation bias.

What do I want to remember for next time? How good it felt to have my own ideas! This is the first time I ever felt like I really made these ideas my own. I was nervous about putting so many things into my own words. But I did it. I think I made it work. Now I have a better sense of how to use sources to think (and even to revise).

Summarizing your own argument?

Compare these last two paragraphs to the last paragraph of Harley's original draft (→ see page 283). Harley no longer brings in new evidence but instead summarizes her argument and ends with a hopeful statement. (Notice how this draws on what she wrote in her statement of purpose.) How might her summary here help readers?

How to get to your claim?

Compare this paragraph to the last paragraph of Harley's original draft (→ see page 283). By revising her thesis statement and using it to organize her writing (→ see pages 222–225), Harley can now address her thesis statement's claim. How persuaded are you by this conclusion? What might you recommend to Harley to make it more persuasive?

consciously seeking a broad range of information will get caught in a vicious circle, only looking for and believing information that confirms what they already believe.

Writers claim that cognitive bias affects all that we believe, not just politics. For example, three researchers in behavioral and political sciences from Stony Brook University claim that "cognitive biases influence a wide range of health-related attitudes, from broad, national decisions about health reform to individual decisions about caffeine consumption and smoking" (Strickland, Taber, and Lodge 1). For these writers, the result is that "Although fair-mindedness and objectivity are desirable qualities of thought, particularly for weighty issues such as gun control, health care reform, and affirmative action, evidence has shown that human information processing often does not operate in that manner" (6). In a different article, two of the writers I just cited also note that "In the extreme, if one distorts new information so that it always supports [what one already believes], one cannot be rationally responsive to the environment; similarly, manipulating the information stream to avoid any threat to [what one already believes] is no more rational than the proverbial ostrich" (Tabor and Lodge 767). A quick library database search finds many similar articles describing experiments that demonstrate our confirmation bias and how this bias usually prevents us from truly having good reasons to believe what we do. (See, for example, Edwards and Smith; Balcetis & Dunning [who offer evidence that confirmation bias even affects what we are capable of seeing]; or Nickerson).

What "confirmation bias" and "selective exposure" show us is that none of us is perfect. Unless we have very careful and purposefully sought out the broadest possible information on any topic and paid it serious attention, our information will always be biased, narrow, and self-perpetuating.

For the sake of dinner table conversations—and for all other conversations that involve difficult topics—we do need to be civil. We do need to show others that we respect their opinions and beliefs, and we need to listen well. But if that is all we do then we can still believe that our own ideas are better than anyone else's and we won't achieve what civility is meant to achieve: better discussion about controversial matters. Bringing awareness of confirmation bias together with civility helps us be aware that our own ideas are rarely as well-informed as we think. If we are aware of that, then maybe we will listen more closely to others and really be able to figure out together how to solve our problems.

CITED PAGE IN MLA FORMAT

A WORKS-CITED PAGE IN MLA FORMAT

In a paper written in MLA style, the last page or pages will look like the page to the right.

NOTE!

Only include in your works-cited list the sources you cited in your paper. Do not include sources that you read but did not cite.

- ❑ Put the works-cited list after the last page of the paper.

- ❑ The works-cited list starts on its own page.

- ❑ Use the same margin measurements as the rest of the paper (→ see pages 355 and 357).

- ❑ Number each works-cited page at the top right of the page (as you do each page in MLA format; → see page 355). The number on the first page of the works-cited list follows the number of the last page of the paper. For example, if the last page of the paper is 8, the first page of the works-cited list will be 9.

- ❑ **Works Cited** is centered at the top of the page.

- ❑ The listings are arranged alphabetically by the author's last name. (If a listing starts with the title of a source, place it into the whole list alphabetically, using the first letter of the title. If the title begins with **A**, **An**, or **The**, alphabetize by the second word of the title.)

- ❑ If you list two or more sources by the same author, alphabetize them by the source titles. List the author only once; start all subsequent entries by the same author with three hyphens and a period.

- ❑ If you have two authors with the same last name, alphabetize by the first name.

- ❑ Double-space the entries.

- → Starting on page 368, we show how to make the individual listings that go on such a page.

Use hanging indentation

So that readers can scan the alphabetic list easily and quickly, MLA style asks that all lines under the first line of a citation entry be indented $1/2$-inch (or $1 1/2$-inch from the left margin).

What do you think of Harley's sources?

As you look through Harley's works-cited list, what thoughts do you have about the quality of her research and the sources she chose?

Works Cited

Balcetis, Emily and David Dunning. "See What You Want to See: Motivational Influences on Visual Perception." *Journal of Personality and Social Psychology,* vol. 91, no. 4, 2006. *PsycARTICLES*, doi: 10.1037/0022-3514.91.4.612.

Calhoun, Cheshire. "The Virtue of Civility." *Philosophy and Public Affairs,* vol. 29, no. 3, 2000, pp. 251-75. *JSTOR*, doi: 10.1111/j.1088-4963.2000.00251.x.

Davetian, Benet. *Civility: A Cultural History*. Toronto UP, 2009.

Edwards, Kari and Edward E. Smith. "A Disconfirmation Bias in the Evaluation of Arguments." *Journal of Personality and Social Psychology,* vol. 71, no. 1, 1996, pp. 5-24. *Westlaw,* doi: dx.doi.org.ezproxy.lib.uwm.edu/10.1037/0022-3514.71.1.5.

Ferree, Myra, et al. "Four Models of the Public Sphere in Modern Democracies." *Theory and Society*, vol. 31, 2002, pp. 289-324. *JSTOR,* www.jstor.org/stable/658129.

Gómez, Manuel N. "Imagining the Future: Cultivating Civility in a Field of Discontent." *Change*, March/April 2008, pp. 11-17.

Haidt, Jonathan. *The Righteous Mind: Why Good People Are Divided by Politics and Religion*. Pantheon, 2012.

Nickerson, Raymond S. "Confirmation Bias: A Ubiquitous Phenomenon in Many Guises." *Review of General Psychology,* vol. 2, no. 2, 1998, pp. 175-220. *PsycARTICLES*, doi: dx.doi.org.ezproxy.lib.uwm.edu/10.1037/1089-2680.2.2.175.

Schwind, Christina, et al. "Preference-inconsistent Recommendations: An Effective Approach for Reducing Confirmation Bias and Stimulating Divergent Thinking?" *Computers and Education,* vol. 58, 2012, pp. 87-96. *Elsevier*, doi: dx.doi.org.ezproxy.lib.uwm.edu/10.1016/j.compedu.2011.10.003.

Stone, Geoffrey R. "Civility and Dissent During Wartime." *Human Rights,* vol. 33, no. 1, 2006, chicagounbound.uchicago.edu/cgi/viewcontent.cgi?article=8028&context =journal_articles.

Strickland, April A., et al. "Motivated Reasoning and Public Opinion." *Journal of Health Politics, Policy and Law,* Dec. 2011. *CINAHL Plus*, doi: dx.doi.org.ezproxy.lib. uwm.edu/10.1215/03616878-1460524.

Taber, Charles S. and Milton Lodge. "Motivated Skepticism in the Evaluation of Political Beliefs." *American Journal of Political Science,* vol. 50, no. 3, 2006, pp. 755-69. *Academic Search Complete*, doi: 10.1111/j.1540-5907.2006.00214.x.

1"

1/2"

1"

1"

MLA DOCUMENTATION FOR IN-TEXT CITATIONS

In-text citations guide readers to the works-cited page to learn the source information. By giving a page number, in-text citations tell readers exactly where in a source to find the words or ideas being referenced.

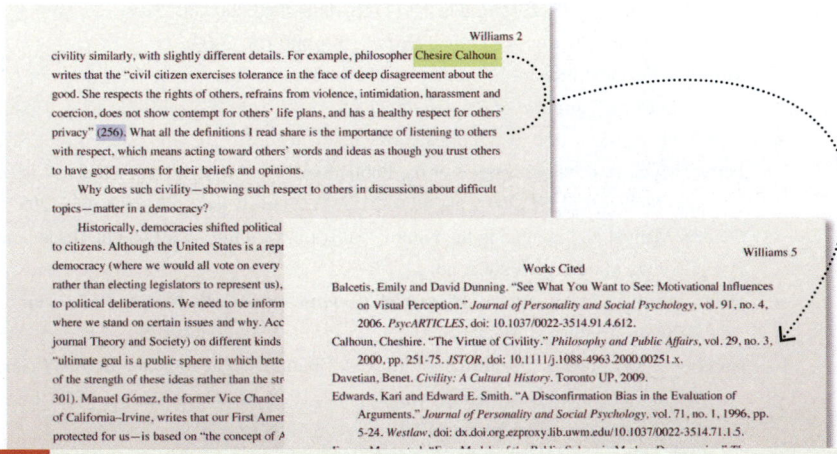

IN-TEXT CITATIONS IN MLA STYLE

In-text citations in MLA style generally contain two elements:

1

The name of the author of the words or ideas being quoted, summarized, or paraphrased. The name can appear within the sentence containing the quotation or within parentheses at the sentence's end.

2

The page number(s) of or some other reference to the words or ideas being cited. The number of the page from which quoted words come goes at the end of the sentence, in parentheses.

In her article on two nineteenth-century women preachers, Patricia Bizzell argues that "a conjunction between the female sex and moral activism is traditional in Methodism" (379).

or

One writer on nineteenth-century women preachers argues that "a conjunction between the female sex and moral activism is traditional in Methodism" (Bizzell 379).

VARIATIONS ON THE MLA IN-TEXT CITATION PATTERN

NO AUTHOR IS NAMED

If no author is named, use the work's title:

To "watch the rejects crash and burn" is why we watch *American Idol,* according to *Rolling Stone* magazine ("Idol Worship" 7).

→ If a company name or government organization is listed as author, see page 378.

YOU CITE TWO OR MORE SOURCES BY THE SAME AUTHOR

When you cite two or more works by the same author, each in-text citation should give the particular work's name in your sentence or in the parenthetical reference.

If you give the work's name in the parenthetical reference, do not use the full title, to save space; instead, use the title's first main noun and any adjectives that come before it (but not articles).

Here is a citation for a first source:

That meat from cows fed on grass is more nutritious than that from corn-fed cows is just one of the many arguments Pollan makes (*Omnivore's Dilemma* 68).

Here is how the second source is cited:

Because his research shows just what chemicals go into a commercial potato, Pollan cannot bring himself to eat one (*Botany* 235).

If you need to put the author's name, the work's title, and a page number into the parenthetical citation, put a comma between the author's name and the title and put a space between the title and page number:

(Pollan, *Botany* 235)

YOU CITE SOURCES BY AUTHORS WITH THE SAME LAST NAME

So readers can find the right citation in your works-cited list, use authors' full names in your sentences or use each author's first initial and full last name in the parenthetical citation. (If both authors have the same first initial, use their full first names.)

Here are examples from the same paper:

Richard Rorty argues that our understanding of what knowledge is has changed over two hundred years.

Amélie Oksenberg Rorty shows how Aristotle's *Rhetoric* draws on understandings of how people communicate, the psychology of audiences, the character of communicators, and politics.

These examples avoid ambiguity through their parenthetical citations:

Some philosophers argue that our understanding of what knowledge is has changed over the last two hundred years (R. Rorty).

Aristotle's *Rhetoric* draws on understandings of how people communicate, the psychology of audiences, the character of communicators, and politics (A. Rorty).

THE SOURCE YOU CITE HAS TWO AUTHORS

List the names in the order they are given in the source. Use *and* between the two names, whether you use the names in your sentence or in parentheses at sentence end:

As "much an activist as an analytical method" is how Moeller and Moberly describe McAllister's approach to computer games.

Reviewers describe McAllister's approach to computer games as "much an activist as an analytical method" (Moeller and Moberly).

THE SOURCE YOU CITE HAS THREE OR MORE AUTHORS

If the work you cite has three or more authors, use only the first author's name, followed by the expression **et al**, putting a period after *al*. (*Et al.* is Latin for *and others*.)

Fine et al. offer a two-year study of such a class in "Before the Bleach Gets Us All."

or:

When a ninth-grade world literature class is offered at high honors level for everyone, without tracking, students "who never expected to be seen as smart" come to see themselves as capable and sharp (Fine et al. 174, 175).

THE SOURCE YOU CITE HAS A CORPORATE AUTHOR OR IS A GOVERNMENT DOCUMENT

If there are common abbreviations for terms in the author name, use them in the parenthetical citation. If a name is long and can't be abbreviated, putting it in the sentence will read less awkwardly than putting it within the parentheses.

According to a Keweenaw National Historical Park booklet, in the early twentieth century, in the copper mines of Michigan's Upper Peninsula, the "division of labor often followed ethnic lines" (United States, Dept. of the Interior, National Park Service).

Because the writer explains the quotation is from a booklet, readers do not expect a page number; they will look in the works-cited list under *United States, Dept. of the Interior*.

Also notice that, in the parenthetical citation, each of the governmental units is mentioned, in order, just as they would be in the works-cited list.

→ See pages 378 and 379 on the works-cited list entries for corporate and government authors.

THERE IS NO PAGE NUMBER

Some print sources have no page numbers. If the paragraphs or sections are numbered, include them in the citation; otherwise, make the author or source title clear:

The Museum of Modern Art's pamphlet, "The Changing of the Avant-Garde," argues that architecture after World War II was shaped by "pop culture, the first stirrings of the information age, and the radical politics of the 1960s."

The words make clear the source is a pamphlet; readers won't expect a page number and will look for "The Changing of the Avant-Garde" in the works-cited list.

Some online sources, like e-books, have location numbers; these numbers change from device to device, so do not use them. Instead, if the source has chapters, use them:

Linden describes people born unable to feel pain, which sounds like a wonderful ability—but he notes that without an ability to feel pain "we do not learn to recoil from sharp blades, boiling liquids, or damaging chemicals" (ch. 6).

The works-cited entry for this in-text citation does not tell the kind of book cited:

Linden, David J. *Touch: The Science of Hand, Heart, and Mind*. Viking, 2015.
   E-BOOK

YOU CITE TIME-BASED MEDIA, LIKE TELEVISION OR VIDEO

Cite the time or range of times of the passage you reference. Give the hours, minutes, and seconds as displayed in your media player, separating the numbers with colons:

In her TED Talk on "How Humans Could Evolve to Live in Space," Lisa Nip suggests we can use "synthetic biology to change the genetic makeup of any living organisms"—including humans (00:11:09).

YOU CITE PART OF AN EDITED COLLECTION OR ANTHOLOGY

Use the name of the author who wrote the words you quote—*not* the name of the collection's editor. For example, if you cite an article by Tania Modleski in a collection edited by Amelia Jones, use Modleski's name in your in-text citations:

Tania Modleski's article "The Search for Tomorrow in Today's Soap Operas" examines the different pleasures women find in soap opera narratives.

One scholar examines the different pleasures women find in soap operas (Modleski).

YOU CITE TWO OR MORE SOURCES IN ONE SENTENCE

Your first option, if you refer to the different sources in different parts of the sentence, is to put a citation after each reference:

While some research finds a link between violent games and children's aggressive behavior (Provenzo 12), many recent studies challenge a direct connection between gaming and real-world behaviors (Jones 144).

Your second option, if your sources support one main point, is to put them all into the parentheses, separated by semicolons:

Although there is agreement that hundreds of languages were spoken in the Americas before Europeans arrived, there is disagreement over the number of linguistic families into which the languages fit (Crystal 403-08; Wade 113-18).

YOU REFERENCE AN ENTIRE SOURCE

If you need to refer to an entire source in your writing, do not include page numbers. Instead, put only the author's and the work's names, or refer to the source in the parentheses at the end of the sentence.

Oliver Sacks's *Seeing Voices* argues that sign languages are indeed real languages, so when people who are deaf learn to sign, they gain the same neurological benefits as people who can hear gain when they learn to speak.

An increase in childhood sports injuries seems related to increased competition (Gorman).

YOU CITE AN ENCYCLOPEDIA OR DICTIONARY

If you cite a reference work with a named author, set up your citation and works-cited entry as you would for a part of a book, using the author's name. If you cite a reference work with no listed author, put the citation into your works-cited list alphabetically by the title. Because reference work sections are usually arranged alphabetically, you do not need to give a page number.

Mad cow disease, the popular name for bovine spongiform encephalopathy (a fatal neurological disorder), appears to be transferable to humans, in whom it is called Creutzfeldt-Jakob disease; mad cow disease spreads when cows are fed the processed remains of cattle who have the disease ("Bovine Spongiform Encephalopathy").

YOU QUOTE WORDS THAT ANOTHER WRITER QUOTED

Use *qtd*. *in* (for *quoted in*) before the source reference to show where you found the quoted words:

Elizabeth Durack argues that *Star Wars* "and other popular media creations take the place in modern America that culture myths like those of the Greeks or Native Americans did for earlier peoples" (qtd. in Jenkins 153).

Readers will look for the corresponding works-cited item under *Jenkins*.

MLA DOCUMENTATION FOR WORKS CITED

These pages show you how to create the individual citations for the Works Cited list that goes at the end of all research papers written in MLA style.

MLA STYLE FOR CHANGING MEDIA

In 2016, the MLA revised its approach to documenting sources, publishing its changes in the eighth edition of the *MLA Handbook*. Because how we read, write, publish, and exchange texts has changed with the Internet, the MLA states that writers "need a system for documenting sources that begins with a few principles rather than a long list of rules" (8).

The new principles help writers figure out how to document any source, old or new, without needing to be told the exact format for a new source: "A work in a new medium thus can be documented without new instructions" (3).

MLA PRINCIPLES FOR DOCUMENTATION

1 "Cite simple traits shared by most works" (3)

Citations grow out of the features *all* sources share: an author and a title. Then other information—shared by different kinds of sources—is added to the citation.

2 "Remember that there is often more than one correct way to document a source" (4)

When writers need to decide whether to include more or less information, the MLA says that the writer's purposes should guide the decision.

3 "Make your documentation useful to readers" (4)

Following the MLA guidelines helps readers because the guidelines help readers find sources.

AN IMPORTANT CONCEPT: "CONTAINERS"

→ See pages 370–371 on this concept used in MLA citations.

WORK CITED ABOVE

MLA Handbook. 8th ed., Modern Language Association of America, 2016.

BOOK—CORPORATE AUTHOR AND PUBLISHER ARE THE SAME

TO MAKE MLA WORKS CITED PAGES

first

COLLECT THE INFORMATION YOU NEED FOR EACH OF YOUR SOURCES.

To know what information to collect, you need to know whether your source is a stand-alone source, is a source inside a container—or is a source inside a container inside a container.

→ See pages 370–371 about stand-alone sources and containers.

→ See pages 124–139 for the information to collect for your source.

second

CONSTRUCT A CITATION FOR EACH SOURCE, FOLLOWING THE MLA PATTERN.

Follow the pattern to construct your listing element by element, starting with the author, moving on to the title, and so on, step by step, until you have a full citation.

→ The pattern is on pages 372–373.

→ The pattern for sources in containers inside other containers is on page 374.

third

CONSTRUCT YOUR WORKS CITED PAGE

When you have all your individual citations, put them together into the Works Cited page.

→ See pages 362–363 for how to format the Works Cited page.

CONCEPTS NECESSARY FOR MLA CITATIONS: "STAND-ALONE SOURCES" AND "SOURCES IN CONTAINERS"

STAND-ALONE SOURCES

A stand-alone source exists as a self-contained whole, such as:

SOURCES IN CONTAINERS

Some sources exist only inside other texts that contain them:

A scholarly article...

can have an online journal as its **container**:

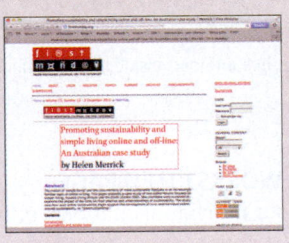

A television episode...

can have a series as its **container**:

 Look across these three categories to determine which fits your source; knowing the category of your source helps you build your source's citation.

SOURCES IN CONTAINERS, IN CONTAINERS

Some sources exist only inside other texts that in turn are contained in other texts:

A scholarly article...

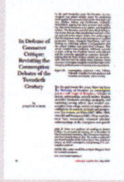

↓
can have
a journal as its **container**...

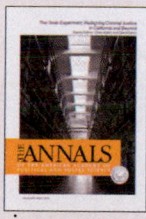

↓
which can have
an online database as its **container**.

A video...

↓
can have
a series as its **container**...

↓
which can have
a website as its **container**.

MLA DOCUMENTATION FOR WORKS CITED
THE PATTERN FOR MLA CITATIONS

The pattern to the right lists the nine elements—in the order they go into a citation—that can be included in an MLA works-cited citation. All citations will include—minimally—a title, a publication date, and some of the other elements. Almost no citations require all the elements listed.

Read the information about each element linked from the opposite page to learn how to include the element.

Note, too, that the pattern shows the punctuation that follows each element. However, all citations end with a period, even if they do not end with a location.

The citations below show how different citations use different elements of the pattern shown to the right; the pattern elements are underlined:

Brown, James. *Ethical Programs: Hospitality and the Rhetorics of Software.*
1   2

U of Michigan P, 2015.
7   8

BOOK

Young, Vershawn Ashanti. "Readings on Rhetoric and Performance."
1   2

Text and Performance Quarterly, vol. 31, no. 4, 2011, pp. 451-53.
3   6   8   9

ARTICLE, IN SCHOLARLY JOURNAL

Weingarten, Judith. "Writing Tablets from Ancient Palmyra." *Zenobia: Empress of the East,*
1   2   3

30 Mar. 2016, judithweingarten.blogspot.com/2016/03/writing-tablets-from-
8   9

ancient-palmyra.html.

POST, ON BLOG

ABOUT THE BLUE SUBTITLES UNDER CITATIONS IN THESE PAGES

The blue subtitles describe the kind of source being cited—but if the blue subtitles contain a comma, the information following the first comma indicates the source's container; the information following a *second* comma indicates a second container.

THE PATTERN FOR MLA CITATIONS

1 **AUTHOR.**
→ Pages 377–379 explain how to format author names and work with differing kinds of authors.

2 **SOURCE TITLE.**
→ Pages 380–383 show how to format source titles.

3 **CONTAINER TITLE,**
→ Pages 380–383 show how to format container titles.

4 **OTHER CONTRIBUTORS,**
→ Page 384 explains when and how to list other contributors.

5 **VERSION,**
→ Page 385 explains when and how to include a version.

6 **NUMBER,**
→ Page 386 explains when and how to include a number.

7 **PUBLISHER,**
→ Page 387 explains when and how to include publisher information.

8 **PUBLICATION DATE,**
→ Pages 388–389 explain how to include publication date information.

9 **LOCATION.**
→ Pages 390–391 explain what a "location" is and when and how to include a location.

MLA DOCUMENTATION FOR WORKS CITED
IF YOUR SOURCE IS INSIDE A CONTAINER THAT IS INSIDE ANOTHER CONTAINER

THE PATTERN FOR MLA CITATIONS WITH TWO CONTAINERS

START WITH THE CITATION FOR THE FIRST SOURCE AND ITS CONTAINER, put a period, and then add (in order) whichever of the following elements is necessary to describe the second container:

3 **SECOND CONTAINER TITLE,**

4 **OTHER CONTRIBUTORS,**

5 **VERSION,**

6 **NUMBER,**

7 **PUBLISHER,**

8 **PUBLICATION DATE,**

9 **LOCATION.**

→ The information that goes into elements 3–9 is formatted exactly as for the basic MLA pattern on pages 372–373.

For example, if you found the second source listed on page 372 (whose first container is a journal) inside an online database, the citation would have additional information:

Young, Vershawn Ashanti. "Readings on Rhetoric and Performance."
1   2

Text and Performance Quarterly, vol. 31, no. 4, 2011, pp. 451-53.
3   6   8   9

Communication & Mass Media Complete, doi: 10.1080/10462937.2011.604426.
3   9

ARTICLE, IN SCHOLARLY JOURNAL, IN DATABASE

Note that for such citations you put a period after the citation for the first source and its container; then begin the citation for the new container.

MLA DOCUMENTATION FOR WORKS CITED
WHAT SOURCES NEED WHICH ELEMENTS?

Very few sources will use all nine elements of the basic MLA citation pattern. Remember that a source *inside a container inside another container* will also need all the second container's elements.)

- ■ You *probably* will find this element for a source of this kind; *most* citations for a source of this kind will include the blue elements noted.

- ■ You *might* find this element for a source of this kind, or you can include information here if it fits your purposes.

Legend for the table below: **B** = blue (probably) ■, **R** = red (might) ■

SOURCE	AUTHOR, pp. 377–379	SOURCE TITLE, pp. 380–383	CONTAINER TITLE, pp. 380–383	OTHER CONTRIBUTORS, p. 384	VERSION, p. 385	NUMBER, p. 386	PUBLISHER, p. 387	PUBLICATION DATE, pp. 388–389	LOCATION, pp. 390–391
ARTICLE IN JOURNAL, MAGAZINE, OR NEWSPAPER	B	B	B			B		B	B
BLOG, ENTIRE	B	B	B				R	B	B
BLOG, SINGLE ENTRY	B	B	B					B	B
BOOK	B	B		R	R		B	B	
COMIC OR GRAPHIC NOVEL PUBLISHED AS PART OF SERIES	B	B	B	R	R	R	B	B	
COMIC OR GRAPHIC NOVEL PUBLISHED AS STAND-ALONE	B	B		R	R		B	B	
ESSAY OR OTHER PART IN BOOK	B	B	B	B			B	B	
MOVIE		B		R			B	B	
PODCAST	B	B	B	R				B	B
SOCIAL MEDIA POST	B	B	B					B	B
SONG	B	B	B				B	B	B
TELEVISION EPISODE	R	B		R			B	B	
TELEVISION SERIES	R	B		R			B	B	
VIDEO ONLINE	R	B	B					B	B
WEBPAGE	B	B	B					B	B
WEBSITE	R	B					B	B	B

MLA DOCUMENTATION FOR WORKS CITED
FIGURING OUT A CITATION IF THERE ISN'T A MODEL

If you cannot find—here or in the MLA Handbook—*a model for the citation you need, what do you do?*

Follow the MLA's advice, given on page 3 of the *Handbook*: "The writer examines the source and records its visible features, attending to the work itself and a set of universal guidelines. A work in a new medium thus can be documented without new instructions" (3).

Below we describe how we followed the MLA's "universal guidelines," as a suggestion for how you can do similarly should you need to.

EXAMPLE: AN ADVERTISEMENT

The *MLA Handbook* does not give a citation example for an adverisement in a magazine.

And so we turned to the guidelines we've taken from the MLA and have described throughout these pages, and we were able to develop this citation, which should enable any reader to find the source:

Walgreens. Advertisement for Vitamin Angels program. *O: The Oprah Magazine*. Apr. 2016. pp. 44–45. Advertisement.

ADVERTISEMENT, IN MAGAZINE
UNTITLED SOURCE
UNEXPECTED SOURCE

Here's how we came up with a citation:

1 An advertisement does not usually list any single person as author, but the *MLA Handbook* does describe how a text "may be created by a corporate author—an institution, an association, a government agency, or another kind of organization" (25). We believe we can therefore use the corporation behind the advertisement as the author.

2 An advertisement does not have a title. The *MLA Handbook* does state, however, "When a source is untitled, provide a generic description of it, neither italicized nor enclosed in quotation marks, in place of a title. Capitalize the first word of the description and any proper nouns in it" (28–29). In the citation above, you can see the description we came up with for this advertisement, based on the information in the advertisement.

3 The advertisement appears in *O: The Oprah Magazine*, so our citation lists that magazine as our source's container, adding to the citation the information one includes about a magazine: its date and the source's page numbers.

4 The MLA states that for "unexpected" kinds of texts, a writer can add a description at the end of the citation: To help our readers know exactly what sort of text we cite, we add **Advertisement.** to the end of our citation.

1 AUTHOR.

The author pattern is consistent for citations of all texts in all media. Keep in mind that *author* can mean a single person, several people, or an organization; when an organization—any group, committee, or business—is responsible for a text, you have a *corporate author*.

THE PATTERN FOR WHEN AUTHORS ARE HUMANS

The first author listed is written with the last name first, followed by a comma, and then the first name.

Last Name, First Name.   **Singh, Amardeep.**

If the writer you cite uses a middle name or initials, those follow the first name.

Phelps, Louise Wetherbee.   **Mitchell, W. J. T.**

If your source has more than one author, list the authors as they are listed in the source; see below for how to format differing numbers of authors.

In a citation, there is a period after the author's name or the list of authors' names.

NO AUTHOR NAMED

If you cannot find an author's name, start the citation with the source's title. (Consider, though, whether there might be a corporate author.)

"Revenant." *Merriam-Webster Dictionary.* www.merriam-webster.com/
dictionary/revenant. Accessed 2 Apr. 2016.
DICTIONARY—ONLINE
ONLINE SOURCE—NO SOURCE DATE, SO ACCESS DATE GIVEN

"Io in Motion." *NASA on The Commons.* 2 Apr. 2007. www.flickr.com/
photos/nasacommons/5278071978. Photograph.
PHOTOGRAPH—NO AUTHOR NAMED

ONE AUTHOR

Chernysheva, Natalia. *Le retour.* 2015, vimeo.com/63082999.
VIDEO ONLINE

Peacay. "1930s Modern Publicity." *Bibliodyssey,* 24 Apr. 2014,
bibliodyssey.blogspot.com/2014/04/1930s-modern-publicity.html.
POST UNDER PSEUDONYM, ON BLOG

TWO AUTHORS

Add the second author as shown to a one author pattern.

Ahern, Kati Fargo, and Jordan Frith. "Speaking Back to Our Spaces: The
Rhetoric of Social Soundscaping." *Harlot,* no. 9, 2013, harlotofthearts.
org/index.php/harlot/article /view/150/122.
ARTICLE, IN SCHOLARLY JOURNAL ONLINE

Author information continues on the next two pages.·······>

THREE OR MORE AUTHORS

Use the name of the first author followed by a comma. Then put **et al.** (meaning "and others").

Fine, Michelle, et al. "Before the Bleach Gets Us All." *Construction Sites,* edited by Lois Weiss and Michelle Fine, Teachers College, 2000, pp. 161-79.
ESSAY, IN EDITED COLLECTION

Nelson, Scott, et. al. "Crossing Battle Lines: Teaching Multimodal Literacies through Alternate Reality Games." *Kairos,* vol. 17, no. 3, 2013, kairos.technorhetoric.net/17.3/praxis/nelson-et-al/index.html.
ARTICLE, IN SCHOLARLY JOURNAL ONLINE

PSEUDONYM

Use the pseudonym as the author's name, spelled exactly as the pseudonym appears. If you know the name of the person using a pseudonym, you can add it in parentheses.

   In citing a tweet, include the @ symbol.)

Alice Addertongue (Benjamin Franklin). Letter to the editor. *The Pennsylvania Gazette,* 12 Sept.1732. The Papers of Benjamin Franklin, vol. 1, American Philosophical Society / Yale University, franklinpapers. org/franklin/framedVolumes.jsp?vol=1&page=243a.
LETTER TO THE EDITOR
SOURCE WITH TWO PUBLISHERS

@manwhohasitall. "TODAY'S DEBATE: What unique skills do men bring to the boardroom?" 22 Mar. 2016, 4:00 p.m. twitter.com/ manwhohasitall/status/712383569415397376.
TWEET

A CORPORATE AUTHOR

Start with the corporate author's name exactly as listed in the source (but omit A, An, or The).

   If the same organization is both author and publisher, begin the entry with the work's title and put the organization only as publisher.

   Some sources (like advertisements) may seem to have no author, but the organization responsible for the source can be listed as author.

→ If you have a government author, see the opposite page.

Hunter College Women's and Gender Studies Collective. *Women's Realities, Women's Choices: An Introduction to Women's Studies.* 4th ed., Oxford UP, 2015.
BOOK—CORPORATE AUTHOR

Médecins Sans Frontières (MSF). 2016, www.msf.org.
WEBSITE—CORPORATE AUTHOR

"Six Extinctions In Six Minutes." *Shelf Life,* American Museum of Natural History, episode 10, 21 Dec. 2015. www.youtube.com/ watch?v=AZuwOgcS1W0
VIDEO—CORPORATE AUTHOR AND PUBLISHER ARE THE SAME

The Changing of the Avant-Garde: Visionary Architectural Drawings from the Howard Gilman Collection. Museum of Modern Art, 2002.
BOOK—CORPORATE AUTHOR AND PUBLISHER ARE THE SAME

Wisconsin League of Conservation Voters. "The Nelson Award." *Wisconsin Gazette.* 24 Mar. 2016, p. 25. Advertisement.
ADVERTISEMENT—CORPORATE AUTHOR

A GOVERNMENT AUTHOR

Begin the entry with the name of the country or state; then put a comma and the name of the government agency. Between the country or state and the agency names, list (separated by commas) the organizational units of which the agency is a part. Arrange the names from the largest government entity to the smallest. (Note that you omit The from the names.)

United States, Census Bureau. "Veteran Statistics: Alabama." 10 Nov. 2015. www.census.gov/library/infographics/veterans-statistics.html. Chart.
GOVERNMENT DOCUMENT—FEDERAL
CHART

United States, Department of the Interior, National Park Service. "Cape Lookout National Seashore." 2007. Brochure.
GOVERNMENT DOCUMENT—FEDERAL
BROCHURE

Montana, Department of Fish, Wildlife, and Parks. "2016 Montana Fishing Regulations." 2016. Booklet.
GOVERNMENT DOCUMENT—STATE
BOOKLET

United Nations High Commission for Refugees. "Global Appeal 2016–2017." www.unhcr.org/pages/49c3646c4b8.html.
GOVERNMENT DOCUMENT—INTERNATIONAL

AN EDITED COLLECTION

Put editor (or editors for multiple editors) after the names that begin the citation.

If the book has more than two editors, follow the pattern for a book with multiple authors.

Le Faye, Deirdre, editor. *Jane Austen's Letters*. 3rd ed. Oxford UP, 1995.
BOOK—EDITED

Bechdel, Alison, editor. *Best American Comics 2011*. Houghton Mifflin, 2011.
BOOK—EDITED
GRAPHIC NOVEL—EDITED COLLECTION

Hocks, Mary, and Michelle Kendrick, editors. *Eloquent Images: Word and Image in the Age of New Media*. MIT P, 2003.
BOOK—EDITED WITH TWO EDITORS

COMICS, GRAPHIC NOVELS, FILM, TELEVISION, AND OTHER MEDIA PRODUCED BY MANY PEOPLE

If you wish to focus on a particular person's contribution, start with that person's name followed by a label describing the person's contribution; otherwise, omit an author and begin with the source title.

Coates, Ta-Nehisi, writer. *Black Panther: A Nation Under Our Feet, Book 1*. Illustrated by Brian Stelfreeze, Marvel, 2016.
COMIC BOOK—WITH FOCUS ON WRITER AND ADDITION OF OTHER CONTRIBUTOR

Cheadle, Don, actor, director, and writer. *Miles Ahead*. Bifrost Pictures, 2015.
FILM—WITH FOCUS ON CONTRIBUTION OF ONE PERSON

Miles Ahead. Bifrost Pictures, 2015.
FILM

Bela, Dalila, actor. "Trials and Tubulations." *Odd Squad,* season 1, episode 29, 1 Sept. 2015.
TELEVISION EPISODE—WITH FOCUS ON CONTRIBUTION OF ONE PERSON

MLA

2 SOURCE TITLES

3 CONTAINER TITLES

To follow MLA conventions accurately, you need to understand the following distinction:

STAND-ALONE SOURCES

→ Pages 370–371 also explain about stand-alone sources and sources in containers.

Sometimes you cite a whole book, a whole website, a film, an album, or a computer game.

In such cases, you have **a stand-alone source**.

Stand-alone sources do not have containers: they are self-contained.

In such cases, your citation will include element 2 from the MLA pattern for works-cited lists but not element 3.

SOURCES IN CONTAINERS

→ Pages 370–371 also explain about stand-alone sources and sources in containers.

Some sources live within larger texts:

- A journal article is contained within a journal.
- A webpage is contained within a website.
- An essay is contained within a collection.
- Poems are generally contained within a printed or online collection of many poems.
- A television episode is contained within a series.
- A song is contained within an album.

In such cases, you have **a source in a container**. In such cases, your citation will include both element 2 and element 3 from the MLA pattern for works-cited lists.

Your citation needs to include only one title, that of the stand-alone source:

2 SOURCE TITLE.

Your citation needs to include a source title followed by the container title:

2 SOURCE TITLE.
3 CONTAINER TITLE,

THE PATTERN FOR FORMATTING STAND-ALONE SOURCE TITLES AND CONTAINER TITLES

ITALICIZE STAND-ALONE AND CONTAINER TITLES.

Put **a period** after stand-alone source titles:

WHOLE BOOKS:	*Crow Lake.*	*Autobiography of a Face.*
FILMS:	*1916: The Irish Rebellion.*	*In Jackson Heights.*
ALBUMS:	*Marvin Gaye: What's Going On.*	*Music in Exile.*
GAMES:	*The Elder Scrolls V: Skyrim.*	*Minecraft.*

Put **a comma** after container source titles:

NEWSPAPERS:	*Washington Post,*	*Daily Mining Gazette,*
JOURNALS:	*Journal of Experimental Medicine,*	*Journal of American History,*
MAGAZINES:	*TIME,*	*National Geographic,*
TELEVISION SHOWS:	*Buffy the Vampire Slayer,*	*Shots Fired,*
WEBSITES:	*The Mary Sue,*	*Anime News Network,*

THE PATTERN FOR FORMATTING SOURCES IN CONTAINERS

PUT QUOTATION MARKS AROUND THE TITLES OF SOURCES THAT ARE IN CONTAINERS.

Put a period after the last word of the title, inside the final quotation mark. (If the title ends with a question mark or exclamation point, use that.)

ESSAY IN A BOOK:	"Meno."
SONG FROM AN ALBUM:	"Me Voy Enamorando."
ARTICLE IN A NEWSPAPER:	"The Global Journey of the Zika Virus."
ARTICLE IN A JOURNAL:	"Cloudshine: New Light on Dark Clouds."
ARTICLE IN A MAGAZINE:	"My Guide to a Better Night's Sleep."
TELEVISION EPISODE:	"Trials and Tubulations."
WEB PAGE ON A WEBSITE:	"A Bookling Monument."

THE PATTERN FOR CAPITALIZING TITLES

ALL TITLES FOR ALL SOURCES IN ALL MEDIA HAVE THIS PATTERN:

1 Capitalize all the words of the title except for:

articles (*a, an, the*)

prepositions (*to, at, by, for, from, in, of, with*)

conjunctions (*and, but, for, or*)

the word **to** when it is part of an infinitive (as in *to read* or *to write*)

2 Capitalize the first and last words, even if the words are one of the exceptions above.

3 If there is a subtitle, put it after a colon and capitalize it as you would the title.

Scribbling the Cat: Travels with an African Soldier • *The Quick and the Dead: Artists and Anatomy*

"Lucky Catch: Tongue Fishhook Injuries" • *"Like a Thesis: A Postmodern Reading of Madonna Videos"*

TITLES FOR STAND-ALONE SOURCES

Note that the titles are always italicized and followed by a period. Also note that sometimes no author is cited, because stand-alone sources produced by many people (such as a film, television show or website) do not have a single author. However, if the purpose of your writing about such a source is to focus on one of the people involved, you can put that person's name in the author position, as in the example to the right about the film *In Jackson Heights*.

Marvin Gaye. *Marvin Gaye: What's Going On.* Tamla Records, 1971.
ALBUM

Lawson, Mary. *Crow Lake.* Delta Trade, 2002.
BOOK

The Elder Scrolls V: Skyrim. Bethesda Game Studios, 2011.
COMPUTER GAME

Frederick Wiseman, director. *In Jackson Heights.* Moulins Films, 2015.
FILM WITH FOCUS ON DIRECTOR

Cosmos: A Spacetime Odyssey. Cosmos Studios, 2014.
TELEVISION SERIES

@paulaakpan and @harrietevs. *The "I'm Tired" Project.* 2016. www.instagram.com/theimtiredproject.
WEBSITE—INSTAGRAM

All Day. allday.com. Accessed 25 Mar. 2016.
WEBSITE—WITH NO DATE OF PRODUCTION

TITLES FOR STAND-ALONE SOURCES IN CONTAINERS

Bruegel, Pieter, the Elder. *The Triumph of Death.* Museo Nacional del Prado, 1562–1563, www.museodelprado.es/coleccion/obra-de-arte/el-triunfo-de-la-muerte/d3d82b0b-9bf2-4082-ab04-66ed53196ccc.
PAINTING, ONLINE

TITLES FOR SOURCES IN CONTAINERS—AND THEIR CONTAINER TITLES—AND *THEIR* CONTAINER TITLES (IF THERE IS ONE)

Ahmad, Leila. "Self-Driving Cars Will Eliminate Accidents." *Daily Cardinal,* 28 Mar. 2016, p. 5.
ARTICLE, IN NEWSPAPER PUBLISHED DAILY

Owens, Jill. "Ethan Canin: The Powells.com Interview." *Powells.com Blog,* 21 Mar. 2016, www.powells.com/post/interviews/ethan-canin-the-powellscom-interview.
INTERVIEW, ON BLOG

"Ingrid Bergman in *Gaslight,* 1944." *George Cukor papers,* 1944. *Margaret Herrick Library Digital Collections,* digitalcollections.oscars.org/cdm/singleitem/collection/p15759coll13/id/12/rec/13.
PHOTOGRAPH, IN ARCHIVE, IN ONLINE COLLECTION
PHOTOGRAPH—UNTITLED

Goodman, Robert B. "Men blast granite to build tunnels for a hydroelectric project in Australia, 1963." *Found,* National Geographic, 21 Aug. 2015, natgeofound.tumblr.com.
PHOTOGRAPH, ON TUMBLR

Bragg, Melvyn. "Bedlam." *In Our Time,* BBC, 17 Mar. 2016, www.bbc.co.uk/programmes/b0739rfg#in=collection:p01dh5yg.
PODCAST, FROM WEBSITE

Kilwein Guevara, Maurice. "Pets." *Poema,* U of Arizona P, 2009, p. 48.
POEM, IN BOOK BY ONE AUTHOR

Simone, Nina. "Please Don't Let Me Be Misunderstood." *The Lady Has the Blues,* Tomato Records, 2003.
SONG, ON ALBUM

UNTITLED SOURCES

If you need to cite an e-mail, use the subject as the title. Capitalize the title as in the pattern on page 382.

To cite a tweet, put the whole tweet within quotation marks as the title. Use the tweet's capitalization.

If you cite an untitled review of a book or other text, follow the model shown to the right.

Bill Gates. "Windows Usability Systematic Degradation Flame." Received by Jim Allchin. 15 Jan. 2003.
E-MAIL

@CDCGov. "The best way to prevent #Zika is to prevent mosquito bites. http://1.usa.gov/1QbHwpF." 23 Mar. 2012, 12:00 p.m. twitter.com/CDCgov/status /712685452298289153.
TWEET

Haas, Christina. Review of *Literacy and Racial Justice: The Politics of Learning after Brown v. Board of Education,* by Catherine Prendergast. *African American Review,* vol. 38, no. 3, Fall 2004, pp. 537-39.
REVIEW OF BOOK, IN JOURNAL

4 OTHER CONTRIBUTORS,

A PIECE FROM AN EDITED COLLECTION

Because the people who edit collections play central roles in producing the collections, their roles are always entered in citations.

Lebowitz, Fran. "Pointers for Pets." *Living with the Animals,* edited by Gary Indiana. Faber, 1994, pp. 61-64.
ESSAY, IN EDITED COLLECTION

Chen, Lynn. "You Are What You Eat." Art by Paul Wei. *Secret Identities: The Asian American Superhero Anthology*, edited by Jeff Yang et al. New Press, 2009, pp. 100–106.
GRAPHIC NOVEL, IN EDITED COLLECTION

Colby, Richard. "Writing and Assessing Procedural Rhetoric in Student-produced Video Games." *Computers and Composition*, edited by Carl Whithaus, special issue on multimodal assessment, vol. 31, pp. 43–52. *ScienceDirect*, doi:10.1016/j.compcom.2013.12.003.
ARTICLE, IN SCHOLARLY JOURNAL, IN DATABASE
ARTICLE, IN SCHOLARLY JOURNAL—SPECIAL ISSUE

A TEXT TRANSLATED FROM ANOTHER LANGUAGE

Like editors, translators play central roles in the production of these texts, and their roles are noted in citations, as shown to the right.

Mina, Hanna. "On the Sacks." *Literature from the "Axis of Evil,"* translated by Hanadi Al-Samman. New Press, 2006, pp 179-206.
SHORT STORY, IN EDITED BOOK
SHORT STORY—TRANSLATED

Grossman, David. *See Under: Love.* Translated by Betsy Rosenberg. Washington Square, 1989.
BOOK—TRANSLATED

OTHER KINDS OF CONTRIBUTORS

Include other contributors relevant to your purposes. Examples of other kinds of contributions include:

Adapted by
Directed by
Illustrated by
Introduction by
Narrated by
Performance by
Uploaded by

Dillard, Annie. *The Abundance: Narrative Essays Both Old and New.* Foreword by Geoff Dyer. HarperCollins, 2016.
BOOK—WITH CONTRIBUTOR FOREWORD

Keegan, Marina. *The Opposite of Loneliness: Essays and Stories.* Introduction by Anne Fadiman. Scribner, 2014.
BOOK—WITH CONTRIBUTOR INTRODUCTION

Moore, Alan, writer. *Watchmen.* Illustrated and lettered by Dave Gibbons, colored by John Higgins, DC Comics, 1987.
GRAPHIC NOVEL

5 **VERSION,**

If, in collecting citation information about your source, you discover that there are multiple versions of the source, identity the particular version you cite.

In a citation that includes version information, the version information usually begins with a lowercase letter. However, if the version information follows directly behind an italicized title with a period, the version information begins with a capital letter.

If your source is an edited version, in your citation note that with **ed.**, as in the different versions below. Also see below for examples of the different versions sources can have.

VERSIONS IN PRINT

Print sources (including those you find online) can appear in different editions, labeled by a date, number, or other descriptor.

The Bible. Introduction and notes by Robert Carroll and Stephen Prickett, authorized King James Version, Oxford UP, 1998.
BIBLE—KING JAMES VERSION

Coutin, Anne-Sophie. *Essential Obstetric and Newborn Care.* 2015 ed., Médecins Sans Frontières, 2015, http://refbooks.msf.org/msf_docs/en/obstetrics/obstetrics_en.pdf.
BOOK—ONLINE
BOOK—VERSION BY YEAR

Macchiavelli, Niccolo. *The Prince.* Translated by Harvey C. Mansfield, 2nd ed., Chicago UP, 1998.
BOOK—TRANSLATED
BOOK—SECOND EDITION

Norman, Don. *The Design of Everyday Things.* Revised and expanded ed., Basic Books, 2013.
BOOK—REVISED AND EXPANDED EDITION

Hugo, Victor. *Les Misérables.* Abridged ed., Fawcett, 1982.
BOOK—ABRIDGED EDITION

VERSIONS IN OTHER MEDIA

Note that the titles are always italicized and followed by a period.

Morrison, Van. *Moondance.* Expanded ed., Rhino, 2013.
ALBUM—EXPANDED EDITION

Watchmen. Director's cut, Warner Home Video, 2009.
FILM—DIRECTOR'S CUT

Martin, Alan C. *Tank Girl One.* Illustrated by Jamie Hewlett, anniversary ed., Titan Books, 2009.
GRAPHIC NOVEL—ANNIVERSARY EDITION

6 NUMBER,

PERIODICALS: VOLUME AND ISSUE NUMBERS

Periodicals—magazines and journals that are published regularly every month or season—often track their publications by year: *Volume* 1 is all the issues published in the periodical's first year, *Volume* 2 in the second year, and so on. The *Number* of an issue then refers to when in the year it was published: *Number* 1 appeared first, *Number* 2 second, and so on.

If you find only a volume number or only a number, give whichever you find.

→ Page 45 shows where to find volume and issue information.

French, R. M. "Using Guitars to Teach Vibrations and Acoustics." *Experimental Techniques*, vol. 29, no. 2, 2005, pp. 47-48.
ARTICLE, IN SCHOLARLY JOURNAL

Borrero, Luis Alberto. "Moving: Hunter-gatherers and the Cultural Geography of South America." *Quaternary International*, vol. 363, 30 Mar. 2015, pp. 126–33. *Science Direct*, doi:10.1016/j.quaint.2014.03.011.
ARTICLE, IN SCHOLARLY JOURNAL, IN DATABASE

Kampf, Ronit and Esra Cuhadar. "Do Computer Games Enhance Learning about Conflicts? A Cross-national Inquiry into Proximate and Distant Scenarios in Global Conflicts." *Computers in Human Behavior*, vol. 52, Nov. 2015, pp. 541–49. *Social Sciences Full Text*, doi: 10.1016/j.chb.2014.08.008
ARTICLE, IN SCHOLARLY JOURNAL, IN DATABASE

"Vaccination: A Jab in Time." *Economist*, vol. 418, no. 8982, 26 Mar. 2016, p. 67.
ARTICLE, IN POPULAR MAGAZINE PUBLISHED WEEKLY

NUMBER INFORMATION FOR OTHER KINDS OF TEXTS

Television shows have season and episode numbers; graphic novels and comic books can have volumes and numbers.

Whenever you cite a source number, precede it with a descriptive term (like vol., no., season, or episode).

"eps1.7_wh1ter0se.m4v." *Mr. Robot*, season 1, episode 7, Universal Cable, 12 Aug. 2015.
TELEVISION EPISODE

Liu, Marjorie, writer and Sana Takeda, illustrator. *Monstress*. No. 4, Image Comic, 2015.
COMIC BOOK

Vaughan, Brian K., writer, and Fiona Staples, illustrator. *Saga*. Vol. 5, 2015.
COMIC BOOK

7 **PUBLISHER,**

A publisher does the work of taking the author's words, pictures, or sounds and getting them to readers: This can be a traditional press, a museum, a production company, a library…

PATTERNS FOR PUBLISHERS' NAMES

- From the publisher's name, omit any business words like *Company* (Co.), *Corporation* (Corp.), *Incorporated* (Inc.), or *Limited* (Ltd.).

- If your source was published by an academic press, replace *University* with U and *Press* with P:
  University of California Press → U of California P • MIT Press → MIT P
  Kent State University Press → Kent State UP • Syracuse University Press → Syracuse UP

- Otherwise, put the publisher's name exactly as you find the name in your source:
  Random House • HarperCollins • Penguin Press • Riverhead Books • Picador • Verso

→ Page 125 shows where to find the publisher information in a book; page 132 shows where to look for publisher information in a website.

TWO OR MORE PUBLISHERS

If you find two or more names given as the publisher, and they both seem equally responsible, include both, formatted as shown at right.

Sherman, Claire Richter. *Writing on Hands: Memory and Knowledge in Early Modern Europe*. Trout Gallery / Folger Shakespeare Library, 2001.
BOOK—TWO PUBLISHERS

Invisible Man: Gordon Parks and Ralph Ellison in Harlem. Steidl / The Gordon Parks Foundation / The Art Institute of Chicago, 2016.
BOOK—THREE PUBLISHERS
BOOK—CORPORATE AUTHOR AND PUBLISHER ARE THE SAME

PUBLISHERS FOR NON-PRINT MEDIA

For films, television series, or other sources produced by several companies, the MLA recommends to name as publisher the company with primary responsibility.

A blog network serves as the publisher of the blogs it hosts.

What Happened, Miss Simone? Directed by Liz Garbus, Moxie Firecracker Films, 2015.
FILM

Greg Laden. "Are Engineers More Likely To Be Terrorists, And If So, Why?" *Greg Laden's Blog: Culture as Science, Science as Culture*, Science Blogs, 2016, scienceblogs.com/gregladen/2016/03/25/are-engineers-more-likely-to-be-terrorists-and-if-so-why.
POST, ON BLOG, PUBLISHED BY BLOG NETWORK

8 PUBLICATION DATE,

A date in a citation helps readers judge the relevance of a source and also find the source. Because different kinds of sources are produced under different time frames, different kinds of sources need different formats for how the publication is presented.

SOURCES THAT NEED A YEAR IN THE CITATION

A book's citation generally only needs to show a year to help readers find the particular edition you cite. Similarly, some journals only need a year for date information because the number information focuses in on a specific issue.

Austen, Jane. *Pride and Prejudice*. Scribner's, 1918. *Google Books*, books.google.com/books/about/Pride_and_Prejudice. html?id=s1gVAAAAYAAJ
BOOK, IN GOOGLE BOOKS

Sengupta, Somini. *The End of Karma: Hope and Fury Among India's Young*. W.W. Norton, 2016.
BOOK

Hawhee, Debra. "Rhetoric's Sensorium." *Quarterly Journal of Speech*, vol. 101, no. 1, 2015, pp. 2–17.
ARTICLE, IN SCHOLARLY JOURNAL

SOURCES WITH A YEAR PLUS A MONTH OR SEASON IN THE CITATION

Because periodicals—journals, magazines, newspapers—are published regularly (as often as daily or weekly), readers need a date in the citation if they are to find your source.

Different kinds of periodicals will need different kinds of dates in citations: You can't go wrong if you use the date as you find it listed in the source.

Wortham, Jenna. "We're More Honest with Our Phones Than with Our Doctors." *New York Times*, 23 Mar. 2016, www.nytimes. com/2016/03/27/magazine/were-more-honest-with -our-phones-than- with-our-doctors.html.
ARTICLE, IN NEWSPAPER PUBLISHED DAILY—ONLINE

Cobb, Jelani. "The Matter of Black Lives." *New Yorker*, vol. 92, no. 5, 14 Mar. 2016. www.newyorker.com/magazine/2016/03/14/where-is- black-lives-matter-headed.
ARTICLE, IN POPULAR MAGAZINE PUBLISHED WEEKLY

"Saving Africa's Rhinos: Pooches v. Poachers." *Economist*, vol. 418, no. 8976, 13 Feb. 2016, p. 40.
ARTICLE, IN POPULAR MAGAZINE PUBLISHED WEEKLY

Miklósi, Adám. "The Science of a Friendship: How Dogs Became Our Closest Animal Companions." *Scientific American Mind*, May–June 2015.
ARTICLE, IN POPULAR MAGAZINE PUBLISHED BI-MONTHLY

Ken, Stephanie Wong. "Blood on the Tracks: An Interview with Living Legend Buffy Sainte Marie." *Bitch*, no. 68, Fall 2015, pp. 73–75.
ARTICLE, IN POPULAR MAGAZINE PUBLISHED SEASONALLY INTERVIEW

SOURCES WITH A DATE AND TIME IN THE CITATION

If you cite an online source that includes a time as well as a date, put both in your citation. Choose either a consistent twelve- or twenty-four-hour format for times.

Werner, Sarah. Comment on "How to Destroy Special Collections with Social Media." *Wynken de Worde*, 2 Aug. 2015, 10:59 a.m., sarahwerner. net/blog/2015/07/how-to-destroy-special-collections-with-social-media.
COMMENT, ON BLOG POST

"19,300 Women Transformed by Fistula Surgery Since 2009." *Fistula Foundation*, 5 Mar. 2016, 5:30 p.m., *Facebook*, www.facebook.com/ fistulafoundation/photos/a.138870922878394.26855.13875495622332 4/907569836008495/?type=3&theater. Graph.
CHART, ON FACEBOOK

INCLUDING THE DATE YOU ACCESSED A SOURCE

Online sources can be changed or deleted; sometimes they appear without publication dates. Giving the date you accessed the source helps readers understand the source's time period and the version you cite. When you include an access date, put it at the at the end of your citation; do still include any information you have about the source's publication date.

sunagainstgold. "FAQ." *I am a Food Blog,* iamafoodblog.com/faq. Accessed 27 Mar. 2016.
ONLINE SOURCE—NO DATE
POST, ON BLOG—UNDATED

A. C. Smith. "The Waif." *A Selection of Australian Poetry and Prose*, librivox. org/a-selection-of-australian-poetry-and-prose. Accessed 2 Apr. 2016. Audiobook.
AUDIOBOOK
ONLINE SOURCE—NO DATE
POEM, IN COLLECTION, ONLINE

"Bovine Spongiform Encephalopathy (BSE)." *Encyclopædia Britannica,* www.britannica.com/science/bovine-spongiform-encephalopathy. Accessed 2 Apr. 2016.
ARTICLE, IN ONLINE REFERENCE WORK
ONLINE SOURCE—NO DATE

THE PATTERN FOR FORMATTING DATES

The MLA's convention for formatting a date is to use no commas by putting the date in the order of day–month–year:

1 Jan. 2017	29 Feb. 2016	1 Mar. 1963	15 Apr. 1984	18 May 1926
22 July 1929	23 Aug. 1961	22 Sept. 1955	10 Nov. 1956	3 Dec. 1951

If a month's name is longer than four letters, abbreviate it in your works-cited list. The MLA's preferred abbreviations are shown here:

Jan.	Feb.	Mar.	Apr.	May	June
July	Aug.	Sept.	Oct.	Nov.	Dec.

9 **LOCATION.**

Location information depends on the kind of source; check these pages for the information to include for your source. (Some citations—generally stand-alone sources where the publisher information is all readers need to find the source—do not need locations.)

TWO OPTIONS EXIST FOR ONLINE SOURCE LOCATIONS

DOI

DOI stands for **digital object identifier**. The DOI system gives a publication a unique identifying number—the DOI—that provides a persistent link to the source. DOIs are more stable and shorter than URLs; if you have both a DOI and a URL, use the DOI.

In a citation, put **doi:** and then the DOI information.

→ See page 137 on finding DOIs in sources.

Stell, Gerald. "Uses and Functions of English in Namibia's Multiethnic Settings." *World Englishes*, vol. 33, no. 2, 2014, pp. 223-241. *Education Research Complete*, doi: 10.1111/weng.12082.
ARTICLE, IN SCHOLARLY JOURNAL, IN DATABASE

United States, Department of the Interior, U. S. Geological Survey. "Geologic Map of Alaska." Scientific Investigations Map 3340, 2015, doi: 10.3133/sim3340.
MAP
GOVERNMENT DOCUMENT—FEDERAL

URL (OR A PERMALINK)

As you enter URLs into reference lists, first remove http:// or https://. Then make sure your word processor does not automatically hyphenate the URL: This can "break" the URL, since a reader will try to use the hyphen as part of the URL. Instead, if you have a long URL and need to break it across lines, break it before a slash or other hyphenation.

You do not need to list a URL in a reference if you provide the DOI for your source.

Friedman, Jane. "Four Lessons for Authors on the Current State of Publishing." 14 Mar. 2016, janefriedman. com/4-lessons-publishing.
BLOG POST—INDIVIDUAL BLOG

"Omi Kuni-ezu." 1837. *Stanford Digital Depository*, Stanford University Libraries, purl.stanford.edu/hs631zg4177. Accessed 25 July 2016. Map.
MAP, IN ONLINE LIBRARY SPECIAL COLLECTION
REPUBLISHED SOURCE—SHOWING ORIGINAL PUBLICATION DATE

A permalink is a stable web address, usually available on blogs and sometimes given with databases; if you can find a permalink for a source, use it instead of a URL.

SOURCES WITH LOCATIONS THAT ARE NUMBERED PAGES

If your source is part of a book or is a journal article, include the page numbers in your citation, following the pattern below.

Saulitis, Eva. "Wondering Where the Whales Are." *Leaving Resurrection: Chronicles of a Whale Scientist*, Boreal Books, 2008, pp. 140–52.
ESSAY, IN COLLECTION OF ONE AUTHOR'S WRITING

Russell, Joshua Kahn. "Anger Works Best When You Have the Moral High Ground." *Beautiful Trouble: A Toolbox for Revolution,* edited by Andrew Boyd, OR Books, 2012, pp. 96–97.
ESSAY, IN EDITED COLLECTION

SOURCES THAT NEED TWO LOCATIONS

If your source is inside a container inside another container, your citation might include two locations. This generally will happen for sources where you need to give an article's page numbers and then a URL or doi for the online container.

"Traveling Notes in Italy: Pompei." *The Builder*, vol. 7, no. 309, 6 Jan. 1849, pp. 2–4. *Internet Library of Early Journals–Bodlein Library*, www.bodley.ox.ac.uk/cgi-bin/ilej/image1.pl?item=page&seq=1&size=1&id=bu.1849.1.6.7.x.x.2
ARTICLE, IN POPULAR MAGAZINE, IN ONLINE ARCHIVE

Hoel, Aud Sissel. "Measuring the Heavens: Charles S. Peirce and Astronomical Photography." *History of Photography*, vol. 40, no. 1, 2016, pp. 49–66. *Taylor & Francis Online*, doi: 10.1080/03087298.2016.1140329.
ARTICLE, IN SCHOLARLY JOURNAL, IN DATABASE

LOCATIONS FOR OTHER KINDS OF SOURCES

If you cite a live performance or lecture, or a physical object in a museum or other space, include the name of the venue and the city. (If the city name is in the venue name, you do not have to repeat it.)

Turrell, James. *One Accord.* 2001, Live Oak Friends Meeting House, Houston.
ARTWORK–PHYSICAL OBJECT

Lupton, Carter. "Beyond the Veil: Diversity in Arab and Muslim Women's Clothing." Lunch and Lecture Series, 5 May 2014, Milwaukee Public Museum.
LECTURE

D'Angelo. 7 Feb. 2015, Apollo Theater, New York.
MUSICAL PERFORMANCE–LIVE

THE PATTERN FOR PAGE NUMBERS FOR PERIODICAL ARTICLES

Place a comma after the date of the periodical and then put the page number or numbers. End the citation with a period. Give the page numbers for the entire article, even if you refer to only a small portion of an article. Use p. for *page* and pp. for *pages*.

p. 52.   pp. 721-86.   pp. 237-58.   p. B5.   pp. 21-28.   pp. 237-358.

(Note that if the ending page is above 100, you list only the last two digits of the page number unless more are necessary for clarity.)

MLA DOCUMENTATION FOR WORKS CITED
CITING SOURCES WHEN YOUR PROJECT ISN'T A RESEACH PAPER

According to *The MLA Handbook*, how to cite sources in a research project that does not take the form of a paper "is not yet a settled matter" (128). Nonetheless, the MLA states that you should still offer citation information "that enables a curious reader, viewer, or other user to track down your sources and giving credit to those whose work influenced yours" (128). To those ends, the MLA has some suggestions:

CITING SOURCES IN RESEARCH PROJECTS YOU PUT ONLINE
The suggested options include:

- Putting links to sources in your project itself, when a source is named.
- Putting a full works-cited list, with links to sources, at the end of the project or on a linked webpage.

CITING SOURCES IN A SLIDE PRESENTATION
The suggested options include putting citations on:

- Any slide that uses anyone else's written or visual sources.
- A works-cited slide at the end of the presentation.
- A printed works-cited handout for your audience.
- A works-cited webpage, for which you provide the URL.

CITING SOURCES IN A VIDEO
The suggested options include putting citation information:

- At the bottom of any screen that uses anyone else's written or visual sources. Such information might be the name of the person being interviewed, the producer and title of a video clip, the name and title of any photographs.
- In a full works-cited listing in your closing credits.

PART 9
APA, CSE, AND CMS DOCUMENTATION

...beliefs about the nonver...

...Nonverbal Behavior, 29(2), 105-123. doi:10.100...

...shdan, E. (1998). Smiles, speech, and body posture: How wor...

status and power. Journal of Nonverbal Behavior, 22(4), ...

www.springer.com/psychology/personality+&+social+...

Cohen, H. (1980). You can negotiate anything. New York, NY:...

Dunbar, N., & Abra, G. (2008). Observations of dyadic powe...

Conference Papers—International Communication As...

icahdq.org/

Dunbar, N., & Burgoon, J. (2005). Perceptions of power an...

interpersonal relationships. Journal of Social & Per...

doi:10.1177/0265407505050944

...Knott, G. (1979). Nonverbal communication during ear...

CONTENTS

WHERE ARE WE IN A PROCESS FOR COMPOSING?

Understanding your project
Getting started
Asking questions
Shaping your project for others
Drafting a paper
Getting feedback
Revising
Polishing

Ensuring that you have used your sources with integrity: Using APA, CSE, or CMS styles to cite sources conventionally and build bibliographies

APA DOCUMENTATION

GUIDE TO APA DOCUMENTATION MODELS

PAGES FROM A PAPER IN APA FORMAT

Nonverbal Power Displays by Doormen

Christine Wysocki

University of San Diego

Abstract

This paper reports the results of a study conducted by a research team into the nonverbal behavior of doormen and security personnel at eight establishments within the city limits of San Diego. The initial hypothesis was that doormen are likely to speak with strong, stern voices, have a large physical appearance, use direct body orientations, and adopt or adapt various artifacts that signal or exert the power necessary to establish and maintain their authority and control over approaching patrons. The results of the study mostly confirmed the initial hypothesis, with two exceptions: The doormen did not uniformly employ a strong, stern tone of voice, and the doormen did not use the advantage of a higher plane of orientation in order to establish and maintain relations of power.

Title page

Approximately halfway down your title page, center the following information without bolding or italicizing it: your paper's title, your name, and your institution. (In a paper to be published, you would also include an "author note"; see the *APA Publication Manual.*)

Abstract

The APA requires a separate abstract page for papers going to publication; if your teacher asks you to include it, put it on a separate page (following the title page and numbered as page 2). Abstracts average 150–250 words but can be shorter. An abstract is a summary of the paper, reporting (without evaluation) what was studied, why it was studied, and the results of the study.

Running Head

At the top left of every page—including the title page—put a running head containing your title in all capital letters. The running head title should be no more than fifty characters; if you have a title that has two phrases separated by a colon, only put the part of the title before the colon into the running head. *Only on the title page* should the running head be preceded by "Running head:"

Repeat your title

Center your title above the body of your paper. Do not bold or italicize it.

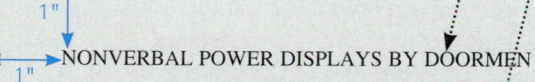

NONVERBAL POWER DISPLAYS BY DOORMEN   3

Nonverbal Power Displays by Doormen

According to some researchers, nonverbal cues may contribute up to 65% of what we understand in any communication exchange (Knott, 1979). Even before people speak, they transmit nonverbal messages, so that verbal and nonverbal communication are always entwined in any given situation. Understanding the roles the nonverbal—or what is often referred to as "paralanguage"—plays in overall communication can help us to become better communicators.

Although people control only a part of the nonverbal messages they send, it is possible to extend the conscious control one has of what one nonverbally projects—the nonverbal signals one sends—in any given situation. In other words, those who seek to project an image of power can learn to take on certain behaviors and appearances in order to affect others.

This paper reports on a study of a group of people, doormen at nightclubs, whose work necessitates that they project an image of pow[...]

enters a club, doormen need others to accept t[...]

authority. Through observations and interview[...]

doormen use, and do not use, to do their jobs.

The perceived or actual social distances bet[...]

interactive behaviors (Carney & LeBeau, 2005;

The content of the introduction: How does your research relate to others' research?

In an APA paper, the introduction lays out the problem under consideration, saying why the problem is worth addressing and how it relates to previous research—which you can see here as Christine first describes other research to situate her own work and then states this paper's specific focus.

APA

Power relations are also present in bodily orientation—or proxemics. If a person moves close to another, or violates another's personal space, the other can become stressed and react in a variety of ways, including but not limited to, increased anxiety, discomfort, and aggressiveness (May, 2000). Likewise, standing in the center of a small space, such as a doorway, or blocking others' access to a destination signals to others that movement is not possible without negotiation or struggle (Nadler, 1986). Perceived power can also be influenced by posture and the plane of interaction: Elevation provides the most power, followed by postural orientation and rank (Schwartz, Tesser, & Powell, 1982). Conversely, as Tiedens and Fragale's study on body orientation mimicry and posture shows, a complimentary (open/closed versus closed/closed) posture results in higher likeability and an easing

Finally, what one wears or carries—consider example, wearing a uniform can deliver authority ditioned [in our society] to regard with awe anyt way, its authority can be enhanced (Cohen, 198

Based on this intial research, we hypothesize that, to establish and maintain their authority and control over approaching patrons, doormen are likely to speak with strong, stern voices; have a large physical appearance; use direct body orientations; and use various artifacts that signal or exert power.

> **The content of the introduction: What is your hypothesis?**
>
> After you have introduced the problem on which your paper focuses and have provided background for it, state your hypothesis or the main question guiding your research.

Method

Three research methods were used in the collection of data.

The first method was based on a series of observations conducted by four researchers at eight establishments in the city of San Diego. The eight establishments studied were Pacific Beach Bar & Grill, The Field, Cabo Cantina, Typhoon, Tavern, The Marble Room, Stingaree, and Sandbar. The

> **THE METHOD SECTION**
>
> In this section you describe in detail how you conducted your study. You give this information so readers can evaluate the appropriateness of your approaches, which then enables them to judge the validity of your results.
>
> Describe in detail who or what you studied, by characteristics, number, and place where you performed your study. When you describe the characteristics of a group, emphasize the characteristics that might bear on your results.

Beach Bar & Grill, The Field, Cabo Cantina, Typhoon, Tavern, The Marble Room, Stingaree, and Sandbar. The researchers unobtrusively observed doormen at these different locations and recorded in detail the interactions between doormen and patrons. Data was collected about the doormen's use of vocal tones, haptics, physical appearance, body orientation, and use of artifacts. Researchers did not initially in[...] of objectivity.

Passive voice

Because the APA style reports research that any researcher anywhere should be able to replicate, the identity of the person doing the research shouldn't matter—and so passive voice is used to put emphasis on what was done rather than on who did it.

→ See pages 308–309 and 445 for more on passive voice.

The second method of da[...] ers and the doormen at the eigh[...] into the ways the doormen use[...] allowed for a more direct collection of data.

The last method of data collection was face-to-face interviews conducted with individual doormen at four of the different establishments. The interviewers gathered data about the degree to which doormen were cognitively aware of their behaviors in establishing power.

Results

Based on our observations, we drew the following results.

In terms of vocal tones, four out of five of the doormen used softer vocal tones with females. Speaking with men, six out of eight doormen used more [...]

THE RESULTS SECTION

In this section, summarize the data you collected and whatever analysis you performed that supports your conclusions. If you have results that run counter to your initial hypothesis, be sure to mention this.

In their physical appearance, five out of eight of [...] observed that doormen also responded to patrons depe[...] a possible threat due to physical stature and gender: D[...] of a male-female couple, and were more courteous to [...] than, theirs.

The body orientation of doormen was shown through how six doormen stood on the same level as the patrons, while only one sat on a stool and one stood on a raised platform.

[...] wore some sort of attire that signified the particular estab-[...] e wore jackets with writing that announced their position [...] ther half wore all-black clothing. Three out of

Formatting in APA style

- Double-space the paper throughout, including titles and quotations.
- The "preferred" typeface for APA papers is Times New Roman, in 12-point size. Use the same typeface throughout the entire paper.

A REFERENCE LIST IN APA FORMAT

- Put the reference list at the end of the paper, starting on its own page.
- Use the same margin measurements as the rest of the paper (➔ see pages 394–395).
- Put the running head and page number on each reference list page at the top (as on every APA formatted page; ➔ see page 395). The number on the first reference list page follows the number of the paper's last page. For example, if the last page of the paper is 7, the first page of the reference list will be 8.
- **References** is centered, top.
- Arrange listings alphabetically by authors' last names. (If a listing starts with a title, insert it using the title's first letter. If the title begins with **A**, **An**, or **The**, alphabetize by the second word of the title.)
- If you list two or more sources by the same author, order them by the date, with the most recent first. If there are multiple authors, alphabetize subsequent sources for these authors by the second author's name.
- Double-space the entries.
  - ➔ See pages 402–419 for creating individual entries.
- So readers can scan the list easily, indent by 1/2 inch all lines underneath the first of each entry. This is called *hanging indent*.

NONVERBAL POWER DISPLAYS BY DOORMEN   8

Carney, D., Hall, J., & LeBeau, L. (2005, Summer). Beliefs about the nonverbal expression of social power. *Journal of Nonverbal Behavior, 29*(2), 105–123. doi:10.1007/s10919-005-2743-z

Cohen, H. (1980). *You can negotiate anything.* New York, NY: Bantam Books.

Dunbar, N., & Abra, G. (2008, May). *Observations of dyadic power in interpersonal interaction.* Paper presented at the annual meeting of the International Communication Association, Montreal, Canada. Retrieved from http://www.icahdq.org/

Dunbar, N., & Burgoon, J. (2005, April). Perceptions of power and interactional dominance in interpersonal relationships. *Journal of Social & Personal Relationships, 22*(2), 207–233. doi:10.1177/0265407505050944

Knott, G. (1979, October). Nonverbal communication during early childhood. *Theory into Practice, 18*(4), 226. Retrieved from http://search.ebscohost.com.ezproxy.lib.uwm.edu/ login.aspx?direct=true&db=a9h&AN=5201824&loginpage=Login.asp&site=ehost-live

Krumhuber, E., Manstead, A., & Kappas, A. (2007, Spring). Temporal aspects of facial displays in person and expression perception: The effects of smile dynamics, head-tilt, and gender. *Journal of Nonverbal Behavior, 31*(1), 39–56. doi:10.1007/s10919-006-0019-x

May, S. (2000, Winter). Proxemics: The hula hoop and use of personal space. *Communication Teacher, 14*(2), 4–5. Retrieved from http://search.ebscohost.com.ezproxy.lib.uwm.edu/login.aspx?direct=true&db=ufh&AN=31746491&loginpage=Login.asp&site=ehost-live

1/2"

398   PART 9 DOCUMENTING: APA

APA DOCUMENTATION FOR IN-TEXT CITATIONS

THE PATTERN

IN-TEXT CITATIONS IN APA STYLE

Whether you are citing books, periodicals, or electronic sources, in-text citations in APA style generally contain three elements:

1

The name of the author of the words or ideas being quoted, summarized, or paraphrased. The name can appear within a sentence containing quoted words, or it can appear in parentheses at the sentence's end.

2

The date when the source being cited was published.

3

The page number(s) of or some other reference to the cited words or ideas. The number of the page from which quoted words come goes at the end of the sentence, in parentheses. Note that **p.** goes before the page number.

You can arrange these three APA elements in two ways to create an in-text citation:

Discussing nineteenth-century women preachers, Bizzell (2006) argues that "a conjunction between the female sex and moral activism is traditional in Methodism" (p. 379).

One writer on nineteenth-century women preachers argues that "a conjunction between the female sex and moral activism is traditional in Methodism" (Bizzell, 2006, p. 379).

→ Pages 400–401 list variations on this pattern for APA in-text citations.

PUNCTUATION IN APA IN-TEXT CITATIONS

- The parentheses that contain page numbers go at a sentence's end, followed by the punctuation that ends the sentence.
- When you include an author's name in the parentheses with the year and page number, put a comma between each element.
- If the words you quote run across several pages, use **pp.** to cite them like this: **(pp. 23–25)** (**pp.** stands for *pages*).
- If the quoted words are from nonconsecutive pages, cite them like this: **(pp. 45, 76)**.

VARIATIONS ON THE APA PATTERN FOR IN-TEXT CITATIONS

NO AUTHOR IS NAMED

If no author is named, use the work's title:

To "watch the rejects crash and burn" is why we watch *American Idol*, according to *Rolling Stone* magazine ("Idol Worship," 2007, p. 7).

THERE IS NO PAGE NUMBER

Give a paragraph or part number (if there is one); otherwise, give the author's name.

The World Health Organization names obstetric fistulas as a global problem; over two million women suffer from them (2006, para. 64).

(Readers will look in the references for a listing under *World Health Organization*.)

YOU CITE TWO OR MORE SOURCES BY THE SAME AUTHOR

Give the date of each source in your citation.
    This cites the first source from an author:

That meat from cows fed on grass is more nutritious than that from corn-fed cows is one of Pollan's many arguments (2006, p. 211).

    This cites a second source by the author:

Because his research shows what chemicals go into a commercial potato, Pollan cannot bring himself to eat one (2001, p. 98).

A SOURCE HAS TWO AUTHORS

List the names in the order they appear in the source. Use *and* between the names in an in-text citation, but use an ampersand (**&**) in parenthetical references:

As "much an activist as an analytical method" is how Moeller and Moberly (2006) describe McAllister's approach to computer games.

As "much an activist as an analytical method" is how reviewers describe McAllister's take on computer games (Moeller & Moberly, 2006).

YOU CITE TWO AUTHORS WITH THE SAME LAST NAME

Include the authors' initials in your citations so readers know which citation to check.

R. M. Rorty (1979) argues that we ought no longer to think of our minds as "mirrors" that only reflect what is already in the world.

A. O. Rorty (1996) shows how Aristotle's *Rhetoric* brings together conceptions of communication, the psychology of audiences, communicators' character, and politics. These examples use their parenthetical citations to avoid ambiguity:

Some philosophers argue that our conception of what knowledge is has changed in the last 200 years (R. M. Rorty, 1979).

Aristotle's *Rhetoric* brings together conceptions of communication, the psychology of audiences, the character of communicators, and politics (A. O. Rorty, 1996).

A SOURCE HAS THREE, FOUR, OR FIVE AUTHORS

The first time you cite the source, list each author's name. After that, list the first author's name followed by *et al.* (Latin for *and others*.) Put a period after *al*.

What happens when a ninth-grade class is offered at the honors level for all students, without tracking? Fine, Anand, Jordan, and Sherman (2000) offer a two-year study of such a class.

Later in the same paper:

As a result of their study, Fine et al. (2000) argue that students "who never expected to be seen as smart" come to see themselves as capable and sharp (pp. 174, 175).

A SOURCE HAS SIX OR MORE AUTHORS

Include only the first author's name, followed by *et al.* (Latin for *and others*.) Put a period after *al.*

Statistical data is "easily misinterpreted" (Walpole et al., 2006, p. 217).

Walpole et al. (2006, p. 217) argue that statistical data is "easily misinterpreted."

A SOURCE HAS A GROUP OR CORPORATE AUTHOR OR IS A GOVERNMENT DOCUMENT

Write out the name of the group author.

When organizing catalogs, librarians typically follow a set of guidelines established by the American Library Association (2004).

When organizing catalogs, librarians typically follow established guidelines (American Library Association, 2004).

YOU CITE TWO OR MORE SOURCES IN ONE SENTENCE

List the sources (separated by semicolon) in alphabetical order by author's last name.

The words used to describe race and ethnicity shape the way people respond to calls for diversity or justice (Adams, 2000; Fletcher, 2007).

Adams (2000) and Fletcher (2007) argue that language plays a vital role in shaping how people respond to calls for diversity and justice.

YOU CITE A CLASSICAL SOURCE, SACRED TEXT, OR OTHER SOURCE WITH NO DATE LISTED

Use the author's name followed by a comma and *n.d.* (for *no date*).

Early in its history, rhetoric was defined as the use of the available means of persuasion (Aristotle, n.d.).

You can also use the date of translation, if known, preceded by *trans.*

Early in its history, rhetoric was defined as the use of the available means of persuasion (Aristotle, trans. 1954).

If you cite a sacred text such as the Bible or the Koran, you do not need to provide a reference list entry. The first time you cite the work, identify the version you are using.

John 11:7 (Revised Standard Version)

YOU CITE ELECTRONIC SOURCES

If your source includes paragraph numbers, use that number preceded by *para.*

Some researchers have used a concept of "virtual wives" to describe technology in personal life (Clark-Flory, 2007, para. 12).

If the source does not number paragraphs, cite the nearest main heading and number the paragraph of your quotation relative to that heading.

Some researchers have used a concept of "virtual wives" to describe technology in personal life (Clark-Flory, 2007, Introduction, para. 1).

Because personal e-mails cannot be retrieved by readers, do not include them in a reference list. Cite them in your text only.

Austin's famous Congress Avenue bats first appeared in 1980 (E. C. Lupfer, personal communication, March 17, 2003).

APA DOCUMENTATION FOR REFERENCE LIST ENTRIES

The following pages show you how to format entries in the reference list that goes at the end of any APA-style paper. The essential pattern is shown here:

THE PATTERN

Four elements make up any citation in the reference list of an APA-style paper:

Author's Name. (Date of Publication). *Title of text.* Publication information.
1   2   3   4

The publication information about a text includes who published a text and where. For example, here is a citation for a book:

Boo, K. (2012). *Behind the beautiful forevers: Life, death, and hope in a Mumbai undercity.*
1   2   3

     New York, NY: Random House.
     4

(Note the indenting in the example: This is standard when formatting your list of references, as we describe on page 398.)

The APA distinguishes works to be cited as periodicals and nonperiodicals. (Nonperiodicals are books and any other kind of source not published on a regular schedule.) We follow the same distinction in the pages that follow.

Note that when you cite a book, periodical, or webpage, the format of the citation—the capitalization of the title of a book, the inclusion of a periodical's issue number, or the listing of a URL—tells a reader what kind of text you are citing. When you cite a text that isn't a book, periodical, or webpage, you may also need to indicate what kind of text it is.

1 MAKE AN INDIVIDUAL LISTING FOR EACH WORK YOU ARE CITING

Do you know the kind of source you have?

YES   NO ···▶ Go to pages 62–65.

Have you collected the expected citation information for your source?

YES   NO ···▶ Go to pages 124–139.

Go to the page with the citation pattern for the kind of source you have.

PERIODICAL   NONPERIODICAL

Page 404   Page 406

- Follow the pattern to construct your listing part by part, starting with the author, moving on to the title, and so on.
- If a part of your citation varies from the pattern, follow the page references to see the format for the variation.

2 CONSTRUCT YOUR REFERENCE LIST

When you have all your individual citations, put them together into the reference list.

➔ See page 398 for details on how to format the reference list.

APA REFERENCE LIST ENTRIES
FOR PERIODICAL SOURCES

1 ARE YOU SURE YOU ARE WORKING WITH A PERIODICAL?
See pages 60–65 to check.

2 DO YOU HAVE ALL THE NEEDED INFORMATION FOR YOUR CITATION?
See pages 130–131 to check.

3 THE PATTERN

Here is a sample APA citation for an article from a periodical, followed by a detailed pattern.

Jeffries, M. P. (2014) Hip-hop urbanism old and new. *International Journal of Urban and Regional Research, 38*(2), 706–715 doi:10.1111/1468-2427.12106

Author's Name. (Date). Title of article.

The pattern for an author's name is on page 408.

WHAT TO DO WHEN YOU HAVE

• no author named: page 408
• one author: page 408
• two to seven authors: page 408
• eight or more authors: page 408
• two or more works published by the same author in the same year: page 409
• a government author: page 409
• a corporate author: page 409
• a work signed *Anonymous*: page 409

The pattern for the article title is on page 412.

WHAT TO DO WHEN YOU HAVE

• a letter to the editor: page 414
• a review: page 414

The pattern for date of publication is on page 410.

WHAT TO DO WHEN YOU HAVE

• a monthly magazine article: page 410
• a daily newspaper article: page 410

WHAT COUNTS AS A PERIODICAL?
A periodical is a publication published at regular intervals: every week, every month, every season. Journal, magazine, or newspaper articles, *including those published online,* are periodicals.

Include a digital object identifier (**doi**) if you see one with your source. See page 416.

Periodical Name, Volume(Issue), Pages. doi:

If the periodical name begins with **A** or **The**, you can leave off those words.

Italicize the periodical name.

The pattern for the volume and issue numbers is on page 415.

WHAT TO DO WHEN YOU HAVE

- no issue number: page 415
- only a date: page 415
- a daily newspaper: page 415
- a weekly or biweekly journal or magazine: page 415

Give the inclusive page numbers: **37–52** or **121–145**.

If you cite a newspaper article, put **p.** (for single-page articles) or **pp.** (for multipage articles) before the page numbers: **p. J3** or **pp. C2–C5**. If the pages are discontinuous, put a comma between the numbers: **pp. B1, B4**.

APA REFERENCES LIST ENTRIES
FOR NONPERIODICAL SOURCES

1 ARE YOU SURE YOU ARE WORKING WITH A NONPERIODICAL?
See pages 60–65 to check.

2 DO YOU HAVE ALL THE NEEDED INFORMATION FOR YOUR CITATION?
See pages 124–129 to check.

3 THE PATTERN

Here is a sample APA citation for a nonperiodical, followed by a detailed pattern.

Berger, J. (1992). *About looking.* New York, NY: Vintage.

Author's Name. (Date). *Source title.*

The pattern for an author's name is on page 408.

WHAT TO DO WHEN YOU HAVE

- no author named: page 408
- one author: page 408
- two to seven authors: page 408
- eight or more authors: page 408
- an edited collection: page 409
- a government author: page 409
- a corporate author: page 409
- a work signed *Anonymous*: page 409
- a screen name: page 409

The pattern for titles is on page 412.

WHAT TO DO WHEN YOU HAVE

- an essay or chapter in a book: page 412
- an essay in an online collection: page 412
- an article from a reference book: page 412

Put the year in parentheses, followed by a period. If you have no publication date, put **n.d.** (for *no date*) inside the parentheses, without quotation marks.

WHAT COUNTS AS A NONPERIODICAL?

Nonperiodical sources include books, parts of books (such as essays and chapters in books), films, videos, CDs, audio recordings, and reports—*including those that are published online.*

Place of publication: Publisher.

The pattern for the place of publication is on page 411.

WHAT TO DO

- about the state where the source was published: page 411

- when the source was published in another country: page 411

From the publisher's full name, you can leave off words such as **Press** or **Company**. Note that a colon precedes the publisher's name and that a period follows it.

IF YOUR SOURCE IS ONLINE:

The pattern for online sources is on page 416.

YOU MAY NEED TO INCLUDE ADDITIONAL INFORMATION HERE IN YOUR CITATION IF

- you are citing a report from the Education Resources Information Center (ERIC): page 414

- the work is translated: page 414

- a book is a second (or later) edition: page 414

- the work is in more than one volume: page 414

- the work is a review: page 414

- you are citing software, visual sources such as charts or photographs, film and television shows, interviews, conference papers, or sound recordings: pages 418–419

APA DOCUMENTATION FOR REFERENCE LIST ENTRIES
Author's Name

The pattern for author names is consistent across differing texts and media.

THE PATTERN

The first author listed is always written with the last name first, then a comma, and then the initials. (If an author's first name is hyphenated, include the hyphen with the initials.)

Last Name, Initials.   Singh, A. R.   Chen, K.-H.

If a work you are citing has more than one author, list the additional names in the order in which they are given in the source. All authors are cited last name first. Use an ampersand (**&**) before the last author's name.

Phelps, L. W., & Emig, J.   Fine, M. T., Weis, L., Pruitt, L. P., & Burns, A.

Note that, in a reference list entry, there is a period after the author's name or the list of authors' names.

NO AUTHOR NAMED

If you cannot find an author's name, start the entry with the name of the book or article.

Idol worship. (2007, February 8). *Rolling Stone*, 1016, 7.
MAGAZINE ARTICLE

Ultimate visual dictionary (Rev. ed.). (2002). New York, NY: Dorling Kindersley.
REFERENCE WORK

ONE AUTHOR

Xavier, J. (2007, June 11). Timo Veikkola (Nokia): A vision for the future. Message posted to http://julianax.blogspot .com/2007/06/timo-veikkola-nokia-vision-of-future.html
BLOG POST

TWO TO SEVEN AUTHORS

In reference list entries, include the names of up to seven authors. Separate names and initials with commas, and use an ampersand (**&**) before the last author.

Levitt, S. D., & Dubner, S. J. (2006). *Freakonomics: A rogue economist explores the hidden side of everything.* New York, NY: HarperCollins.
BOOK

DeVoss, D. N., Cushman, E., & Grabill, J. T. (2005). Infrastructure and composing: The when of new-media writing. *CCC, 57,* 14–44.
ARTICLE, IN SCHOLARLY PERIODICAL

EIGHT OR MORE AUTHORS

List the first seven names, insert an ellipsis, and then list the last author's name.

Liu, X., Zhang, L., You, L., Yu, J., Zhao, J., Li, L., Wang. Q., . . . Wu, H. (2011). Differential toxicological effects induced by mercury in gills from three pedigrees of manila clam ruditapes philippinarum by nmr-based metabolomics. *Ecotoxicology, 20*(1), 177–186.
ARTICLE, IN SCHOLARLY PERIODICAL, MORE THAN EIGHT AUTHORS

TWO OR MORE WORKS PUBLISHED BY THE SAME AUTHOR IN THE SAME YEAR

List the works in alphabetical order by title, and use lowercase letters (**a**, **b**, **c**, etc.) following the year to distinguish the works.

Helfand, G., & Walker, C. J. (Eds.). (2001a). *Mastering APA style: Instructor's resource guide.* Washington, DC: American Psychological Association.
BOOK

Helfand, G., & Walker, C. J. (Eds.). (2001b). *Mastering APA style: Student's workbook and training guide.* Washington, DC: American Psychological Association.
BOOK

Your in-text citations will also need the lowercase letters so readers know which of the two sources you are citing.

AN EDITED COLLECTION

Adams, M. (Ed.). (2000). *Readings for diversity and social justice: An anthology on racism, sexism, antisemitism, heterosexism, classism, and ableism.* New York, NY: Routledge.
BOOK, EDITED

If you are citing only a piece from an edited collection and not the whole collection, create the citation following the pattern for an essay or chapter in a book shown on page 415.

ANONYMOUS AUTHOR

Use **Anonymous** as the author only if the work is so signed.

Anonymous. (n.d.). How to be an anarchist. Retrieved from http://www.wikihow.com/Be-an-Anarchist
WIKI POST

A CORPORATE AUTHOR

A corporate author is an organization, corporation, or association. Start with the name of the corporate author exactly as it is listed (but omit **A**, **An**, or **The**).

American Counseling Association. (2007). *Basic facts about clinical depression* [Brochure]. Alexandria, VA: Author.
BROCHURE

Employee Benefit Research Institute. (2007). *How are retirees doing financially in retirement?* (Issue Brief No. 302). Washington, DC: Author.
REPORT FROM A PRIVATE ORGANIZATION

A GOVERNMENT AUTHOR

Start with the name of the government branch responsible for the publication.

National Center for Educational Statistics. (2005). *Comparative indicators of education in the United States and other G8 countries: 2004.* Washington, DC: U.S. Department of Education Center for Educational Studies.
REPORT
GOVERNMENT AUTHOR, FEDERAL

A SOURCE PUBLISHED UNDER A SCREEN NAME

Provide the "real" name if you have it, followed by the screen name in brackets; otherwise, give only the screen name.

Moore, S. J. [Skrillex]. (2015, Sept. 24). TokyÜ there. Retrieved from https://www.youtube.com/watch?v=uFjwNGxqkb4
YOUTUBE VIDEO
SOURCE WITH SCREEN NAME

APA REFERENCE LIST ENTRIES
Date of Publication

The pattern for date of publication is consistent across differing texts and media.

Place the copyright date or year of publication in parentheses, followed by a period.

(Year of Publication). **(2007).**

If you find more than one copyright date for a book, use the most recent one.

For monthly magazines, newspapers, and newsletters, give the year, then the month.

(2006, July).

Include the day for periodicals published daily, like newspapers: **(2007, August 23).**

A BOOK THAT HAS BEEN REPUBLISHED

Use the standard book pattern, but add the original publication date at the end.

Johnson, S. (2002). *Emergence: The connected lives of ants, brains, cities, and software.* New York, NY: Touchstone-Simon. (Original work published 2001)
BOOK, REPUBLISHED

A BOOK THAT HAS NO PUBLICATION DATE

Put **n.d.** (for *no date*) where the year of publication usually goes in a citation.

Baudrillard, J. (n.d.). *Simulations.* New York, NY: Semiotext(e).
BOOK, NO PUBLICATION DATE

MAGAZINE ARTICLE

Include the month of publication following the year.

Ehrenreich, B. (2000, April). Maid to order: The politics of other women's work. *Harper's,* 59–70.
ARTICLE, IN POPULAR MAGAZINE

NEWSPAPER ARTICLE

For newspapers and other daily periodicals, include the month and day of publication following the year.

Lipton, E. (2007, September 2). Product safety commission bears heavy scrutiny. *Austin American Statesman,* p. A11.
ARTICLE, NEWSPAPER

Rood, L. (2011, March 5). More information on attorney discipline. *Des Moines Register.* Retrieved from http://www.DesMoinesRegister.com/article/20110306/NEWS/103060335/More-information-on-attorney-discipline?odyssey=tab|topnews|text|News
ARTICLE, NEWSPAPER, ONLINE

APA REFERENCE LIST ENTRIES
Place of Publication

The pattern for place of publication is consistent across differing texts and media.

THE PATTERN

Put the place of publication after the title of the book, followed by a colon.

Place of Publication: Boston, MA: Cambridge, England: Santa Monica, CA: Calumet, MI:

If more than one place of publication is listed, use the first one.

EXAMPLES

Merrell, F. (1991). *Unthinking thinking: Jorge Luis Borges, mathematics, and the new physics.* West Lafayette, IN: Purdue University Press.
BOOK

Wardlow, G. D. (1998). *Chasin' that devil music: Searching for the blues.* San Francisco, CA: Miller Freeman.
BOOK

INCLUDE THE STATE
The convention for adding the state is to use the two-letter abbreviation used by the U.S. Postal Service.

Eisner, W. (1996). *Graphic storytelling and visual narrative.* Tamarac, FL: Poorhouse.
BOOK

Hargittai, I., & Hargittai, M. (1994). *Symmetry: A unifying concept.* Bolinas, CA: Shelter Publications.
BOOK

Harris, S. L. (1990). *Agents of chaos: Earthquakes, volcanoes, and other natural disasters.* Missoula, MT: Mountain Press.
BOOK

A BOOK PUBLISHED IN ANOTHER COUNTRY
Put the name of the city of publication, a comma, and then the country name.

Yanagi, S. (1989). *The unknown craftsman: A Japanese insight into beauty.* Tokyo, Japan: Kodansha.
BOOK, PUBLISHED IN ANOTHER COUNTRY

Bourriaud, N. (2004). *Relational aesthetics.* Dijon-Quetigny, France: Les Presses du Réel.
BOOK, PUBLISHED IN ANOTHER COUNTRY

APA REFERENCE LIST ENTRIES
Titles

The pattern for titles is consistent across differing texts and media.

THE PATTERN

BOOK TITLES

1 Capitalize only the first word of the title and the first word of the subtitle.

2 Capitalize any proper nouns within a title.

3 Italicize the entire title. If you are not using a computer, underline the title.

4 Put a period after the title. (If the title ends with a question mark or exclamation point, use that instead.)

The title of the book.

Crow Lake.

The diving bell and the butterfly.

If the book has a subtitle, put the subtitle after a colon and capitalize its first word.

Scribbling the cat: Travels with an African soldier.

The quick and the dead: Artists and anatomy.

A country doctor's casebook: Tales from the north woods.

THE PATTERN

TITLES OF BOOK PARTS, PERIODICAL ARTICLES, AND WEBPAGES

1 Capitalize only the first word of the title and the first word of the subtitle.

2 Do not italicize or put quotation marks around the title.

3 Put a period after the last word. (If the title ends with a question mark or exclamation point, use that instead.)

4 Follow the pattern below for finishing:

PARTS OF BOOKS

List the chapter title, followed by the word **In** and the editor's name, followed by (**Ed.**) and the book's title.

At the corner of progress and peril. In K. Merida (Ed.), *Being a black man: At the corner of progress and peril.*

JOURNAL ARTICLES

Put the name of the journal—in italics—after the article title.

Article title. *Journal Name*

Will the next election be hacked? *Rolling Stone*

WEBPAGES

Put the name of the website—in italics—after the name of the webpage.

Article title. *Website name.*

Project description. *The Nora Project.*

A BOOK

Petherbridge, D., & Jordanova, L. (1997). *The quick and the dead: Artists and anatomy.* Berkeley, CA: University of California Press.
BOOK

Vaillant, J. (2012). *The tiger: A true story of vengeance and survival.* Retrieved from http://www.barnesandnoble.com
BOOK ON AN E-READER

AN ESSAY OR CHAPTER IN A BOOK

Makhan, J. (1998). Island ecology and cultural perceptions: A case study of Lakshdweep. In B. Saraswatie (Ed.), *Lifestyle and ecology.* New Delhi, India: Indira Gandhi National Centre for the Arts. Retrieved from http://www.ignca.nic.in/cd_08012.htm
ESSAY, IN ONLINE BOOK

Plato. (1961). Meno (W. K. C. Guthrie, Trans.). In E. Hamilton & H. Cairns (Eds.), *The collected dialogues of Plato* (pp. 353–385). Princeton, NJ: Princeton University Press.
ESSAY, IN EDITED BOOK
ESSAY, TRANSLATED

Parry, D. (2012). The digital humanities or a digital humanism. In Matthew K. Gold (Ed.). *Debates in the digital humanities* (pp. 429–437). Minneapolis, MN: Minnesota University Press.
ESSAY, IN EDITED BOOK

AN ESSAY IN AN ONLINE COLLECTION

Badger, M. (2004, June). Visual blogs. In L. J. Gurak, S. Antonijevic, L. Johnson, & J. Reyman (Eds.), *Into the blogosphere: Rhetoric, community, and culture of weblogs.* Retrieved from http://blog.lib.umn.edu/blogosphere/visual_blogs.html
ESSAY, IN ONLINE COLLECTION

AN ARTICLE FROM A REFERENCE BOOK

Reference works rarely give the names of article authors. Put the title in place of the author in these cases.

Islam. (1989). In *The New York Public Library desk reference.*
ARTICLE, IN REFERENCE BOOK

Bovine spongiform encephalopathy. (2007). In *Encyclopaedia Britannica.* Retrieved from Encyclopaedia Britannica Online: http://www.search.eb.com/eb/article-9002739
ARTICLE, IN ONLINE REFERENCE BOOK

SOCIAL MEDIA PHOTO OR GRAPHIC

Provide the title of the photo or graphic; if there isn't one, provide a description of the item in brackets.

U.S. Census Bureau. (2015, October 7). [Percent of the population 25 and older with a Bachelor's degree or higher by sex, 2005–2014] [Infographic]. Retrieved from https://www.facebook.com/uscensusbureau/photos/pb.202626512363.-2207520000.1445995198./10152987169942364/?type=3&theater
INFOGRAPHIC, FROM SOCIAL MEDIA
GOVERNMENT AUTHOR, FEDERAL

Additional Information

REPORT FROM THE EDUCATION RESOURCES INFORMATION CENTER (ERIC)

Polette, N. (2007). *Teaching thinking skills with picture books, K–3.* Portsmouth, NH: Teacher Ideas Press. Retrieved from ERIC database. (ED497152)
REPORT, FROM ERIC

A WORK WITH A TRANSLATOR

Burgat, F. (2008). *Islamism in the age of al-Qaeda* (P. Hutchinson, Trans.). Austin, TX: University of Texas Press.
BOOK, TRANSLATED

A BOOK IN A SECOND OR LATER EDITION

Rubenstein, J. M. (2004). *The cultural landscape: An introduction to human geography* (8th ed.). Upper Saddle River, NJ: Prentice Hall.
BOOK, IN A SECOND OR LATER EDITION

WORK IN MORE THAN ONE VOLUME

Goldman, B. A., & Mitchell, D. F. (2007). *Directory of unpublished experimental mental measures* (Vol. 9). Washington, DC: American Psychological Association.
BOOK, MULTIVOLUME

A BOOK REVIEW

Julius, A. (2007, September 2). A people and a nation [Review of the book *Jews and power,* by R. R. Wisse]. *The New York Times Book Review,* p. 27.
REVIEW, OF BOOK

AN ABSTRACT

Lacy, E., & Leslie, S. (2007). Library outreach near and far: Programs to staff and patients of the Piedmont Healthcare System. *Medical Reference Services Quarterly, 26*(3): 91–103. Abstract obtained from Library, Information Science & Technology Abstracts database.
ABSTRACT, JOURNAL ARTICLE

LETTER TO THE EDITOR

Delaney, J. (2007, August 28). Helping the world's sexually abused children [Letter to the editor]. *The Washington Post,* p. A12.
LETTER TO THE EDITOR

Periodical Volume and Issue

THE PATTERN

VOLUME AND ISSUE NUMBER

The volume number, italicized, follows the name of the periodical; there is a comma between the two. If there is an issue number, put it in parentheses after the volume number, with no space before the parentheses. Issue numbers are not italicized.

Volume(Issue) *5*(2) *27*(11)

EXAMPLE

Watts, S. (1995, June). Walt Disney: Art and politics in the American century. *The Journal of American History, 82*(1), 84–110.
ARTICLE, IN SCHOLARLY PERIODICAL

WHEN THERE IS NO ISSUE NUMBER

Lawrence, R. (2000). Equivalent mass of a coil spring. *Physics Teacher, 38,* 140–141.
ARTICLE, IN A PERIODICAL PAGINATED BY VOLUME

WHEN THERE IS ONLY A DATE
Many popular magazines only list a date.

Birnbaum, C. A. (2007, September). Cultivating appreciation. *Dwell,* 196+.
ARTICLE, IN POPULAR MAGAZINE

A DAILY NEWSPAPER
Daily newspapers do not have volumes and issues; they are cited only by the date.

Rozek, D. (2006, November 10). Girls' squabble over iPod over: And in the end, neither will get music player. *Chicago Sun-Times,* p. 3.
NEWSPAPER ARTICLE

A WEEKLY OR BIWEEKLY JOURNAL OR MAGAZINE
If a weekly or biweekly journal or magazine does not have volume and issue numbers, cite only the date.

Gorman, C. (2006, September 18). To an athlete, aching young. *Time, 168*(12), 60. Retrieved from Expanded Academic ASAP database.
ARTICLE, IN WEEKLY JOURNAL, RETRIEVED FROM ONLINE DATABASE

Schlei, R. (2007, September 6). Faithful comrade: A monumental affair [Review of the book *Loving Frank* by N. Horan]. *Shepherd Express,* 48.
REVIEW, OF BOOK, IN WEEKLY JOURNAL

APA DOCUMENTATION FOR REFERENCE LIST ENTRIES
For Online Sources

In APA style, reference list entries for online sources include the same information as print sources, in the same order—but with the addition of information (at the citation's end) that enables readers to find online sources.

PATTERN 1

GIVE THE SOURCE'S URL.

As you find and track sources, copy a source's URL into your running source list (→ see pages 140–141). When you put the source into your reference list, create the citation following the patterns on pages 404–407—but put Retrieved from, followed by the URL.

Dieterle , B. (2015) [Review of the book *Toward a composition made whole* by Jody Shipka]. *Kairos, 19*(2). Retrieved from http://kairos.technorhetoric.net/19.2/reviews/dieterle/index.html
REVIEW OF BOOK, ONLINE

As you enter URLs into reference lists, make sure that your word processor does not hyphenate them. This can "break" the URL, since readers will use the hyphen as part of the URL. If you have a long URL and need to break it across lines, break it before a slash or other punctuation. (Always keep http:// together, however.) Do not put a hyphen at the break, and do not put a period after the URL.

PATTERN 2

GIVE THE SOURCE'S DOI.

DOI stands for **digital object identifier**. The DOI system was developed by international publishers, who recognized that URLs can change and so do not ensure readers can find sources. With the DOI system, a publication is given a unique identifying number—the DOI—that provides a persistent link to it. You can find DOIs at the top of journal articles or in the citation information provided by databases. (→ See pages 136–137.)

To put a DOI into a reference list citation, create the citation as you would following the patterns on pages 404–407, then insert doi: followed by the DOI.

Stell, G. (2014). Uses and functions of English in Namibia's multiethnic settings. *World Englishes, 33*(2), 223-241. doi:10.1111/weng.12082.
ARTICLE, FROM DATABASE

You do not need to list a URL in a reference if you provide a source's DOI.

CITING AN ENTIRE WEBSITE

In APA style, if you refer to an entire website, you can give the address of the site in the text, without an entry in the reference list:

The state of Hawaii's website feels like entering an online game (https://portal.ehawaii.gov).

CITING ONLINE ARTICLES

Cite online articles as you would any other article, but include the URL or DOI if one exists. When you cite articles from databases, give either the article's DOI for the article or find the stable URL provided by the database (→ see pages 136–137); you do not need to list the database name.

Flora, C. (2005, November). Tough love. *Psychology Today*. Retrieved from http://www.psychologytoday.com/articles/200511/tough-love
ARTICLE, ONLINE VERSION OF PRINT SOURCE

Kelly, S., & Nardi, B. (2014). Playing with sustainability: Using video games to simulate futures of scarcity. *First Monday, 19*(5). doi:http://dx.doi.org/10.5210/fm.v19i5.5259
ARTICLE, ONLINE ONLY

Franzen, L., & Smith, C. (2009). Acculturation and environmental change impacts dietary habits among adult Hmong. *Appetite, 52*(1), 173–183. doi:10.1016/j.appet.2008.09.012
ARTICLE, FROM DATABASE

CITING DISCUSSION LISTS OR MAILING LISTS

For retrievable postings— discussion groups, mailing lists— use the format shown right.

McLaughlin, B. (2007, September 4). Webinar for environmental benchmarking survey [Message posted to AAUP-L mailing list]. Retrieved from http://ucp.uchicago.edu/mailman/listinfo/aaup-l
DISCUSSION GROUP OR MAILING LIST POST

CITING BLOGS AND WIKIS

Because a wiki page's date is the "last modified" date, not the date of publication, the APA recommends putting **n.d.** for the date. Include the retrieval date for a wiki because the information is likely to change.

Godin, S. (2015, September 30). Susdat. [Web log post]. Retrieved from http://sethgodin.typepad.com/seths_blog/2015/09/susdat.html
BLOG POST

Carnivorous plant. (n.d). Retrieved Otober 26, 2015, from http://www.gardenology.org/wiki/Carnivorous_plant
WIKI POST

A YOUTUBE OR OTHER ONLINE VIDEO

What You Can Do. (2015). Space and the sea. [Video file]. Retrieved from https://www.youtube.com/watch?v=vekFEPnuXhM
VIDEO ON YOUTUBE

A TWEET

Include the full text of the tweet, including any URLs and punctuation.

MaryLeeShark. (2015, September 30). Your fact of the day: An adult great white shark's liver is as big as a whole human. -;() . [Tweet]. Retrieved from https://twitter.com/MaryLeeShark/status/649261132398612480
TWEET

A FACEBOOK POST

Give the post (up to the first 40 words) as the title.

Fistula Foundation. (2015, July 13). High rates of maternal mortality and obstetric fistula are representative of the global inequalities that exist in access to basic health care and human rights. Share if you agree! [Facebook status update]. Retrieved from https://www.facebook.com/fistulafoundation?fref=ts
FACEBOOK POST

CITING EMAIL

Readers cannot retrieve personal e-mail; the APA says not to include citations for email in a Reference list (→ see page 401 on in-text citations for e-mail).

APA REFERENCE LIST ENTRIES
For Other Kinds of Sources

You may need to create references for other types of sources, including visual and multimedia sources. In APA style, a note or identifying description usually helps clarify the type of source you are citing.

As the examples on these two pages show, you can help readers by describing the medium of a source that is not usual:

Author's Name. (Year). *Title* [Medium]. Place of Publication: Publisher. Online information (if necessary).

NONPERIODICAL

As the examples on these two pages show, you can add to the citation, in brackets, **Chart, CD, Computer software, Television series, Television episode, Motion picture**—whatever information will help readers know the source kind if it is not a print or online alphabetic text.

SOFTWARE

Cite software as you would a book without a named author (→ see page 408)—but include **Computer software** in brackets after the title. If there is a publisher, include the name and date of publication; for software you have downloaded, give the date of the download and the URL.

PsychMate (Version 2.0) [Computer software]. (2007). Philadelphia, PA: Psychology Software Tools.

SOFTWARE

SOUND RECORDING

Camera Obscura. (2009). Away with murder. *On My Maudlin Career* [CD]. London, England: 4AD Records.

MUSIC OR AUDIO RECORDING

WORKING WITH UNUSUAL SOURCES

The APA has this recommendation: "In general, a reference should contain the author name, date of publication, title of the work, and publication data." If you cannot find in these pages a sample exactly like what you need, the APA recommends that you "choose the example that is most like your source and follow that format. Sometimes you will need to combine elements of more than one reference format."

VISUAL SOURCES

Sander, N., Abel, G. J., & Bauer, R. (2014). *The global flow of people* [Chart]. Retrieved from http://www.global-migration.info/?_ga=1.22066875 .1833179927.1399505154
CHART, ONLINE

Cubitt, C. (2006). *Church* [Photograph]. Katrina: A gallery of images. Retrieved from http://www.claytoncubitt.com/publish/katrina
PHOTOGRAPH, ONLINE

Adams, A. (ca. 1930). *Factory Building, San Francisco* [Photograph]. Santa Fe, NM: Museum of Fine Arts.
PHOTOGRAPH

CONFERENCE PRESENTATION, LECTURE, OR PUBLIC TALK

Use this format if you need to cite a conference presentation or similar lecture or speech that has not been published.

Kleinberg, S. L. (2005, June). *The changing face of Texas in the twenty-first century: Perspectives on the new immigration.* Paper presented at Gateway on the Gulf, a Humanities Texas Institute for Texas Teachers, Galveston, TX.
PRESENTATION OR LECTURE

AN INTERVIEW YOU CONDUCT

The APA does not consider an unpublished interview to be checkable data and so an interview should not go in the reference list. You may, however, give an in-text citation for the interview.

Some music composers believe digital technologies slow down their composing processes because they offer so many options (M. Boracz, personal communication, October 18, 2015).

FILM AND TELEVISION

Gibney, A. (Director). (2005). *Enron: The smartest guys in the room* [Motion picture]. New York, NY: Magnolia.
FILM, VIDEOTAPE, OR DVD

Hanson, H. (Writer), & Yaltanes, G. (Director). (2005, September 13). Pilot [Television series episode]. In B. Josephson & H. Hanson (Producers), *Bones*. New York, NY: Fox Broadcasting.
TELEVISION SHOW OR SERIES

TIP

FINDING INFORMATION ABOUT FILMS

The *Internet Movie Database* (http://www.imdb.com) gives you access to the information you need for citing films.

CSE DOCUMENTATION

CSE

GUIDE TO CSE DOCUMENTATION MODELS

THE PATTERNS

CSE REFERENCES

FOR BOOKS

Number. Author's Last Name Followed by Initials. Title of the book. City of Publication (State): Publisher; Year.

19. Stewart J. Calculus. Boston (MA): Brooks/Cole; 2002.

FOR ARTICLES FROM PERIODICALS

Number. Author's Last Name Followed by Initials. Article title. Periodical.Date;Volume(Issue): Pages.

17. Richie DJ, Lappos VJ, Palmer PL. Sizing/optimization of a small satellite energy storage and attitude control system. JOSR. 2007 Jul-Aug;87(52):940-952.

FOR ONLINE SOURCES AND ELECTRONIC MEDIA

Number. Title of source [Kind of electronic medium]. Edition. Place of Publication: Publisher; date of publication [date updated; date cited]. Notes.

44. WebElements: chemistry nexus [Internet]. Sheffield (UK): University of Sheffield; c1993-2007 [cited 2007 Jun 18]. Available from: http://www.webelements.com/nexus/

When you cite a book, periodical, or webpage, the format of the citation—the punctuation of the title, the inclusion of a periodical's issue number, or the listing of a URL—tells readers what kind of text you are citing. When you cite a text that isn't a book, periodical, or webpage, indicate what kind of text you are citing, in brackets after the title (as in the pattern for online sources).

DETAILS OF THE PATTERNS

AUTHOR'S NAME

An author's name is listed last name first, with initials for first and middle names. If there are two initials, they are not separated by space or periods. A period separates the author's name from the title.

TITLES OF BOOKS AND PARTS OF BOOKS

1 Capitalize only the first word and any proper nouns.

2 Do not italicize or underline book titles.

3 Put a period after the title.

JOURNAL TITLES

Journal titles in CSE are always abbreviated according to the ISO (International Organization for Standardization). For example, the full title of the journal in the example numbered 17 to the left is the *Journal of Spacecraft and Rockets*. The CSE manual has guidelines for abbreviations. Your school's library has this manual.

DATES

If you cannot find a date but can figure it out from other information, set the date in brackets: **[2002]**. If only a copyright date is available, use that with a **c** for *copyright*: **(c1962)**. If there is a publication date and a copyright date, with more than three years between them, give both dates: **(2007, c1962)**. If there is no date of publication, use the words *date unknown* in brackets: **[date unknown]**. With a website, the copyright or publication date will be a span of years. In this case, use an en dash: **(c1993–2007)**. For multiple years of publication, separate the years by an en dash: **(2004–2005)**. (The box to the right explains en dashes.)

ONLINE SOURCES AND ELECTRONIC MEDIA

References for Internet sources and electronic media do not differ significantly from what is required for print sources. There is still an author or organization who is responsible for the content, a title, a place of publication, and a date of publication. Additional information will be the URL and access date, and with some media, technical information.

Always put the medium in brackets after the title:

[Internet]

[DVD]

CSE also notes dates of updates (which are most applicable to websites) and dates accessed for Internet sources. In some cases, a date of update will not be provided, but you should always note the date of access, especially for materials that change frequently, such as a blog or wiki.

In a CSE citation, notes include URLs as well as technical information. See the examples for audio and video recordings and CD-ROMs for examples of technical notes.

→ See sample references on pages 423–424.

→ See sample references on pages 423–424.

EN DASHES

hyphen: -   en dash: –

CSE style specifies that you use an en dash (instead of a hyphen) in dates. On Macintosh computers, you can make an en dash by holding down the Option key as you click the hyphen key; on Windows computers, hold down the ALT key while typing 0150.

CSE LIST OF REFERENCES

In CSE's citation-name system, writers complete the list of references and then create the in-text citations. The reference list (called *References*, *Cited References*, *Literature Cited*, or *Bibliography*) is arranged alphabetically by author and then numbered:

References

1. Amann RI, Ludwig W, Schleifer KH. Phylogenetic identification and in situ detection of individual microbial cells without cultivation. Microhi01 Rev. 1995;59:143-169.

2. Barns SM, Fundyga RE, Jeffries MW, Pace NR. Remarkable arched diversity detected in a Yellowstone National Park hot spring environment. Proc Natl Acad Sci USA. 1994;91:1609-1613.

3. Dojka, MA, Harris JK, Pace NR. Expanding the known diversity and environmental distribution of an uncultured phylogenetic division of bacteria. Appi Environ Microbiol. 2000;66:1617-1621.

→ See page 420 for information on how to format CSE style references.

CSE IN-TEXT CITATIONS

The numbers alphabetically assigned to these end references are then used for in-text references, regardless of the sequence in which the works appear in the text:

> Early studies [2] used molecular methods to reveal remarkable microbial diversity in the sediment of Yellowstone hot springs.

or:

> Early studies (2) used molecular methods to reveal remarkable microbial diversity in the sediment of Yellowstone hot springs.

In order to avoid ambiguity, citation numbers appear immediately after the relevant word, title, or phrase rather than at the end of a sentence. Usually, the citation number appears as a superscript, but it can also be set in parentheses. Set the citation number with one space both before and after, except when followed by a punctuation mark. This spacing makes the citation number easier to see.

When there are several in-text citations occurring at the same point in the text, put them in numerical order so that a reader can find them easily in the list of references. Separate the numbers by commas; if the numbers are consecutive, they can be joined by a hyphen:

> Researchers have studied brucellosis for the better part of a century [3,5,16-18,43], finding that transmission. . .

CSE SAMPLE REFERENCES

NO AUTHOR NAMED
Start with the work's title.

8. Handbook of geriatric drug therapy. Springhouse (PA): Springhouse; c2000.

MORE THAN ONE AUTHOR

17. Sebastini AM, Fishbeck DW. Mammalian anatomy: the cat. 2nd ed. Burlington (NC): Carolina Biological; 2005.

A CORPORATION OR ORGANIZATION AS AUTHOR
Start with the abbreviated name of the corporate author as it appears in the source.

3. [CCPS] Center for Chemical Process Safety. Guidelines for safe and reliable instrumented protective systems. Indianapolis (IN): Wiley; 2007.

AN EDITED BOOK
Put **editor** or **editors** after the name(s) at the start.

2. Celesia GC, editor. Disorders of peripheral and central auditory processing. Atlanta (GA): Elsevier; 2013.

A GOVERNMENT AUTHOR
GPO stands for *Government Printing Office.*

6. [GPO] US Government Printing Office. Style manual. Washington (DC): The Office; 2015.

AN ESSAY OR CHAPTER IN A BOOK

8. Feynman RP. The making of a scientist. In: Leighton R, editor. Classic Feynman: All the adventures of a curious character. New York (NY): Norton; 2006. p. 13-19.

A REVISED OR LATER EDITION OF A BOOK
Add the edition after the title.

22. Tufte ER. The visual display of quantitative information. 2nd ed. Cheshire (CT): Graphics Press; 2001.

AN ONLINE BOOK

7. Ebert D. Ecology, epidemiology, and evolution of parasitism in Daphnia [Internet]. Bethesda (MD): National Library of Medicine (US), National Center for Biotechnology Information; 2005 [cited 2007 Sep 4]. Available from: http://www.ncbi.nlm.nih.gov/entrez/query.fcgi?db=Books

AN ARTICLE IN A DAILY NEWSPAPER

24. Revkin AC. Cooking up a fable of life on melting ice. New York Times. 2007 Jul 22;Sect. 2:11.

A VOLUME IN A SERIES
The series information goes in parentheses at the end.

9. Honjo T, Melchers F, editors. Gut-associated lymphoid tissues. Berlin (Germany): Springer-Verlag; 2006. (Current Topics in Microbiology and Immunology; vol. 308).

A TECHNICAL REPORT
Include the performing and/or sponsoring organization. (The example shows the performing organization [the group that performed the research], the University of Washington Department of Statistics; the sponsoring group funded the research.)

14. Krivitsky P, Handcock M, Raftery AE, Hoff P. Representing degree distributions, clustering, and homophily in social networks with latent cluster random effects models [Internet]. Seattle (WA): University of Washington Department of Statistics; 2007. No. 517. Available from: http://www.stat.washington.edu/www/research/reports/

Note: Often, the very end of the citation acknowledges the funding; for example: (Sponsored by the Nuclear Regulatory Commission). The report number goes at the end of the citation (before the URL if there is one). If there is a contract number, include it.

A CONFERENCE PRESENTATION
Include the location and dates.

2. Braun F, Noterdaeme JM, Colas L. Simulations of different Faraday screen configurations for the ITER ICRH Antenna. In: Ryan PM, Rassmussen D, editors. Radio frequency power in plasmas: 17th topical conference on radio frequency power in plasmas; 2007 May 7-9; Clearwater (FL). Melville (NY): [AIP] American Institute of Physics; 2007. p. 175–178.

A JOURNAL PAGINATED BY VOLUME

8. Donovan SK. When is a fossil not a fossil? When it is a trace fossil. Lethaia. 2015;(48):145–146.

AN ONLINE ARTICLE

24. Spiesel S. Can a rollercoaster really scare you to death? and more. Slate [Internet]. Aug 28 [cited 2007 Sep 3]. Available from: http://www.slate.com/id/2172960/fr/flyout

A WEBPAGE

5. DNA Interactive [Internet]. Cold Spring Harbor (NY): Cold Spring Harbor Lab; c2003 [cited 2007 Aug 12]. Available from: http://www.dnai.org/

AN ONLINE DATABASE

3. Catalysts and catalysed reactions [Internet]. London (UK): RSC Publishing. 2002 [updated 2007 Aug; cited 2007 Sep 5]. Available from: http://pubs.rsc.org/Publishing/CurrentAwareness/CCR/CCRSearchPage.cfm

A BLOG POSTING

4. Isis the Scientist [screen name]. Idiosyncracies of Academia – Part 1 in a Never-Ending Series. In: Isis the Scientist [Web log]. [posted 2015 Jan 27; cited 2015 Sep 2].

CMS DOCUMENTATION

CMS

GUIDE TO CMS DOCUMENTATION MODEL

IN-TEXT CITATIONS AND FOOTNOTES

The sample sentence below contains a quotation as it would appear in a paper's body, with a superscript number at its end. The note to that sentence follows, linked by the number. (This sample is numbered 12 because eleven references precede it.) Notes can appear as footnotes at the bottom of each page or can be compiled into one list starting on a new page at the paper's end.

> In *Marriage, a History*, Stephanie Coontz states that, "whether it is valued or not, love is rarely seen as the main ingredient for marital success."[12]
>
>   12. Stephanie Coontz, *Marriage, a History: From Obedience to Intimacy or How Love Conquered Marriage* (New York: Viking, 2005), 18.

SUBSEQUENT NOTE ENTRIES

After the first reference to a book or other source, CMS conventions say that writers should put into a footnote the following:

- the author's last name

- the title of the work (or a shortened version if the title is long)

- a page number

Some writers, however, use only the author's name and the page number if there will be no ambiguity as to which source is being cited. The footnote could thus read

10. Coontz, *Marriage*, 99.

or

10. Coontz, 99.

If a reference is to the same work as in the preceding note, you can use the abbreviation **Ibid**. (*Ibid*. is a shortened form of the Latin word *ibidem*, which means *in the same place*.)

11. Ibid., 103.

BIBLIOGRAPHY

If the writer of these sample citations were to include a bibliography listing at the paper's end, the citation would be:

Coontz, Stephanie. *Marriage, a History: From Obedience to Intimacy or How Love Conquered Marriage.* New York: Viking, 2005.

(Notice, in this case, that the listing has the same formatting as MLA style.)

CMS SAMPLE REFERENCES

BOOKS

For a note:

16. J. H. Plumb, *The Italian Renaissance* (New York: Mariner Books, 2001), 86.

In the bibliography:

Plumb, J. H. *The Italian Renaissance.* New York: Mariner Books, 2001.

AN ESSAY OR CHAPTER IN A BOOK

For a note:

8. F. J. Byrne, "Early Irish Society (1st–9th Century)," in *The Course of Irish History*, eds. T. W. Moody and F. X. Martin (Lanham, MD: Roberts Rinehart, 2002), 55.

In the bibliography:

Byrne, F. J. "Early Irish Society (1st–9th Century)." In *The Course of Irish History*, edited by T. W. Moody and F. X. Martin, 43–60. Lanham, MD: Roberts Rinehart, 2002.

ARTICLES FROM PERIODICALS

For a note:

31. Ingrid Kleespies. "Tourism: Soviet-Style." *Kritika: Explorations in Russian and Eurasian History* 16, no. 2 (2015): 446.

In the bibliography:

Kleespies, Ingrid. "Tourism: Soviet-Style." *Kritika: Explorations in Russian and Eurasian History* 16, no. 2 (2015): 444–50.

A JOURNAL ARTICLE RETRIEVED FROM AN ELECTRONIC DATABASE

The citation follows the form for a journal, but the URL for the article is included.

For a note:

23. James Ramsey Wallen, "What Is an Unfinished Work?," *New Litrary History* 46, no. 1 (2015): 127, accessed June 14, 2015, doi: 10.1353/nlh.2015.0000

In the bibliography:

Wallen, James Ramsey. "What Is an Unfinished Work?" *Chronicle of Higher Education New Litrary History* 46, no. 1 (2015): 125–42. Accessed June 14, 2015. doi: 10.1353/nlh.2015.0000

ONLINE SOURCES (OTHER THAN DATABASES)

For a note:

4. Lauri Goodling, "MOAR Digital Activism, Please," *Kairos* 19, no. 3 (Summer 2015), accessed September 21, 2015, http://kairos.technorhetoric.net

In the bibliography:

Goodling, Lauri. "MOAR Digital Activism, Please." *Kairos* 19, no. 3 (Summer 2015). Accessed September 21, 2015. http://kairos.technorhetoric.net

NO AUTHOR NAMED

Start the citation with the work's title.

For a note:

    4. *Broad Stripes and Bright Stars* (Kansas City, MO: Andrews McMeel, 2002), 15.

In the bibliography:

Broad Stripes and Bright Stars. Kansas City,
    MO: Andrews McMeel, 2002.

TWO OR THREE AUTHORS

In a note, put all of the authors' full names. For subsequent references, give the authors' last names only. In the bibliography, give full names.

For a note:

    2. Larry J. Reynolds and Gordon Hutner, eds., *National Imaginaries, American Identities: The Cultural Work of American Iconography* (Princeton, NJ: Princeton University Press, 2000), 56.

In the bibliography:

Reynolds, Larry J., and Gordon Hutner, eds.
    National Imaginaries, American Identities: The Cultural Work of American Iconography. Princeton, NJ:
    Princeton University Press, 2000.

FOUR OR MORE AUTHORS

In a note, give the name of the first author listed, followed by *et al.* List all the authors in the bibliography.

For a note:

    3. James Drake et al., *James Drake* (Austin, TX: UT Press, 2008), 40.

In the bibliography:

Drake, James, Bruce Ferguson, Steven Henry Madoff,
    and Jimmy Santiago Baca. *James Drake*. Austin, TX: UT
    Press, 2008.

A CORPORATE AUTHOR

Start with the name of the corporate author as it appears in the source.

For a note:

    14. Brady Center to Prevent Gun Violence, *Guns and Hate: A Lethal Combination* (Washington, DC: Brady Center to Prevent Gun Violence, 2009), 13.

In the bibliography:

Brady Center to Prevent Gun Violence. *Guns and Hate: A
    Lethal Combination*. Washington, DC: Brady Center to
    Prevent Gun Violence, 2009.

A GOVERNMENT AUTHOR

List the full agency or department name as author.

For a note:

    11. Centers for Disease Control, "Get the Facts About Tuberculosis," (Washington, DC: United States Government Printing Office, 2014), 9.

In the bibliography:

Centers for Disease Control. "Get the Facts About
    Tuberculosis." Washington, DC: United States
    Government Printing Office, 2014.

AN EDITED BOOK

Put *ed.* (or *eds.* for multiple editors) after the names that begin the citation.

For a note:

    34. J. Peter Burkholder and Claude V. Palisca, eds., *Norton Anthology of Western Music*, Vol. 1, *Ancient to Baroque* (New York: Norton, 2005), 550.

In the bibliography:

Burkholder, J. Peter, and Claude V. Palisca, eds. *Norton
    Anthology of Western Music*. Vol. 1, *Ancient to Baroque*.
    New York: Norton, 2005.

A RELIGIOUS TEXT

Citations for religious texts appear in the notes, but not in the bibliography.

    13. Qur'an 18:16–20.

AN ARTICLE FROM A REFERENCE BOOK

Well-known reference materials are not usually listed in a CMS bibliography, so you need to know only the footnote format. Start with the name of the reference work, and then list its edition. Put **s.v.** (*sub verbo*, Latin for *under the word*) and then put the title of the entry you are citing in quotation marks:

    9. *Riverside Dictionary of Biography*, 2004 ed., s.v. "Aaron, Hank (Henry Lewis)."

AN ARTICLE FROM AN ONLINE REFERENCE

The access date should be included in the citation only for sources that are frequently updated, such as Wikis. (And, as with reference works in print, there should be no listing in the bibliography.)

    17. Wikipedia, s.v. "Deadwood, South Dakota," last modified June 8, 2015, http://en.wikipedia.org/wiki/Deadwood%2C_South_Dakota.

AN E-MAIL

If you refer to e-mails in the text of your paper, you do not need to provide a note. E-mails are not listed in a CMS bibliography.

In an e-mail message to the author on February 6, 2016, Marilyn Cooper noted. . . .

If you do need to include a note:

    14. Marilyn Cooper, e-mail message to author, February 6, 2016.

A WEBPAGE

For a note:

    19. New York Historical Society, **"Galleries,"** *New York Divided: Slavery and the Civil War*, http://www.slaveryinnewyork.org/tour_galleries.htm (accessed September 2, 2015).

In the bibliography:

New York Historical Society. "Galleries."
    New York Divided: Slavery and the Civil War. http://www.slaveryinnewyork.org/tour_galleries.htm (accessed September 2, 2015).

A BLOG POSTING

Like e-mails, blogs can be cited in the text and are not listed in the bibliography:

In the October 27, 2014, blog post titled "Digital Scholarship and Book History," Sarah Werner discusses...

For a note:

    8. Sarah Werner, "Digital Scholarship and Book History," In the *Wynken de Worde Blog*, October 27, 2014, http://sarahwerner.net/blog/2014/10/digital-scholarship-and-book-history/.

PART 10
EDITING AND PROOFREADING YOUR WORK

CONTENTS

10 EDITING AND PROOFREADING

WHERE ARE WE IN A PROCESS FOR COMPOSING?

Understanding your project
Getting started
Asking questions
Shaping your project for others
Drafting a paper
Getting feedback
Revising
Polishing   Editing and Proofreading

PART 10 **EDITING AND PROOFREADING YOUR WORK**

Questions you might have about editing and proofreading:

What is Academic English?

→ See pages 430–431.

What are some effects of globalization on English?

→ See pages 432–433.

What if I grew up in a home where we didn't speak or write "standard English"?

→ See page 431.

My teacher tells me I am editing when I should be revising. What's the difference?

→ See page 434–435.

How do I edit?

→ See page 435.

How do I proofread?

→ See page 435.

What are the most common grammatical errors I should be trying to catch in my writing?

→ Pages 436–460 address the aspects of sentences that give writers the most trouble.

THE WPA OUTCOMES* FOR PART 10 INCLUDE:

Rhetorical abilities: Understanding levels of formality needed for different contexts and audiences.

Writing processes: Developing flexible strategies for editing and proofreading.

Using conventions: Developing knowledge of linguistic structures, including grammar and punctuation; understanding why conventions for tone and mechanics vary.

*See page 15.

ACADEMIC ENGLISH

The following paragraph comes from a publication (by Dr. Terry Myers Zawacki, Eiman Hajabbasi, Anna Habib, Alex Antram, and Alokparna Das) titled *Valuing Written Accents: Non-native Students Talk about Identity, Academic Writing, and Meeting Teachers' Expectations*:

> Many of the [students] felt confused when they first began writing in the American academy because they were translating the "richness" of their language into English, thinking that the American academy, like their native countries, held language itself to a high esteem. Hanyan from China said, "In English, I try to use big words, but I don't use them correctly, so it makes my paper look weird." Most of them talked about how they used long, involved sentences when they first arrived, but were then surprised when their professors told them to "keep it simple"; Ayesha echoed her professors' words by emphasizing the importance of the three Cs: be complete, be concise, be clear.

PARTS 10 AND 11 OF THIS BOOK DESCRIBE SENTENCE-LEVEL CONVENTIONS OF ACADEMIC ENGLISH

The students quoted above describe learning to write in *Academic English* (which can also be called *Standard Written English* or *Edited American English*). What the students describe is common for all writers entering a new writing context, whether or not they are comfortable English speakers.

Academic English is yet another variety of English, as we describe on pages 432–433—and (unless you make a living as an academic) Academic English is not much used in most people's day-to-day lives.

Learning to write Academic English, you face the challenges and opportunities we all face whenever we need to write a new kind of text: We have to learn the textual conventions, style preferences, and reader expectations of the new context.

These new exigencies may at first seem uncomfortable, but you carry adaptable tools from your previous speaking, reading, and writing experiences. Through growing up, you know how to shape your language for different audiences (such as your friends, your parents, people at work); you understand how to play with the language varieties you use regularly. Bring that play and inventiveness to Academic English.

When you need to write for a discipline or academic area new to you, analyze writings of the kind you need to produce. Ask those who write in the area to give you sample texts they consider effective *and* well written. Use the strategies on the opposite page to understand what makes this type of writing successful.

THE ORGANIZATION OF ACADEMIC WRITING IN ENGLISH

→ See pages 216–225 for information about the organizational features of academic writing across disciplines.

UNDERSTANDING HOW WRITING IS ORGANIZED IN A NEW DISCIPLINE

Use the questions below to help you analyze and so understand how to organize writing of the kind you need to produce:

- Look for background information. What kind and how much background information does a writer provide before launching into the argument?

- Look for supporting evidence. What kinds of supporting evidence are provided? How is this supporting information used?

- Where in the document does the main argument appear?

- How is the text organized? How does the writer signal this organization? With headings? With transitional phrases?

- Are headings standard from one document to another or are they author-created? What function do they serve? If they are standard headings, what information appears in each section of the document?

- Are ideas repeated? If so, which ideas and where does the repetition appear?

- How does the writer make important information stand out? Bullet points? Numbering? Headings? Bold text?

THE STYLE OF ACADEMIC WRITING IN ENGLISH

→ See pages 296–297 and 312–313 for information about the stylistic features of academic writing across disciplines.

UNDERSTANDING HOW WRITING IS STYLED IN A NEW DISCIPLINE

Analyze writing of the kind you need to produce, using the questions below to help you understand—and be able to reproduce—the style.

- What is the tone of the text? Is the vocabulary formal or informal? Does it use words that are subjective and judgmental or objective?

- Is the text simple and direct or more dense and involved? To determine this, look at the length of sentences.

- Does the writer rely more on noun phrases and technical terms or on a variety of verbs?

- When the writer uses the verb *to be*, is it followed by adjectives or complex noun phrases?

- Are there parts of the text in which the writer uses more informal language and a more personal style? If so, in what sections?

IF YOU GREW UP SPEAKING A LANGUAGE OTHER THAN ENGLISH...

If English is your second or third (or more) language, look for boxes like this in Parts 10 and 11. In these boxes are strategies for editing that can help you learn some conventions and styles unique to formal written English. Also check TIP boxes for issues that challenge anyone not comfortable with the conventions of academic English.

VARIETIES OF ENGLISH

I been thru a lot of struggles to get where I'm at today.
I've struggled to accomplish what I have.

My brother was into skydiving and he got me hooked on this stuff.
My brother, who is a skydiving fan, introduced me to the sport.

I became boring.
I became bored.

I will climb machine to the junction. I cannot trek.
I will ride my motorcycle to the junction. I can't walk the short distance.

Reading the top line in each quotation set above, some might say, "That's not good English!" By *good English*, they mean what is often called **Standard English**, represented by the second statement in each set. Standard English—and its grammatical rules—is what is taught in schools and used in many formal situations.

Standard English is a historical accident: it grows out of the language practices of the economically and politically advantaged when English usage began to be standardized several centuries ago. In this part of our book, we follow the guidelines of Standard English, as is expected in most academic writing.

But keep in mind that English—Standard English and English as it is used anywhere—changes, precisely because people use it. Today, as transportation and communication technologies bring once-distant communities closer, pushes toward *variety* meet pushes toward *standardization*, as we describe on the opposite page.

For example, the third and fourth examples above show *variety*: The third starts with Singaporean English and the fourth with Nigerian English. Because English is spoken in so many countries, many varieties have emerged, such as (adding to those above) Indian English, Caribbean English, Malaysian English, and so on. Language experts call these **world Englishes**. Each group of speakers uses English to fit their culture and needs—just as, starting in the sixteenth century, people in the British colonies (including what is now the United States) changed the language as it was then spoken and written in England.

Standardization steps in because businesses now operate worldwide and media have a twenty-four-hour worldwide news cycle. Some believe using one language can ease such broad communication. English has taken on that role in business, science, and to some extent, the Internet. English has taken on that role not because it is superior but simply because English was in the right place at the right time. And, possibly, English will be displaced by another language in the future when English no longer holds political or economic advantage.

Two tendencies push and pull each other to shape all language use:

LANGUAGE VARIETY

People use their language in different contexts for different purposes—and so different language varieties develop. People fixing cars tend to use different sets of words than people treating diseases. Occupations can become so specialized—as law has, for example—that they have their own language patterns.

Similarly, different communities shape local vocabularies and grammars. For example, the Gullah people, who live on islands off the southern states from North Carolina south to Florida, hold on to African words and speech patterns; these words and patterns have been brought into and have changed English in the area.

Depending on the influence that different groups have, and how much they interact with others, their words and language patterns can be accepted into the standard variety of a language, as the words of computer programming—*interface*, *platform*, and *input*—have become part of our day-to-day talk.

LANGUAGE STANDARDIZATION

In formal practice, languages tend to become standardized. In any language, one set of grammatical practices and speaking patterns will be favored more than others, as we noted on the opposite page.

Some argue that such standardization supports wider communication among speakers of a language's different varieties. Standard forms of a language are thus often used in the media (think of how network television news reporters speak or of the writing in big-city newspapers) and in schooling, which is often meant to provide people from different backgrounds with a common culture and an ability to speak across their differences.

As you move through the next pages, be mindful of how context shapes language use; you'll see the symbols below:

✔ = what readers expect in formal writing

✘ = what readers do not expect in formal writing but which may be fine for other contexts

EDITING AND PROOFREADING

WHAT ARE REVISING, EDITING, AND PROOFREADING?

As you write a paper, you move through stages. In the initial stages, you find and arrange ideas—and then you arrange them into an overall argument. Once you have a full first draft, you move into a middle stage of writing, revision.

Only after you have revised writing to have a solid argument do you move into the later stages of editing and proofreading.

REVISING

When you revise, you attend to large-scale persuasive aspects of a text: organization and style. You start revising once you have close to a full draft.

→ See pages 290–293 for more on revising.

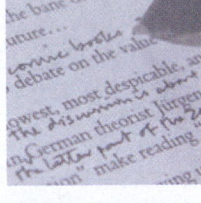

EDITING

When your overall argument is solid and unlikely to change, you focus on editing. In editing, you attend to sentences and other large details: Are sentences readable? Have you documented all your sources?

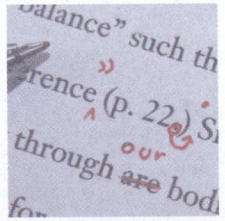

PROOFREADING

When proofreading, you check spelling, punctuation, and other mechanics. While you can pay attention to these details throughout the development of a paper, you also want to do this *as your very last step*. Whenever you revise or edit you can make mistakes, and you want to be sure to catch them once and for all.

TO EDIT, ASK . . .

Are my sentences easy to read? Will they engage readers?

❏ For easy-to-read sentences, See pages 314–315.

❏ Are my verbs active? Are my nouns concrete? See pages 325–326.

Are my sentences grammatically appropriate for my audience and purpose?

❏ A sentence's subject and verb agree in person and number. See pages 436–439.

❏ Verb tenses meet academic conventions. See pages 442–443.

❏ The tenses of verbs change only when necessary. See pages 440–441.

❏ The voice and level of formality are consistent. See pages 444–445.

❏ There are no sentence fragments, run-ons, or comma splices—except for those I can justify rhetorically. See pages 446–451.

❏ Each pronoun has a clear antecedent with which it agrees in person and number. See pages 452–453.

❏ Modifiers in sentences are placed so readers can tell easily what is being modified. See pages 454–455.

Have I integrated my quotations of others' work into my writing—while making it clear when I am using others' ideas or words?

❏ See pages 188–203.

Have I documented my sources according to expected conventions?

❏ See Part 9 of this book.

Have I removed any biased language?

❏ See pages 330–339.

TO PROOFREAD, ASK . . .

Have I followed conventions for spelling, capitalization, and other mechanics?

❏ For spelling, see page 531.

❏ For capitalization, see page 532.

❏ For other details of mechanics, See pages 530–535.

Did I omit words?

Only careful proofreading helps you find accidentally omitted words.

Have I used the right word?

Wrong words have one of two causes: A spell-checker suggests an incorrect replacement word (**their** instead of **there**) OR you are not yet familiar enough with the conventions of formal writing or of a discipline to know the expected word.

❏ For the first kind, use spell-checkers attentively and proofread carefully.

❏ For the second kind, find someone who knows your audience's expectations; ask that person to read for any such words.

Is my punctuation conventional?

❏ Check that you have apostrophes in possessives and contractions. See pages 456–457.

❏ Do you have commas before coordinating conjunctions in compound sentences? See pages 502–503.

❏ Are there commas after nonessential information at a sentence's beginning? See page 460.

Are quotations punctuated conventionally?

❏ Pages 524–525 offer a chart to help you punctuate quotations.

MAKING SUBJECT–VERB AGREEMENT

In sentences that fit with academic expectations, the subject and verb have the same person and number. The information to the right helps you figure this out for your own sentences.

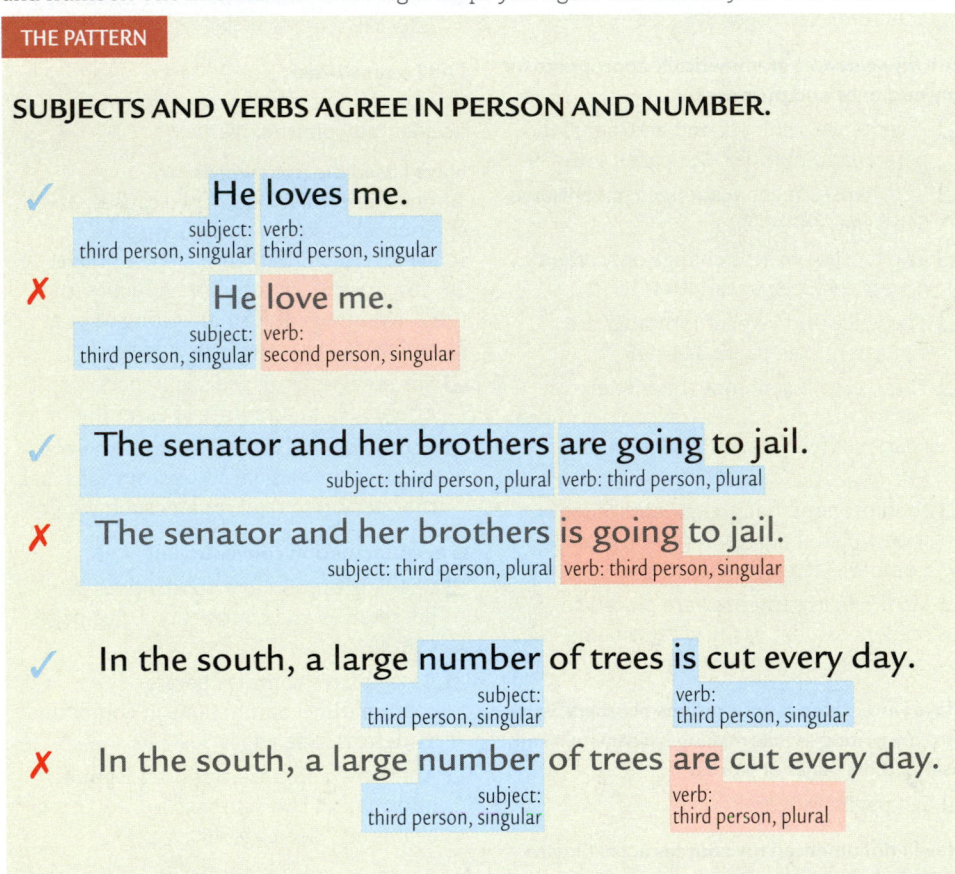

THE PATTERN

SUBJECTS AND VERBS AGREE IN PERSON AND NUMBER.

✓ He loves me.
subject: third person, singular   verb: third person, singular

✗ He love me.
subject: third person, singular   verb: second person, singular

✓ The senator and her brothers are going to jail.
subject: third person, plural   verb: third person, plural

✗ The senator and her brothers is going to jail.
subject: third person, plural   verb: third person, singular

✓ In the south, a large number of trees is cut every day.
subject: third person, singular   verb: third person, singular

✗ In the south, a large number of trees are cut every day.
subject: third person, singular   verb: third person, plural

✓ = what readers expect in formal writing
✗ = what readers do not expect in formal writing but which may be fine for other contexts

HOW TO EDIT FOR SUBJECT–VERB AGREEMENT: PERSON

1 Identify a sentence's subject. (See below.)

2 Determine the subject's person: Is it first, second, or third person? (➔ See page 438.)

3 Find the sentence's verb, and identify its person: Is it first, second, or third person? (➔ See page 443.)

4 Do the subject and verb have the same person?

YES? Your sentence is fine.

NO? Use the information on pages 443 and 469–470 to create the appropriate verb.

HOW TO EDIT FOR SUBJECT–VERB AGREEMENT: NUMBER

1 Identify a sentence's subject. (See below.)

2 Determine the subject's number: Is it singular or plural? (➔ See page 438.)

3 Find the sentence's verb, and identify its number: Is it singular or plural? (➔ See page 443.)

4 Are the subject and verb the same number?

YES? Your sentence is fine.

NO? Use the information on pages 443 and 469–470 to create the appropriate verb.

1 IDENTIFYING A SENTENCE'S SUBJECT

The information on pages 482–483 can help you identify the subject of a sentence.

Sentences that contain prepositional phrases, however, can confuse writers: The prepositional phrases add words that may look like the subject. To identify the subject:

1 Underline any prepositional phrases (➔ see pages 472–473 and 484) or other descriptive phrases that come immediately before the verb.

In the south, a large number of trees is cut every day.

The record that he set for driving across country is thirty-one hours.

2 Rewrite the sentence *without* the phrases you underlined. This should put the subject next to the verb.

In the south, a large number is cut every day.

The record is thirty-one hours.

Help with subject–verb agreement continues on the next page . . .

2 DETERMINING THE SUBJECT'S PERSON

Use the grid below to determine the person of the subject you've identified.

	SINGULAR	PLURAL
FIRST PERSON	I	we
SECOND PERSON	you	you
THIRD PERSON	he, she, it	they
	All nouns are third person:	
	woman, dog	women, dogs
	The President of the United States furniture, justice	

3 DETERMINING WHETHER THE SUBJECT IS SINGULAR OR PLURAL

Use the information about noun plurals on page 457 to help you determine the subject's number. Keep an eye out, however, for the following kinds of subjects:

COMPOUND SUBJECTS JOINED BY *and*

Compound subjects joined by *and* are usually plural:

Leela and Joe work on their homework together.

There are exceptions:

- If the compound subject names what we consider to be one object or activity—as with *peanut butter and jelly* or *drinking and driving*—it is singular. (Company names using *and* are also singular, as with a law firm named *Black and Bland*.)

- If the compound subject refers to the same person or thing, then it is singular:

  My best friend and advisor is my father.

- If the compound subject is preceded by *each* or *every*, then it is singular:

  Each dog, cat, and pet ferret is to be registered.

  Every girl and boy deserves health insurance.

COMPOUND SUBJECTS JOINED BY *or*, *nor*, *either . . . or*, OR *neither . . . nor*

The number of the subject is determined by the noun closest to the verb:

A dog or crows get into our garbage every week. Because **crows** is closest to the verb and is plural, the subject of this sentence is plural.

Crows or a dog gets into our garbage every week. Because **a dog** is closest to the verb and is singular, the subject of this sentence is singular.

SUBJECTS THAT USE INDEFINITE PRONOUNS

The indefinite pronouns (→ see page 464) **anybody**, **anyone**, **anything**, **each**, **everybody**, **everyone**, **everything**, **nobody**, **no one**, **someone**, **somebody**, and **something** are singular:

Everyone in my class is late with homework! • Everything has gone wrong.

The indefinite pronouns **both** and **many** are plural:
Both motorcycles were broken. • Many have visited our town.

The indefinite pronouns **all**, **any**, **none**, and **some** can be singular or plural, depending on the noun or pronoun to which they refer:

| SINGULAR | All my money goes to rent. | Some of his dinner was overcooked. |
| PLURAL | All my nieces go fishing. | Some of his books were lost. |

COLLECTIVE NOUNS

Nouns referring to collections of people—**audience**, **class**, **committee**, **crowd**, **family**, **group**, **public**, **team**—are usually singular, because the collection is usually described as acting as one unit.

The audience was delighted by the performance.

When such a noun refers to its members acting individually, however, it is plural:

The audience were looking at each other.

CLAUSES AND PHRASES

When a sentence's subject is a clause or a phrase, the subject is singular:

What frustrates me is my math homework.

Going to the dentist makes me nervous.

If the verb is a form of **be** and the word or words following it (which are called the **subject complement**) are plural, then the verb is plural even if the subject is singular:

What frustrates me are inconsiderate drivers.

WATCH OUT FOR THIS!

Phrases such as **along with**, **in addition to**, and **together with** can sound as though they build compound nouns—but they do not. The subject of the sentence below is **Hasan**; **together with Kim** is an adjectival phrase.

Hasan, together with Kim, is driving to Appleton.

USING VERB TENSES CONSISTENTLY

CONSISTENT VERB TENSES CREATE COHERENCE

If you shift verb tenses in a sentence, you shift from one sense of time to another. Readers can be confused by such shifts because readers might not then know if the actions of a sentence happened in the past, present, or future.

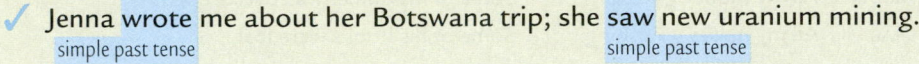

✓ Jenna **wrote** me about her Botswana trip; she **saw** new uranium mining.
   simple past tense   simple past tense

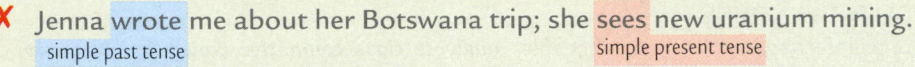

✗ Jenna **wrote** me about her Botswana trip; she **sees** new uranium mining.
   simple past tense   simple present tense

→ See page 443 for a list of all verb tenses.

A CONSISTENT TENSE FOR WRITING ABOUT FICTION

When you summarize the plot or describe the actions in fiction, write as though the events happen in an eternal present: Put all descriptions in present tense.

In Colette's novels *Cheri* and *The Last of Cheri*, the character Léa <u>works</u> hard to appear and act young at the start; by the end she <u>is</u> gray-haired and stout.

BUT SOMETIMES YOU NEED TO CHANGE TENSES . . .

Because writing often involves describing relations among events that occured at different times, you sometimes need to change tenses, as this example shows:

A new study <u>offers</u> some relief to parents who <u>worry</u> that their children <u>will never eat</u> anything but chocolate milk, gummi vitamins, and the occasional grape. Researchers <u>examined</u> the eating habits of 5,390 pairs of twins between eight and eleven years old and <u>found</u> children's aversions to trying new foods are mostly inherited. The message to parents: It's not your cooking, it's your genes.

PRESENT TENSE
The present tense verbs describe how a study can ease parental worries now.

PAST TENSE
The past tense verbs describe the actions that had to have taken place before the study could be useful now, in the present.

FUTURE TENSE
The future tense describes parents' fears about their children's future actions.

USING PRESENT PERFECT AND PAST PERFECT TO SHOW TIME DIFFERENCES

Writers can show relationships between actions or states by shifting from simple or progressive present tense to present perfect; they can also shift from simple or progressive past tense to past perfect. The perfect tenses signal that the action or state they describe occurred before the action or state in the other tense.

Present perfect maintains a present focus; past perfect maintains a past focus.

SWITCHING TENSES WHEN THE TIME FOCUS IS THE PRESENT

The homeless can be roughly divided into two groups: those who have had homelessness forced upon them and want nothing more than to escape it and those who have chosen it for themselves and now accept it or, in some cases, embrace it.

PRESENT TENSE

PRESENT PERFECT TENSE

This sentence focuses on a present distinction; for that distinction to be possible, however, the people being described had to have become homeless in the past.

SWITCHING TENSES WHEN THE TIME FOCUS IS THE PAST

In 1965, Thorazine was introduced. This drug is responsible for much of the homeless problem we see today. Before it was introduced, people diagnosed with mental illness, particularly schizophrenia, had been considered incurable and had been confined to mental institutions.

PAST PROGRESSIVE TENSE

PAST PERFECT TENSE

This sentence focuses on a distinction that occurred in the past. The writer uses the past progressive tense to describe how a drug was introduced in the past; the writer then uses the past perfect tense to show conditions that happened even further in the past than the drug's introduction.

HOW TO EDIT FOR SHIFTS IN VERB TENSES

1 Using different colored pencils or pens (or different colored highlighting on the computer), highlight each verb tense in its own color.

2 Where you see shifts, ask if readers will understand why the tense shifts.

3 If you need to clarify verb tense for readers, do one of the following:

- Add words or time expressions that signal a tense shift.
- Change one verb to present or past perfect to indicate that an action or state occurred prior to the other.
- Change the tense of the verb to maintain a consistent time focus.

USING VERB TENSES IN ACADEMIC WRITING

THE SIMPLE PRESENT is used to . . .

- describe the present situation.
  Conservationists at the Masai Mara work hard to protect the wildebeest from poachers.

- generalize.
  Studies show that chronic stress contributes to heart attacks and other diseases.

- describe the contents of a book, movie, or other text.
  In his thesis, "Intimate Relationships with Artificial Partners," Levy conjectures that robots will become so human-like that people will fall in love with them.

THE PRESENT PROGRESSIVE is used to . . .

- describe actions happening at the moment of speaking.
  Women are dying from complicated pregnancies at almost the same rate as 1990.

- compare two present actions. One action is described in simple present, the other in present progressive.
  When strict parents are not watching, their children often engage in reckless actions.

THE PRESENT PERFECT is used to . . .

- describe actions begun in the past but not completed.
  The once vanished gray wolf has made a comeback in the Northern Rockies.

- describe actions begun at an unspecified past time.
  Over half of adolescents have tried alcohol and drugs at least once.

- introduce a topic.
  Once a disease of the Western world, breast cancer has become a global concern.

THE SIMPLE PAST is used to . . .

- describe completed events or states.
  Charles M. Schulz drew "Peanuts" for nearly half a century.

- report past research or events, summarize research results, and give narrative examples.
  Steven C. Amstrup of the United States Geological Survey led a recent study of polar bears.

THE PAST PERFECT is used to . . .

- compare two past events. The past perfect signals the event that happened first.
  The protesters demanded the freedom and democracy for which their parents had fought.

FORMING THE TENSES OF ENGLISH VERBS

SIMPLE TENSES

Simple present: Describes actions taking place at the time a sentence is written or for actions that occur regularly.

Simple past: Describes actions completed in the past.

Simple future: Describes actions not yet begun.

PROGRESSIVE TENSES

Describe actions that continue—or will continue—over time.

PERFECT TENSES

Describe actions that have been (or will have been) completed.

PERFECT PROGRESSIVE TENSES

Present perfect progressive: Describes an action begun in the past, continuing in the present, and that may continue into the future.

Past perfect progressive: Describes a stretched-out action completed before some other past action; this tense usually appears in sentences that describe that other past action.

Future perfect progressive: Describes a stretched-out action that will occur before some specified future time.

THE PATTERN

	SINGULAR	PLURAL
SIMPLE PRESENT		
Only the third person singular changes to the *−s* form.		
first	I ask.	We ask.
second	You ask.	You ask.
third	She/He/It asks.	They ask.
SIMPLE PAST		
All persons and numbers use the past form of the verb.		
	I/We/You/You/She/He/It/They asked.	
SIMPLE FUTURE		
All persons and numbers use *will* + the simple form of the verb.		
	I/We/You/You/She/He/It/They will ask.	
PRESENT PROGRESSIVE		
Use the appropriate simple present form of *be* + the present participle.		
first	I am asking.	We are asking.
second	You are asking.	You are asking.
third	She/He/It is asking.	They are asking.
PAST PROGRESSIVE		
Use the appropriate simple past form of *be* + the present participle.		
first	I was asking.	We were asking.
second	You were asking.	You were asking.
third	She/He/It was asking.	They were asking.
FUTURE PROGRESSIVE		
All persons and numbers use *will be* + the present participle.		
	I/We/You/You/She/He/It/They will be asking.	
PRESENT PERFECT		
Use the appropriate simple present form of *have* + the past participle.		
first	I have asked.	We have asked.
second	You have asked.	You have asked.
third	She/He/It has asked.	They have asked.
PAST PERFECT		
All persons and numbers use *had* + the past participle.		
	I/We/You/You/She/He/It/They had asked.	
FUTURE PERFECT		
All persons and numbers use *will have* + the past participle.		
	I/We/You/You/She/He/It/They will have asked.	
PRESENT PERFECT PROGRESSIVE		
All persons and numbers use *have been* + the present participle.		
	I/We/You/You/She/He/It/They have been asking.	
PAST PERFECT PROGRESSIVE		
All persons and numbers use *had been* + the present participle.		
	I/We/You/You/She/He/It/They had been asking.	
FUTURE PERFECT PROGRESSIVE		
All persons and numbers use *will have been* + the present participle.		
	I/We/You/You/She/He/It/They will have been asking.	

AVOIDING SHIFTS IN STYLE AND VOICE

STYLE: SHIFTS IN LEVELS OF FORMALITY

Even academic writing has levels of formality. Convention says to use only one level throughout a piece of writing.

✓	FORMAL WRITING	Coltrane plays saxophone tenderly and searchingly; his searching is perhaps the most salient characteristic of both his work and his life.
✓	LESS FORMAL WRITING	Saxophones can whisper or shriek, breathe warmth or spit fire— and a quick listen to John Coltrane's 1965 album, *Transition*, will disabuse anyone of the misimpression that the saxophone is limited to that canned sound you heard during the credits of *L.A. Law*.
✗	MIXED LEVELS	Coltrane plays saxophone tenderly, but there is a searching quality to it and sometimes his changes can really bug a listener.

STYLE: SHIFTS BETWEEN DIRECT AND INDIRECT DISCOURSE IN VOICE

✓	DIRECT DISCOURSE	**Direct discourse** quotes another's words exactly. "Are you going to the store?" Harriet's sister asked.
✓	INDIRECT DISCOURSE	In **indirect discourse**, you report what someone else said. Harriet's sister wanted to know if we were going to the store.
✗	MIXED	A convention of formal written English is not to shift between direct and indirect discourse in one sentence. Harriet's sister asked are we going to the store.

TIP PURPOSEFUL SHIFTS

Sometimes shifts make sentences do what you need them to. To be sure you use shifts only when necessary, follow this rule: *When you check your writing and find any of the shifts we describe here, remove the shift—unless you can give a solid reason why it is necessary.*

VOICE: SHIFTS BETWEEN ACTIVE AND PASSIVE VOICE

Is the subject of a sentence performing an action or being acted upon? If the subject is performing an action, the sentence is in **active voice**; if the subject is being acted upon, the sentence is in **passive voice**.

ACTIVE VOICE

Amanda fed the macaw.
subject

We caught and ate the mice that came into our camp.
subject

PASSIVE VOICE

The macaw was fed by Amanda.
subject

The mice that came into our camp were caught and eaten.
subject

Who ate the mice? The sentence doesn't say…!

✓ **CONSISTENT VOICE**

Jade fed the macaw even though David had fed it earlier.

When we had no food, we caught and ate the mice that came into our camp.

✗ **MIXED VOICE**

Jade fed the macaw even though it had been fed earlier by David.

When we had no food, the mice that came into our camp were caught and eaten.

Active voice uses action verbs, which convey movement and energy (→ see page 325). Passive voice uses forms of **be**; passive voice may also need a prepositional phrase to explain who performed the action (…*fed by David*)—so passive sentences tend to be wordy.

The passive voice is useful, however, when writers want to avoid naming who performed an action—as in the passively voiced sentence about the mice above. Scientific and technical writing often uses passive voice because it may seem fact-based and objective: Writers present their research and conclusions without attribution so that the writing appears to be unshaped by individual bias.

→ For more on uses of active and passive voices, see pages 308–309.

AVOIDING SENTENCE FRAGMENTS

A sentence fragment is an incomplete sentence: Because Vered said so. • Where I watched. A capital letter at the beginning and other conventional punctuation do not turn words into a sentence. A sentence, grammatically, is an independent clause (➔ see page 485).

Vered said so. • In the hospital I watched my father sleep.

STEPS FOR DETERMINING IF YOU HAVE A SENTENCE—OR A FRAGMENT

The phrase that might be a fragment:	Danced in the streets.	The computer on the desk.	Unless there is old wiring in the house.	Nevertheless, they plotted.
1 Is there a subject? ➔ See pages 482–483.	NO. This is a fragment. To fix fragments lacking subjects, go to page 447.	YES, there is a subject: **The computer**. Move to the next step.	YES, there is a subject: **there**. Move to the next step.	YES, there is a subject: **they**. Move to the next step.
2 Is there a predicate? ➔ See pages 482–483.		NO. This is a fragment. To fix fragments that have no predicates, go to page 448.	YES, there is a predicate: **is**. Move to the next step.	YES, there is a predicate: **plotted**. Move to the next step.
3 Do the words make up a dependent clause without an attached independent clause? ➔ See page 449.			YES. This is a fragment. To fix fragments that are dependent clauses, go to page 449.	NO. THIS IS A SENTENCE.

FIXING FRAGMENTS THAT LACK SUBJECTS

Fix fragments that lack subjects with one of the following two approaches:

ADD A SUBJECT TO THE FRAGMENT

These phrases are fragments because they lack subjects:

Danced in the street.

Sensing their delight in winning.

To add a subject, ask *Who is doing the action?* and then give that information:

Mary and Elaine danced in the street.

Christa was sensing their delight in winning. [OR] Christa sensed their delight in winning.

As with the second example, note that you may have to modify the verb when you add a subject.

or

ADD THE FRAGMENT TO A SENTENCE

Often people inadvertently write fragments in longer descriptions:

Mary and Elaine won the guitar contest last June. They were so happy they threw a party. Danced in the street.

The *danced in the street* fragment can be joined to the sentence before it with a coordinating conjunction:

Mary and Elaine won the guitar contest last June. They were so happy they threw a party and danced in the street.

→ We discuss coordinating conjunctions on pages 474 and 502–503.

Go to the next page to learn about fixing fragments missing predicates and fragments that are dependent clauses.

FINDING FRAGMENTS

If you are uncertain whether a phrase is a sentence or not, try saying it aloud with *I believe that . . .* in front of the phrase. If the result sounds odd to you, it probably is a fragment and worth checking with the steps to the left.

FIXING FRAGMENTS THAT LACK PREDICATES

Fix fragments that lack predicates with one of the following two approaches:

ADD A PREDICATE TO THE FRAGMENT

These phrases are fragments because they lack predicates:

The computer on the desk.

Only the lonely.

To add a predicate, ask *What is happening to the objects named in the fragment?*—and then give that information:

The computer on the desk was broken.

Only the lonely know how I feel tonight.

or

ADD THE FRAGMENT TO A SENTENCE

Just as with fragments that lack subjects, fragments without predicates often occur when people write descriptions:

Nobody was out walking after midnight. Only the lonely.

The *only the lonely* fragment can be joined to the sentence before it by making it into the subject:

Only the lonely were out walking after midnight.

Or you can use a conjunction to join the fragment to the end of the sentence:

Nobody was out walking after midnight, except for the lonely.

→ We discuss conjunctions on pages 474–477.

FIXING FRAGMENTS THAT ARE DEPENDENT CLAUSES

Fix such fragments with one of the three approaches below.

JOIN THE DEPENDENT CLAUSE TO AN INDEPENDENT CLAUSE

Rather than build a road, they installed a tram over the trees.

Although my family lived under the Nazi regime for only one year, I will never forget the fear and humiliation I experienced that year in Vienna.

When the people of this part of Peru were building their cities, there was only one other urban complex on earth.

or

REMOVE THE SUBORDINATING CONJUNCTION TO MAKE A SENTENCE

We lived under the Nazi regime for only one year.

or

INSERT A DEPENDENT CLAUSE BEGINNING WITH A RELATIVE PRONOUN INTO AN INDEPENDENT CLAUSE

All the men who regularly sit in hot tubs showed signs of infertility.

Talib Kweli began recording with Mos Def, whom he met in high school.

THE PATTERN

IDENTIFYING DEPENDENT CLAUSES

Dependent clauses begin in one of two ways:

SUBORDINATING CONJUNCTIONS BEGIN DEPENDENT CLAUSES

rather than build a road

although we lived under the Nazi regime for only one year

when the people of this part of Peru were building their cities

→ See page 476 to learn about subordinating conjunctions.

RELATIVE PRONOUNS BEGIN DEPENDENT CLAUSES

who regularly sat in hot tubs • whom he met in high school

→ See page 465 to learn about relative pronouns.

Anytime you see a phrase that begins with a subordinating conjunction or a relative pronoun, it cannot stand on its own as a sentence; each example above is a fragment.

AVOIDING COMMA SPLICES AND FUSED SENTENCES

Comma splices and fused sentences are examples of **run-on sentences**. Run-on sentences result when you join two independent clauses with unconventional or no punctuation.

THE PATTERN		
✗ COMMA SPLICE	Flower was one of the meerkats on the Animal Planet documentary series *Meerkat Manor*, she died after being bitten by a cobra.	
	A comma splice has a comma between its independent clauses.	
✗ FUSED SENTENCE	Flower was one of the meerkats on the Animal Planet documentary series *Meerkat Manor* she died after being bitten by a cobra.	
	A fused sentence has no punctuation between its two clauses.	
✓ WITH A PERIOD	Flower was one of the meerkats on the Animal Planet documentary series *Meerkat Manor*. She died after being bitten by a cobra.	
✓ WITH A COLON	Flower was one of the meerkats on the Animal Planet documentary series *Meerkat Manor*: She died after being bitten by a cobra.	
✓ WITH A SEMICOLON	Flower was one of the meerkats on the Animal Planet documentary series *Meerkat Manor*; she died after being bitten by a cobra.	
✓ WITH A COMMA AND A COORDINATING CONJUNCTION	Flower was one of the meerkats on the Animal Planet documentary series *Meerkat Manor*, but she died after being bitten by a cobra.	
✓ WITH A SEMICOLON AND A CONJUNCTIVE ADVERB	Flower was one of the meerkats on the Animal Planet documentary series *Meerkat Manor*; however, she died after being bitten by a cobra.	
✓ MAKE ONE INDEPENDENT CLAUSE DEPENDENT	Flower, who was a meerkat on *Meerkat Manor*, died after being bitten by a cobra.	

→ Page 511 explains about joining independent clauses with colons.

→ Page 512 explains joining independent clauses with semicolons.

→ See pages 474 and 502–503 to learn about coordinating conjunctions.

→ Pages 486–487 explain conventions for joining independent clauses into compound sentences.

UNDERSTANDING WHY RUN-ON SENTENCES HAPPEN

Sometimes hurried writing or writing what we hear in our heads results in run-ons. Being able to recognize other reasons for run-ons can help you keep an eye out for them.

COMMA SPLICES

When you write two closely connected thoughts, a comma can just seem the natural way to connect them:

Children play daily, adults play nightly.

Anne Frank's diary is hard to read, she was so young and had so much before her.

Any of the fixes listed to the left will conventionalize those sentences:

Children play daily; adults play nightly.

Anne Frank's diary is hard to read, because she was so young and had so much before her.

Comma splices also come easily with conjunctive adverbs (➜ see page 477):

J. K. Rowling received twelve rejections, now she can laugh because of her success.

But, formally, conjunctive adverbs require semicolons before and commas after them:

J. K. Rowling received twelve rejections; now, she can laugh because of her success.

FUSED SENTENCES

Like comma splices, fused sentences are often the result of two sentences whose ideas relate closely; and, as in the example about Anne Frank to the left, fused sentences often happen when the second clause begins with a pronoun (➜ see pages 464–465) that connects the two thoughts:

Russell Wilson was the twelfth pick in the thirty-ninth draft round he went on to the Super Bowl.

Use any of the fixes listed to the left to make a fused sentence into a formal sentence:

Russell Wilson was the twelfth pick in the thirty-ninth draft round, and he went on to the Super Bowl.

Russell Wilson was the twelfth pick in the thirty-ninth draft round; nonetheless, he went on to the Super Bowl.

HOW TO FIND COMMA SPLICES

Look for longer sentences that have a comma in the middle. Change the comma to a period to see if the two parts of the longer sentence are individual sentences that can stand alone (using the tip on the bottom of page 447). If they can stand alone, you have a comma splice.

HOW TO FIND FUSED SENTENCES

Look for longer sentences that have no punctuation. Convert the possible fused sentence words into a question by adding *isn't it?* or *doesn't it?* (or similar words) to the end. For example, if you are concerned about the words *Our professor teaches us well she teaches with passion*, ask *Our professor teaches us well she teaches with passion, doesn't she?* The question should sound weird to you, indicating that you have a fused sentence that should be *Our professor teaches us well and she teaches with passion* or one of the other possible fixes.

WORKING WITH PRONOUN REFERENCE AND AGREEMENT

TO USE PRONOUNS CONVENTIONALLY, UNDERSTAND **ANTECEDENTS**

The person or thing to which a pronoun refers is its **antecedent**. In the sentences below, the antecedent is underlined.

The dog wasn't gray; it was black.

Marina came prepared: She brought a toolbox.

Computers change time: They speed it up.

Jamshed and I worked and then we ate lunch.

AVOIDING VAGUE PRONOUN REFERENCES

Check your writing for sentences in which a pronoun could have two antecedents. Revise the sentences to remove the ambiguity.

✗ Marisa told Tania that she had passed the class after all.

✓ Marisa told Tania, "I passed the class after all."

✗ After Lupita put the book in her bag, she couldn't find it.

✓ After Lupita put it in her bag, she couldn't find the book.

PRONOUN AGREEMENT

Conventionally, pronouns must agree in person, number, and gender with their antecedents.

AGREEMENT IN NUMBER

✗ If a person wants to be a good citizen, they should vote.
    singular   plural

✓ **If people want to be good citizens, they should vote.**
    plural   plural

AGREEMENT IN PERSON

✗ If people want to be good citizens, you should vote.
    third person   second person

✓ **If people want to be good citizens, they should vote.**
    third person   third person

AGREEMENT IN GENDER

✗ If Tamika wants to be a good citizen, he should vote.
    feminine   masculine

✓ **If Tamika wants to be a good citizen, she should vote.**
    feminine   feminine

PRONOUN PERSON AND NUMBER

	SINGULAR NUMBER	PLURAL NUMBER
FIRST PERSON	I, me, my	we, us, our
SECOND PERSON	you, your	you, your
THIRD PERSON	she, he, it, one, anyone	they
	her, his, him, its	them, their

HOW TO EDIT FOR PRONOUN REFERENCE AND AGREEMENT

Circle every pronoun in your paper and draw an arrow to each pronoun's antecedent.

1 If you *can't* find an antecedent, insert one be forehand or change the pronoun to a noun.

2 If the pronoun could have two different antecedents, edit the sentence to clarify the antecedent, as we show to the left.

3 If you *can* find an antecedent, be sure it agrees with your pronoun, as shown above.

AVOIDING DISRUPTIVE AND DANGLING MODIFIERS

Modifier is the collective name for adjectives, adjectival phrases, adverbs, and adverbial phrases. Modifiers make writing concrete and engaging—if readers can tell what words are being modified. Unfortunately, writers can easily put modifiers in odd places.

THE PATTERN

PUT MODIFIERS CLOSE TO THE WORDS THEY MODIFY

✗ Covered in chocolate icing, my friends will love this cake.

✓ My friends will love this cake covered in chocolate icing.

✗ The Great Comet of 1577 was seen by Europeans passing close to Earth.

✓ Passing close to Earth, the Great Comet of 1577 was seen by Europeans.

TIP

HOW TO CHECK FOR DISRUPTIVE AND DANGLING MODIFIERS

Modification slips are easy to produce—and easy to fix. Fixing them requires finding them, however, and finding them takes time and careful reading. To check modifiers:

1 Underline every modifier in your writing; draw a line from each to the word it modifies.

2 Move modifiers that are far from the words they modify closer to those words.

3 If the underlined word is a limiting modifier (→ see the TIP on page 455), is it placed so that the sentence means what you desire?

4 If you cannot find a noun to which the modifier refers, you have a dangling modifier. Choose one of the options on the facing page to fix it.

FIXING DISRUPTIVE MODIFIERS

Disruptive modifiers disrupt a sentence's grammatical elements. In the sentence below, a long phrase separates the sentence's subject and predicate, disrupting reading:

Palenquero, although its grammar is so different that Spanish speakers cannot understand it, is thought to be the only Spanish-based Creole language in Latin America.

This phrase placement makes the sentence easier to read:

Although its grammar is so different that Spanish speakers cannot understand it, *Palenquero* is thought to be the only Spanish-based Creole language in Latin America.

FIXING DANGLING MODIFIERS

Modifiers dangle when they seem to hang in a sentence, unable to modify anything logically. For example, unless the writer of this sentence has an unusual dog—

While reading, my dog rested her head on my knee.

—the sentence describes an impossible situation: The position of the modifier *While reading* implies that the dog can read.

In addition, the person we assume is reading is not made explicit as a noun in the sentence. Because there is no such noun, the sentence cannot be fixed by moving the modifier closer to the (nonexistent) noun.

Because dangling modifiers cannot be fixed by being moved, two other options exist for fixing them:

1 Revise the dangling modifier to make explicit the noun to be modified:

As I was reading a book, my dog rested her head on my knee.

2 Revise the rest of the sentence so that the noun appears elsewhere:

While reading, I was warmed when my dog rested her head on my knee.

PAY PARTICULAR ATTENTION TO LIMITING MODIFIERS

Limiting modifiers are words such as *almost, even, hardly, just, nearly, not, only,* and *simply.* They can be placed almost anywhere in a sentence—and that makes them dangerous. Their placement can change a sentence's meaning.

For example, this sentence says Luther thought about donating his collection but didn't:

Luther almost donated his entire collection of LPs to the auction.

This sentence says that Luther *did* donate a large part of his collection:

Luther donated almost his entire collection of LPs to the auction.

Check your limiting modifiers to be sure your sentences say what you want.

USING APOSTROPHES WITH POSSESSIVE FORMS (but not with plural forms)

Both plurals and possessives usually add an **-s** at the end of a noun. The difference is that possessives always have an apostrophe; plurals do not.

MAKING NOUNS POSSESSIVE
A possessive noun comes before another noun, and its possessive form—the addition of **-'s**—indicates possession or some other close association with the noun it precedes.

POSSESSIVES USING SINGULAR NOUNS
Add **-'s** to the end of the noun even if the noun ends in **-s**:
a cell's wall • my life's story • Luis's award • the grass's height • a potato's texture

POSSESSIVES USING PLURAL NOUNS
If the plural noun does not end in **-s**, add **-'s**.
the children's choir • the media's analysis • the deer's diseases

If the plural noun *does* end in **-s**, add only an apostrophe.
the boxes' interiors • the Kennedys' compound • the grasses' heights

POSSESSIVES USING COMPOUND NOUNS
The last word in a compound noun becomes possessive, following the above guidelines:
a NASCAR driver's car • the school nurse's office • some swimming pools' depths

POSSESSIVES USING TWO OR MORE NOUNS
If the object in question is owned jointly by the nouns, make the last noun possessive:

Abbott and Costello's "Who's on first?" routine was developed in the 1930s.

If each of the two nouns has possession, make both possessive:

Abbott's and Costello's lives had very different endings.

PROOFREADING FOR PLURALS AND POSSESSIVES
Circle every noun ending in **-s**. Ask yourself if the noun is possessive or plural; based on your decision, check that you have the conventional form.

If you have any questions about a noun's plural form, a dictionary will show it to you.

MAKING NOUNS PLURAL

In English, a noun's ending usually indicates whether it is singular or plural.

SINGULAR	PLURAL	
-s		
a boy	the boys	If a noun ends in an **-o** preceded by a *vowel*, it usually takes an **-s** to make it plural.
the site	many sites	
freedom	seven freedoms	With compound hyphenated words, add **-s** to the main noun, even if that noun is not at the end of the word.
my radio	their radios	
father-in-law	fathers-in-law	
-es		
a box	six boxes	Nouns that end in **-s**, **-sh**, **-ch**, and **-x** add **-es** to become plural.
my church	our churches	
one potato	two potatoes	If a noun ends in an **-o** preceded by a consonant, the plural forms usually ends in **-es**.
-ies		
the summary	several summaries	Nouns that end in **-y** lose the **-y** and add **-ies** to become plural.
a boundary	the boundaries	
-ves		
my life	our lives	With nouns that end in **-f** or **-fe**, replace the **-f** or **-fe** with **-ves** to become plural.
a calf	six calves	
other endings		
one medium	the media	Sometimes the plurals of words that derive from other languages take their plural form from the original language.
the analysis	the analyses	
one criterion	three criteria	
his child	his children	
changed form		
one man	many men	Words that have been in use since the beginning of language often change their forms to make plurals.
a mouse	three mice	
no change		
one moose	two moose	Many names for large animals keep the same form in both singular and plural.
one deer	many deer	

USING ARTICLES CONVENTIONALLY

KNOW THE DIFFERENCE BETWEEN COUNT AND NONCOUNT NOUNS

Count nouns refer to objects that exist distinctly as countable units: *dogs, chairs, words, toes, plates, books, glances.* Count nouns refer to what you can perceive with your senses.

COUNT NOUN SINGULAR	a woman	the dog	his emotion
COUNT NOUN PLURAL	the women	the dogs	their emotions

Noncount nouns name what can't be cut into parts or counted: They name abstractions (*education, happiness*) and also collections of objects (*furniture, silverware, rice, coffee*).

NONCOUNT NOUN	justice	weather	anger

THE PATTERN

COUNT AND NONCOUNT NOUNS AND ARTICLES

Singular count nouns *always* need an article or another adjective (*this, that, my, each*) in front of them.

ARTICLE OR OTHER ADJECTIVE	SINGULAR COUNT NOUN

A snowstorm hit our town this week.

The teacher gave an apple to each child.

Plural count nouns do not need articles—but can have other adjectives.

PLURAL COUNT NOUN

Anger shows on bodies and faces.

How did we come to associate teachers with apples?

or

ADJECTIVE	PLURAL COUNT NOUN

Our winters have big snowstorms.

Of all the kinds of nouns, only **noncount nouns** can stand alone without an article. They cannot be counted, they cannot be used with quantifiers (*one, two, many*) or made plural. Use *much* (not *many*), *little* (not *few*), *amount of* (not *number of*) before these nouns.

NONCOUNT NOUN

Privacy is under attack online.

You can study anger in psychology.

PROOFREADING FOR ARTICLES

Here are two common mistakes in writing—and advice for proofreading for them.

MISSING *a* OR *an*

Underline all singular nouns that appear in your writing without an article or adjective. Decide whether the noun is countable or uncountable. (Many nouns can be either, depending on their contexts.)

❑ If what you've underlined is a noncount noun, it does not need *a*, *an*, or an adjective in front of it.

❑ If what you've underlined is a count noun, it must be marked in some way:

If the count noun refers to an indefinite or unspecified person, place, or thing, add *a* or *an*:

> When I was young, I used an abacus instead of a calculator in math class.

If a noun is used as a representative of a class of nouns rather than of a particular individual member of that class, add *a* or *an*:

> An abacus is a Chinese counting device.

If the noun refers to all members of the group or is general, make the noun plural and use no articles.

> For some math problems, abacuses work as well as calculators.

MISSING *the*

We use *the* when we know readers will understand exactly what object is meant by a noun we use (→ see page 467). To be sure you have used *the* when you should, underline all singular nouns that appear without an article or adjective. If the noun fits one of the three categories described below, it is "specific," so put *the* before it.

1 Shared knowledge. For example, because two people who live together can be expected to know that they have children, one could send this e-mail to the other:

> Can you pick up the kids from school?

(Can you pick up kids would mean Pick up some kids, any kids…!)

2 Second mention. After a singular count noun is first used, readers will know what is meant by the second reference—and so *the* goes before its later uses:

> Depo-Provera, a contraceptive, may cause serious side effects. Some drug companies, however, have promoted the contraceptive outside the U.S. with no warnings about its side effects.

first mention

second mention

3 If a noun is followed by a relative clause or a prepositional phrase that modifies it, and if there is a count noun in the clause or phrase, put *the* before the count noun:

> He described the ways in which the sound of music calms him.

→ See pages 472–473 and 484 to learn more about prepositional phrases.

USING COMMAS WITH INTRODUCTORY PHRASES

To understand this particular use of commas, understand the difference between **a phrase** and **a clause**. Clauses contain subjects and predicates (➜ see pages 478 and 482–485); phrases do not.

THE PATTERN

IF THE INTRODUCTORY PHRASE BEGINS WITH A PREPOSITION

Academic convention says to use a comma after any introductory phrase that begins with a preposition (➜ see pages 472–473 and 484) and is longer than three or four words.

✓ In August, I returned to New Orleans to observe the changes following Hurricane Katrina.

✗ In August I returned to New Orleans to observe the changes following Hurricane Katrina.

✓ Out of desire not to be home alone on their computers, people come to this university library to work among others.

✗ Out of desire not to be home alone on their computers people come to this university library to work among others.

IF THE INTRODUCTORY PHRASE BEGINS WITH A PARTICIPLE OR INFINITIVE

Academic convention says to use a comma after any introductory phrase that begins with a participle or an infinitive (➜ see page 469).

✓ Vaulting and rolling over walls, *Parkour* practitioners propel themselves through cities.

✗ Vaulting and rolling over walls *Parkour* practitioners propel themselves through cities.

✓ To think like a computer scientist, you do not have to play *Dungeons and Dragons*.

✗ To think like a computer scientist you do not have to play *Dungeons and Dragons*.

GRAMMAR, PUNCTUATION, AND MECHANICS

CONTENTS

WHERE ARE WE IN A PROCESS FOR COMPOSING?

Understanding your project

Getting started

Asking questions

Shaping your project for others

Drafting a paper

Getting feedback

Revising

Polishing   Checking the details

PART 11 **GRAMMAR, PUNCTUATION, AND MECHANICS**

11 GRAMMAR AND PUNCTUATION

Questions you might have about grammar, punctuation, and mechanics:

What is grammar?
→ See page 462.

What are the basic parts of sentences?
→ See page 478.

I did not grow up speaking English. What are particular aspects of English grammar to which I should pay attention when I write?
→ See Part 10 as well as pages 463, 466, 470, and 472.

I've had different people tell me that my writing might strengthen if I learned to use different kinds of sentences. What are other kinds of sentences I could use?
→ See page 479.

What is a comma splice? How do I fix comma splices?
→ See page 503 (as well as pages 450–451).

I think I use commas too much. How do I know when NOT to use commas?
→ See pages 508–509.

I'm not sure about punctuation when I quote others' writing. Help?
→ See pages 495 and 524–525.

A friend says I shouldn't rely on a spell-checker. Why not?
→ See page 531.

THE WPA OUTCOMES* FOR PART 11 INCLUDE:

Writing processes: Developing flexible strategies for editing and proofreading.

Using conventions: Developing knowledge of linguistic structures, including grammar and punctuation; understanding why conventions for tone and mechanics vary.

* See page 15.

GRAMMAR

To use Academic English grammar, understand the pieces and patterns of academic writing. In Part 11, we look at a sentences' pieces and then at sentence patterns.

THE PARTS OF SPEECH
The parts of speech are the pieces out of which all sentences are built:

Alice walks.
NOUN · VERB

She walks.
PRONOUN · VERB

The smiling woman walked happily yesterday.
ADJECTIVES "The" is also an article. · NOUN · VERB · ADVERBS

Alice and Omar walk and talk.
NOUN ↑ NOUN · VERB ↑ VERB
CONJUNCTION · CONJUNCTION

After saying goodbye, Alice walked into the store.
ADJECTIVAL PREPOSITIONAL PHRASE "After" is the preposition. · NOUN · VERB · ADVERBIAL PREPOSITIONAL PHRASE "into" is the preposition.

NOUNS: describe the person, place, thing, or idea being discussed

PRONOUNS: a certain kind of noun that refers back to an earlier mentioned noun

VERBS: describe what the person, place, thing, or idea is doing

ADJECTIVES AND ARTICLES: give more details about nouns

ADVERBS: give more detail about how an action is done (where, when, or in what manner)

CONJUNCTIONS: help us talk about more than one noun or action at a time

PREPOSITIONS: allow us to describe how the actors and actions in a sentence are placed in space or time; prepositions appear always as the first word of a phrase; the phrase can serve as an adjective or adverb.

GRAMMAR—PARTS OF SPEECH
NOUNS

Nouns name people, animals, places, things, and ideas or concepts.

any NOUN is . . .

SINGULAR OR	PLURAL	and	COMMON OR	PROPER
one	many		just any thing	a specific one
person	persons		person	Phillip Andrews
woman	women		woman	Tia Patrón
dog	dogs		dog	Lassie
city	cities		city	Milwaukee
tree	trees		tree	*Ficus benjamina*
religion	religions		religion	Buddhism

IF YOU GREW UP SPEAKING A LANGUAGE OTHER THAN ENGLISH . . .

→ English differentiates between two kinds of nouns—count and noncount nouns—that challenge many writers. See page 458.

WORKING WITH PLURAL NOUNS

Most nouns make the plural form by adding an **–s** to the end of the singular form, but as you can see above not all do.

→ See page 457 to learn about irregular plural noun forms.

WORKING WITH PROPER NOUNS

Note above that proper nouns have their first letters capitalized.

GRAMMAR—PARTS OF SPEECH
PRONOUNS

Pronouns take the place of nouns in many different ways.

PERSONAL PRONOUNS — I, me, he, him, she, her, it — we, our, they, their

Personal pronouns refer to specific people or things. In writing, you must first name the person or thing; then you can refer to the person or thing later with a pronoun:

Jenna came prepared: **She** brought her briefcase. (*She* and *her* are both feminine.)

The dog wasn't gray; **it** was black. • Sara and Lia walked to the beach where **they** ate lunch.

Jamshed and **I** worked for a while, and then **we** ate lunch.

The person or thing to which the pronoun refers is called the pronoun's **antecedent**. (Note that *I* does not have an antecedent; readers will understand the person to whom *I* refers.)

→ In formal and Academic English, a pronoun agrees in person, number, and gender with its antecedent. To learn more about this common problem for writers of formal English, see pages 452–453.

INTERROGATIVE PRONOUNS — who, which, what

We use interrogative pronouns to ask questions about people, places, things, or ideas. When we build such questions, there is a noun implied by the question.

Who climbed the stairs? (That is, someone climbed the stairs. *Who* was that someone?)

Which man spoke to you? • **Which** people were there?

POSSESSIVE PRONOUNS — my, mine, his, her, its — our, their

Possessive pronouns indicate close relationship or ownership. As with personal pronouns, you need to make clear to readers the person or thing for which the pronoun stands in. (Again, as with *I*, the antecedent of **my** is understood.) Like adjectives, possessive pronouns tell us about the noun they precede: They tell us who **possesses** the noun.

Eva lost **her** backpack. • The dog leaned into **my** hand—**its** nose was cold! • **Our** car broke down.

Jonathan and Mack got on the same train even though **their** destinations differed.

INDEFINITE PRONOUNS — one, each, every, another, anybody, none, no one, neither, either, both, few, some, many, most, all

Indefinite pronouns function like adjectives and help us communicate when we do not want to or cannot be specific. Indefinite pronouns give readers a rough—indefinite—idea about the noun, not specifying, for example, exactly which person or how many did something.

Each woman brought a book. • **One** could climb the stairs. (*person* is implied after *One*.)

Few people complained. • **Some** dogs like to swim. • **Most** homes here are old.

RELATIVE PRONOUNS   who, whoever, whom, which, that, what, whatever

Relative pronouns allow us to combine sentences that are about the same person, place, thing, or idea. Using them, we can help readers see the connections between two sentences:

The man was tired. The man climbed all the stairs. • **The man who climbed all the stairs was tired.**

(The single sentence implies more strongly than the two separate sentences that the man was probably tired because he climbed the stairs. Note that *who* replaces *The man*.)

The buildings burned. The buildings were old. • **The buildings that burned were old.**

■ ■ ■

Relative pronouns function as the first words of clauses (→ page 478) that give additional information about a noun. Clauses made with relative pronouns are called **dependent clauses** (→ page 449) because they are not sentences by themselves; to make a sentence with such a dependent clause, join it to an **independent clause** (→ page 485).

DEPENDENT CLAUSE: **who climbed all the stairs** • INDEPENDENT CLAUSE: **The man was tired.**

SENTENCE: **The man who climbed all the stairs was tired.**

→ For more on using relative pronouns, see pages 449 and 488.

DEMONSTRATIVE PRONOUNS   this, that   these, those

These pronouns help us be specific about a person or object we want to discuss.

This woman is my friend. • **That dog belongs to Mavis.**

These people went to the museum. • **Those buildings are on Washington Street.**

In the examples above, the demonstrative pronouns function like adjectives, telling readers exactly what person or thing is meant. Below, the pronouns function like nouns:

This is the most important issue of our time: Are we running out of oil? • **That is my best pen.**

RECIPROCAL PRONOUNS   each other, one another

Use reciprocal pronouns when you want to show people or objects acting on each other.

The survivors helped one another. • **The dogs chased each other.**

ADJECTIVES

With adjectives, we can describe the specific qualities of people, places, objects, and ideas.

WHICH ONE? WHAT KIND?

Adjectives allow us to specify exactly which people, places, objects, or ideas we want to consider or discuss.

She wore red shoes. • The green shoes are comfortable.

HOW MANY?

Adjectives help us say how many people, places, objects, or ideas are at stake.

Four of these potatoes will feed three people.

HOW DO THEY COMPARE?

Adjectives help us specify which people, places, objects, or ideas we mean by allowing us to make comparisons.

Please hand me the smallest book.

The larger of the two books contains less information than the smaller.

PLACEMENT OF ADJECTIVES

1 Adjectives usually come before the nouns they modify:

Use only the sharpest tools to prune your trees. • Last night we saw a brilliant green aurora.

There is no biological reason for this condition.

The jubilant procession danced through the narrow streets.

2 Adjectives come after the verbs *appear*, *be*, *feel*, *look*, *seem*, *smell*, *sound*, and *taste*:

She was not at her sharpest. • The frog looked a brilliant green in the sun.

The reason is purely biological. • The team sounded jubilant after their win.

→ See pages 454–455 to learn how to avoid some problems writers often have with placing adjectival phrases.

IF YOU GREW UP SPEAKING A LANGUAGE OTHER THAN ENGLISH . . .

→ Page 499 offer help in using multiple adjectives.

ARTICLES

Articles are a special kind of adjective. There are three articles: *a*, *an*, and **the**.

THE INDEFINITE ARTICLES *a* AND *an*

A and **an** have the same function: We use them before a noun that does not refer to a known or specific person, animal, place, thing, or idea.

■ ■ ■

Use these indefinite articles before nouns when you make general statements:

A computer is useful for homework.

A birthday happens only once a year.

Also use indefinite articles before nouns when your writing does not concern a particular person or thing of its kind:

An hour passes quickly when you are focused on your work.

■ ■ ■

Use **a** before nouns (or adjectives placed before nouns) that begin with a consonant sound; use **an** before nouns (or adjectives placed before nouns) that begin with a vowel sound.

A knife is useful on a camping trip.

An octopus is an unusual pet.

Note that, at the beginning of words, **h** and **u** can sometimes sound like vowels and sometimes like consonants. Use the sound of the word following the article to determine whether to use **a** or **an**:

An honest person returned my wallet.

A history book was on the table.

THE DEFINITE ARTICLE *the*

The is used when your reader or listener will know or be able to figure out exactly which person, animal, place, thing, or idea you discuss.

■ ■ ■

To decide whether to use the definite or indefinite article, consider the context in which you write or speak. If you know for sure that your readers or listeners will know the exact person or thing to which you refer, use **the**:

The rosebush needs water.

If you are standing in your yard speaking with neighbors and there is only one rosebush, everyone will know exactly which rosebush you mean.

GRAMMAR—PARTS OF SPEECH
VERBS

Verbs describe what the nouns of a sentence do in time. Verbs are about actions (whether of body or of mind) or about states of being in the present, past, or future.

AT THE PRESENT TIME: **The man runs.** • **The man is running.**

IN THE PAST: **The man ran.** • **The man was running.**

IN THE FUTURE: **The man will run.**

THE PATTERN

IN ENGLISH, VERBS CHANGE THEIR FORMS TO INDICATE:

TIME (OR TENSE: PAST, PRESENT, OR FUTURE).

Some tenses are shown above. (→ For more on English verb tenses, see pages 440–443.)

WHO IS DOING THE ACTION (OR BEING ACTED ON).

This is called the person of the verb.

FIRST PERSON:	I run.	I was thinking.	We will play.
SECOND PERSON:	You run.	You were thinking.	You will play.
THIRD PERSON:	She runs.	He was thinking.	It will play.

→ The person of the verb has to agree with the verb form; see pages 436–439.

HOW MANY PEOPLE ARE DOING THE ACTION.

This is called the number of the verb.

SINGULAR:	I am thinking.	You, Kris, forgot.	She has run.
PLURAL:	We are thinking.	You three forgot.	They have run.

→ The number of the verb has to agree with the verb form; see pages 436 and 439.

VOICE.

There are two voices:

ACTIVE: The person, animal, place, object, or idea named by the noun is performing the action described by the verb: **You run.** • **She will play.**

PASSIVE: The person, animal, place, object, or idea named by the noun has the action of the verb performed on it: **The record was played.** • **The store was run by two sisters.**

→ For more on the voice of English verbs, see pages 308–309 and 445.

MOOD.

There are three moods:

INDICATIVE, for facts, opinions, and questions: **The song plays for twenty minutes.**

IMPERATIVE, for commands and requests: **Run!** • **Please think.**

SUBJUNCTIVE, for wishes and hypothetical situations: **I wish we could play.**

FORMING THE TENSES OF ENGLISH VERBS

Except for the verb **be**, all English verbs have five forms.

	BASE FORM	-S FORM	PRESENT PARTICIPLE	PAST	PAST PARTICIPLE
REGULAR VERB	walk	walks	walking	walked	walked
IRREGULAR VERB	sing	sings	singing	sang	sung
IRREGULAR VERB	ride	rides	riding	rode	ridden

THE BASE FORM
Use the base form to find a verb in a dictionary and to build all a verb's tenses. If you place **to** in front of the base form, you make what is called **the infinitive**.

THE -S FORM
This form is the third person singular present tense of any verb.

THE PRESENT PARTICIPLE
The present participle, made by adding **-ing** to the base form, is used with a helping verb to build any verb's progressive tenses. (If a verb's base form ends in **-e**, the **-e** is dropped before the **-ing**.) The present participle can be used as an adjective: **Let sleeping dogs lie.**

THE PAST FORM
The past form is used for the simple past tense. Because English has been formed from so many other languages, many frequently used verbs have irregular past forms. A dictionary will show you the past form of any verb.

THE PAST PARTICIPLE
With a helping verb, the past participle is used to construct the perfect tenses of any verb. For regular verbs, the past participle is the same as the past form; for irregular verbs, you will need to check a dictionary to learn the past participle.

→ See page 443 to see all the verb forms.

INFINITIVES

Infinitives are made by putting the word **to** in front of the base form of a verb:

to walk • **to talk** • **to eat** • **to dream** • **to argue**

Infinitives can function as nouns, adjectives, or adverbs:

To walk is good. • **To talk, one must have language.** • **He lives to eat.** • **He likes to argue.**

MAIN VERBS AND HELPING VERBS

In the patterns on page 469, note that—except for the simple present and simple past—verb tenses are constructed from a main verb and a helping verb (➔ see page 443).

The main verb is one of the five forms of a verb described on the previous page; a helping verb is one of the forms of the irregular verbs **be**, **have**, and **do**.

THE FORMS OF HELPING VERBS

BASE FORM	PRESENT			PAST		
	SINGULAR	PLURAL	PARTICIPLE	SINGULAR	PLURAL	PARTICIPLE
be	I am	We are	being	I was	We were	been
	You are	You are		You were	You were	
	He/She/It is	They are		He/She/It was	They were	
have	I have	We have	having	I had	We had	had
	You have	You have		You had	You had	
	He/She/It has	They have		He/She/It had	They had	
do	I do	We do	doing	I did	We did	done
	You do	You do		You did	You did	
	He/She/It does	They do		He/She/It did	They did	

MODAL HELPING VERBS

Helping verbs also include the verbs called **modals**, whose form never changes: *can, could, may, might, must, ought to, shall, should, will, would*. Modals help us express abilities, possibilities, necessity, intentions, requests, or obligation.

ABILITY, POSSIBILITY, REQUEST: You could have gone running with us last night. • Can you play with our band this weekend?

POSSIBILITY, REQUEST: May I think a little longer about it? • Conrad might run in the race.

OBLIGATION: You must think about a vacation. • The senator ought to run harder in this election.

INTENTIONS: I shall play over the weekend. • You should run over to school. • Jamshed will practice his violin every day.

IF YOU GREW UP SPEAKING A LANGUAGE OTHER THAN ENGLISH . . .

How verb tenses change and how they are used differs considerably from language to language, so—no matter what your home language—pay particular attention to the information about verbs on these pages and on pages 436–443.

ADVERBS

Adverbs are most often used to show when, how, or where the action of a verb takes place. Adverbs can also modify adjectives or other adverbs.

ADVERBS OF TIME

Adverbs of time describe when something happened; they can also describe for how long and how often something happens.

She wants food now. He slept all winter. She plays sometimes.

ADVERBS OF MANNER

Adverbs of manner describe how something happened. They are usually formed by adding **–ly** to the end of an adjective.

He shook wildly. He rolls the ball happily. She rested lazily. She waited patiently.

ADVERBS OF PLACE

Adverbs of place describe where or the direction in which something happened.

He walked forward. She worked uphill. She sat down. He jumped high.

PLACEMENT OF ADVERBS

Adverbs generally follow the verb or the object.

She drives the car carefully. The number of scholarships has dropped considerably.

CREATING EMPHASIS WITH PLACEMENT OF ADVERBS OF MANNER

Adverbs of manner generally go after the verb or object, as noted above—unless you want to emphasize the manner in which something is done. In such cases, you can place adverbs of manner before the verb.

The lion carefully approached the elephants. The man repeatedly claimed his innocence.

For even more emphasis, you can start a sentence with an adverb of manner.

Belatedly the soldiers received their new protective bodywear.

PLACEMENT OF ADVERBS OF TIME

Adverbs of time that express how often something happens usually go before the verb.

Small refinements in energy production are rarely considered newsworthy.

When an adverb tells the exact number of times something happens, it usually goes at a sentence's end.

The city's alternative newspaper is published weekly.

PREPOSITIONS

Prepositions help us express a relationship in time or space between (usually) two nouns in a sentence.

PREPOSITIONS START PREPOSITIONAL PHRASES

on the Web   in Asia and Europe

at almost the speed of light   to the first year of parenthood

PREPOSITIONAL PHRASES SERVE AS ADJECTIVES OR ADVERBS WITHIN SENTENCES

Would you put your health records on the Web?
In this sentence, *on the Web* is an adverbial prepositional phrase.

My cellphone works in Asia and Europe.
In this sentence, *in Asia and Europe* is an adverbial prepositional phrase.

Einstein's special theory of relativity describes particle motion at close to the speed of light.
In this sentence, *at almost the speed of light* is an adjectival prepositional phrase.

Anna and Otto wrote a guide to the first year of parenthood.
In this sentence, *to the first year* is an adjectival prepositional phrase—and so is *of parenthood*.

Prepositions functioning like adverbs can go anywhere in a sentence, depending on the emphasis you want to give. Prepositions that function like adjectives generally go right after the noun they modify.

IF YOU GREW UP SPEAKING A LANGUAGE OTHER THAN ENGLISH . . .

KNOW THAT PREPOSITIONS ARE IDIOMATIC.
Certain verbs are followed by certain prepositions: *He was listening to music. We rely on each other.* Checking a verb in the dictionary will tell you which prepositions follow it.

Similarly, certain nouns and adjectives are followed by certain prepositions: *He has an interest in anthropology. She puts emphasis on the importance of rules.* Again, checking nouns and adjectives in the dictionary will tell you which prepositions follow them.

PREPOSITIONS DESCRIBING RELATIONSHIPS IN TIME

The prepositions *at*, *on*, and *in* are conventionally used for certain time relations:

TIME WITH *at*
- exact time: at 3 p.m., at midnight
- meal times: at dinner, at breakfast
- parts of the day, when no article is used for the part of the day: at night, at daybreak, at noon (compare: in the morning, in the evening)
- age: At 21 you are legally considered a full adult.

TIME WITH *on*
- days of the week: on Monday, on Tuesdays
- parts of the day, when the day is named: on Friday evening, on Saturday morning
- dates: on July 28th, on September 22nd

TIME WITH *in*
- seasons: in spring, in summer
- months: in April, in the third month
- years: in 2056, in 1956
- durations: in ten minutes, in one day, in a month

PREPOSITIONS DESCRIBING RELATIONSHIPS IN SPACE

at, by, in, on

show an object's settled position or position after it has moved

I arrived at the Baghdad airport.

In this town most people work at the call center.

They carry their children on their backs.

to, onto, into

show the direction of movement toward a point, surface, or area

They brought their babies to the clinic.

She placed the crown onto his head.

Walking into his office is like walking into a zoo.

by, along, through

show the direction of movement next to or past a point, surface, or area

We drove by the ocean.

From castles along the Rhine River, German princes regulated river traffic.

Omero Catan, a salesperson from New York, drove the first car through the Lincoln Tunnel after waiting in line for 30 hours.

from, out of

show the direction of movement away from a point, surface, or area

The *joropo* is a waltzy musical form from Venezuela.

After the airplane crashed, she had to walk out of the jungle.

CONJUNCTIONS

Conjunctions connect words or groups of words. There are four kinds of conjunctions, each of which helps you express different kinds of relations between the words you are connecting.

THE PATTERN

COORDINATING CONJUNCTIONS

Coordinating conjunctions can connect nouns (including pronouns), adjectives, adverbs, prepositions, clauses, and sentences.

Use a coordinating conjunction when you want a reader to see that the words you are connecting have equal—coordinate—emphasis. These are the coordinating conjunctions, together with the relations they show:

and	addition	Jacob and Ali went to the store. Loretta cooked and ate dinner.
for	cause	The dog is wet, for she swam. I am hungry, for I forgot to eat.
but, yet	contrast	Jacob went to the store, but Ali stayed home. Loretta cooked dinner, yet she did not eat right away.
or	choice	Jacob or Ali can go. • Loretta can cook dinner or eat out.
so	effect	I am hungry, so I will eat. The dog is wet from the rain, so I will dry her.
nor	exclusion	José doesn't swim, nor do I.

To connect individual words—such as nouns (including pronouns), adjectives, adverbs, and prepositions—**or phrases,** use this pattern:

WORD OR PHRASE	COORDINATING CONJUNCTION	WORD OR PHRASE

To connect sentences, use this pattern:

INDEPENDENT CLAUSE	**,**	COORDINATING CONJUNCTION	INDEPENDENT CLAUSE	**.**

CORRELATIVE CONJUNCTIONS

Correlative conjunctions are like coordinating conjunctions in that they help you give equal emphasis to the words you are connecting—but correlative conjunctions come in two parts, and readers always expect to see both parts:

both . . . and, not only . . . but also
addition

Both Miguel and Rav are on vacation.
She did both her English and her math work.

either . . . or, whether . . . or
choice

I could hire either Paul or Shawna.
I want either to go out for dinner or to sleep.
Either you will eat at home, or you will go out.

just as . . . so
equality

Just as the bread's smell brought back memories, so too did its taste.

neither . . . nor
exclusion

Neither this car nor that one is running.
Neither will Noor go out, nor will she stay in!

To connect individual words—such as nouns (including pronouns), adjectives, adverbs, and prepositions—**or phrases**, use this pattern:

WORD OR PHRASE	CORRELATIVE CONJUNCTION, PART 1	WORD OR PHRASE	CORRELATIVE CONJUNCTION, PART 2

To connect sentences, use this pattern:

CORRELATIVE CONJUNCTION, PART 1	INDEPENDENT CLAUSE		CORRELATIVE CONJUNCTION, PART 2	INDEPENDENT CLAUSE	
		,			**.**

SUBORDINATING CONJUNCTIONS

Subordinating conjunctions join two sentences. The sentence following the conjunction is subordinate to—less emphasized than—the other sentence.

as, because, since cause or reason	I am angry because he told lies. Since you left, our group has no women.
so that effect or result	He packs a lunch so that he can save money. So that you can travel, you must get a passport.
if, even if, provided that, unless condition	You couldn't get in even if you wanted. If you want, he can bake the cake.
although, even though, though contrast	He took the test even though he had not studied. Although she was tired, she went out.
where, wherever location	Nan sings wherever there is karaoke. Wherever Heather goes, laughter follows.
after, before, once, since, until, when, whenever, while time	She went to the movies after she had dinner. While it rains, the city cannot fix the road.

Putting a subordinating conjunction in front of a sentence turns the sentence into a dependent clause.

When you put the dependent clause at the beginning of a sentence, put a comma after it:

| SUBORDINATING CONJUNCTION | INDEPENDENT CLAUSE | , | INDEPENDENT CLAUSE | . |

When you join two sentences by putting a subordinating conjunction between them, you need no comma:

| INDEPENDENT CLAUSE | SUBORDINATING CONJUNCTION | INDEPENDENT CLAUSE | . |

CONJUNCTIVE ADVERBS

Independent clauses can be joined with a semicolon and conjunctive adverb to show the relationships listed here:

also, besides, furthermore, moreover	addition	We don't need a car; besides, we can't afford one. The city paved our street; moreover, they put up a new sign.
however, instead, likewise, nevertheless, nonetheless, otherwise, similarly, still	comparison and contrast	We could eat; otherwise, we should go home. Their team went into the game with a three-point advantage; nonetheless, they lost.
accordingly, consequently, hence, then, therefore, thus	result or summary	The jury found her not guilty; thus, she was freed. She went home with a migraine; consequently, she missed the lecture.
finally, meanwhile, next, now, then	time	The first expedition set out; meanwhile, the second expedition gathered its equipment.

When you use conjunctive adverbs, start with an independent clause followed by a semicolon; then, put the conjunction (followed by a comma) and then put the second independent clause.

GRAMMAR—PARTS OF SPEECH
BUILDING SENTENCES

THE PARTS OF SPEECH (→ see pages 462–477)

NOUNS: Society, Diffusion, Knowledge, members, Magazine, Cyclopedia, practices, audience
PRONOUNS: its
ARTICLES: THE

ADJECTIVES: nineteenth-century, Useful, working-class
ADVERBS: Really
CONJUNCTIONS: and
PREPOSITIONS: of

VERBS: published, distributed, worried
HELPING VERBS: were
ADVERBS: widely
CONJUNCTIONS: and

NOUN PHRASES

The nineteenth-century Society for the Diffusion of Really Useful Knowledge

The Penny Magazine and *The Penny Cyclopedia*

its members

the reading practices of its working-class audience

VERB PHRASES

published and distributed widely

were worried

SUBJECTS

The nineteenth-century Society for the Diffusion of Really Useful Knowledge

its members

PREDICATES

published and distributed widely *The Penny Magazine* and *The Penny Cyclopedia*

were worried about the reading practices of its working-class audience.

CLAUSES: two kinds, INDEPENDENT . . .

The nineteenth-century Society for the Diffusion of Really Useful Knowledge published and distributed widely *The Penny Magazine* and *The Penny Cyclopedia*

and DEPENDENT

because its members were worried about the reading practices of its working-class audience.

A SENTENCE (all sentences are independent clauses)

The nineteenth-century Society for the Diffusion of Really Useful Knowledge published and distributed widely *The Penny Magazine* and *The Penny Cyclopedia* because its members were worried about the reading practices of its working-class audience.

THERE ARE 4 SENTENCE FUNCTIONS

1 **WE MAKE STATEMENTS:** Such sentences are called **declarative sentences** and are the main sentence kind you see in all writing.
In the fifth and sixth centuries, Ireland was the center of high culture in Europe.

2 **WE ASK QUESTIONS:** Sentences that ask questions are called **interrogative sentences** and matter in all writing. In academic writing, authors often use questions to set up the problems they want to address.
How lethal was the flu of 1918? • How is it to live in the most notorious prison in the country?

3 **WE COMMAND:** Sentences that tell someone to do something are called **imperative sentences**; you find them in instruction sets and manuals. (They begin with the implied subject *You*.)
Watch out that the temperature of the beaker's contents does not rise above 275°.

4 **WE ARE EMOTIONAL:** With such **exclamatory sentences** you express strong feeling; these sentences end with exclamation points.
If the electrons are not seen, we have interference!

THERE ARE 4 SENTENCE PATTERNS.

All American English sentences are built following one of the following patterns:

1 **SIMPLE SENTENCES** appear in all writing and build the other patterns:
Dogs bark. • Children love robots. • They tracked the experiment and wrote their report.

2 **COMPOUND SENTENCES** join two simple sentences. Compound sentences matter in formal writing because they help you express relationships among your sentence's elements.
An autumn wind gusts up to thirty miles an hour; a winter wind gusts up to fifty miles an hour.

3 **COMPLEX SENTENCES** allow you to express complicated relations among the elements you describe and so are important in academic and other formal writing.
In this chapter I examine the development of Piaget's thought, which has three main features.

4 **COMPOUND-COMPLEX SENTENCES** result when you combine a compound sentence with a complex sentence. These sentences tend to be long and are used almost exclusively in academic writing.
In the Sung and Yuan dynasties of the twelfth to fourteenth centuries C.E., the Chinese school led the world in solving equations; the triangle we call Pascal's was already old in China in 1300 C.E.

GRAMMAR—SENTENCE PATTERNS
SIMPLE SENTENCES

Two words can make a sentence. The first word names a person, place, thing, or idea; the second word describes what that person, place, thing, or idea is, was, or will be doing.

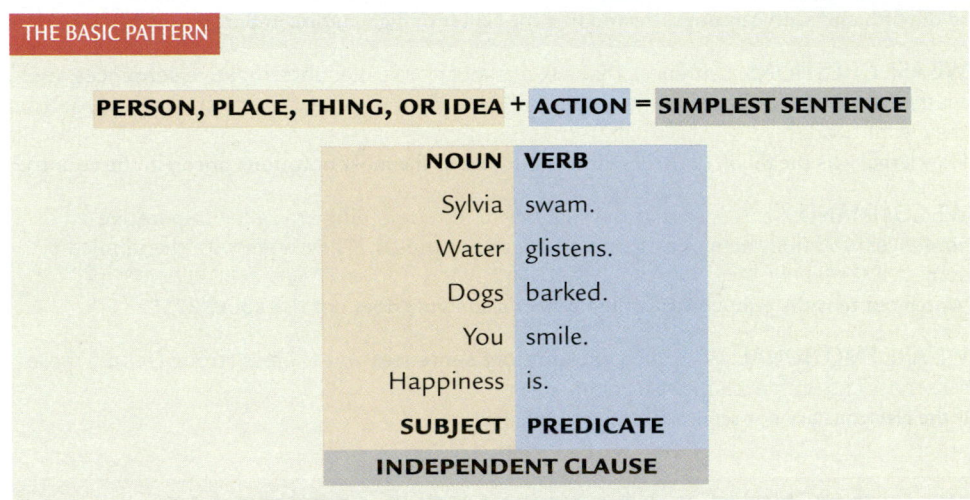

THE BASIC PATTERN

PERSON, PLACE, THING, OR IDEA + **ACTION** = **SIMPLEST SENTENCE**

NOUN	VERB
Sylvia	swam.
Water	glistens.
Dogs	barked.
You	smile.
Happiness	is.
SUBJECT	**PREDICATE**
INDEPENDENT CLAUSE	

You can add descriptions to the nouns and verbs in the most basic sentences.

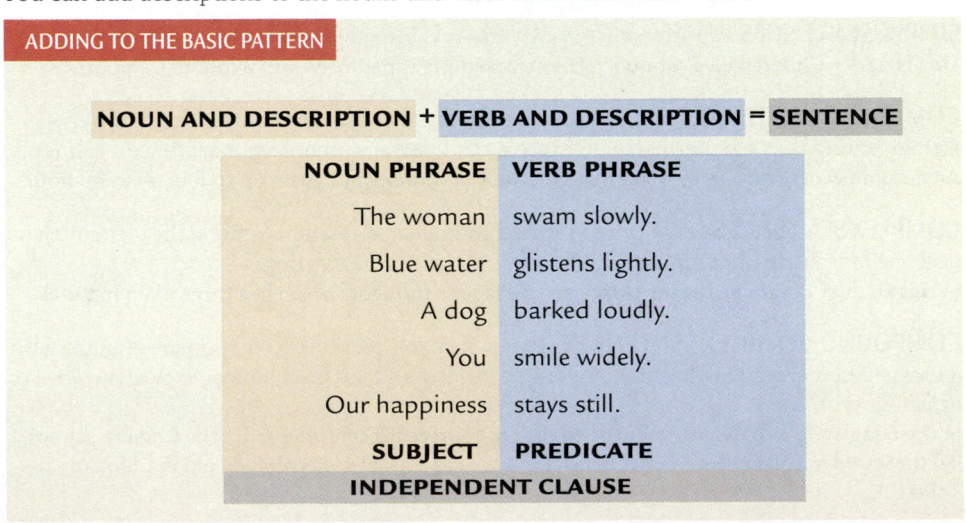

ADDING TO THE BASIC PATTERN

NOUN AND DESCRIPTION + **VERB AND DESCRIPTION** = **SENTENCE**

NOUN PHRASE	VERB PHRASE
The woman	swam slowly.
Blue water	glistens lightly.
A dog	barked loudly.
You	smile widely.
Our happiness	stays still.
SUBJECT	**PREDICATE**
INDEPENDENT CLAUSE	

To the nouns and verbs in the most basic sentences you can also add objects, which are the persons or things acted on by the subject.

ADDING TO THE BASIC PATTERN

NOUN PHRASE + **VERB PHRASE** + **OBJECT (NOUN PHRASE)** = **SENTENCE**

SUBJECT	PREDICATE
The woman	quickly walks her barking dog.
An irritated man	slapped a whiny mosquito.
The chair legs	dented the floor.
The wind	easily moves the lake water.
She	shifted her weight.
You	warily watch the changing weather.
I	make the bed.
Our happiness	fills me.

INDEPENDENT CLAUSE

→ To learn more about
nouns, see pages 463 and 456–457.
verbs, see pages 468–470 and 436–445.
subjects, see pages 482–484.
predicates, see pages 482–484.

→ A subject and predicate together form a clause (page 478); when they can stand alone as a sentence, they are independent clauses (page 485).

→ The words that help us say descriptive things about nouns are adjectives (page 466). Articles are the words *a, an,* and *the* and are a special kind of adjective (page 467).

→ The words that help us say descriptive things about verbs are adverbs (page 471).

→ When nouns and verbs have descriptive words added to them, as above, they are called (respectively) noun phrases and verb phrases (page 478 in addition to this and the previous page).

SUBJECTS AND PREDICATES

To move from writing simple sentences to writing compound, complex, and compound-complex sentences, writers need to understand subjects and predicates.

SUBJECTS

Subjects are the word or words in a sentence that name who or what is performing some action. Subjects can be composed of one word (in which case it is always a noun) or multiple words (in which case they are some combination of nouns and articles, conjunctions, and/or adjectives).

> Yang smiles.
>
> Michael and the new student went to lunch together.
>
> Their sad songs filled the valley and echoed in the air.

SUBJECT

→ To learn more about the kinds of words that make up subjects, see pages 463–465 for nouns and pronouns, page 466 for adjectives, page 467 for articles, and pages 474–477 for conjunctions.

SUBJECT-VERB AGREEMENT

→ In formal English, the subject of a sentence agrees with the verb in person and number. To learn how this works, see pages 436–439.

PREDICATES

Predicates are the words in a sentence that describe the action taken by the subject. Predicates can be made of one word (in which case it is always a verb) or multiple words (in which case they are some combination of verbs and adverbs, conjunctions, or noun phrases that are objects).

> Yang smiles.
>
> Michael and the new student went to lunch together.
>
> Their sad songs filled the valley and echoed in the air.

PREDICATE

→ To learn more about the kinds of words that make up predicates, see pages 468–470 for verbs, page 471 for adverbs, pages 478 and 480–481 for noun phrases, and pages 474–477 for conjunctions.

COMPOUND SUBJECTS AND PREDICATES

You can use the patterns on the preceding pages to build more detailed sentences. One way to do this is to use a kind of word called a **conjunction** to build:

SUBJECTS THAT DESCRIBE MORE THAN ONE PERSON, PLACE, THING, OR IDEA

You can substitute any of the following subjects for any of the noun phrases in the simple sentence patterns on the preceding pages (as long as you make the verb agree):

Sylvia and Luisa walk.

Neither the air nor my heart moved.

Dogs or coyotes barked last night outside my window.

Paul, Tonio, and I make the beds.

SUBJECT   **PREDICATE**

The subjects above are called **compound subjects** because they are compounded out of multiple nouns.

→ Note that the form of the verb sometimes has to change when you change the subject of a sentence; see pages 436–439 and 468–470.

PREDICATES THAT DESCRIBE MORE THAN ONE ACTION

You can substitute any of the following predicates for any of the verb phrases in the simple sentence patterns on the preceding pages (as long as the subject and predicate agree in number):

Sylvia walks or runs.

My heart jumped and stilled.

The dogs both barked and snored loudly.

Paul makes the bed and sweeps the floor.

SUBJECT   **PREDICATE**

The predicates above are called **compound predicates** because they are made of multiple predicates.

→ To learn more about conjunctions, which enable you to build compound predicates, see pages 474–477.

USING PREPOSITIONAL PHRASES TO MAKE MORE DESCRIPTIVE SUBJECTS AND PREDICATES

Prepositions are words that allow you to say more precisely where a noun is in space or time or where the action of a verb takes place. Prepositions do this by being the first word of **prepositional phrases**, which show where one noun is in relation to another or where the action of a verb takes place relative to some noun. Prepositional phrases thus allow you to make subjects and predicates that can be very descriptive.

MORE DESCRIPTIVE SUBJECTS

As parts of subjects, prepositional phrases function like adjectives: They tell your readers more about the nouns you are using:

The dog on the sidewalk was barking.

The air in the tent shimmered.

Hiro, on the telephone, sounds less serious.

Children at school tend to be quieter.

SUBJECT   **PREDICATE**

MORE DESCRIPTIVE PREDICATES

As parts of predicates, prepositional phrases function like adverbs: They tell your readers more about the action being described by the verb, such as where or when the action happens or happened:

Sylvia walks into the store.

My heart jumped at the sound of your voice.

The dogs hid underneath the table.

Sudawat studies the book over the course of the day.

SUBJECT   **PREDICATE**

→ To learn more about prepositions, see pages 472–473.

→ To learn more about adverbs, see page 471.

INDEPENDENT CLAUSES

Consider what *independent* and *dependent* mean: Something that is independent can stand alone; something that is dependent cannot.

Independent clauses can be sentences, and dependent clauses cannot.

THE PATTERN

AN INDEPENDENT CLAUSE CAN STAND ALONE AS A SIMPLE SENTENCE

SUBJECT + PREDICATE = INDEPENDENT CLAUSE

Nazila bikes.

Dogs and coyotes bark in the lonely night.

The cell was large and unevenly shaped.

The fast growth of cities causes trouble for mapmakers.

Ambassador Dodd came from a farm family of seven children.

When an independent clause stands by itself, it is a simple sentence. When it is combined with dependent clauses (as we show on the next pages), you build complex sentences.

→ See page 449 to learn more about dependent clauses.

GRAMMAR—SENTENCE PATTERNS
COMPOUND SENTENCES

Compound sentences are made up of two or more simple sentences joined by punctuation or conjunctions—or both punctuation and conjunctions.

THE FUNCTIONS OF COMPOUND SENTENCES

When you write with compound sentences, your sentences can show readers more complex relations among events than simple sentences allow. Compound sentences show up frequently in academic writing.

Because compound sentences are made up of two independent clauses joined together, they show that the writer wants to give equal emphasis to both clauses.

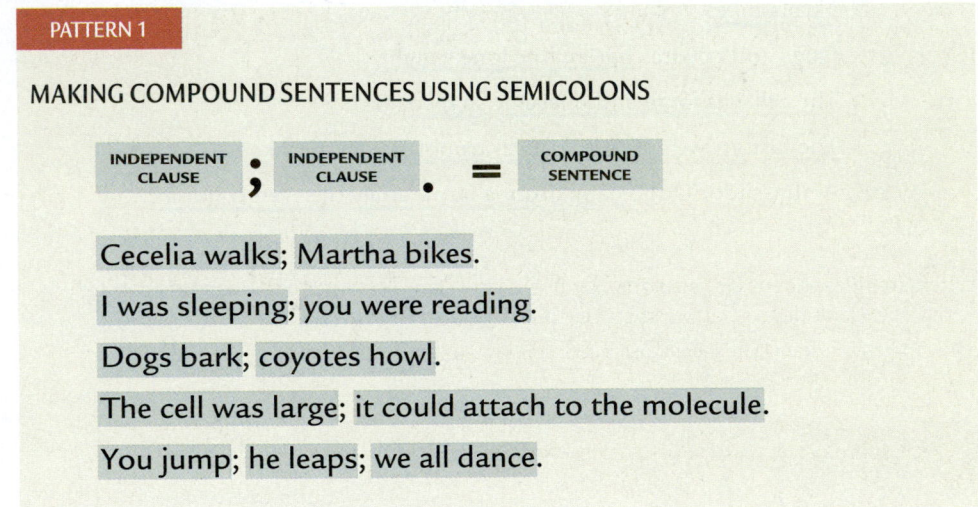

PATTERN 1

MAKING COMPOUND SENTENCES USING SEMICOLONS

INDEPENDENT CLAUSE **;** INDEPENDENT CLAUSE **.** **=** COMPOUND SENTENCE

Cecelia walks; Martha bikes.

I was sleeping; you were reading.

Dogs bark; coyotes howl.

The cell was large; it could attach to the molecule.

You jump; he leaps; we all dance.

This pattern implies that the events described in the joined independent clauses happened at the same time and are of equal importance.

→ To learn more about using semicolons to join two independent clauses, see page 512.

MAKING COMPOUND SENTENCES USING COMMAS AND COORDINATING CONJUNCTIONS

| INDEPENDENT CLAUSE | , | COORDINATING CONJUNCTION | INDEPENDENT CLAUSE | . | = | COMPOUND SENTENCE |

Cecelia walks, and Martha bikes.

I was sleeping, while you were reading.

Dogs bark, but coyotes howl.

The cell was large, but it could attach to the molecule.

This pattern uses **coordinating conjunctions**.

→ To learn more about coordinating conjunctions and the relations they can help you build between independent clauses, see page 474.

MAKING COMPOUND SENTENCES USING SEMICOLONS, CONJUNCTIVE ADVERBS, AND COMMAS

Some kinds of conjunctions take the following pattern for joining independent clauses (note the comma after the conjunction):

| INDEPENDENT CLAUSE | ; | CONJUNCTIVE ADVERB | , | INDEPENDENT CLAUSE | . | = | COMPOUND SENTENCE |

Cecelia walks; meanwhile, Martha bikes.

I slept; instead, you read.

It rained while we were there; moreover, it was cold.

She was found innocent; accordingly, she will go free.

This pattern uses **conjunctive adverbs**.

→ To learn more about conjunctive adverbs, see page 477.

GRAMMAR—SENTENCE PATTERNS
COMPLEX SENTENCES

Complex sentences combine one independent clause with at least one dependent clause.

THE FUNCTION OF COMPLEX SENTENCES

Complex sentences show readers more complex relations among events than simple sentences because complex sentences are made of two clauses, one of which—the independent clause—will always have more emphasis than the other.

PATTERN 1

COMPLEX SENTENCES WITH ADJECTIVE CLAUSES

RELATIVE PRONOUN + PREDICATE = ADJECTIVE CLAUSE

which was in the street

whose shape kept changing

Adjective clauses allow you to give additional information about subjects, and so they help you write expressive sentences. Adjective clauses are inserted into independent clauses to make **THE FIRST KIND OF COMPLEX SENTENCE**:

The bicycle, which was in the street, is missing.

The cell whose shape kept changing has been identified.

→ To learn more about relative pronouns, see page 465 (and also page 449).

→ To learn more about the punctuation of adjective phrases when you weave them into independent clauses, see pages 504–507. Pay close attention to this: Punctuating adjective phrases can cause writers trouble.

WATCH OUT FOR THIS!

Adjective clauses can look like independent clauses because they have a similar structure to sentences: There is a word and then a predicate. But, in formal English, relative pronouns cannot take the place of nouns—and so adjective clauses cannot stand alone as sentences.

NOT SENTENCES

which <u>was in the street</u>

whose shape <u>kept changing</u>

SENTENCES

The bicycle <u>was in the street</u>.

The cell's shape <u>kept changing</u>.

If, in the adjective clauses to the left, you were to replace the relative pronouns with subjects, you would have sentences.

ALSO SENTENCES

Whose shape kept changing?

Sometimes, if you put a question mark at the end of an adjective clause—and you capitalize the first letter of the relative pronoun—you can make interrogatory sentences out of adjective clauses.

When you do this, you are changing the function of the pronoun, and so you are changing the type of the pronoun, from a relative pronoun to an interrogative pronoun.

→ To learn more about interrogative pronouns, see page 464.

COMPLEX SENTENCES WITH ADVERB CLAUSES

SUBORDINATING CONJUNCTION + **SUBJECT** + **PREDICATE** = **ADVERB CLAUSE**

after it rains

while the cell's shape changed

Adverb clauses help writers express complex ideas and so are important in academic writing. Add adverb clauses to independent clauses to make **THE SECOND KIND OF COMPLEX SENTENCE**, which express subtle relationships.

After it rains, we will go for a bike ride.

While the cell's shape changed, it could not be identified.

→ To learn more about subordinating conjunctions, see page 476.

WATCH OUT FOR THIS!

Adverb clauses are not independent clauses, so they cannot stand alone as sentences.

NOT SENTENCES	SENTENCES
after it rains	It rains.
while the cell's shape changed	The cell's shape changed.

→ The phrases above are fragments of sentences that can be turned into sentences. To learn more about sentence fragments, see pages 446–449.

If you remove the subordinating conjunctions or correlative adverbs, you make sentences out of the fragments to the left.

COMPOUND-COMPLEX SENTENCES

Compound-complex sentences are a sure sign of academic writing. Knowing how to mix compound and complex sentences into compound-complex sentences helps writers build sentences for the widest range of contexts and purposes.

THE PATTERN

Compound-complex sentences consist of two or more independent clauses, at least one of which contains a dependent clause. The sentences can be joined in any of the ways compound sentences can be made.

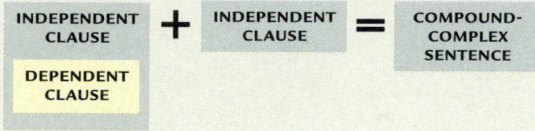

Because compound-complex sentences are composed of many parts, they tend to be long:

Young people who came of age during the Progressive Era years of 1910 to 1914 had grown up during a time of optimism and change, and they believed in a living wage for workers, reduced corporate power, and equitably distributed wealth.

Below you can see the parts of this compound-complex sentence:

- An independent clause, which is a complex sentence because it contains the dependent clause *who came of age in the Progressive Era years of 1910 to 1914.*
- A comma after the first independent clause.
- The conjunction *and.*
- A simple sentence.

Young people who came of age during the Progressive Era years of 1910 to 1914 had grown up during a time of optimism and change, and they believed in a living wage for workers, reduced corporate power, and equitably distributed wealth.

PUNCTUATION

Before writing, there was no punctuation: People simply spoke, not thinking of what they said as being words, much less as being divided up by punctuation. People simply put sounds together in different orders, and they understood each other.

After the invention of writing, many centuries passed before punctuation (or even spaces between words) was invented. What seems to have given rise to punctuation was the need for speakers to read printed words aloud to listeners, as in churches. Imagine reading this passage aloud if you hadn't had time to figure out the passage beforehand:

most punctuation marks are composed to be seen but not heard these subtle often understated devices are quite important however for they are the meter that determines the measure within the silent voice of typography punctuation directs tempo pitch volume and the separation of words periods signify full stops commas slow the reader down question marks change pitch quotation marks indicate references

Punctuation is thus an important part of writing to communicate: It shows readers how you are shaping your ideas, where you are putting emphasis, and when you are using others' words.

There is considerable room for you to choose how to punctuate in order to reach the audiences for whom you write—but the information in the following pages will help you make informed decisions.

THERE ARE TWO MAIN KINDS OF PUNCTUATION MARKS—

PUNCTUATION THAT GOES WITHIN SENTENCES
- commas
- semicolons
- colons
- parentheses
- dashes
- brackets
- hyphens
- slashes
- quotation marks
- apostrophes

PUNCTUATION THAT GOES AT THE END OF SENTENCES
- periods
- exclamation points
- question marks

— AND A THIRD KIND YOU MIGHT NOT THINK OF AS PUNCTUATION:

CAPITALIZATION
Capitalization is form of punctuation that is not really a mark, but, like all punctuation, capitalization helps readers understand where sentences begin and end.

COMMAS, now, have four main uses.

1

MAKING NUMBERS, PLACE-NAMES, AND DATES CLEAR

To learn how and when to use commas in sentences like the following—

Virginia's population was 1,000,000 in 1830.

If you visit Emily Dickinson's house in Amherst, Massachusetts, you won't see anything that truly belonged to Emily Dickinson.

Abraham Lincoln was shot the night of April 14, 1865, and died the following morning.

→ GO TO PAGE 494.

2

INDICATING WHEN YOU ARE QUOTING (EXACTLY) THE WORDS OF SOMEONE ELSE

To learn how and when to use commas in sentences like the following—

"The real problem with having a robot to dinner," argues Ellen Ullman, "is pleasure."

—or to learn about the following kinds of sentences (in which you aren't quoting someone else's words directly)—

Ellen Ullman argues that pleasure (or the lack of it) is why people don't have robots to dinner.

→ GO TO PAGE 495.

3

SEPARATING WORDS THAT ARE PARTS OF LISTS IN SENTENCES

To learn how and when to use commas in sentences like the following—

The stinking, reeking water roiled down the street.

She caught a cab, her breath, and then the flu.

He was livid, he was angry, and he was mad.

→ GO TO PAGE 496.

4

BUILDING SENTENCES THAT CONTAIN MULTIPLE PARTS

To learn how and when to use commas in sentences like the following—

Her father, who was born in Saudi Arabia, always longed for the hottest days in August.

Can you bring me the ladder, which is in the backyard?

He looked up at me, and he burst into tears.

→ GO TO PAGE 500.

COMMA USE 1

MAKING NUMBERS, PLACE-NAMES, AND
DATES CLEAR

NUMBERS

When you are writing numbers, use commas
to separate the digits in numbers higher
than 999.

1,000 (but 999) 2,304,504 $87,000,000,000

Note that the commas separate the long
numbers into groups of three, *moving from
the right to the left*:

In 1889 more than 3,000,000 acres in the
Indian Territory, now Oklahoma, were opened
to non-Indian homesteaders; a territory that
had held virtually no non-Indians in 1880 had
730,000 in 1900.

Large money amounts work the same way:

On the $65,000,000 bond sale, Morgan and
Belmont made a perfectly legal profit somewhere
between $1,500,000 and $16,000,000.

BUT!

Note that numbers representing years have
no commas. It is also conventional not to
use commas in street addresses:

20419 West Second Street

PLACE-NAMES

In writing a location and a larger place of which it is part—such as a neighborhood in a city,
a city in a state, a state or province in a country—separate the place-names with commas:

Neighborhood, city: **Algiers, New Orleans** • *City, state:* **Houghton, Michigan**

State, country: **Oregon, United States** • *Province, country:* **Tangier, Morocco**

In 1948, Adrian Piper, an artist and philosopher, was born in Harlem, New York City.

To finish his Ph.D. at the University of California, Davis, he had to leash a rattlesnake.

To put a multiline address onto one line, put commas between the sections:

Please send your donations to Habitat for Humanity/Metro Jackson, P.O. Box 55634, Jackson,
MS 39296.

DATES

Only one of the common formats for written
dates in the United States requires a comma:

1 February 17, 1951

When you write a date in month-day-
year order, put a comma after the day:

On January 26, 1950, the Constitution of
India was adopted.

2 17 Feb. 1951

This format is for citing online sources
in the MLA style:

Sutliff, Amileah. "SXSW Explores Concept
of Creative Safe Spaces." *Daily Cardinal*,
28 Mar. 2016, p. 7.

→ See page 389 for more information on this use
of dates.

3 February 1951

If you write only the month and year, no
comma is needed between them:

In February 1912 La Follette delivered
an angry, rambling, and—according to
some—drunken speech, extinguishing
whatever chances he had had for the
nomination.

COMMA USE 2
INDICATING WHEN YOU QUOTE (EXACTLY) SOMEONE ELSE'S WORDS

When you embed someone else's spoken or written words into your own, use commas to separate the words you quote from the phrases that signal you are quoting:

"I've got to sing," he said, hoarsely.

WHEN YOU DON'T BREAK UP THE SENTENCES YOU QUOTE
You can put quoted words at the beginning or at the end of a sentence.

"Keep the hard hat on," she said to me.

As the poet W. H. Auden put it, "The chances are that, in the course of his lifetime, the major poet will write more bad poems than the minor."

In the first case, notice that the comma goes inside the quotation mark and before the *she said* phrase. In the second, the comma goes after the (equivalent of the) *she said* phrase, before and outside the quotation mark.

WHEN YOU DO BREAK UP THE SENTENCES YOU QUOTE
You can break up others' words for effect:

"Why," asks Jonathan Burt, "should the rat be such an apt figure for horror?"

Note the placement of the two commas.

WHEN YOU DON'T QUOTE A WHOLE SENTENCE
Use no comma *before* the quoted words because the quoted words are not sentences.

In describing his cityscapes of Paris, Fox Talbot says that photography "chronicles whatever it sees," noting the complex and jumbled array of chimney pots and lightning rods.

WHEN YOU QUOTE SEVERAL SENTENCES
If the sentences all follow the signalling phrase, put a comma after the phrase:

The cop observed, "In the older generations we didn't even drink a beer. If your mom and dad smelled a beer on you, oh my God, you might have to stay in for a year."

If you put the signalling phrase between the sentences, put a comma before the phrase:

"It was the sociological nadir of the American spirit," a Pepsi executive recalled. "Protests. Woodstock. Drugs. A surly and sullen generation occupying the dean's office, burning it down—whatever it was. It was all that sixties stuff."

WHEN YOU DON'T QUOTE WORDS EXACTLY
When you do not quote someone's exact words, you use indirect quotation. In indirect quotation, you do not use quotation marks or commas. Very often, *that* introduces the words that are being indirectly quoted.

INDIRECT QUOTATION
Mr. Quiring told me that essays and stories come to a preordained ending out of a writer's control.

DIRECT QUOTATION
In class, Mr. Quiring said, "Essays and stories come to a preordained ending organically—completely out of a writer's control!"

→ See pages 188–203 for help in thinking about how and why to incorporate the words of others in your academic writing.

→ See pages 524–525 for more information on using quotation marks to punctuate quotations.

COMMA USE 3
SEPARATING WORDS THAT ARE PARTS OF LISTS IN SENTENCES

In official grammar-speak, a list of words—such as *dogs, tables, justice, snow,* and *imagination*—is referred to as a series.

Only two? No commas.

If you list only two nouns, verbs, adjectives, phrases, or clauses in a sentence, this is the pattern:

 **and**

For example:

She ran and dove into the water.

or

The audience sing-along was flaccid and unenthusiastic.

Three or more? Commas!

If you combine three or more nouns, verbs, adjectives, phrases, or clauses, this is the pattern:

 **,**  **,** **and**

For example:

She grinned, ran, and dove into the water.

or

The audience sing-along was short, flaccid, and unenthusiastic.

This pattern can be expanded to include any number of items:

In the past week we had rain, hail, snow, and a desire for springtime.

NOUNS IN LISTS

ONLY TWO NOUNS? NO COMMAS.

A hat and gloves are necessary for winter.

We find ourselves entering a realm of fantasy and paradox.

THREE OR MORE NOUNS? COMMAS.

When you make a list of three or more nouns, put a comma after each item in the list—except the last:

A hat, gloves, and boots are necessary for winter.

After spending the bulk of the afternoon talking with patients who had no idea what year, month, or day it is, I myself felt rather disoriented.

Mr. Armstrong pleased most of the audience; he has timing, charisma, and plenty of eyeliner—and he's not afraid to sweat.

The player is then set loose in a huge, colorful fantasy world with cities, plains, oceans, mountains, forests, rivers, jungles, deserts, and (of course) dungeons.

Other writers who scholars have argued had temporal lobe epilepsy include Tennyson, Lear, Poe, Swinburne, Byron, de Maupassant, Molière, Pascal, Petrarch, Dante, Teresa of Avila, and Saint Paul.

VERBS IN LISTS

ONLY TWO VERBS? NO COMMAS.

The infant burped and grinned.

I learned to shovel coal and haul clinkers at an early age.

THREE OR MORE VERBS? COMMAS.

When you make a list of three or more verbs, put a comma after each item in the list—except the last:

On that rooftop, she sees, imagines, and remembers.

All day long the contents of my heart would slide down my arm, past my sleeve, and into my phone.

Most birds are idiots. They fly into airplanes, smash into cars, and fling themselves at pigs with reckless abandon.

Lawrence North High School basketball center Greg Oden passes, blocks, shoots, scores, rebounds, and smiles.

When a couple is good at fighting, they defuse tension, approach things with humor, and genuinely listen to the other side, while avoiding getting nasty, personal, or defensive.

→ The ability to use commas as we describe on these pages is important in building parallelism, which is a form of list building. See page 318–319 to learn about parallelism.

PHRASES AND CLAUSES IN LISTS

ONLY TWO PHRASES AND CLAUSES? NO COMMAS.

Furious, Buffmeier crossed the parking lot and went into his shack.

THREE OR MORE PHRASES AND CLAUSES? COMMAS.

Furious, Buffmeier walked through the front door, exited to the back, crossed the parking lot, and went into his shack.

Gilligan's work emphasizes relationships over rules, connection over isolation, caring over violence, and a web of relationships over hierarchy.

The Egyptians mummified their dead in a complex process that involved pulling the brain through the nostrils with an iron hook, washing the body with incense, and, in later dynasties, covering it with bitumen and linen.

BUT!

Use semicolons—and not commas—between a series of phrases that themselves contain commas:

The four common principles that ran through much of this thought through the end of the Cold War were a concern with democracy, human rights, and, more generally, the internal politics of states; a belief that American power can be used for moral purposes; a skepticism about the ability of international law and institutions to solve serious security problems; and, finally, a view that ambitious social engineering often leads to unexpected consequences and thereby undermines its own ends.

WHEN CAN YOU OMIT COMMAS?

Sometimes writers want to emphasize the length of time that goes into a series of actions, so they link the words or phrases of a series with *and* or *or*:

Instead, we arrange the platters of food and remove bread from the oven and fill cups with grape juice and wine.

The example at the left is correct, as is the example below (which creates a quicker sense of the time involved in all the actions):

Instead, we arrange the platters of food, remove bread from the oven, and fill cups with grape juice and wine.

ADJECTIVES IN LISTS

When you list together two or more adjectives, you have three choices:

, OR **and**

Use a comma or *and* to separate two adjectives if you can change their order without changing the meaning of the sentence. For example, the meaning of

He was a thin, dapper fellow who preferred a suit and vest to ordinary clothes.

isn't changed when it is written as

He was a dapper, thin fellow who preferred a suit and vest to ordinary clothes.

or as

He was a thin and dapper fellow who preferred a suit and vest to ordinary clothes.

In these examples, *thin* and *dapper* are called **coordinate adjectives**, the name for adjectives whose order can be changed without the meaning of the sentence changing.

, AND **and**

When you have three or more adjectives whose order can be changed without changing the meaning of the sentence, use the same pattern as with lists of nouns, verbs, phrases, and clauses. Put a comma after each of the adjectives except the last:

Reappropriate.com is a political, current-events, and personal blog written from the perspective of a loud and proud Asian American woman.

We have come to know zero intimately in its mathematical, physical, and psychological embodiments.

NEITHER **,** NOR **and**

If you cannot rearrange the adjectives in a sentence without changing the meaning of the sentence, do not put a comma between them, *no matter how many adjectives you are using:*

The prize for my banana costume was a radio designed to look like a box of frozen niblets corn.

This sentence does not have a comma between *frozen* and *niblets* because, in the United States, we would not say *niblets frozen corn* or *niblets and frozen corn*.

Here is another example:

Three huge gray whales swam by.

Because *three* is describing how many *huge gray* whales this writer saw, *three* goes before the other adjectives.

Adjectives that cannot be rearranged are called **noncoordinate adjectives**, and they do not have commas between them.

COMMA USE 4

BUILDING SENTENCES THAT CONTAIN
MULTIPLE PARTS

Here is a paragraph of simple sentences:

There was a racist bombing of a church in Alabama. This happened in 1963. *ID* magazine published an article about race in industrial design. The article discussed only one female African American designer. Her name is Madeleine Ward.

Here are those sentences joined into one:

In 1963, in response to a racist bombing of a church in Alabama, *ID* magazine published an article about race in industrial design, but they discussed only one female African American designer, Madeleine Ward.

The ideas are more tightly woven together in the single sentence, and (some would argue) they suggest more strongly than the individual sentences that something is wrong with the magazine article if it discusses only one female African American designer.

If you decide that the audience and purpose motivating your writing require using sentences like the single-sentence example, then your sentences will need commas. When you write such sentences, which complicate the basic subject-verb-object structure, commas set off the sentence's parts and help readers see and better understand how the sentence's parts relate to each other.

There are two patterns for building sentences that contain multiple parts:

1

USING COMMAS TO ADD ONE SENTENCE ONTO THE END OF ANOTHER

To learn how and when to use commas in sentences like the following—

Her body seems distracted, but her mind is not.

Every limb was broken, and he ended up a triple amputee.

Music has got to be useful for survival, or we would have gotten rid of it years ago.

Will I get a second chance, or am I supposed to remain a suspect for the rest of my life?

One woman in each tent started dinner, and the other finished securing the tent and sleds for the night.

St. Sebastian was condemned to be shot by arrows, but a tradition says that he survived this torment only to be stoned to death.

→ GO TO PAGE 502 TO SEE THIS PATTERN.

2

USING COMMAS TO ADD ADDITIONAL INFORMATION TO THE MAIN IDEA OF A SENTENCE

To learn how and when to use commas in sentences like the following—

A parrot that cannot talk or sing is, we feel, an incomplete parrot.

Kudos are due to Dwyane Wade, who pretty much single-handedly won the NBA Finals.

Without raising his voice above a murmur, this artist-thinker gives the condition of exile an existential, universalist weight.

The freshwater vertebrates, originally found in the slow waters of East India, are fast replacing the lab rat as a prime model for studies in genetics and development.

→ GO TO PAGE 504 TO SEE THIS PATTERN.

→ The kinds of sentences we discuss here are part of the style of most academic writing; see pages 296–297 and 312–313 to learn about other aspects of the style of academic writing.

USING COMMAS TO ADD ONE SENTENCE ONTO THE END OF ANOTHER

THE PATTERN

When you combine two sentences, one convention of written English is to put a comma and then a coordinating conjunction between the two:

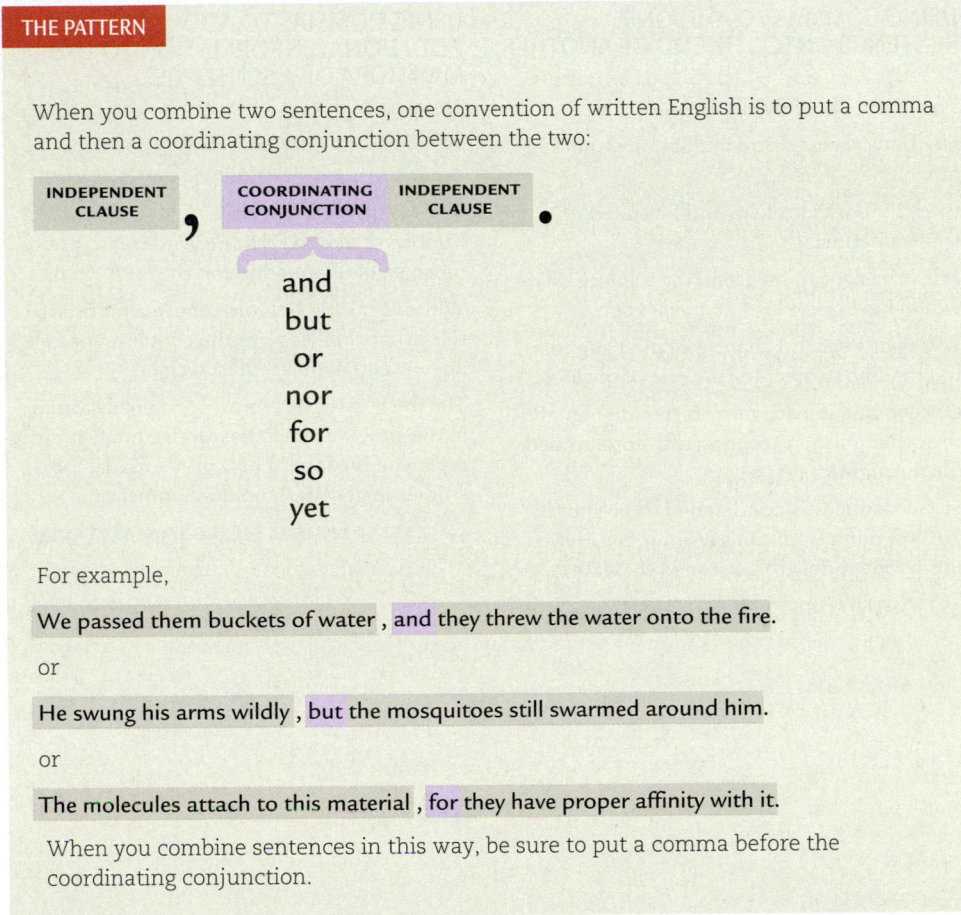

For example,

We passed them buckets of water **, and** they threw the water onto the fire.

or

He swung his arms wildly **, but** the mosquitoes still swarmed around him.

or

The molecules attach to this material **, for** they have proper affinity with it.

When you combine sentences in this way, be sure to put a comma before the coordinating conjunction.

Below are more examples. Note how each follows this pattern:

| independent clause | + **,** + | coordinating conjunction | + | independent clause | • |

I tried to draw him out, but it saddens Hugh to discuss his childhood monkey.

My brain has an itch, and dubstep scratches it.

The sweaters I've made aren't impressive specimens, but they've taught me a lot.

We can turn a blind eye to the polluted air in China, but it's only a matter of days until we breathe it.

Part of Goldstein's work was concerned with the effects of brain damage, and he found that, whenever there was extensive damage, there tended to be an impairment of abstract-categorical capacity.

Twenty years later there were 3,000 factory hands at Baldwin, and by 1900 there were more than 8,000.

You do not need a parachute to skydive, but you do need a parachute to skydive twice.

Several selective pressures may act similarly and simultaneously on trees, so it is difficult to tease apart the contributions those pressures make to tree evolution.

It sounds like something you'd read on a movie poster, but sometimes the sins you haven't committed are all you have to hold on to.

Like most Kenyans, I was not taught about my culture or about the things my parents learned from their parents in school, yet I was taught about the American Revolution, Niagara Falls, and the Second World War.

BE CAREFUL . . .

If you were to take these sentences—

In this section I focus on fluorescent biological samples. The techniques may be applied to material science.

—and combine them with a comma but no coordinating conjunction—

In this section I focus on fluorescent biological samples, the techniques may be applied to material science.

—you would have **a comma splice.** Writing teachers notice comma splices—so if you have been making this error without knowing it, now is the time to learn how to keep your writing teacher smiling at you.

Here is one version that will make a writing teacher put away the red pen:

In this section I focus on fluorescent biological samples, but the techniques may be applied to material science.

You can avoid comma splices by following the pattern shown on these pages, joining two sentences with a comma and a coordinating conjunction.

→ There are other strategies for mending comma splices; see pages 450–451. For more on coordinating conjunctions, see page 474.

USING COMMAS TO ADD ADDITIONAL INFORMATION TO THE MAIN IDEA OF A SENTENCE

THE PATTERN

You can add additional information to a sentence at the beginning, middle, or end.

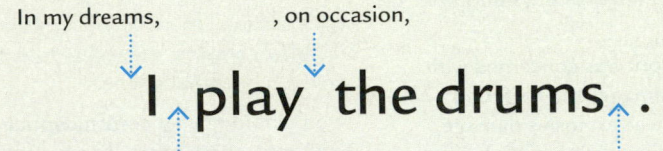

You can add the suggested insertions (some of which are adjective phrases, some adverb phrases) to the sentence above to build the following:

In my dreams, I play the drums.

I, who have no musical sense, play the drums, to the delight of my neighbor downstairs.

I play, on occasion, the drums.

Notice the pattern of comma use around the inserted information:

- When you add information at the **beginning of a sentence**, put a single comma after what you add.
- When you add information in the **middle of a sentence**, put a comma before and a comma after what you add.
- When you add information at the **end of a sentence**, put a comma before what you add.

WHAT DO WE MEAN BY ADDITIONAL (OR "NONESSENTIAL") INFORMATION?

Each of the additions to the sentence *I play the drums* brings something new to the sentence, but if you took away all the additions, you would still understand the sentence's basic idea.

If you can remove information from a sentence without harming a reader's ability to understand the main point, then the information is additional, or **nonessential** or **nonrestrictive** (which are the grammatical terms for such information).

If you can remove a phrase from a sentence without changing the basic meaning of the sentence, separate the phrase from the rest of the sentence with commas.

NONESSENTIAL INFORMATION AT THE BEGINNING OF A SENTENCE

These examples show ways you can start a sentence with a nonessential phrase. Notice the comma in each:

Unlike many other producers who step to the mic, Kanye is also an extremely talented emcee who flexes a relaxed but focused flow.

At the time of her husband's assassination, Mary Todd Lincoln had already buried two young sons.

Because data are always ambiguous, it can be years before physicists feel confident enough to publish potentially controversial results.

As unions waxed stronger after 1886, the number of strikes to enforce union rules grew steadily.

Once upon a time, I was one of those nerds who hung around Radio Shack and played with LEDs, resistors, and capacitors.

Even in the harsh penal environment of early America, some colonies had laws against feeding lobsters to inmates because it was thought to be cruel and unusual, like making people eat rats.

If you use only one or two introductory words, you can omit the comma:

On Wednesday we conduct the experiment.

NONESSENTIAL INFORMATION AT THE END OF A SENTENCE

These examples show some of the many ways you can end a sentence with a nonessential phrase. Notice where the comma is in these examples:

I used to play that song over and over in the dark when I was nine, the year I really became aware of my own existence.

Ray has exceptionally large glasses like an underwater mask, as if he never knows when he'll have to do some welding or shield himself from a solar eclipse.

Shani Davis stood out as a rare African American in a mostly white sport, supported by a single mother who helped bulldoze any barriers she sensed were in front of him.

Knitting is a skill that has come in handy throughout my life, mostly because I am so afflicted with the Protestant work ethic that I can't bear to watch television unless I am doing something productive with my hands.

Dogs are said to be the first domestic animals, displacing pigs for primal honors.

NONESSENTIAL INFORMATION IN THE MIDDLE OF A SENTENCE

Short interjections of words can add a conversational tone to writing; these interjections remind readers that a person wrote the words, so interjections can help writers build relations with their readers. Put a comma before and after such interjections:

Dirt, it seems, is an important ingredient in particle physics experiments.

Some sequels, as we all know, are better than the originals.

Let me clarify two points that will, I hope, make clear our disagreement.

■■■

When you use explanatory words and phrases such as *though* and *for example*, they should be set off by commas:

Once I'm awake, though, I tend to lie there wondering if I've made a terrible mistake.

Among Plains tribes, for example, certain forms of design knowledge, such as quill embroidery and beadwork, are sacred.

BUT!

Do not put a comma after *though* if the word introduces a phrase:

Though she had already been executed, Joan of Arc was acquitted on July 7, 1456.

■■■

The following sentences have phrases that come after nouns (nouns that are very often names) and that explain what the noun is; put a comma before and after all such phrases:

Aunty Lau, an accomplished weaver, teaches Hawaiian culture in the schools.

My son, who is eleven, has a memory like wet cement.

Lascelles Brown, an athletic Jamaican butcher who had briefly dabbled in boxing, first got interested in bobsledding after seeing the 1993 Disney film *Cool Runnings*, based on Jamaica's 1988 Olympic team.

Scissors, a mundane object to which we are introduced in kindergarten, are a sophisticated tool requiring opposable thumbs and some dexterity.

The Space Shuttle, on track and on schedule, came into view just after 5:53 Pacific time.

Nature, when abused, may react eventually like a tiger whose tail has been pulled.

We know from research that dogs, even kennel-raised puppies, do much better than generally more brilliant wolves or human-like chimpanzees in responding to human cues in a food-finding test.

STEPS FOR DECIDING IF INFORMATION IS ESSENTIAL OR NOT

		EXAMPLE 1	EXAMPLE 2
1	For a sentence about which you are unsure, describe to yourself exactly what is most important to you in the sentence: *What exactly is it that you want your readers to take away from your sentence?*	Your sentence emphasizes some events that took place in New York City.	Your sentence focuses readers' attentions on society's responses to women who died in the Vietnam War.
2	Identify in the sentence the information that may or may not be essential.	All of this took place in New York City, which is cruelly, insanely expensive.	This website is dedicated to women who died in the Vietnam War.
3	Remove the information you identified in step 2.	All of this took place in New York City.	This website is dedicated to women.
4	Ask yourself this question about the shortened sentence: *Does it give your readers exactly what you want them to take from the sentence?*	If you want to emphasize that the events you are describing took place in New York City and not to emphasize the cost of being in New York City, the answer is **yes**.	If you want to focus readers' attentions on society's responses to women who died in the Vietnam War—and not on all women—the answer is **no**.
5	If the answer is *yes*, then the information you identified in step 2 is nonessential and should be separated from the rest of the sentence with commas. If the answer is *no*, then the information you identified in step 2 is essential and should not be separated with commas.	**YES?** Use commas: All of this took place in New York City, which is cruelly, insanely expensive.	**NO?** DON'T use commas: This website is dedicated to women who died in the Vietnam War.

WHEN NOT TO USE COMMAS

We list here kinds of sentences in which people are often tempted to use commas—but for which the conventions of formal writing say not to.

BEFORE INFORMATION ESSENTIAL TO A SENTENCE

delete

I am writing about the woman, who was nominated for president by the Republican Party in 1964.

I am writing about the woman who was nominated for president by the Republican Party in 1964.

Read the sentence without the part following the comma; if the sentence loses the meaning you want it to have, then you **do not** need the comma.

→ For more information on making this decision, see pages 504–507.

BETWEEN TWO CLAUSES THAT ARE NOT INDEPENDENT CLAUSES

delete

Some people look at war, and see nothing but violence and chaos.

Some people look at war and see nothing but violence and chaos.

→ If you need help determining whether you are writing independent clauses, see pages 449 and 485.

BEFORE "THAN"

Some scientists argue that there is no clearer indication of global warming, than Greenland's melting glaciers.

delete

Some scientists argue that there is no clearer indication of global warming than Greenland's melting glaciers.

BEFORE OR AFTER PARENTHESES

delete

A political career, (or a legal one) is the surest ticket to a historical legacy.

A political career (or a legal one) is the surest ticket to a historical legacy.

or

A political career, or a legal one, is the surest ticket to a historical legacy.

The convention is to use parentheses or commas around parenthetical comments, but not both.

AFTER A SUBORDINATING CONJUNCTION

delete

Although, scientists no longer consider Pluto to be a planet, many still seek that little celestial body in their telescopes.

Although scientists no longer consider Pluto to be a planet, many still seek that little celestial body in their telescopes.

→ Page 476 lists and explains subordinating conjunctions.

BEFORE THE FIRST ITEM IN A LIST OR AFTER THE LAST ITEM

delete

E-mail spammers endure, legal harassment, exclusion from polite society, and the disgust of nearly every computer user.

E-mail spammers endure legal harassment, exclusion from polite society, and the disgust of nearly every computer user.

Many accidents of geography, history and biology, created our lopsided world.

delete

Many accidents of geography, history, and biology created our lopsided world.

→ See pages 496–499 for the conventional uses of commas with lists.

BETWEEN A SENTENCE'S VERB AND ITS SUBJECT OR OBJECT

Everything good, is bad for you.

Everything good is bad for you. *delete*

One of the dominant themes in American science policy this past year was, how we can maintain a competitive edge in a global economy. *delete*

One of the dominant themes in American science policy this past year was how we can maintain a competitive edge in a global economy.

If you include more than one word in a subject, it can be tempting to put a comma after it because you might read the sentence out loud with a pause after the subject—which can suggest that a comma should go there. The same temptation can happen with long objects: If you were reading it out loud, you would probably pause before the object. But in writing, the convention is not to put commas in these places.

COLONS have three main uses

1

USING COLONS IN CERTAIN CONVENTIONAL PATTERNS

SALUTATIONS

In formal or business letters, colons are used after the greeting at the beginning of the letter:

Dear Sir or Madam: • **Dear Dr. Lucchesi:**

MEMO HEADINGS

In workplaces, memos (less formal than letters) are used to inform others of project progress, meetings, or other events. The top of a memo will usually look like this:

To: The members of the Research Committee

From: Ralph Bunker

Re: Next Steps

(**Re:** means *regarding*; think of it as being like the subject heading of an e-mail.)

TIME

To write a time, use a colon between the hour, the minutes, and the seconds (if you include them):

12:32 P.M.   **4:50:32 P.M.**

I awoke just before the alarm went off, at 5:59:59 A.M.

She ran her first mile in 4:35 and her second in 4:50.

BETWEEN TITLE AND SUBTITLE

When you are writing the title of any communication—book, article, movie, television show—that has a subtitle, put the title, then a colon, then the subtitle:

Katherine Dunham: Dancing Queen

Wind: How the Flow of Air Has Shaped Life, Myth, and the Land

CITATIONS FROM THE BIBLE

Put a colon between the chapter and verse:

Matthew 6:5 • **Deuteronomy 5:17** • **Psalm 46:9**

2

USING COLONS TO PREPARE READERS FOR INFORMATION AT THE END OF A SENTENCE

Use a colon at the end of a sentence to introduce an explanation:

If the three prongs of the suburban American dream are family, job, and house, there is a ghostly, underdiscussed consequence: yardwork.

The networked information economy holds out the possibility of reversing two trends in cultural production central to the project of control: concentration and commercialization.

Use a colon to introduce an example:

Writers ought to consider how the defense- and commercially tied history of computers shapes the thinking encouraged by the design of the software we use for writing: How many word-processing or webpage-composing software packages do you know that encourage scribbling, doodling, or writing outside the margins?

Use a colon to introduce a list:

I improvised with my equipment: fashioning together a hook and a line, making my own harpoons, or gathering up cast-off pieces of net from the fishermen.

→ When you put a list at the end of a sentence, punctuate it just as you would any other list; see pages 496–499.

3

USING COLONS TO LINK TWO SENTENCES

WHEN THE SECOND SENTENCE EXPLAINS OR SUMMARIZES THE FIRST

If you are joining two sentences where you could lead into the second sentence with *for example* or *that is*, use a colon between them:

Her illness confined her to a sofa, and so she did the one thing she could think to do on a sofa: She started writing.

There's a reason that freedom of the press was enumerated in the First Amendment: It's more fundamental to our liberty than even guns.

Some journals—and some teachers—request that the sentence following the colon start with a capital letter.

WHEN THE SECOND SENTENCE IS A QUOTATION

If you use a sentence to introduce a quotation, use a colon between them:

In order to write today's novel, movie, or song, I need to use and rework existing cultural forms, such as story lines and twists. This characteristic is known to economists as the "on the shoulders of giants" effect, recalling a statement attributed to Isaac Newton: "If I have seen farther it is because I stand on the shoulders of giants."

SEMICOLONS have two main uses;
those uses are:

1

JOINING SENTENCES

Be sure you have two complete sentences (that is, independent clauses), and then join them with a semicolon. The first letter of the word following the semicolon is not capitalized, unless it is a proper noun.

The father didn't move out; he just moved to a different bedroom.

The ceiling, freshly painted, was luminous as the sky; I almost thought I could smell the paint.

My fears were powerful and troubling and annoyingly vague; I couldn't establish exactly what it was that frightened me.

The highway went for miles between high mud walls and canebrakes; the black tracery of date palms rose above them, against the brilliant night sky.

You can use semicolons to join multiple sentences:

Work made people useful in a world of economic scarcity; it staved off the doubts and temptations that preyed on idleness; it opened the way to deserved wealth and status; it allowed one to put the impress of mind and skill on the material world.

→ To be sure you are joining complete sentences, read about independent and dependent clauses, pages 449 and 485.

2

USING SEMICOLONS TO JOIN LIST ELEMENTS THAT ARE COMPLICATED OR CONTAIN THEIR OWN PUNCTUATION

In complicated sentences, commas might not be enough to help readers see lists:

Istanbul's steep hills and harbor views remind you of San Francisco, its overcrowded streets recall Bombay, its transportation facilities evoke Venice, for you can go many places by boats, which are continually making stops.

Instead, with semicolons separating the items, it is easier to see the separate items:

Istanbul's steep hills and harbor views remind you of San Francisco; its overcrowded streets recall Bombay; its transportation facilities evoke Venice, for you can go many places by boats, which are continually making stops.

If you are building a list using items that contain their own punctuation, use semicolons to separate the items:

As the leech began to suck, it released several other substances into his ear: a powerful anticoagulant, which prevented his blood from clotting; a vasodilator, which opened his vessels, helping to increase blood flow; and a spreading factor, which moved these chemicals quickly into tissue farthest from the bite, liquefying any hardening blood.

ELLIPSES...
have two main uses.

1

USING ELLIPSES TO SHOW A PAUSE OR AN INTERRUPTION IN SPEECH THAT YOU ARE QUOTING

Because readers cannot hear words that you quote but can only see your transcription of them on a page, use ellipses to signal, visually, where someone you are quoting paused:

In an interview with Powells.com's Dave Weich, chef and writer Anthony Bourdain said: "I knew already that the best meal in the world, the perfect meal, is very rarely the most sophisticated or expensive one. . . . Context and memory play powerful roles in all the truly great meals in one's life."

Put a space after the ellipsis.

■ ■ ■

In contexts less formal than the academic one, writers sometimes use ellipses to show hesitation or surprise; the following sentence, for example, comes from a science magazine for general audiences:

In the grand tradition of linking raunchy music with irresponsible sexual activity comes a new study touting a link between sexual risk taking and listening to . . . gospel music.

→ You can also use dashes to show hesitation in speech that you are quoting; see page 516.

2

USING ELLIPSES TO SHOW YOU HAVE OMITTED WORDS FROM A QUOTATION

IN A PROSE QUOTATION

If you need to drop words from a sentence you are quoting, use ellipses. Here are words from an interview with George Lucas, showing where words have been dropped:

When I was younger, I had a collection of history books that I was addicted to, a whole series about famous people in history. . . . I collected a whole library.

Put a space before and after the ellipsis.

IN A QUOTATION OF POETRY

If you must drop one or more lines from poetry you quote, use a line of periods (with a space between each) to show where you have dropped lines; the line of periods should be as long as the poem's longest lines.

William Butler Yeats often uses slight shifts in repeated sentence structure to build emotinal energy, as in these lines from "Maid Quiet":

The winds that awakened the stars

Are blowing through my blood.

. . . .

Now words that called up the lightning

Are hurtling through my heart.

(PARENTHESES
have four main uses.

1

USING PARENTHESES TO EXPLAIN ABBREVIATIONS

Through use, long titles—of organizations, laws, and objects—often get abbreviated into acronyms. Acronyms are usually composed of the first letters of the title's main words, as **United States of America** is abbreviated **USA**.

If you are writing about something that has an acronym, don't assume that all your readers will know the acronym. The first time you mention the organization, law, or object, put the acronym in parentheses following the full name. After that, use the acronym:

The builders closely followed the Americans with Disabilities Act (ADA) when they constructed the entry to the building; the ADA requires that all buildings be accessible to people with a range of abilities.

San Francisco's Museum of the African Diaspora (MoAD) has a different goal than many other museums: The staff of MoAD work to put together exhibitions that represent the global impact of Africans—in South America, Central America, Europe, and Asia.

2

USING PARENTHESES FOR NUMBERS IN LISTS

If you are including a numbered list in your writing, use parentheses to indicate the steps:

The steps for checking writing that you think is done are (1) edit for readability, (2) check spelling, (3) check grammar, and (4) proofread.

The networked information economy improves the practical capacities of individuals along three dimensions: (1) It improves their capacity to do more for and by themselves; (2) it enhances their capacity to do more in loose commonality with others, without being constrained to organize their relationship through a price system or in traditional hierarchical models of social and economic organization; and (3) it improves the capacity of individuals to do more in formal organizations that operate outside the market sphere.

Note the punctuation above: If the steps are short, put a comma after each one; otherwise, put a semicolon.

3

USING PARENTHESES FOR IN-TEXT CITATIONS

Readers of academic research writing expect—whenever they find a source used in the writing—to also find information enabling them to check the source themselves. Conventionally, then, writers include the quoted author's name as well as the page number of the quoted words; readers can then look to the list of works cited at the essay's end to find the bibliographic information that enables them to find the cited work:

In Carruthers's argument, a sacred book is given a bejeweled cover to signify to readers that one's memory, growing out of the book, was "a storehouse, a treasure-chest, a vessel, into which the jewels, coins, fruits, and flowers of text are placed" (246). But, by the twelfth century, for those who could not afford treasure chests, the same books could also appear in "cheap and decorative binding" (Foot 118).

Notice that, if the author's name is included as part of a sentence, it is not noted in the parentheses; if the author's name is not included, then it is put in the parentheses along with the page number.

→ The example above is for MLA citation style, about which there is more on pages 364–367. For APA style, see pages 399–401.

4

USING PARENTHESES TO ADD INFORMATION

You can use parentheses to insert comments or additional information into a sentence. When you do this, you are adding **parenthetical remarks**. Many writers use this strategy to add humor to a sentence:

Sometimes in the morning Mrs. Murrow asks me if I heard the cobras singing during the night. I have never been able to answer in the affirmative, because in spite of her description ("like a silver coin falling against a rock"), I have no clear idea of what to listen for.

This afternoon, Johnny Depp is wearing a white undershirt tucked into gray tweed slacks hiked a tad too high (in the style of certain retirement-aged Italian gentlemen).

You can also use parenthetical information to add dates, definitions, a URL, or anything else you think will help readers understand:

Katherine Dunham's dance piece "Southland" (1951), which was a protest against lynching and depicted a lynching on stage, created a lot of controversy in America.

Traditionally, a hysterectomy (removal of the uterus) was the primary way to treat fibroids, and it remains the only permanent cure.

DASHES

and their four main uses.

1

USING DASHES TO EMPHASIZE INFORMATION AT THE END OF A SENTENCE

Sometimes writers want to put particular emphasis on a word or phrase. Should you choose to do this, using a dash to set off a word or phrase at the end of a sentence helps to emphasize that word or phrase:

I stood in my empty room. In place of the bed was—shame?

War does not determine who is right—only who is left.

She danced by herself in the corner to a Brenda Lee record, but it was obvious she couldn't dance—she had the white girl's embarrassing habit of brandishing an invisible tambourine.

2

USING DASHES TO INDICATE A RESTATEMENT OR A CHANGE IN TONE

To make writing sound conversational and to add particular emphasis to phrases that might otherwise sound out of place because of the explanation or emotion they provide, writers will use dashes:

The wall-to-wall carpet—roughly the color of brains—was frayed and worn.

It dawned on him that he knew plenty of Americans—he was one himself—who held apparently contradictory beliefs, such as faith in both medicine and prayer.

3

USING DASHES TO SET OFF EXPLANATORY INFORMATION

Sometimes writers use dashes to put more emphasis on infomation, which could also be set off by commas:

A jay can store up to five acorns—depending on their size and his—in his throat.

The trailer's owners—Della Busby, a shovel-jawed woman with short bangs like Bettie Page's and a raspy smoker's growl, and her husband, Tim—had refused the corporation's buyout offer.

4

USING DASHES TO SHOW HESITATION IN SPEECH

When writers are transcribing speech or are trying to emulate speech for readers, they use dashes to show where a speaker has hesitated or changed direction in mid-sentence:

On the witness stand, Michael Eisner responded to a lawyer's question by saying, "I think you're getting into an area that—that—I just want to say that this is ill-advised . . . ."

[BRACKETS]
have two main uses.

1

USING BRACKETS INSIDE PARENTHETICAL COMMENTS

Sometimes writers need to put parenthetical information inside other parenthetical information. When this is the case, the convention is to put the embedded information inside brackets instead of inside another set of parentheses:

(For further discussion, see Abdo [2000] and Burgat [2003].)

Khubz marquq (also called *lavash tannour* [mountain bread]) is a flat bread with a slightly tangy taste.

2

USING BRACKETS TO INSERT INFORMATION INTO A QUOTATION

Anytime writers use the words of someone else, the words are removed from their full context; sometimes, then, writers have to fill in information or change words so that readers can understand the quotation.

If writers need to do this in the middle of a quotation, the convention is to put the changed or added information inside brackets so that readers can see where the original has been changed. For example, here are words as they were originally spoken by Anthony B. Pinn, a professor of humanities and religion at Rice University in Houston:

What you get with mega-churches is a kind of caricature of the social gospel thrust. In terms of the hard issue of social justice, such churches tend to be theology-lite.

Here is how a magazine article quoted those words, in order to fit them to its needs:

What you get with mega-churches is a . . . caricature of the social gospel thrust. In terms of . . . social justice, [they] tend to be theology-lite.

→ If you need to leave words out of quotations, use ellipses, a punctuation mark explained on page 513, to show the omissions.

HY PHENS have two main uses.

1

USING HYPHENS FOR CLARITY

A precise reader sees considerable difference between these two sentences:

He was a big city man.

He was a big-city man.

The first is about a man from the city who is big; the second is about a man from a big city. When using two words as an adjective, put a hyphen between them if you wonder whether others will read your words as you intend.

■ ■ ■

When you use the prefixes *re-*, *anti-*, and *pre-* with verbs, use a hyphen between the prefix and the verb if, without the hyphen, a different meaning is made.

I resent her letter.

I re-sent her letter.

■ ■ ■

Use hyphens if the first word of a compound word you are making begins with the same letter as the second:

doll-like   non-native

2

USING HYPHENS IN COMPOUND WORDS

When writers put together two or more words to make one new word, the result is a compound word:

Operating on an off-the-shelf Linux-based computer, MooBella's fresh-on-the-spot system changes traditional ice-cream vending machines, which spit out months-old bars.

The longer a compound word has been in use, the more likely it won't have a hyphen in it (think of *bathtub*, *earthquake*, *bookshelf*, or *website*); conversely, the newest compound words most likely have hyphens.

Some compound words, however, do conventionally keep their hyphens:

Dr. Bonnez treated dairy cows, which grow grapefruit-sized warts. He still has a block of 20-year-old cow warts in his freezer.

When compound words are used as adjectives before nouns—such as *20-year-old* and *grapefruit-sized* above or in the term *nineteenth-century art*—they tend to be hyphenated.

To be safest, check a dictionary.

■ ■ ■

When you write out numbers between 21 and 99, a hyphen is conventional:

twenty-three • one hundred twenty-three

one thousand two hundred and ninety-four

SLASH / SLASHES have three main uses.

1

USING SLASHES IN PAIRED TERMS

Some terms in English are hard to separate:

on/off switch	and/or
a pass/fail class	an either/or situation

It is the preferred convention for writing in humanities disciplines **not** to use such terms, but sometimes a slash is the only way to give readers the sense you intend:

If all writing is a form of quotation—as blogs invariably include a mix of "original" text and text copied from other websites—we need to question the "original"/"copied" dichotomy.

If you need to use a slash in this way, do not put spaces on either side of the slash.

2

USING SLASHES TO INDICATE LINE BREAKS IN QUOTED POEMS

Because line breaks in poems indicate poets' rhetorical choices, be careful to reproduce line breaks when you quote poems.

These lines come from a poem by Charles Simic:

Like the sound of eyebrows
Raised by a villain
In a silent movie.

Here is a quotation using those lines:

Simic can create striking metaphors, as in these lines from "The Wooden Toy," where the toy is quiet, "Like the sound of eyebrows / Raised by a villain / In a silent movie."

Note that there is a space on either side of each slash.

3

USING SLASHES WITH DATES AND FRACTIONS

DATES

In informal and business writing in the United States, the convention is to write dates with slashes, giving the month, day, and year:

11/10/56	10/31/2009

Note that there are no spaces around the slashes and that you can use two or four digits for the year.

FRACTIONS

Put a slash between the two numbers of a fraction:

1/2   2/3   15/16

There are no spaces between the numbers and the slash.

"QUOTATION MARKS have six main uses," instructs my writing professor.

1 **USING QUOTATION MARKS FOR TITLES OF SHORT WORKS**
For sentences like the following—

The radio is playing The Romantics' "That's What I Like About You."

→ GO TO PAGE 521.

2 **USING QUOTATION MARKS TO INDICATE YOU ARE USING A WORD AS A WORD**
For sentences like the following—

And by "malignant" and "addictive" I do not mean evil or hypnotizing.

→ GO TO PAGE 521.

3 **USING QUOTATION MARKS TO INDICATE TECHNICAL TERMS AND WORDS FROM OTHER LANGUAGES**
For sentences like the following—

"Malar" means relating to the cheek.

→ GO TO PAGE 522.

4 **USING QUOTATION MARKS TO SHOW IRONY**
For sentences like the following—

To quantify the "benefit" side of the equation, a dollar amount is assigned to each saved human's life.

→ GO TO PAGE 522.

5 **USING QUOTATION MARKS TO INDICATE DIRECT QUOTATION**
For sentences like the following—

David Foster Wallace believes that "fiction writers as a species tend to be oglers" (21).

→ GO TO PAGE 523.

6 **USING QUOTATION MARKS TO INDICATE SPEECH**
For sentences like the following—

The woman at Macy's asked me, "Would you be interested in full-time elf or evening and weekend elf?"
    I said, "Full-time elf."

→ GO TO PAGE 523.

QUOTATION MARKS USE 1

USING QUOTATION MARKS FOR TITLES OF SHORT WORKS

Use quotation marks to indicate the name of a show or exhibition—

"Goya's Last Works," at the Frick, isn't large, but neither are grenades.

—the titles of poems and musical pieces—

I had to study why Van Halen moved (certain) people as much as the Beatles, but, folks, they did, in the same way Whitman did. "Hot For Teacher" is "Song of Myself" with crappier words but much better lead guitar.

—and the titles of essays—

"The Making of Americans" was a work that Stein evidently had to get out of her system—almost like a person having to vomit—before she could become Gertrude Stein as we know her.

—or the titles of almost any work that is not book length.

→ Information on how to indicate the titles of book-length works is on page 530.

QUOTATION MARKS USE 2

USING QUOTATION MARKS TO INDICATE YOU ARE USING A WORD AS A WORD

Sometimes, writers need to refer to a word as a word. If ever you need to do this, put quotation marks around the word:

"Doctor" comes from the Latin word *docere,* "to teach."

The term "preservation" usually comes up in reference to buildings, not to the graffiti that covers them.

What one generation identified as charisma in their famous writers would now be labeled "alcoholism."

His student asked him how to use "until" according to English conventions.

Franziska often spews repetitive insults using the word "fool."

→ The use of quotation marks for this function goes back to the days of typewriters. With computers, italics can replace quotation marks; see page 530 on using italics.

→ Because quotation marks are almost always interwoven with other punctuation, it is tricky to use them as academic readers and readers of published works expect. On pages 524–525 we go over the little but important details of using quotation marks in expected ways.

QUOTATION MARKS USE 3
USING QUOTATION MARKS TO INDICATE TECHNICAL TERMS AND WORDS FROM OTHER LANGUAGES

Use quotation marks to indicate technical terms and words from other languages:

Ringed seals, ivory gulls, and other birds and mammals whose lives are ice-oriented are called "pagophylic."

During the thirteenth century, the Dutch instituted a "wind brief," a tax paid to the lord or king over whose fields the wind blew before reaching a mill.

Consider, for example, a form of creativity that seems strange to many Americans but that is inescapable within Japanese culture: "manga," or comics.

As I explain in the pages that follow, we come from a tradition of "free culture"—not "free" as in "free beer" (to borrow a phrase from the founder of the free software movement), but "free" as in "free speech," "free markets," "free trade," "free enterprise," "free will," and "free elections."

→ The use of quotation marks for this function goes back to the days of typewriters. With computers, italics can replace quotation marks; see page 530 on using italics.

→ Because quotation marks are almost always interwoven with other punctuation, it is tricky to use them as academic readers and readers of published works expect. On pages 524–525 we go over the little but important details of using quotation marks in expected ways.

QUOTATION MARKS USE 4
USING QUOTATION MARKS TO SHOW IRONY

Writers sometimes want to distance themselves from words: They need to use particular words, as in the examples below, but want to show that they don't agree with the word choice. In such cases, writers can put quotation marks around the words.

Look, for example, at how novelist Janet Frame, in her autobiography, uses quotation marks to let readers know how she feels about the sincerity of the women who visited her mother after her sister's death:

They sat patting and arranging their "permanent" waves.

Here are sentences from scientists commenting on how others have characterized scientific practice:

How can an experiment be "wrong"?

The problem I am posing here is not one of individual morality, of individual scientists doing "dirty" work or "clean" work; rather, the problem is institutional.

In each case, the quotation marks let readers know that the writers question the characterizations of experiments and other scientific work contained in the punctuated words.

→ Because quotation marks are almost always interwoven with other punctuation, it is tricky to use them as academic readers and readers of published works expect. On pages 524–525 we go over the little but important details of using quotation marks in expected ways.

QUOTATION MARKS USE 5
USING QUOTATION MARKS TO INDICATE DIRECT QUOTATION

Over the centuries, conventions have developed in different languages for indicating to readers that writers are quoting the words of others. In English, quotation marks—placed on either side of the words being quoted—have become the expected way of doing this, even if a writer is quoting only one word from someone else:

Fukasawa's approach to designing electronic gadgets, based on over 25 years' experience, has been called "anti-technical" because it dispenses with unnecessary buttons, displays, and other high-tech signifiers.

A comparison to make a point is Sarah Vowell's claim that "Going to Ford's Theatre to watch the play is like going to Hooter's for the food."

At the time the Wright brothers invented the airplane, American law held that a property owner owned not just the surface of his land, but all the land below, down to the center of the earth, and all the space above, to "an indefinite extent, upwards."

→ Because quotation marks are almost always interwoven with other punctuation, it is tricky to use them as academic readers expect. On pages 524–525 we go over the details of using quotation marks in expected ways.

QUOTATION MARKS USE 6
USING QUOTATION MARKS TO INDICATE SPEECH

When you wish to suggest to your readers that the words you are writing were spoken out loud by someone else, quotation marks are the customary strategy in English:

"He was going to write the definitive book on leeches," she says. "It was his primary ambition in life."

"Reading ability is a proxy for intelligence in American culture," said Dr. Sally E. Shaywitz of Yale University School of Medicine, a pediatrician who is an expert on dyslexia.

"You have to listen to music before you go out on a mission and get real hyped," says Sgt. Junelle Daniels, a twenty-five-year-old generator mechanic from Miami who is gearing up for a second deployment. "If not, you start thinking, 'What if? What if this happens? What if that happens?' You start to get the fear."

Note that indicating speech is sometimes the same as indicating a direct quotation.

→ Because quotation marks are almost always interwoven with other punctuation, it is tricky to use them as academic readers and readers of published works expect. On pages 524–525 we go over the little but important details of using quotation marks in expected ways.

→ In academic writing, any time you quote someone else, the expectation is that you will provide the source of the quotation; see pages 194–199 for how to do this.

USING QUOTATION MARKS AND OTHER PUNCTUATION WHEN YOU INCLUDE OTHERS' WORDS IN YOUR WRITING

To quote others' words in the patterns that readers of academic and other formal texts expect, pay close attention to these details in the examples below:

- The use of a comma or period at the end of the quotation. (Note also that, whether a comma or period is used, it is included inside the quotation mark.)
- The capitalization of the words at the beginning of the quotation.

THE PATTERN	QUOTING A COMPLETE SENTENCE
AT THE BEGINNING OF YOUR WRITING	"Most of what we teach is wrong," said Johndan Johnson-Eilola.
IN THE MIDDLE OF YOUR WRITING	Johndan Johnson-Eilola said, "Most of what we teach is wrong," while speaking at a recent conference.
AT THE END OF YOUR WRITING	Johndan Johnson-Eilola said, "Most of what we teach is wrong."
WITH IN-TEXT CITATION (MLA STYLE)	Johndan Johnson-Eilola said, "Most of what we teach is wrong" (77).

→ To learn more about in-text citations in MLA style, see pages 364–367; in APA style, see pages 399–401; in CSE style, see page 422; in CMS style, see pages 425–428.

→ Quotations that take up more than four lines in a paper are conventionally treated as **block quotations**; see page 196.

→ See page 198 for help with choosing the words to use to introduce or explain the words you quote.

QUOTING PARTS OF A SENTENCE

"A natural sense of geometry" is innate in babies, argues cognitive psychologist Elizabeth Spelke.

All babies have "a natural sense of geometry," argues cognitive psychologist Elizabeth Spelke.

Cognitive psychologist Elizabeth Spelke argues that all babies have "a natural sense of geometry."

All babies have "a natural sense of geometry," argues cognitive psychologist Elizabeth Spelke (qtd. in Talbot 92).

If you quote only part of a sentence, don't capitalize the first word, unless the quoted words start your sentence.

Note also that the quoted words in these examples do not have commas before them.

QUOTING A SENTENCE THAT ENDS WITH A QUESTION MARK OR EXCLAMATION POINT

"Why did wealth and power become distributed as they are now, rather than in some other way?" Jared Diamond asks at the beginning of his book.

Jared Diamond asks, "Why did wealth and power become distributed as they are now, rather than in some other way?" at the beginning of his book.

At the beginning of his book, Jared Diamond asks, "Why did wealth and power become distributed as they are now, rather than in some other way?"

"Why did wealth and power become distributed as they are now, rather than in some other way?" Jared Diamond asks at the beginning of his book (15).

NOTE: If you quote a sentence that ends with an exclamation point, the punctuation pattern is the same as when the sentence ends with a question mark.

APOSTROPHES' three main uses are:

1

USING APOSTROPHES TO MAKE PLURALS OF CERTAIN WORDS

Use apostrophes to make plurals of lowercase letters; otherwise, readers might confuse the plural with a word:

Is it "cross your is and dot your ts," or the reverse?

Is it "cross your i's and dot your t's," or the reverse?

Use an apostrophe to make plurals of uppercase letters if the addition of an **-s** without an apostrophe would make a word:

She earned As throughout school but could never rise above an entry-level position.

She earned A's throughout school but could never rise above an entry-level position.

But: He never earned higher than Cs or Ds in school, yet he's a well-known newscaster.

2

USING APOSTROPHES TO MAKE CONTRACTIONS

Apostrophes show where letters have been taken out of phrase to make a contraction:

I am = I'm	we are = we're
I would = I'd	we have = we've
you are = you're	they are = they're
she is = she's	do not = don't
he is = he's	did not = didn't
it is = it's	cannot = can't

One odd pattern to learn:

will not = won't

I'm sure that we didn't leave the window open, but shouldn't we go back and check?

We've got time; he won't expect us until late.

3

USING APOSTROPHES TO MAKE POSSESSIVES

Seeing a word ending with an apostrophe and **-s**, readers assume the word is a possessive.

This blog's message is "Stop Buying Crap."

Uncovery Channel's new reality television show is *Could We Dream Some More, Please?*

→ To learn more about the possessive case, see page 456.

→ To learn more about the possessive case, see page 456.

TIP

LEARN THE DIFFERENCE BETWEEN *it's* AND *its*

it's = it is   its = the possessive form of the pronoun it

It's going to rain. (It is going to rain.)

Democracy can be said to be its own biggest threat. (its is a stand-in for *democracy's*)

PERIODS have two main uses.

1

USING PERIODS WITH SOME ABBREVIATIONS

Abbreviations shorten words.

Company → Co.   Doctor → Dr.

et cetera → etc.   Incorporated → Inc.

Mister → Mr.   Monday → Mon.

These abbreviations are made of the first letter of the word and the last letter, or are truncated versions of the words (**Mon.** for **Monday** or **Co.** for **Company**). When an abbreviation is made this way, it will most likely have a period after it.

■ ■ ■

Name abbreviations customarily use periods:

John Fitzgerald Kennedy → John F. Kennedy

Mary Francis Kennedy Fisher → M. F. K. Fisher

Put a space after each period

■ ■ ■

Some abbreviations are the first letters of word series:

a.m. → **ante meridiem** (Latin for *before noon*)

R.S.V.P. → **respondez, s'il vous plait** (French for *Please respond*)

U.N.I.C.E.F. → United Nations International Children's Emergency Fund

The USPS requests that we abbreviate state names this way, without periods:

MI   CA   RI   AK

2

USING PERIODS TO END SENTENCES THAT MAKE STATEMENTS OR COMMANDS

Of the four kinds of sentences (→ page 479), two of them, declarative and imperative sentences, conventionally end with periods.

These are **declarative sentences**, which make statements:

Water buffalo do not exist in Africa.

Smaller species of exploding ants are more likely to combust than larger ones.

Neil Burger's movie *The Illusionist,* based on a short story by Steven Millhauser, is a delicate film, almost a fairy tale.

Though armed with a sharp, venom-coated barb on their tail, stingrays use the weapon only defensively, and attacks on humans are extremely rare.

These are **imperative sentences**, which make commands:

Mix the sliced pears and walnuts together.

Fasten your seat belt by sliding the metal notch into the buckle.

Use a period after most abbreviations.

USING PERIODS WITH QUOTATION MARKES

→ Using periods with quotation marks requires careful attention. See pages 524–525.

Do you know the two main uses of
QUESTION MARKS?

1

USING QUESTION MARKS TO END SENTENCES THAT ARE QUESTIONS

Of the four functions that sentences can have (→ page 479), asking questions is one; sentences that ask questions are called **interrogatory sentences:**

What is education?

Have you ever browsed a sperm bank catalog?

You bought the CD or DVD, and that means you own it, right?

If prisons are meant to make troubled men and women into citizens, he wondered, might there be a social cost to bad prison design?

BUT!

The examples above are **direct questions**; there are also **indirect questions**, in which a writer describes someone else asking a question, without direct quotation. *These end with a period, not a question mark:*

I heard her ask whether the mail had arrived.

He asked how the test had gone.

2

USING QUESTION MARKS TO SHOW DOUBT ABOUT DATES AND NUMBERS

If you have doubts about a date or quantity, or if your sources describe doubt about a date or quantity, put **(?)** after the date or quantity.

In this photograph, Reynolds is seen with his mother in 1928 (?).

Witness reports put the number of people trapped in the building at 180 (?).

USING QUESTIONS MARKS WITH QUOTATION MARKES

→ Using question marks with quotation marks requires careful attention. See page 525.

EXCLAMATION POINTS

have one main use, really and truly

USING EXCLAMATION POINTS TO INDICATE TO READERS THAT A SENTENCE CARRIES EMOTIONAL WEIGHT

It is customary in written American English to put a single exclamation point after a sentence when the sentence is an exclamation—

Yikes! Oh no!

—a strong command—

Help!

Don't touch that burner!

Don't go beyond the perimeter!

—or is meant by its writer to encourage a strong emotional response in a reader—

Each treehouse is built in two main pieces: the playhouse and the log. The log is a real, old, fallen tree that we hollow out using a chainsaw!

Age is absolutely no barrier in today's world. In fact, some 30 percent of students today are "non-traditional," meaning us, of course!

Your age is not an issue unless you choose to make it one; don't!

In academic writing, exclamation points are almost nonexistent because such writing is meant to appeal primarily to reason. In most other kinds of writing, the exclamation point is also rare, because people who grow up speaking American English tend to think that exclamation points are a sign of youth or silliness—especially when several sentences in a row have them or when a single sentence ends in many of them.

There are exceptions: In blogs, for example, writers sometimes use them excessively, as a self-conscious indication that they know exclamation points are dangerous but still potent:

It's not that we know we aren't writing well—and so tack on some exclamations!!!—it's that we know what we're saying doesn't deserve to be written at all.

→ Using exclamation points with quotation marks requires careful attention. See page 525.

MECHANICS

USING ITALICS AND UNDERLINING

Italic type

Italic type was developed during the Italian Renaissance, and over time those who used printing presses developed specific uses for it.

Until computers were developed, those who did not have access to printing presses but who instead used typewriters—like most college students—could not use italic type. A convention developed to use underlining wherever a printer would use italics.

If you cannot use italics as we discuss below, use underlining.

FOR THE TITLES OF BOOKS AND OTHER LONG PUBLICATIONS

Use italics for the titles of books, magazines, journals, newspapers, websites, feature films, radio and television shows, book-length poems, comic strips, plays, operas and other musical performances, ballets and other dance performances, paintings, sculptures, pamphlets, and bulletins.

Marilyn's book will be titled *The Animal Who Writes*.

Little Nemo was a popular comic strip of the early twentieth century.

→ See page 521 to learn about using quotation marks with the titles of shorter publications.

FOR FOREIGN TERMS

The environmental studies professor, who is from Pakistan, was first educated in a *madrassah*, or Muslim school.

China is shifting resources away from state-directed scientific research into initiatives designed to stimulate *zizhi chuangxin* (indigenous innovation).

You do not need to italicize commonly used foreign expressions and abbreviations:

cum laude	ex officio	et al.	e.g.
in vitro	vice versa	vis-à-vis	i.e.

FOR SCIENTIFIC NAMES IN LATIN

It is conventional to put the Latin names of organisms in italics.

Foot-and-mouth disease (*Aphtae epizooticae*) is a highly contagious and sometimes fatal viral disease of cattle and pigs.

The Bengal tiger is *Panthera tigris tigris* and the Siberian tiger is *Panthera tigris altaica*.

FOR REFERRING TO WORDS AS WORDS

When you need to discuss a word in its functions as a word, you can italicize it. (In this case, if you cannot italicize, use quotation marks.)

The English articles are *a*, *an*, and *the*.

FOR EMPHASIS

Do this sparingly. This kind of visual emphasis works only when it can stand out against large passages that receive no visual emphasis.

Sacks said, "I didn't just care for these patients. I *lived* with these patients."

SPELLING

It is now an expected sign of formal documents that the words are all spelled according to conventions that have developed over time and that are recorded in dictionaries.

CHECK A DICTIONARY

Spelling is the attempt to put spoken language into consistent patterns on the page, using just the twenty-six characters of the English alphabet. Because English developed out of many different languages, the spelling of a word often results from an attempt in the past to use the English alphabet to translate sounds made in other languages.

English spelling can therefore be vexing, even if your home language is English. There are some spelling rules for English, but all have considerable exceptions and variations, and many people find them confusing.

The best advice we can give you when you are trying to spell a word is to use a dictionary.

USING SPELL-CHECKERS

Spell-checkers only check spelling; they cannot tell if you are using the wrong word or have made other mistakes.

To use spell-checkers well, follow these steps:

1 After you have a complete draft, use a spell-checker to catch obvious spelling errors.

2 Use the items listed to the right under "*What spell-checkers miss*" to find specific kinds of mistakes.

3 Proofread the whole text at least one more time.

WHAT SPELL-CHECKERS MISS

- **Incorrect words that are spelled correctly.** In the sentence *He might loose his job*, all the words are spelled correctly, but *loose* should be *lose*. The Glossary (pages 536–543) shows words that are commonly confused.

- **Homonyms.** *Peace* and *piece* are homonyms: They are words that are spelled differently but sound the same. When writing quickly, it is easy to use a homonym in place of the word you want. The Glossary contains some common homonyms.

- **Possessives used as plurals—and vice versa.** If you are writing about more than one dress, it is easy to write *dress's* instead of *dresses*.

  → See page 456 to learn about possessives.
  → See page 457 to learn about plurals.

- **Pronouns that do not match their antecedents.**

  → See pages 452 and 464 to learn about pronouns and antecedents.

- **Words that are missing.** Spell-checkers do not catch words left out of a sentence. Read your work out loud, slowly, so you hear if you have left out any words.

- **Misspelled names.** Spell-checkers rarely check for proper nouns because there are so many. Misspelling the name of an author or major figure is not only embarrassing, but readers can also interpret this as a sign you were not paying close and careful attention while you were writing. Anytime you use a proper noun, check its spelling by looking up the name in a newspaper, magazine, biographical dictionary, or through an online search.

CAPITALIZING WORDS
Conventionally, capital letters are
used in many ways:

THE FIRST WORDS OF SENTENCES
We must become spies on behalf of justice.

A combination of ego and gin stood between
me and my ability to learn from my mistakes.

THE FIRST WORD IN A DIRECT QUOTATION
She said, simply, "No."

Chris Magnus, Chief of Police in Richmond,
California, has said, "There's a mentality
among some people that they're living some
really violent video game."

DAYS, MONTHS, AND PUBLIC HOLIDAYS
On Tuesday, we'll be home late.

My family could celebrate Hanukkah,
Christmas, and Kwanzaa.

NAMES OF PEOPLE
Capitalize first and last names, whether you
use one or both.

Heidi worked until the early morning.

Thomas Pynchon begins his novel *Gravity's
Rainbow* with the sentence, "A screaming
comes across the sky."

NAMES OF CITIES, STATES, AND COUNTRIES
Capitalize these names when they are nouns
and when they are adjectives.

Seattle has changed since I was born there.

The Waifs are an Australian band.

NAMES OF ORGANIZATIONS
My brother volunteered with Habitat for
Humanity.

"Doctors Without Borders" is the English
name for the organization started in France,
Médecins Sans Frontières.

PROFESSIONAL TITLES
Whether they are spelled out or abbreviated,
capitalize all professional titles when they
come before a person's name.

It was Colonel Peacock in the kitchen with
the knife.

Professor Yunus won the Nobel Prize.

Surgeon General Joycelyn Elders said, "When
hope dies, moral decay can't be far behind."

TITLES OF ARTWORKS
The artworks can be paintings, sculptures,
photographs, musical compositions, and
songs.

Art historians do not know who posed for the
Mona Lisa.

I wish I knew all the words to that Mose
Allison song "Your Mind Is on Vacation, But
Your Mouth Works Overtime."

TITLES OF BOOKS AND OTHER WRITINGS
Arundhati Roy's book, *The God of Small Things*,
won the Booker Prize.

"The Moral Equivalent of War" is an essay by
William James.

→ See page 521 to learn when to use quotation marks
around titles; see page 530 to learn when to italicize
titles.

NUMBERS

WRITING NUMBERS

In MLA style, spell out numbers that can be expressed in one or two words, using hyphens, as in the examples below. Give the numerals for longer numbers.

seven	sixty-one	1,347
forty-one dollars	$77.17	ten miles
twenty-two years	250 years	352 miles

In APA style, use numerals for the numbers 10 and above; for numbers preceding a unit of measurement; and for dates, mathematical functions, and fractions:

seven	61	1,347
41 dollars	$77.17	10 miles
22 years	3 times as many	5 grams

Spell out numbers preceding other numbers expressed in numerals; otherwise readers might have trouble, as in the first sentence below, where it is possible to misread the two numbers as 10,250.

The game is run from 10 250 gigabyte servers.

The game is run from ten 250 gigabyte servers.

SPELL OUT NUMBERS THAT BEGIN SENTENCES

7% of eligible voters don't have ready access to proof of citizenship.

Seven percent of eligible voters don't have ready access to proof of citizenship.

USE NUMBERS CONSISTENTLY

If you spell numbers out or use numerals in a series, do so consistently.

League of Legends has twenty-seven million daily and 67 million monthly players.

League of Legends has 27 million daily and 67 million monthly players.

DATES AND TIMES

Use numerals for dates and times.

President John F. Kennedy was shot and killed on November 22, 1963, at 12:30 p.m.

PAGES AND OTHER PARTS OF BOOKS

Use numerals for pages, chapters, and other book divisions.

In his book *The Uses of Disorder*, Richard Sennett defines adulthood as when people "learn to tolerate painful ambiguity and uncertainty" (108).

ADDRESSES AND PHONE NUMBERS

Use numerals for addresses and phone numbers.

Grauman's Chinese Theatre is located at 6801 Hollywood Boulevard in Hollywood. For showtimes, call (323) 464-8111.

DECIMALS AND PERCENTAGES

Use numerals for percentages, and use the percentage sign (%).

In 1650, only 1% of all babies were born to unmarried women. By 1800, it was 24%, and furthermore, 40% of women getting married were already pregnant.

(If the percentages come at the beginning of a sentence, however, use words for both the number and the percentage sign.)

SCORES AND STATISTICS

Use numerals for scores and statistics.

In 2015, 44% of all online gamers were women, down from 48% percent a year earlier.

The most lopsided score ever in college football occured in 1916, when the Georgia Tech Engineers beat the Cumberland College Bulldogs by a score of 222–0.

ABBREVIATIONS

TITLES

Dr. and *St.* (*Saint*) are abbreviated before a name but not after.

. . . said Dr. Robert Cantu.

. . . said Robert Cantu, a doctor specializing in neurosurgery.

Prof., Sen., Gen., Capt., and other titles can be abbreviated when placed before a full name (i.e., first and last names, or initials and last name) but not before the last name when it is given alone:

Sen. Hattie Wyatt Caraway

Sen. H. W. Caraway

Senator Caraway

Put suffixes, academic, and professional titles—*Sr., Jr., J.D., Ph.D., M.F.A., R.N., C.P.A.*—after names. (The periods are often left out of abbreviated titles.)

Ralph Simmons, Ph.D., will speak.

Ralph Simmons, PhD, will speak.

COMPANY NAMES

If a company name contains an abbreviation, write the name as the company does:

Charlie and the Chocolate Factory, distributed by Warner Bros. Studios, is based on a novel by Roald Dahl.

MEASUREMENTS

In a paper's body, spell out measurement units such as *foot, percent, meter*—but abbreviate them in charts, tables, and graphs.

HMS Titanic was 883.75 feet long and 92.5 feet wide.

PLACE-NAMES

Spell out the names of continents, rivers, countries, states, cities, streets, and so on, except in these two cases:

1 You can use U.S. as an adjective, but not as a noun:

U.S. soldiers

soldiers from the United States

2 To put a full address in a sentence, write it as you would on an envelope, using the state's postal abbreviation.

Please send your applications to Habitat for Humanity International, 121 Habitat St., Americus, GA 31709.

Otherwise, spell out the state name:

Habitat for Humanity International's head office is in Americus, Georgia.

DATES

Spell out months and days of the week.

"Statistically, you are more likely to have an accident on Monday, November 27, than any other day of the year," the insurance official said.

For dates, these abbreviations are customary:

399 BC	**399 BCE**
1215 CE	**AD 1215**

BC (*Before Christ*), **BCE** (*Before the Common Era*), and **CE** (*Common Era*) are placed after the year. **AD** (*Anno Domini*, "Year of Our Lord") goes before the year. *BCE* and *CE* are currently the most favored abbreviations.

TIMES

The conventional abbreviations for time of day are *A.M.* or *a.m.* for before noon and *P.M.* or *p.m.* for afternoon.

ACRONYMS

An acronym is a word formed by the initial letters of a phrase or title.

PC   personal computer

NPM   National Poetry Month

BBC   British Broadcasting Corporation

If you use an acronym that readers might not know, spell it out first, put the acronym in parentheses, and then use the acronym for all later references.

Folding At Home (FAH) is Stanford University's distributed computing project to study and understand protein folding, protein aggregation, and related diseases. So far, almost 500,000 users have donated processing time to FAH's projects.

LATIN EXPRESSIONS

Some Latin expressions, commonly used in academic writing, appear only as abbreviations:

cf.   *compare*   e.g.   *for example*

et al.   *and others*   etc.   *and so forth*

i.e.   *that is*   n.b.   *note well*

IN DOCUMENTING SOURCES

Different documentation styles use different abbreviations for words like *anonymous*, *editor*, or *no date*. Check your style manual for any abbreviations you need to use.

→ See page 527 for how to use periods with abbreviations.

→ See page 527 for how to use periods with abbreviations.

TIP

MAKING ABBREVIATIONS PLURAL AND POSSESSIVE

To make an abbreviation plural, put **-s** after it.

Analysts estimate that more than 6,000 PCs become obsolete in California every day.

To make an abbreviation possessive, put **-'s** after it.

IBM's earning forecast was grim.

ABBREVIATIONS IN DIFFERENT DISCIPLINES

Different disciplines—from mathematics to the social sciences—use abbreviations differently. The advice we offer on these pages is general, so if you are writing for a specific discipline, ask someone familiar with the field (or a reference librarian) for help in learning the field's conventions.

GLOSSARY OF GRAMMATICAL TERMS AND USAGE

In this glossary, we provide definitions of **grammatical terms** (shown in blue) and **guidelines for usage**. We also list **homonyms** (words that are spelled differently but sound the same) and other words that writers can easily confuse.

As you use this glossary, just as you use this handbook, keep in mind that the guidelines for usage are not strict rules but are, rather, academic and professional conventions developed over time. When you follow these conventions, readers will tend to see your writing as academic and professional.

One further note: In academic and professional writing, words considered colloquial, nonstandard, or informal (as we label them in this glossary) are usually avoided by writers.

a/an   **A** and **an** are indefinite articles because they indicate general objects (*a book, an apple*) rather than specific objects (*the president*). (See pp. 458–459.)

a lot/alot   **A lot** and **alot** are often used in informal writing to mean *many* or *much*. In academic writing, *many* or *much* are expected, instead of **a lot**. **Alot** is nonstandard.

accept/except/expect   **Accept** is a verb meaning "to receive." **Except** is usually used as a conjunction or preposition meaning "other than," but it can also be used as a verb meaning "leave out." **Expect** is a verb meaning "to regard something as likely."

active voice   In a sentence or clause in active voice, the subject of the clause or sentence performs the action. See **passive voice**. (See also pp. 308–309, 445, and 468) *We installed a new operating system on the computer.*

ad/add   **Ad** is a shortened form of *advertisement*; **add** is a verb meaning "to join or combine."

adjective   An adjective is a word that modifies a noun or pronoun. (See p. 466.) *I like salty snacks.*

adjective clause   An adjective clause is a subordinate clause that modifies a noun or pronoun. Adjective clauses are also called *relative clauses* because they begin with a relative pronoun. (See p. 488.) *The park allows only dogs that are on leashes.*

adverb   An adverb is a word that modifies a verb (*talk quietly*), another modifier (*very inexpensive*), or a whole clause or sentence (*Fortunately, we had an umbrella*). (See p. 471.)

adverb clause   An adverb clause is a subordinate clause that modifies a verb, another modifier, or a whole clause or sentence. (See p. 490.) *We did not leave until all of the trash had been picked up.*

advice/advise   **Advice** is a noun meaning "an opinion." **Advise** is a verb meaning "to give an opinion or advice."

affect/effect   **Affect** is usually used as a verb meaning "to influence," and **effect** is a noun meaning "a result." Sometimes **affect** is used as a noun meaning "an emotional state or feeling," and sometimes **effect** is used as a verb meaning "to bring about."

agreement   Agreement refers to the correspondence of one word to another in gender, number, or person. For example, a verb should agree with its subject (*The mechanic knows how to fix the engine*) and a pronoun must agree with its antecedent (*The fast food workers are on strike for their pay*). (See pp. 436–439 on subject-verb agreement.)

all ready/already   **All ready** is an adjective phrase meaning "ready to go." **Already** is an adverb that means "before" or "previously."

all right/alright   **All right** means "acceptable" and is all right to use in academic writing. **Alright** is considered nonstandard.

all together/altogether **All together** means "in one place" or "in unison." **Altogether** means "entirely."

allude/elude **Allude** means "to refer to." **Elude** means "to escape."

allusion/illusion An **allusion** is an indirect reference to something. An **illusion** is a false or misleading impression.

among/between Use **between** when referring to two objects; use **among** when referring to three or more objects.

amount/number **Amount** is used for quantities of things that can be measured but not counted, such as *energy*. **Number** is used for quantities of things that can be counted, such as *bananas*.

an See **a/an**.

antecedent An antecedent is the noun or pronoun referred to by a pronoun. (See p. 453.) In the following sentence, *Rav* is the antecedent of *his*: *Rav was on his way to pick up his grandchildren.*

any more/anymore **Any more** means "no more." **Anymore** means "now." Both are used in negative constructions. (*I don't want to hear any more lies; I don't believe you anymore.*)

anybody/any body/anyone/any one **Anybody** and **anyone** are indefinite pronouns that have the same meaning. **Any body** and **any one** are usually followed by the noun each modifies (*any body of water, any one incident*).

anyway/anyways **Anyway** is used to support a point that was just made and is the standard form, but the nonstandard **anyways** is often used in informal writing and conversation.

apt/liable/likely **Apt** and **likely** are interchangeable, but **apt** specifically means "having a tendency to." *He is apt to make mistakes like that.* **Liable** means "in danger of" and is best used only in contexts describing a dire situation. *You are liable to start a fire if you light a match near a gas tank.*

article Articles are always followed by a noun. *A, an,* and *the* are articles. (See pp. 458–459.)

as/like Use **as** instead of **like** before dependent clauses, which contain a noun and a verb (*She saw the parade as she walked out the door.*). Use **like** before a noun or pronoun (*He ran like a cheetah.*).

assure/ensure/insure **Assure** means "promise," **ensure** means "make certain," and **insure** means to "arrange for compensation in case of damage."

at/where Using **at** with **where** is unnecessary and makes for wordy writing, as in *We are right at where we started.*

auxiliary verb See **helping verb**.

awful/awfully **Awful** is an adjective that means "awe inspiring" but more commonly means "really bad." **Awful** and the adverb form **awfully** should not be interchanged and do not require intensifiers such as "very" or "extremely." *We heard an awful sound and were awfully frightened.*

awhile/a while **Awhile** is an adverb and **a while** is a pairing of an article and noun. Consequently, **awhile** cannot be used as the object of a preposition (**a while**, however, can), and **a while** cannot be used to modify a verb. *We waited awhile because Mario said he would be back in a while.*

bad/badly **Bad** should be used only as an adjective; **badly** is the adverb. *I sing badly.*

being as/being that Both **being as** and **being that** are colloquial and should not be used in academic writing.

beside/besides **Beside** means "next to." **Besides** means "except." *No one, besides Betty, would sit beside Archie.*

between See **among/between**.

bring/take **Bring** describes movement from a more distant location to nearby. **Take** describes movement away from. *Bring me that box so I can take it with me to work.*

but/however/yet **But**, **however**, and **yet** can all be used to indicate a contrast. Using them together in the same sentence will make it wordy.

can/may In academic writing, **can** indicates the ability to do something, while **may** indicates permission to do something. Informally, these words are often used interchangeably.

capital/capitol A **capital** is the main governmental city of a state or country. *Annapolis is the capital of Maryland.* A **capitol** is the building in which government bodies meet. *The senator gave a press conference on the steps of the capitol.*

case Case is the form of a noun or pronoun that indicates its function. Nouns change case only to show possession. (See p. 456.) *A dog ran into the street.* (subject). *A woman grabbed the dog.* (object of preposition). *The dog's life was saved.* (possessive noun).

censor/censure   To **censor** is to ban or silence. To **censure** is to reprimand publicly.

cite/sight/site   **Cite** is a verb meaning to "reference specifically." **Sight** is used as a verb meaning "to view" and as a noun meaning "vision." **Site** is usually used as a noun to mean "location," but it can also be used as a verb to mean "to locate."

clause   A clause is a group of words containing a subject and a verb. A **main** or **independent clause** can stand alone as a sentence (see p. 485), but a **subordinate** or **dependent clause** acts as a part of speech and cannot stand alone (see pp. 449 and 488–490).

comma splice   A comma splice occurs when two independent clauses are joined by a comma. (See pp. 450–451.) *José did not approve of our choice, he wanted to hire the other candidate* (incorrect, because only a comma joins the two clauses). *José did not approve of our choice; he wanted to hire the other candidate* (correct, because now a semicolon joins the clauses).

common noun   A common noun names a general person, place, or thing. Common nouns are not capitalized unless they are the first word of a sentence. (See p. 463.) *Did Johnny Depp portray a pirate in that movie?*

complement/compliment   To **complement** something is to complete it. To **compliment** is to flatter. Because they are spelled so similarly, they are often confused.

complex sentence   A complex sentence is a sentence that contains at least one subordinate clause attached to an independent clause. (See pp. 488–490.) *Despite the heat, we had a good time at the festival.*

compound sentence   A compound sentence contains at least two main clauses. (See pp. 486–487.) *We ate dinner, and we went for a walk.*

compound-complex sentence   A compound-complex sentence contains at least *two independent clauses* and *a subordinate clause*. (See p. 491.) *Though my parents are Italian, I have not visited Italy and I do not speak the language.*

conjunction   A conjunction is a word that links and relates parts of a sentence. (See pp. 474–477.) *Eric arrived late, but the movie had not started yet.* See **coordinating conjunction**, **correlative conjunction**, and **subordinating conjunction**.

conjunctive adverb   A conjunctive adverb is an adverb (such as *however, besides, consequently,* or *therefore*) that relates two main or independent clauses. (See p. 477.) *Our car is broken; consequently, we had to carpool with neighbors.*

conscience/conscious   **Conscience** is a noun meaning "a sense of right or wrong." **Conscious** is an adjective meaning "awake."

continual/continuous   **Continual** is an adjective meaning "recurring." **Continuous** is an adjective meaning "constant." *That continual noise is a continuous bother.*

coordinating conjunction   A coordinating conjunction is a word (such as *and, but, or, for, nor, yet,* and *so*) that links two grammatically equal parts of a sentence. (See pp. 474 and 502–503.) *I brushed my teeth and went to bed.*

correlative conjunction   Correlative conjunctions are two or more words (*neither…nor, either… or, not only…but also*) that work together to link parts of a sentence. (See p. 475.) *Not only were we excited, but we were also a little bit afraid.*

could of   **Could of** is often used in informal writing; use *could have* in academic writing.

count noun   A count noun names things that can be counted. (See p. 458.) *goats, shoes, computers*

criteria/criterion   A **criterion** is a singular noun that means "a measure" or "a condition." **Criteria** is the plural form of **criterion**.

dangling modifier   A dangling modifier does not have a clear connection to the word it modifies. (See pp. 454–455.) *Spicier than expected, she spat out the soup.* (The wording says that *she* is spicier than expected!)

data/datum   **Datum** is a singular noun that refers to a piece of information or a fact. **Data** is the plural of **datum**, and although it is often used as a singular noun, it should be treated as a plural noun and take a plural verb.

declarative   A declarative sentence is a statement. (See p. 479.) *The measurements were incorrect.*

dependent clause   See **subordinate clause**.

differ from/differ with   To **differ from** means "to be unlike." To **differ with** means "to disagree with."

different from/different than   Different from is preferred in academic writing, except in situations where **different from** would be wordy.

direct object   A direct object is the noun, pronoun, or noun clause naming the person or thing that receives the action of a transitive verb. (See p. 481.) *The chef threw the meatloaf in the trash.*

discreet/discrete   Discreet means "careful" or "prudent." **Discrete** means "separate."

disinterested/uninterested   Disinterested is an adjective that means "impartial." It is often used incorrectly in place of **uninterested**.

double negative   A double negative is the use of two negatives to convey one negative idea. It should be avoided in academic writing. (See p. 313.) *I don't have no time to go with you.*

due to the fact that   Due to the fact that is a wordy substitute for **because**.

each other/one another   Each other should be used for two things; **one another** should be used for more than two things.

effect   See **affect/effect**.

elicit/illicit   Elicit is a verb that means "to bring out." **Illicit** is an adjective that means "unlawful." These words are often incorrectly used in place of each other.

emigrate from/immigrate to   Emigrate is a verb meaning "to leave one's country." **Immigrate** is a verb that means "to settle in another country."

ensure   See **assure/ensure/insure**.

etc.   Etc. is an abbreviation for the Latin *et cetera* and is used to shorten a list of items. **Etc.** is mostly used in informal writing.

every body/everybody/every one/everyone   Everybody and **everyone** are both collective nouns referring to all parties under discussion. **Every body** and **every one** are both adjective-noun combinations that refer to individuals within the larger group.

except   See **accept/except/expect**.

except for the fact that   Except for the fact that is a wordy substitute for *except that*.

expect   See **accept/except/expect**.

expletive   *There* and *it* are expletives, or "dummy subjects" that are used to fill a grammatical slot in a sentence. (See p. 314.) *It is very clear.*

explicit/implicit   Explicit is an adjective used to describe what is stated, obvious, and/or visible; **implicit** is also an adjective, used to describe what is not stated, obvious, or visible: *The assignment was explicit about how many pages we should write; implicit was how many sources we should cite.*

farther/further   Farther refers to distance, while **further** refers to time or another abstract concept.

fewer/less   Fewer is used for things that can be counted, while **less** is used for things that cannot be counted.

fragment   A fragment is a group of words that is capitalized and punctuated like a sentence but lacks a subject and predicate. Fragments are used in some forms of writing, such as fiction and advertising copy, but they are usually not acceptable in academic writing. (See pp. 446–449.) *A representative who cares.*

further   See **farther/further**.

gender   Gender is the classification of nouns or pronouns as masculine and feminine. (See pp. 452–453.)

good/well   Good can be used only as an adjective, while **well** can be used as both an adjective and an adverb. *His last album was good. He sings well. Is your mother well?*

hanged/hung   Hanged is a verb that specifically refers to an execution. **Hung** is used in all other instances. *In the past, criminals were often hanged. The noose hung from the gallows.*

have/of   Have, rather than of, should be used after auxiliary or helping verbs such as *could, should, would, might,* and so on.

he/she; s/he   Academic audiences prefer writing that is gender inclusive (unless a distinction of gender is necessary). (See p. 335.)

helping verb   Helping verbs are also known as *auxiliary verbs*. These verbs (forms of *be, do,* and *have*) join with other verbs to indicate tense and mood. *Modal verbs* can also be used as helping verbs. (See pp. 469–470.) *By Friday, she had collected enough signatures to be listed on the ballot.*

herself/himself/myself/yourself These *–self* pronouns refer to or intensify nouns or other pronouns. They are often used colloquially in place of personal pronouns, but not usually in academic writing.

hopefully **Hopefully** is an adverb that is often used to modify a sentence, but it is considered nonstandard.

if/whether **Whether** is clearer than **if** when you are posing an alternative. *Whether your vote matters depends on the integrity of the electoral process.*

illusion See **allusion/illusion**.

immigrate See **emigrate from/immigrate to**.

impact **Impact** is used as a noun referring to a violent collision and, less commonly, as a verb meaning "to collide violently." The use of **impact** as a noun to mean "an effect" or as a verb to mean "to have an effect on" is prevalent, but it is considered nonstandard.

imperative An imperative sentence expresses a command. The subject of an imperative sentence is often implied. (See p. 479.) *Be quiet!*

implicit See **explicit/implicit**.

imply/infer **Imply** is a verb meaning "to suggest." **Infer** is a verb meaning "to conclude."

in regards to **In regards to** is a wordy substitute for *regarding*.

incredible/incredulous **Incredible** is an adjective that means "unbelievable." **Incredulous** is an adjective that used to mean "not believing." *Our incredulous minds could not fathom the incredible sight before us.*

independent clause An independent—or main— clause is a group of words with a subject and predicate that can stand alone as a sentence. (See p. 485.)

indirect object An indirect object is a noun, pronoun, or noun phrase that names the person or thing that is affected by the action of a transitive verb. *The waiter served us fresh coffee.*

interjection An interjection is a word that expresses strong emotion. *Ouch! That hurt!*

interrogative An interrogative sentence asks a question. (See p. 479.) *What did you do this weekend?*

intransitive verb An intransitive verb does not take an object. *I just wanted to participate.*

irregardless/regardless **Irregardless** is often used as a substitute for **regardless**, but using **irregardless** in that way is considered nonstandard.

irregular verb An irregular verb does not take *–ed* or *–d* to form its past tense or past participle. (See p. 469.) *slept, swam*

it is my opinion that **It is my opinion that** is a wordy substitute for *I believe that*.

its/it's **Its** is the possessive form of **it** and does not take an apostrophe. *As the fish swam, its fins undulated.* **It's** is the contraction of **it is**. *It's a sad day when the Cubs lose.*

-ize/-wise The suffix **-ize** turns a noun or an adjective into a verb (*motorize*). The suffix **–wise** turns a noun or an adjective into an adverb (*clockwise*).

kind of/sort of/type of These three constructions are used to classify things. Informally or colloquially they are used to mean *somewhat* or *rather*. *That kind of soup makes me sick.*

knew/new **Knew**, a verb, is the past tense of "to know." **New** is an adjective meaning "fresh, not seen before."

lay/lie **Lay** is a verb that means "to place," and it takes a direct object. **Lie** means "to recline" or "to position" and does not take a direct object.

leave/let **Leave** and **let** are interchangeable only when followed by "alone." **Leave** means "go" and **let** means "allow."

less See **fewer/less**.

lie See **lay/lie**.

linking verb A linking verb connects a subject to a complement.

literally **Literally** means "actually" or "just as the words say." It is often used colloquially to intensify a word.

loan/lone A **loan** is money that is borrowed; **lone** is an adjective meaning "single, isolated."

loose/lose **Loose** is an adjective meaning "not tight." *His pants were so loose he couldn't walk.* **Lose** is a verb meaning "to misplace" or "to be defeated." *Don't lose your homework.*

lots/lots of   Lots and **lots of** are often used as substitutes for *many*, but they are considered nonstandard.

main clause   See **independent clause**.

may/can   See **can/may**.

may be/maybe   **May be** is a verb phrase. **Maybe** is an adverb.

media/medium   **Medium** is a singular noun referring to a means of conveying information. **Media** is the plural of **medium** and takes a plural verb. *The media portray…*

might of   See **have/of**.

modifier   A modifier is a word, phrase, or clause that describes another word. Modifiers are adjectives (see p. 466), adverbs (see p. 471), adjective clauses (see p. 488), and adverb clauses (see p. 490).

must of   See **have/of**.

noncount noun   A noncount noun names things that cannot be counted. (See p. 458.) *electricity, history, peace*

nonrestrictive modifier   A nonrestrictive modifier is not essential to the meaning of the word, phrase, or clause it modifies and should be set off by commas or other punctuation. (See pp. 504–507.) *My uncle, Misha, used to work on Wall Street.*

noun   A noun names a person, place, or thing. (See p. 463.)

number   See **amount/number**.

object   An object is the receiver of an action within a sentence, clause, or phrase. (See p. 481.)

OK/O.K./okay   OK, O.K., and **okay** are all okay for informal writing but are less okay in academic writing.

owing to the fact that   **Owing to the fact that** is a wordy substitute for *because*.

parallelism   Parallelism is the practice of putting similar elements in a sentence in a similar grammatical pattern. (See pp. 318–319.) *Her resume stated that she had trained and supervised employees, analyzed and evaluated software, and organized and maintained records.*

parts of speech   There are eight parts of speech, or groups of words classified by their grammatical functions and meanings: nouns, pronouns, verbs, adjectives, adverbs, prepositions, conjunctions, and interjections. (See pp. 462–477.)

passed/past   **Passed**, a verb, is the past tense of "to pass." **Past** is a noun or adjective, describing something that happened prior to the present moment.

passive voice   Passive voice is indicated by a clause with a transitive verb that acts upon the subject. (See pp. 308–309, 445, and 468.) *The issue was called to our attention by the maintenance crew.*

peace/piece   **Peace** is a state of harmony. A **piece** is a part of something.

people/persons   Use **people** to refer to a general group, unless it is necessary to emphasize individuals within the group. In that case, use **persons**.

per   The Latin word **per** means "for each." It is best used in familiar phrases such as *miles per gallon*.

phenomena/phenomenon   **Phenomenon** is a singular noun meaning "observable fact" or "unusual event." The plural form of **phenomenon** is **phenomena**, which takes a plural verb. *Among the phenomena that were discussed were alien abductions and reincarnation.*

phrase   A phrase is a group of words that does not contain both a subject and a predicate. (See pp. 446–447, 478, 480–481, 484, 472–473.) *A lovely day*

plenty   **Plenty** is often used as a colloquial substitute for *very*.

plus   **Plus** is often used informally to join clauses or sentences. In formal writing, use *and, also, moreover, furthermore,* or another conjunctive adjective instead.

possessive case   The possessive case indicates ownership. (See p. 456.) *her shoes, Tran's car*

precede/proceed   **Precede** and **proceed** are both verbs, but *precede* means "come before" and *proceed* means "continue."

predicate   The predicate is the part of a clause that expresses the action or tells something about the subject. The predicate includes the verb and its complements, objects, and modifiers. (See pp. 448 and 480–484.)

prejudice/prejudiced   **Prejudice** is a noun meaning "bias." **Prejudiced** is an adjective meaning "biased" or "intolerant."

preposition   A preposition is a part of speech that shows relationships or qualities. (See pp. 472–473 and 484.)

prepositional phrase   A prepositional phrase is a phrase formed by a preposition and its object. A prepositional phrase includes the modifiers of the object. (See pp. 472–473 and 484.)

pretty   **Pretty** is often used as a colloquial substitute for *very*. Avoid using **pretty** to mean *very* in academic writing.

principal/principle   **Principal** can be a noun, meaning "the head of a school" or it can be an adjective, meaning "the most important element." **Principle** is a noun meaning "a rule or standard."

pronoun   A pronoun is a part of speech that stands for other nouns or pronouns. Classes of pronouns include: **possessive pronouns**, **personal pronouns**, **demonstrative pronouns**, **indefinite pronouns**, **relative pronouns**, **interrogative pronouns**, **reflexive pronouns**, and **reciprocal pronouns**. (See pp. 464–465.)

pronoun case   Pronouns that act as the subject of a sentence are in the **subjective case** (*I, you, he, she, it, we, they*). Pronouns that act as direct or indirect objects are in the **objective case** (*me, you, him, her, it, us, them*). Pronouns that indicate ownership are in the **possessive case** (*my, your, his, her, its, our, their*). (See pp. 464–465.)

proper noun   A proper noun is a noun that names a particular person, place, thing, or group. Proper nouns are capitalized. (See p. 463.) *Anthony Bourdain, Dublin, Yom Kippur*

question as to whether/question of whether   These phrases are both wordy substitutes for *whether*.

raise/rise   The verb **raise** means "lift up" and takes a direct object. The verb **rise** means "get up." It does not take a direct object.

real/really   **Real** is an adjective, while **really** is an adverb. These words are often used incorrectly in place of each other.

reason is because   **Reason is because** is often used to explain causality. *Reason is* and *is because* are less wordy.

reason why   **Reason why** is a redundant construction to avoid in academic writing. Instead of *The reason why he went to Malaysia is for work*, you can write *He went to Malaysia for work*.

relative pronoun   A relative pronoun initiates clauses. *That, which, what, who, whom,* and *whose* are relative pronouns. (See p. 465.) *The woman who makes those funny, furry purses will have a booth at the fair.*

restrictive modifier   A restrictive modifier is essential to the meaning of the word, phrase, or clause it modifies. Unlike a nonrestrictive modifier, it is not set off by punctuation. (See pp. 504–507.) *My uncle who lives in Canada is visiting next week.*

rise/raise   See **raise/rise.**

run-on sentence   A run-on sentence occurs when two main clauses are fused together without punctuation or a conjunction. (See pp. 450–451.) *I don't like Wednesdays they are too far away from the weekend.*

sentence   A sentence is a grammatically independent group of words that contains at least one independent clause. (See pp. 478–491.)

set/sit   The verb **set** means "to put" and it takes a direct object. **Sit** means "to be seated" and does not take a direct object.

shall/will   **Shall** is very formal, and is most often used in first person questions, while **will** can be used in the future tense with all persons.

should of   See **have/of.**

simple/simplistic   Although it is often used as such, **simplistic** is not a synonym of *simple*. **Simplistic** means "crude" or "unsophisticated," while **simple** means "easy."

since   **Since** most commonly refers to time, but it can also be used as a synonym of *because*. Keep in mind, though, that some readers prefer that **since** not be used as a synonym of *because*.

sit/set   See **set/sit.**

some time/sometime/sometimes   **Some time** refers to a period of time, while **sometime** refers to an unspecified time. **Sometimes** means "occasionally."

somebody/some body; someone/some one Somebody and someone are indefinite pronouns that mean the same thing. **Some body** and **some one** are adjective-noun combinations.

sort of See **kind of/sort of/type of.**

subject A subject is a noun, pronoun, or noun phrase that identifies what the clause is about and is connected to the predicate. (See pp. 447 and 480–484.)

subject-verb agreement See **agreement.**

subjunctive mood The subjunctive mood expresses a wish, a condition contrary to fact, a recommendation, or a request. (See p. 468.)

subordinate A subordinate relationship is a relationship of unequal importance, in either grammar or meaning. (See pp. 316–317 and 449.)

subordinate clause A subordinate clause, also called a *dependent clause,* is a clause that cannot stand alone but must be attached to a main clause. (See pp. 316–317 and 449.)

subordinating conjunction A subordinating conjunction is a word that introduces a subordinate clause. Some subordinating conjunctions are *after, although, as, because, before, if, since, that, unless, until, when, where,* and *while.* (See pp. 476–479.)

such Such means "of the previous kind" (*such behavior, such praise*), but it is often used informally as a synonym for *very.*

sure Sure is often used as an adverb to mean *certainly,* but it is more properly used as an adjective.

sure and/sure to; try and/try to Sure to and try to are correct; do not add *and* after *sure* or *try.*

take See **bring/take.**

than/then Than is a conjunction expressing difference. *I would rather watch a movie than go out tonight.* Then is an adverb expressing time. *First we went to church, then we went shopping.*

that/which That introduces a restrictive or essential clause, while **which** is usually used to introduce nonrestrictive or nonessential clauses.

their/there/they're Their is a possessive pronoun (see p. 456); there is most commonly used as an expletive (see p. 314); and **they're** is a contraction of *they are* (see p. 526).

to/too/two To is a preposition, while **too** is an adverb. **Two** is a number.

transition A transition is a word or phrase that notes movement from one unit of writing to another. (See pp. 244–245 and 306–307.)

transitive verb A transitive verb is a verb that takes a direct object.

try and/try to See **sure and/sure to.**

unique If something is **unique,** it is one of a kind and can't be compared to anything else. Consequently, it is not necessary to use words such as *most* to modify **unique.**

usage/use/utilize Utilize and usage are often used in informal writing as synonyms for **use.**

verb A verb is a word that shows action or characterizes a subject in some way. (See pp. 468–470.)

well/good See **good/well.**

weather/whether Weather is a noun describing whether it is sunny, raining, hot, or cold outside. **Whether** is a conjunction that can mean "if" or can introduce a set of opinions.

which/that See **that/which.**

who/whom Who is the subject pronoun, while **whom** is the object pronoun. *Who is that in the yard? With whom did you dance?*

who's/whose Who's is a contraction of *who is,* while **whose** is a possessive. *Who's there? Whose shoes are those?*

will/shall See **shall/will.**

-wise/-ize See **-ize/-wise.**

would of See **have/of.**

you You is primarily used to directly address the reader, but it is often used informally to refer to people in general.

your/you're Your and you're are not interchangeable. **Your** is the possessive form of *you. Your conscience will rest easier after you vote.* **You're** is the contraction of *you are. You're a citizen, and so you are expected to vote.* (See p. 456 on possessives; see p. 526 on contractions.)

CREDITS

TEXT CREDITS

14 Nov. 2015. **357:** Ferree, Myra, William A. Gamson, Jürgen Gerhards, and Dieter Rucht. "Four Models of the Public Sphere in Modern Democracies." *Theory and Society* 31 (2002): 289–324. JSTOR. Web. 10 Dec. 2015. Originally Published by Springer Publishing. **357:** Gómez, Manuel N. "Imagining the Future: Cultivating Civility in a Field of Discontent." *Change* (March/April 2008): 11–17. Taylor and Francis. Print. **357:** Haidt, Jonathan. *The Righteous Mind: Why Good People Are Divided by Politics and Religion.* New York: Pantheon, 2012. Random House Publishing. **357–359:** Stone, Geoffrey R. "Civility and Dissent During Wartime." *Human Rights* 33.1 (2006): n. pag. Web. 10 Dec. 2015. **359:** Calhoun, Cheshire. "The Virtue of Civility." *Philosophy and Public Affairs.* Volume 29, Issue 3, pages 251–275, July 2000 (Summer, 2000): 251–75. JSTOR. Web. 14 Nov. 2015. **359:** Haidt, Jonathan. *The Righteous Mind: Why Good People Are Divided by Politics and Religion.* New York: Pantheon, 2012. Random House Publishing. **359:** Schwind, Christina, Jürgen Buder, Ulrike Cress, and Friedrich W. Hesse. Preference-Inconsistent Recommendations: An Effective Approach for Reducing Confirmation Bias and Stimulating Divergent Thinking?" *Computers and Education* 58 (2012) 787–96. Elsevier. Web. 18 Nov. 2015. **361:** Strickland, April A., Charles S. Taber, and Milton Lodge. "Motivated Reasoning and Public Opinion." *Journal of Health Politics, Policy and Law.* Dec. 2011. Duke University Press. **361:** Taber, Charles S., and Milton Lodge. "Motivated Skepticism in the Evaluation of Political Beliefs." *American Journal of Political Science* 50.3 (2006): 755–69. JSTOR. Web. 18 Nov. 2015. Midwest Political Science Association. **430:** Zawacki, Dr. Terry Myers, Eiman Hajabbasi, Anna Habib, Alex Antram, and Alokparna Das. *Valuing Written Accents: Non-Native Students Talk About Identity, Academic Writing, and Meeting Teachers' Expectations.* Issue II, Second Edition. Diversity at Mason series. From the Diversity Research Group, George Mason University. Copyright © 2007 by the Diversity Research Group, George Mason University. **330, 331:** Ozeki, Ruth. *My Year of Meats.* Penguin Books (March 1, 1999).

PHOTO CREDITS

2: Jocic/Shutterstock. **4:** Destina/Fotolia; Pixelbliss/Fotolia. **5:** Kitch Bain/Fotolia; Md3d/Fotolia. **6:** PhotoSerg/shutterstock; Volodymyr Burdiak/Shutterstock. **7:** dcwcreations/Shutterstock; 123RF/Anton Starikov. **8:** Karandaev/Fotolia. **10:** Chatchawanak/Fotolia. **13:** Kenneth Man/Fotolia. **16:** Poco Bw/Fotolia. **18:** Arto/Fotolia. **20:** Rawpixel/Fotolia. **22:** Beeboys/Fotolia. **26:** Dmitry Lobanov/Fotolia. **28:** Rido/Fotolia. **33:** Ljupco Smokovski/Fotolia. **34:** Alex/Fotolia; Alex/Fotolia. **35:** Semprevivo/Fotolia; Jeff Greenberg/PhotoEdit, Inc. **36, 40, 42, 44:** Alex/Fotolia. **45:** Three Rocksimages/Fotolia. **50, 54, 56, 60, 66:** Alex/Fotolia. **76, 77, 79, 82, 83, 85:** Portland State University. **92, 94:** Alex/Fotolia. **97:** Tom Wang/Fotolia. **98:** Olly/Fotolia. **118:** Piotr Marcinski/Fotolia. **122:** Minerva Studio/Fotolia. **131:** Courtesy of Chain Camera Pictures. **135:** U.S. Dept of Commerce. **138:** Charlesknoxphoto/Fotolia. **140:** Alphaspirit/Fotolia. **143:** Vladimirfloyd/Fotolia. **144, 146, 148:** Alphaspirit/Fotolia. **149, 151, 153, 155:** International Society for Human Rights. **151, 153, 155:** Physicians Against Landmines. Center for International Rehabilitation. **158:** Syda Productions/Fotolia. **165:** Der Mensch als Industriepalast (Man as Industrial Palace) (1926), Fritz Kahn. Chromolithograph. Courtesy of the National Library of Medicine. **166:** Reproduced from Government of Manitoba with permission from Manitoba Water Stewardship Division. **170:** Courtesy of Persuasive Games LLC. **187:** Copyright © World Health Organization, 2004. **188:** Alphaspirit/Fotolia. **204:** Syda Productions/Fotolia. **206:** Vladstar/Fotolia. **208:** Syda Productions/Fotolia. **211:** Andres Rodriguez/Fotolia. **212:** Mike Clark/Fotolia. **213:** Friedrich Stark/Alamy; Friedrich Stark/Alamy; Krsmanovic/Fotolia; Jeff Greenberg/PhotoEdit, Inc.; Sean Ellis/Getty Images; David McLain/Aurora Photos. **215:** Vivian Seefeld/Fotolia. **216:** Ioannis Pantzi/Fotolia. **232:** Yuri Arcurs/Fotolia. **240:** lukasvideo/Fotolia. **256:** Twixx/Fotolia. **257:** Shmuel Yosef, Copyright © 2011, Courtesy of Kehinde Wiley; Library of Congress Prints and Photographs Division [LC-DIG-ppmsca-08762]; Library of Congress Prints and Photographs Division [LC-DIG-ppmsca-08762]. **261:** Library of Congress Prints and Photographs Division [LC-DIG-ggbain-11032]. **265:** Fotolia/www.doglikehorse.com. **266:** Yuri Arcurs/Fotolia. **270:** Yanlev/Fotolia. **284:** Dinostock/Fotolia. **286:** Andres Rodriguez/Fotolia. **289:** Odua Images/Fotolia. **290:** Kastanka/Fotolia. **294:** Alphaspirit/Fotolia. **298:** Guz Anna/Fotolia. **300:** Sergio/Fotolia. **310:** Beaubelle/Fotolia. **322:** Cornotomo/Fotolia. **330:** Djma/Fotolia. **340:** Pun/Fotolia. **344:** Ryanking999/Fotolia. **349:** Serkucher/Fotolia. **429:** Se media/Fotolia. **430:** Matthew Benoit/Shutterstock. **432:** Destina/Fotolia. **434:** Kastanka/Fotolia. **465:** Pathdoc/Fotolia. **599:** Fancy/Alamy. **Tab1:** Oneinchpunch/Fotolia. **Tab2:** Ssilver/Fotolia; Pathdoc/Fotolia. **Tab3:** Berc/Fotolia; Ljupco Smokovski/Fotolia. **Tab4:** Fotolia; Tom Wang/Fotolia. **Tab5:** Diego Cervo/Fotolia; Vladimirfloyd/Fotolia. **Tab6:** BlueOrange Studio/Fotolia; Andres Rodriguez/Fotolia. **Tab7:** Buchachon/Fotolia; Fotolia/www.doglikehorse.com. **Tab8:** Samuii/Fotolia; Odua Images/Fotolia. **Tab9,** front both tabs: Anne Frances Wysocki; **Tab9, MLA,** back: Serkucher/Fotolia. **Tab10:** Red2000/Fotolia; Se media/Fotolia. **Tab11:** Ra2 studio/Fotolia; Pathdoc/Fotolia.

INDEX

QUESTIONS ABOUT RESEARCH